D1498893

Concepts and Cases in Retail and Merchandise Management

Concepts and Cases in

Retail and Merchandise Management

Nancy J. Rabolt
San Francisco State University

Judy K. Miler
University of Tennessee, Chattanooga

Fairchild Publications New York

Library of Congress Catalog Card Number: 96-85746

ISBN: 56367-086-0
GST # R 133004424

Printed in the United States of America

Concepts and Cases in Retail and Merchandise Management

Table of Contents

Cases

Chapter Three
Merchandise Characteristics 62

Cases

Chapter Four
Merchandise Planning, Buying, Control, and Profitability 83

Cases

Chapter Five
Sourcing 122

Cases

Chapter Eight
Personal Selling and Customer Relations   192

Cases

Preface

Merchandising is based on decision-making, therefore, understanding the complexity of decision-making and sharpening critical thinking skills is paramount in preparing students for their place in business management. Skills need to be developed to provide potential professionals the capability to successfully function in the increasingly complex world of retailing. Case study analysis is a proven means of sharpening critical thinking for effective decision-making. Working in the industry has reinforced our belief that actual experience is the best teacher, and if this is not available, simulated experience, such as case studies, can be an excellent substitute. Analyzing case studies have proven to be a much better and more enjoyable way to learn about businesses and their problems and successes than just reading about them.

Purpose of this Book

The major purpose of this book is to provide a merchandising-based case book that identifies and presents critical management issues in contemporary retailing and related manufacturing. It should provide an aid in preparing and developing future retail executives to meet the many changes they will encounter in the next century. Several benefits distinguish this case book from other retail, marketing, or merchandising case books. First, the authors have attempted to present a comprehensive book that covers all aspects of retail and merchandise management from a conceptual and case perspective. Second, most of the cases have been selected to represent commonly encountered beginning and middle management business problems, such as those a beginning professional would encounter. Third, we have presented both qualitative and quantitative types of cases, because both arise in the business environment.

And last, because the manufacturer and retailer are becoming closer partners today than ever before, and in many cases the retailer is also a manufacturer or the manufacturer is also a retailer, the authors felt that it was important to present more manufacturing/retailing problems than other case books have in the past. As a result, quite a few of the cases stress the integrative nature of the manufacturer and retailer working to meet the consumer's needs and wants today. Additionally, almost all of the cases presented are customer service driven, which serves to emphasize the importance of satisfying the customer from both the manufacturing and retailing perspective, because the customer is the one who actually drives the business.

It was not our intention to rewrite a basic retail, merchandising, or management textbook, but to highlight and emphasize the major concepts and principles of retail and merchandising management, so that they may be used to analyze the cases we are presenting without the use of any other source. It was our intention, however, for our case book to stand alone as a practical learning tool for merchandising management decision-making. Some may wish to use the book as a supplement to a larger text, for example, in a merchandising management class and others may use it alone in an upper division case analysis class.

Contents and Chapter Objectives

There are both new and original cases, and also those that have been previously published. Authors are from the profession, as well as academia, and they have written from retail, manufacturing, marketing, and merchandising perspectives. There are a total of 95 cases in the book (including three two-part cases). To ensure that we covered all the major topics that are vital to retailing and merchandising, a combination of real and simulated cases were used in this book. Propriety sometimes dictated that company and personal names used in the cases be changed. We are pleased that there is such a vast array of material covered in the cases. Many major companies are profiled, such as Esprit, Gap, Wal-Mart, Retail Technologies International, Fuller Brush, Banana Republic, Nordstrom, and Saks Fifth Avenue.

All cases are incorporated in the chapter introductions as an example of a concept and/or principle. For ease in using the numerous cases, we have compiled a list of case summaries that starts on page XXXIX, which highlights the major concepts and/or principles contained in the cases, chapter by chapter. The case numbers and titles identify the cases for easy reference.

Multiple objectives are presented at the beginning of each of the twelve chapters in the book. They represent the major focus of the chapter introduction, as well as the cases contained within the chapter. Additionally, the opening abstract to each chapter summarizes the concepts and principles that are contained in the introductions.

As a beginning, Chapter One identifies the major types of retailers and their characteristics and differences, emphasizing the diversity and complexity of retail formats today. This chapter also describes retail ownership and retail format trends.

Chapter Two relates image, identity, and retail positioning to companies and products. It stresses the importance of retail differentiation and successful merchandising. The relationship between competition, positioning, and target marketing in today's complex marketplace is also discussed.

Chapter Three presents major merchandise characteristics, such as style, fashion, price, and quality, as related to image. Branded vs private-label merchandise is also discussed in addition to the concepts of licensing, knockoffs, and counterfeiting.

The importance of merchandise planning and forecasting is highlighted in Chapter Four, while the relationship of planning, pricing, productivity, and profit to buying is also examined. Dollar, unit, and assortment planning and their importance in merchandise management is considered. The critical role of standards and controls in successful retail management is also stressed.

Chapter Five examines the challenges and opportunities of domestic and international sourcing. This chapter emphasizes the importance of careful merchandise source selection. Centralized and decentralized buying, along with other types of buying origination and ordering, are also presented. Lastly, an explanation of the use and importance of buying offices and markets to retailers is given.

The importance of good retail-vendor partnerships is stressed in Chapter Six, and the role of negotiation between buyer and seller is explored. Major problems between vendors and retailers and potential resolutions are also presented. Additionally, the types of orders that retailers utilize are discussed.

Chapter Seven presents methods of communication between retailers and customers and analyzes their effectiveness. Promotional mix is defined and related to media selection. Also, the types and importance of advertising, promotional planning, and budgeting are presented.

The importance of customer service and the role of personal selling at retail is emphasized in Chapter Eight. The concepts of good customer service, compensation, selling incentives, and product knowledge are examined. The importance of product knowledge in the selling process is explained. The methods and importance of effective sales training and evaluation of retail sales personnel are also discussed.

Chapter Nine describes retail management's role and responsibilities. A discussion of the methods and importance of effective training and evaluation of retail management personnel along with an explanation of organizational structure, delegation of authority, and chain of command is also contained in this chapter.

As other recent textbook authors have also thought, we believe that technology is an essential factor in today's business environment, which warrants a separate chapter. Chapter Ten emphasizes the importance of technology at the consumer, retail, and manufacturing levels, and describes the major technological systems that aid retail merchandising. The interaction of technology at the manufacturing and retail levels is also examined.

Chapter Eleven describes entrepreneurship and presents characteristics of successful entrepreneurs. The process and challenges of starting your own business is also explained, and the role of leadership is examined.

When this book was being conceived, the authors debated whether or not ethics warranted its own chapter. As we received and reviewed cases, we found out that our first instincts had been correct. Ethics is such an important issue today in the business environment that we ended up having more cases that shared some ethical dimension than any other facet. Therefore, we concluded that a chapter focusing on ethics was indeed a good idea. Chapter Twelve explains ethics and social responsibility of retailers and manufacturers, while distinguishing between business and personal ethics. Ethics in sourcing and selling are explained, as are the legal considerations within which retailers and manufacturers operate.

Instructor's Guide

An Instructor's Guide accompanies this book. To help direct the resolution to the cases, this instructor's manual gives a thorough analysis of the cases, suggested answers to selected case study questions, and pedagogy on chapter discussion questions. However, some study questions from the cases can be answered with the alternative analysis presented for the major question or through the material in the case and/or the chapter introductions. Also provided is teaching strategy for using the recommended formats in the How to Use section, found on p. XXI. The instructor's guide is arranged by chapter and contains:

1. Teaching objectives

2. Case analyses

3. Study question answers and/or suggestions

4. Chapter discussion question suggestions

Acknowledgments

There are many people to acknowledge and to extend our sincere appreciation and gratitude for their help in making this book a reality. First, we would like to thank the many friends and colleagues who are members of the American Collegiate Retailing Association and the International Textile and Apparel Association. From these two professional organizations we were able to draw support, as well as find the majority of the case authors. We would like to sincerely thank all the contributing authors for their submissions in this endeavor. Without their active participation, we would not have a book at all. A complete listing of authors, (called "About the Authors") along with short biographies and their professional affiliations may be found at the end of the book. We thank you all!

For their thoughtful, constructive, and helpful reviews of the manuscript, both the authors and the editors gratefully acknowledge the following people: Marianne Bickle, Colorado State University; John Donnellan, University of Massachusetts, Amherst; and Faye Gibson, University of North Carolina, Greensboro. We also wish to thank the publishers and authors of the copyrighted cases we wished to use, who are also listed in the About the Authors section.

A special thank you to Sidney Packard and Nathan Axelrod, for pioneering the predecessor to this book about 20 years ago.

To our Fairchild editors, Pam Kirshen Fishman and Olga Kontzias for their belief and support in this project and us, we wish to express our appreciation. To Martin Schwabacher for finding all the photographs, evaluating all the figures and tables, we extend our sincere appreciation. For her assistance in obtaining the text permissions for this book, we are grateful to Gabrielle Heitler. For his design of the book, we would like to thank David Jaenisch. Special indebtedness and gratitude must be extended to editor Susan Jeffers Casel who understood our trials and tribulations, worked with us every step of the way, kept us on track, and guided us in the right direction with her astute comments. With her help, the manuscript and the book were greatly improved.

We would also like to thank our students, who were wonderful critics and willing case testers; our colleagues at San Francisco State University and the University of Tennessee at Chattanooga, who lived through all this with us; and our close friends and family, who supported us emotionally and understood our anxieties, needs, and tight schedules. Specifically, we extend our gratitude to Dennis David, for his computer support and his constant good humor; and to Dan Baker, for his always willing and objective perspective and great grammatical skills.

We would also like to extend special appreciation to our parents George and Anne Kuchler, who early on instilled the value of education; and Newton Scott and Nell Stine Miler, whose love and support through the years has helped in the realization of achievement and knowing that almost anything is possible.

And last, but not least, the marvel of technology: fax, e-mail, and overnight delivery that allowed co-authors on opposite sides of the country to communicate and collaborate with relative ease to complete this book.

Nancy J. Rabolt
Judy K. Miler

How to Use This Book

The challenges and opportunities facing retailers and manufacturers today are tremendous because of the rapidly changing business environment that surrounds all of us. Because of this pace of change, students need to be prepared to meet these challenges and opportunities head on. Preparation is necessary to think and act quickly and efficiently to be able to meet the changes that will be encountered in the workplace. Critical, innovative thinking is paramount, and case study analysis will help position you into life-like business situations that simulate those that may be encountered in future careers.

An overview of today's retail merchandising and management concerns is provided through the concepts and issues examined in this book. Twelve major topical areas of concern to current and future retail professionals—like yourself—are presented in the chapter introductions and the related cases. The cases in this book are based on real business situations or amalgams of real situations. These involve both individuals and groups, independent and corporate businesses, retailers and their suppliers, along with domestic and international settings. The cases help exemplify to students the challenging and exciting nature of merchandising, from both a retail and a manufacturing perspective. They also support the reality that retailing and manufacturing are more interrelated (and more interdependent) today than ever before, as they must work together cooperatively toward success, particularly in the apparel manufacturing and retail industries.

Concept Overlap

Business decisions are often complex, overlapping several areas and affecting more than one facet of business or industry. Problems can stem from a myriad of sources. Likewise, the cases presented in certain chapters could very well have been placed in other chapters or sections. It may be helpful to use the case summary table (p. XXXIX), which illustrates this overlap. Concepts addressed in one case may appear in several chapters; therefore, this list shows the position of each case in its chapter in addition to secondary chapter usage. For example, *Case 23, The Knockoff,* is discussed in Chapter Two under the concept of fashion image, but also is related to the issues in Chapter Twelve. The chapter introductions make reference to cases in other chapters with similar applications. This serves to emphasize the fact that decision-making related to a specific business function may be a more complex effort than it first appears, as well as reinforcing the interdependence and interrelationship of all aspects of retailing and manufacturing.

Chapter Structure

The twelve chapters in the book are arranged in six parts, which are:

1. Chapter objectives

2. Chapter text with key terms in bold

3. Cases with major question for analysis and additional study questions

4. Chapter references

5. Key terms listed

6. Chapter discussion questions

The list of chapter objectives are those goals that the authors intended that particular chapter to accomplish, through the presentation of the material in the introductions and in the cases.

The introductions to the chapters provide information pertinent to the concepts and principles related to the chapter topic. References have been made to appropriate cases within the introduction and at times cases from other chapters are also referred to because they are examples of these concepts and principles in action (as discussed previously). Some information provided in the introduction, however, does not have an illustration in a case, but has been included to provide a more complete overview of the major topic or concept.

Key terms are bolded and defined within the introduction and are listed alphabetically at the end of the introduction. These terms are important components in the overall understanding of the chapter topic and are highlighted to bring attention to them. A glossary at the end of the book provides definitions for all key terms at a glance. Most of these terms are used in the cases but sometimes are not defined there, so the glossary will help a student to look up quickly a term that is in question. Because the cases are taken from the workplace, common business language is used. In some instances a term may be used in a case that is introduced in a later chapter, again making the glossary important to use for full understanding of the case.

The 95 cases (which include three two-part cases, for a total of 98 cases) that appear in this book all contain a major problem for you to analyze. These problems relate directly to the major concepts in the introductions of the chapters. Each case also has several study questions that should stimulate further inquiry pertaining to the chapter concepts/principles and/or the specific problems presented in the cases themselves. Discussion of and investigation into these additional study questions may also help lead you to an approach to use for the analysis of the cases.

The chapter discussion questions found at the end of each chapter may be used for debating and discussing a concept, which can incorporate several of the cases and concepts in the chapter. Additionally, they may be used to compare and contrast the various issues raised within all the chapters, as well as being helpful in formulating strategies to solve the cases.

Chapter references provide sources used in the introduction, in addition to other readings and information that might be helpful to prepare an analysis of individual cases. Tables and figures (including photographs and diagrams) are used to supplement and support material in the chapter introductions as well as the actual cases themselves. This supporting evidence either highlights and reinforces the concepts/principles and data explored in the chapter introductions or presents vital statistics and data that are actually necessary in understanding and solving the case.

What Is a Case?

A case is a written description of a business situation or problem. It generally provides factual information about a company's background, which often includes organizational or financial data related to the present situation. The use of case analysis in teaching was developed by the Harvard Business School in the 1920s with the purpose of introducing the highest possible level of realism into teaching management decision-making. A case raises contemporary issues and provides information to analyze from a business perspective. Also, often included in a case is information that is outside of the immediate company, which is related to the socio-cultural, political, legal, technological, and competitive environments. Data related to such industry sectors as apparel or fashion are described to give the reader a better understanding of the circumstances surrounding the situation. It is your job to propose solutions to the problems. In some circumstances, the case authors have purposely presented cases with no readily identifiable problem, just facts to sift through to arrive at the problem. In this book, however, each case poses at least one specific problem to be solved or analysis to be undertaken.

The Value of the Case Method of Inquiry

The case analysis method is different from other teaching/learning situations that you are probably more familiar with, such as lectures or demonstrations. There is no memorization of facts or other material presented by the instructor. The case study method is an active, problem-solving way of learning in which you have to think about the problem, use the facts provided in the case, and then decide on the most appropriate action to take. External environmental factors (those outside the company) should also be considered, along with the specific internal facts about the company and the situation. Analyses are reliant on critical thinking, logic, and sound integrative reasoning. A form of experience in handling a variety of problem situations can be gained through this process, providing preparation for the reality of the workplace.

The cases themselves can also help you to improve your reading, writing, and speaking abilities, which are vitally important for good communication in business. Additionally, exposure to others' thoughts and reasoning (such as those characters portrayed in the cases) can open your mind to other views. Most of the cases in this book are descriptions of real situations in a company; some, however, are an amalgam of several companies. In these cases, a name for the company has been created; therefore, you will not recognize the company name. In other cases, companies have requested that their firm's name not be used and because of this we have changed the names of their organizations. The facts are real, however, and you are to use them in your analysis. Primarily, this book focuses on cases about retailers and manufacturers of apparel; nevertheless, other related products available to the consumer today are also included.

Case Analysis

When analyzing a case, you should assume the role of the challenged individual in the case and react as you believe that person should to best remedy the problem. As in all problem situations, there never is a single solution, nor a right or wrong answer. Therefore, your fellow classmates may come up with different recommendations and devise other solutions than you. However, your recommended course of action (the best alternative) relies on a justification for that recommendation. It should be based on the facts contained within the case, along with the basic concepts and/or principles of retail and merchandise management provided in the chapter introduction.

Often it may seem that you don't have enough information to solve the case problem. Welcome to the real world of business! Often decision-makers do not have all the information needed for a "good" decision. But they must make a decision with the information available at the time. Later, when more information becomes available, it may appear that the decision was not the best; but most of us do not have a crystal ball and we must do the best we can with the information and data we have at that time.

Common Questions and Difficulties with Cases

Case analysis takes time. More time is required in doing cases properly than just answering questions. There are often numerous variables to consider within a case, and sometimes the solutions are not obvious. Sometimes there is more information offered than is necessary, and at other times it seems that there may not be enough data given. You may be assured, however, that there is enough information in all the cases in this book to propose viable solutions.

Frustration can occur when trying to solve a case, because very often there is not just one answer to remedying the situation at hand. Here, a thorough analysis of the facts presented helps to determine the best solutions. You—the case analyst—must also realize that the more knowledge you bring to the solving of a case, the more thorough a job you can do. Just as in the real world, the more knowledge and information accumulated, the better a problem can be resolved or a decision made. Caution must also be taken because there is a definite difference between identification of the problem to be solved in the case and identification of the central or major issue raised by the problem. The problem is the specific situation to which a resolution must be identified. The major retailing concepts or principles involved in the problem, are such issues as image, advertising, customer service, selling or buying principles.

When a group approach to case analysis is used, students must understand that participation by everyone is absolutely necessary for this approach to be effective. Assuming that you are a part of a management team charged with a problem to solve may also help to motivate everyone in the group to participate.

It is also important to remember that using common sense may help you to realize what is relevant for solving a case. Logic is another tool you will find helpful. Used in tandem with management concepts and principles, logic will also assist you in formulating your plan of action and your arguments and justifications for the selection of the best alternative solution.

A Recommended Approach for Students

Not all case analyses can be approached exactly the same way, but generally we recommend the following approach to analysis of the cases found in this book:

- Read the case completely through, along with the major question.

- Reread the case and any accompanying illustrations or data carefully and do the following:

  1. Clearly **define the immediate problem** to be solved, if it is not already done for you.

  2. **Identify the major concept(s) and/or principles** raised by the problem.

  3. **Develop several alternative solutions** to the problem and that could be applied to the situation.

  4. **Evaluate each alternative** by listing its advantages and disadvantages. (This may include consistency with company mission or strategy, long-term implications, resources available, or impediments.)

  5. **Identify the recommended solution** along with any further justification.

  6. **Develop a recommended course of action** if needed.

There are two types of major questions used with the cases. In most instances, the major issue(s) of the case is incorporated into the major question. In some cases, however, these major issues have purposely not been identified in the major question. This was done so that you, the case analyst, can do so. One question type involves the use of a narrowly defined and specific question. The other question type uses a more general inquiry approach. For example, in Chapter One, *Case 2, Creative Wear's Short Life,* the major question asked is: What could Suzanne have done differently in the planning, merchandising, and production of Creative Wear to ensure more success? In Chapter Three, *Case 21, The Fabric Problem,* the major question presented is: What should Robert do? In this book, the first type of specific question is used much more often, however, the generalized questions are also used.

Some cases present information about a business situation before any action has been taken in regard to a specific business problem. Other cases present a situation that needs some remedial action, or rather, the major question asks you to recommend alternative action(s) that are different than what has already transpired in the case. Additionally, you should not judge the complexity of a case by its length. A case may be short, but the problem and issue(s) and subsequent analysis may be much more complex than those for a longer case.

As stated earlier, there is sufficient information within each case and each chapter introduction for you to determine alternatives to case solutions and to choose the most appropriate course of action. You should be realistic and explicit when recommending alternatives. Specific action and outcomes should be identified. However, if desired, further investigation of the problem can be done with the suggested readings at the end of the chapters. This might result in a more thorough, studied response to the topic, time permitting.

The study questions might also be considered as a way of leading to the identification of issues or determining your approach to the analysis. Some of these queries might take you in a different direction than the main case question, but also might raise some important issues that may be discussed either within the class or within your case analysis group.

An instructor's guide is available to teachers, which provides the authors' analysis and justification for the recommended alternative. Your analysis and recommended course of action may differ and can be justified if based on sound logic and use of the facts. Certainly other analyses are warranted, particularly with the passage of time and changing environments that can (and often do) affect the situation. For example, the enactment of a law may change the circumstances of the described situation and a different decision may benefit customers, employees, or the company. Most of the analyses found in the instructor's guide are taken from the real circumstances and provide the actual decision and justification for it. Sometimes the actual decision is not the best, but this is pointed out with the author's recommended alternative solution.

The Role of the Student and Instructor in Case Analysis

As indicated earlier, the case study method is probably different from other learning activities that you as a student have been involved in, for example, lecture and discussion. The case study method is student—not teacher—oriented. In a case analysis situation, the instructor's primary role is to guide students in the analysis process, keeping them on track, sometimes interjecting ideas, judging the quality of the discussion, and at times acting as a devil's advocate to provide a new viewpoint. The specific role of the student and instructor varies depending on the method used for "solving" the case study. The next section examines the various types of methods used for case analysis.

Case Study Methods

There are different structural approaches to accomplishing case analyses. These methods include: 1) individual; 2) group or collaborative; 3) brainstorming; and 4) role playing. In addition to these methods, the actual case analysis can be presented either narratively (orally) or as a written paper. Students can do individual analyses on their own, with whatever resources are available (in this case, the teacher role above does not apply), or stu-

dents can come together in small groups or one large group in which everyone participates in discussion. In this method, no one should just sit and listen. Everyone must prepare before the discussion for this collaborative method to work, and this preparation should include carefully reading the case and the chapter introduction for needed background. Then each student should outline an analysis, as suggested earlier, which will be presented to the group. Some of you may have more experience in the workplace than others from which to draw upon for further input, and all group members can learn from hearing about your experiences. As in most group situations, some individuals will be more productive than others. But group members should respect and consider each other's opinions and contributions. A group leader, recorder, and spokesperson can be assigned or elected, which automatically gives three members an active role, and perhaps some leadership experience. The leader should guide and direct the group's case analysis. The recorder should act as secretary, writing all information down, including the proposed solution. The spokesperson can then present the group's conclusions to the instructor and the remainder of the class or the other groups. Varying the roles of group members gives variety to the group dynamics and stimulates different perspectives. These variations can be initiated by the instructor, or can be done voluntarily by the group itself.

In addition to these variations, a single case can be done by all the groups in a class and then all solutions can be heard and a consensus reached for the best, most appropriate solution. Another possibility is that different groups solve different cases, so that more material and issues are covered during the class.

The brainstorming method of case analysis is another group method, which is based on oral discussion. It is unstructured and is the most informal. Here, the instructor or a student leader plays the role of the facilitator, who directs the group through the stages of analysis. Essentially, any input from all participants is used, and the consensus is reached for selection of the best alternative solution.

Role playing is another effective approach to case analysis. It also is a group method, and can be fun and exciting. It is the dramatization of a structured case, which is enacted by members of a group who are chosen as actors. This method may not be suitable for all cases, but could be quite practical and useful for those cases in which there is a situation that can be "played" out and in which there are not too many characters. In some instances, background information may have to be reviewed, and data could be presented as reports or charts. The actors would then proceed with solving the case and the class would evaluate the recommendation(s) proposed.

A case study solutions form is given for use in helping to guide the analysis and ensure consistency and completeness in the evaluation of cases. In addition to this, a sample case and step-by-step analysis with solutions to the case problem is presented to help illustrate how to approach case study analysis.

Concepts and Cases in Retail and Merchandise Management

Sample Case Study
The Classification Conundrum

Castle's Department Store, which has an annual sales volume of $120 million, is located in Atlanta, Georgia. The climate there usually ranges from mild to hot almost all year long, with a few cold days during the winter months. The annual temperature range is an ideal 70 degrees Fahrenheit. These conditions are perfect for most sports, and tennis in particular, which is fast becoming the number one sports activity among young professionals in Atlanta.

While the area surrounding Atlanta is still predominantly agricultural, such big industries as textiles, paper, chemicals, pharmaceuticals, as well as all media-related industries, such as television, radio, and publishing, are becoming a larger part of the area's economy. All in all, the influx of a younger, more professional population and their growing families has been good for Castle's. This change in the demographics of the area, however, has brought a younger, more affluent group of customers to the store and has required that the store's management "think fashion" somewhat differently than its competitors because Castle's has always been known as "the best apparel store in town."

Kate Butler has been Castle's women's sportswear buyer for the past three years, having come to Atlanta from Minneapolis, where she had been an assistant buyer of activewear. She is very happy at Castle's, is doing a good job, and is well-thought of by upper management.

During the annual Atlanta Womenswear market, Kate bought something new for Castle's—an off-white tennis dress with lace details for non-tennis players—an *après* tennis outfit. Previously, similar dresses had sold very well in smaller markets and had done especially well at the shops at private tennis clubs. Kate just "knew" that this dress would be a hit and so she bought it. When the merchandise arrived, she first called the visual merchandise department and arranged to have a mannequin display placed at the entrance to her department. When the mannequin display was in place, she and her assistant finished ticketing the goods and then they arranged a good-sized sample assortment on a T-stand next to the display. When Kate looked at the display and the assortment, she knew she would have a "hot" seller in no time. She was mulling over the possibility of advertising the dress, when Janice Reed, the junior dress department buyer, stormed into her office.

As it happened, the location of the display and the T-stand abutted one side of the junior dress department. Janice had practically fallen over the display and new merchandise and after looking it over, strode into Kate's office.

"Hey, Kate, where do you come off selling those off-white dresses in the sportswear department? You're practically flaunting them in my face!" Janice said angrily.

Kate looked at Janice calmly. "If you'll look closely, you'll see that they are not really dresses at all. They are tennis outfits, as their labels clearly state. I bought them from Miss California, one of my key resources."

Janice persisted. "Well, it's bad enough that you're carrying them right next to my department, but they're also priced $5 lower than similar dresses that I'm overstocked with already!"

"Janice, you know that sportswear prices are generally lower than dress prices," Kate answered. "You know they have a different labor setup and sportswear workmanship is not as costly as dresses are. Anyway, Janice, you remember when you bought that big line of pantsuits from Radioline? They were definitely sportswear items, but I went along with it even though I knew that they would hurt my business. Why don't you just sit down and I'll go get us both a—." Kate abruptly stopped, when she saw that Janice's face was red with anger. She was not going to be pacified, regardless of what she may have done in the past. She saw those tennis dresses as a potential threat to her department, especially because the numbers of tennis "buffs" were growing steadily and showing no signs of abating.

Accordingly, Janice sought Jessica Cunningham, the ready-to-wear merchandise manager and discussed the full impact of Kate's purchase of the so-called tennis "outfit." Jessica listened carefully and after Janice finished, she promised to check into the matter at once.

Jessica then called Kate into her office and listened to her side of the story, which included her reasons for buying the dress and the necessity of the display and T-stand.

Jessica is relatively new to Castle's, having come from New York City, where she had been the dress buyer for a large chain department store. Generally, she is regarded as an astute merchandiser and she has not been known to play favorites among the buyers under her supervision.

Major Question

If you were in Jessica Cunningham's place, what would you do in regard to the sportswear buyer's purchase of the tennis "dresses" and the dress buyer's objections?

Study Questions

1. What classifies a dress as a "dress?" When would a dress be classified as something other than a dress?

2. Do you think the display and the T-stand of tennis outfits will negatively impact the junior dress department sales? Why or why not?

3. Should the junior dress buyer be more reasonable about this purchase, given her own past history of purchasing pantsuits? Why or why not?

A Step-by-Step Solution to the Sample Case

(Using the sample form starting on p. XXXIII.)

Major Question and Immediate Problem

The junior dress buyer discovers that the neighboring sportswear department is selling a "tennis" dress at a lower price than similar dresses found in the junior dress department.

Major Concept and/or Principle

A basic merchandising principle: A merchandise classification belongs to the store, not to any individual buyer.

Alternative Solutions

1. Leave the situation as it is now—status quo.
   Advantages
   - It is the easy way out—let it be.
   - A buyer should be able to use her own resources that provide merchandise for her department and/or classification.
   Disadvantages
   - This provides unfair competition for the junior dress department.
   - Customer confusion may arise as to price and merchandise location.

2. Transfer the similar dresses from the junior dress department to the sportswear department, after the junior dress department takes a markdown of $5 to bring the merchandise in line with the sportswear department's price on the tennis dresses.
   Advantages
   - It is an easy, simple solution
   - Customers get the best buys, building good customer relations. No more confusion because only one department is selling the like items.
   Disadvantages
   - Dresses belong in a dress department— this is self-evident and customers generally look for dresses in a dress department.
   - There is usually better quality in the dress market than in sportswear—so this would be lowering those standards and it is important to maintain quality standards.

3. Transfer the tennis outfits from the sportswear department to the junior dress

department, but first taking a markup of $5 to bring the merchandise in line with the dress department's price on similar goods.

Advantages
- It is an easy, simple solution.
- Customers will not be confused because the merchandise will be selling in one department only.
- Dresses belong in a dress department.

Disadvantages
- Customers are not receiving the best possible price.
- It is a sportswear item and should be sold in the sportswear department.

4. Take the merchandise from both the junior dress and sportswear departments and sell it in the activewear department.

Advantages
- It is a natural place for such outfits to be sold.
- It is neutral ground and avoids conflict between the two buyers.

Disadvantages
- The activewear buyer is not the buyer who has the responsibility to buy such fashion merchandise.

- The sales associates in the activewear department are untrained to sell the level of fashion that sportswear does.
- The activewear department does not have the facilities, such as dressing rooms, for trying on these tennis dresses.

Recommended Solution, Justification, and Course of Action

(Alternative A.) Leave the situation as it is now—status quo. These are the days of "scrambled merchandising" and customers are accustomed to competition within stores and departments. A buyer usually has the right to buy the offerings of what manufacturers consider a trend in their markets, particularly from their key vendors. This sets a precedent (knitted dresses, pantsuits, golf dresses, knitted suits, two-piece dresses, and so forth) which favors the maintenance of stock in both the sportswear and junior dress departments.

Bring both buyers into the merchandise manager's office and tell them of the decision to let the tennis dresses remain where they are. If need be, listen to both sides again, but remain firm in this decision, because it is the fairest way to go.

Case Study Analysis Form

Name _____

Date _____ **Case Study Number** _____

Case Study Title _____

Major Question and Immediate Problem _____

_____

_____

_____

Major Concept and/or Principle _____

_____

_____

Alternative Solution 1 _____

_____

_____

_____

_____

_____

Advantages

_____

_____

_____

_____

_____

_____

_____

_____

Disadvantages

_____
_____
_____
_____
_____
_____

Alternative Solution 2 _____

_____
_____
_____
_____

Advantages

_____
_____
_____
_____
_____
_____

Disadvantages

_____
_____
_____
_____
_____
_____

Alternative Solution 3 _____

_____

_____

_____

_____

_____

Advantages

_____

_____

_____

_____

_____

_____

_____

Disadvantages

_____

_____

_____

_____

_____

_____

_____

Alternative Solution 4 _____

_____

_____

_____

_____

_____

Advantages

_____

_____

_____

_____

_____

_____

_____

Disadvantages

_____

_____

_____

_____

_____

_____

_____

Recommended Solutions, Justification, and Course of Action _____

_____

_____

_____

_____

_____

_____

_____

_____

_____

_____

_____

_____

_____

Concepts and Cases in Retail and Merchandise Management

Case Summaries

Case	Title	Major Concept(s) and/or Principle(s)
1	*The Fuller Brush Company: Rediscovering the Magic*	• Revitalizing an older retail concept • Non-store retailing: door-to-door selling • Direct marketing • Entrepreneurship • Changing retail image • Strategic market planning • Competitiveness • Environmental influences
2	*Creative Wear's Short Life*	• Non-store retailing: house parties • Direct marketing • Entrepreneurship • Product/company image • Vertical integration • Niche merchandise
3	*Where Did All the People Go?*	• Retailer makeup of mall • Mall competition • Market research to determine customer base
4	*Mike Young: The Dynamics of Independent Retailing*	• Small independent store ownership • Sole proprietorship/informal partnership • Buying/balancing merchandise for a small store • Evaluating career opportunities
5	*Cironi's Sewing Center Loses a Franchise*	• Legal aspects of franchise ownership • Power structure of business • Representing manufacturer's brands in the marketplace • Analysis of selling costs, sales, profits, and market share of brands

Concepts and Cases in Retail and Merchandise Management

1

Retailing Formats and Structures

Chapter Objectives

- Identify major types of retailers and their characteristics and differences.

- Emphasize the diversity and complexity of retail formats today.

- Describe the differences in terms of retail ownership.

- Identify trends in retailing formats.

Businesses have a myriad of formats in which to market their products and to own companies in today's complex, highly competitive business environment. Technology has created new formats that are challenging older formats. More and more apparel companies are mixing retailing and manufacturing, are becoming more vertically or horizontally integrated, and are streamlining operations. Retailers are merging and eliminating non-profitable units. Only those formats that truly meet consumer needs in a profitable manner are surviving. The distinction between retailer types today seems harder to verbalize because of the blending of retail formats, and many standard definitions are no longer appropriate.

Retailing Classifications

There are many retailing formats used today with overlaps in categories as one store can fall under several formats. For example, a department or specialty store can be part of a chain. Also, an independent or conglomerate-owned store can be a chain. A discount store can be found in the form of a department store. At times, new terms for old formats become popular; therefore meanings can change over time. Is a mass merchandiser a discounter? Is an off-price store a discount store?

The U.S. Bureau of Census classifies retailers into a system of four-digit **SIC (Standard Industrial Classification) codes.** These codes identify general types of retailers such as apparel and department stores. For example, apparel stores are listed under code 56 with specialty women's clothing stores listed under 5621. Department stores are listed under 5311. Some stores are placed under several SIC categories. For example, Wal-Mart and

Kmart are both considered family clothing stores (SIC 5651) and also department stores (SIC 5311). Today, the use of such terms as off-price retailer, mass merchandiser, warehouse store, or catalog showroom are different from SIC designations such as variety store, family clothing store, and general merchandise store. Marshall's and T.J. Maxx are listed under the heading "variety store," but we think of them as off-price stores. (These store types are defined later in this chapter.) Thus, it is somewhat challenging to use the SIC system for today's fast-changing retail formats because more and different varieties spring up so rapidly the SIC system cannot keep pace with these variations. The SIC system is important to understand, however, because there is a wealth of data and information published by business and government agencies, which use this classification system. Other methods of classification of retailers are based on ownership, merchandise mix, and service.

Types of Ownership

A **sole proprietorship,** which is a company owned by one person, is fully controlled by the owner, and all benefits and costs accrue to that individual. A **partnership** is a firm owned by two or more persons, each of whom has a financial interest. A **corporation** is different because it allows capital to be raised through the sale of company stock, and does not allow legal claims against individuals as in sole proprietorships and partnerships.

An **independent store** is a single unit owned by an individual. There are over 1.5 million independent retailers in the U.S. today. The relative ease of entry into the marketplace of independent stores creates a great deal of competition, and in the 1990s only the strong are surviving. The Small Business Administration (SBA) estimates that one-third of all new retail firms fail within the first year of business. The trend in ownership of department stores today is fewer and fewer independent stores, as they are being bought out by conglomerates. See *Case 4, Mike Young: The Dynamics of Independent Retailing,* for an illustration of the trials and tribulations of small, independent store ownership. Dillard's and Nordstrom remain two of the few

independent department stores left. For our purposes here, independent means it is not owned by a large conglomerate, but the majority of stocks or holdings is owned by a family. For example, Nordstrom is a public corporation, but the majority of stock is owned by the original family and the corporation is still run by the family.

A **chain** is defined as multiple retail units under common ownership and usually has centralized buying and management. The Limited, for example, is a chain. The parent company, The Limited, Inc., owns several chains including Express, Victoria's Secret, Structure, Lerner New York, Lane Bryant, Abercrombie and Fitch, Henri Bendel, Cacique, and Bath & Body Works. Some define a chain as the same ownership having at least two stores; however, chains generally have more than two outlets. Department stores are often chains, for example, Macy's and Nordstrom; but they may not have the same degree of corporate control as such chains as Gap or The Limited. Macy's is organized in the "hen and chick" format, in which there is a flagship or main store. Macy's Herald Square in New York City is the flagship in this case, and has many branches—or chicks—in other locations. Nordstrom's decentralized district level buying also differentiates it from chains such as Kmart where central buying is done through headquarters. (See Chapter Five for more on different types of buying arrangements.)

Retail concepts are sometimes licensed or franchised—for example, Benetton and Esprit stores, and recently Nicole Miller stores. In some instances, the company owns some, but not all of the stores. The Nicole Miller SOHO (New York) and Crocker Galleria (San Francisco) stores are owned by the company while other Nicole Miller stores are licensed to independents outside the company. This arrangement is known as franchising. A **franchise** is a contractual arrangement between a franchisor (the entity selling its name) and a franchisee (the owner). A franchise combines independent ownership with franchisor management assistance, which includes a well-known name and image. The franchisee pays royalties for the privilege of using the company name. This licensing (franchising) of stores is similar to a designer licensing his or her name to a manufacturer that produces a product and then places the designer's name on the product for an agreed upon price and/or percentage of profit. The potential problems with lack of control over one's business that is franchised is shown in *Case 5, Cironi's Sewing Center Loses a Franchise.*

Merchandise Mix/Service

Retailers are further defined by the type of product or merchandise mix and service level they provide their customers. Still another major delineation is that the retail format can be stored or non-stored. The next sections explore the many varieties of both stored and non-stored formats.

Stored Retailers Precise definitions of retail formats are blurring and changing over time. For years, *Stores* magazine listed the Top 100 Department Stores and Top 100 Specialty Stores. Their definition of a department store included furniture. Saks Fifth Avenue was listed as a specialty store because it carried apparel for family members, but did not carry furniture. Then, such fashion stores as Saks appeared on the Department Store list, not the Specialty Store list; thus, the definition seems to have changed overnight. The meaning of the term factory outlet has also changed. Factory outlets used to be attached to the factory. Today we see outlets far from production sites; however, they still sell overruns and often seconds. Some manufacturers are seeing the outlet as a new venue to sell merchandise to a specific target customer, and are producing extra inventory specifically to be sold in their outlets. Esprit, for example, does this; identical merchandise as that at retail, is held in their storeroom until a certain agreed upon date for release onto the outlet floor. A similar concept is operative at the retail level. Nordstrom Rack—Nordstrom's clearance outlet—sells their own markdown merchandise, and more. The Rack has its own buyers who purchase comparably priced merchandise (to the markdown prices of Nordstrom products) from vendors that are different from those selling to the Nordstrom stores. They are appealing to the Rack customer who is looking for a "bargain." The traditional retailing that we are most familiar with are stored retailers. The following is a listing of the most common types of stored retailers:

- **Department stores** are large units that carry an extensive assortment of merchandise organized into separate departments. U.S. Bureau of Census uses three criteria to define department stores: 1) at least 25 employees; 2) must carry dry goods and household items, family apparel, furniture, and home furnishings; and 3) $10 million in sales, with some stipulations. Both the traditional department store like Macy's and the full-line discount store, such as Kmart, qualify for this definition. However, today we often refer to other specialty stores such as Nordstrom and Saks Fifth Avenue as department stores—even though they don't carry furniture.

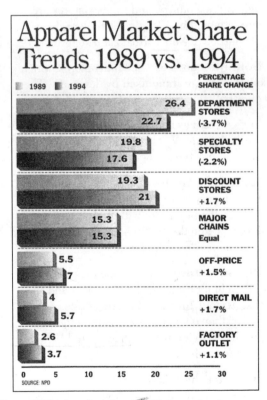

Figure 1.1 This bar chart from *WWD* shows that department and specialty stores had the largest percentage of market share, but they are now losing share to discount, off-price, direct mail, and factory outlets.

- **Specialty** (or **limited assortment**) **stores** sell a limited type of merchandise, for example, shoes, electronics, or apparel. Generally, this type of store provides the customer with special services not often seen in department or discount stores. Gap is an example of a highly successful specialty apparel company. Some specialty stores have become so successful at beating the competition in their specialized product, that they are considered **category killers,** or some call them **big box stores.** These stores, such as Toys "R" Us, are specialty discounters that focus on one product and have the best selection at the best price, which effectively "kills" the competition. Variety and discount stores find it difficult to compete with Toys "R" Us, because of their price and selection. Because of competition from category killers, small independents are closing in malls throughout the country, and big box stores are replacing them, for example, Lechmere, Home Depot, Barnes & Noble, Ross, and so forth.

- **Boutiques** are small specialty stores, which are often owned or franchised by designers. These can offer both accessories and apparel.

- **Variety stores** sell a wide assortment of popularly priced goods. Woolworth and Thrifty are examples of this type of operation.

- **Mom and pop stores** are small, privately owned, independent stores that are owned and operated by the proprietor with perhaps a few employees. Often these stores are run by a husband and wife, hence "mom and pop."

- **Discount stores** sell merchandise at prices lower than other traditional department and specialty stores due to lower operating costs. Generally, they offer self-service and large quantity purchases to lower costs. Kmart and Wal-Mart are considered discount stores.

- **Mass merchandisers** are large discount stores that serve the mass market. Discounters have begun to use the term in an effort to "trade up." Kmart, Wal-Mart, Target, and Sears are sometimes referred to as mass merchandisers.

10 Key Reasons Why Women Have Decreased Department Store Shopping

1	Other stores have merchandise they like better	63%
2	Other stores more conveniently located.	63%
3	Other stores show combination of outfits better.	63%
4	Other stores easier to shop because of layout.	61%
5	Other stores take less time.	58%
6	Too many departments to shop.	57%
7	Crowded racks makes apparel seem less valuable.	56%
8	Shopping ambience not as nice as other stores.	53%
9	Level of service inferior to other stores.	51%
10	It is much more confusing than others.	48%

Figure 1.2 This figure shows the percentage of respondents who cited the above reasons why they have decreased department store shopping in the last 5–10 years. These results are based on interviews with 500 female shoppers.

- **Off-price stores** sell brand-name merchandise at lower than department store prices due to low overhead and such special purchases as overruns or end-of-the-season merchandise. T.J. Maxx, Ross, and Marshall's are examples of this type of retailer.

- **Catalog showrooms** sell merchandise from a catalog or floor samples in a warehouse-style operation. Service Merchandise and Best are typical of this type of operation.

- **Warehouse stores** are discounters that offer food and other items in a no-frills setting. They often concentrate on special purchases of brand-name goods. Generally they are characterized by a lack of such customer services as credit card usage or bagging. Many times these operations require a "membership fee," which the consumer must pay before being able to shop at the store. PriceCostco, Sam's Club, and Pace are considered warehouse stores.

- **Factory outlets** are manufacturer-owned stores that sell the manufacturer's closeouts, overruns, canceled orders, discontinued items, and irregulars. Today, there are many examples of this type of retailer, from Liz Claiborne to Hanes and Nike.

One of the challenges of retailers today is to become a **destination store,** which is a type of retailer that a customer shops because only it can provide the product or service that the customer wants. *Discount Store News* defines this as a "magnet" for customers, distinguishing it from other retailers that customers also patronize. Customers make special efforts to go to destination stores. Because we are in such an over-stored environment, that is, there are more stores than the marketplace can support, consumers generally shop at whatever store is most convenient for them. Formerly, department stores were destinations; now, however, the mall often is the destination. *WWD* research has shown that women have decreased department store shopping because of the merchandise, location, confusing layout, and lack of service. However, there are some destination stores left—those that have some outstanding feature. Bloomingdale's flagship store in New York City is a good example, as it is one of the largest tourist attractions in New York. Customers and tourists alike shop Bloomingdale's because of the exciting atmosphere and the store's image of having the newest trendy merchandise. Other successful destination stores are PriceCostco, Pace, or other warehouse outlets because of their price advantage image and their (generally) convenient locations with ample parking facilities.

Non-stored Retailers As technology expands, we are seeing more non-conventional ways to sell merchandise, for example, TV home shopping networks, and such interactive types of retailing as the Internet. See Chapter Ten for discussion on technology in retailing. Other examples of non-stored retailers are:

• **Mail order,** a conventional form of non-store retailing, continues to grow as busy two-income families are finding less and less time to shop the stores. However, as interactive retailing grows and the cost of paper and postage continue to increase, a

Figure 1.3 Cover of a Spiegel catalog, a popular mail-order (non-store retailing) business, which primarily sells designer and upper-end merchandise. Spiegel, once known for value-oriented merchandise, has successfully repositioned itself to the upper-end market. In addition to twice-yearly fall/winter and spring/summer catalogs, sale catalogs, and an annual Holiday catalog, Spiegel also targets specific markets with specialized catalogs, for example, *Together,* for a younger, more outdoorsy, coordinated look; *E Style,* which was developed with *Ebony,* for African-American women; and *For You,* which targets the size 14+ woman.

slowing of mail order will probably occur. Mail order can be an extension of a store's business for example, Williams-Sonoma and Bloomingdale's by Mail, or can be such stand-alone operations as Spiegel and Lands' End. As the market becomes more and more specialized and targeted, successful mail order is serving the needs of specific niches. Because of this trend, such general merchandise catalogs as Montgomery Ward and Sears are disappearing.

Figures 1.4–1.5 Michael Jordan (above) wearing the T-shirt (featuring a muscular bull) that was sold by temporary retailers who took advantage of a hot opportunity after the NBA championship in 1996. (See *New York Times* article below.) *Photo courtesy of Reuters/Sue Ogrocki/ Archive Photos.*

• **Direct marketing,** which is a broad term that includes many forms of non-personal communication, for example, mailed catalogs, flyers, radio, magazine, and newspapers. It also includes forms of personal communication, such as telemarketing and TV home shopping, in which customers call "800" numbers to order merchandise. This type of retailing increased tremendously in the 1980s and continues to take market share from conventional retailers.

• **Home parties,** which consist of merchandise showings in the home to "guests" or customers. Examples of successful home-party companies are the venerable Tupperware, Mary Kay Cosmetics, and Sarah Coventry companies.

• **Kiosks,** which are small stationary facilities that generally have the capability of customer ordering of merchandise through a computer.

• **Temporary retailers,** which are generally small vendors who set up tables or carts and sell a variety of goods—often one-of-a-kind—made by the seller or artist. They usually set up on street sidewalks or walkways of malls. Some larger retailers are even experimenting with temporary stores. For example, during the 1996 Olympic games in Atlanta, Georgia, a huge store was housed under a

---

As the Bulls Celebrate, Merchandisers Are Tagging Along

By RICHARD SANDOMIR

Most people resist wearing caps with tags flapping from them. But the Chicago Bulls celebrated their fourth National Basketball Association title Sunday night with headgear bearing the manufacturer's name, Logo Athletic.

It's a post-game ritual: Sweaty champions don official locker-room caps and T-shirts — a designation that costs their makers extra fees — within minutes of their triumphs.

Starter made the official shirts, plus those featuring a muscular cartoon Bull worn by players during a parade yesterday in Chicago.

Logo and Starter are 2 of 23 companies licensed by the N.B.A. to produce championship caps, T-shirts, watches, garbage cans, coins, license plates, pins, pennants and other items for retailers, from Foot Locker to QVC. It is a rapid-response retail universe that reacts quickly to the flush of victory.

"It used to be a two-week market, but with our manufacturing capabilities, it's down to three days," said Tom Shine, the president of Logo.

The Bullish frenzy "is already double what we did for the Cowboys" after the Super Bowl in January, said Robin Wexler, a Starter Spokeswoman.

A flood of goods began shipping soon after the Bulls won Game 6 over Seattle, with at least 70 percent of the merchandise destined for the Chicago area.

Logo has manufactured 500,000 caps and 300,000 T-shirts. Pro Player said its eight championship T-shirt designs will generate $6 million in retail sales.

Starter's demand is stronger than for the Bulls' 1993 title, Wexler said.

Sportswon — an Oberlin Park, Kan., special-promotion retailer that leases stores for short periods to sell championship goods — has 27 outlets hawking Bulls regalia in the Chicago area.

"We'll stay open as long as we keep selling," said Tom Healy, manager of the 8,000-square-foot store on State Street. "The demand is overwhelming."

Sportswons stayed open for 40 days after the 1993 championship.

Manufacturers are relieved that the Bulls won. Logo, Starter and Pro Player began manufacturing last week before the Bulls lost Game 4 to the SuperSonics.

Wexler said that Starter gambled and never stopped production.

"Friday night after Seattle won Game 5, I was getting a little worried," said Doug Kelly, the president of Pro Player.

Had the less-marketable Sonics won the title, all those hastily made Bulls' goods would have had to be destroyed.

"The good guys won — in terms of volume," Shine said.

---

climate-controlled tent that could be disassembled after the games concluded. (An example of successful temporary retailing is shown in Figure 1.5.)

• **Door-to-door selling,** also referred to as direct-to-home selling, includes personal contact with consumers in their homes or offices and telephone solicitations. Cosmetics, household goods, encyclopedias, and vacuum cleaners are often sold direct to consumers without a retail store middleman. Amway and Fuller Brush are examples of door-to-door retailing.

For further examples of non-stored retailing, see *Case 1, The Fuller Brush Company: Rediscovering the Magic; Case 2, Creative Wear's Short Life;* and *Case 6, Wish Book.*

Malls and Shopping Centers

With the return of many veterans after World War II, the starting of families and the construction of suburban housing, regional shopping centers—or malls—were built by developers to serve consumers moving to suburban communities. Large department

Figure 1.6 The Mall of America in Bloomington, Minnesota, the largest U.S. mall (4.2 million square feet), is a retail/entertainment complex with 14 movie theaters, 50 restaurants, a bi-level miniature golf course, and the nation's largest enclosed theme park with an indoor roller coaster. In addition to all the entertainment offered at the mall, there are four anchor department stores and over 400 specialty shops. This mall competes with Disney World and the Grand Canyon as a major tourist attraction, drawing more than forty million domestic and foreign travelers each year.

stores have traditionally served as **anchor stores** for the malls. These are large retail centers that attract considerable numbers of people, and are located at the ends of the mall (hence the term "anchor"). Today, however, other formats are adopting the anchor role, for example, Borders Books, which is a "big box store." The remainder of the mall generally consists of specialty and/or chain stores. As discussed in the previous section, the mall has become the shopping destination as people go to the mall, rather than to individual stores, to shop. The Mall of America outside Minneapolis is a good example of this because it includes not only Macy's, Bloomingdale's, Nordstrom, and Sears as anchor stores, plus many small retail stores, but also a full amusement park for the family. In urban settings, we

Figure 1.7 Trump Tower, a vertical mall in Manhattan, encompasses upscale retail establishments, as well as other businesses, and a luxury apartment complex located above the mall.

are seeing more vertical malls that consist of multiple shopping levels. Examples are Water Tower Place in Chicago, San Francisco Center, and Trump Tower in New York.

An increase in **factory outlet malls** that sell factory overruns and/or seconds and irregulars is also occurring today. Malls and shopping centers have similar concerns and problems to retailers in attracting a certain target market and the need for appropriate promotion. *Case 3, Where Did All the People Go?* describes an unsuccessful mall that is considering a change of format to the popular outlet mall concept.

Another trend in the 1990s is the revitalizing of **strip centers,** or neighborhood shopping centers, as they are luring such national retailers as Ann Taylor and Gap. Strip centers, sometimes called "string streets" or "strip malls," are composed of a relatively small number of stores set beside each other, with the largest tenant perhaps a grocery store, variety store, or drugstore. Usually the remainder of the stores are convenience stores. These strip centers are not enclosed as are larger malls. However, as regional mall construction slows and rents stay high, retailers are finding viable opportunities in new and remerchandised strip centers. Another change in some of these centers is the trend toward category killers and big box stores replacing small specialty stores. These big stores bring increased traffic to centers that had found it hard to compete with larger, neighboring, enclosed centers. Additionally, some anchor department stores have eliminated some categories and changed their merchandise selection as they rethink how this type of competition affects them.

International Retailing

Successful U.S. retailers are going global—that is, opening stores internationally. As the world becomes smaller and as the U.S. market becomes saturated with retailers in an already very over-stored environment, companies are looking to overseas markets as a way to increase their business. As some companies expand by merging or taking over other companies, others grow simply through internal growth, and international expansion is a natural growth step. Sears and J.C. Penney Company, Inc. (JCPenney) have been international for many years, with Sears

Figure 1.8 Outlet malls, composed of factory outlets of many well-known manufacturers such as Adidas, and retail-manufacturers such as Ann Taylor, are becoming popular throughout the U.S. This highly successful outlet mall (Woodbury Common) is located 30 minutes outside of New York City and is designed with stand-alone buildings, which give the effect of a small village. Along with the many outlet stores, there are also restaurants and other services including a bank with ATMs.

having a very different and chic image in Mexico. Gap has stores in Great Britain and Canada, Barney's in Japan, and Ralph Lauren in Europe. Levi Strauss has used European markets as testing grounds for such domestic action as their recent opening of Levi's stores in the U.S. Similarly, we see more and more Japanese and European retailers in the U.S. Also overseas investors are buying parts or all of such American companies as Brooks Brothers, Saks Fifth Avenue, Talbot's, and Ann Taylor.

Normally market research is done in an international location before opening a new store, just as it is done at home, and local preferences are taken into consideration. However, some retail formats successfully "export" to other countries intact with few if any changes from their U.S. formula because other countries prefer the American format. Williams-Sonoma and Toys "R" Us are examples (Williams-Sonoma's Tokyo store is slightly smaller in size because of high rent.) To succeed in international markets a domestic company usually

needs a proven, well-developed business, the commitment to adapt to the local environment, recruiting and training local employees, and the necessary capital for this type of expansion. Category killers are thought of as having real potential for international success. Mexico, Europe, and Asia are the areas holding the most opportunities for U.S. companies.

Mergers and Integration

Mergers and diversification are common to sustain or enhance sales growth. Mergers are arranged combinations of business. They can take the form of horizontal or vertical integration. **Horizontal integration** can be thought of as one company buying or forming another company that is different than its customer or supplier. Horizontal mergers can include specialization and diversification mergers. Specialization mergers combine like businesses. The 1980s brought a plethora of mergers. For example, The Limited's acquisitions in the 1980s include Henri Bendel, Victoria's Secret, Lane Bryant, Lerner New York, and Abercrombie & Fitch. R.H. Macy bought I. Magnin and Bullock's from Federated; next, Federated bought all of R.H. Macy; and then Federated bought Broadway Stores, which owned Emporium, Broadway, and Weinstock's. In the 1980s, Broadway Stores were called Carter Hawley Hale, which owned Neiman Marcus, among other specialty stores. It's hard to keep track of who owns what at any time. Diversification mergers take place with a combination of different types of companies, such as Kmart and Waldenbooks. Another example of this type of merger (which was not successful) is Mobil Oil buying Montgomery Ward many years ago. After attempts to make Montgomery Ward profitable, Mobil sold the company. Often there are disastrous results when a retailer is bought by a non-retail company as they have no experience managing a retail-type of business. Another example of this is Hooker (an Australian company) that purchased Bonwit Teller, which Hooker eventually closed.

Amongst all the merger mania, the mid-1990s brought a sudden turnaround with The Limited spinning off three major divisions. This was fol-

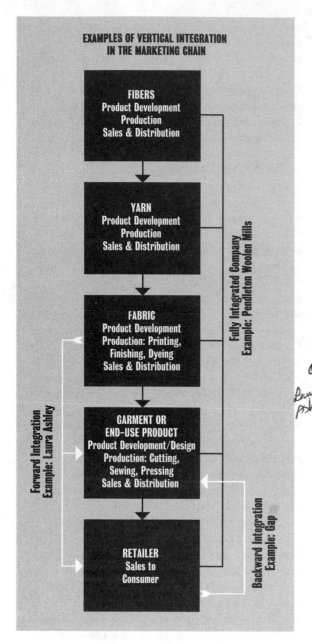

EXAMPLES OF VERTICAL INTEGRATION
IN THE MARKETING CHAIN

FIBERS
Product Development
Production
Sales & Distribution

YARN
Product Development
Production
Sales & Distribution

FABRIC
Product Development
Production: Printing,
Finishing, Dyeing
Sales & Distribution

**GARMENT OR
END-USE PRODUCT**
Product Development/Design
Production: Cutting,
Sewing, Pressing
Sales & Distribution

RETAILER
Sales to
Consumer

Fully Integrated Company
Example: Pendleton Woolen Mills

Forward Integration
Example: Laura Ashley

Backward Integration
Example: Gap

Figure 1.9 Three examples of vertical integration in the apparel/retail industry are shown in this diagram. Developing private-label merchandise to sell in Gap's retail stores is an example of backward integration. Laura Ashley, an illustration of forward integration, added retail stores as a vehicle to sell products that the company designs (including the design and production of their fabric). Pendleton Mills is fully integrated as it is responsible for all levels of production and distribution from fiber to retail store.

lowed by Melville also splitting into three divisions, and Kmart shedding its specialty stores. Retailers in the mid-1990s cleaned house and shed less profitable units. For example, Federated closed I. Magnin soon after their R.H. Macy buyout (Macy's owned I. Magnin) and then Federated closed all Broadway Stores upon purchase of that chain. Store closures are a retailing fact of life in the 1990s and are anticipated to continue into the next century as companies become more streamlined, keeping only profitable units. Additionally, this type of downsizing often occurs before or after entering a Chapter 11 bankruptcy situation.

Vertical integration is another form of merger or diversification. Horizontal integration is generally more common in the apparel industry; however, there is a tendency for companies to become more vertical as this type of integration helps to increase margin, as profits are kept in-house. Vertical integration involves a company acquiring another company or developing a function that serves as either its supplier or its customer. When it serves as its supplier, it is called **backward integration;** when serving as its customer, it is called **forward integration** (see Figure 1.9). As an example of backward integration, The Limited acquired Mast Industries, which manufactures The Limited's apparel. Forward integration is when manufacturers have retail outlets for their products. Levi's opening their own retail stores is an example of this trend. There is also a tendency for smaller manufacturers to open their own retail outlets. ABS USA, a Los Angeles bridge sportswear firm, has ten stores in California, New York, and New Jersey. One of the main functions of the retail store is to test market a collection. Some manufacturers have only one retail store because they want to stay close to their customer. An example of this is Japanese Weekend, a small San Francisco maternity apparel company, which has one retail store in the downtown area. Some manufacturers open stores in the upper-end markets to provide a presence, thereby enhancing their image. Leon Max, David Dart, and Rampage are other California wholesale companies that are opening retail stores.

As designers have become more and more disillusioned with department store presentations and operations, they have begun opening their own retail stores too. Opening their own retail locations affords designers complete control of the presentation of their merchandise to the public. Armani has opened his EmporioArmani shops across the country and a limited number of his Armani boutiques; others include Ralph Lauren, Calvin Klein, Todd Oldham, Anna Sui, Jean-Paul Gaultier, Gianni Versace, and many other European designers as evidenced by boutiques on Rodeo Drive in Beverly Hills and Madison Avenue in New York City. In addition to designers opening their own boutiques, designers and manufacturers are also opening factory outlet stores in outlet malls across the country, as mentioned earlier. This 1980s craze is "settling down" in the 1990s because consumers often do not see the deep discounts that they expected. However, like the upper-end boutiques, the manufacturer/designer has an opportunity to offer a full range of their lines with merchandise presentation under their control. Of course, their original purpose was to create an outlet for overruns and seconds.

Private-Label Merchandising

A major phenomenon in the fashion business is the blending or blurring of retailing and manufacturing. In addition to manufacturers becoming retailers as they develop their own retail formats, retailers are also becoming manufacturers with their private label development. Examples of this are The Limited and Gap as they sell only their private labels. Private-label development is a form of vertical integration as the retailer becomes the manufacturer and eliminates the buying level from the business. Gap eliminated Levi Strauss as a vendor when Gap went to a completely private-label operation. The Limited has carried some vendors in their larger stores when they have experimented with new looks, but as a rule they sell exclusively The Limited-labels, which are often interpretations or knockoffs of popular European styles. This private-label concept has become increasingly popular and an important part of department store inventories. Macy's Charter Club, Nordstrom's NOL (Nordstrom's Own Label), and BP (Brass Plum) are examples of successful private labels. See *Case 7, The Limited Knows No Global Bounds,* for an example of private-label development.

Summary
Retailers are classified by ownership, merchandise mix, and selection. They can be stored or non-stored, carry general goods to very specific niche merchandise, and cater to upper-end or mass markets. Trends include an increase in global retailers, large specialized category killers, and integrated companies. Also, small independent formats are closing due to strong competition from both chain stores and category killers.

References
Anderson, A. (1994). *Retailers on retailing: Lessons from the school of experience (International trends in retailing).* New York: Arthur Anderson & Co.

Department stores: Losing the battle to keep it simple. (1995, October 5). *WWD*, pp. 1, 8–10.

Dickerson, K. (1995). *Textiles and apparel in the global economy.* Englewood Cliffs, N.J.: Prentice-Hall.

Entertainment anchors: New mall headliners. (1989, August). *Chain Store Age Executive,* pp. 54–65.

Malkin, N. (1994, July 24). L.A.'s vertical retailers. *WWD*, pp. 8–9.

Reda, S. (1994, November). Global expansion: Will retailers get burned? *Stores,* pp. 20–24.

Reda, S. (1995, May). Do power centers make sense? *Stores,* pp. 20–26.

Reda, S. (1995, June). When vendors become retailers. *Stores,* pp. 18-21.

Reitman, J. (1994). *Beyond 2000: The Future of Direct Marketing,* Lincolnwood, IL.: NTC Business Books.

Specialty shops—Is the shift booming to landslide? (1989, March 27). *Inside Retailing (A special report from Inside Retailing),* pp. 1–2.

Specialty stores under siege. (1995, September). *WWD, A business newsletter for specialty stores,* pp. 1, 3.

The great mall makeover. (1995, August 19). *WWD*, pp. 8–9.

Top 100 retailers. (1996, July). *Stores*, pp. S2–S24.

Top 100 specialty stores. (1996, August). *Stores*, pp. S3–S23.

Key Terms

anchor store

backward integration

big box store

boutique

catalog showroom

category killer

chain

corporation

department store

destination store

direct marketing

discount store

door-to-door selling

factory outlet

factory outlet mall

forward integration

franchise

home parties

horizontal integration

independent store

kiosk

mail order

mass merchandiser

mom and pop store

off-price store

partnership

SIC (Standard Industrial Classification) codes

specialty (or limited assortment) store

sole proprietorship

strip center

temporary retailer

variety store

vertical integration

warehouse store

Case 1
The Fuller Brush Company: Rediscovering the Magic

James W. Camerius, Northern Michigan University

Once upon a time, not too long ago, a doorbell would ring almost anywhere in America, a housewife would answer it, and there would stand a well-groomed, smiling gentleman. "I'm your Fuller Brush Man," he would say, stepping back deferentially. "And I have a gift for you."

The Fuller Brush Man has been around since 1906, but he hasn't been knocking on many doors recently. The sales force of The Fuller Brush Company, 30,000 in the 1950s, had dropped to 10,000 by the 1990s. Market penetration was less than 1%, while company research showed that more than 80% of all Americans knew who the Fuller Brush Man was. The company that instituted door-to-door selling of fine quality brushes and household cleaning products over 90 years ago was rebuilding its sales force and changing its marketing strategy. In 1991, management announced that it was abandoning door-to-door sales in favor of a word-of-mouth network similar to that used by competitors like Avon and Amway.

The Company and Its Products
In 1995, the Fuller Brush Company, Inc. had corporate offices, and manufacturing and distribution facilities in Great Bend, Kansas. It made over 425 different products, including household and commercial cleaning chemicals, brushes, brooms, mops, and personal care products. The business was divided into industrial and consumer divisions. In the consumer division, it had more than 100 trademarks in the U.S., Canada, and Puerto Rico and sold products under such brand names as

"Fuller Life" and "Oceanesce." Products were sold to consumers though independent sales representatives, mail order catalogs, and retail outlet stores.

In the industrial division of the business, Fuller manufactured high quality, industrial strength cleaning and janitorial products for use in restaurant and food service establishments, rest room sanitation, and other specialty cleaning applications. These products were sold exclusively through janitorial supply, paper supply, and food distributors. The company also produced high quality, engineered brushes. It had the capability of manufacturing any of its products on a private-label basis, and had contracts to supply other large companies in the household and personal care industries.

The Legacy of Alfred C. Fuller

The Fuller Brush Company was founded as the Capital Brush Company in 1906 by Alfred C. Fuller (1885–1973), a 21-year-old entrepreneur from Nova Scotia. The company was an instant success with sales amounting to $8,500 at the end of that first year. The firm was producing 32 different types of mops and brooms. Fuller's credo was: "Make it work. Make it last. Guarantee it no matter what." His early influence was considered "mystifying" and continued to inspire the management team in "building upon Fuller's 90-year reputation as a pioneer of the direct selling industry and developing and executing a strategy for the company's growth in the upcoming decades." Operating on an initial capital of $400, Fuller turned out brushes in the basement of his sister's New England home on a machine he had designed. He made brushes at night and sold them door-to-door by day.

In the next two decades sales grew exponentially, rising from $87,000 in 1916 to $800,000 in 1918. By the 1920s, the firm had established the identity of "The Fuller Brush Man." In 1922, Norman Rockwell painted the Fuller Brush Man for a *Saturday Evening Post* magazine cover. In the years that followed, the character appeared in several popular comic strips, including "Blondie," "Mutt and Jeff," and "Mickey Mouse." He inspired Arthur Miller to write, "Death of a Salesman." "The Fuller Brush Man" and "The Fuller Brush

Woman," starring Red Skelton and Lucille Ball respectively, were featured attractions at the movies. Sales volume was $15 million in 1923.

The firm grew despite the fact that many small towns and suburban communities near major metropolitan areas enacted ordinances to protect local merchants by regulating or forbidding door-to-door selling. The first such ordinance was enacted in Green River, Wyoming, in 1933; hence all comparable enactments by municipalities became known as "Green River" ordinances. While constituting a local problem for some Fuller representatives, such local laws did not limit the use of door-to-door selling as a strategy by the firm on a national basis.

Fuller was credited in 1948 by the *New Yorker* magazine with pioneering the concept of door-to-door selling. As a form of non-store marketing, door-to-door selling is a marketing strategy that uses salespeople to make sales at the consumer's residence (or sometimes place of work) rather than in a retail outlet.

When Fuller's oldest son Howard joined the company, he made a number of changes. As president, Howard Fuller built a machine shop that handled millions of dollars of subcontracts during World War II. He expanded the product line to include a total of 200 items, from a basic stock of brushes to toiletries, vitamins, and household chemicals. He also introduced a short-lived female sales force known as "Fullerettes." With a mixture of pride and regret, Alfred C. Fuller later recounted how Howard had elbowed him aside to take over active direction of the company and then did away with many of his original ideas. Howard was killed in an automobile accident in 1959 and another son, Arvard F. Fuller then became president.

Two Decades of Changing Hands

Sales, which had reached a low of $5 million in 1932, had rebounded to $15 million by 1939 and reached $109 million by 1960. In December, 1968, the Sara Lee Corporation (then operating as Consolidated Foods, Inc.) purchased the Fuller Brush Company from the family. Four years later, the manufacturing plant was moved from Hartford, Connecticut, to a new facility in Great Bend,

Kansas. Six different chief executives were to lead the firm while it was under Sara Lee control. Each tried something different to update the organization; however, none led it to the success it once had and Sara Lee Corporation announced its intent to divest itself of Fuller in 1989. The following year it was sold to Fuller Industries, which felt there was potential in the Fuller name and put in place the investment support necessary for a vision of a dynamic new organization.

In 1990, Fuller sales/marketing offices were moved to Boulder, Colorado. W. Steven Coggin, whose experience included a seventeen-and-a-half-year career at Avon Products, Inc., became executive vice president. While at Fuller, Coggin put emphasis on coordinating the marketing strategies of the firm. The retail stores operated by the firm were remerchandised, an existing catalog was revised, the pricing strategy was changed, several new products were introduced, and major new incentive and motivational programs were launched for sales representatives. The basic theme, "It's Fuller & You Together in a Whole New Light," was used as a motivating message for the national sales conference.

The mission of Fuller Brush was a management statement of corporate purpose: "To generate profit and provide opportunity and growth for all Fuller associates by meeting the needs of our customers through quality products and services. The scope of our marketplace will be limited only by our associates' creativity." The charge, as management perceived it, was to revitalize this legend in American business. Steven Coggin noted, "The goal is to turn Fuller into a totally contemporary and 20th-century company." Coggin left Fuller in late 1990 to become executive vice president of Melaleuca, Inc., another direct selling organization.

John Aplin, a former academic, was named president and chief executive officer of Fuller in the fall of 1990. Aplin's first goal toward boosting revenues at the company would be to revitalize the firm's direct selling force. Plans were put in place to expand the product line of cleaning products, personal care items, and giftware; however, John Aplin sought employment elsewhere in early 1991.

Stuart A. Ochiltree, former president of the direct sales group at Avon Products, Inc., was appointed president and chief executive officer in January, 1991. As part of a plan to bring the company into the 21st century, Ochiltree's challenge was "to build upon Fuller's 90-year reputation as a pioneer of the direct selling industry and to develop and execute a strategy for the company's growth in the upcoming decades." Ochiltree referred to the changes as a "renaissance." He had a five-point plan:

1. "Only the Best" was emphasized. It called for a narrowing of the product line to focus on superior quality, environmentally safe brushes, and home-care products. Perfume, gifts, and jewelry were eliminated. The product line would be reduced from some 300 to 70 different products within a year.

2. "A New Image" was instituted where consumers would see "a new look, new prices, and a new focus on helpful problem solving information." In October, 1991, the company issued a new catalog/sales brochure entitled, "Enjoy the Fuller Life."

3. "Restoring the Tradition of Service" enhanced customer service by putting more emphasis on sales representative training programs and introducing an "800" number for increased customer feedback. The Fuller Homecare Institute also was launched as a clearinghouse of information on cleaning up spills and stains, and to position Fuller in customers' minds as "America's cleaning expert."

4. "An Opportunity to Grow," a new marketing plan and commission structure, was developed to increase the earning opportunities for sales representatives. It was one of marketing's most controversial approaches, a multilevel sales structure or "network marketing" as Ochiltree preferred to call it. Representatives earned commissions not only from product sales, but also from signing up other representatives. Distributors who get in at the top can earn handsome incomes just by selling start-up kits to new recruits. They receive a portion of the proceeds when their recruits sign up new people. Similar plans were successful in other direct selling organizations, for example, Amway International, Avon, Mary Kay Cosmetics, and

Tupperware. "The traditional door-to-door system basically had its day in the 1950s, 1960s, and perhaps the 1970s," said Stuart Ochiltree. "We believe [network marketing] is the only way to achieve the kind of expansion that Fuller needs," he noted.

5. "Integrated Access" called for the integration of the alternative distribution channels that Fuller had used to reach consumers. Consumers would have access to Fuller products and service "whenever and however" they wanted them.

Ochiltree explained how this five-point plan was directly relevant to current dominant consumer trends. "Today's consumers are looking for products and companies they know and trust," he noted. The charge, as management perceived it, was to revitalize this legend in American business. The company had sales of $50 million in 1990. By 1994, sales had dropped to $26.6 million.

In October of 1994, Fuller Brush Co. was sold to CPAC, Inc., a N.Y. manufacturer and seller of prepackaged chemical formulations, supplies, and equipment systems to the imaging industry. CPAC's strategic goal was to become a world leader in the manufacture, packaging, and distribution of specialty chemicals. In January, 1995, CPAC management also signed an agreement to license the trademarks and formulas of Stanley Home Products. Similar to the Fuller Brush line, Stanley's products included 250 different cleaning and personal care items, sold through a network of 16,000 distributors via a "hostess" or "party plan." Stanley had over 50 trademarks in the U.S., Canada, and Puerto Rico. The Fuller and Stanley acquisitions were a major step toward diversification by CPAC and "continuing with its successful strategy of emphasizing the growth of consumable product lines and seeking expanded marketing avenues." CPAC, Inc.'s net sales for the fiscal years ending March 31, 1993, 1994, and 1995 were $39.9 million, $43.8 million, and $58.6 million.

Direct Marketing Industry

Sales from direct selling to homes showed little or no growth throughout the 1980s. Major issues that impacted the marketplace included many more women entering the labor force and the rise in the crime rate in urban areas. People had become more and more concerned about their safety and security, and in many cases, if the customer was home, he or she wouldn't open the door to strangers. Therefore, the company experimented with other types of distribution. In 1987, when Fuller was owned by the Sara Lee Corporation, a mail-order catalog was published, but was discontinued three years later. Also in 1987, the first Fuller Brush retail store opened in Mesquite, Texas, and eventually the firm opened seven stores in factory outlet malls. In some cases, however, these proved to be unprofitable, as well as detrimental to the morale and effectiveness of the field representatives in the areas where the stores existed. "In order to try to push sales, management entered into an aggressive price-cutting program in the stores," noted Steven Coggin. "They ultimately cut prices in the stores to the point where representatives in the area could buy products from the stores cheaper than they could buy from the company." Even a maid service called Dallas Dusters was instituted. After several years of experimenting with various forms of distribution and services, the company decided to focus on basic direct selling.

The sales representative's compensation is straight commission. It varies from 35 to 50 percent of sales. "Even the most gung-ho representative is lucky to bring home $20,000 a year, hardly an awe-inspiring income for the 1990s," indicated CEO Ochiltree. Also, traditional turnover rates of 100% or more annually have continued to plague the company.

In 1991, the profile of a Fuller representative was similar to that of an Avon sales representative: a woman, 30 years or older, with an average household income of $40,000. Additionally, the company has increased its efforts to develop opportunities with the Hispanic and African-American communities, as well as women and couples.

Currently, Fuller competes with other direct marketers and firms manufacturing similar items which are sold in retail stores. It also competes in the recruiting of independent salespersons from other direct selling organizations. In 1995, the total domestic market for cleaning and personal care products grew to an estimated $37 billion. The personal care products alone were estimated at $21.5 billion annually. Sales of consumer (household) cleaning products were approximately $10 billion, and brushes and brooms comprised roughly $.2 billion in sales. Fuller's key competitors are Avon and Amway, with worldwide sales volume of $3.9 billion and $3.2 billion respectively. These are followed by Tupperware at $1.2 billion and Mary Kay at $600 million, compared with Fuller at $26 million.

Like so many other direct selling companies, Fuller does not have a lot of information on its ultimate consumers. Management does know, however, that the customer is traditionally over 35 years of age. Corporate experience with the catalog shows that there is a large number of people out there who want Fuller products and can't get them, but were delighted to find a Fuller Brush catalog in their mail. Steven Coggin concluded that "Fuller Brush had been stranding customers for 25 years." People know and remember the company, know the quality of its products, but do not know how or where to buy Fuller products.

Major Question

What recommendations would you suggest to aid and assist in revitalizing Fuller Brush?

Study Questions

1. Review the marketing strategy of The Fuller Brush Company. What can management expect to gain by changing from a strategy employing door-to-door selling to one which used Ochiltree's terms, "network marketing"?

2. Identify and discuss the characteristics and degree of involvement in the alternative marketing strategies used or considered by Fuller Brush management other than direct selling.

3. Review the changes in today's marketing environment that may impact Fuller Brush marketing strategy in the future.

4. If you were a sales representative of the firm, what changes in the business would you expect from a change in leadership of the company? If you were a customer how would you interpret it? Suggest forms of leadership that might give more direction to the organization.

References

Berg, E.N. (1989, May 18). At Fuller Brush, new ways to get foot in the door. *New York Times,* p. 1.

Coggin, W.S. (1990, August 23). Interview with executive vice president, Fuller Brush Company: Boulder, CO.

Hannon, K. (1986, October 20). A foot in the door. *Forbes,* pp. 134+.

Howard, N. (1975, August 25). Can ailing Fuller Brush Co. revive that oldtime magic? *Advertising Age,* pp. 49–50+.

Kiley, D. (1987, September 7). Fuller Brush Co.: Modernity knocks. *Adweek's Marketing Week,* p. 20.

Knock, knock no more. (1992, February 3). *Time,* p. 43.

Case 2
Creative Wear's Short Life

Connie Ulasewicz, CU Productions
Nancy J. Rabolt, San Francisco State University

Creative Toys is a successful private company in California owned and founded by Suzanne Montgomery. Her philosophy is to provide for the whole child and to help the child develop self-esteem by producing enjoyable and educational products. These products are made in the U.S., are unconditionally guaranteed, and can be returned by customers for any reason. Toys are sold only through home parties and catalogs, which are distributed by independent "customer representatives" similar to

Avon and Amway. Company representatives buy samples to show and demonstrate to customers at the parties. Creative Toys carry a high price point, are of high quality claiming to last "forever," and are available only through this distribution avenue. The Creative Toy customer is willing to pay high prices. Typically, she is a grandmother with high discretionary income or a mother who wants products for her children that are educational, good quality, and unique or special. She is not a Toys "R" Us customer, but is a savvy shopper who recognizes high quality and good value.

Suzanne felt her customer would be a good prospect for high-quality children's apparel, a similar market to Hanna Andersson (an upper-end Swedish catalog carrying high-quality, functional children's apparel). The apparel could be sold in the same venues as the toys. Because the apparel business is in many ways different from the toy business, Suzanne hired Heather Hilstead and Jasmine Jones, consultants with extensive apparel production experience, to advise her on this new apparel end of the business. Suzanne wanted the following aspects incorporated into her apparel lines:

- A similar markup to what is achieved in her toy business (a 72 percent markup).

- The same type of educational element for the clothes as the toys have.

- Special or unique qualities in the clothes to satisfy her savvy customer.

Suzanne did not want her very visible Creative Toys logo to be incorporated into the apparel line because she was afraid that if the apparel line was unsuccessful, by association it could damage the good reputation of Creative Toys. She was not willing to take this risk, so a new name and logo, Creative Wear, was developed for the apparel line.

Even though her customer is used to paying high prices for the toys, Suzanne wanted a lower-price point in the apparel because her customer, who is a smart shopper, is aware of the competition in the apparel business (e.g., department stores, discount stores, off-price stores, factory stores, and so forth). Therefore, prices on the apparel needed to be comparable to the local retail store competition but lower than would be expected relative to the high toy prices. However, Suzanne is used to a high markup in her toy business and she demanded a comparable markup in the apparel line. To beat the retail store competition, Suzanne wanted special features in the clothes such as a gusset in each shirt for easier maneuverability for active children and a special jacquard (patterned) knit collar rather than a plain, solid collar. A tab system, similar to the Sears "Geranimal" concept, was incorporated into the garments so children could mix and match appropriate pieces. Also, instead of screen printing patterns directly onto plain T-shirts, Suzanne had screen prints specially made and appliquéd onto the T-shirts, a feature found in higher quality apparel. Many items also had appliquéd logo patches.

The apparel collection consisted of two separate lines: one for boys and one for girls. The boy's line had pants, shorts, T-shirts, polo shirts, jackets, and a licensed cap and socks. The girl's line included jumpers, dresses, shorts, pants with a feminine ankle bow, T-shirts, and vests.

Similar to toy samples, sales reps purchased apparel samples. These were in the form of "kits." Suzanne had a full-time merchandiser who planned the lines and the kits. Reps did not buy samples of all garments in the catalog; the kits merely gave a representative look of the collection. For example, a kit might include one color of shorts, T-shirt, and jacket. The company provided all reps with fabric swatches of four solid colors and two prints along with sketches of other items produced by a CAD (computer-aided design) system. Reps were not required to purchase the sample kits, but some did. Many felt the fabric samples, CAD sketches, and catalog pictures were sufficient to show customers, especially in the light of the added costs the reps would have to incur to purchase the kits.

Developing the catalog to include the apparel line was problematic because the photo shoot for apparel had to be scheduled far earlier than the toys. The apparel shoots had to wait until all the various pieces arrived from the different manufacturing sites. Toy styles didn't change often; therefore, many toy pictures were reused in new catalogs. On the other hand, the apparel line was more demanding because color pallets change each season necessitating new shoots for each season.

To keep prices down and to achieve Suzanne's required markup, Heather and Jasmine sourced the jackets in Peru, T-shirts in Los Angeles, and the pants and jumpers in Mexico. As a result, pieces came into the warehouse at different times. After all the pieces arrived, workers assembled the items into packages to be sent to the customer representatives. The warehouse, which was set up for toys that all came in as a unit at one time, had to be rearranged to accommodate the apparel kit assembly, which was also a time-consuming process. Additionally, there was a scheduling problem for the warehouse. The toy business is essentially a Christmas business with December the busiest time in the warehouse. The Spring apparel line required a January delivery of the apparel sample kits to reps. This necessitated a December 15th delivery date to the warehouse so that kit assembly could be accomplished. This definitely interfered with the normal smooth operations of the toy distribution at the warehouse.

Manufacturers were very pleased to produce the apparel sample line because it was easy: one size (size 4), one color and a large order. The problem was that the reps didn't buy the sample kits as anticipated, leaving the company with a huge inventory of a one-color/one-size product. However, after the reps showed the samples and pictures to customers, they loved the line. Orders came in, and the production had a great sellthrough, with a 62 percent markup, appearing very successful. Especially successful were the higherend products with special features. But the sample making was a losing proposition. After two seasons of production, Suzanne decided to discontinue the extensive apparel line and concentrate on the toys.

Major Question

What could Suzanne have done differently in the planning, merchandising, and production of Creative Wear to ensure more success?

Study Questions

1. What should Suzanne do with the huge sample inventory?

2. What potential problems are there in combining toys and apparel in the same company? How are they the same and how are they different?

Case 3
Where Did All the People Go?

K. Denise Threlfall, Old Dominion University

Westridge Mall, generally busy in the 1980s, has endured a huge decline in business from 1988 to the present. After watching an anchor store close because of bankruptcy, satellite merchants began leaving the mall property, too. A major renovation was conducted, and the updated mall itself is a beautiful complex, complete with a historic carousel and a small food court on the second level. Still, many nationally recognized retailers (such as The Limited, Casual Corner, and Gap) found it necessary to pack up and leave their spaces in this mall because business continued to decline. This retail space has often been referred to as a "third mall in a two-mall market," and nothing that has been attempted by mall management seems to bring the consumer base back to its original success level.

Currently, the mall has over a 50 percent vacancy rate of the over one hundred lease spaces available within the structure. Another major anchor (a large regional department store) recently left the property, leaving only one general merchandise retailer in the anchor position. This retailer owns its space, rather than leasing it, and will probably stay in the mall no matter what evolves around them. Many of the newest stores to lease space are "mom and pop" single entrepreneurial ventures, and these retailers are lured in by the cheaper lease rates. Their offerings are unique and often serve only a limited consumer target market. This has left Westridge Mall with a very poor retail image, and many consumers choose to drive quite a distance past this area just to shop at other regional malls, shopping centers, and factory outlets. The mall property has lost almost all of its regular customer base and cannot compete with the other malls in market share.

After contracting with a market research team, Westridge's mall management realized they were servicing a greatly diversified group of consumers who were frequenting the mall. A large majority of those who regularly shopped or dined during the daytime hours were older adults. The most prevalent themes emerging from this market segment were issues of limited disposable income and safety concerns. Others identified as patrons of this center were mothers with small children, because the historic carousel rides are a selling point to entertain their little ones. Very few young adults or couples were surveyed in this sample of over eight hundred, and this relatively absent market segment was hypothesized as possibly the missing link to the mall's success. There wasn't any specific thing identified to bring this consumer group into the area and entice them to spend their money. Mall management then found themselves with a dilemma—how to keep the older customer population satisfied (without compromising their perceived safety level) while still attracting the young adult consumer.

Additional demographic findings from the market research revealed that Westridge Mall borders two cities with major military populations in each one. These transient groups have often been blamed for the mall's decline, although other area retailers realize their patronage as a means of steady income. Also within a few miles of the mall is the state's largest employer—a shipbuilding and repair business. Thousands of shipyard employees and their families live and work within a ten-mile radius of this mall, yet these employees do not contribute to the mall traffic. With numerous consumer opportunities to capture, there still hasn't been any significant increase in customer traffic at this retail "ghost town" mall.

Although there is a four-screen movie theater within Westridge Mall, there is still no other apparent family entertainment draw to this facility. Four fast-food retailers are included in the mall's food court, with three of the outlets owned and operated by the same individual. Competition for the food offerings is nonexistent. Thus, prices are high and choices are limited. The surrounding area near the mall mainly consists of used car dealers and furniture stores. Most family restaurants in the area—with the exception of fast-food retailers—also closed their establishments after the mall began its consumer decline. Unfortunately, this leaves Westridge Mall in an unsupported retail area with no apparent draw to consumer traffic. Family entertainment opportunities or sports-related concepts were suggested by those surveyed as a way to provide the area with a possible surge in the local and tourist retail customer base.

Major Question
As the marketing management for this retail property, what would you do to improve Westridge Mall's success?

Study Questions
1. Based on the trends in retailing today, what would be the most appropriate format choice for this mall to rebuild consumer traffic, considering space utilization, demographics, and existing structure modifications?

2. What promotional and/or merchandising activities should be employed by mall management to match the current retail format, and how will these enhance the customer base as well as overcome the existing negative retail image?

3. What other successful format changes would be appropriate for the surrounding retail area? How would they complement the choices previously made for the mall in question 1? What issues would have to be considered? Are these ideas actually possible, considering the current situation?

Case 4
Mike Young: The Dynamics of Independent Retailing

Sandra Skinner Grunwell, Western Carolina University

Mike Young felt fortunate that, during his last semester in college, Jane Weiss, a friend who had known him for years, asked him to enter into a joint venture in opening Joffree's, a privately owned apparel store. Throughout college, Mike had been employed by a men's specialty store and over a four-year period had worked his way up to assistant manager. In addition, he had done the store's displays each week and assisted in buying merchandise.

As part of their agreement, Jane Weiss, an accountant for the past 20 years, would provide the financial backing for the business venture and would handle its financial operation. Mike's major responsibilities would include buying, merchandising the store, and promotions. Mike would also oversee the renovation of the store site. They both agreed to co-manage the business and to split the profits 60/40 (Jane and Mike, respectively). The business was legally formed as a sole proprietorship, although informally it would function as a partnership.

Jane and Mike selected the name, Joffree's, because it had an upscale image, befitting the merchandise to be carried. The store would carry both men's and women's better-quality, fashion-forward merchandise and would cater to the middle to upper-middle income customer. Mike spent untold hours his last semester in school planning the selection of vendors and merchandise for both the men's and women's divisions. When it was time to go to market to make actual selections, Jane went with Mike.

From *Retailing Concepts, Strategy, and Information* (3rd ed.) by Carol Anderson. Reprinted by permission of West Publishing Company. Copyright © 1993. All rights reserved.

They could find the selection there that would meet the needs of their target market. Since Jane was actually funding the venture and she had the accounting background, she felt she should be there to oversee the spending. Also, Jane wanted to gain an understanding of what "shopping the lines" entailed.

Mike informed Jane he preferred to shop the market by spending the first day or two looking over the vendor lines to feel out what was being offered in terms of style, quality, and price. During this process he took notes and picked up any written information vendors had available on their lines. In the evenings he analyzed each vendor's line and decided specifically what he would purchase. He followed this procedure to avoid impulse buying, to avoid buying duplicates, to ensure he purchased a model stock, and to have better control over how much he was spending.

When they arrived at market, Jane was impressed with the professional manner in which Mike handled the purchasing procedure. At first she just observed and listened. However, by the second day Jane was ready to buy and began making some impulse purchases against Mike's wishes. That evening Mike tried to work her purchases into the overall plan he had for merchandising the store. On the third day, Jane was still committing to goods not in the plan.

By the end of the fourth day at market, they had bought significantly more than they had budgeted. Mike feared that this would affect the money allotted to him for the purchase of the men's wear lines. When he confronted Jane regarding these concerns, she told him there was still enough money available to stock the men's department and not to worry. After four very long days at market, they drove home excited about their purchases and turned their thoughts to what needed to be done to renovate the chosen store site.

Because Mike also had a strong background in merchandise display and a good eye for design and layout, Jane left the preparation of the store up to him. Mike was provided a budget to undertake basic renovations including painting, carpet, wall decor, lighting, store facade, signage, fixtures, mannequins, and props. He was excited to be given the freedom and flexibility to design the store and took on the project with much enthusiasm.

When the time came to return to market for the purchase of the men's wear lines, Mike went alone since Jane did not have an interest in its selection. Mike was somewhat intimidated to be going to market totally on his own because he knew his purchase decisions would affect the initial success of the store. However, he was relieved Jane would not be there making impulse decisions and confusing his merchandising plans. Although Mike worked the market as systematically as he had before, previewing the lines before making actual purchases, he missed Jane being there to support him in his decisions. He found himself working late into the evenings on his purchase plans until he was sure of his decisions.

Upon returning home he met with Jane to inform her of how the market had gone and gave her copies of the purchase orders. Then he turned his efforts to renovating the store interior and planning the store's grand opening. He hadn't heard from Jane in over a week, so he decided to give her a call. When she answered, she told him she had been analyzing the expenditures for the men's wear lines and was concerned that Mike had overspent. He reminded her that he had stayed within the agreed budget and that the overspending was in the purchase of women's wear.

Jane responded that she felt they needed to lower initial overhead because they were spending themselves too thin. She told Mike to cancel the men's wear orders and just go with women's wear for the first six months or so, until they saw how things went. Mike was disappointed. Not only had he put many hours into the planning of the men's wear merchandise, it was the area of the store he was to manage. When he expressed his concerns to Jane, she said there would be plenty for the both of them to do managing the women's apparel. Although it would take some rethinking and rearranging of the store interior, Mike knew they had ample merchandise to stock the store because of their overbuying in the women's lines. The next day he called the men's wear vendors and canceled his orders.

Soon the women's wear purchases were arriving at the store and Mike's excitement returned. He stayed at the store round the clock, receiving the merchandise, pressing it, tagging and pricing it, and arranging it on the racks. He prepared ads for the newspaper and radio and planned for the store's grand opening. Besides some special events at the store, a grand opening fashion show and dinner were being sponsored by the local Professional Women's Association. Each person attending would get a gift certificate that could be applied to any purchase at Joffree's.

The store opened June 1, and the customer traffic was exceptional. All of Mike's promotional activities and public relations efforts were paying off. Soon after, the fashion editor of the local newspaper sought them out and did a two-page spread on fashion trends for fall, using their merchandise and giving the store credits. Business boomed through August, then sales began to slow down. At first, neither Mike nor Jane thought much about the decline in sales because September is typically a slow month in retailing. In fact, when Mike went to market in October, Jane relented and allowed him to pursue a line of men's wear. But, October and November remained slow.

To combat the slow days, Jane would, on the spur of the moment, have half-off sales. This bothered Mike because there was no promotion of the sales and regular customers were becoming wary of buying at full price. He felt Jane's half-off sales caused business to suffer even more as regular customers would come in, try on merchandise, and then ask about the next sale. In addition, Jane didn't carry her weight in the store. She came in late, left early, or did not come in at all. Mike had to cover her hours and work his own. In fact, Mike came in early to clean and straighten the store, worked the store 10:00 a.m. to 6 p.m., closed the store, and worked on his merchandise plans in the evening.

As the end of November drew near and Christmas merchandise was arriving, Mike felt the store needed strong promotions to get it back on its feet. He knew December should be the biggest selling month, and he wanted to do what he could to turn around the downward spiral in sales. His efforts seemed to work. December was an excellent month for sales; and, for the first time in months,

Mike was able to draw a full week's salary at the end of December.

January brought mixed news for Mike. H.B. Men's Wear, one of the men's wear manufacturers he had pursued in October, agreed to accept Joffree's as a customer provided the store committed to the required $10,000 minimum order. To make this feasible for Joffree's, H.B. Men's Wear offered lenient payment terms, 2/10, net 90. The merchandise would arrive in February. Jane consented to the vendor terms, and Mike began revamping the store to add the new line.

One afternoon in late January while Mike was managing the store alone, one of his better customers, Eva Hanley, came into the store. As they were chatting, Eva told him she had a business proposal she wanted to discuss with him. She said she had been observing the store's operations for some time and, although she felt the store was teetering between success and failure, she felt Mike was exceptionally qualified to operate a retail business, if given the right backing.

She was interested in opening a combined men's and women's upscale apparel store in a nearby city and would like for him to be her partner. Like Jane's initial offering, Mike would be in charge of buying and merchandising, while Eva, who had been a corporate accountant for the past five years, would provide the financial backing and oversee the financial operation. Both would co-manage the store. The proposed store site was three times the size of Joffree's and would necessitate an assistant buyer, a promotions manager, and a sales staff and would legally incorporate. Mike would be paid an agreed-upon guaranteed salary, written into a contractual agreement.

Mike told Eva he would need to think about her offer and would get back to her within two weeks. When she left, Mike began to wonder if this was the break he needed. The idea of a steady income sounded great after the salary losses he had experienced over the past retail quarter. He would also have a staff to assist with the store's operation. Eva was nearly 20 years younger than Jane and was very interested in maintaining an active role in the

business. The store was a much bigger undertaking, yet he felt he had acquired invaluable experience in opening Joffree's.

Mike decided to make a list of the pros and cons of staying with Joffree's or accepting the proposed offer. That Jane would be left with a $10,000 order from H.B. Men's Wear for which he was responsible weighed on his mind.

Major Question

If you were Mike, would you take Eva up on her offer and why?

Study Questions

1. What are the advantages/disadvantages of working for a small, independently owned store?

2. How would you suggest Mike protect himself from similar problems occurring in the future?

3. How does working for a large and a small store differ?

Case 5
Cironi's Sewing Center Loses a Franchise[1]

Gary B. Frank, University of Akron
J.B. Wilkinson, Youngstown State University

It started out as a beautiful spring day. Tony Cironi had spent the morning servicing sewing machines at East High School. He had deliberately timed his arrival to coincide with a visit to the school by Verna Robbins, educational supervisor of the home economics division of Consolidated School District.

From *Cases and Problems in Contemporary Retailing* by Mason, Mayer, & Ezell. Reprinted by permission of Dame Publications, Inc., Houston, TX. Copyright © 1992. All rights reserved.

[1]The authors wish to thank Bob Barnes, owner of Barnes Sewing Center in Akron, Ohio, for technical information regarding sewing centers.

Over the previous four years, Tony had sold over 500 Elna sewing machines to the school district and now the biggest contract yet was coming up. As part of a special state appropriation, the district had received funding for 150 replacement sewing machines. Tony felt he had an inside track because of his demonstrated ability to perform to contract specifications, and Verna would know when the winning bidder would be announced. Sure enough, as Tony was leaving the building, he saw Verna outside the administrative office. She motioned him over and said, "Tony, I just heard that yours was the winning bid! Congratulations! We think a lot of you here. I'm glad that you're going to get the business!"

After a start like that, what could spoil the day? Tony drove back to his store the long way—through the park. This was a big sale—over $80,000. Even though he had cut his price to rock bottom, he could anticipate a gross profit of $10,000, and ongoing service revenues from the school district would be at least $1,000 a year. But, when he got back to the store and opened his mail, he got the shock of his life—White Sewing Machine Company was canceling his franchise!

A month earlier, Tony and Herb Hanson, the national sales manager for White Sewing Machine, had a major altercation. Herb had just popped in, introduced himself, and initiated a conversation about how to increase sales of White sewing machines. Tony had responded, "How can I? You're distributing the best-selling White sewing machine model to Jo Ann Fabric Stores for $97 a machine while I pay $140." Herb said, "That's a different machine!" That is when Tony blew up. "To hell it's different! It's the same machine! You just slapped a different model number on it, sprayed it a different color, and let Jo Ann Fabrics label it. But customers aren't fooled—Jo Ann Fabric salespeople make sure of that. And why should customers pay $200 at my store for a machine they can get at Jo Ann Fabrics for $149?" The conversation deteriorated after this point, and Herb left in a huff.

Two weeks later, Herb called and asked if he and the new district sales representative could stop by to discuss a new sales strategy for White sewing machines. That afternoon, Herb started off the discussion with a compliment, "Tony, you're doing a great job of selling the Elna sewing machine. No other dealer in the U.S. does as good a job. But, as you know, we only distribute Elna in this area. Our primary concern is the White sewing machine. It is made in Cleveland, Ohio, and customers in this area are very brand loyal to us. We believe that you are not selling as many White sewing machines as you could. You really are not advertising and promoting our machine like you should. Also, you are not carrying our new knitting machine. All dealers are supposed to carry the full product line. So, what we want to do today is work out an advertising campaign for the next six months and get a commitment from you to actively sell our products, including the new knitting machine."

Tony took a deep breath and said, "I do advertise White! And in terms of sales, I push the product as much as I can. I try to treat fairly all the brands I carry. But newspaper advertising in this town is expensive, and some brands are more profitable than others. Also, the advertising I do for Bernina is paid 100 percent by Bernina, up to 3 percent of my gross sales for the brand. You pay only 50 percent of my advertising cost, up to 3 percent of gross sales for the brand. If you want me to increase my advertising for White sewing machines, you should change your policies. As far as the knitting machines go, forget it! I don't sell any knitting machines in the store!"

After this, the meeting broke up. Herb suddenly remembered that he and the new district sales representative had a late afternoon appointment with a prospective new dealer back at the Cleveland office. He told Tony that he would be back within the week.

As Tony read and re-read the letter from White, several thoughts raced through his mind. Although the letter did not give any reason for terminating his franchise, events over the past month provided some clues. Clearly, White Sewing Machine Company felt that he was "short-changing" the White brand of sewing machines. Yet Tony felt that he had been fair to White when allocating the advertising budget. After all, the gross profit margin on a White machine was lower than some of his other brands of machines (see Tables 1.1 and 1.2).

On the other hand, Tony had to admit, even to himself, that he did not sell as many White machines as some of the other dealers in the area (see Table 1.3). Part of the problem had to do with White's practice of supplying Jo Ann Fabrics with a popular machine model for distributor branding. Also, the other dealers that carried White machines often discounted their prices, using White sewing machines as a price leader to generate store traffic. Most of the other sewing machine dealers carried other types of products, such as vacuum cleaners, to make up for what they lost on White. As a result, Tony had been hard pressed to realize a 30 percent gross margin on the White brand. Many customers shopped around and compared prices. If they decided to buy a White machine, they often bought it at a lower price somewhere else, even though the dealer from which they bought could not service or repair sewing machines.

Uppermost in his mind, though, was concern about his *winning* bid for the school district contract. Verna Robbins had specified a sewing machine with the following features: ability to fit into the existing cabinets, a free arm, and a drop-in bobbin. This last feature was an absolute *must* in her mind. Past experiences with students losing a removable bobbin case or switching bobbin cases between machines had convinced her that a drop-in bobbin (stationary bobbin case) was a non-negotiable requirement. A replacement bobbin case typically cost $8.95. Switching bobbin cases between machines usually causes expensive repairs since a bobbin case must be *balanced* for a particular machine. The only machine in his store that could meet these specifications was an Elna model. Consequently, he had put in a bid for 150 Elna machines. But Elna was distributed by White in this area! and, according to the letter from White, his franchise for the White and Elna brand would be canceled within thirty days!

Tony was deeply disturbed. He began to question himself. How could he deliver on his bid if he was no longer a dealer for Elna? How would he get parts to repair the Elna machines that he had already sold the school district? He wondered if White had the legal right to cancel his Elna franchise. If so, should he attempt to re-negotiate his franchise agreement with White? Why would White do this to him? Was it a sound business decision for them? Was it an ethical decision on their part? Or were they just trying to pressure him? He considered his relative power in this situation—after all, he was the largest independent sewing machine dealer in the area. Most importantly, he wondered what he should do now. As Tony pondered these questions, he reached for a copy of his Elna dealer agreement. Both the Elna and White dealer agreements were virtually the same. As he read his dealer agreement, several clauses seemed to leap out at him.

The supplier hereby grants the dealer the nonexclusive right to purchase from supplier for resale to consumers Elna sewing machines and sewing machine parts, supplies, and accessories. Dealer agrees to maintain a stock of current Elna sewing machines and parts, supplies and accessories, and an organization and facility as necessary, in supplier's judgment, to provide adequate and proper sales, sales promotion, and services of Elna products at dealer's location at:

_____.

The term of this agreement shall be of an indefinite duration. This agreement may be terminated by either party upon thirty (30) days' written notice to the other party.

Dealer shall provide prompt, competent, and efficient servicing on all Elna sewing machines sold by it or otherwise brought into its place of business for servicing. Dealer shall comply with warranty servicing policies as published by the supplier and shall provide customer servicing in accordance with the supplier's published procedures for premium sales, educator sales, courtesy sales, and school sales.

The supplier reserves the right from time-to-time to sell and offer to sell Elna sewing machines and sewing machine parts and accessories directly

Table 1.1	Cironi's Advertising Expenditures by Brand	
	$ Expenditures	Percent of Advertising Budget
Baby Lock	$ 3,150	15.0%
Bernina	6,562	31.2
Elna	3,150	15.0
Necchi	1,400	6.7
Pfaff	5,552	26.4
Singer	420	2.0
White	788	3.7
Total	$ 21,022	100.0%

Table 1.2	Gross Profit Margin by Brand
	Gross Profit Percentage
Baby Lock	45.0%
Bernina	50.0
Elna	30.0
Necchi	40.0
Pfaff	45.0
Singer	12.0
White	30.0

in the same general marketing area served by the dealer. The supplier also reserves the right to appoint such sewing machine dealers in the same general marketing area served by the dealer as the supplier, in its discretion, deems desirable.

The dealer is not and shall not be deemed to be a joint venturer, partner, agent, server, employee, fiduciary, or representative of the supplier. The dealer shall conduct its entire business under this agreement at its own cost and expense.

This agreement may be terminated by either party, with or without cause, subject to the applicable provisions of state law, if any, upon thirty (30) days' written notice to the other party. The supplier may terminate this agreement if the dealer shall fail to comply with any of the terms hereof, or if a petition in bankruptcy shall be filed by or against the dealer, or if the dealer shall reorganize or shall make an assignment or conveyance of its property for the benefit of creditors, or if a receiver shall be appointed with authority to take possession of any of the property of the dealer, or if the dealer fails to pay any amount due to the supplier, or if the dealer fails to conform to the business system or the standard of conformity and quality for the products and services promulgated by the supplier in connection with the business system. The termination of this agreement shall not release either party from the payment of any sum then owing to the other.

Table 1.3	Local Area Sales and Market Shares for Household Sewing Machines	
	Sales	Area Market Share
LOCAL AREA DEALERS	$800,000	
Cironi's Sewing Center	300,500	37.6%
White	15,000	1.9
Elna	60,000	7.5
Pfaff[1]	70,500	8.8
Necchi[1]	20,000	2.5
Bernina[1]	75,000	9.4
Baby Lock[1]	40,000	5.0
Singer	20,000	2.5
Akron Sewing Machine	200,100	25.0
White	40,000	5.0
Elna	9,600	1.2
New Home[1]	10,500	1.3
Singer	140,000	17.5
Mollie's Sewing and Knitting Boutique	150,800	18.8
White	40,000	5.0
Elna	10,400	1.3
Riccar[1]	15,400	1.9
Singer	85,000	10.6
Jo Ann Fabrics (4 stores)	148,600	18.6
Singer	81,400	10.2
Distributor Brands[2]	67,200	8.4

[1]*Exclusive dealership.*
[2]*Brands made exclusively for Jo Ann Fabrics by manufacturers (i.e., Sonata made by Singer).*

Major Question

What would you advise Tony to do upon reviewing the cancellation letter from White Sewing Machine Company?

Study Questions

1. Is White making a good business decision?

2. What are the bases of power of White Sewing Machine Company? What are the bases of power of Cironi's Sewing Center? Which party has the most power in this case? Why?

Case 6
Wish Book

Melvin Morgenstein and Harriet Strongin, Nassau Community College

---

On August 2, 1985, Montgomery Ward & Company held a news conference in Chicago. Bernard F. Brennan, president and chief executive officer, announced that Montgomery Ward, the company that had invented the mail order business, was closing its catalog operation. Montgomery Ward would issue its last catalog in December 1985, thus ending 113 years in mail order retailing.

The first mail order catalog was a one-page flyer printed and distributed in Chicago by an enterprising young salesman named Aaron Montgomery Ward. The year was 1872. Lee's surrender at Appomattox had ended the Civil War only seven years earlier. The first transcontinental railroad link was only three years old. Homesteaders were still carving out their farms and ranches in the West, and cowboys were still driving cattle herds north to Abilene, Kansas, along the Chisholm Trail. Custer's Battle of Little Big Horn was still four years in the future.

From *Modern Retailing Management Principles and Practices (3rd ed.)* by Morgenstein and Strongin, eds. Reprinted by permission of Prentice-Hall, Inc., Upper Saddle River, NJ. Copyright © 1992. All rights reserved.

When Ward's first catalog appeared, nearly 75 percent of the U.S. population lived in rural areas. It is nearly impossible today to imagine the isolation and drabness of farm life in the late nineteenth century. The telephone wasn't invented until 1876, the radio not until the 1890s. Roads were poor and travel by horse or on foot was slow. In 1890, only four automobiles were on the road in the United States. The electric light bulb was invented in 1879, but many rural areas went without electricity until the Rural Electrification Assistance Act was established in 1935.

Montgomery Ward's mail order catalogs soon became the mainstay of the farm family. Few of America's small towns had much in the way of retailers, often just a general store or a dry goods store with a very limited selection of merchandise. "Monkey Wards" filled the gap. The great "wish book" provided everything the family needed—including entertainment and a window on the outside world. Between its paper covers, one could find everything from long woolen underwear and whalebone corsets to yard goods for a new dress and, just maybe, a pair of kid-leather shoes.

Of course, the catalog had more than just clothing—the Ward's customer could send away by mail for a plow or a barrel of nails, for a set of china or the latest in ice boxes, for a cradle or a coffin.

For decades, the catalog business flourished, as did Montgomery Ward's chain of retail stores. A century after that first catalog, Montgomery Ward was the sixth-largest retailer in the United States. The company had 365 retail stores, 150 distribution centers, and over 100,000 employees. The twice-a-year catalog had multiplied into 20 separate books each year, with a circulation of 5 million. Catalog operations were supported by nearly 200 company-owned catalog stores and over 1,200 independent catalog sales agencies.

The Montgomery Ward catalog, reflecting its origins, continued to appeal to the small-town and rural customer, even though urban singles and suburban young marrieds had become the major buyers of goods and services. The catalog was still being published as a multiproduct book, with no differentiation by audience. Most of the newer mail order retailers (and there were many) tended to produce specialized catalogs that carried only selected merchandise categories. Even the venerable Spiegel, Inc., made a highly successful move from an all-purpose catalog to a mail order business specializing in apparel and home furnishings.

In 1974, Mobil Oil Company bought Montgomery Ward & Company for $1.7 billion. The acquisition was part of a diversification strategy common among oil companies at the time. What Mobil bought, according to some analysts, was a dinosaur—a company that was too large, too slow-moving, and out of touch with the times. The catalog operation had fallen to third place, behind longtime competitors Sears, Roebuck & Company and behind JCPenney, which hadn't even entered the mail order business until 1962. Mobil invested over $600 million in an attempt to improve Montgomery Ward's performance, but the company continued to have lackluster results. The catalog operations lost heavily for 10 years, with losses of over $260 million in the six years from 1979 through 1984.

By the middle of 1985, despite the fact that catalog sales were rising, Montgomery Ward's management decided that the operation could not be profitable in the foreseeable future. Even though the direct-mail market in the United States was booming and was expected to exceed 32 billion in 1985, revenues and profits of Ward's catalog division were not growing as rapidly as those of other divisions. Montgomery Ward's management decided to discontinue the catalog operation. The action would free up nearly $1 billion in capital, money that was badly needed to finance Montgomery Ward's five-year plan to revamp their retail stores into a nationwide chain of specialty stores.

Today, nearly 7,000 different mail order catalogs are produced by more than 250 companies. Not one of them carries the name of the company that started it all—Montgomery Ward.

Major Question

Considering the cause of the failure of the Montgomery Ward catalog operation, how could the downward trend have been reversed?

Study Questions

1. What factors have led to the enormous growth of the mail order business in the U.S.? Do you think the industry will continue to grow? Why or why not?

2. Why do you think specialty catalogs are more popular today than multiproduct catalogs such as Montgomery Ward?

Case 7
The Limited Knows No Global Bounds

Richard Leventhal, Metropolitan State College

The Limited was created in 1963 by Leslie Wexner when he borrowed $5,000 from his aunt to start a women's retail store; today it sells more women's clothing and accessories than any other merchant in the world, including such giants of retailing as Sears, JCPenney, and Kmart. Leslie Wexner has seen both good and bad times with The Limited, but he has emerged as a billionaire as the value of his company's stock has skyrocketed.

More than 2,400 Limited stores serve seven different segments of the market. Overall, it has achieved astounding results; in the later part of the 1980s, on the average, sales rose 55 percent a year and net income increased by a phenomenal 64 percent annually.

Leslie Wexner is a retailing prodigy. In an industry showing signs of complacency, he has developed a more limber form of fashion retailing—an empire vertically integrated like a major oil company and standardized like a fast-food chain. He bypassed the industry's traditional, slow-moving production system, with its innumerable middlemen, and created his own global manufacturing and distribution network.

From *Retailing Concepts, Strategy, and Information (3rd ed.)* by Carol H. Anderson. Reprinted by permission of West Publishing Company. Copyright © 1993. All rights reserved.

Specialty fashion chains like The Limited are the new wave in retailing. Others include Gap, a California chain, and Benetton, an Italian franchisor. They cater to the insatiable taste of younger Americans for fresh, affordable apparel—exuberantly reinterpreted classics rather than designer novelties.

But none can match the size of The Limited fed by Wexner's unrelenting acquisition strategy. (Wall Street analysts maintain what one calls "the Wexner watch" waiting for him to gobble another major chain of stores.) No other fashion retailer so dominates the suburban shopping malls where American consumers now spend vast quantities of their time and money.

In 1983, the Limited's president was on a trip through Italy; she spotted teenagers in Florence buying bulky yachting sweaters. The sweater was copied by The Limited—in retail trade parlance it was "knocked off"—and, under the The Limited's private label, Forenza, sold millions. (Forenza, shrewdly named to evoke a nonexistent Italian designer, was one of the best selling sportswear brands in the country.) This is a perfect example of how The Limited is able to spot trends in other countries and transport them to the United States. What took place in 1983 is constantly being repeated in the 1990s. (The following is an example of the process).

Monday night in Columbus, Ohio, in a windowless conference room deep in the recesses of The Limited's giant distribution center, the weekly merchandise meeting for the 600 stores of The Limited Stores division, the company's flagship chain, has been called to order. Similar conferences for the six other divisions are under way elsewhere in the center and in New York. These sessions are the first step in the process that determines what millions of American women will be wearing.

On the agenda this particular Monday evening in September is nothing less than the mounting of a spring offensive. The debate rages concerning a new line of safari clothing, a look already implanted in yuppie-consciousness by Banana Republic, a San Francisco-based retailing phenomenon owned by Gap. The executives go on to examine the clothing on the conference table. The safari jacket from Banana Republic is a natural. The soft, flower-printed shirt from Laura Ashley in London adds the right feminine note to the khaki jacket. The tan cotton pants from Europe are a perfect match. With a touch here and there, these garments will form the basis for a new line—hardly original but not a total knockoff, either.

The promising new line is named Outback Red. Its advertising trademark: a pouting, red-headed model wearing a safari coat and an Australian outback hat. But before committing The Limited to full production, Verna Gibson, the president of The Limited division, wants to check its sales appeal.

In late November, samples of the collection—sweaters, shirts, skirts, pants, vests, and shorts—appear in a handful of stores in southern cities. Every evening after closing, cash registers are checked to determine which colors and styles are moving and how customers are reacting to the price tags.

After the Thanksgiving weekend, the results are in. Certain adjustments must be made. Pleated pants, for example, have outsold those with plain fronts. But overall, the new line is a hit. Wexner and his staff decide to distribute Outback Red nationally. He wants 500,000 garments in the stores within 10 weeks. "You can't patent anything in the clothing business," he says. "So you've got to get stuff to the consumer first if you want to be successful."

Producing a collection of such magnitude so fast would be impossible for most retailers. They are dependent on middlemen such as Seventh Avenue (New York) wholesalers, importers, and independent buying offices. A department store might have to allow ten months for delivery of such a vast order.

The Limited, however, has an edge. In 1978, Wexner took on a huge debt to buy Mast Industries, an importer and contract manufacturer. Mast has interests in a dozen factories in Asia and long-standing relationships with 190 factories around the world. It also has coordinated global transport. "Mast is The Limited's trump card," says the president of a competing specialty chain. "It's light years ahead in terms of understanding how to get things done in the Far East."

If fabric must be moved from China to Korea, a Mast employee is on hand to get cloth through customs. If Columbus is desperate for a shipment of pants, a Mast executive in Hong Kong gets them on the next plane out; The Limited's merchandise fills an average of three U.S.-bound 747s a week.

Outback Red presents Mast with a formidable challenge: to track down hundreds of thousands of yards of khaki-colored fabric at a reasonable price. Mast finds the material at a mill in China. The bolts of fabric are shipped to Hong Kong for dyeing, finishing, and printing. Then the piece goods are distributed for manufacturing— pants to Hong Kong, shorts to Mauritius, shirts to Sri Lanka.

While Third World sewing machines are stitching to The Limited's beat, Leslie Wexner is circling the globe in his new Gulfstream jet. In Tokyo, he introduces his company to Japanese institutional investors. After checking with Mast suppliers in Hong Kong and touring his factories in Mauritius, he heads for Jerusalem. There, Wexner discusses with government officials a plan to set up three apparel plants near the Golan Heights to be owned jointly by The Limited and Chinese and Israeli interests.

In late January, Mast employees begin loading the Outback Red line onto jets for the journey to California and New York. After clearing customs, the goods are transferred to a fleet of tractor-trailers owned by The Limited and operated by Walsh Trucking, a New Jersey-based company, and rushed to the distribution center in Columbus. The journey from the Far East to Columbus has taken six days, too many for Wexner. He wants an airfield south of Columbus designated an international port of entry, which would cut that time in half.

In cartons and hanger packs, the Outback Red line moves steadily along a computerized freeway of conveyor belts. Workers attach price tags while Madonna sings accompaniment. Sorters separate the clothes into stacks destined for individual stores. Packers heft the stacks into boxes—to the tune of Willie Nelson's "On The Road Again." On a conveyor belt that looks like a ski slope, the boxes slide toward computerized selected trucking bays.

In an average of forty-eight hours, a garment passes through the distribution center. Most retailers are plagued by inventories that languish in less-automated warehouses for weeks on end. Such schedules may suffice for the industry's traditional selling seasons—fall-winter and spring-summer— but The Limited has abandoned this approach, feeding fresh merchandise into its stores at the rate of two shipments per week. Wexner believes that women are more inclined to visit a store regularly if they know there will be something new to look at. "People don't buy what they already have," Wexner has stated.

On the first Monday in February, Outback Red goes on sale in 600 chrome-and-glass stores from coast to coast, and the presentation is everywhere the same. Twice a month, merchandisers meet in Columbus to choose displays for the next two weeks. Blueprints and photographs accompany the props and furniture dispatched to the stores; no deviation is allowed. "We don't want 100 managers out there deciding what the stores should look like," declares Verna Gibson.

All over America, racks of Outback Red trousers and skirts stand just to the left of entranceways. In the window, amid palm trees and bushes, incredibly lifelike mannequins in flower printed shirts recline in tan wicker chairs.

The Limited does not release sales figures for its brands. The first evidence of a new line's success or failure appears on the price tag. Industry analysts who travel the country, visiting the stores, report no markdowns on Outback Red, whose prices range from about $20 for a shirt to about $50 for a jacket. A retail industry analyst is quoted as saying: "This could be a $500 million line, which would make it the fourth largest women's sportswear brand in the United States."

Major Question[1]

How does The Limited get its product to the consumer faster than conventional manufacturer selling to retailers?

---

[1]Please note: Do not use alternative analysis format for this case.

Study Questions

1. Discuss the international nature of The Limited's business operation.

2. Discuss how operations of The Limited (a chain) are different from department stores and small independent stores in terms of product acquisition.

3. Not only is the Limited a vertically integrated company, but the parent company, Limited, Inc., is horizontally integrated. Explain how the vertical structure can benefit other subsidiaries.

4. Why would Verna Gibson want to check the potential for sales appeal for the Outback Red line before she commits to production?

5. Why would The Limited test market the new Outback Red line in November in southern cities?

6. Why would markdowns on the Outback Red line indicate that consumer acceptance is not as it was anticipated to be?

Chapter Discussion Questions

1. If you were starting a new business, what format would you choose? Why?

2. What are the advantages and disadvantages of conventional formats, for example, department and discount stores? Compare to new niche companies and such new formats as on-line services.

3. In the future, do you think all retailing and manufacturing will merge into large vertical companies?

4. Compare and contrast the various retailing formats illustrated in the cases. Are there any that you believe will not survive into the next century? Which ones do you think will thrive? Why?

2 Merchandise/Store Positioning

Chapter Objectives

- Relate image, identity, and retail positioning to companies and products.

- Stress the importance of retail differentiation and successful merchandising.

- Discuss the relationship between competition, positioning, and target marketing in today's complex marketplace.

- Illustrate how changes in the population relate to redefining target markets and image.

In today's fiercely competitive environment, companies must clearly articulate their identity, evidenced by a developed image in the marketplace. Businesses must differentiate their products from their competition to maintain success. Knowing who the target customers are and what level of fashion merchandise they want helps to clarify the image a retailer or manufacturer wants to present. Additionally, market research is essential to understand in order to profile a specific target market. Understanding how changes in the demographic and psychographic makeup of society affect business is vital in decisions to maintain or change one's image at both the product and retail level. The trend toward vertical integration, with retailing and manufacturing done by the same company brings a double need for clarity in image and positioning.

Image and Identity

With the trend toward consolidation of retail stores because of bankruptcy and takeovers, and the redundancy of retail offerings that are found in many stores, a clear image, merchandise differentiation, and a distinct market position are all vital for success in today's over-stored, competitive retail environment. Image differentiation in the marketplace presents both challenges and opportunities to today's retailers. Not only is it important to convey a clear image to consumers, retailers and manufacturers must also understand their ultimate customers: who they are, what their needs and desires are, what they think and feel, and what is affecting them and their purchasing habits.

Company Identity

A company must possess a clear **identity** before it can be conveyed to its customers. All personnel including owners, managers, and sales staff must be aware of and understand a consistent, well-articulated company mission, including the nature, purpose, and direction of the company. After this identity is made clear, it is easier to identify a target market and to choose appropriate communication channels to reach that market. Who the company is and what that company stands for influences the type of merchandise offered and subsequently the type of customer the company is trying to reach. A "fuzzy" or unstable image breeds trouble for retailers and manufacturers. Esprit is an example of a manufacturer that had problems deciding on its identity. Doug and Susie Thompkins were two owners who had different visions for their company. He wanted the image to remain young and exciting, but she also wanted to respond to demographic changes and appeal to the career woman. Such mixed messages resulted in a confused customer and declining sales. When Susie took majority ownership of the company, she decided that the design direction should include more than just the "young look." However, the "Susie Thompkins line" (at price points targeted to working women) was not successful after several years in production.

The **image** that a company possesses is the perception customers have of it. Because perceptions vary among consumers, not all customers perceive a particular company in the same way. Some find upscale, sophisticated stores quite intimidating and do not even enter the store because they perceive a situation in which they would be most uncomfortable. It may be the pristine appearance of the store, it may be the intimidating look of the sales personnel, or it may be the prices displayed in the window that create such an image or impression. On the other hand, stores that are crowded with merchandise with much promotional signage convey the image of a discount store or of lower-quality merchandise. This image might discourage a more upscale consumer, who is used to the ambience of a quiet, laid-back specialty store.

Fashion Image

A company's fashion image is based on its merchandise, promotion, and environment. Jernigan and Easterling (1990) differentiate fashion images with the terms advanced fashion, updated fashions, exclusive, trendy, traditional fashions, and classics. Some stores and manufacturers specialize in one of these fashion levels, while others (for example, department stores) offer more than one fashion level depending on the department focus. The **fashion cycle,** or **product life cycle,** which represents the adoption level of consumers of a particular style and the stages of a product's life cycle, is the traditional analysis of fashion stages. Retailers and manufacturers place themselves in a fashion position by targeting the consumer adopters as the innovators, early conformists, mass market conformists, late fashion followers, or laggards. (See Figure 2.1, The Fashion Cycle.)

Research has indicated that these categories are difficult, however, to utilize in terms of identifying and differentiating consumers at each level; therefore, for the sake of analysis, retailers and manufacturers might choose to use the more broad categories of **fashion leaders** and **fashion followers.** A company that is always showing the newest, latest styles is seen as **fashion forward,** which appeals to fashion leaders. This can be very

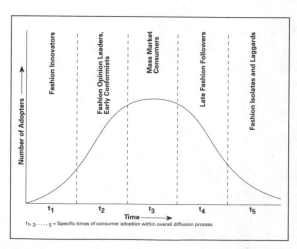

Figure 2.1 The fashion cycle.

risky because consumers do not always accept the new styles; also, fashion with such narrow appeal is generally produced in limited quantities, and is expensive and exclusive. If the store does not have an image for fashion leadership, it can be very perilous to bring in new fashion items as a large proportion of their offerings. Additionally, customers will not find the more traditional or classic styles they expect from the store and therefore can get mixed messages of the store's image. In *Case 9, Frustration in the Men's Wear Department,* this dilemma is illustrated by a cautious divisional merchandise manager who is hesitant to allocate a large portion of a men's wear department to an untested style.

After consumers accept a new (or fashion forward) style, it is usually translated into a more affordable item with less-expensive fabrication and detailing that is produced and sold by other companies at lower-price points. This less expensive, more affordable item is generally referred to as a **knockoff.** Knockoffs are a way of life in the fashion industry and are indicative of general consumer acceptance and adoption of styles. See *Case 23, The Knockoff* in Chapter Three for an illustration of a buyer/vendor conflict that is caused by the retailer's copying the vendor's popular style.

Toward the end of the fashion cycle, acceptance of a style wanes and now only laggards are accepting and purchasing a style at discount or resale stores. The fashion has generally ended with an excess; that is, the knockoff manufacturers are left with unwanted stock that they must sell. Usually, they give great deals to retailers at off-prices to move the merchandise out. Similarly, retailers usually put the style on sale to make way for newer, more profitable, more fashionable merchandise. *Case 82, Amber's Wave* in Chapter 11, illustrates the possible end of a style's product life cycle as sales reps document slow sales on new merchandise that is seen as too similar to previous looks from the company. Fashion is acceptance. If consumers don't buy an item, it is not being accepted for some reason and therefore, it is not "in fashion." It may be a style at the end of the fashion

cycle, which people are tired of and they are looking for something new and exciting; or it may be too new, too fashion forward for the store's clientele. Of course, there are many other reasons related to the quality, color, brand, and so forth, which can contribute to the reason why merchandise is not purchased. (See Chapter Three for a discussion of these issues.)

Changing Image
Image serves as a filtering function in the customer's evaluation of a company. Performance must be consistent with the image the retailer or manufacturer wants to project. Customers will overlook minor shortcomings, for example, a mistake made in a transaction, in a company that holds a positive image, gives good service, and provides good quality merchandise. But if problems continue to happen, the firm will lose that positive image. This happened on a large scale when many department stores reduced the number of sales associates available to help customers. Consequently, the overall image of department stores has changed from full service to limited or self service; with this image change has come a change in store patronage. If customers do not receive service but still pay high prices, why not go to lower-priced, self-service stores? Therefore, such stores as Target and Wal-Mart are doing very well and expanding, while many department stores are going out of business or reorganizing with the help of Chapter 11 bankruptcy court protection from their creditors.

Retailers and manufacturers often find that they wish to change their image and offerings or even their location because of events occurring around them. Increased competition may force a company to change in order to differentiate itself from that competition. A changing neighborhood may lead a store to relocate or change to merchandise that is more suitable to its clientele. Local clientele can be lost with store location changes, so there are definite risks with major changes. Often, however, there are more risks involved with no change. *Case 8, The Big Move,* presents a fabric store owner who is confronted with a decision to move to a new location with better amenities and higher costs or stay in a building badly in need of repair and remodeling.

New ownership often brings changes and new images, sometimes beneficial, other times not. Ownership by Gap brought complete, successful store makeovers for Banana Republic, which eliminated the safari decor and the original travel concept and added higher-priced, well-tailored merchandise. It is not an easy task to change an image and not all attempts are successful. After an image is established, it is hard to change customer perceptions. It is possible to change from one image to another but it can be very difficult and can take a great deal of time and promotion to acquaint the public with the change. Macy's did it in the 1970s when they abandoned their bargain basement and replaced it with the Cellar, an upscale kitchen and housewares concept. Spiegel, once known for value-oriented merchandise, now carries upper-end, well-known brands. Changed images imply changed target markets and companies risk the loss of the old market before gaining the new one. This problem is presented in *Case 10, Off With the Old—On With the New*, which is an example of a change in ownership that leads to an altered company image. In this case, an elegant, high-end department store with long-time loyal customers brings in a new owner who has new—and different—ideas for the store.

Established, successful companies often think that all they need to do is more of the same to maintain success. That, unfortunately, does not always work in today's fast-paced, quick-changing society and marketplace. Formats that are on the rise include the super specialists or niche companies, and price-oriented companies. Those with high overhead and high prices are finding it a more difficult environment in which to be profitable. The demise of B. Altman in the 1980s and I. Magnin in the 1990s, as well as the Chapter 11 filing by Barney's are evidence of this (some say Barney's case was different as it was precipitated by ownership politics and aggressive expansion). Businesses must change with the times to survive. In some instances that means using

New Team at Altman's To Keep Its Traditions

B. Altman & Company, which has occupied its site on 34th Street and Fifth Avenue since 1906, has a new set of officers since its sale last year by the Altman Foundation. They held a breakfast conference this week to report that its traditions will continue and to show, through displays and models, the directions the New York store's two main areas, home furnishings and fashion, will take next fall.

"We're better known for our home furnishings than fashion, for reasons we do not yet completely understand," said Anthony C. Conti, the new chairman, who promised expansion into the fashion area.

Jack Schultz, the new president, described the store's style as "updated classic, somewhat traditional." He said special attention would be given to the working woman's needs through service and specialized merchandise from Europe, the Far East and the United States.

A new Ralph Lauren shop will open in the store's home furnishings area in September, said Anita Gallo, vice president for fashion direction. Other major themes running through home furnishings will be an emphasis on 18th- and 19th-century styles, including furniture, printed and woven damask fabrics, embroidered linen and cotton sheets and English silver serving pieces.

Gold accents will be stressed in dinner services and accessories, Miss Gallo said. Flowered pillows and platters will express a romantic theme. Pottery, glassware and rugs with primitive look represent another direction.

In fashion, suits will constitute an important category, geared especially to the working woman. Long jacket styles and knits were included in the fashion presentation. Store executives believe the one-piece dress will be significant and daytime separates will look more coordinated.

For men, classicism prevails, as in a one-button suit shown in a muted gray glen plaid with a white shirt and red tie. A navy double-breasted blazer was shown with gray flannel pants as Miss Gallo observed that more men are wearing sports coats to work. Polo coats were presented for both men and women.

Figure 2.2–2.4 Two *New York Times* articles, originally published on June 12, 1986 (left) and November 18, 1989 (right), illustrate the hazards of failing to change with the times. After 124 years as a landmark institution on Fifth Avenue in Manhattan, the posh but old-fashioned B. Altman & Company department store was forced to close its doors. Above right: shoppers packed B. Altman's on November 24, 1989, to take advantage of the going-out-of-business sale. *Photo courtesy of Fred R. Conrad/NYT Pictures.*

No Bidder To Rescue B. Altman

6 of 7 Stores to Close After One Last Sale

By ISADORE BARMASH

B. Altman & Company, the 124-year-old department store whose flagship establishment on Fifth Avenue was one of the first to cater to Manhattan's carriage trade, will be closed, a bankruptcy court decided yesterday.

After a month on the auction block and a decade of decline, the New York-based retailer failed to attract any acceptable bidders and will shut six of its seven stores after a clearance sale starting Friday, the start of the Christmas shopping season.

The closing of the stores, expected by Jan. 29, ends an era of dignified retailing in lush surroundings that began fading with the demise of New York City retailers like John Wanamaker, Best & Company and Arnold Constable. These stores boasted rich wood paneling, high ceilings with chandeliers and wide, carpeted aisles. Their merchandise was mostly higher-priced than the competition. . . .

The decision to close the Manhattan store and five branches on Long Island and in New Jersey and Pennsylvania was made yesterday in New York by Federal Bankruptcy Judge Tina Brozman in approving a request of the L. J. Hooker Corporation, the owner of Altman's. . . .

The closing of Altman's reflects the pressures that certain retailers have experienced in the last several years, particularly because of a decline in the women's apparel business.

In big city after city, the quiet, slow-paced retailing emporiums that catered to the affluent have either disappeared or adopted a snappier, more contemporary atmosphere. . . .

Today, only some large specialty stores, like the Saks Fifth Avenue chain, Brooks Brothers and Tiffany & Company have the traditional ambience, combined with a disdain for anything too modern or radical in fashion. . . .

Aside from the severe drain of merchandise created by Hooker's decision not to finance new merchandise so that goods could be delivered only when paid for in cash, Altman's suffered from a competitive weakness. It became saddled with an eroding image because of its failure to remodel sufficiently, a reluctance to enrich its merchandise with more diversity and an inability to project a clear image to the customer.

"You can hardly call it a strong carriage-trade store, or, an attraction to the affluent anymore, not anything like Saks," said a retailing executive in another city who asked not to be identified. "Altman's lost its way years ago and never found it again."

technology to streamline operations to remain cost effective. Other times it means changing a target market to coincide with societal, economic, and demographic changes. In *Case 17, Hilo Hattie: A Shifting Customer Base*, a Hawaiian manufacturer/retailer is coping with a reduced tourist trade, and has to decide if it should target local trade rather than tourists exclusively. When the customer base changes, it is vital that a company make appropriate changes to survive and thrive.

Product Differentiation/Positioning

Image must differentiate a company from others in the marketplace, that is, it must be different from competition. No two retailers or manufacturers are alike; each has its own unique personality or image, which emphasizes such factors as price, quality, physical environment, customer service, employee attitude, fashion, level of merchandise, or unique or convenient location. These factors create a certain image that attracts a certain type of customer. The success of Nordstrom in competing with other department stores is attributed mainly to their reputation for excellent customer service—not only the perception of it, but the reality. Customers found the best customer service at Nordstrom and therefore were lured away from other department stores that were clearly losing the customer service battle. Indeed, customers of some stores have difficulty merely finding sales associates to help them. (For more on Nordstrom's customer service, see *Case 64, parts 1 and 2* in Chapter Eight).

Retailers cannot be all things to all people. They must clearly target their customer and position themselves by differentiating their business from others. At a time when demand is greater than supply, many similar companies can be successful by merely offering certain types of merchandise. This has been the case at times throughout history, for example, after a war when previously scarce items finally became available. However, retailers and manufacturers are finding themselves in trouble if they compete for the same customer and cannot differentiate themselves from others in the marketplace. The closing of Gimbel's and Ohrbach's in 1986, and Broadway Stores in 1996 was due in part to their inability to establish clear identities. Consumers could not differentiate these two stores from others in the market. Each store must be clearly different or unique to the consumer.

The term **positioning** refers to the image of a company relative to its competition in the marketplace. For example, where is Mervyn's positioned relative to Macy's, Nordstrom, or JCPenney? They see themselves in direct competition with JCPenney but below Macy's or Nordstrom in terms of fashion, even though they carry some of the exact same brands. The Limited, Inc. grew tremendously in the 1980s with acquisitions and the development of stores that target specific population segments. For example, Express grew out of The Limited's concept, but is geared to a younger, trendier market. For a time, however, they both tended to compete for the same customer, but eventually went back to differentiating their customers. A similar situation is analyzed in *Case 11, Cannibalization in Product Development and Retailing,* in which one arm of a company begins cannibalizing another as they compete for the same customer with no **product differentiation.** Differentiated products, as the term implies, are products that are different from others in the market.

Competition

Companies competing or vying for the same consumer business is called **competition,** and is an important consideration when deciding whether to open a store in a new area. Is there too much competition in one area? Or is competition good for everyone? After an area is saturated, that market may have difficulty sustaining all the establishments, and many times stores will be forced out of business. On the other hand, a new store can bring more shoppers into an area and often can bring new customers to established stores. Of course, those businesses have to stay on their toes and not rest on past successes. Additionally, competition can be too much for some small stores. When Wal-

Mart moves into areas that have been serviced by small, independent retailers, many of these will leave the area or will simply go out of business as the competition becomes too much for them to combat. Such large stores with huge buying power can achieve profits on small margins that small retailers cannot. An illustration of this issue is *Case 13, The Small Store Dilemma,* in which a small store's future is threatened by a large store and shopping center that is relocating into the area. A small store may be in trouble in such a situation if it cannot offer something better than the new competition, such as better selections (wide or deep), lower prices, or better customer service. This is what competition is about: the one that does the best job survives. *Case 12, Burlington Vermont—Church Street Marketplace* carefully analyzes other retailers in an area to determine if there is a large enough consumer market for a new upscale boutique.

Niche Merchandise

Meeting the needs of a specific population **niche** (a narrowly defined customer segment) is one way of differentiating a product or store. Because niches have very specific needs, niche retailers offer deep assortments of one particular type of merchandise. A company could also serve a niche by defining its market in narrow geographic terms; that is, a retailer might serve only one small neighborhood, meeting many of its needs. Golf is a niche that is becoming more popular with aging baby boomers, retirees, and has growing popularity with women—an untraditional golf market. The need for this niche merchandise is described in *Case 15, Women's Golf Apparel: An Important Niche,* in which an established men's golf apparel manufacturer must decide whether or not to enter into the women's market. *Case 14, Trend Decisions: Prototype of a New Line* explores a growing niche—large-size, fashionable women. In this case, fashion trends summarized by reporting services must be interpreted for the large-size career woman. Not all trends will meet the needs of this distinctive niche.

Figure 2.5 Niche merchandise is illustrated here with Ralph Lauren's Polo golf line.

Market Research

The collection and analysis of data relating to such issues as store location, target-market profiling, the determination of the target consumer's needs and wants, company image, promotion, and so forth is called **market research.** Research provides data on which to base decisions and thus reduces some risks. Market research should be a continuous process providing information for planning and decision-making. *Case 8, The Big Move,* considers the types of information obtained from a fabric store's

target market to help make the decision on whether or not to move from one part of town to another.

Target Marketing

Target marketing (customer segmentation) is one of the most basic and important components of market research. A **target market** is the group of customers that a company seeks to serve. A target market is often identified by demographic and psychographic profiles. **Demographics,** used to identify and count groups of people, include population factors of age, gender, income, education, marital status, religion, family size, life-cycle stage, ethnicity and mobility, among others. Demographic variables are investigated and used by retailers because they are often linked to marketplace needs and are relatively easy to access. Some demographic trends in the U.S. are:

- *Slowing population growth.* Families are becoming smaller; households, however, will grow as more people live alone, more people delay marrying, and as there are more divorces. Also non-family units will increase. *Implications for retailers:* A slowing population is generally a negative for retailers. Nevertheless, as the number of households increase, there is an increased market for home furnishings.

- *Aging population.* There are more older people who are living longer. The median age of the population will rise to 36 by the year 2000. The **baby boomers** are those 76 million Americans born after World War II (between the years 1946 and 1964). Although they have an orientation toward the home, they are active in sports, exercise, and healthful living. The fastest growing population segment is the over-85 age group, but young seniors, age 55–64, will also increase. The over-50 group—or **silver streakers**—are not ready to retire from life. *Implications for retailers:* The "graying of America" has led to a redefinition of "old" and the search for beauty at any age. The Body Shop, with its lotions and potions, is popular with most segments of the population. Sharper Image's high-tech toys is targeted to well-off, educated baby boomers. (See *Case 16, A Void in Gap's Apparel,* for an example of a company targeting the younger ages versus the boomers.) Older seniors are not as conservative with their savings as in the past. They are traveling, buying second homes, luxury cars, electronics, clothing, and gifts. They like "Made in USA" items, natural fibers, and recognizable brand names. Such senior programs as mall walking and discounts at slower times (or on slower days) are popular and will bring seniors to the stores. To meet the needs of this market, retailers also need to include clearer and larger labels and signage, added seating in stores, and better-lighted parking lots. Retirement communities will increase, consequently, adding new markets or increasing an existing market for such areas.

• *An increase in teens and young adults.* In the 1980s and early 1990s, there were fewer young people as the 16- to 24-year-old group declined in numbers. However, Price Waterhouse estimates a return to an increase in the number of teenagers to the year 2001, increasing three times the pace of other segments of the population. They have baby-boomer parents, often live in two-income families with fewer children than in the past, and have their own money. *Implications for retailers:* There should be a renewed interest in fashion, but this is also coupled with an increase in crime and consequently there will be more controlled-access malls. Teens spend their money freely because most of it is discretionary. Additionally, they influence their parents' spending. With fewer teenagers, retailers found themselves without an adequate source of labor and many retailers turned to older adults who are more stable and knowledgeable than this younger group. Now, with increasing numbers of teenagers, there will a larger pool of younger, entry-level workers.

• *More working women who have children in daycare.* Women account for two-thirds of the labor-force growth. Generally, working women think independently when making purchases, often seeking individualism and affirmation of their own personal identity. *Implications for retailers:* Busy, working women need convenience. Merchants who offer services and help to reduce the number of trips to the mall or store will benefit from this group. Banking (ATMs) in grocery stores, more sales assistance during lunch hours and after working hours, special services, catalog, in-home shopping, and individualized products all meet their needs. Responsible, conscientious child care facilities are also needed, especially at (or close to) the workplace.

• *Increased education.* The baby boomers are the most educated generation ever. One in four has completed four years of college. *Implications for retailers:* The college-educated consumer segment differs in its buying behavior from other workers with similar incomes. They tend to be more independent, less influenced by advertising; they are, however, receptive to ethical, informative advertising. Consumers will continue to be sophisticated and discriminating in their shopping, and will demand an informed sales force.

• *Migration to the sunbelt.* The population movement to the South and West (California, Nevada, Arizona, New Mexico, Texas, and Florida) will lead to population declines in the North and Central parts of the country. Today's U.S. population is extremely mobile, as each year about one-sixth of all Americans move, either to a different location in the same area or to a different region altogether. *Implications for retailers:* Many retailers cater to local groups. With high mobility, some will find their consumer base soon gone. Those businesses in areas of rapid growth should be prepared to meet the needs of newcomers. Flexibility and constant market research are important. After a move, consumers often seek out a recognizable chain to fill their needs. JCPenney, Sears, Target, Wal-Mart, Gap and other chains have an advantage as customers know what to expect from these establishments—no matter where they are located. The same holds true for recognizable national brands. Easily utilized national credit also becomes even more important.

• *Increased cultural pluralism.* The U.S. is becoming more ethnically diverse as minorities are growing seven times faster than the European-

American (white) majority. This is occurring as immigration increases and the birthrate of minorities remains higher than the white majority. *Implications for retailers:* Some retailers are targeting specific ethnic groups by advertising in their language in addition to bilingual signage in the stores. Also, carrying specific ethnic products and hiring sales associates who speak the language in areas with large ethnic populations make certain centers important destinations for their customers. For example, Vons in Los Angeles carries a large selection of Mexican foods; JCPenney uses the JCPenney Spanish USA Shopping Guide in Miami; the Aberdeen Centre near Vancouver carries traditional Chinese medicines, movies, and activities.

• *Increased but unequal income growth.* Income distribution is becoming more polarized as the middle- and low-income groups (as measured by real purchasing power) are declining while the highest-income groups are growing. The increase is due to the maturing of the population, the increase in dual-income households, and higher levels of education. *Implications for retailers:* Many retailers have upgraded both their stores and merchandise as they cater to the higher-income consumer. Such upper-end stores as Nordstrom and Saks are doing well with this change in demographics. On the other hand, Wal-Mart, Target, and warehouse retailers on the low-end of the price structure are also doing well. To meet this competition, upscale retailers are adding outlets or close-out centers to capture the "value-oriented" market. Many middle-of-the-road retailers are either in trouble or trading up.

In addition to demographics, **psychographics,** which are data related to activities, interests, and opinions of the target consumer, are an important tool for retailers and manufacturers. Psychographics are generally thought of as **lifestyle**—or how people spend their time and money. One prominent method used to analyze lifestyle is SRI International's Values and Lifestyle (VALS) program, which has helped marketers predict consumption patterns based on consumer attitudes and psychological states. Similar to

demographics, this type of information affects how retailers and manufacturers make decisions about products and services they offer. Some major lifestyle trends are:

• *Blurring of male and female roles in society.* Women are entering such traditional male-dominated careers as law enforcement, construction, banking, and so forth. At the same time, more men are electing to stay home as technology allows for telecommuting. *Implications for retailers:* Retailers are beginning to see more men shopping in general and at hours of the day when formerly only women used to shop. To capture this market, adjustments must be made to accommodate this new customer.

• *Importance of time management.* As more households consist of both men and women working, effective use of time becomes even more important as decisions are made as to what activities are vital enough to warrant participation. Leisure activities are also becoming more precious and important. *Implications for retailers:* As individuals and families are finding they are "time poor," they want to spend less time in stores. In addition to offering more microwavable and prepared foods, supermarkets are becoming one-stop establishments with ATMs and other services. Even clothing items can be bought while shopping for the week's groceries.

• *Life simplification and a return to traditional values.* Back-to-basics and good value are the consequences of some demographic changes, which include stagnant incomes. Many people are spending more time at home where it is familiar and safe. *Implications for retailers:* The home entertainment and home repair industries are elated at these trends as people spend more time at home and more money improving their homes. As consumers look for basics and value, such retailers as Gap, L.L. Bean, Lands' End, and Eddie Bauer should do very well.

• *Generational differences in the marketplace.* **Generation X** (also called baby busters and post-baby boomers) have distinctly different values from baby boomers. The baby busters are just entering the mainstream marketplace and mostly have been ignored by retailers. They are angry and alienated from the boomers and generational values will clash as expectations and allegiances are different. *Implications for retailers:* Generation Xers may be hard to reach as they can be turned off by normal promotions. Also, they can clash with older baby boomers in the workplace.

• *Interest in the environment.* Generally, as society becomes more affluent with basic needs met, we concentrate more on our surroundings. Consumers are demanding more natural, pure products. Recycling is becoming prevalent in communities. *Implications for retailers:* "Green marketing" is a strategic approach taken by many companies today as consumers show more and more interest in recycling and safe manufacturing processes and products. Such companies as The Body Shop communicate this type of message to their market. Target, Gap, Wal-Mart, Patagonia, Levi Strauss, Esprit, among many others, have taken special interest in environmentally friendly products and processes, in addition to environmental awareness programs, to which consumers are responding positively.

All these trends (both demographic and psychographic) have implications for retailers and manufacturers, including what type of merchandise to produce and offer for sale, where to locate production sites and stores, what services to offer, and what type of formats to provide for busy consumers. *Case 16, A Void in Gap's Apparel* illustrates the demographic trend of baby boomers—the largest age group in society—who are aging. Gap used to appeal to this group in the store's beginnings in the 1970s; but is Gap appealing to this group now? *"Experts say it's losing [the] baby boomer"* as the store is carrying younger styles that are more attractive to Generation Xers. *Case 15, Women's Golf Apparel: An Important Niche* is an application of the psychographic trends of men's and women's roles and interests blending and the use of quality leisure time. Another example is *Case 17, Hilo Hattie: A Shifting Customer Base,* which presents a change in a store's target market that is caused by fewer people traveling to Hawaii. Such demographic, psychographic, and societal changes must be addressed by retailers if they want their businesses to thrive.

Summary

Product differentiation is a vital part of competing in the marketplace. Many once strong retailers that have lost their uniqueness are no longer in business today. Niche merchandise, which serves a specific market, is one way that companies differentiate themselves from others. Image and identity must be clearly communicated to a retailer's consumers. Additionally, market research can identify consumer changes in makeup and needs.

References

Baby boomers: A \$33B market. (1996, May 8). *WWD,* Special report: WWD tracking the trends 1997, pp. 17, 19.

Jernigan, M.H., & Easterling, C.R. (1990). *Fashion merchandising and marketing.* New York: Macmillan.

Retailing in the nineties: The age of information. (1996, May 8). *WWD,* Special report: WWD tracking the trends, 1997, pp. 2, 18, 19.

Rath, P., Peterson, J., Greensley, P., & Gill, P. (1994). *Introduction to fashion merchandising,* Albany, N.Y.: Delmar.

Key Terms

baby boomer	lifestyle
competition	market research
demographics	niche
fashion cycle	positioning
fashion followers	product differentiation
fashion forward	product life cycle
fashion leaders	psychographics
generation X	silver-streakers
identity	target market
image	target marketing (customer segmentation)
knockoff	

Case 8
The Big Move

Paula R. King, Southeast Missouri State University

Marian Shaw owns a profitable independent fabric store and sewing machine dealership in Dallas, Texas. The family owned and operated store is located in an upscale strip shopping center in a wealthy residential area. Neighboring businesses include an exclusive antique dealership, a gourmet food shop, a hairdresser, and a grocery store that offers valet parking to its customers. Marian sells mostly imported silk and wool fabrics, plus patterns and sewing supplies, in addition to imported sewing machines. The services offered by the store include sewing machine repairs, sewing machine training, and a wide range of sewing classes such as couture techniques, French hand sewing, machine embroidery, and working with leather and suede.

Marian's sales staff is composed of trained, well-educated, knowledgeable sewers, all of whom work part-time in sales and teach classes. Marian's customers are a mixture of neighborhood residents, maids who work in neighborhood homes, sewing hobbyists from the metropolitan area, and local sewing and design professionals who own the brand of machine that Marian sells and services.

The strip shopping center in which Marian's store is located is an aging adobe-style structure that is in need of repairs and remodeling. The property owner plans to remodel to his tenants' specifications, but after doing so, he will raise the rent substantially. Parking at and around the center is difficult; lot space is limited because of the heavy traffic associated with the grocery store and gourmet food shop. Additionally, access to the parking lot from the very busy street (especially during noon and rush hours) is a problem.

Marian recently received information from a developer who is building new retail space less than a mile south of her present location in a growing area filled with new homes and young upper-middle class families. She has noticed an increase in customers from this area. Most are non-working mothers in their late twenties or early thirties, with two or three preschool-aged children. Several have expressed an interest in fabric for home decor, and in sewing classes that focus on children's wear or home decorating projects.

The developer has a very appealing visual presentation of the attractive new space and has offered each new tenant an attractive financial package. Merchants will be responsible for the cost of exterior signage, and the cost of constructing and decorating the interior of their retail space. However, by using the developer's own contractors, merchants will be able to defer payment for remodeling costs and rent until the second year of business. At that time, a lump-sum payment for remodeling and first-year rent will be due. Businesses already planning to locate in the new center include a chain supermarket, gift shop, dance studio, and a franchise sandwich shop.

Marian is very tempted by the thought of new, remodeled store space in a new, growing area of Dallas; however, she doesn't want to make an uninformed decision to move. Her family members are enthusiastic about the new location and its possibilities for growth, but staff at the store feel less certain that old customers will continue to shop in a new location.

After a great deal of thought, Marian decided to conduct some simple market research before making up her mind. As a first step in her research, she analyzed her store mailing list, which interested customers sign up on when they shop. To Marian's surprise, most of the names on the list were in the zipcode area that included the new location. To confirm that residents of the new area were a major part of her customer base, Marian mailed a sale brochure with a coupon for savings on selected sewing notions to all the customers on the mailing list. Returned coupons showed that most of the customers who responded to the mailing were from the new area.

Major Question

Should Marian move her store to the new location or stay in the old one through the remodeling process? Should she adjust her image and product assortment to better accommodate customers from the new area in either location?

Study Questions

1. Did Marian's coupon research and zip code analysis give her enough data upon which to base her decision to move or stay?

2. What other information about both the old area and the potential new area would be valuable for a small retailer to know?

3. What is the profile of the fabric customer? How does it differ from department store customers? How does it differ, or is it similar, to Marian's current strip shopping center neighbors?

Case 9
Frustration in the Men's Wear Department

Nancy J. Rabolt, San Francisco State University
Judy K. Miler, University of Tennessee

Jim Safford is the men's suit buyer for the Langley Department Store, Milwaukee, Wisconsin, and has been in this position for five years. He was employed directly after graduation from the University of Michigan where he earned an MBA. After completion of the Langley Training Program, he was an assistant buyer, then an associate, and finally a buyer, all within two years. His first buying assignment was in the men's furnishings department where he performed admirably for four years. His record was so good that management decided to give him the new assignment of buying men's suits, a department with declining sales. Despite this, Jim felt that this was a step toward a position on the

upper management team, an achievement that would take another year or two. In fact, it was common knowledge among personnel that he was a young man slated for higher management, so his thoughts were not just reveries.

Jim tackled his job with enthusiasm, care, and understanding. He gave the opportunity all it was worth—a lifetime career that was going to lead to big things. Unfortunately, Jim was the victim of circumstance, and soon some of the glitter began to fade. Despite all his efforts—which included advice from the buying office, peers in the field, and friendly manufacturers—business continued to lag. The trend toward sportswear hurt his business; losses of volume were suffered up to 10 percent per year; and, after five years, the department's projected volume for the next year was 60 percent of what it was when Jim took over. Management was not deeply disturbed because they were aware of the fashion trend and had industry records that reflected similar regional and national results.

Despite management's support, Jim was grim and never ceased to search for the key to build the department and again assume the position of a man on the rise. Finally, during January of this year, the message came across loud and clear. The market, optimistic for the first time in years, reported a trend toward men's suits and a new silhouette, the revival of the double-breasted, English "soft" suit—just what the doctor ordered as medicine to accelerate business. Jim visited the market and shopped it thoroughly. He spoke to all sources of information and learned of heavy manufacturer production concentrating on the new style, other stores' plans for strong promotions, and fashion magazine support. He was convinced—this was it. And he made up his mind that 80 percent of his suit budget should be put behind the trend.

Fortunately, his divisional merchandise manager, Dan Powers, was in the market and was able to meet him for dinner. As Jim enthusiastically presented his plan to Dan, he outlined the following:

• Men's suit orders must be given four to six months in advance of delivery.

- The lead time requires an early decision; it is not possible to purchase needed goods after the season starts. Failure to take an early stand means a serious loss during the best-selling period of the year.

- The new styling is not revolutionary; it is highly wearable.

- Competition is going all-out for the first good news in years.

- Coop ad money is available and strong promotional efforts will not exceed last year's budget substantially.

- Customers are looking for styling that is wearable but fashionable. Moreover, the styling fits right into the Langley customers' taste level.

Powers listened carefully and then replied, "It all sounds great; but fashion is acceptance, anything less is an opinion. I suggest that we plan one early strong promotion, about 20 percent of your open-to-buy, which is an important investment." Jim was annoyed, "You were a fashion merchandiser of women's apparel; you just don't understand the men's business." One word led to another, and an impasse developed. Both men were angry and finally Powers said, "I've made my decision, and I will not countersign any order beyond 20 percent of the OTB." With those words, he got up and said, "That is final. Good night."

Jim was terribly upset. He understood the meaning of fashion and knew the difference between opinion and acceptance. But he also felt that even modest success would bolster the department's sagging volume. In fact, he worked up a chart proving that a markdown of 15 percent of net sales would still allow for a profitable season. He knew that the department needed stimulation, the store needed newness, and the sales personnel needed the lift of a new fashion development. He considered going over Powers' head to the general merchandise manager, who was regarded as a logical thinker. His main arguments would be:

- He is a seasoned buyer who should be the selector of merchandise. After all, he is being paid to evaluate the market, study customers, and stock merchandise.

- Retailing demands that merchandisers take some risk. Staying with the tried-and-true does not reflect fashion leadership or allow profits from early trends.

- The element of risk in this case is minute.

Before taking his next step and trying to convince Powers's boss with his arguments, Jim thought he would discuss the issues with friendly peers. He called several of his colleagues, explained the situation, and asked for advice on how to approach the problem.

Major Question
If you were one of Jim's colleagues, how would you advise him?

Study Questions
1. Why would promoting a new style or trend at the beginning of a season be a safe way for a retailer to test it?

2. Discuss the risks associated with the introduction of new styles and the maintenance of a store's fashion image.

3. What does Powers mean when he said "fashion is acceptance, anything else is an opinion"?

4. What type of stores show fashion leadership? How does the merchandise differ relative to non-fashion forward stores?

Case 10
Off with the Old—
On with the New

Carolyn Olsen, Southeast Community College

Rikers and Samson was an elegant downtown specialty establishment in Des Moines, Iowa. Branches of the store were in Lincoln and Omaha in Nebraska, and Sioux Falls in South Dakota. The least expensive garment available in their stores was $500, and their target market was the well-to-do, over-forty set in both town and country. The stores exuded an elegant image that attracted the more sophisticated and well-to-do customer who enjoyed shopping as an experience. Shoppers were made to feel like a welcome part of the establishment, and courtesy charge cards were faithfully sent to each customer by the associates. Many of the customers were so loyal that they allowed their associates to send them $5,000 to $10,000 in orders just on approval. High levels of personalized customer service along with expensive, beautiful clothing made Rikers and Samson THE place to shop.

For years, Mssrs. Rikers and Samson and their sons, daughters, nieces, and nephews had operated the family business. But as the families aged and many moved away from the Midwest, the directors (composed of the remaining Rikers and Samson family members) had decided to take Al Black into the business. Mr. Black brought with him years of expertise in retail, as well as some much needed capital. Because of the capital investment, all of the stores soon proudly carried the names of Rikers, Samson and Black!

Mr. Black did indeed bring with him fresh new ideas not only for remodeling the stores but also for the advertisement of the designer merchandise. He ordered nationally distributed advertisements featuring models in clothing from the stores staged at outdoor sites. These advertisements were very

well-received and as a result, customer traffic and sales volume increased. Soon, the stores were remodeled and updated with a fresh young image and look to them, and the employees were excited and upbeat about working with the beautiful merchandise in such lovely and elegant surroundings.

Mr. Black had a daughter who was very interested in retail and he soon established her as the manager of the Sioux Falls branch store. Her experience was not in management, but she did have a business degree and had worked in retail during her high school and college years. Mr. Black had the utmost confidence in her abilities and very soon, she had talked her father into letting her go to the various markets to do some of the buying. Consequently, the store merchandise slowly began to change in both cut and quality. The board of directors complained about some of her purchases, and consequently, Mr. Black advised her to take a lower profile in buying for awhile. However, Mr. Black had long-range plans for the future and these plans included his daughter and her buying strategies. Quietly establishing the store in Sioux Falls as a pilot store, he and his daughter began to purchase clothing for a younger and not-so-affluent clientele. Mr. Black allowed his daughter to make the decisions for purchasing at the Sioux Falls branch and paid for her buying trips to Texas, California, and New York.

After three years had passed, the board of directors in Des Moines could see that Mr. Black had indeed made their stores current and more active. As they no longer were suspicious of his every move, the time had come for Mr. Black to put his long-range plans into action. Large advertisements appeared in the Omaha, Des Moines, and Lincoln newspapers announcing that Rikers, Samson and Black would now also be targeting the under-forty customer. Follow-up articles in the papers featured interviews with Mr. Black talking about the changes that would soon appear in the stores.

Mr. Black assured the three communities that the new clothing and different styles had already been well received by the customers in a pilot store. The clothing would be less expensive but of good quality, and the under-forty customers would be made to feel more welcome in the stores. In fact, service was being updated to accommodate the younger executive woman.

In accordance with the plan, the newspapers soon carried headlines of Rikers, Samson and Black "Steps Toward Success." One of the major steps was the forced turnover of all sales associates over the age of forty. The public was assured personally by Mr. Black that none of these loyal associates was being fired. Instead, each of them had either been offered a buy-out plan or early retirement. Some had found new and challenging positions elsewhere when they decided they were not ready to quit working. It was known, however, that some of the displaced sales associates were unhappy and some lawsuits were being brought against the store for discrimination.

In late September, all of the stores were closed for one week and the grand opening was set for Saturday, October 1. It was a busy "football" Saturday across the Midwest and it seemed that Mr. Black's plan had worked because the stores were mobbed with customers. Then the backlash began. Following the grand opening, letters to the newspapers in all three cities complained of the shoddy service by unskilled, hastily trained sales associates. Additionally, complaints were made about the poor quality of clothing found in Rikers, Samson and Black. Letters, however, were not only arriving at the newspapers in these cities—bags of mail were also arriving at the individual stores. This mail included piles of cutup Rikers, Samson and Black courtesy charge cards, along with very angry letters concerning the loss of "my favorite associate" and cries of "if you are catering to the "under-forty customer, you don't want me!"

Mr. Black was very dismayed by the loss of so many loyal customers at one time. He immediately launched an advertising campaign in an attempt to bring back the customer base that the store had had for so many years. The advertisements denied that the stores were not welcoming the more mature customer; they were just changing their present focus to broaden their customer attraction. The wealthy, more-mature customers answered this claim by continuing their boycott of the stores.

Mr. Black had not planned on these events. His accountants soon reported to him a cashflow problem. Although business was brisk from the younger crowd, none of them were spending $7,000 to $10,000 in one shopping excursion as the older, more-established customers often had done.

The cash flow problem soon became very acute. His daughter's store was the furthest in debt for she had hidden her actual sales figures from her father's scrutiny. To stay in business, she had borrowed $25,000 from the corporation to make her store appear more economically sound. Soon, even the orders from manufacturers were shipped only COD. The stores were beginning to default on their payments, and sales associates were quitting each day. Something was going to have to happen soon.

Major Question
You are a business consultant who specializes in retail stores. Mr. Black has come to you for help. Can you save his stores? How?

Study Questions
1. What can be done to bring back the older, more affluent customers, or is it too late?

2. How can a store successfully appeal to a young, trendy customer at the same time as the older, more affluent, conservative customer?

3. What are the problems with changing a store's product mix and ultimately its image?

Case 11
Cannibalization in Product Development and Retailing

Evelyn Brannon, Auburn University

Sharron Peebles is an apparel product manager (APM) employed by the nation's largest women's specialty store operator. The ad recruiting for her position read:

> *Join an exciting company known for leadership in the development and global sourcing and production of apparel. We are a technology-based company looking for people with a "Yes We Can" philosophy—hands-on, fast-paced entrepreneurs to work together in product teams. Be part of bringing apparel from computer image to production spec to order to delivery at the most exciting retail stores in America. You will need a minimum of five years' apparel product development experience.*

Sharron's division is responsible for product development and sourcing for each of eleven store chains in the corporation. Some of the retail chains specialize in women's wear. Other chains carry men's wear, children's wear, lingerie, or accessories. The retail chain stores are mostly in malls but there are a few free-standing units in high traffic urban areas. Each chain has its own product development/sourcing team headquartered at a centralized location. The offices and workspace of each division are separate but all employees share public spaces, conference rooms, halls and elevators, and the cafeteria.

The company scours the world for "hot" items that can be translated into private-label products to be produced domestically and overseas. The buyers for the chains (who are headquartered at another site) do much of the design research by shopping in the U.S., Europe, and Asia. They send their "samples" to the APM. The APM's job is to:

• Turn the garments into specification drawings—fully detailed line drawings developed on an in-house CAD system.

• Select the color(s) for the item based on the seasonal color palette for that product development group.

• Swatch the design with suitable fabric by working with the fabric coordinators who track fabric trends and availability.

• Supervise patternmaking and fittings to translate the sample into the size standards used by that chain.

• Work with others on the team to coordinate items into a line plan.

• Coordinate the sourcing and scheduling of that item with associates at domestic and overseas manufacturing facilities and determine the delivery date with the buyers.

• Prepare detailed specifications for transmittal to the manufacturing facilities where the item will be made so that the stores will receive the item exactly as expected and on schedule.

Sharron relies on the management information system that links her product development/sourcing group with the buyers and with overseas associates. Through this system, computers are linked electronically to all the offices in the corporation. The system also provides access to information that Sharron uses for writing the specifications of the products. In her computer workspace she has access to CAD and to the forms for conveying product decisions.

Sharron's division, BasicOne, targets the fashion-conscious young woman from 18 to 25 with moderately priced, stylish clothes in the misses size range. There are two other chains in the corporation with a similar target:

1. CareerOne, a chain specializing in moderately priced careerwear.

2. EuroOne, a chain with hipper, more European-flavored styles.

The problem is that these three chains are cannibalizing each other in two ways:

1. Style research done for EuroOne is finding its way into the other two chains before the styles can be debuted in EuroOne stores. This practice is eroding the fashion leadership position of EuroOne. It also means that there is little design differentiation between the three chains. For example, all three chains tend to select samples from the same two or three bridge lines and designers. DKNY was particularly popular one season. Other seasons have seen similar leggings and tunics at all three chains. These items had slightly different trim and were offered in different colors, fabrics, and prices, but were essentially the same styles.

2. All three chains are crossing customers—that is, the same customers shop all three stores.

Overall, the chains are experiencing deteriorating sales, inconsistent quality, problems with pricing strategy, and a sagging reputation for fashion products. In terms of the corporation, this downswing has resulted in falling prestige in financial circles, tumbling stock prices, and store closings. The problem with stock prices affects Sharron directly because she participates in an employee stock ownership program.

However, there are opportunities for change. Each division/chain has a weekly meeting attended by buyers and APMs where new product ideas are generated. The meetings are open to employees at all levels including store presidents and corporate managers. The participants bring swatches, samples, photos, concept boards, and magazine photos to back up their new product proposals. This corporation is known for quick response and the ability to change fashion direction rapidly.

All three chains live on fast-turning fashion. No sooner does a trend appear on runways than it is available in these three stores at very moderate prices. The speeding up of the fashion cycle plus the availability of the fashion in all three chains has caused confusion in the mind of the consumer in regard to what is "in" and what is "out" at any given time. This has led to a slow down in consumer purchases, which is indicated by falling sales.

Major Question

How can Sharron battle the cannibalization of her line by CareerOne and EuroOne? How can the three chains differentiate their products and target markets?

Study Questions

1. What type of cooperation can the three chains do to lower costs without cannibalizing each other in terms of merchandise offerings?

2. What type of promotions, merchandise presentations, and service appropriate to each chain's target, would you recommend for each of the three chains?

3. Are there other recommendations you can suggest to help retain product differentiation between the three chains?

Case 12
Burlington, Vermont— Church Street Marketplace

Pauline Sullivan, The University of Vermont

Zeppa Masseau, a fashion designer who manufactured high-priced women's apparel, including an evening line, recently sold her business in San Francisco and then moved to Burlington, Vermont. After living in Burlington for almost a year, Zeppa noticed a lack of sophisticated women's clothing for sale. In fact, she regularly traveled to Montreal and Boston to shop for herself.

Zeppa is considering opening her own upscale women's fashion boutique. She thinks that there is a market for designer clothes in Burlington. Moreover, she is exploring an opportunity to develop her own private label line to sell in her store. Currently, Zeppa is evaluating a downtown location for her store. In Burlington, the Church Street Marketplace offers merchants services, and she is researching what services she will receive if she locates there.

Burlington, Vermont

Burlington, Vermont's largest city, is a picturesque community of 39,000, located on the shore of Lake Champlain. It is located in Chittenden county (population 131,761), 60 miles from the Canadian border and 90 miles from Montreal. The city is ranked as one of the best places to live in the United States according to several national publications. It is an urban area surrounded by tranquil countryside and the Green Mountains. It has all the amenities of an urban area, including Vermont's only state university and several other colleges. In the downtown area, there are the Flynn Theater, Memorial Auditorium, a movie theater, and many restaurants serving diverse cuisines. Such cultural activities as plays, concerts, a jazz festival, and museum exhibits are regularly featured in Burlington.

Church Street Marketplace

The Church Street Marketplace is an upscale pedestrian mall with 300,000 square feet of retail space located along four city blocks in Burlington's downtown central business district. The Church Street Marketplace is managed by the Marketplace Commission, a seven-person management organization that is part of the City of Burlington. The Marketplace Commission uses a shopping center model of management to maintain, operate, and promote the downtown area. The Church Street Marketplace attracts approximately three million visitors annually. Seasonal promotions and cultural activities in the Burlington area, for example, First Night and Discover Jazz, generate customer traffic for the Church Street Marketplace (see Table 2.1).

The Church Street Marketplace charges retail property owners common area fees, which generate most of its $700,000 operating budget. Supplemental

Table 2.1   Annual Promotions for the Burlington Area

Event	Traffic Generated	Month
Green Mountain Chew-Chew	60,000	June
Sidewalk Sale	NA	August
Pepsi at Noon	NA	July & August
Arts Alive	1,000	June
Discover Jazz	40,000	June
Americana Unlimited Antiques Festival	NA	June
Fourth of July	30,000	July
Champlain Valley Festival	NA	August
Fall Foliage (Vermont)	3,000,000	September–October
Marketfest	10,000	October
Vermont Mozart Festival	NA	October–March
First Night	20,000	December 31

security, in addition to the Burlington Police Department, is provided. In addition to promotions, the Marketplace uses cooperative advertising dollars for newspaper, radio, and television advertising on several local stations. Cooperative advertising is paid for by the Marketplace and local merchants. Burlington has three local television stations, one daily newspaper, six radio stations, and two weekly newspapers. The television stations reach Quebec.

Church Street Marketplace is a successful operation with almost 100 percent occupancy. Stores range in size from 200 to 14,000 square feet on the first floor. Retail stores in the downtown area include clothing, shoes, jewelry and accessories, books, gifts, cards, home furnishings, music and videos, as well as a department store and many restaurants. Such national chains as Gap, The Limited, Express, and Victoria's Secret operate stores in downtown Burlington. Recently, the Body Shop, Nature Company, and Ann Taylor opened on the Church Street Marketplace. Also, vendors operate carts on the Marketplace.

Generally, stores on the Church Street Marketplace operate 10 a.m.–6 p.m. Monday through Saturday, and noon to 5 p.m. on Sunday. Some stay open later on Friday. The Marketplace is active all year long and has been compared to Boston's Faneuil Hall or New York's South Street Seaport.

The consumer market for Church Street Marketplace encompasses local college students, medical staff, attorneys and legal staff, bank employees, government workers, and retail/restaurant employees. Average family income in Burlington (1995) is approximately $40,000.

Canadian/U.S. Cross-border Shopping

Many Canadians, with an average family income of approximately $46,000 Canadian ($34,000 U.S.), travel to Burlington specifically to shop and are considered part of its secondary market area. Most of these tourists come from Quebec, which is primarily a French-speaking province. They shop in the U.S. for better prices, selection, days and hours of operation, staff friendliness, and service quality in bars and restaurants.

Recent research results show Canadians who cross-border shop have younger spouses, more children under 18 living at home, speak English and are more educated than those who do not shop in the U.S. Cross-border shoppers make 4.87 annual trips to the U.S. to shop and spend an average of $235.95 Canadian ($174.60 U.S.) per trip.

Approximately 90 percent of the cross-border shoppers reported buying textile and apparel products in the U.S. These cross-border shoppers visit a variety of shopping areas and store types. They shop the downtown area, malls, and shopping strips including chain, department, and discount stores. Most cross-border shoppers reach their U.S. destination by automobile and live within two hours of the Canadian/U.S. border. Primarily, cross-border shoppers learn about U.S. shopping information on Canadian and U.S. television stations.

The number of Canadian cross-border shoppers, however, has decreased 14 percent within the last year, while the number of U.S. citizens shopping in Canada has increased almost four percent during the same time period. A low Canadian dollar (approximately $.74 U.S.) has made shopping in Canada as attractive as U.S. shopping. Additionally, a majority of noncross-border shoppers cited the low exchange rate as a deterrent to shopping in the U.S.

Canadian and U.S. Apparel Purchasers

There are differences between Canada and the U.S. regarding industry structure for apparel products. Although comparable products are sold in both countries, brand names and prices differ. For example, a tailored European-cut women's suit jacket can be found in a Canadian discounter for $49 Canadian ($36 U.S.) and a similar jacket by an American designer can be found at a U.S. discounter for $61 Canadian ($45 U.S.). Canadian shoppers purchase more private-label and store-brand merchandise than U.S. shoppers. Canadians perceive private- and store-brand merchandise as higher quality and more prestigious than regularly branded apparel products.

In particular, shoppers from Quebec are more fashion forward than Vermonters in their apparel purchases. Vermonters tend to be more functional—relative to weather conditions—in apparel selection.

The Competitive Environment

Approximately 40 women's apparel stores operate in the greater Burlington area. Nineteen of these stores are located in Burlington's central business district. However, only five stores carry career apparel and more sophisticated day-into-evening clothing. There is no upscale fashion boutique like the one Zeppa is proposing. Table 2.2 lists the stores and the products that are offered in these stores.

Henrietta's caters to the business woman with a merchandise selection that is broad and somewhat deep. However, the store does not project a sophisticated image. Window designs are boring. Bella appeals to the more fashion-oriented woman, whereas St. Savior attracts a more conservative shopper. VT Apparel, which carries fancy dresses for less formal evening events, has a unique artistic image but does not sell formal evening apparel. North's Department Store has a department devoted to eveningwear but their selection is shallow and narrow. Also, the styles are conservative and stock turnover is slow. Table 2.3 describes and compares store attributes. Henrietta's, Bella, St. Savior, and North's Department Store all carry narrow selections of eveningwear.

Table 2.2   Product Category Competition in Burlington

Store	Price Range	Product Categories	Major Labels
Henrietta's	Moderate	Business Suits Sportswear Dresses Evening Accessories	Harvé Bernard Kenar Oleg Cassini Nightline Oasis Maggie Boutique
Bella	Moderate- Prestige	Sportswear Dresses Evening	Nicole Miller BCBG French Connection Item
St. Savior	Moderate- Prestige	Business Suits Sportswear Evening Accessories	Angel Heart Trio Kenar Rialto Cynthia Rowley Laundry Datiani
VT Apparel	Moderate	Sportswear Dresses Accessories	Newfield Westerwear Bonnie Strauss
North's Department Store	Moderate- Prestige	Business Suits Sportswear Evening Accessories	Maggie Boutique Late Edition Nicole Paris LA Glo Liz Claiborne Zum

Table 2.3   Analysis of Competition in Burlington

Attribute	Henrietta's	VT Apparel	Bella	St. Savior	North's
Years in Business	20	10	8	12	50
Marketplace Location	no	yes	no	no	yes
Store Front Appealing	no	yes	yes	yes	no
Window Displays	poor	good	good	good	poor
Merchandise Assortment	broad/ deep	narrow/ shallow	narrow/ shallow	narrow/ shallow	narrow/ deep
Merchandise Quality	variable	good	good	good	variable
Instore Displays	boring	good	creative	good	poor
Interior Design	conservative	conservative	exciting	conservative	boring
Interior Scents	none	none	none	none	none
Interior Sounds	none	rock	world beat	classical	none
Instore Traffic Flow	poor	good	good	good	good
Knowledgeable Personnel	no	yes	yes	yes	no
Friendly Personnel	no	yes	yes	yes	no
Sales Service	acceptable	good	good	good	poor

Major Question

Should Zeppa open up an upscale fashion boutique in Burlington?

Study Questions

1. What market segments might attract an upscale apparel boutique in Burlington?

2. Is the Church Street Marketplace an appropriate location for this boutique? What is the image of Church Street Marketplace? Would Zeppa's boutique be well positioned in this shopping area?

3. How important is the Canadian market to the success of this store?

4. What merchandising strategies should the boutique use to attract Canadians customers?

References

Sullivan, P. (1995). *A Pilot study of Canadian cross-border shopping: Implications for the Vermont retail trade.* Hatch Project HA488, Vermont Agricultural Experiment Station.

Sullivan, P., & Lavoie, D. (1995, winter). *Metropolitan Montrealer's cross border shopping practices,* paper presented at ACRA, New York.

Case 13
The Small Store Dilemma

Nancy J. Rabolt, San Francisco State University
Judy K. Miler, University of Tennessee

Juan Romano is a small apparel speciality store owner in Dubuque, Iowa. He has had the store for fifteen years, and while it has not been an easy road to success, he very much enjoys his work and lifestyle in this middle American city. Prior to having his own business, Juan had worked for several major apparel retailers as a buyer and divisional merchandise manager. Life has been good to him, and he gives back to his community through philanthropic involvement and donations, granting him respect as a Spanish-American businessman in Dubuque.

The annual sales volume of the store is in the neighborhood of $500,000, which yields a comfortable living. Juan's store sales personnel consist of one full-time salesperson and two part-timers, a student at the local community college and a retired school teacher. The customers are in the middle to slightly above average income range. They are not fashion leaders in the sense that they want the latest market offerings, but they are fashion conscious and highly selective. Juan's store sells a full range of men's and women's clothing: from sleepwear to outerwear, sportswear and a small amount of seasonal, special-occasion merchandise. He has built up a loyal customer base of professional men and women who live and work in the area. Juan offers his customers the service they want, with the prices and styles they desire.

Juan enjoys the daily running of the store. It adds up to a most pleasant and profitable occupation—that is, until six months ago when Juan learned that one of the major chain stores in the state, with a national reputation, had filed plans to build and anchor a shopping center approximately one-quarter mile from his store. The shopping center will be ready for occupancy in eight months. This has Juan quite upset as he knows that the ladies' sportswear and dress departments will be in direct competition to the merchandise classifications he carries, because he has shopped this major chain store himself, looking for inspiration of lines to purchase for his store.

Even though Juan already knows the character and practices of the department store that will be moving into Dubuque, he starts an in-depth investigation. He travels to the nearest branch and studies it for a day. The store's departments offer a wider assortment of styles than Juan's store, maintain depth beyond his ability, have interesting and compelling regional advertising, including television spots, offer personal selling service, including personal shoppers, maintain liberal return policies, and accept any credit card under the sun.

Needless to say, Juan is more than a bit upset and disturbed by his findings. He knows that there is a possibility that he will not be able to stand the hard-hitting competition, let alone the pressure. One of his neighbors, the owner of a children's shop, remarked the other day, "I don't know what I'm going to do—look for another location? I don't know how to stand up to the competition."

Juan's full-time salesperson, Sara Cummings, keeps repeating, "I'm not afraid of them. They're big, but our customers are loyal. They've been our customers for years, and they like us and our merchandise." If Juan could only believe this, there would be no reason to fear the new store taking his customers away.

Juan, however, knows the threat is real and he must begin to prepare a proactive course of action. His store's location is in a strip shopping area with no strong pull from adjoining stores. They are all small retailers like himself. The strength has to come from within. Steps must be taken to ensure continued success. As a small store operation, Juan knows that he cannot obtain exclusivity of styling, preferential delivery, buy in promotional quantities or use conventional promotional power like the big stores.

Juan visits his Dallas buying office, an operation that handles small specialty shops, but feels that their advice is inadequate to meet the situation. As a matter of fact, he is somewhat annoyed by the president's major suggestion, which was to visit the market more often. This is very unrealistic. As a small store operator, how can he leave the store to visit New York, Dallas, or Atlanta more frequently? Not only is it too costly, as he does not have the volume to support more frequent purchasing, but he cannot see how it will position him better to meet the other challenges the new store is going to present.

Major Question

If you were Juan, what course of action would you take to combat the big, new competition moving into your store's area?

Study Questions

1. Today, many small, independent apparel stores are suffering from competition of large, national chains. Discuss some strategies that a small

retailer could implement to help secure the maintenance of the store's market share when faced with new competition.

2. In what ways can a small store excel compared to a large department store?

3. If two stores carry the same merchandise, how can one store differentiate itself to ensure customer loyalty?

Case 14
Trend Decisions: Prototype of a New Line

L. Susan Stark, San Francisco State University

Joan Walters, a division of Sue J, Inc., is located outside of San Francisco and sells to Nordstrom and Dillard's, as well as many small specialty stores. The manufacturer's line serves the 30+ woman who is conservative, likes comfortable-fitting, easy-care garments. The firm specializes in pants and has one of the best-fitting pants in the market. Typical fabrications are polyester and rayon; 48 percent of the designs are for the misses market, 35 percent for petites, and 17 percent for women's. Generally, this customer is regarded as a fashion follower who is one year behind the current trends, buys moderately priced clothing, and never buys anything too trendy. In the past, one of the big sellers at Joan Walters has been jumpsuits, which is currently being revived and restyled. The company also makes blouses, skirts, and some blazers.

Recently, the company was approached by Delta Burke Designs to be the exclusive designer/producer of the separates segment of the new Delta Burke Collection. Delta Burke is a company that plans to focus on beautiful, affordable designs for the larger-sized woman. The company envisions their target customer as a career woman, who dresses to express her womanly attributes with a romantic flair, rather than cover up her size. The price points, fabrication, styling, and quality of the line would follow Joan Walter's line. The spokes-woman, Delta Burke, is a larger-sized comic actress (who is also a former Miss Florida) with a perceived romantic Southern background. She is known for dressing in a conservative, yet feminine manner. Delta Burke Designs has requested five prototypes for the line.

Claudia Siegel, the President of Joan Walters, must give her design team guidelines for fabrication, colors, and silhouettes for the Burke prototypes. Paula Powers and Nancy Hamlow make up the design team with some input from Claudia, as well as several student interns. Paula has been with the company for two years after coming from a small fashion-forward sportswear company in New York. She was instrumental in wooing the Delta Burke Design people and is excited about the prospects of working this line. Her long-range goal is to update the Joan Walters' company. Nancy, the other main design team member, is more conservative and proposes "safe" designs for their conservative customer. After examining three major fashion forecaster reports, Paula and Nancy noted the following six trends for the Fall season:

• *The Romantics:* soft colors with bright high-lights, ruffles, and flared edges dominating; a draped and flowing silhouette, with waistline shaping in full or tiered skirts.

• *The Active Life:* body-hugging clothes that allow freedom for active sports like biking and aerobics; sturdy practical clothing for hiking and other sports; neutral colors, with some dramatic, hard-edged emphasis; knits, Lycra, and nylon are important materials.

• *Retro Art:* styling that is based on the fit and shape of the 1940s and 1950s; career dressing mainly; shapely, with exaggerated fit and a conservative attitude; many suits in wool using neutral colors, navy important; suiting materials with some silky fabrics for contrast.

• *Whimsical Minds:* floaty, flirtatious, gauzy fabrics, with a lighter-than-air feeling; layering with soft, thin fabrics; garments do not seem to touch the body.

• *Ethnic Minds:* printed fabrics that bring in various cultures—African, Bali, Indian, Middle Eastern—used with diaphanous, full clothing styles, generally wrapped and draped; mixture of fabrications with many bright colors and interwoven metallic threads.

• *Natural Lines:* clothing inspired by nature in neutral colors and natural fibers; soft clothing in loose-fitting, comfortable shapes and body covering, soft lines; little dramatic emphasis, easy fit, which often uses layering.

Both team members developed their own ideas for the line separately and came together in a meeting to share ideas. Their goal was to come to a consensus for the line to deliver to Claudia for approval before going to Delta Burke Designs. However, they could not agree on just one trend for the Delta Burke line. Paula's idea was to produce a line around the romantic trend with soft colors and flaring silhouettes because this styling addresses the romantic nature of the customer. Nancy felt that the natural trend was more suited to the larger-sized woman. The loose fit camouflages the figure and is comfortable and appropriate for work, more so than the romantic trend.

Major Question
With which of the design team members do you agree, if either? How should that trend be interpreted for the Delta Burke Collection prototypes?

Study Questions
1. Which of the five trends are most flattering for the larger-sized figure?

2. How do fashion-forward, mass-fashion, and fashion-follower manufacturers use the information provided by fashion forecasters?

3. What is the relationship between the manufacturer of the apparel and the company whose name appears on the label, such as Delta Burke?

Case 15
Women's Golf Apparel: An Important Niche

Carol F. Tuntland, California State University

Apparel manufacturers and retailers continue to look for growth opportunities and profits as we head into the 21st century. Niche markets are an important source for both growth and profit. Segmenting the cusomer into smaller customer groupings allows the marketer to target the customer more specifically. One popular niche market is golf apparel. The game is played around the world and there are 27 million golfers in the U.S., as well as millions of players in Japan and England. Other countries in Europe and Asia have excellent courses, and the game is even attracting new players in Africa.

Golf became a popular sport for men at the turn of the century, and professional golf, as a sport, was recognized early in the century. Women also took up the sport, but, for the first part of the twentieth century, there were only a handful of women professionals. After World War II, however, women's professional golf began to make significant strides. Babe Didrickson Zaharias and Patty Berg were among a group of eleven female golfers who established the Ladies Professional Golf Association (LPGA) in 1950.

The 50th anniversary Women's Open Championship was held at The Broadmoor in Colorado Springs, Colorado, with a field of 150 professionals and amateurs competing for $175,000 in prize money. Other major tournaments include the Nabisco Dinah Shore in Rancho Mirage, California, and the Tournament of Champions in Lake Worth, Florida. Prior to the Open Championship at The Broadmoor, 19 tournaments had been played in the U.S. and were documented on America Online. Prize money for these tournaments ranged from $75,000 to $180,000 awarded per tournament to professional and amateur LPGA players.

Clothing fashions for golf began to develop in the late 19th century and have continued to be important throughout the 20th century. In addition to the equipment needed to play the sport, apparel is very important to many golfers. Golfing apparel continues to retain its own distinct image. One such apparel item is *plus fours*. These full, baggy pants, which end just below the knee were popularized by the Duke of Windsor in the 1920s. They are still an identity item for some well-known male golfers at the end of the 20th century.

Golf shirts and shorts have been fashionable since the 1950s for both men and women and continue to be popular with golfers. Apparel styling for men and women is dictated, to a degree, by the rules of the Professional Golf Association (PGA) and the LPGA. Male golfers buy more apparel at pro shops, while female golfers frequently purchase their apparel from department and specialty stores. Employees at two pro shops have speculated that women do not purchase golf apparel at pro shops because they like a greater variety than most pro shops carry. These employees also thought that women do not buy specific labels in golf apparel in the same way that men do, but will mix and match labels and styles.

A well-known golf apparel manufacturer, T-Off, is attempting to increase its market share of the golf apparel market. This manufacturer produces men's golf shirts, shorts, and caps, and women's placket shirts and sweatshirts. A specialty of T-Off is the apparel embroidery logo business that they do for numerous golf courses across the country.

Profiled in *Bobbin* magazine, T-Off has been very successful for the last two years and expects to become a major golf apparel manufacturer in the U.S. A vertical manufacturer of golf shirts and other shirtings, the company has reengineered itself for success in the years ahead by offering quick delivery, small-order flexibility, a variety of shirt colors, and embroidery options. For golf shops that buy small quantities of merchandise, these options provide variety without a requirement to invest inventory dollars in only one partic- ular style or color. Additionally, the option to purchase a variety of colors and styles provides more flexibility in planning and producing a good mix of women's apparel for pro shops.

One of the methods T-Off uses to advertise its golf apparel is to sponsor professional golfers. In fact, the company considers this the heart of its marketing plan. For this advertisement campaign, T-Off recruits and sponsors well-known PGA play- ers. This year, two golfers wearing T-Off's apparel have finished in the top four places at national tournaments and have been photographed in its apparel at the end of the tournaments. The expo- sure has gained T-Off national recognition and has increased sales. The sponsored players vary from year to year, as does the level of sponsorship.

The company sponsors no LPGA or Seniors players at this time; however, when questioned about additional sponsorships, the company presi- dent mentioned that the company will probably begin to sponsor some members of the Seniors tour as well-known PGA players join the seniors group.

Recently, T-Off's product development man- ager, Beau Richards, met with the president of T-Off, Dominic Pascal, to discuss a proposal to begin manufacturing a line of LPGA sportswear. Because the company is looking for ways in which to increase its market share, Beau thought this market was a natural add-on. Also, because the company already does a small amount of women's golf separates, it would not be too difficult to expand the line and sponsor a couple of profes- sional women golfers. The response from Dominic, however, was not positive. Dominic said that he would like his wife to start playing golf and he knows more and more women are playing. However, he had no plans to sponsor any LPGA players because, in his words to Beau, "So few women play yet, and I just don't think it would be a very good move."

Major Question

Should T-Off develop and manufacture a complete line of women's golf apparel and sponsor LPGA players?

Study Questions

1. Do "so few women" play golf? How would one research golf to find information about female golfers?

2. What questions should be asked to determine the need for a women's golf apparel line? Where would you market a women's golf apparel line?

3. If you owned a sports apparel manufacturing company, would you sponsor LPGA players as part of your advertising campaign?

4. How would you research the competition for this product?

Case 16
A Void in Gap's Apparel (Experts Say It's Losing Baby Boomer)

Gavin Power, Levi Strauss & Co.

Has the Gap Inc. gotten too young?

Victoria Miller, a fashionable, 37-year-old mul- timedia designer, thinks so. "Gap is gearing more to a younger audience these days," says Miller. "It's OK if I'm looking for basics like shirts and stuff, but it's hard to find dressier things. I feel like I'm at the far end of their demographic."

In explaining the recent poor sales at its core 810-store Gap division, the San Francisco clothing company blames the general downturn in the apparel business, as well as a barrage of copycat products from competitors. Gap also lays some fault on its own doorstep, saying its merchandise has been bland in recent seasons.

Retail experts agree. But there are those who also wonder whether Gap may be making a tactical mistake in trying too hard to appeal to teenagers

---

and the twenty-something set, especially given indications that Gap attire is "uncool" to some Generation Xers. "Saturday Night Live," for example, has a running skit that mocks the chain and several alternative magazines have lampooned its celebrities-in-khakis advertising campaign.

The apparel merchandise change at Gap's core stores—which account for more than half of Gap's annual sales of about $4 billion—seems to correspond with the company's flagging sales. Business began to slow significantly in the second half of 1994 and the slump has continued (into 1995).

For the fiscal first quarter ended April 29, Gap's earnings dropped 21 percent to $50 million, while sales at stores open at least a year—known as same-store sales—fell 2 percent, compared with a 7 percent gain in the year-earlier period. Analysts expect Gap to show another big decline in profits for the second quarter. Just last week the company said that same-store sales fell 4 percent in June, leading several brokerage houses to cut their earnings estimates. The stock has been among the most volatile in the retail sector.

Some analysts and consultants say the company is alienating the baby boomer who can't find enough grown-up clothing at Gap stores and may suffer sticker shock at Banana Republic—Gap's upscale division. "Gap really made a shift to a younger customer last year," said Helen Bulwik, president of Seagate International, a retail consultancy based in Oakland. "A great deal of their square footage is now focused on a very young woman—things like short shorts and skimpy skirts. The boomer customers are not finding a whole lot that appeals to them. There's a gap at the Gap, and it's hurting them."

Robert Buchanan, retail analyst at NatWest Securities Corp, in New York, also has noticed the merchandise shift over the past year. "They have a more youthful approach in the stores these days, and I'm not sure that's been their historical strength." A visit to Gap's flagship San Francisco store on Market Street shows a decidedly youthful bent. There are ample assortments of short floral skirts, denim overalls, and tight-fitting denim vests. There is little in the way of blazers, blouses, and light summer slacks.

Diane Arnold, a 26-year-old executive assistant, says she is beginning to have a hard time shopping at Gap, traditionally one of her favorite stores. "I went there the other day to buy a skirt for work, but I couldn't find anything appropriate," said Arnold. "I think they used to have more casual things you could wear to the office."

Gap, arguably the best-managed retail company in the industry, has hit rough spots before. In 1992, sales growth slowed dramatically and earnings dropped for the first time in eight years. But the following year Gap rebounded, posting record sales and earnings. The question now is whether Gap can pull itself out of the doldrums with the deftness it has displayed in the past.

Warren Hashagen, senior vice president of finance at Gap, said the company made no conscious decision to target young customers. He said teenage customers are important, but added, "Our intent is to also appeal to the customer who can wear our product in an office environment. Whether we've done an adequate job is open to debate." Hashagen said Gap does recognize that there's a large opportunity in casual work clothes, and not just khaki pants and denim shirts which it and so may other retailers have been pushing. He said Gap's fall selections will feature blazers, dresses, and other fashionable merchandise.

Offsetting the weakness at Gap's core stores are better results at its other divisions. Banana Republic now has 192 stores and is said to be performing well. Hashagen defended the chain's prices, saying it was never intended as a mass-market operation. He said the price points—neckties run from $30 to $38, while a pair of silk slacks costs $129—are reasonable given the quality and tailoring.

Even if adults aren't buying much for themselves, they're definitely purchasing more for their kids, which is helping GapKids. The division has 326 stores in the U.S. and is expected to grow to 361 in the next two years.

Gap is putting a lot of stock in its Old Navy Clothing Co. discount chain, which was rolled out in 1993 and has grown to nearly 70 stores. The company plans to open an additional 50 outlets this year. Gap believes Old Navy, which offers basic clothing priced 30 percent lower than regular Gap clothing, will be the most aggressive vehicle of growth over the next decade.

Internationally, Gap has stores in Canada, England, and France and will move into Germany and Japan within the next decade.

Major Question

Should Gap gear its merchandise to a specific demographic group? If so, which? If not, why?

Study Questions

1. If you were a consultant to Gap, Inc. what changes would you make in the company to provide for continued growth?

2. What are the target markets of Gap, Inc.'s divisions: Gap, GapKids, Banana Republic, Old Navy?

3. What image does Gap have? Is it a strong image? Who are its competitors and how is Gap different from those competitors?

4. Can a store like Gap appeal to both 20-year-olds and 40-year-olds at the same time? If so, how does that affect advertising, store display, merchandise offerings and service?

Case 17
Hilo Hattie: A Shifting Customer Base

Aileen Geronimo and Karen H. Hyllegard, University of Hawaii

Hilo Hattie is the largest manufacturer and retailer of men's and women's Hawaiian or "Aloha" wear in Hawaii. The company maintains three retail stores (in Kauai, Maui, and Hawaii), and two production/retail centers (in Honolulu and Hilo). In addition to its company-manufactured Hawaiian apparel, Hilo Hattie's retail outlets also sell assorted Hawaiian souvenirs and jewelry for both the tourist and *Kama'aina* (local resident) markets.

Tourism Industry

Tourism is Hawaii's main source of revenue, and thus the future of the industry is a constant concern for many Hawaii businesses. Hawaii's tourist industry is clearly going through changes that may affect Hilo Hattie's sales. Unfortunately, however, because tourism is affected by occurrences in other parts of the world, the state and local businesses have limited control over the industry's growth and development. For example, the many natural disasters and economic troubles that have plagued the state of California (Hawaii's primary source of U.S. visitors), the Kobe earthquake in Japan, and the devaluation of the Mexican peso, which makes Mexico a better-value beach vacation for price-conscious Americans, have all contributed to a recent decline in Hawaii's tourism.

Pomare, Ltd.: History and Background

In 1963, James Romig created Pomare, Ltd., a conglomerate of Hawaiian and resortwear businesses. Romig got his start wholesaling clothes to retailers in 1960, expanded into manufacturing in 1966, and then into retailing in 1967 on the island of Kauai. Although the original retail shop was located far from the hotels, the partners came up with a unique means of ensuring customer traffic. They arranged for tour buses to stop at their store on the way to and from the airport and hotels—offering tourists a quick and easy means of purchasing gifts and souvenirs. This strategy proved to be very successful and led to the opening of more retail stores throughout the Islands.

Pomare, Ltd. continued to grow throughout the 1970s, and in 1979, Romig purchased Hilo Hattie, an existing Hawaiian-wear manufacturing and retailing business owned by the Margolis family of Hilo. The company's original owners took the name Hilo Hattie for its label from the performer Clara Nelson. Clara "Hilo Hattie" Nelson was a well-known performer of the comic hula, a satire of

Hawaiian dance. When "Hilo Hattie" performed, she dressed in a custom-made Hawaiian *mu'umu'u* and a straw hat, contributing to the tourists' notion of "Hawaiian" dress. Romig obtained the right to use the Hilo Hattie label and decided to continue using the brand name because it exemplified the Aloha spirit and the "fun" image he wanted his company to project. He also believed that Hilo Hattie was more recognizable than the old name, Hawaiian Wear Unlimited.

In 1983 an 80,000 square foot flagship store was established in Honolulu. This store houses Hilo Hattie's corporate offices, 55 percent of the company's manufacturing operations (the manufacturing branch in Hilo accounts for the remaining 45 percent), and a retail outlet. One of the unique features of this facility is the garment production space located within the selling area, which allows customers to observe the assembly of Hilo Hattie's Aloha wear. In 1987, Romig sold his other resortwear stores to focus more of his attention on his growing Hilo Hattie operations.

Hilo Hattie's Merchandise Mix

Hilo Hattie sells a variety of merchandise, including Aloha wear and other apparel items, jewelry (the second largest merchandise classification), and souvenirs (e.g., candy, coffee, key chains, placemats, hats, leis, and so forth). The merchandise assortment is broad and deep, especially in regard to Hawaiian apparel. For example, Aloha shirts for men can be found in both wild or subdued prints, bright or pastel colors, and an array of sizes—from extra small to double-extra large. The same variety of fabric colors and prints can be found in women's garments, for both long and short *mu'umu'us,* although sizes range from only small to large. Most of Hilo Hattie's garments are fairly simple in terms of styling and construction.

"Aloha" is a Hawaiian word spoken as a greeting or to extend a welcome. It generally implies warmth, friendliness, and the pride of the Hawaiian people. Although not indigenous to the native population of Hawaii, "Aloha wear" refers to those clothing items that are recognized as hav-

ing originated in Hawaii. Today's Aloha wear consists mainly of the *holoku,* a women's formal dress; the *mu'umu'u,* a chemise-like dress that was originally worn as an undergarment; and the Aloha shirt for men. Many Hawaii residents frequently wear *mu'umu'us* or Aloha shirts for both social and work occasions, particularly on Fridays, which are officially known as "Aloha" Fridays in Hawaii.

Today's Aloha shirt is worn by both tourists and local residents. For instance, many state and local government officials and business owners regularly wear Aloha shirts—rather than business suits—to the office. The Aloha shirts marketed to local residents for business wear are generally more subdued than the shirts marketed to tourists. To create a more subdued look, the Aloha "business" shirt is often constructed using the reverse side of fabrics, and the fabrics tend to have small geometric prints rather than large floral prints—more like the traditional Polynesian designs.

All of Hilo Hattie's brand-name merchandise is made in Hawaii but most of the Company's fabrics are produced in Japan. The actual fabric prints are designed and approved by Hilo Hattie; however, the artwork is generally contracted out locally, and the production prints and dye colors for the initial fabric samples are worked up in Japan. Print designs are reviewed continually by a design committee to ensure that the company's merchandise keeps pace with current fashion trends and new styles are introduced quarterly.

Price and Distribution

The use of advanced production techniques enables Hilo Hattie to maintain high-quality merchandise and lower costs, which are reflected in the moderate prices of their retail brand name apparel. A basic, short polyester *mu'umu'u* starts at $16, whereas the fancier styles average $45 to $50. A long *mu'umu'u* costs between $65 and $70, and Aloha shirts retail from $16 to $60. Hilo Hattie sells its Aloha wear only through its five company-owned retail stores. It also sells other brand-name apparel products at its retail stores.

Promotional Channels and Activities

Hilo Hattie's promotional mix focuses on print advertising in all major tourist magazines, and such promotional activities as shell lei greetings, entertainment, demonstrations, complimentary drinks, and traditional sales events at all stores. Information about Hilo Hattie's stores can also be found in the tourist-guide pamphlets provided by hotels and rental car companies. Flyers containing shuttle bus schedules to and from the Hilo Hattie stores are distributed to all tour agencies.

One of Hilo Hattie's most successful promotional activities, "Three for Free," was created in cooperation with other companies in the tourist industry. In 1976, when Hawaii's economy was suffering from a recession, Romig entered into a cross-promotional program with the Kodak Hula Show and the Dole Cannery Tour in an effort to boost sales. Hilo Hattie, Kodak, and Dole worked together to transport tourists to and from their three locations free of charge. This kind of cooperation proved to be good for business, and today Hilo Hattie continues this service, which enhances its image of a fun Hawaiian shopping experience. Hilo Hattie's other promotional activities include free transportation for large groups, breakfast orientations for tour groups, and a stop on the Old Town Honolulu Trolley Tour.

Competition

Hilo Hattie is the only manufacturing and retail chain of Aloha wear in the state of Hawaii; thus, the company has no direct competition in terms of "concept-to-consumer" operations. However, there are many department stores and specialty stores throughout Hawaii that sell Aloha wear.

Local department stores generally have a broad and shallow assortment of Aloha wear merchandise; these stores cater to all types of customers in all socio-economic groups, and are a popular source for Aloha wear with the local market. Hilo Hattie's main competitors in this category include Liberty House, JCPenney, Sears, and Woolworth, all of which have multiple stores in Hawaii. The Aloha wear sold in these stores is similar in terms

Table 2.4	Average Department Store Prices for Selected Aloha Wear		
	Long *Mu'umu'u*	Short *Mu'umu'u*	Aloha Shirt
Liberty House	$84–$200 +	$40–$76	$30–$62
JCPenney	$55–$200	$50–$80	$26–$65
Sears	$60–$102	$40–$98	$16–$54
Woolworth's	$20–$52	$20–$31	$10–$45

of style, selection, fabric content, and sometimes brand names, but prices tend to vary from store to store. The average prices for Aloha wear in Hawaii department stores are provided in Table 2.4.

Specialty store competition includes Reyn's, Watumull's, and Princess Kaiulani Fashions, which are all local Hawaii businesses. Reyn's and Watumull's are retail chain stores, whereas Princess Kaiulani Fashions is an independent manufacturer, wholesaler, and retailer of women's Hawaiian wear and eveningwear.

Reyn's formerly sold only Aloha shirts; however, the company recently added a women's wear department. Their assortment of Aloha shirts is fairly broad and deep, but the assortment of women's wear is narrow and shallow. Reyn's caters to both Hawaii residents (specifically businessmen and women) and tourists. The fabric prints are more subdued compared to some of Hilo Hattie's garments.

Watumull's caters primarily to tourists, offering a wide selection of stylish Aloha wear. Watumull's has multiple shops in Waikiki, a popular spot for Japanese tourists.

Princess Kaiulani Fashions' focus is on production and wholesaling finished goods to Liberty House; however, the company also maintains a retail showroom, located one mile from Hilo Hattie's store in Honolulu. Princess Kaiulani caters mostly to local residents. Their merchandise and prints are more subdued and more fashionable than Hilo Hattie's, but the assortment is shallow and narrow. The average prices for Aloha wear at these specialty stores are provided in Table 2.5.

Table 2.5	Average Specialty Store Prices for Selected Aloha Wear Items		
	Long *Mu'umu'u*	Short *Mu'umu'u*	Aloha Shirt
Reyn's	$125–$175	$100–$150	$45–$60
Watumull's	NA	$30–$105	$30–$70
Princess Kaiulani	$90–$170	$60–$110	NA

Target Market

Hilo Hattie has a simple, yet unique, system for tracking customer characteristics. Upon entering a Hilo Hattie store each customer is given a color-coded shell lei which classifies the customer by method of transportation (e.g., tour group or individual or local resident) and identifies the specific tour company and group (e.g., U.S. Mainland vs Japanese tourist). The color of each lei signals the sales personnel as to the corresponding customer identification number which is recorded for each sale. This system provides Hilo Hattie with information on the type and amount of purchases made by various customer groups. Today, the majority of Hilo Hattie's customers are tourists. Hilo Hattie's fashion center in Honolulu alone attracts 2,000 visitors a day and the company's showrooms host 1,000,000 visitors per year, making Hilo Hattie one of Hawaii's most-visited attractions.

Hilo Hattie's main target customers are westbound visitors, or U.S. residents, who visit Hawaii during the winter season. The majority of these tourists range from 40 to 50 years of age, are male-female couples, and many are repeat visitors. First-time visitors frequently purchase matching male-female attire with bold Hawaiian prints. Repeat visitors, on the other hand, tend to favor Hawaiian apparel made from more subdued colors and prints, as well as more fashionable styles—similar to those worn by local Hawaii residents. However, the number of westbound visitors (predominantly U.S. mainland residents) to Hawaii has declined.

Secondary customers are eastbound visitors, whose numbers are increasing. Japanese tourists account for the majority of these eastbound visitors, with modest growth seen in other such emerging markets as Korea, Taiwan, China, Hong Kong, and Singapore. However, Japanese tastes are somewhat different from other eastbound visitors and their preferences for apparel goods lean toward high-quality, fashion items. Young Japanese tourists, both males and females from age 20 to 30 tend to be very brand conscious and are frequently found shopping at Chanel, Giorgio Armani, and other designer boutiques in Waikiki. Therefore, the young Japanese is not a target market for Hilo Hattie compared with other Asian tourists.

The length of stay for eastbound tourists averages six days, whereas the length of stay for westbound tourists averages ten days. On average, Japanese tourists spend $300 per day while vacationing in Hawaii, U.S. tourists spend $120 per day, and other foreign visitors spend $85–$140 per day.

Hilo Hattie's strong promotional efforts aimed at the tourist market has led many Hawaii residents to perceive Hilo Hattie as a retailer that caters strictly to tourists. Local residents perceive Hilo Hattie's merchandise as "loud and touristy," not suitable to their preferences for more subdued colors and prints. Therefore, customers in the *Kama'aina* market are not presently viewed as a target for Hilo Hattie.

Major Question

What recommendations would you make for changes in Hilo Hattie's business to combat the possible negative impact of the current shift in Hawaii's tourism?

Study Questions

1. As a vertically integrated company, what advantages does Hilo Hattie have over its competitors?

2. Is Hilo Hattie's Oahu business location an advantage or disadvantage in Hawaii's Aloha wear market?

3. What are some of the strengths and weaknesses of Hilo Hattie's promotional strategy?

4. Is Hilo Hattie's method of product distribution sufficient for future sales growth?

5. What are the advantages and disadvantages to Hilo Hattie's current target market?

6. How do Hilo Hattie's prices compare to its main competitors' prices?

References

A report on the economic conditions in Hawaii. (1995, July/August). *Business Trends*. Honolulu, HI.: Economics Department of the Bank of Hawaii.

The garment business conglomerate of Jim Romig. (1969, February). *Hawaii Business*, pp. 35–36, 38.

Hilo Hattie FACT SHEET. Honolulu, HI.: Pomare, Ltd.

History highlights of Hilo Hattie. Honolulu, HI.: Pomare, Ltd.

Lynch, R. (1991, July 10). Industry honors Hilo Hattie's. *Honolulu Star Bulletin*, p. E1.

Ronck, R. (1994, March 18). Hilo Hattie's is for visitors and locals alike. *Honolulu Advertiser*, pp. C1, C3.

Steele, H.T. (1984). *The Hawaiian shirt*. New York: Abbeville Press.

Yoneyama, T. (1990, March). Pomare's piece de resistance. *Hawaii Business*, pp. 85–87.

Chapter Discussion Questions

1. What stores have closed lately? Analyze their images and positioning in the market. Were they clearly differentiated, offering superior merchandise and service to the public? Why do you think they went out of business?

2. Discuss successful retailers and manufacturers that offer niche merchandise and/or services. How do they differ from traditional department and specialty stores? What are the keys to successful niche merchandising?

3. Discuss the fashion level of The Limited, Gap, Saks Fifth Avenue, Nordstrom, Neiman Marcus, Bloomingdale's, Macy's and other popular stores. How would you position them in terms of fashion leadership?

4. What demographic and psychographic changes have you become aware of in the population where you live?

5. How can small stores compete with larger stores that have more power?

Merchandise Characteristics

Chapter Objectives

- Present and exemplify such major merchandise characteristics as style, fashion, price, and quality as related to image.

- Differentiate levels of fashion and explore the concepts of licensing, knockoffs, and counterfeiting.

- Relate the advantages and disadvantages of branded vs private-label merchandise and dis-

The characteristics of merchandise offerings of a manufacturer or retailer are defined by its mission, image, and target market. Customers expect to find certain price, quality, and fashion levels, in addition to their favorite brands at the stores they patronize. Brands are recognizable labels, whether they are store, manufacturer, or designer labels, which have specific expectations of performance defined as value by customers. These expectations are based on consistency of the defining characteristics. Successful companies understand their customers' preferences and strive to maintain their business by meeting those needs. Dominance in one or more characteristics helps a manufacturer or retailer stand out from its competition and gain the all-important competitive edge.

Characteristics and Types of Merchandise

Part of the image of a company is based on the type of merchandise they offer. Retailers and manufacturers must decide on the characteristics of their merchandise offerings. Among the many questions to be asked and decisions to be made are:

- Will the company offer soft or hard goods?

- At what price and quality level will the products be offered?

- Will the products be private label or branded?

- Will the products be basic or fashion goods? If they are to be fashion goods, at which fashion level will they be offered?

After these decisions are made (among many others), there are also marketing considerations and decisions to be evaluated. A company (retail or manufacturer) must decide how to market the merchandise (whether it be fashion or basic goods, soft or hard goods, private or branded). Merchandise can be marketed as **convenience goods** (for example, pantyhose), **shopping goods** (which are evaluated more by the consumer and include most clothing purchases), **specialty goods** (which are particular brands), or **impulse goods** (which by their very nature are purchased with little or no planning). Obviously, the nature of the goods themselves (i.e., hard, soft, basic, fashion, and so forth) helps in making all these determinations, but merchandise characteristics can also identify and build (or hinder) the reputation of the business in the eyes of the consumer.

Soft Goods vs Hard Goods

Early American retailers sold general merchandise or dry goods. The term "dry goods" referred to bolts of fabric, while "wet goods" referred to rum, the two chief imports of Colonial days. Dry goods are now referred to as **soft goods,** which include apparel and linens. **Hard goods** include home furnishings, appliances, electronics, and so forth. A company's merchandise mix can include either one or both types of merchandise. In the last decade, department stores have tended to decrease or even eliminate hard goods while increasing soft goods, which have higher turnover and profitability. Other retailers began selling strictly hard goods in mass, and departments stores found it difficult to compete with their limited stocks. Because soft goods were consistently the majority of traditional department store sales, they frequently decided to drop many hard goods and to build up their apparel lines. JCPenney and Sears are two examples of the trend toward emphasizing soft goods over hard goods.

Price Levels

Price level is another characteristic of merchandise and store positioning. Certain stores are thought of as selling merchandise at certain prices. For example, discount stores sell lower-price point merchandise than regular-price stores,

while traditional department stores—which are regular-price oriented—sell merchandise at higher price levels. Prices of merchandise take into account more than just the merchandise; price also takes into account the services offered by the retailer and other non-price bases, for example, the store's environment, location, and level of customer service. Therefore, the same product may be found at two different retailers at two very different prices. Retailers with a monopoly position have the most freedom to determine prices; that is, with no competition, they can ask any price despite merchandise cost. For example, shops at airports are notorious for this because of their excessively high prices due to the relative absence of any competition. In a competitive situation, which is the case in most of today's retail environment, prices are affected by consumer demand and competitors' prices. Often apparel and other types of retailers meet their competitor's prices to make an individual sale and will also lower prices of branded goods when another store does. (See Chapter Four for more discussion on pricing policies and strategies.) Consumer prices are also affected by government regulations through the Robinson-Patman Act, which regulates the price retailers pay to suppliers. (See Chapter Twelve for discussion of this related issue.)

Some manufacturers and designers try to protect their reputations by selling only to full-price retailers and not to discounters. Similarly, some retailers try to protect their image by not selling any product that is also sold at a discounter. *Case 18, "With It" or Without,* describes such a department store policy.

The price of goods is generally related to the quality and style level of the goods. Apparel is designated as designer, bridge, better, moderate, or budget, generally in respectively descending price and quality. Designer goods carry a designer name. These vary by price and exclusivity levels; **designer collections** consist of the designer's high-end couture lines and ready-to-wear lines shown to the press twice a year, while the **bridge** (or **secondary**) **lines** are somewhat

Figure 3.1 Donna Karan showing her collection. She is one designer who takes an active role in how her line is sold at retail.

more affordable and may be licensed to another manufacturer. For example, Giorgio Armani's black label, his top line, carries the label "A Milano Borgonuovo 21" (his home address). In this line, men's and women's suits average $1900. The white label line, "LeCollezioni," in which suits are made with less expensive fabric, averages $1500. Both the black and white labels are found in Armani boutiques. His Emporio Armani labels—considered his bridge line—are less expensive and are found in stores with this name, while A/X Armani, his lowest price lines are found in A/X boutiques, as well as in department stores. Similarly, Calvin Klein has price variations within his offerings, with his popular bridge line, CK. Bridge lines are often similar to the quality and price of **better goods.** Bridge goods, which carry a designer name and high price, may not necessarily be as high quality as better goods, however. This is because the status of the designer name, and not necessarily the quality, is the reason for the popularity; thus, the product can command a higher price. **Moderate goods**

are lower in price and quality than better goods and are sold at many department stores, while **budget** (or **popular**) **goods,** are even lower-priced and are offered at discount department stores and mass merchandisers. Budget goods may also be referred to as **opening price point** because they are the beginning price that a retailer offers.

Style and Fashion Levels

Retailers often classify merchandise as basic or fashion. **Basics** (also known as **staples**) generally have a stable customer demand. Some examples of basics are pencils, shoelaces, jeans, T-shirts, and hosiery. Although some basics are seasonal, this type of merchandise is often **non-seasonal** as it sells all year long. At times, basics become so popular that they take on a "fashion" of their own. This happened in the 1980s with women's blazers and in the 1990s with Gap's "basic" look.

    Fashion goods are thought of as something new, in demand, or popular—at any particular time. They are less stable, have a short life span, and therefore are more risky (financially) than basics. Generally, they are also **seasonal**; that is, they sell best during either the Spring or Fall season. As demand for fashion goods is not easily predictable, buying mistakes can be made and there can be more markdowns at the end of the season for fashion goods than for basics, which change less from season to season and can demand a more stable price. Fashion level is another characteristic of merchandise. **Mass fashion** appeals to the majority of consumers and is produced and distributed at moderate or opening prices at both discount and department stores. Consumers who buy mass fashion are not fashion leaders, but still want to be in fashion. **High fashion** is produced and priced for that small percentage of the population who want something new and different from mass fashion, with the added panache of exclusivity. High fashion products are generally high-priced because of these factors.

Figure 3.2 Levi's apparel is an example of basic merchandise that never really goes in or out of style.

Figure 3.3 An example of fashion goods, Giorgio Armani's black label (his top couture line) is offered exclusively through his boutiques.

Each retailer has to determine the proportion of fashion to basics that will meet its customer's needs. Gap is a retailer that sells mostly basics; sometimes, however, they offer fashion goods. Buying decisions related to stock and merchandise assortments often consider both basics and fashion groups together—not in isolation. (More on assortment planning may be found in Chapter Four.) Fashion items are often matched with basics in merchandise groupings that sell well together as discussed in *Case 19, Bottom Out on Basics.*

Merchandise Quality

The **quality** of merchandise is a major consideration in product selection and offerings by both retailers and manufacturers when determining merchandise positioning or the company's reputation, as well as the needs and wants of their market. Quality is often thought of as "degree of excellence." In apparel it is determined by many aspects, which are comprised of many aesthetic and functional features. Aesthetics include appearance, fit, design, fabrication, construction, and details or decoration. Functional features include such attributes as durability and serviceability.

Consumers' perceptions of quality may be as important as the actual quality. It is difficult to judge some aspects (for example, durability) at the point of sale because some items must be "tested" before a true evaluation can take place; that is, many times apparel has to be worn and in some cases washed before a true evaluation can take place. Therefore, extrinsic characteristics are often used to judge quality. Extrinsic features include such factors as price, brand, reputation of the retailer or manufacturer, and country of origin.

Branded merchandise (discussed in the next section) is known for a certain expected quality. Private labels may be of comparable quality, but are often not as well known. If expected or perceived quality is not achieved, reputations and customers can be lost. Such was the situation in *Case 20, The Super Shell.* By changing contractors and their selection of fabric, a store's successful private-label shell lost its appeal when the fit of

Table 3.1	Relationship of Styling and Price in Women's Wear		
Market	Styling	Brand Example	Price Range
Designer collection	Unique, top-name designer fashion	Donna Karan	Designer (high-end)
Designer bridge	Designer fashion	DKNY	Bridge
Misses or petite	Adaptations of fashions	Liz Claiborne	Better to budget
Contemporary	Trendy	BCBG, The Limited	Better to budget
Junior	Youthful, trendy	Guess?	Moderate to budget (low-end)

the garment was distorted because of an unstable new fabric.

Quality control is done at either the fabric manufacture, garment manufacture, or retail levels. Specifications of private-label merchandise are usually checked by the retailer against approved samples before being distributed to the stores. Some large retailers and manufacturers, such as JCPenney and Levi Strauss, perform extensive textile testing on products based on standards set by the American Association of Textile Chemists and Colorists (AATCC) and the American Society for Testing and Materials (ASTM). Normally, the manufacturer is responsible for checking the quality of materials before production—but not always. This is illustrated by *Case 21, The Fabric Problem,* in which fabric flaws were discovered after a garment was produced.

The relationship between quality and price, often thought of as **value,** is another important factor in merchandise selection. Off-price goods (discussed in Chapter One) can offer many consumers good value because they are often brand-name goods that are being sold at lower prices. However, as these often are late-in-the-season goods, they do not offer fashion timeliness and may not be of value to every consumer. Generally, however, a good value is defined as a high-quality product at a low price, which is seen as a "true bargain." On the other hand, an expensive, but poor-quality product is seen as overpriced. Sometimes goods that carry a designer name can fall into this category. Figure 3.4 illustrates the relationship between value and price.

Cost per wear can also be used as a measure of value. An expensive item that is worn very often has a lower cost per wear and may be seen as a bargain or a good value, while an inexpensive

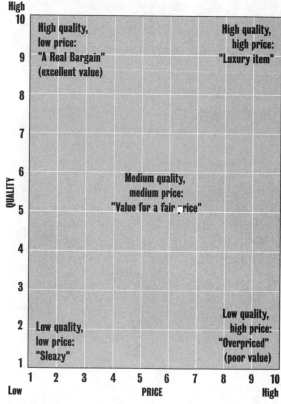

Figure 3.4 This figure, a "value grid," shows the relationship between quality and price.

item that is never worn has little value. This, of course, is evaluated after purchase, but consumers should try to keep this factor in mind when purchasing merchandise. Additionally, retailers selling "good value" should communicate all the quality features of the merchandise to their customers.

Branded and Licensed Merchandise

A **brand** has been defined as "a known name associated with a specific product or group of products carrying with it an expectation of such perceived values as style and image, quality, price, fit, reliability, consistency, and confidence that you'll look good." A brand is produced and controlled by the manufacturer. Branded merchandise dominates most merchandise categories

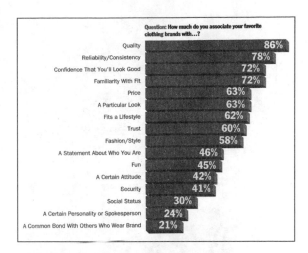

Figure 3.6 This bar chart shows the relationship between brand merchandise and various consumer perceptions about the product. *Source: Kurt Salmon Associates*

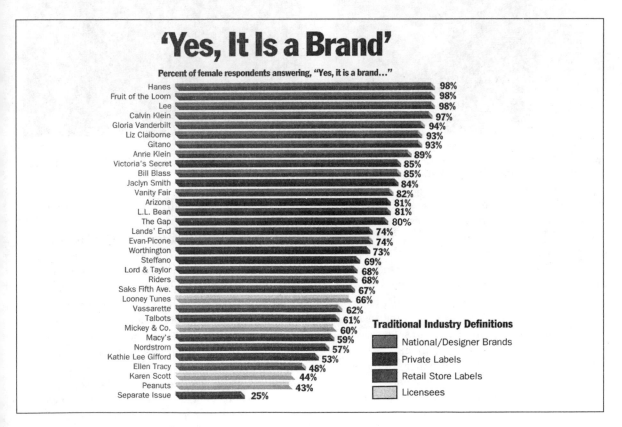

Figure 3.5 Today, not just national/designer brands, but private-label, store-label, and licensed merchandise are often seen by consumers as brands, as shown in this bar chart. *Source: Kurt Salmon Associates*

Figure 3.7–3.8 The tuxedo dress (left) that Yves St. Laurent claims was knocked off by Ralph Lauren. St. Laurent subsequently filed suit against Lauren. Ralph Lauren's version of the tuxedo dress is on the right.

today, and in fashion apparel it is especially important in intimate apparel, hosiery, and footwear. A brand should set the product or company apart from its competition.

Consumers generally pay more for brands because they feel they are worth more than non-brands. Many consumers prefer branded merchandise because they make shopping easier; that is, the reputation of brands means they are a known entity, with an established fit and quality, and the manufacturer and retailer that sell these products stand behind them. As time and convenience are important factors in busy consumers' daily lives, brands become even more valuable. A popular brand has a loyal customer base, which is

a very valuable commodity today that is worth protecting.

Companies often register their brand names or logos as trademarks. Levi's has several trademarks including the red tab stitched into the patch pocket seam, the arcuate stitching on the back pocket of its 501s, and the name Levi's. Some designs are copyrighted, but as most fashion is an interpretation and not original design, few companies register or enforce copyrights. Many, however, attempt to protect their trademarks from counterfeits (see Chapter Twelve for more discussion on this and related concepts). While counterfeits are illegal copies of trademarked goods, knockoffs (also discussed in Chapter Two) are copies or interpretations of popular styles at lower-price levels. Often referred to as "style piracy," knockoffs are a way of life in the fashion industry. Many manufacturers are referred to as knockoff companies, as they do no real designing on their own. Instead, they shop the market, find the most sought-after styles, and then "reinterpret" them or simply copy the style and put their own label on the merchandise. Some companies knock themselves off, that is, they produce a similar version of their own popular item in a lower cost fabrication and generally lower-cost construction techniques, but they keep the "flavor" of the original design. Often referred to as a secondary line, these products are sold in a different market, at different stores, and to different consumers. *Case 23, The Knockoff,* is an example of a buyer who finds a manufacturer to knockoff a popular style of shirt, which then threatens her store's relationship with the vendor who produced the original design.

Licensed goods, which carry the name of a famous person, character, or company are an important part of the fashion industry. In this arrangement, a company allows a marketer to sell a product with its registered trademark or logo (for example, Mickey Mouse nightshirts). Manufacturers seek to become licensees because of the high recognition of the trademarks. While couturiers make little or no profit on their couture collections, large profits frequently are made on licensed secondary lines, accessories, and fragrances. Advertising of the licensed product reinforces the sale of the principal product and vice versa. Corporate licensing increases brand awareness and allows for brand extension into other product categories. For example, in the mid-1990s Tommy Hilfiger, well known for men's wear, quickly broke into the women's industry by licensing his name out. Licensing involves many areas today including cartoon characters, sports figures, celebrities, designers, TV programs, music, and so forth. Pierre Cardin is the designer known for the most number of licenses with over 700 products that are licensed. The success of licensed products, however, depends on the continued quality of the product and often the continued success of the designer's collec-

Figure 3.9 Disney Babies is a line licensed by the Disney Corporation. Manufacturers seek to become licensees due to the high recognition of the trademark. Licensees generally pay a percentage of the profits to the licensor.

tions. Just because a designer's name appears on a product does not mean that the designer had anything to do with the design. Such designers as Bill Blass and Geoffrey Beene, however, participate in the design and development of their licensed products, while others have little (if any) input.

With all the competition today with private and designer labels, manufacturers of existing brands are finding they must continue to strive for their brands to thrive. Popular one year, a brand can fade away the next. According to large denim makers in the U.S., the following strategies are important to maintain brands: 1) advertise; 2) develop a unique relationship with the stores; 3) have up-to-date systems response; 4) bring value to the market; 5) license; 6) go international; 7) once it's built, protect it (Ozzard, 1995). In *Financial World's* 1995 brand survey, Coca-Cola was seen as the world's most valuable brand worth an estimated $39 billion; Levi's ranked 15th. Other recognized, valuable apparel brands include Hanes, Fruit of the Loom, Benetton, Wrangler, and Lee. Table 3.2 lists the top 20 brands in a 1995 Kurt Salmon Associates (KSA) apparel brand study.

The list in Table 3.2 is interesting as it shows a lack of distinction between national brands (Levi's) and designer labels (Calvin Klein), store brands (Gap), and private labels (Jaclyn Smith). It appears that—at least in the minds of consumers—a brand is a brand is a brand, regardless of ownership or traditional definitions. KSA's study also found that younger consumers and those who are more affluent are more brand conscious than older and less-affluent consumers.

Private-Label Merchandising

The distinction between brands and private labels is becoming fuzzy, if not disappearing altogether. What is important is the consumer's perception of a brand, which now includes store and private labels as discussed in the previous section. A recent *WWD* study indicates consumers refer to labels as "brand" or "not a brand." Sometimes there is little or no difference in these products as manufacturers or contractors that produce brands also produce private labels for retailers at the same time; they just put different labels on the merchandise. Generally, consumers are not aware of this situation and they judge the product exclusively by the label—thus illustrating the importance of image and reputation.

Store brands and **private labels** are produced and named by the retailer that sells them. Store brands literally carry the name of the store. Private labels may carry names other than the store's name, for example, Charter Club and Aeropostale, which are Macy's private labels. Some names refer to such real people as Kmart's

Table 3.2	Top 20 Brands	
1. Hanes	11. Arizona
2. Levi's	12. Vanity Fair
3. Lee	13. Guess?
4. Liz Claiborne	14. Reebok
5. Gap	15. Jaclyn Smith
6. Nike	16. L'eggs
7. Calvin Klein	17. Chic
8. Fruit of the Loom	18. Jones New York
9. Victoria's Secret	19. Jockey
10. Wrangler	20. Anne Klein

Source: Friedman (1996)

Jaclyn Smith and Wal-Mart's Kathie Lee collections, while others are made to sound like designers, for example, The Limited's Forenza and JCPenney's Stafford.

Private and store brands have advantages for retailers. They are generally knockoffs and therefore more profitable than national brands as there is no advertising to add to costs and no middlemen involved because the retailer manufacturers them. As national brands saturate the market, stores begin to look alike; therefore, a private/store label is one way a retailer can differentiate itself from its competition. While national brands are sold to many stores, private labels are found only in one store—the store that created them—and they lend a sense of identity to the retailer. Despite the fact that branded merchandise dominates most categories, private labels' share of the market is increasing faster than traditional brands. Additionally, private/store labels may constitute all or part of a retailer's offerings. For example, both the Gap and The Limited's chains sell 100 percent private-label merchandise. Retailers change the proportion of private vs branded merchandise over time. Two illustrations of this trend are Gap and Barney's. Gap started out selling Levi's jeans, but today sells only its own label jeans; Barney's currently carries about 30 percent private labels, but hopes to increase that number.

Figure 3.10 Kathy Ireland's private-label exercise wear, which is sold exclusively at Kmart. She is an example of a model whose highly recognizable name has made this apparel line successful.

Department stores often have a percentage of private-label merchandise, with most of their goods being branded. Retailers need to find the right balance for themselves between branded and non-branded merchandise. There is a danger of putting too much stock into brands and/or private labels as a buyer may not be able to capitalize on new trends or "hot" resources in the market. *Case 22, To Brand or Not to Brand,* which describes a men's department that may be overbranded, is an example of a store's relying too heavily on branded merchandise.

Retailers with private labels are essentially becoming manufacturers as the merchandise is developed for the store by its product development department. Manufacturing, however, is not their expertise and sometimes private-label retailers can find themselves with new challenges. One such

challenge is sourcing for production. *Case 39, A Color Coordination Conundrum* in Chapter Five presents potential quality problems that can plague a retailer with private-label sourcing. Another challenge is marketing a retailer's own brand. Such stores as Gap, Talbot's, Crate & Barrel, Nike Town, The Limited, Ann Taylor, and Tiffany's have been very successful when using their own names as their brands. Department stores, however, do not always have the same success creating their own brands, with some exceptions. Customers purchasing from Tiffany's, for example, have a product with a name that has a certain reputation. This doesn't necessarily hold true for department stores unless that store has a clearly perceived image of quality. Two notable examples of department stores that have successfully marketed their own store brands are Bloomingdale's (Bloomingdale's Own) and Neiman Marcus.

Summary

The characteristics of merchandise help to define its image and reputation. Consumers look for certain levels of fashion, quality, and price to meet their needs. Nationally branded merchandise is thought of as having high quality with a known reputation. Private or store labels offer more value to consumers and generally are profitable for retailers who are responsible for their manufacture. Some store labels have become as well known as nationally advertised brands and, consequently, the distinction to the consumer between national and private brands is less distinct. As retailers develop their own labels, the distinction between manufacturer and retailer also is becoming less defined.

References

Abend, J. (1995, June). Private labels, brands square off. *Bobbin,* pp. 66–75.

Brown, P. (1992). Ready-to-wear analysis. New York: Macmillan.

The consumer says they are all brands. (1995, November). *WWD, Infotracs Supplement,* pp. 10–15.

Diamond, J., & Diamond, E. (1994). *Fashion apparel and accessories.* Albany, N.Y.: Delmar.

Friedman, A. (1996, January 17). Survey: Brands stay strong. *WWD*, p. 16.

Frings, G. (1996). *Fashion from concept to consumer.* Upper Saddle River, N.J.: Prentice-Hall.

Ozzard, J. (1995, October). How to build a brand. *WWD, Denim Network Supplement*, pp. 10–11.

Private label jeans mount aggressive attack on market. (1996, February). *Stores*, pp. 68-69.

Rath, P.M., Peterson, J., Greensley, P., & Gill, P. (1994). *Introduction to fashion merchandising.* Albany, N.Y.: Delmar.

Stamper, A., Sharp, S.H., & Donnell, L. (1991). *Evaluating apparel quality.* New York: Fairchild Publications.

Wingate, I., Gillespie, K., & Barry, M. (1984). *Know your merchandise.* New York: McGraw Hill.

Wolfe, M.G. (1989). *Fashion.* South Holland, IL.: The Goodheart-Wilcox Co, Inc.

Key Terms

basics	non-seasonal
better goods	opening price point
brand	popular goods
bridge	private label
budget goods	quality
convenience goods	quality control
designer collection	seasonal goods
fashion goods	secondary line
hard goods	shopping goods
high fashion	soft goods
impulse goods	specialty goods
licensed goods	staples
mass fashion	store brand
moderate goods	value

Case 18
"With It" or Without

Nancy J. Rabolt, San Francisco State University
Judy K. Miler, University of Tennessee

One of the hottest manufacturing houses in the New York market is "With It," which makes junior-size apparel that is very "in." Its styling is casual, young, and a symbol of being "with it" for high school and college students alike. The company motto being sung by fans is: "If you are not *With It*, you are out."

The company is owned by two relatively young men who had once been top ready-to-wear buyers for Macy's—John Sung and Bill Lipe. It is apparent that they know the business because they anticipate the latest trends and "hot" styles, and their use of marketing and positioning the business is very savvy. They have brought "With It" to a dominant name-brand recognition level in an extremely short period of time. Part of their business philosophy is to sell only to regular price stores, which they rigidly enforce. Discounters are not considered as accounts, not even as a way of dumping end-of-season merchandise. When "With It" was conceived, an underlying principle was that their merchandise would never be discounted. This strategy enables them to maintain a certain level of status in the minds of their target consumer, which in turn keeps the retail price up and generates a high level of profit for the regular-priced retailer. Irregulars and closeouts, however, are disposed of at the plant level, but the labels are always cut or removed and these garments are not sold to any regular-price customers.

The level of success has been ongoing. From the day John and Bill started the business five short years ago, some retailers, impressed with the acumen and record of the maker, opened "With It" shops within their stores, a strategy suggested by John and Bill. "With It" works closely with the retailers to set up these shops.

Main Street, California's largest department store chain, is one of the biggest users of "With It." They virtually ton out the goods, never seeming to have enough merchandise. The junior sportswear buyer, Carol Baker, has had a great working partnership with John and Bill for three years.

One store policy concerning resource criterion is that Main Street will never share a resource with a discount store within its trading area, so the exclusive sales policy followed by "With It" fits right in with Main Street philosophy. Two weeks ago, however, a comparison shopper for Main Street reported that The Mart, a twenty-six store discount chain, was carrying the "With It" jeans line. The labels, although cut, had not been removed and were easily identifiable as "With It" merchandise. A customer complaint involving a pair of jeans priced at $10 less at The Mart was the stimulus for the investigation.

Carol Baker, the buyer, called "With It" collect to find out why The Mart has the line. She got John on the phone. Excitedly she explained, "We do a great job. I can't understand how you can ship to a discounter and hurt us. It doesn't make sense, particularly because you're familiar with our store policy and you've told me it's your policy, too. It doesn't matter that you are a very profitable line for our stores, management looks at the long-term meaning to our customers. They'll refuse to allow me to carry your goods any longer."

John explained, "Don't get excited, Carol. We don't ship The Mart any part of our regular line. Any merchandise they have is irregular or last season's goods. The labels are removed or cut to show that they're not current or regulars. One more point, we have a big successful operation; but, like all manufacturers, we always own goods that must be sold, which are closeouts or are less-than-perfect. They are job lots, the kind most of our buyers can't use. This merchandise represents a lot of stock that must be liquidated and if we can sell it—we do. We don't want to hurt loyal customers and it represents too much money to sell for waste—to rag men—so we will sell to retailers who do not buy our regular line of merchandise.

"What you don't realize," John continued, "is that The Mart has given us an open order. Anytime we have $10,000 worth of goods, we ship what we want without notice. The price is cheap, but it gives us a pipeline to dispose of unwanted goods. Frankly, this arrangement is as important as any we have that sells at regular retail levels. I'm sure you understand that business is business. We want to keep our great working relationship with you and we want it to remain profitable for both of us, but this is one situation that we can't change. We will, however, make sure all labels are completely removed in the future, rather than just cut, if that will help."

"John," Carol replied, "what you say, I guess, makes sense. Our policy, though, is not to stock goods from manufacturers represented in discount stores, with or without labels, different styles, closeouts, or whatever. The problem is bigger than my department; it's one that I must take to a higher level. I'll be back in touch with you after my boss returns from Europe in a week. I don't want to go to the general merchandise manager, as he is apt to be tough and stick to the book. I just hope that he doesn't see the Comparison Office report and that no more complaints come in before my boss returns."

Carol is concerned and worried because she does not want to lose "With It"—one of her major vendors. The records show that 15 percent of her department volume is "With It" merchandise and they are a key resource that she does not feel can be replaced. Even worse, the store has built up a trade for the label, and competition would love for her to give up the line so they could take her "With It" business. However, she understands that rules are rules and policy must be followed. But sometimes, rules are bent to fit circumstances. Hopefully, this situation fits into the latter. Anxiously, Carol starts to prepare a plan to present to her boss, who will return from Europe tomorrow.

Major Question

What strategy should Carol suggest to her boss, which would best help her keep the "With It" line?

1. Does lower price always mean lower quality? Or lower fashion level?

2. How can one store retail the same product for $10 less than another and still be profitable?

3. If a retailer loses an important label at a vital price level, how can a replacement be found?

Case 19
Bottom out on Basics

Laura Neumann, Eagle's Eye

Anne Strahan, a buyer for a television retailer—Shop TV—has purchased a 100 percent polyester private-label apparel line. The fabric is made in Korea and the garments are made by a U.S. apparel manufacturer. The fabric mill requires four weeks for production and four weeks for transportation and U.S. Customs clearance. The apparel manufacturer—a la Mode—requires a minimum of eight weeks for production of new items and four weeks for reorders. Added together, a la Mode needs 12 to 16 weeks for production. Lead time from concept to commercialization requires a minimum of 6 months. A la Mode does not stock extra fabric in the U.S. warehouse for several reasons. One reason is that Shop TV is the manufacturer's only customer. If Shop TV does not purchase the fabric, the manufacturer is left warehousing unwanted fabric. Additionally, fabric colors change from season to season and the company would be guessing as to which colors should be stocked in what quantities.

A la Mode delivers merchandise to Shop TV twelve months a year—both basic and novelty/fashion. Basics consist of seven items that run all year with two color pallets—Spring and Fall. Novelty items are more fashion forward and change from month to month. Each month there are approximately nine novelty items including print and solid colors. The basic items are the volume business while the novelty items are ordered in smaller quantities until the item has proven to sell well (i.e., approximately 90 percent sell-through) with a low return rate (i.e., 27 percent or less). However, one must be careful in using sell-through as a tool of comparison in electronic retail. On the retail floor, the buyer knows when the merchandise becomes available for sale to the end-use consumer. Therefore, information is fairly accurate on how much and how quickly merchandise is sold. When the retail outlet is television, a number of factors make the reliability of sell-through data suspect. For example, sell-through data are altered when (because of the popularity of a product line) customers call and order products without any on-air prompting—that is, they order without seeing the product on-air. This can leave inventory broken in both size and color. A show host who is knowledgeable and excited about selling the product can also alter the sell-through data. Additionally, return rates are a major factor in accurate analysis of sell-through information. When comparing styles sold in an electronic retailing setting, it is possible that a garment with a 90 percent sell-through could be more successful than a garment with a 100 percent sell-through because total sales volume is higher.

Shop TV will only sell merchandise that has been delivered to the warehouse and has been approved through its quality assurance department. Customers order by the telephone using a customer service representative or the customer can use Shop TV's automatic order entry system with any touch-tone phone by following a series of computer-generated commands. The automatic order entry system lists all the colors and sizes available when the customer enters a style number. After Anne keys the purchase order in the computer and generates the manufacturer's order, the colors for the next season are in the computer. Therefore, customer service and the automatic entry system can identify the new garments and colors that will be available to the customers for the next season. Customers can then put their name on a list to reserve the product for when it is received at the warehouse and ready to ship to the end-use consumer. Numerous customers order garments without ever seeing the product.

Four new colors for Spring are to be debuted on a 24-hour fashion program. Anne ordered less quantity than usual in the basics because management said the division had too much inventory carried over from the previous Fall. Management's evaluations frequently create inventory problems for retail buyers. Management is correct that too much money was tied up in unsold Fall merchandise; however, Anne knows that Fall merchandise will not sell in Spring. If dollars for Spring are decreased because of unsold Fall inventory, it is possible that there would be a low-dollar volume for Spring merchandise. That was the case for Shop TV's apparel buyers.

In February, Anne began to worry about the quantity of basics she would have available to sell on the upcoming fashion extravaganza planned for March. Primarily, she was worried because after the new Spring merchandise entered the warehouse and passed quality assurance, many Spring basics would be tagged as already sold to customers through the reserve list. Secondly, Anne has also worried about making the show's dollar volume projection, which is based on sales-per-hour show, because merchandise sold on the reserve list is not recorded as sold during the on-air show. Thirdly, she was worried that the customers would become frustrated and refuse to buy the novelty items because the new basics were sold out. Typically, customers purchasing a novelty item also purchase a basic shell, pant, or jacket to complete the outfit. Therefore, Anne was concerned that the manufacturer would not be able to deliver more Spring basics in time to fill all the customer orders received during the show. If merchandise is sold out during the show, the customers can reserve certain items in the hope that the buyer will reorder the item and the manufacturer will deliver another shipment within 45 days of the show. Generally, 45 days is impossible turn-around time for a la Mode. However, it is sometimes possible if they have fabric and the garment is a basic body that the contractors have experience sewing (for example, a pull-on pant or shell).

Major Question

How would you solve Anne's potential problem of little merchandise but many customers who want to buy?

Study Questions

1. How would this scenario change if fabric was sourced from the U.S.?

2. What different considerations in production and ordering are there between a regular, stored retailer and an electronic retailer?

3. How can an electronic retail buyer project sales?

4. What can Shop TV do with the leftover Fall inventory?

5. Would you recommend that Shop TV promote branded merchandise? If so, how?

Case 20
The Super Shell

Betty K. Tracy, California State Polytechnical University
Terry Faraone, California State University

Nine Months, a 60-million dollar business, is a specialty maternity retailer with 250 of its own stores. It is a vertical operation with its own domestic production company. Nine Months designs five seasonal lines for its own stores and also manufactures limited styles for department stores under different labels. Its production company (the manufacturing arm of Nine Months) includes a production pattern room, designers and staff, and a production manager who deals with contractors, negotiates costs, and works with fabric and trim buyers. Having its own production capabilities is beneficial to the operation of the Nine Months retailing business. Because the production company is located geographically close to the retail headquarters and also to some of its stores, it does well with Quick Response. Merchandise can be ordered closer to the season, which provides more accurate forecasting. This helps the business with cash flow, helps keep inventory low, and allows for more available floor space for a current season. Based on profit margin projections, Nine Months acquires its merchandise from either its own production company or its offshore suppliers. Currently, the merchandise mix in the Nine Months stores is about 85 percent private label. Each store is full service and carries all classifications, including lingerie, foundations, dresses, in addition to casual and career sportswear. The typical store is small (approximately 800 square feet) and usually located in a shopping mall.

Nine Months is successful in its niche market and appeals to the moderate customer. It has maintained its market share over the last eight years but wants to increase sales. It is considering increasing the number of store sites, enlarging the store sizes of key stores, and adding more styles to its lines.

For the Spring season, Nine Months produced a 500-unit test cut of a short sleeve, solid-colored shell for the career sportswear line in its own domestic production company. This shell was manufactured in a woven cotton and was produced in several key colors. The shell was a hot seller with well above a 15 percent weekly sell-through at $40 each. This item had the best sell-through in the company and was the pivotal and strongest piece in the newly emerging career sportswear line.

Sarah Connely, the career sportswear buyer for Nine Months, was excited at the sell-through and success of the shell. (She referred to it as The Super Shell.) She felt that if she redesigned the shell into a key item for the Fall and Cruise seasons, she would receive a salary bonus and possibly a promotion. Nine Months had relayed to Sarah an interest in increasing sales and felt she could be a star in the company with a really hot item. Based on the early test, Sarah projected that she could sell approximately 15,000 units at the same $40 retail. Because it was for the Fall and Cruise seasons, she changed the sleeve length to long and the fabric to a woven rayon challis. She felt the Nine Months customer would want this

item for career use, as well as after work. To make it a pivotal piece, she decided that it should be available in colors to mix and match the career sportswear line. She predicted that multiple sales would result from the possible combinations of pieces within the line, all centering around the modified shell. Sarah talked to the Nine Months in-house production company personnel to obtain the revised shell design cost. Previously, Sarah had bought casual tops from offshore sources and now sought price quotes from them, also. She did find an Asian source that gave her a greater profit margin than her own production staff had been able to give her. To maximize the profit potential, she chose to go with the Asian source and not use the Nine Months domestic production company.

Sarah traveled to Hong Kong and met with Ling Manufacturing, a new resource for her. A total of 20,000 units was purchased and divided into two deliveries. Sarah requested that Ling Manufacturing deliver 10,000 units for the Fall season and the remaining 10,000 units for the Cruise season. Mr. Ling purchased a rayon challis fabric for the entire order, which Sarah approved. He was able to get a good price for the fabric because of the size of the order, which enabled him to lower his garment cost. The fabric was dyed and finished to the color palette that Nine Months had selected for each season. Through her negotiations with Ling Manufacturing, Sarah achieved a cost that would give her an initial markup of 70 percent vs 55 percent from her own production company. Sarah was excited about the prospect of increased sales and profit for Nine Months and the potential boost to her career.

Ling Manufacturing produced patterns and first samples based on a garment which Sarah brought with her. The samples, after some corrections, were accepted and approved by Sarah, and the shell went into production. As agreed, the Fall delivery of 10,000 units hit the stores in July, but the initial selling was very disappointing and did not meet projections. Sarah rationalized that it was too early in the season for strong sales results. However, as the season progressed the key item shell continued to produce dismal sales. She contacted stores for input as to why the shell wasn't selling, and all the store managers said, "It doesn't fit." Sarah could not understand this because the redesigned item was based on the strong-selling, Spring season, short-sleeve shell specifications and she herself had approved the new production patterns that Ling had produced. She decided to send a size range to Carolyn Wilson, the Nine Months production patternmaker. Carolyn spec'd the garments and determined that the overall sleeve and body length were too long. Next, Sarah requested production patterns from Mr. Ling. The garments were compared to the patterns and it was decided that the patterns were indeed correct. It was found that the rayon challis fabric was not dimensionally stable, and the garments had "grown" while hanging in stock. This elongation caused additional problems because the style lines became distorted as the garment grew in length. Obviously, the fabrication chosen was not suitable for the silhouette.

Sarah now had the first 10,000 units for Fall season consuming floor space, because they were not selling well. This decreased sales in other areas because the inventory was unbalanced and the garments were not easily mixed and matched. It also reduced the cash flow needed to maintain successful future buying seasons. Additionally, the remaining 10,000 units were to be cut from the same already purchased fabric, perpetuating the fit problem. This also compounded the space and cash flow situations. Sarah decided she must find a way to move the troublesome shell and generate some income from this Fall line. Because Sarah had negotiated the contract and approved the fabric, she wanted to correct the situation without involving Ling Manufacturing.

Major Question

How would you recommend that Sarah move the first 10,000 shells for the Fall season? How can she salvage the second half of the order?

Study Questions

1. Should Sarah have sourced offshore for the key item in a new line?

2. What type of quality control can a company establish to ensure the fabric and other materials used will meet company specifications?

3. What other safeguards should Sarah use when choosing a new vendor for the first time, especially for a key item?

Case 21
The Fabric Problem

*Diane Cantua and Nancy J. Rabolt,
San Francisco State University*

Robert Rossi is a fabric sales representative carrying a line of wool fabrics of various types. He has set up an account with Jordan Luce, a new customer, who is new in the business. Jordan has always wanted to produce some of her own designs, and her husband—a wealthy doctor—is backing her venture. She will sell her designs in a small boutique that is owned by a friend. She was on her way toward this goal when she ordered six colors of wool jersey from Robert.

Because Jordan is a new customer, Robert very carefully explained the trade practices of the fabric business. On her request, he even took samples of fabric to her house for Jordan to choose. During this time, he showed her the Worth Street Rules, which itemize textile trade practices. The American Textile Manufacturers Institute (ATMI) revised these rules in 1986. They include provisions for buyers' rights, sellers' rights, quality, and grading fabrics. Some of the provisions are outlined in Table 3.3. Robert did not give Jordan a contract outlining these conditions because they are normal business practice and are understood within the industry. Essentially, Robert indicated to Jordan that even though the fabric may be given a cursory glance as a quick inspection, the buyer or cutter should inspect the goods in sufficient light before cutting. It was explained that if there was a problem, for example, wrong color, color blotching, color streaking, yarn defects, or any other defect,

Table 3.3	Summary of Revised Worth Street Rules

BUYERS' RIGHTS

If the buyer is going to reject or cancel a fabric order, the seller must be notified:
- Within ten days after the defect is known.
- Within three months after passing title.
- Prior to cutting.

SELLERS' RIGHTS

- If fabric has been invoiced but not shipped and the buyer is five days late in payment on previously shipped fabric (this could be 30, 60, or 90 days after delivery), the seller has the right not to deliver the fabric.
- Delivery by the mill within 15 days of a specified delivery date is acceptable.
- "If you cut it you own it" rule has been somewhat modified. New rules allow a converter to dye or print a fabric and still make a claim for defects, but they deny an apparel manufacturer that right if the fabric is cut. It is assumed that a cutter or the contractor will be able to see defects in a fabric as it is laid up.

Jordan should call immediately and a replacement bolt would be sent. After Robert reiterated this to Jordan, she carefully selected the fabrics that she wished to order. This order consisted of two bolts each of Plum Red, Chocolate Brown, Emerald Green, Sapphire Blue, Mustard Yellow, and True Black. Later that week, twelve bolts of wool fabric were shipped with COD terms.

Jordan took the fabric to her cutter and sewer, but neither of them inspected the goods. Long-sleeve dresses were constructed from the six colors of wool fabric. When the dresses were complete, Jordan took them to the store. She was very proud and happy. As the dresses were being displayed in the store, however, Jordan noticed color streaks in the four chocolate-brown dresses. She became very upset, removed the dresses from the floor, and called Robert immediately demanding that she be reimbursed for the fabric and all labor costs involved in constructing the brown dresses. All the other dresses were fine and they continued to be displayed in the boutique.

Robert reminded Jordan of their conversation and explained again that after the fabric was cut, the buyer owned it. It also was explained to her that reimbursement for labor charges was not industry practice and he was not prepared at all to do that. She was not satisfied with these answers. Two days later, Jordan's husband telephoned Robert and threatened to sue him and the fabric company. He is a powerful man in the community and is used to always getting his own way. He claimed that Robert did not give Jordan a contract that outlined the conditions of sale. Before hanging up the phone, he threatened, "If there are any legal loopholes my lawyers will find them!"

Major Question

What should Robert do?

Study Questions

1. What else could Robert have done to ensure that Jordan understood and abided by standard industry policy?

2. How is the fabric business different from the apparel business in regard to returns?

Case 22
To Brand or Not to Brand

Nancy J. Rabolt, San Francisco State University
Judy K. Miler, University of Tennessee

Jones Department Store is one of the few remaining privately owned department stores left in the still thriving downtown area of Philadelphia. The store has been passed down from generation to generation of Jones' family entrepreneurs for over 100 years and still remains in the same location on which it was originally built. While tradition has been discarded by many long-term retailers, Jones

Department Store has kept their merchant family traditions alive and it has served them well, as generations of Philadelphians have continuously made Jones their preferred place to shop. Locals still make it a day to come downtown to shop and lunch at Jones'.

Bruce Gregory is the recently hired buyer of men's furnishings on the main floor of Jones Department Store. Store sales volume is over $50 million a year. The men's furnishings department, as is the case in many major stores, is a well-developed, well-trafficked section that alone brings in approximately one million dollars a year. A major sales contributor, furnishings is an important department.

Bruce has been studying the operation with extreme care—not only because he is new, but also because he has been advised by his divisional merchandise manager that he is going to be called upon soon to make several important merchandising decisions. The owners hired Bruce partially because they knew that some improvements need to be made in furnishings and he comes with experience in that area. Bruce had been a men's furnishings buyer in a major New York City store prior to coming on board with Jones, and is up-to-date on market trends and developments.

One of the aspects that surprised Bruce is the dominance of brand names in his inventory. Practically all of the merchandise stocked is from nationally known manufacturers. When this fact came to his attention, he spoke to several of the salespeople about it. Their remarks indicated that the store's policy favored heavy concentration on labels and that most of the brands had been carried for many years. He also learned that the customers seemed to prefer major brand names, as indicated by a continuous department sales growth. However, he also learned that, on many occasions, Jones's had been beaten out by other stores because new styling that was available from small, private-label resources, was not available from the larger, branded resources that concentrate on traditional, classic looks. He recognized that overbranding can be prohibitive—shutting the door to new creativity. He studied the classifica-

tions and could readily see that at least six items that deserved to be included in stock were absent: pocket squares, cuff links, sunglasses, formalwear accessories, leather nail grooming kits, and Jones signature merchandise for those loyal Jones customers.

Now he knew that he had to take a stand in regard to introducing private-label merchandise. He realized that the department produces well, but is not realizing its full sales potential. Another disturbing element is that the store has shut itself off from the benefits of newness in the market. As a buyer, he concluded that if things remained as is, he would have a narrow selection of merchandise offerings from relatively few resources. His market associations would be of no real value; and, from a selfish point of view, he would lose all his meaningful contacts that he worked hard over the years to develop. "Besides," he wondered, "how long will it be before customers recognize that Jones is standing still in a new, exciting market and then shop elsewhere?"

Bruce is quite concerned, now that he has analyzed the department's situation and feels some changes should be made in regard to merchandise assortment and private labeling. The aphorism, "a new broom sweeps clean" is very much on his mind. He knows that he must take special care when confronting his boss because logically his superior would conjecture:

• You are new and do not understand the operation, and our policy favors carrying name-brand merchandise.

• Which resources would you discard?

• Our customers depend upon specific brands; to a large degree they mean customer patronage.

Bruce is well aware that he cannot make a presentation in regard to his recommendations without data that prove his thesis, "It is possible to be overbranded."

Major Question
What steps would you recommend to Bruce? How would you present your findings to management?

1. What are the advantages and disadvantages of using national branded sources?

2. What control in merchandise selection does a buyer have when buying from national brands? Who makes the decision to carry a national brand?

3. Compare the level of fashion, quality, price, and degree of advertising of several successful national brands with the hottest new fashion of today.

4. How does the type of merchandise vary the importance of branded vs unbranded or private label merchandise?

Case 23
The Knockoff

Nancy J. Rabolt, San Francisco State University
Judy K. Miler, University of Tennessee

Gold & Silver, Inc., a women's fine jewelry and casual clothing store is a unique type of retailer with an unusual, but highly successful merchandise mix. Currently, it has the best small independent retail financial record in the U.S. Profits on sales and returns on capital investments outstrip any comparable retail organization in the country. This enviable record is the result of careful planning, risk-taking, and imaginative controls by management and staff.

Merchandise policies and procedures are one type of control management abides by. One aspect requires management to keep detailed records on merchandise to the lowest tracking level possible, for example, color and size. Another of the merchandising policies that works is to establish in-depth stock of the most wanted items, promote on a consistent basis, and extend the selling period as long as possible.

Jeanette Jildor is the women's shirt buyer. She has been with Gold & Silver for almost six years, and has done quite well with her department. As any good, aggressive buyer would, she is looking

for her chance to shine through finding the "hot," new shirt of the year. Armed with well-thought out and approved plans, Jeanette went to market in search of her "find." She visited several resources before she discovered her "star" shirt. There was no doubt in Jeanette's mind that this long-sleeve, solid shirt with the crested pocket was just the new look she'd been searching for to make her year! It was also gratifying that the manufacturer was already a highly respected supplier and a key resource to Gold & Silver.

What made it even more interesting, however, was the fact that the shirt was not being pushed by the sales rep. Jeanette saw the sales potential herself by relating the crested pocket on the shirt with the current popularity of crested blazers. She figured that this look was a natural winner.

Working with the manufacturer to her advantage, Jeanette was able to get assurances from the vendor on the quality of the fabric and workmanship, the colorfastness of the crest emblem, reorder capability, and delivery guarantees. As added insurance to these favorable factors, and as a safeguard to her strong position on the shirt, Jeanette also secured a promise from the resource that no similar merchandise would be shipped in quantities to support a promotion within her trading area for two months. This promise was not hard for the resource to make, because most buyers were just sampling the shirt or did not buy the style at all. The manufacturer was excited that someone found the shirt more exciting than even they had originally thought it to be. Consequently, both the vendor and Jeanette were very pleased with the sale and the commitment Jeanette was going to take with the shirt.

She advertised—and was on target—the style took off. Week after week there was an ad that invited mail and telephone orders; the latter was supported by a 24-hour phone ordering service. She "milked" the item through every means possible. The sales during the season were just short of phenomenal, three thousand a week, with no abatement. It just kept rolling along, to the delight of Jeanette, her merchandise manager, upper management, and the manufacturer.

The resource was most cooperative in supplying even more mechandise than Jeanette had originally anticipated and planned. They put aside production orders for other styles to help Jeanette fill her promotional needs. Sales were soaring, with seemingly no end in sight. After three months of record-breaking sales, however, Jeanette decided that the "party" would probably end in a couple of weeks. She couldn't imagine the life of the shirt being much longer, as she had never experienced such success in her life as a buyer.

Deciding to act on her hunch, Jeanette visited the manufacturer, talked to the decision makers, and advised: "You've made my season, which will be over soon. However, have you considered the volume potential if we reduce the retail price from $30 to $19.99, a level that will open up a new customer group, develop individual multiple sales, and, above all, extend the selling season? I think that we need to plan on promoting the shirt to conclude the season and end with a bang."

The resource balked. "You've had your party, now it's our turn. We're going to make it a basic shirt and get the distribution we missed on the first selling round. You showed us the way, now we want to capitalize on an item that can have a successful run for several years."

"Be realistic," Jeanette responded. "Sure, your name is nationally known, but don't you know that the style is going to be knocked off at lower prices? If you don't take action, others will."

The manufacturer again disagreed, replying, "Apparently you're not aware that one of the largest men's brand houses features a shirt that has been at one price for twenty years, despite knockoffs."

The conversation ended in a stalemate, with no conclusions or agreements drawn. Knowing that she wanted to do what she had planned, a day or two later, Jeanette took the shirt to another resource that she used regularly. Jeanette explained her success with the shirt and how she now wanted to position it promotionally in her store to conclude the season. The manufacturer was interested and listened intently. The sales manager called the production manager in to get her input.

After close inspection, the production manager said, "We can make this style at a cost of $9.75, or less, depending on what you want to change about the shirt." Jeanette did not want to change anything about the styling, because the crested pocket really was what made the shirt.

Jeanette took a position. She placed a verbal order on the spot for promotional depth at $9.75 in a narrow range of colors suitable for the current time of year. She also indicated that she would send a confirming written order countersigned by her merchandise manager tomorrow. Jeanette said her goodbyes and happily left the resource feeling good about her new "find."

Three weeks later she advertised the shirt at $19.99. The stock consisted of the original shirt marked down to $19.99 and the knockoff received five days previously. Again, she was right in her prediction for success. The momentum continued at peak levels for several weeks. Her real problems centered around forecasting just how long this could continue and what quantity should be committed for reorders.

The national brand house from which Jeanette originally purchased the crested shirt watched events at Gold & Silver. They resented the store's course of action and made their feelings known in the market and to other retailers. A letter was received by Jeanette's divisional merchandise manager, which stated, "We have decided to cancel any future business arrangements with you and are taking steps to sell to additional stores in your area, to those retailers from whom we previously declined to sell, as negotiated with you." Jeanette's merchandise manager is upset and disturbed by the letter, because a major sportswear promotion was in the works for the next season, and this resource was to be a major player in that promotion. He wants them back—and soon.

Major Question

If you were Jeanette, what would your recommended course of action be in regard to the resource's choice to terminate business with Gold & Silver? How would you go about luring them back to your store?

1. How often do you think national brands are copied or knocked off? Is that illegal?

2. What is the difference between a counterfeit and a knockoff?

3. At what level of fashion is a popular style knocked off? Who buys the original and who buys the knockoff?

4. Do you think Jeanette was right in knocking off a style from one of her major branded manufacturers, then selling it, along with the manufacturer's style at a reduced retail price?

Chapter Discussion Questions

1. How do price and fashion level relate to the quality and value of a product?

2. How do retailers determine their merchandise mix based on these characteristics?

3. Which is "safer" — fashion or basics? Which is more profitable? How does a retailer determine the mix of fashion and basic goods? Use case examples to support your argument.

4. What are the advantages and disadvantages of carrying national and private brands?

5. List your favorite brands and then identify them as national, store, or private label. Why are these you favorite brands? What makes them distinct from other merchandise on the market?

6. When is it appropriate to knock off a popular style? What is the relationship between national brands, private labels, and knockoffs?

Merchandise Planning, Buying, Control, and Profitability

Chapter Objectives

- Highlight the importance of merchandise planning and forecasting.

- Distinguish between dollar, unit, and assortment planning and consider their importance in merchandise management.

- Stress the critical role of standards and controls in successful retail management.

- Relate planning, pricing, productivity, and profit to buying.

Careful planning and control, using the most accurate information available guides a retailer to profit. Any plan, however, should always be regarded as a flexible and adaptable guide that is not written in stone, and which allows for all the revisions that constantly occur in the retail business. The merchandising division is responsible for the buying of the goods that a retailer sells. This division is also responsible for the planning, pricing, and ultimate profitability of the retailer through the sales generated. Dollar and unit planning and controls are the major means of merchandise management that lead to the profit goal. Today, through technology, more detailed and accurate planning and control can be accomplished, which is faster than ever before, due to the information that is available literally at our fingertips. The better the planning and controls, the more the retailer will achieve the goals that have been set. Monitoring, and, in many cases, adjusting plans (up or down) is necessary because retailing is dynamic. Even the most experienced buyers or planners cannot always accurately predict, for example, how many customers purchase or how much they will purchase.

Merchandising and Profit

Merchandising is one of two of the necessary retailing functions, without which the business could not exist. **Merchandising** is the buying and selling of goods and/or services for the purpose of making a profit. The first and foremost aspect of merchandising is satisfying the customer's wants and needs. Doing such, however, requires preparation and planning. Additionally, the type of retail organization plays an integral part in achieving the set goals. Controls also play a major role in helping to ensure the profitability the retailer is looking to achieve. Prior to establishing controls, however, the merchandise that the customer needs and wants must be bought.

Buying

One of the major functions of the merchandising division of a retail organization is **buying.** It is the purchasing of goods and/or services for the retailer to sell to the ultimate consumer. This function can be separated out as a division, as is most often the case in large organizations, or it may be combined with the operations function, as it often is in smaller companies. The individual given formal authority to undertake the purchasing for a retailer is the **buyer.**

Most experts agree that buying is both an art and a science. As an art, aesthetic and visual principles are considered. As a science, the mathematics of budgeting are primary in forecasting (or predicting) the needs and wants of the retailer's customers. Some of the skills can be taught, others are an inherent part of the buyer and what that person is as an individual—including the knowledge and experience an individual brings to a buying position.

Buying, of course, is also undertaken at the manufacturing level. In that context, however, it is usually referred to as **purchasing** and refers to obtaining the materials to make the end product. The individual given buying authority at the manufacturing level is either given the title buyer, **purchasing agent**, **merchandiser**, or **sourcing agent**. Many of the techniques and preparation for purchasing (including the information that is gathered and analyzed) are often the same or very similar from either a retailing or manufacturing perspective. Also, because of the complexity of the apparel and retail environments today, often the retailer and manufacturer are one and the same, and buying is undertaken at both levels. In some cases buying from vendors, as well as manufacturing, is done by the same individual. Additionally, the buyer is sometimes the designer and/or merchandise planner for private-label merchandise. A good example of a retailer that is also a manufacturer is The Limited. To muddy the waters a little more, The Limited calls this position a "buyer," but all the apparel these "buyers" purchase is really private-label manufactured items.

Today, buying merchandise for retailers—whether stored or non-stored, small-independent operations or large chains—has become a complex effort that requires major preparation and planning, time, and effort. Gone are the days of buying by the seat of one's pants, so to speak. Also gone are the glamorous days when buyers had unlimited expense accounts and travelled to exotic markets, enjoyed the luxury of time, and received other benefits that made their job one to be envied. There are still plenty of benefits to a buying career, such as travel and opportunities to meet and work with a variety of people; however, the buyer's job has changed somewhat from years gone by. The world has become smaller, there are more resources from which to select merchandise, and change occurs more rapidly, so the very nature of buying has altered. A buyer must act and react faster and there is more information to use in operating and managing a retail business than ever before. Consequently, in some cases, the challenges are even greater than in the past, making the job even more exciting.

Merchandise Planning and Forecasting

Planning is a critical element of retailing and merchandising. Successful merchants must plan their businesses in today's sophisticated retail environment. People and products, or, in other words, the target customer and the merchandise, along with the desired profit must be anticipated and planned, for these three are inherently related. Running a business by the seat of your pants can rarely result in profit. **Planning** is a means of control that helps provide the buyer with information to make the best decisions in purchasing, which hopefully results in a profit. Some large retail organizations today have merchandise planners whose sole responsibility is to predict, distribute, and control merchandise at their stores. **Profit** results when operating expenses are less than the gross margin. **Gross margin** is the difference between the net sales and the cost of goods sold and usually is an indicator of profit. A retailing business is planned either manually or more and more frequently today by computer. Using computer technology to plan and track a business is a time-savings method that is within the reach of almost all businesses, and which allows for better and faster planning than in the past. Computer technology enables easy tracking of **stock keeping units (SKUs)** allowing the retailer to continuously keep up with sales and inventory levels along with other merchandise specifics. An SKU is the smallest unit level of merchandise and includes style, color, size, and any other information that needs to be tracked.

Planning involves determining what, for whom, and how much to buy. Also considered are where to buy, what method of buying to undertake (centralized vs decentralized), as well as what type of buying in which to partake (regular, off-price, promotional, and so forth). There are so many options available today, that generally, this is not an easy task.

The preparation (or forecasting) and planning for buying and **merchandise planning**, directly involves the five "rights" of merchandising that Mazur (1927, p. 66) brought to our attention many

Figure 4.1 Textile reps showing their fabric lines to apparel designers and manufacturers. Because fabric and color decisions are made at least a year in advance textile companies must be able to successfully forecast future merchandise trends.

years ago. These are: purchasing the *right merchandise*, at the *right time*, at the *right place*, in the *right quantities*, and at the *right price*.

Forecasting is predicting the styles and trends to purchase for the customer. It is a part of the buyer's job that is dependent on a lot of work and effort, due to the dynamic nature of the retail environment. Forecasting the right merchandise, as well as the expected or right amounts to be sold, is a crucial part of the merchant's job. The better a buyer or retailer is able to forecast, the better the likelihood that the projected sales and resultant profit will be obtained. Forecasting involves decision-making that uses as much input as possible.

Scanning the **environmental factors,** from both an internal (inside) and external (outside) perspective, impacts the buyer's decision-making.

External environmental factors include aspects of technology, the economy, society, and culture, along with political and legal issues that affect the business and the customer being considered. Internal environmental factors include information from store records to the store's particular culture and vendors. Data that are gathered from within and/or outside the company supply the retailer with a wide range of information to interpret, to analyze, and on which to act. The more information the buyer is able to synthesize, the better s/he will be at projecting the needs and wants of the consumer.

Figure 4.2 shows two pages from a trend book provided by Promostyl USA. Organizations such as this compile information and forecast the major trends in colors and styling for an upcoming season in apparel, accessories, cosmetics, and home fur-

NATUREL
pour le teint • for the complexion
NATURAL

ÉLÉGANCE
pour la bouche • for lips
ELEGANCE

ARTIFICIEL
pour les cheveux • for hair
ARTIFICIAL

MÉTALLIQUE
pour le regard • for eyes
METALLIC

Après la paleur évanescente de l'hiver dernier, les tendances beauté de cette saison mettent l'accent sur la couleur et sur l'éclat : les lèvres reviennent à l'élégance des rouges opaques, le teint naturel donne "bonne mine", les cheveux adoptent la couleur artificielle, le regard brille comme du métal. Ces quatre point forts sont développés en quatre grandes orientations beauté.

Beauté d'hiver
Winter beauty

After the evanescent palor of last winter, this season's beauty trends focus on color and brilliance : lips return to the elegance of opaque hues, natural complexions give a healthy glow, hair adopts artificial color, eyelids shine like metal. These four key point are developed for four major beauty orientations.

Figure 4.2 This page from the *Promostyl Color Forecasting Book* is an example of forecasting beauty trends.

nishings. Such information is available for purchase from numerous sources or may be provided to member stores by the buying offices of corporations, such as Federated Stores by their buying office. *Case 25, Forecasting Fashion in Menswear,* examines the complexity of forecasting the right merchandise trends from a menswear buyer's perspective.

The history of the retail organization, including the past performance records, can also be of significant help in planning. Measured results, such as sales and profit or loss of past years, may aid the planner in predicting the future with more precise accuracy. In *Case 26, The Inexperienced Buyer,* a novice buyer must make a multifaceted sales planning decision based on last year's poor sales, a current and strong open-to-buy position, and a single key market trend about which she does not feel confident.

Retail planning can be long-range and/or short-range, as well as top-down or bottom up. **Long-range planning** entails looking toward the future for a business and projects goals of five or more years. If a retailer considers how to diversify a business over the next ten years, then long-range planning is a necessity. **Short-range planning** involves looking at the most immediate concerns and setting goals of the business to achieve them. Two examples of short-range planning include such subjects as what to do about a sale that is a week away or how to meet a sales plan for the week. How much of the planning is done and by whom is dependent on the size and type of retailer, as well as how the retailer operates.

Top-down planning involves goal setting at the highest level of the organizational structure and management, then filtering the goals down to the other levels. For example, a corporation and its president plan the company's total sales goal, then it is broken down by division (e.g., women's and children's), and to the category (e.g., women's apparel) or department level (e.g., junior's) and the buyer. Next, the buyer breaks the sales down from a department (or category), to the classification (e.g., junior sportswear), sub-classification (e.g., junior tops), and perhaps even to the brand, price, style, size, and color. Generally, merchandise is

planned to (at least) five levels. These five levels are further explained below:

1. A **division** is the largest breakdown of merchandise for a retailer. It contains categories, departments, classifications, and sub-classifications. Examples of divisions are: soft goods, hard goods, women's and children's.

2. A **category** is a major grouping of merchandise that includes all types of departments, classes, and sub-classes that a particular type of customer would shop, for example, women's or men's apparel.

3. A **department** is a segment of a retailing establishment that groups classifications of merchandise together that are complementary to one another, such as a junior department or a men's department.

4. A **classification** (**class**) is a group of items (or the same general type of merchandise that are housed within a department), for example, sportswear or eveningwear.

5. A **sub-classification** (**sub-class**) is the term used to describe a group of merchandise within a classification that is closely related in styling, such as bottoms or tops under the classification of sportswear.

The level to which detailed planning is done is dependent on the type and importance of merchandise to the buyer and retailer. **Bottom-up planning** involves goal setting at the lowest levels of management—and even sometimes non-management—then filtering plans up the organizational structure to the highest management level. It is planning from the lowest level to the highest level. An example of bottom-up planning is when sales volume is being predicted by the department manager, who then tells the store manager, who finally relays this to the company's operations manager.

Dollar and Unit Plans

A major portion of the buyer's role involves planning what merchandise to purchase. The buyer relies on **dollar plans** and **unit plans,** or what may also be referred to as the **merchandise budget,** to guide them in making the best purchases. These plans forecast the merchandising activities for a department or store for a specific period of time. The buyer usually has direct involvement in creating the merchandise budget. Dollar planning is regarded as the money budget preparation of retail dollars to meet sales plans. This plan is quantitative and results in the planned purchases. **Unit planning** refers to the physical units and most often to the assortment planning and qualitative aspects. This type of plan involves decisions about what types of merchandise (or mix) should be bought and stocked by a retailer down to the number of pieces in inventory. Dollar and unit plans usually include calculations in dollars and/or percentage figures that relate to net sales.

Unit and dollar merchandise planning covers two six-month time frames within a calendar year, Spring/Summer (February–July) and Fall/Winter (August–January), and are referred to as **six-month plans.** An example of a six-month plan may be seen in Figure 4.3. This plan presents the projected sales, beginning and end of the month stocks, reductions, retail and cost planned purchases, along with other critical elements for planning. These elements include: initial and maintained markup, gross margin, operating expenses, expected net profit, and turnover. Last year's actual sales, a plan for this year, and actual sales figures are all recorded on the plan. For an example of how a six-month plan has been developed, but which needs to be revised, see *Case 28, Phillips Department Store: Developing a Six-Month Plan.*

Planning, whether the dollars and/or units, includes five progressive steps, which are:

1. Planning the retail sales.

2. Planning the inventory or stock (beginning of the month and end of the month).

3. Planning the reductions (markdowns, employee discounts, and shortages).

4. Planning the markup (retail minus cost).

5. Planning the purchases (needs to meet projected sales).

These five steps are explored in the next sections.

Sales Planning

The first step in developing the merchandise budget is **sales planning,** which is the estimation of the sales that a retailer will make over a period of time. If sales history is available, planners can use these figures as a base, and the sales from year-to-year and season-to-season are planned, based on increases or decreases to a set figure. If no past sales figures are available and original sales plans are being created from scratch, then more work and research in sales planning will be necessary. Environmental information, trends, and industry data need to be collected and analyzed to help estimate first-time sales. The accuracy of the sales plan is important, because all other merchandise plans are based on this, and consequently, if it is unrealistic, then the other plans will most likely be as well. A **sell-through** plan often is also developed, which sets a certain percentage of the amount of merchandise sold as a goal to achieve.

Inventory and Assortment Planning

Inventory (stock) planning is accomplished after sales planning, and entails the determination of the stock levels necessary to meet the sales plan. (The terms inventory and stock are used interchangeably.) **Beginning of the month (BOM)** and **end of the month (EOM)** inventory levels are calculated for each month of plans, as a means to ensure that enough merchandise will be stocked to cover the planned sales. The planner must remember that the planned BOM for a month is also the planned EOM for the preceding month. There are four methods of inventory planning that can be used to arrive at the "right" beginning of the month stock levels. These methods are briefly described below:

1. **Basic stock method,** which relies on having a minimum level of stock no matter what, as a reserve stock level and also enough stock to meet projected sales each month. Basic stock is equal to

SIX-MONTH MERCHANDISING PLAN

DEPARTMENT NAME _____   DEPARTMENT NO. _____   PERIOD COVERED _____

	LAST YEAR	PLAN		LAST YEAR	PLAN
Initial Markup	....	....	Gross Margin	....	....
Reductions	....	....	Operating Expense	....	....
Maintained Markup	....	....	Operating Profit	....	....
Cash Discount	....	....	Season Turnover	....	....
Buyer	....	....	Date Prepared	....	....

Spring	Fall	Sales +			E.O.M. +			Reductions -			B.O.M. =			Retail Purchases			Cost Purchases		
		Last Year	Plan	Actual	Last Year	Plan	Actual	Last Year	Plan	Actual	Last Year	Plan	Actual	Last Year	Plan	Actual	Last Year	Plan	Actual
Feb.	Aug.																		
Mar.	Sept.																		
Apr.	Oct.																		
May	Nov.																		
June	Dec.																		
July	Jan.																		
Total																			

Figure 4.3 An example of a six-month merchandise plan form.

the average stock for the season minus the average monthly sales.

2. **Percentage variation method** determines stock for a high turnover rate (six or more per year). It allows for stock fluctuation and is based on the premise that the variation of monthly stock from average stock should be half as much as the percentage variation in monthly sales from average sales.

3. **Stock-to-sales-ratio (SSR) method** arrives at a planned stock level that is based on what should be on hand at any given time, rather than on an average stock basis. It may be arrived at by multiplying the planned sales for the month by the BOM stock-to-sales ratio.

4. **Week's supply method** is used when calculating a needed stock level by week. With this method, planned stock is equal to the average stock in a week's supply multiplied by the planned weekly sales.

Different factors help a merchant determine which method of stock planning is best to use. Turnover is one factor that is always considered. **Turnover (TO)** or **stock turn** describes how many times stock is sold and replaced within a period of time. Stock turn rate helps ensure that the amount of merchandise available is adequate to meet the sales. A retailer or buyer must be careful, however, not to have too much more inventory than is needed. There is often a fine line between too much and not enough, or just the "right" amount of inventory. An overstocked position causes problems in *Case 30, Sell! Sell! Sell!*, because there is plenty of merchandise—but not the "right" merchandise—on hand.

Inventory problems that need immediate attention are presented in *Case 31, Inherited Inventory Problems,* in which there is an accumulation of old stock that the buyer's predecessor never moved out and action is needed to bring in fresh, new stock. What kind of action to take can sometimes present problems, and when goals conflict there may be negative repercussions.

An **assortment** of stock (or what particular types of merchandise will be purchased) is determined. Merchandise **assortment planning** regards not only what vendors are to carry, but the number of units and stock levels, price ranges, styles, sizes, colors, fabrics, and even the level of fashion. In essence, it plans the mixture of merchandise. An example of a simple unit and assortment plan by department, classification, and sub-classification that breaks the merchandise down into specific types of styles, level of fashion by percentage and number of units is presented in Figure 4.5.

An assortment is sometimes referred to as a **merchandise mix.** A golf pro-shop wants to make some improvements in its merchandise mix, but is unsure how to do so in *Case 29, Sub-Par Inventory.* Unfortunately, a lack of planning and control in the past provides current problems in stock that may have been otherwise avoidable. Merchandise assortment planning is also considered in *Case 37, A Competitive Dilemma: Advance or Retreat?*

There are two basic systems of developing assortment plans: creating basic stock plans or model stock plans. The type of merchandise being planned for—either basic or fashion—helps the retailer or buyer determine the type of plan to use. **Basic stock planning** involves staple merchandise, while **model stock planning** sets a determination of merchandise levels according to factors important to the buyer, for example, fabric, price, style, and so forth. A model stock plan is for fashion and/or seasonal merchandise within a particular merchandise category.

An effective, salable assortment of balanced stock should be strived for by the buyer. In doing so, two dimensions of stock are considered—the breadth and depth. The **breadth** of merchandise refers to the number of different product lines, styles, or brands that are carried in a retailing establishment. The **depth** refers to the number of units within a product line, style, or brand. Figure 4.4 shows several types of breadth and depth plans—with sizes or colors used for the depth dimension and styles or brands used for the breadth

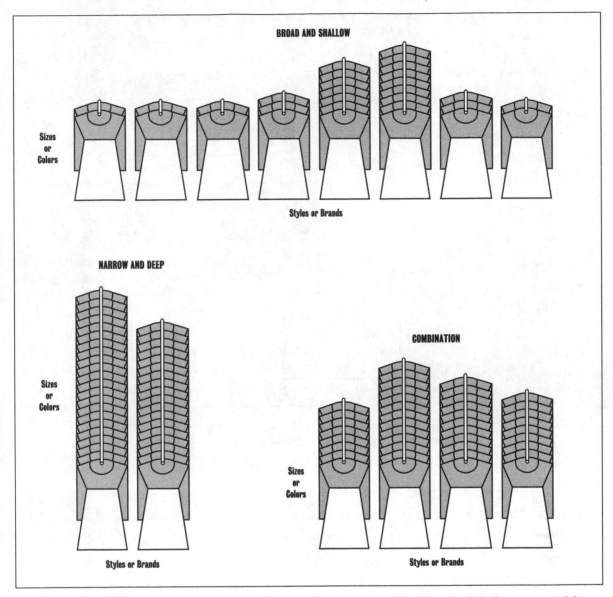

Figure 4.4 This figure shows examples of breadth and depth stock dimensions, including broad and shallow, narrow and deep, and combination.

dimension in an assortment plan. Descriptions of assortments are often presented in terms of breadth and depth. For example, merchandise within an assortment may be described as **broad** (lots of styles), **narrow** (few styles), **deep** (many colors and sizes), or **shallow** (few sizes and colors). An assortment can also be described in combinations, as in narrow and deep (few styles, many colors, and sizes), broad and shallow (many styles, few sizes and colors), and so forth.

Figure 4.5 This unit and assortment plan breaks merchandise down into management control levels, showing both the number of units and the corresponding percentage of stock.

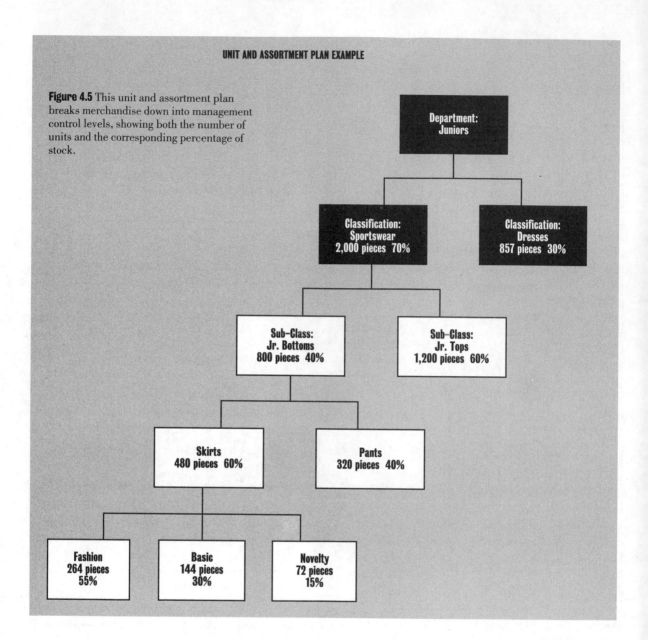

Planning Reductions

A means of lowering or marking down the retail price of merchandise, **reductions** are planned because only rarely can all the merchandise purchased be sold at the originally set retail price. Reductions are a provision used by retailers to reduce the retail price of merchandise and encourage the sale of stock so that it can be replaced with fresh, new goods. Markdowns, markup cancellations, and discounts are all types of reductions that a retailer should plan to incur. **Markdowns** are either **promotional** or **permanent** and these adjust the initial retail price downward temporarily or set a new retail, respectively. **Markup cancellations** adjust the amount of markup that was put on an item originally, thereby lowering the retail price.

Different reasons for reductions help the retailer decide what type of markdown to take. Special events, sales, clearance, old or damaged stock, the competition, or buyer's errors in purchasing or pricing are the more common reasons for markdowns. **Discounts** can also lower the retail price as a concession to employees (i.e., employee discounts) or other special customers.

Planning Markups

Markup (or **markon**) is the difference between the manufacturer's cost and the retail price offered to the customer. To realize profit, a retailer must sell merchandise for more than it costs. Markup is the amount of money added to the cost (or wholesale price) of the merchandise. Not only does markup need to be planned to cover the cost of goods, but the expenses incurred with selling the goods also have to be incorporated into the markup. **Expenses** are the costs expended by a business to generate sales. The markup taken varies dependent on the type of merchandise, type of store, the retail price desired, in addition to the expenses of running the business.

There are published industry averages and standards that may be used as guides for setting markup. For example, an average, healthy markup in apparel is what is referred to as keystone. A **keystone markup** is an amount that equals the cost of the merchandise, or a 50 percent retail markup. That is, the retail is arrived at by doubling the cost. A **short markup** is less than keystone. Also, sales volume (i.e., total sales) may play a role in determining the amount of markup for a retailer to take. A retailer such as Wal-Mart may take less than keystone markups, but makes up for this in the amount of sales volume acquired.

Pricing

The actual setting of the retail price on products is called **pricing**. It is a strategic decision that directly affects profit. Setting the retail price of goods and/or services is much more complicated than it first appears to be. Not only do retailers have to consider all the expenses incurred in the price, but they must also consider the type of merchandise, the competition, and the target customer when determining the best retail price to set on a product. The consumer today is cognizant of the relationship between value and price; however, value today means much more to the customer than just price. It is more situational and varies depending on who the customer is, what merchandise the customer is shopping for, and where the customer is shopping. "Getting your money's worth" is a real, and often major factor in consumer purchase decision-making. Many retailers compete with others for the customer's patronage through price alone. Therefore, setting the right retail price is a very important—and is often the deciding factor—in whether or not a sale is made. This can be a difficult decision to make.

The retail price for merchandise is calculated using a number of important factors. The cost (i.e., wholesale price) of a garment, plus all expenses that need to be figured into the markup are itemized and added into the total retail selling price. The proportional expenses that are included in the markup of a retail price varies from retailer to retailer; however, all these expenses must be included in the markup or part of the cost of merchandise is not being accounted for, and consequently, sales will not cover all the expenses incurred. Expenses include not only the cost of the merchandise, but allowances for markdowns, shortages and theft, salaries and benefits, and business overhead. Also, expected profit should be planned and worked into the markup, so there will be a residual profit after all the expenses are accounted for. No matter what the amount is, the retail price is the sum of the cost and markup.

Deciding on the correct and profitable retail price for a proven seller can be a problem for both a buyer and a retail owner who must consider a cost increase, markup, and gross margin. Such is the problem in *Case 32, How Much for the Good Smell?* A cost increase also warrants a retail increase in *Case 48, Tying One On* in Chapter Six. This case exemplifies the fact that setting retail prices may be dependent on outside factors.

Pricing strategy is the determination of the type of pricing policy a buyer or retailer will use along with the practices the buyer or retailer will employ. It involves understanding not only who the target customer is and what their needs and/or wants are, but also a number of other such factors as the image and identity that a retailer wants to project. (See Chapter Two for more on image and identity.) Additionally, there is usually a direct relationship between the retail price, quality, and style level of merchandise in most customers' minds. (See Chapter Three for more on this subject.)

Merchandise pricing policies are the methods that retailers use to set retail prices on their merchandise in addition to the thought processes behind their pricing. A policy is selected by a retailer to help set the price on merchandise and to also convey a message (or image) to the customer about the retail operation and the merchandise being carried. Psychology often plays a role in determining the type of pricing to use. As mentioned before, both who the customer is and what type of merchandise a retailer wants to sell to that customer play an important role in what price should be the "right" price to place on the merchandise to sell it. Pricing policies and strategies must incorporate the psychology to best match the correct price with the merchandise being sold, so that the customer will feel that the price is fair for the merchandise being bought. (Price and retail image are discussed in Chapter Two.) Pricing determinations are made on such issues as:

• Will price ranges and/or price points be used? That is, will the retail price be determined by keeping the dollar amount between one retail price and another, or will a single, predetermined price be used? For example, at a dollar store everything would sell for one dollar. Another example is a retailer who marks everything at whole and mid-dollar points, for example, $5 and $7.50.

• Will the merchandise be **promotionally priced** (i.e., have a sale price) or **regularly priced** (i.e., not on sale)? A discounter might sell all merchandise at the .49 or .99 cent price point ending to indicate a sale price, while a department store might price and sell all regular merchandise at whole number prices, such as $60 or $100.

• Will the merchandise be **odd priced** (i.e., ending with an odd number or a round number) or **even priced** (i.e., ending with numbers that can be divided evenly)? Odd price point endings, such as .95 or .99 often reflect sale merchandise while .00 or evenly divisible numbers usually indicate non-sale prices.

• Should the merchandise be priced as a **loss leader** (i.e., priced at or below cost) to attract customers?

Pricing and pricing practices are regulated by the Federal Trade Commission (FTC), which helps to protect the retailer and consumer alike from deceptive, unfair, and/or illegal pricing tactics. Several examples of the FTC's involvement in regulating pricing can be found in Chapter Twelve.

Planned Purchases and Open-to-Buy

Planning the dollars and units for the open-to-buy and the planned purchases (needs) must take into consideration the five merchandising rights. These include the determination of the best (right) merchandise desired, the correct (right) quantities, the setting of the best (right) retail prices, the most accurate (right) timing and delivery, and the proper (right) placement of the merchandise.

A **planned purchase** is the difference between what is needed and what is on hand. The amount of planned purchases that is projected is based on the planned sales, BOM and EOM inventory levels desired, and the amount of reductions that are being planned. Failing to plan can cause many merchandising and retailing problems, as it does in *Case 84, Amy's Fashions on First, parts 1 and 2* in Chapter Eleven.

The **open-to-buy** (OTB) is an adjustment to the planned purchases that takes into account what is already **on order** (i.e., what is due in). It is calculated on a frequent basis and aids the buyer in making necessary adjustments throughout the season to help control inventories and profitability. After purchases are placed originally, the OTB is then periodically determined by subtracting the on order from the planned purchases.

Adjusting plans is a means to change what can realistically be done and more accurately ensure that goals will be met. *Case 34, Is the Purchase Worth the Risk?*, involves a buyer who is in an overstocked and overbought position, but is offered an attractive promotional package of merchandise from a vendor. She desperately wants to make the purchase, and then adjusts her plans to allow her to make the buy. Her merchandise manager, however, does not want to approve the purchase based on the adjusted plans, even though the buyer feels the merchandise is just what she needs to stimulate business.

Setting the best, most realistic, reasonable plan is not always easy. A plan needs to be realistic enough to be achievable, yet aggressive enough to be a challenge, which will increase sales and improve profit. In *Case 27, The Planning Impasse*, a buyer disagrees with the merchandise manager who wants to increase the department planned sales. Reworking his aggressive department plans as instructed by his merchandise manager is also a challenge for a new buyer in *Case 28*.

Incorrect and/or poor merchandise planning and purchasing can result in poor sales performance from stock-outs, high markdowns, lost sales, and ultimately a poor bottom line. Successful buyers regularly review and revise their plans throughout the season to act upon changes that may affect their business. To make the best buy, the prepared buyer should purchase goods armed with plans. When planning is not done or is improperly done, disaster can strike. *Case 33, The Assistant Buyer's Costly Mistake* presents the disastrous repercussions of an unprepared assistant buyer who shops the market without plans, against the request of her buyer to prepare them.

Improper planning can also have negative results at the manufacturing level. In *Case 24, Chaos of Cancellations*, sudden cancellations by a buyer (who has been directed to cancel orders by upper management) may result in an exclusive contractor starting all over again, as well as a loss of employees if a resolution to the lost orders is not obtained.

Controls

Measuring and evaluating performance productivity and resulting profitability of a business is reliant on planning and controls. **Controls** are the methods employed to help a retailer track the business to see how it is doing and how effective the merchandising strategies are. Effective control systems have established **standards,** a means of measuring performance through accepted guidelines that help to monitor performance. Consequently, the resulting analyses allow for change to the business that can be based on the information provided with the control. When retailers discuss controls, they usually refer to the financially based aspects of their business and those accounting and merchandising measures that help ensure profitability. Controls can also be records that track data or compare and contrast information.

The importance of maintaining merchandising standards as a control in an effort to run a profitable business is brought to light in *Case 35, The Impossible Goals*. Planning and controlling such specific aspects of a buyer's business as markup, turnover, markdown, and sales as related to improving sales and profitability are also examined. Controls also aid a business in reacting to events that occur, in order for adjustments to be made as needs arise. Usually controls are built into management objectives during the business planning stages. For example, the dollar and unit control of a retailer is often built into the merchandise planning budget.

Merchandise planning is a necessary control for retailers. However, there are tools other than budgets that may also be utilized to control a retailing business and help to make it profitable. Inventories (both periodic and perpetual) are types of retail controls taken to keep track of stock. **Periodic inventory** is a method of stock control in which the retailer physically counts merchandise at designated time periods. Many apparel retailers take periodic inventories twice a year, in July and January. These dates coincide with the end of the six-month planning periods and also correspond to the lowest inventory levels of the year. In contrast,

Table 4.1   Key Vendor Matrix

Vendors	Ranking	$* Pur	$* Sales	% Sell- Through	% MM+	% Mkdowns	$* Mkdowns	% GM
ALL THAT JAZZ	5	40	32.0	80	46	4.0	1.60	36
ALLYN PAIGE	13	23	9.2	40	30	15.0	3.45	28
BLONDIE & ME	10	8	2.0	25	44	9.0	.72	38
BRIOCHE	7	12	6.6	55	50	6.3	9.45	32
BYER TOO	16	17	8.5	50	32	14.0	2.38	30
CITY TRIANGLES	3	9	6.3	70	46	8.0	.72	34
CLE PARIS	8	15	6.3	42	41	7.0	1.05	42
DAWN JOY	19	7	2.1	30	40	22.6	1.58	31
HEARTS DIVINE	12	13	5.5	46	49	16.0	2.08	34
JALATE	18	42	28.6	68	29	55.0	23.10	19
JUMP	20	8	7.2	90	60	36.0	2.88	29
JUST CHOON	2	24	18.0	75	52	4.0	.96	38
LA BELLE	11	29	9.3	32	36	20.0	5.80	22
MARIAN & MARAL	6	10	3.2	32	48	3.5	.35	37
RAMPAGE	14	8	5.4	67	42	22.0	1.76	20
TICKETS	4	30	22.2	74	52	7.2	21.60	32
TRIANGLE BLUES	15	4	6.0	15	34	19.0	.76	26
XOXO	9	22	32.0	15	37	14.0	3.08	31
XTRMZ	17	6	3.6	60	41	9.0	.54	29
YOU BABES	1	30	25.5	85	49	6.0	1.80	35

* Dollars in thousands
+ Maintained Markon

perpetual inventories are stock control methods that provide a continuous record of the movement of incoming and outgoing merchandise. Today, computer technology and point-of-sale cash registers allow retailers to easily maintain perpetual inventories. (See Chapter Ten for more discussion of technology and point-of-sale.)

Records help management follow and guide businesses to success. Retailers generate various reports to help monitor their businesses, which may include many types of planning reports and records. Reports on units, dollars, assortment, pricing, fast or slow sellers, sell-through analysis, vendors, and other information desired are frequently used methods of retail control.

Another aid for control used by numerous large retail chains is a **vendor matrix** or **key resource list.** These matrices or lists are based on the premise that fewer resources or suppliers are better than many, in order for the resources to be as beneficial to the retailer as possible. The matrix or key resource list incorporates the company-approved key vendors from which a buyer is recommended and/or required to purchase. An example of a vendor matrix may be seen in Table 4.1. Pertinent performance information on vendors is contained on the matrix. Such information is reported as dollar purchases, sell-through, the amount of markdowns, markup, and gross margin. Often the vendors are listed according to the most profitable resource, unlike this matrix in which the vendors are alphabetized, but still ranked according to profitability. Sometimes purchasing rules are given to buyers, for example, the 80/20 rule. This guideline instructs the buyer to purchase 80 percent of their department needs from the top 20 percent of their vendors, which helps to ensure proven profitability and vendor consistency in assortment.

Productivity and Profit

The retailer's bottom line and also the objective of most retail businesses, is to realize a profit. The evaluation of a company's profitability is reported on a **profit and loss statement** (**P&L**) or **income statement.** This is also a control that helps to monitor the budget. It summarizes the financial workings of a business during a certain period of time and documents whether or not there is a profit or loss. Profit results when revenues generated exceed the costs incurred in producing those revenues. On the profit and loss statement, net sales are first compared to cost of goods sold to arrive at gross margin. Next, the expenses are subtracted for resulting profit or loss. Such reports as the profit and loss statement can help direct a retailer as to whether or not changes are necessary to a business. In *Case 37, A Competitive Dilemma: Advance or Retreat,* facts and figures are presented on which to base the determination of whether or not a store owner should keep the business as it is or change it. Records that provide information on the maximization of sales potential, productivity, and profitability of the store in general, as well as the separate departments are considered.

The profitability of a business may also be used as a gauge to determine the direction in which a retailer should plan growth, as well as how to specifically plan that growth. *Case 36, Saks Fifth Avenue: A Plan for Profit Rebound* poses the matter of profitability in looking at Saks' one-year actual and long-range, five-year plans. Based on the figures presented, recommendations can be made regarding ways to enhance sales and profitability.

Summary

Forecasting the needs and wants of retail customers through research and careful planning helps to predict sales more accurately, as well as ensuring a retailer's success through profit. The need for effective internal controls in monitoring the dollars, units, and assortments should never be underestimated by a retailer. The closer a retailer monitors and manages a company, as well as adapting to changes that occur in both the external and internal environments, the more profitable and rewarding a business will be.

References

Bohlinger, M.S. (1993). *Merchandise buying.* Needham Heights, MA.: Allyn and Bacon.

Clodfelter, R. (1993). *Retail buying: From staples to fashions to fads.* Albany, N.Y.: Delmar.

Clodfelter, R. (1996). *Making buying decisions: Using the computer as a tool.* Albany, N.Y.: Delmar.

Easterling, C., Flottman, E., & Jernigan, M. (1992). *Merchandising mathematics for retailing.* Englewood Cliffs, N.J.: Prentice-Hall.

Guerreiro, M., & Garrett, L. (1994). *The buyer's workbook.* New York: Fairchild Publications.

Guthrie, K.M. (1996). *Perry's department store: A buying simulation.* Albany, N.Y.: Delmar.

Kotsiopulos, A., & Kang-Park, J. (1994). *Merchandising mathematics.* New York: Fairchild Publications.

Mazur, Paul (1927). *Principles of organization applied to modern retailing.* New York: Harper and Bros.

National Retail Federation. (1979). *The buyer's manual.* Washington, D.C.: Author.

Paidar, M.L. (1994). *Merchandising math: High margin returns for retailers and vendors.* Albany, N.Y.: Delmar.

Perna, R. (1987). *Fashion forecasting.* New York: Fairchild Publications.

Tepper, B.K., & Godnick, N.E. (1996). *Mathematics for retail buying.* New York: Fairchild Publications.

Weeks, A., Miller-Mordaunt, V., Perenchio, M., & Metcalfe, D.A. (1991). *Effective marketing management: Using merchandising and financial strategies for retail success.* New York: Fairchild Publications.

Key Terms

assortment
assortment planning
basic stock method
basic stock planning
bottom-up planning
breadth
broad
buyer
buying
category
classification (class)
controls
deep
department
depth
discounts
division
dollar plan
environmental factors
even priced
expenses

forecasting
gross margin
income statement
inventory (stock) planning
key resource list
keystone markup
long-range planning
loss leader
markdown
markon
markup
markup cancellations
merchandise budget
merchandise mix
merchandise planner
merchandise planning
merchandiser
merchandising
model stock planning
narrow

odd priced
on order
open-to-buy (OTB)
percentage variation method
periodic inventory
permanent markdowns
perpetual inventory
planned purchases
planning
pricing strategy
profit
profit and loss statement (P&L)
promotional markdowns
promotional pricing
purchasing
purchasing agent
records
reductions
regular pricing

sales planning
sell-through
shallow
short markup
short-range planning
six-month plan
sourcing agent
standards
stock keeping unit (SKU)
stock level
stock-sales ratio method (SSR)
stock turn
sub-classification (sub class)
top-down planning
turnover (TO)
unit planning
vendor matrix
week's supply method

Case 24
Chaos of Cancellations

Laura Neumann, Eagle's Eye

Quick Sew, a Southwest apparel manufacturer owned by Rudi Kuchler for 20 years, now produces clothing exclusively for one major TV shopping retailer, Allure. Allure's product lines consist of electronics, jewelry, and apparel/cosmetics. The apparel/cosmetics division carries both branded and private-label merchandise. Quick Sew produces the apparel for Allure's highest-volume private label, which is exclusive to Allure. Quick Sew and Allure have been doing business for two years and have formed a solid partnership. The partnership was formed through a designer, Vicki Shriver, who had been doing business with Allure four years prior to Quick Sew's involvement in production of Allure's apparel. Although selling exclusively to Allure is risky business, Quick Sew has been flourishing while the rest of the retail market has been flat.

Rudi produces both basic and fashion items for Allure's private-label line. His volume business is with basics. Rudi receives large orders for basics approximately four times per year. Spring basics are ordered in February and April; Fall basics are ordered in July and September. Smaller orders for nonbasic, fashion items are received from Allure approximately ten times per year. The slow months for Quick Sew are January and June. Allure's fashion seasons are not categorized in the same way most retailers typically use them, i.e., Spring, Fall, Fall transition, Holiday. Rather, Allure's fashion seasons are known as Spring transition, Spring, Fall transition, and Fall. However, the buyers for Allure use the month of delivery rather than the season as a basis for communicating desired delivery with Quick Sew. Purchase orders for the garments are typically written by the retail buyer four to six months prior to the date Quick Sew must deliver the garments.

Quick Sew has no in-house production; rather, Rudi contracts all the work out. That is, production sewing is done in small factories in outlying areas of the Southwest. Specifically, six contractors have allocated complete production capability to Quick Sew. These contractors are experienced with the required sewing for specific fabrics demanded by Allure and they all have accommodated to Allure's quality and packaging standards. The employees in these factories are well trained and produce an excellent product with a short lead time.

In February, Allure suddenly canceled their Quick Sew orders for the months of May and June because their sales were down and inventory levels were high. The cancellations are driven by Allure's management, who were being pressured by stockholders to show higher profits. Although it is possible to adjust down from preset orders, cancellations are deadly. Quick Sew's contractors have come to rely on Rudi to fill their sewing capacity. If the capacity is not used, the contractors will go elsewhere for business. Rudi has trained these contractors to comply rigidly to Allure's quality and packaging standards. Losing the contractors would mean starting all over and training new sewers again when business picks up.

Major Question
What strategy can Rudi implement to keep the contractors busy during months with no orders?

Study Questions
1. What other differences are there between electronic television retailers and conventional department store retailers?

2. What are the advantages and disadvantages of a supplier being the exclusive source of only one retail account?

Case 25
Forecasting Fashion in Men's Wear

Janice Rosenthal McCoart, Marymount University

On this particular morning, Naomi Hicks was especially anxious to get to work. After several years of assisting in the buying of women's sportswear and dresses at a regional chain of stores called Edmonds, Naomi was beginning a new job as buyer of men's related separates.

Edmonds is situated in the suburbs of a major, eastern city in the U.S. With a central buying structure, it enjoys a reputation for quality apparel, generally a mix of brand-name and private-label merchandise. The chain even has its own import program. Its main competition comes from larger, departmentalized stores like Bloomingdale's, Macy's, and JCPenney.

Edmonds provides personalized service, building customer loyalty that may combat competition. The stores occasionally run sales timed with those of competitors. It is not considered a fashion-forward store; however, it aims for uniqueness in product mix as a defense against the competition.

Paul Clay, the menswear merchandise manager, greeted Naomi. He defines Edmonds' male customers as "age thirty- to sixty-years-old, educated, white-collar, family-men who spend 20 percent of the week in leisure activities." Naomi oversees these classifications: polos, rugbies, crew-neck shirts, workshirts, sport pants, and shorts.

Paul presented two immediate concerns to Naomi. It is time to prepare for the buying of Spring season merchandise, but simultaneously, product information must be assembled and presented to upper management for the store's import of its own merchandise during the following Fall. Naomi learned that Edmonds' theme for its Fall merchandise was "Crew." She is not sure what "crew" means and feels immediately overwhelmed, having to formulate merchandising ideas

for two different seasons. Paul suggested that she compile a list of sources of relevant fashion forecasting information because this is her first buying experience. She draws on her experience as an assistant and using information she remembers from school research sources she compiles a list of information:

1. Color reporting service—for example, Color Projections, Inc.

2. Resident buying office, especially the one serving Edmonds, which is Certified Fashion Guild.

3. Consumer menswear publications, for instance, *Gentleman's Quarterly.*

4. Trade associations, like the National Association of Men's Sportswear Buyers.

5. Historic costume books.

6. European menswear collections, like those designed by Gianni Versace, Romeo Gigli, Nino Cerruti, or Jean Paul Gaultier.

7. Trade publications for the menswear market, for instance, *DNR.*

8. Edmonds' best sellers from last season.

9. Local store competitors.

10. Local art museum.

11. Museums that feature historic costume, such as the Metropolitan Museum of Art.

12. New York's most prestigious stores: Barney's, Bloomingdale's, Bergdorf Goodman, etc.

13. Apparel on local college campuses.

Paul reviewed Naomi's list, but knows that she cannot possibly research all the information contained on the list because time will not allow it. He wants plans by the end of the week and it is Tuesday. He also thought the list lacked order and feels that narrowing the list down and/or rank ordering the information could help Naomi prioritize her research. He asked Naomi to look at the list a second time and rerank the sources for her research and pare the list down, because she will be unable to research everything she has listed.

Naomi is a bit disappointed, as she spent quite a bit of time compiling her list, but knows that if her plans have to be in by Friday, she had better get to work. She does know that the more information she has, the better her decisions will be, so she is somewhat frustrated because she really wants her first buying plans to be great.

Major Question

How should Naomi rank these sources in order of importance, and what information would you eliminate if you were Naomi? Analyze each source for relevance to Naomi's situation.

Study Questions

1. Should any of Naomi's choices be omitted from the list?

2. Did Naomi forget any other sources of fashion information?

Case 26
The Inexperienced Buyer

Judy K. Miler, University of Tennessee
Nancy J. Rabolt, San Francisco State University

Loretta Fall is the women's sportswear buyer for Culver Fashions in Culver City, California. It is July, and she is about to submit a six-month merchandise plan (August thru January) for her department. Loretta has reviewed last year's sales figures and events and has remembered that weather in August and September was most unfavorable for selling. She has also remembered that the heat was constant and this caused consumer lassitude. The computer printout indicates her figures for the two-month period were off about 18 percent from the previous year. She also recalls worrying herself sick to make figures.

This year, Loretta visited the market in June for Fall merchandise and was not impressed with the trends. Although she has been a buyer for only a year, she believes one color trend—heather gray—

may spell trouble because it is a rather dull color and not one that most of her target customers will want to buy. Lately, consumers have been refusing to buy if they do not become excited about the new merchandise. Accordingly, Loretta has bought small amounts of merchandise well below her budgeted figures. She is in a strong open-to-buy position, that is, she has money in her budget for other types of purchases.

Loretta assumes that business will not be adversely affected to the extent of last year. She figures that she can't have such a disastrous Fall season two years in a row. If the market shows real strength with some trends, she could plan a strong increase of sales for the two opening months of the plan with some hustling. If she plans for a decrease, it may be considered as a defensive measure by a new buyer. Should Loretta plan for a strong increase and sales remain flat, she could be strongly criticized and look like an inefficient new buyer. Because she is a fairly new buyer, she is between the devil and the deep blue sea.

The other ready-to-wear buyers are more confident and they don't have the same misgivings about this season. They suffered some losses last year, but they have affirmative feelings about the opportunities for increases this year. Business, this year, they maintain, will be better than last year's disaster.

Loretta considers going to her merchandise manager, George Ramos, to discuss the dilemma with him. Loretta knows George is a fair person, but she knows that he has some misgivings about her being a buyer because he feels she lacks experience. Actually, he hired her after considerable soul searching and at the time shared his misgivings with her. Therefore, Loretta discards the idea of going to George.

Finally, she decides to talk with Matt Washington, a buyer who went through Culver Fashion's buying training program with her. They shared many of the same experiences during that time and Matt has always given her good, solid advice. Also, he is familiar with the current market conditions.

Major Question

If you were Matt, how would you advise Loretta?

1. Discuss the advantages of maintaining an open-to-buy during the selling season. Disadvantages?

2. How else can an inexperienced buyer research fashion trends when planning?

Case 27
The Planning Impasse

Judy K. Miler, University of Tennessee
Nancy J. Rabolt, San Francisco State University

About four months ago, the Midwest Department Store in Sheboygan, Wisconsin, hired a new divisional merchandise manager, Richard Blum, who had a fine record at Marshall Field's in Chicago. He was assigned to the women's apparel departments.

The store had brought in merchandise consultants prior to hiring Richard to determine ways to increase the ready-to-wear volume that was not up to comparable stores. The recommendations included the goal to increase turnover, which ranged from four to a little less than five times per year. This was below the standard of other stores in the region devoted to moderately priced merchandise. One of the strategies suggested was to set up an advertising program featuring specially priced merchandise.

Shortly after he arrived, Richard held a meeting with the six buyers on his staff and outlined his plans. He said, "We are shooting for a minimum turnover of six times with a stock-sales ratio of two

to one. With additional advertising, thorough shopping of the market, and good vendor relations, we should be able to make many good buys and pass them on to our customers."

On July 14, Marjorie Porter, the accessories buyer, was with Richard at the weekly buyer review meeting and presented her merchandise plan (as seen in Table 4.2). Richard scanned the plan and commented: "This plan is okay, but the sales are increased only 10 percent despite twice as many ads, improved displays, and strong store programs. I'd judge that a 10 percent increase would be a pretty poor estimate in view of the cost and efforts to stimulate real volume."

Marjorie was taken aback. She did not understand his concern, and felt that a 10 percent increase was aggressive enough. She thought Richard was overplaying the recommendations of the consulting firm. She defended her plan to him, explaining, "A plan is a flexible tool. If conditions warrant additional increases in sales and open-to-buy, the plan can be changed later. I can't see any reason for being unrealistic and for projecting unobtainable figures."

"Listen," Richard responded, "modest increases indicate to management a lack of confidence and motivation and I don't want to project that. I also feel that you won't be under sufficient pressure to top planned figures. My philosophy is that pressure helps realize goals."

Marjorie retorted, "If I submit high figures, I leave myself vulnerable to downward revision and high markdowns and to me that makes me look worse than exceeding sales. So, I'm not going to look bad and I don't want to play an unfair game, period."

Table 4.2	Marjorie's Six-Month Plan						
	Aug.	Sept.	Oct.	Nov.	Dec.	Jan.	Total
SALES							
LY (actual)	90,000	100,000	70,000	90,000	120,000	60,000	530,000
Plan	99,000	110,000	80,000	99,000	132,000	66,000	586,000
RETAIL STOCK							
LY (actual)	225,000	250,000	175,000	225,000	300,000	150,000	1,325,000
Plan	198,000	220,000	160,000	198,000	264,000	132,000	1,172,000

Richard was surprised that Marjorie was standing her ground. He had never before been challenged by a buyer not to do what he was asking. He did not expect this response. Since his arrival, this was his first real encounter with Marjorie, and he had not established a track record at the store, so he felt vulnerable. He was trying to win over the buyers and impress management with his business knowledge and management skills. He simply could not afford an impasse at this early stage; the results could do him no good and might even make him look ineffective as a manager.

Major Question

What do you think should be Richard's course of action in regard to Marjorie's refusal to increase her plan even more?

Study Questions

1. Who do you think should make the final decision in setting the sales plan? Why?

2. Do you agree or disagree with Richard's response to Marjorie that "modest increases indicate to management a lack of confidence and motivation . . . ?"

Case 28
Phillips Department Store: Developing a Six-Month Plan

D. Michael Fields, Southwest Missouri State University

Corey Matthews sat down at his desk to reflect on the review of his first six-month plan. He remembered the hours he had spent developing the plan, the justification he had for each figure, and the

confidence he had when he submitted it to Jim Edwards, his divisional merchandise manager. Corey could not help the feeling of disappointment. The meeting had not gone as he had anticipated.

After his promotion to buyer of men's sportswear at Phillips Department Store, Corey had sought to write a six-month plan that would impress management with its thoroughness and its lack of need for revision. He knew that management would be watching him closely. Many people in the store were surprised when he had been named to the position after only eighteen months in the management training program. In addition, buying positions in soft lines (i.e., clothing departments) were prized assignments because of the sales growth the area had enjoyed in the past few years. Corey had wanted to justify the confidence that management had shown in giving him the position. He felt like he was viewed as a rising star, and he did not want to do anything to jeopardize that position.

Phillips Department Store was clearly the dominant department store in Minton, a southern city of 400,000. Phillips had recently celebrated its 100th year in Minton. From the initial block square downtown flagship store, the company had added six branches in and around the city and had achieved a regional reputation as the store to go to for upscale fashion merchandise. Phillips faced a typical mix of competitors. On the low end, several discounters had invaded the market and were chipping away at the base of customers for which price was the predominant factor in the purchase decision. On the high-end, a wide range of specialty stores could be found which were attempting to lure Phillips' customers by claiming to offer greater merchandise depth, more available services, and salespeople who were more knowledgeable.

The men's sportswear department had typically been used as a training ground for new buyers who management felt had a great deal of potential. In essence, the position gave the individuals an opportunity to "prove their worth." Even though the department was clearly a soft line (i.e., clothing) department, it was considered an excellent training position because it gave a young buyer soft-line buying experience in a relatively stable merchandise environment. Although there were fashion considerations, the merchandise expectations of the target market (professional and retired men) did not typically vary a great deal from year to year. As a result, a young buyer could gain valuable soft-line buying experience and not be put immediately in a position where the success of the department was dependent on the buyer's ability to match merchandise with the changing fashion tastes of the target market. The position was clearing a *stepping stone* to larger, more prestigious buying positions.

The department was broken down into six broad merchandise classifications to help ensure a proper merchandise mix was maintained. The department's stability caused very little variation in the percentages of department sales among the classifications. A list of the six classifications and their relative percentage of total department sales can be found in Table 4.3. Phillips Department Store buyers also utilized an eight-step process to develop their buying plans (see Table 4.4).

Table 4.3	Phillips Department Store Classifications in the Men's Sportswear Department
Class	Description
A	Sport shirts (20%)
B	Solid slacks (28%)
C	Print slacks (18%)
D	Swimwear (14%)
E	Light outerwear (12%)
F	Leather goods (8%)

Table 4.4   Phillips Department Store: Eight Steps for Developing a Six-Month Merchandise Plan

1. *Determine total department sales for the entire period.* Department sales are to be derived from the sales of the department in the same period for the previous year. Although differences are expected, buyers should be prepared to reference and justify this year's departmental sales figure by using last year's figure as a frame of reference.
2. *Allocate the sales among the classifications in the department.* Where possible, historical records are to be used as the basis for allocating sales among classifications in a department. Buyers should expect to be required to justify any proposed differences that significantly deviate from established trends.
3. *Calculate the departmental sales by month.* All sales are planned to correspond with the same week for the previous year. As a result, a similar pattern of sales is expected. Buyers whose plan is significantly different from the department's established monthly sales percentages should be prepared to justify any differences.
4. *Determine the sales by class, by month.* The sales amount by class, by month is the result of a simple calculation of the sales allocated among the classifications (step 2) by the percentage of sales by month (step 3).
5. *Calculate the reductions amounts by month, by class.* The most appropriate basis for planning the reductions amounts (employee discounts, markdowns, and stock shortages) is the established percentages with

which your department has operated in recent years. Any deviations from established norms will be closely scrutinized by your divisional merchandise manager.
6. *Assign appropriate stock-sales ratios and determine appropriate BOM and EOM inventory levels for each class.* Most departments will utilize a stock-to-sales ratio as a basis for determining the appropriate inventory levels. The beginning-of-the-month (BOM) amount is the calculation of concern since the ending-of-the-month (EOM) figure is equal to the following month's BOM. Although past ratios for BOM inventory levels can serve as a guide, the ratios that will be employed in the present merchandise plan should come as a result of consultation with the divisional merchandise manager.
7. *Calculate the planned purchases for each class.* With the previous steps completed, the planned purchases figure becomes a very straightforward calculation. It is an addition of sales, total reductions, and EOM inventory *less* the BOM inventory count.
8. *Determine the open-to-buy for each class by subtracting all commitments.* The open-to-buy amount for each month of the plan is simply the planned purchases in a particular classification less any commitments for merchandise that have been made in that classification. The commitments will be applied to the month in which the merchandise is scheduled for delivery.

From Corey's knowledge of the process, he recognized the importance of starting the process with the *correct* sales figure. If the departmental sales amount was not correct, then all the figures in the plan would be wrong since all were derived from the initial departmental sales estimate. Sales planning for the merchandise plan is especially critical. The amount of merchandise that will initially be purchased is determined from the *planned* sales figures. However, the amount of merchandise that should have been purchased is ascertained when the *actual* sales figures are recorded. Thus, when the two figures do not agree, some adjustments must be made. In the month that the discrepancy takes place, the ending inventory (and the corresponding next month's BOM inventory) will not match the planned amount. Management expects the planned and actual inventory levels to be brought back in line by the end of the next month. Thus, the variation in the next month is not with the ending inventory but rather with the planned purchases. For example (assuming all other figures are on plan), if October actual sales exceed planned sales by $1,000, then October's ending inventory (and November's beginning inventory) would be $1,000 under the plan. Since management expects the department to be back on plan by the end of November, then November's planned purchases would be increased by $1,000. If the buyer had already spent all his or her November open-to-buy based on the plan (which is usually the case), then he or she would find that they suddenly have an additional $1,000 of open-to-buy available for November.

To Corey's relief, the planned sales estimation seemed very straightforward. Over the past six years, the annual percentage sales increase of the men's sportswear department had hovered in the narrow range between 7.9 and 8.3 percent (see Table 4.5). The only exception to the consistency in sales percentage growth had occurred four years ago when the department recorded only a 3 percent increase. Upon research, Corey discovered that this was the year that a new buyer had been placed in the department and that individual "just didn't work out" and consequently left the store after one year in the department. Corey considered this event to be the result of poor management and not

Table 4.5 Phillips Department Store Men's Sportswear Department Total Department Sales (most recent year first)

Sales	Increase Over Previous Year	Percentage Increase
1,000,000	75,785	8.2
924,215	68,460	8.0
855,755	64,120	8.1
791,635	23,055	3.0
768,580	56,270	7.9
712,310	54,590	8.3
657,720		

an indication of unstable demand. Corey's research showed that, over this span, inflation had pushed up the department's prices at a constant rate of 3 percent a year over the past six years.

To further alleviate his concern, Corey had checked with the store's research department to ensure that there were no forthcoming changes in the competitive market of which he was not aware that might impact his department's sales. In addition, he had raised a similar question at a recent divisional sales meeting. In each case, there was no indication that the competitive market would be going through any dramatic changes in the near future.

Corey was confident that the 8 percent sales increase that he was planning was realistic. In fact, he felt that through improved merchandise selection he could beat last year by an additional 2 percent—although he did not feel comfortable attempting to justify the 10 percent figure to his divisional merchandise manager. With the sales figure determined, the balance of the plan had been very easy to develop. The sales by class across the department remained relatively stable in recent years. In addition, the percentage of sales by month had experienced very little variation. Also, the reductions percentages had been almost constant over the past ten years. Thus, the determination of these figures had been a simple multiplication of the percentages against the appropriate sales figure. The only other component

FEBRUARY (10%)

Sales		$21,600
Reductions:		
Employee discounts (5%)	$1,080	
Markdowns (9%)	1,944	
Shortages (3%)	648	
Total Reductions		3,672
BOM inventory (2.6/1)		(56,160)
EOM inventory		74,520
Planned Purchases		$43,632
Commitments		0
Open-to-buy		$43,632

MARCH (15%)

Sales		$32,400
Reductions:		
Employee discounts (5%)	$1,620	
Markdowns (7%)	2,268	
Shortages (3%)	972	
Total Reductions		4,860
BOM inventory (2.3/1)		(74,520)
EOM inventory		94,500
Planned purchases		$57,240
Commitments		0
Open-to-buy		$57,240

APRIL (25%)

Sales		$54,000
Reductions:		
Employee discounts (5%)	$2,700	
Markdowns (8%)	4,320	
Shortages (3%)	1,620	
Total Reductions		8,640
BOM inventory (2.6/1)		(94,500)
EOM inventory		86,400
Planned Purchases		$54,540
Commitments		0
Open-to-buy		$54,540

MAY (20%)

Sales		$43,200
Reductions:		
Employee discounts (5%)	$2,160	
Markdowns (11%)	4,752	
Shortages (3%)	1,296	
Total Reductions		8,208
BOM inventory (2.6/1)		(86,400)
EOM inventory		71,280
Planned Purchases		$36,288
Commitments		0
Open-to-buy		$36,288

JUNE (15%)

Sales		$32,400
Reductions:		
Employee discounts (5%)	$1,620	
Markdowns (12%)	3,888	
Shortages (3%)	972	
Total Reductions		6,480
BOM inventory (2.6/1)		(71,280)
EOM inventory		71,280
Planned Purchases		$38,880
Commitments		0
Open-to-buy		$38,880

JULY (15%)

Sales		$32,400
Reductions:		
Employee discounts (5%)	$1,620	
Markdowns (13%)	4,212	
Shortages (3%)	972	
Total Reductions		6,804
BOM inventory (2.3/1)		(71,280)
EOM inventory		68,000
Planned purchases		$35,924
Commitments		0
Open-to-buy		$35,924

of the plan, the ratios to be used to determine the BOM inventory levels, had been given to Corey in a memo from divisional merchandise manager Jim Edwards. As a result, Corey felt very comfortable with the results of his first six-month plan. The plan for classification A, sports shirts, can be seen in Table 4.6. (Note: The percentage of sales by month, the monthly percentage of reductions, and the BOM stock-to-sales ratio is indicated in parenthesis in the appropriate location in Table 4.6.)

The first part of the meeting to review the men's sportswear six-month plan with Jim Edwards had gone just as Corey had hoped. He had felt relaxed and confident, and Jim had seemed impressed with his presentation and degree of justification for the figures in the plan. However, Corey was not prepared for Jim's response.

Jim had noted, "It's obvious that you have put a great deal of effort into this plan, but I'm concerned with the sales figure you have used. I think it will be useful as a basis for personnel planning, however, for merchandise planning it's too aggressive. I want you to rework the plan using the last year's sales plus 3 percent."

Apparently sensing Corey's confusion and disappointment, Jim had smiled and said, "I'll tell you what I want you to do. You've got a plan here for sales plus 8 percent. Look at the result if actual sales turn out to be only last year's sales plus 3 percent. Once you've completed your revised plan of last year's sales plus 3 percent, consider the impact if you actually achieve last year's sales plus 8 percent. In both cases, think about the resulting action you would take and the ramifications of those actions. Now, I want you to come into my office tomorrow morning at 10 a.m. and I want you to be able to explain to me why I've asked you to plan sales conservatively in the merchandise plan for your department."

As Corey reflected on Jim's statements, he glanced at the computer on his desk. He knew that developing the revised plan would present no problems. The challenge, however, would be being able to see the logic behind the change. Regardless, he knew he needed to get to work.

Major Question

What explanation should Corey give Jim as to why he should plan sales conservatively for the men's sportswear department?

Study Questions

1. Revise the plan to reflect a 3 percent increase and compare the two plans.

2. What type of environmental factors could be the cause of both increases and decreases in the OTB?

3. After comparing the 8 percent and 3 percent increase plans, which do you think is most realistic and why?

4. Do you believe fashion merchandise should be planned more aggressively than basic merchandise? Why or why not?

Case 29
Sub-Par Inventory

Antigone Kotsiopulos and Molly Eckman, Colorado State University

Golf clubs and golf courses are organized in different ways, but there is typically a person called a "pro" who manages the golf side of the business. This person may also be responsible for the restaurant business, the golf course greens and other areas of the operation such as retail space, typically referred to as the "pro shop." Many golf pros and club managers are unfamiliar with retailing when they accept the position of "pro." Jerry Kyros was typical because he came from a golf background, but knew little about retailing. Jerry was on the college golf team and was recruited by fraternity friends to come to a very small community in the Midwest to run their golf course seven months of the year. The golf course had several potential revenue sources including the driving (practice) range, golf lessons, the restaurant, and the long-term potential of a retail shop. Jerry worked on developing each revenue source and eventually had enough capital to expand his retail sales beyond the basics of golf balls, gloves, towels, and caps to include men's and women's apparel. Within the club house he created a separate room for retail sales and ultimately developed signage, purchased professional fixtures, and even designed a club logo for monogramming. Frequent tournaments were held at the club and typically prizes were gift certificates to be used in the pro shop. Therefore, Jerry felt he had a built-in percentage of golfers who would automatically be looking for golf and related merchandise. If he capitalized on the opportunity he thought he could generate more revenue through multiple sales. A real bonus was that the club was not charging him for rent or utilities, because they wanted some type of retail operation on site and they were already paying his salary. Therefore, any profit he generated was his to retain.

Jerry knew a great deal about golf equipment and men's clothing, but the most difficult market for him to buy for was women's golf apparel. As the rest of his retail business grew, Jerry became more and more frustrated with his inability to derive more profit from this area. The main problem seemed to be markdowns because he would sell some items but not others and good sellers seldom outnumbered the bad. When he went to golf shows to buy merchandise he would talk with the vendors and other store buyers, but most of them were involved with very large, year-around operations. His club was rural, smaller, as well as seasonal. At last he decided to consult with a merchandiser to see what could be done to enhance his overall business potential.

Tammy Baker, the consultant, suggested she visit Jerry's location to get a better idea of his operation. She also asked Jerry to gather any sales data and inventory information from the previous season, which would allow her to examine trends and possible areas for development. Jerry told her he had never kept sales records, other than his daily sales figures. When Tammy visited the pro shop she was able to see part of the problem by merely examining the merchandise that remained at the end of the season, by asking questions about what items Jerry originally had in inventory, and by reviewing purchase orders.

Tammy took notes throughout her examination of the proshop. The total profile of beginning inventory was as follows:

50 percent equipment—golf bags, clubs, head covers, towels, balls, tees
- Merchandise can be easily reordered and carried over to next year if necessary.

- Does quite a bit of special ordering.

- Typically generates his most profitable markups (little need to markdown).

- Biggest competitors are catalog companies.

20 percent men's apparel
- Pretty basic in styles and colors (not trendy).

- Seems to sell well and selection of size ranges is very good.

- Logo merchandise looks good and could probably be developed further.

- Now has logo on shirts and caps only.

10 percent shoes for both men and women
- Has some samples and does most of his business by special order.

- Good markup items.

- Shoes are classic and can be carried over to next season.

20 percent women's apparel
- Area of greatest concern.

- Currently carries no logo merchandise.

Further examination of women's sizes:

Size 3/4
- Most of what remains are fashion colors, stripes, and prints.

- Short styles that remain are full, baggy look.

- Much had to be marked down to move it.

- A dozen pieces remain at the end of the season.

Size 5/6
- Most colors remaining are fashion colors.

- Styles remaining are varied; plaid shorts remain as the matching tops have sold.

- Sold better than 3/4 but still have about a dozen remaining.

Size 7/8

- Total sales in this size looked better, but more was bought than in the two smaller sizes—about two dozen pieces left.

Size 9/10

- Sold well compared with other sizes and has a few pieces left—could probably have sold more if there was more inventory.

Size 11/12

- Again, fashion colors remain.

- Styling of tops and bottoms are full cuts.

- Shorts are cuffed as were those in small sizes.

- Remaining tops tend to be sleeveless.

Size 13/14

- Has three dozen pieces remaining after big markdowns.

- Same styling as 11/12 leftovers.

Jerry buys most of his merchandise at golf shows (which means golf brands and higher prices) and a considerable amount of this merchandise in pre-packs from vendors. Many are packs of 18 units with sizes and colors predetermined. Jerry has an older clientele; apparently not many young women are golfers and those who do golf tend not to buy much at the pro shop (they're obviously purchasing golf apparel elsewhere). He sells no women's accessories.

Major Question

If you were this consultant, what changes would you recommend to Jerry related to his merchandise assortment?

Study Questions

1. What specific changes would you make in the sizing of the women's apparel?

2. Are there any buying strategies, including possible items for negotiation, that you would recommend to Jerry?

3. Would you expand the club logo business? If so, in what classifications?

Case 30
Sell! Sell! Sell!

Judy K. Miler, University of Tennessee
Nancy J. Rabolt, San Francisco State University

Fred Marcus, the men's sportswear buyer of Brody's Department Store, which is located in Portland, Oregon, is going on his first long vacation in many years. Fred had arranged to take Georgette, his wife, on a three-week tour of China as a fifteenth wedding anniversary celebration. John Gross, the assistant buyer of the department (who, incidentally, is number one on the general merchandise manager's list for promotion to buyer) is being given last-minute instructions by Fred.

John is sharp, highly motivated, well educated, and very articulate. He has been at Brody's for four years, starting out as an executive trainee. As the assistant buyer of the men's sportswear department, he is in charge of selling activities but also buys several segments of the department's merchandise, including such active sportswear as skiwear and workout clothing. Everyone—including Fred Marcus—has full confidence in John's ability to handle the department during the buyer's three-week absence.

"John, you have a relatively simple job," Fred was saying. "While you are in charge, all you have to do is sell. You have lots of merchandise. The racks are full, and your last big shipment is due on Monday. Your stocks are at peak."

"Don't worry, Fred, selling is my middle name," John replied assuredly.

"Of course, you can always put through a special order or two," Fred continued, "but, otherwise, stay away from buying anything. We want to maintain our stock-sales relationship just as it is, and our stock turn for the period will come out just as we planned. Remember—the big word is SELL!"

With that, Fred left the department in the care of John. Fred was only gone a few days when Bill Walker, the sales manager of Todd & Todd, a nationally known branded merchandise manufacturer, came in to see Fred and unaware of his absence, he found John in charge. Bill knew John quite well, however, because John had been buying the skiwear for the department and Todd & Todd made a well-known, nationally advertised line of ski clothing.

Bill Walker greeted John cordially but got down to business immediately. "John, I have a sensational deal for you. I can offer you our Todd & Todd men's ski jackets in the latest colors and patterns and in a full size range. These jackets are our regular $150 retail sellers. I can give you a price on these jackets that will enable you to sell them for half price, and you can still get your regular markup."

When John inquired as to the reason for this great giveaway, Bill explained that Todd & Todd was having a temporary cash flow problem and that it had to convert a big part of its current stock to raise cash. To sweeten the deal, Bill further offered to pay the entire cost of an ad in two major newspapers of Brody's Department Store's choice.

Ernest Brenner, the divisional merchandise manager, listened attentively as John laid out the Todd & Todd offer. While he was not too familiar with the exact merchandise, he did know the firm well. "I'll say this to begin with, John," Ernest said, "I've known Todd & Todd for more than twenty-five years, and everything they do or make is on the up-and-up. I agree with your thinking that if we turn this deal down, one of our competitors will take it and seize our market. So, if you feel this merchandise is salable, buy it. I'll approve the purchase order and get you the open-to-buy. But remember, I'm not telling you to buy it. You must use your own judgment."

Burning with the fervor of a possible great merchandising coup, John bought the entire lot of three hundred ski jackets. The merchandise was delivered in twenty-four hours, and the ads were rushed into print. Unfortunately, the promotion, despite the undeniable bargains offered, was one big failure—for no apparent reason other than apathy on the part of the buying public.

Fred returned from his trip to China and plunged right into work, going over the department's sales and inventory reports and reviewing what had occurred during his absence. Within a few minutes, he was able to put his finger on the ski jacket problem immediately and called John into his office.

"John, you have made a serious error buying these jackets. This is unforgivable for someone who is supposed to be a seasoned fashion merchandiser and who is allegedly ready to become a buyer."

Major Question

What should John have done before placing the order?

Study Questions

1. Do you think special purchases should be made for a department even though the department is overstocked? Why or why not?

2. What are the problems with being overbought or underbought?

Case 31
Inherited Inventory Problems

Maryanne Smith Bohlinger, Community College of Philadelphia

Lloyd & Burns, located in a large New England city, has always catered to a well-to-do, conservative clientele. This large women's specialty store does an annual volume of approximately 35 million dollars and prides itself on being a high-quality, personal-service type of retail establishment.

From *Merchandise Buying (4th ed.)* by Maryanne Smith Bohlinger. Reprinted by permission of Prentice-Hall, Upper Saddle River, NJ. Copyright © 1993. All rights reserved.

As a conservative business, however, L&B never really enjoyed the reputation of real fashion leadership. The management determined that a number of the store's competitors were using the "boutique approach" in merchandising to add a high-fashion image to their stores. Management decided that Lloyd & Burns would try its hand at this new merchandising approach in an effort to gain higher fashion recognition.

Shortly thereafter, the "Royal Garb Boutique" was opened, with a buyer responsible for purchasing exclusive, high-fashion types of merchandise. The buyer was provided with an assistant, two full-time salespeople, part-time sales help, and stock personnel.

The "Royal Garb Boutique" was a success. Store volume increased as a result of the addition of the boutique, and L&B was gaining an image as a high-fashion store. After three years the buyer was rewarded with a promotion and took over the buying responsibilities of a much larger department: the women's better coat department.

When Gwen Franklin, an assistant buyer in fashion costume jewelry, heard that a buyer's position was available, and in the Royal Garb Boutique at that, she immediately applied for the position. After several interviews, she was informed that she was to be the new buyer for the boutique. However, Gwen was soon to discover that along with a successful department she was also about to inherit serious inventory problems.

For various reasons, Gwen's predecessor had allowed a large amount of old merchandise to accumulate in the stockroom. The merchandise consisted of expensive blouses, handbags, sweaters, and other accessory items. When Gwen checked the price tickets for the seasonal code, she was amazed to learn that some of the merchandise was more than two years old. She immediately realized that she must take a physical count of all merchandise on hand to determine the condition of the merchandise assortment. She soon discovered that over 25 percent of her dollar stock was tied up in old or slow-moving merchandise. For some reason, her predecessor had allowed old

merchandise to accumulate in stock while new items were being sold.

The Christmas season was rapidly approaching. Gwen realized that almost half her sales volume would occur between November and January. However, she was overloaded with old and out-of-style goods, a limited open-to-buy, expensive markdowns, and limited storage and selling space. She was in trouble inventorywise, budgetwise, and seasonwise. The department's fashion image was in jeopardy.

Major Question
What plan of activities could Gwen follow to help her solve her inventory problems?

Study Questions
1. How could she avoid the recurrence of these problems in the future?

2. What other kinds of inventory problems can occur?

Case 32
How Much for the Good Smell?

David Ehrlich, Ghostwriters

For the past two Christmas seasons, Courtney's, an upscale gift store, has carried a sweet-smelling potpourri in a plastic bag with an attractive ribbon. Heavily scented with cloves, the mixture gives a pleasant holiday aroma to any room, including the store.

Two years ago, the mixture cost $4.50 a bag. Courtney's (the only store in town that carried it) sold 300 pieces for $9.50. Courtney's supply ran out 10 days before Christmas, and it was too late to get any more.

Last year, the manufacturer raised the price to $5.00, so Courtney's raised its retail price to $9.95. Even though the markup was lower than the previous year, the store owner felt there was "magic" in the $10 price. As before, the store had a complete sellout, this time five days before Christmas. Sales last year were 600 units.

This year, the wholesale price has gone up to $5.50, and store personnel are trying to determine the correct retail price. The owner once again wants to hold the price at $10 ($9.95), but the buyer disagrees: "It's my job to push for the highest possible markup wherever I can. This item is a sure seller, as we're still the only store around with it, and we had some unsatisfied demand last year. I think we should mark it $12.50, which will improve the markup to 56 percent. Staying at $10 will penalize us unnecessarily, especially considering the markup would be even lower than last year. Even if we run into price resistance, we'll only have to sell 480 to maintain the same dollar volume."

The owner demurs, saying, "This scent is part of our store's ambiance. It acts as a draw to get people into the store, and its pleasant smell keeps them in a free-spending state of mind. I think we should keep the price at $9.95 despite the poorer markup. And, if we can sell many more at this price, we'll realize the same dollar gross margin as last year. I think we should buy 1,000. Furthermore, if people see us raising a familiar item's price 25 percent, they might wonder whether our other prices are fair."

Major Question

What price would you charge and how many units would you order?

Study Questions

1. What other factors than price should Courtney consider in determining how many units to add?

2. Which prices and quantities purchased would result in the most profit?

Case 33
The Assistant Buyer's Costly Mistake

Faye Y. Gibson, University of North Carolina

Caroline Smith, a bright, aggressive, young graduate of a highly respected university merchandising program was hired as an assistant buyer by Grabel Department Stores, a Southwestern department store group. Having lived in many locations throughout the U.S. as well as in New York, this novice assistant (after being on the job for two weeks) told the senior buyer, June Parker, and the divisional merchandise manager, Bette Baldwin, that the merchandise mix in the junior department should be more sophisticated and updated. This department maintained one of the largest sales volumes and highest gross margins in the store-group, and was recognized as a leader in trendy merchandise selection by the other 100+ stores in this privately owned department store conglomerate. Bette asked for specific vendors, classifications, or styles and categories that should be added. The young assistant had no specific solutions. However, recognizing Caroline's potential, Bette decided to request that Caroline go to market with the buyers and take on added responsibility as soon as possible.

In the meantime, Caroline became very friendly with the son of the general merchandise manager, Don Frazier, and also found the "ear" of Rod Garrison, the executive vice-president of the group. Caroline was considered to be the "up and coming" star in the organization.

Bette, who was well respected in the organization, monitored Caroline's progress and encouraged her to participate in all aspects of the buying process. After six months and upon reviewing the assistant's paperwork, Bette noticed that Caroline was very careless with figures, that she wasted time in the office, and she did not like to analyze sales figures or to correct markdowns. Bette also received complaints from her department managers on the floor about Caroline's work habits. In Bette's absence, Caroline assigned sales associates the work that should have been her responsibility. Many times when visiting stores in the group to access progress or to communicate critical promotional or markdown information to the individual store merchandisers, Caroline forgot some information, took a long lunch with a very special friend, or left early without completing the job. At first Bette covered for Caroline, in addition to correcting her mistakes. Later, Bette requested that all duties assigned to Caroline be in writing and that Caroline prepare and hand in written reports covering her daily activities at each store. Management discussed Caroline's progress and decided that her only problems were immaturity and inexperience. Rod Garrison, the executive vice president, told Bette not to be such a perfectionist and to work harder to develop this "bright young lady" into an astute buyer.

Following the instructions of the executive vice president, Bette began to train Caroline as a junior dress buyer, because that department had a low sales volume and few mistakes could be made in such a department. While mentoring the young assistant, Bette provided specific training and guidelines for preparation of Caroline's first solo buying trip. Caroline was involved in developing the department's six-month merchandise plan (including planned sales, markdowns and purchases). June (the senior buyer) discussed with Caroline the purpose of the vendor matrix—a listing of approved, key vendors adhered to by all Grabel Department Stores' divisions when buying. June also provided specific completion dates (the last dates which all merchandise had to be shipped from the vendor warehouses) for the fourth-quarter selling period, because the selling season is so short and weather conditions affect it so greatly. Caroline was advised not to buy lines that were not approved on the vendor matrix, unless she obtained special permission from the executive vice president. Additionally, June discussed delivery dates (the beginning and ending ship dates for

the third quarter), and she noted price points for specific sub-classes of merchandise, as well as the approximate percentages of the merchandise mix to order for each quarter.

Bette instructed all buyers and assistant buyers to: 1) review all computer printouts of the stores' major vendors in order to pinpoint the best-selling styles, price points, colors, and sizes; and 2) talk to each department manager and the sales associates in each store to discuss "hot" and "slow" seller classifications and these lines that sold well the previous Fall and Holiday seasons. Bette then instructed all buyers and assistants to schedule an appointment with the stores' New York buying office buyer, Anne Tipper, to obtain an update on current market conditions, fashion trends, and new resources. Bette also requested that each buyer and assistant submit a plan for buying trips for both the New York and the Atlanta markets.

Caroline decided that she did not have time to read and analyze computer printouts (which would take all weekend), nor did she take time to talk with the department managers and sales associates. Moreover, she knew what merchandise should sell in the junior dress department because she wore the clothes. Also, because she had to be out of town on a buying trip, Caroline decided to take a day off to pack and prepare for the trip; therefore, she did not have time to submit the required buying plan.

Because Caroline did not have a market plan and had forgotten to schedule an appointment with Anne Tipper (the New York buying office buyer) she decided it would be safe to shop three of the five major vendors approved on the vendor matrix. One of these vendors had a new trendy line of junior dresses and offered Caroline an exclusive, if she bought a specific quantity/dollar figure of the merchandise. Caroline was thrilled with the new find but realized that the buy would be one-fourth of her total budget. Also, the price points were all upper-end; there were only two fabrications in two colors and one delivery date. However, she decided to listen to her instincts, because she loved the styling and the beautiful purple velvet and taffeta fabrics. Surely the customer would pay the prices for these exclusive dresses!

When Caroline returned from market, she assured Bette that the dress selection for Fall and Holiday would be superb. She boasted to everyone of her exclusive buy. The first problem Caroline encountered was a notification that the dresses would be shipped late, and the second problem was that the elegant, rich fabrics were being substituted with less-expensive fabrics. The vendor, however, would adjust the prices.

The dresses were shipped very late and all were of an inexpensive velvet or taffeta or a combination of the two. Worse, all were either in shades of purple or black! Many junior customers did not like the fabrics nor the odd shades of purple; nor did their mothers wish to pay the high prices for a Holiday dress that would be worn only one or two times.

All of the junior dress department managers in the Grabel Department Store Group were very concerned over the late shipments, the poor quality of the merchandise, and the lack of sell-through on the Holiday merchandise. The managers complained to June, who immediately investigated the problem. After reviewing the shipping receipts, June requested that Bette schedule an early performance review with Caroline, even though company policy did not mandate her review for three months. In fact, it was a customary group policy to schedule only one performance review per employee per year. However, at an earlier date, Rod Garrison had granted Bette permission to schedule additional performance evaluations as needed in order to monitor Caroline's progress and foster her development as a buyer.

After the conference with June and after evaluating the problem situation, Bette decided that it would not be feasible to conduct an additional performance review for Caroline during the busy, hectic, and stressful Holiday season. Anyway, Caroline had shown remarkable improvement since the time of her last review, and the fourth-quarter selling period was known for producing large sales volume and high profits. The problem would probably resolve itself.

Later in the season, Don Frazier (the general merchandise manager) called Bette into his office and asked her to explain why sales were down, markdowns high, and gross margin was eroding in the junior dress department. The store manager, Richard Ray, also wanted to know why his junior department looked like a "sea of purple"—after all, his daughter did not like purple nor would she wear velvet or taffeta!

Major Question

If you were Bette Baldwin, how would you explain the sales results, if at all, in the junior dress department to Don Frazier and Richard Ray?

Study Questions

1. Before market trips, what types of information should be compiled, and who should be responsible for collecting and reviewing the information?

2. What pre-planning is necessary for a successful market trip, and who should be responsible for handling this pre-planning?

3. During market trips, what check points are necessary in order to evaluate the progress and to assure that demands and needs of the retailer are met?

4. After the market trip, what check points should be in place to assure that all store needs are adequately covered, and who should be responsible for evaluating the productivity of the trip?

5. Who has the ultimate responsibility for the merchandise mix, sales, and profit for the junior dress department?

6. What types of training for young assistant buyers is usually available in most retail organizations, and who is responsible for scheduling this training?

Case 34
Is the Purchase Worth the Risk?

Judy K. Miler, University of Tennessee
Nancy J. Rabolt, San Francisco State University

Beverly Manners is the coat and suit buyer for ABC Bargain Stores in Kankakee, Illinois. It is a hard-hitting retail organization that features merchandise at low discount prices. The store's slogan is *ABC—Always Better and Cheaper.*

Beverly was a department store buyer for six years prior to her position with ABC and is fully experienced in working retail figures: she can plan, adjust, and achieve. She is a professional in every sense of the word.

Recently, she has been in a bind because of the unavailability of promotional merchandise suitable for the store's needs. The market has been depressed because of poor business; manufacturers have cut back on production so there are just not enough goods to go around. The result has been that few makers have disposable stock and the bargains have dried up because of supply and demand. Beverly has been looking everywhere for goods, and it does not look promising.

A few days ago, however, a manufacturer, who also happens to be an old friend, called her to advise her of the availability of promotional merchandise—stylish winter coats—which could rejuvenate her business considerably. She was very excited and went to tell her merchandise manager, Artie Lang, about the fantastic deal she was being offered. He knew she needed merchandise to promote—even though she was overstocked—so he advised her to fly to New York to check out those goods and the possibility of others. While in New York, she planned to see fifteen to twenty other manufacturers for possible future promotions. "Perhaps," she thought, "if I planned ahead, the results will be better for my future needs."

She arrived in New York and immediately visited Link Brothers, her friend's firm. Inspection of the coats, an overrun made for a large mail-order firm, proved that they were indeed a great deal: 40 percent below original wholesale costs, fashionable, in great colors, and a complete size spread.

She thought it was a bonanza—just what the doctor ordered. There was one problem, however: Link Brothers will only sell the goods on the condition that the entire job-lot of 2500 garments is purchased. "That's a lot of merchandise," she mused, "but because we are in the middle of the season they will probably sell with a short markup. The store needs the business, and this group can stimulate heavy traffic, so other areas will probably benefit as well."

That evening she called Artie, relayed her good news, and outlined the details. Artie was impressed with Beverly's intensity and desire to perk up the business, but he had strong doubts about such a large quantity purchase.

"In the first place," he said, "2500 coats are an awful lot of garments, which represents a big investment of $100,000. Second, business is poor, and your actual BOM stock is 15 percent over your plan. Finally, if the sale is a disaster—and there certainly is no such thing as a sure winner—you'll be in deeper trouble stock wise. Can't you talk Link into a partial purchase with an option to buy the remainder? When sales are realized we can run a fast promotional sale and establish a rate of sale, then unload all of them if we're successful. He's your friend; press him."

"I've tried that," she replied. "I've tried every possible tactic. He's anxious to sell, and he knows he can get rid of the goods in one shipment to any number of stores. He called me first out of friendship, thinking I probably wouldn't want to pass this purchase up."

"Beverly, I see your point, but good business practice dictates that you shouldn't take such a huge risk. You are overbought and don't have a dime of open-to-buy, let alone $100,000 with one vendor."

Furiously, Beverly snapped back, "If I had open-to-buy money, I certainly wouldn't call you since you sure aren't a risk-taker."

"Sorry," he responded, "you'll just have to keep looking for a smaller deal."

After hanging up the phone, Beverly was quite depressed and angry. She has the chance to buy the perfect promotional merchandise, which could make her season, but she can't get Artie's approval. She knows her store's stock position but feels it could be greatly reduced with a successful promotional ad. "That darned merchandise plan— does one have to live and die by it?" she asked herself. "Plans are made to be revised," she thought, "they are not supposed to be set in stone!"

Beverly, being a fighter, does not give up easily. She prevailed on her friend to give her a 24-hour option on the promotional merchandise, which he did, and she promised to call him after returning home. She is now on the plane heading home, and is planning a strong case to overcome Artie's objections.

Major Question

If you were Beverly, what approach would you plan to obtain some open-to-buy from your boss for the purchase?

Study Questions

1. Should Beverly, or any buyer, create OTB for additional purchases when she is overbought? How would you suggest this be done?

2. What controls do you think ABC should institute to avoid further gross departmental overstock positions?

Case 35
The Impossible Goals

Judy K. Miler, University of Tennessee
Nancy J. Rabolt, San Francisco State University

The Norris Department Store of Pittsburgh, Pennsylvania, has an illustrious background. Established eighty years ago, it has grown with the city and currently enjoys a fine reputation as one of the leading stores of the state, with a sales volume of over $50 million a year on moderately priced to better merchandise. Its advertising slogan—*A Complete Store for the Complete Family*—is more than a slogan. The assortment and depth of merchandise and range of prices are more than ample proof of the truth of the slogan.

Although competition gets tougher and tougher every year, Norris Department Store seems to pull through with a profit every year. During the last few years, though, some departments are not contributing much to the overall profit picture and a few departments are even realizing a loss. When one department in particular, the moderately priced dress department—the Miss Norris Department—did not yield a profit for the second consecutive year, management became concerned and scrutinized the department.

After promoting several associate buyers to the Miss Norris Department with no noted success, management finally hired a buyer from New York. Cara Standard was thirty-five years old with a strong background in chain store moderately priced women's wear buying. She was given a handsome salary and a bonus arrangement based on a sales-volume goal. Cara would be the new kid on the block, as all the other buyers and upper management had been with Norris for years. Cara came in knowing this, and felt she had to prove herself to everyone.

From the beginning, it was apparent that Cara knew the market. She was able to add new resources and "hot" selling styles, build price ranges, and increase promotion. In the course of a year and a half, she tacked on a 25 percent sales increase in business.

Management, at first, was exceedingly happy. The department was a flurry of activity on most days of the week. On Saturdays, the department looked like Grand Central Station at rush hour with customers everywhere.

After reviewing the financial records, however, the general merchandise manager, Hank Higgins, called Phil Forrester, the divisional merchandise manager, to his office and said, "Phil, department 345, the Miss Norris Department, is showing a healthy sales increase, but I'm concerned about the bottom line. Your buyer, Cara Standard, certainly has achieved the sales we've been looking for, but at what price? The advertising cost has doubled, the markdowns have gone from 12 to 17 percent, the cumulative markup from 43 to 38.2 percent, and the turnover rate from 5 to 8.5 times a year. It's true that the margin has also increased a little this year, which is good. I feel that expenses are going to be out of line again, and we still won't see any appreciable profit. An increase in sales is good, but not at the cost of profit. I think we better put a brake on Cara before she goes haywire and we end up looking like a discount store."

Accordingly, Phil Forrester called Cara in for a meeting. He began by saying, "Cara, you've been here almost two years, and you've done a great job. I'm not going to give you the numbers; you're a merchant and can read them as well as I can. Sales are super, but we still haven't realized the needed profit. The time has come to pause and take a close look at where we're going. Let's start by reviewing the store, its customers, and the merchandising tactics that are good for the long run. Next, we'll look at your figures and all the expenses to try to get them in line."

Cara's immediate reaction was defensive, and she replied, "I'm confused. First you want sales volume; now that you have it, you're unhappy. That hurts because I've done what you wanted. You know that I'm trying to build a career in this store, and I want to eventually be promoted to divisional merchandise manager. I came in expecting praise, and I hear myself being damned."

"Hold on," Phil said. "I haven't uttered a word of criticism. All I've said is that we should review where we've been and where we're going. We need to take a hard look at your department." Phil continued, "We want a slower turnover, about six times; a higher initial markup; a higher cumulative and maintained markup; a lower markdown rate; and more controlled advertising expenses."

"And less volume," Cara added.

"If necessary," Phil replied, "because we must turn your business around."

The meeting continued, during which Phil assured Cara that she had a place in the store, that management was happy with her and the great sales increases, and that the meeting was designed to prepare plans to ensure future success.

When Cara went home that night, she was quite disturbed. She could not get it out of her mind that someone was trying to do her harm and that, in the long run, she had satisfied no one in higher management. One of her thoughts was that she had too high a salary for the store's comfort and, now that a cure for the department had been developed, she was being eased out. She had seen this happen before at other companies. Her greatest concern was that she was under the impression that she was doing an excellent job and she had been getting ready to request a promotion; now she felt that she was under pressure to try to hold her job.

She thought she had two alternatives: 1) to move on and look for another job; or, 2) to stay at Norris Department Store and, if possible, try to do the job as management requested.

Major Question
If you were Cara and selected the latter alternative, what could you do to try to obtain the goals of the general merchandise manager?

Study Question
1. What can Phil Forrester, the divisional merchandise manager, do in the future to help Cara maintain the merchandise standards and goals he has set for her department?

2. How can a new buyer in a store prevent miscommunication in regard to what management expects and what the buyer thinks is reasonable to expect?

3. Do you feel that Cara, the buyer, was responsible for the overall state of her department? Why or why not?

Case 36
Saks Fifth Avenue: A Plan for Profit Rebound

John Donnellan, University of Massachusetts

Saks Fifth Avenue is a privately held, full-line specialty retailer of upscale fashions that operates more than 50 stores nationwide, many of which are anchors in the country's most prestigious shopping centers. Disappointing 1991 operating results were a major concern to the 12,000 shareholders of Investcorp who bought the New York-based Saks in 1990. Lackluster performance forced Investcorp to abandon its hopes of going public in 1992. Saks was not in a good position for such a venture in that an organization's stock value is driven by its potential for profitability and growth. Investcorp reacted with an aggressive strategy to improve performance by:

- Eliminating 700 jobs.

- Abandoning the unprofitable children's and gift businesses.

- Expanding private-label programs.

Table 4.7   Saks Fifth Avenue: Actual and Projected Sales (1992–1997)

	1992	1993[*]	1994[*]	1995[*]	1996[*]	1997[*]
Sales	$1340	$1447	$1591	$1774	$1981	$2107
Gross Margin $	$518	$582	$644	$720	$807	$860
Gross Margin %	38.7%	40.2%	40.5%	40.6%	40.7%	40.8%
Expenses $	$442	$455	$479	$524	$573	$599
Expenses %	33.0%	31.5%	30.1%	29.5%	28.9%	28.4%
Net Income $	($85)	($14)	$20	$62	$123	$151
Net Income %	−6.3%	−1.1%	+1.3%	+3.5%	+6.2%	+7.2%

Note: The dollar figures in the table are stated in millions. The figures do not reflect finance charge income from charge accounts, or other expenses, such as depreciation and the interest expense on debt. [*]Projected figures for the year.

The results of the strategy were disappointing. Saks' 1992 income statement reflected a net loss of $84.5 million on sales of $1.4 billion. The company projected a smaller, but still significant loss of $14.2 million for 1993.

At this point, Saks developed a five-year, long-range plan to put itself in a more desirable financial position. The plan included a five-year profit increase of $235.7 million, from a 1992 loss of $84.5 million to a 1997 projected profit of $151.2 million, representing a net profit change +13.4 percent, from −6.3 percent in 1992 to +7.2 percent in 1997.

The plan involved a 62 percent sales increase, from $1.3 billion in 1992 to $2.1 billion in 1997. The projections also included incremental gross margin increases from 38.7 percent of net sales in 1992 to 40.8 percent of net sales in 1997. These gross margin increases ranged from as little as .1 percent of net sales to 1.5 percent of net sales. Likewise, operating expenses were scheduled to decrease, from 33.0 percent of net sales in 1992, to 28.4 percent of net sales in 1997. (See Table 4.7.)

The plan was supported by a multi-faceted merchandising strategy that included:

1. The addition of approximately 60 new stores, which were smaller and more targeted than the existing full-line specialty stores; 3,000 square-foot boutiques for large-size customers; and adding Saks-owned A/X Armani Exchange shops. The expansion plans included opening resort stores in such vacation areas as Palm Springs and Santa Fe, as well as international expansion to Canada and Mexico.

2. The sale of private-label goods through a home shopping network.

3. A shift in target market from the traditional customer to a younger clientele.

4. Frequent launches of new cosmetic lines.

5. Exclusive arrangements with such designers as Nancy Heller and Gordon Henderson.

6. Reduced shrinkage.

7. Opening additional Off Fifth—Saks Fifth Avenue clearance stores which, though producing lower gross margins, generate high net profit because of low operating costs.

8. A shift to a merchandising strategy of "dominant assortments," involving a reduced number of vendors but with broadened assortments of such key resources as Donna Karan, Escada, Ferragamo, and Chanel (Moin, 1993a; Moin, 1993b; Zinn, 1991).

Major Question

What recommendations would you make to enhance sales and profitability at Saks? Consider the changes that you've observed in fashion, the economy, and consumer buying habits since the five-year plan was devised.

Study Questions

1. Do you have other suggestions for resort store locations? How might you distinguish resort store assortments from the offerings of the mainstream stores?

2. Discuss the pros and cons of liquidating mark-downs within Saks Fifth Avenue stores vs Saks Fifth Avenue—Off Fifth clearance stores.

3. Discuss the decision to carry deeper assortments of an edited vendor list. What criteria for editing the list do you recommend?

4. What marketing advantages can you identify with exclusive arrangements with selected designers?

5. What type of controls do you recommend to curb internal and external shortage?

References

Moin, D. (1993a, August 31). Saks' 5-yr plan: From red ink to fat profits. *WWD*, pp. 1, 12.

Moin, D. (1993b, September 9). Sak's big plan: New formats, new markets. *WWD*, pp. 1, 5.

Zinn, L. (1991, August 12). Saks Fifth Avenue has Seventh Avenue shaking. *Business Week*, pp. 30–31.

Case 37
A Competitive Dilemma: Advance or Retreat?

Antigone Kotsiopulos and Molly Eckman, Colorado State University

Ken Lincoln owns a clothing store in a Midwest rural community. Ranching and farming families within a 60-mile radius shop at his store, as do many of the 6000 members of the community. Lincoln's Family Apparel is the only store of its kind in the community catering to the entire family. However, there are three women's specialty stores, two shoe stores, a western wear retailer, and a trendy apparel store catering to the youth market. Two general merchandise stores carry limited clothing items as well. Summer brings thousands of tourists through the community as they head to the largest lake in the region, which is just ten miles north of town.

While Ken's business is good, he feels it could be better. He has a valuable Main Street location with ample parking and an effective, hard-working sales staff. Being his own best critic, Ken always looks at what is not up to par. He knows that in an effort to serve a wide range of family needs, he is carrying a little bit of everything using broad assortments of styles, colors, and sizes. He carries national brands but also looks for special purchases at market that would be suitable for his price-conscious consumers. To be the full-service clothing retailer in the area, Ken carries men's, women's, and children's apparel and everything from undergarments through outerwear. This leads to a steady stream of markdown merchandise which attracts perpetual bargain hunters and reduced profits.

Ken's latest concern comes from a local Chamber of Commerce representative who verified that a large chain operation was looking at possible building sites in the community. Ken is familiar with the chain and knows they carry a broad assortment of brand-name clothing at reduced prices, as well as a variety of household items. Ken decided to seriously examine his own business being as unbiased as possible. He looked at all the facts and figures related to his business to objectively determine whether he would keep his business as is, narrow his merchandise assortment, or possibly relocate to another community.

Ken's figures from the previous business year are shown on Tables 4.8 and 4.9.

Table 4.8 Brand Name Merchandise

	Annual Sales ($)	Average Stock ($)	Annual Stock ($)	Cost of Goods sold ($)	Shortage ($)	Markdowns ($)
WOMEN'S APPAREL						
accessories	8,887	2,279	29,627	3,560	249	1,564
blouses/sweaters	40,221	22,345	290,484	19,306	1,006	9,774
dresses	10,553	7,035	91,455	4,643	201	2,712
slacks	8,705	6,696	87,048	3,656	157	2,403
jeans	7,442	1,815	23,595	4,837	193	1,660
skirts	4,378	3,127	40,651	1,839	70	1,173
outerwear	3,615	1,247	16,211	1,746	69	1,038
lingerie	4,083	1,167	15,171	2,050	102	890
MEN'S APPAREL						
accessories	11,667	3,646	47,398	5,483	233	2,998
shirts/sweaters	55,356	26,360	342,680	27,124	996	13,562
slacks	65,422	18,172	236,236	34,019	1,374	16,355
jeans	72,198	34,380	446,940	46,929	1,733	13,284
outerwear/sport coats	12,321	4,928	64,064	6,161	234	2,698
underwear	24,835	10,798	140,374	11,921	621	3,055
CHILDREN'S APPAREL						
accessories	6,278	2,511	32,643	3,202	82	1,726
shirts/blouses	25,384	11,035	143,455	12,184	584	7,615
dresses	6,218	10,363	134,719	3,109	81	1,660
slack/shorts	48,084	60,105	781,365	23,561	817	13,127
outerwear	18,832	7,847	102,011	9,793	226	5,631
underwear	20,745	5,186	67,418	9,750	187	4,875

Table 4.9 Generic Label Merchandise

	Annual Sales ($)	Average Stock ($)	Annual Stock ($)	Cost of Goods sold ($)	Shortage ($)	Markdowns ($)
WOMEN'S APPAREL						
accessories	9,261	2,437	31,681	2,964	204	1,510
blouses/sweaters	53,687	26,843	348,959	21,474	966	11,864
dresses	9,095	8,268	107,484	3,638	191	2,201
slacks	5,924	3,949	51,337	2,488	53	1,499
jeans	3,083	907	11,791	1,541	65	808
skirts	3,506	2,062	26,806	1,473	46	873
outerwear	4,273	1,378	17,914	1,923	64	1,141
lingerie	3,008	912	11,856	1,053	57	596
MEN'S APPAREL						
accessories	8,782	2,927	38,051	30,737	149	1,748
shirts	56,629	22,651	294,463	23,784	849	11,552
slacks	50,326	14,379	186,927	20,130	654	11,222
jeans	63,887	16,381	212,953	31,944	1,342	10,924
outerwear/sport coats	9,285	5,158	67,054	3,993	158	1,894
underwear	21,054	10,527	136,851	7,799	463	2,737
CHILDREN'S APPAREL						
accessories	8,935	4,964	64,532	3,574	80	2,234
shirts	30,347	11,240	146,120	11,835	637	8,254
dresses	7,483	9,354	121,602	3,517	60	1,856
slack/shorts	55,194	55,194	717,522	24,837	773	15,509
outerwear	20,452	5,843	75,959	8,181	143	5,461
underwear	22,539	13,258	172,354	9,241	270	4,846

Major Question[1]

What general assessment and recommendations would you make of the situation after examining the data? (Calculate: stock-sales ratio, turnover, gross margin dollars and percent, shortage and markdown percentages.)

Study Questions

1. Which department did best with branded merchandise, men's, women's, or children's?

2. Which department did best with generic label merchandise?

3. Which department and category of merchandise performed best overall?

4. How can a specialty store like Ken's compete with a large chain store if it comes to town?

---

[1]Please note: Do not use alternative analysis format for this case.

Chapter Discussion Questions

1. Discuss planning as a merchandise control, distinguishing between the three major types of merchandise planning. What part do standards play in retail control?

2. What are the five sequential steps in merchandise planning? Explain exactly what is involved with these planning steps.

3. What direct role does merchandising play in retail profit? Be specific in your explanation.

4. Compare unit and dollar planning. Why are both equally important?

5. What are the advantages of modifying merchandise plans? What are the disadvantages? Justify your opinions with examples from cases in this chapter.

6. Identify and discuss the internal and external sources of information that may be used in determining what merchandise retailers should purchase from vendors.

5

Sourcing

Chapter Objectives

- Examine the challenges and opportunities of domestic and international sourcing.

- Differentiate between centralized and decentralized buying.

- Describe types of buying origination and types of orders.

- Explain the use and importance of buying offices and markets.

- Emphasize the importance of careful merchandise source selection.

There are many sources and suppliers to meet the needs of manufacturers and retailers alike. Understanding who the target customer is helps to guide a retailer to the best resource for goods to supply the customer. In many instances today, manufacturers have become their own retailers, and retailers have become their own manufacturers, but procuring the materials to create the merchandise is still often an arduous task with all the choices available. Both domestic and international sourcing offer challenges and opportunities that must be considered when determining where to buy. Other helpful criteria for determining the best selection of goods for the best price, along with the best supplier, include: 1) the appropriateness of merchandise; 2) the policies of the supplier (i.e., delivery, specs, distribution, advertising, pricing, terms, and so forth); and 3) timing. There are advantages and disadvantages to all sourcing methods. The pros and cons must be weighed against the company objectives to determine just how to supply the desired merchandise and what to supply. Often the sourcing decision may be quite difficult because of the many choices and factors involved in the decision-making. But in many instances, cost advantage is the deciding factor, when all other factors are equal.

Resources and Sourcing

After retailers have planned their needs (i.e., planned purchases), they must then begin the search for the procurement of merchandise to fill their customers' needs and wants. In today's world there is an extensive selection of merchandise available to the retailer, no matter what the classification or category. The number of available sources is so vast and their locations are so varied that it is impossible to list all of them—let alone shop all the resources.

Sourcing is the term used to describe the process of determining how and where goods will be procured. The selection of types of merchandise from the manufacturers and contractors involves decision-making on the part of the retailer as to which resource would be the best from which to purchase. Retailers may select from a variety of types of resources, of which there are several major kinds. These include: manufacturers, wholesalers, middlemen, and cooperatives. **Manufacturers** offer goods for sale that they have produced. Manufacturers are also referred to as **vendors, suppliers,** or **resources,** and these terms often are used interchangeably. **Wholesalers** are resellers of merchandise. Normally, wholesalers buy merchandise in large quantities to break down and then sell the goods in smaller quantities. **Middleman** is a term used to describe an agent who processes goods in one way or another from the manufacturer to the retail distributor. For example, a manufacturer produces a garment and does not do the finishing or packaging but sends the garment to another company (the middleman) for these steps. After finishing and packaging the garment, the product is then shipped directly to the retailer. A wholesaler can also be a middleman, as is a drop shipper or broker. **Drop shippers** take title to merchandise, but do not take actual possession of the goods. A drop shipper just arranges shipment of the goods to the retailer. A **broker** is a middleman who helps negotiate business between the buyer (retailer) and seller (manufacturer).

Today, many retailers produce their own merchandise by manufacturing goods inhouse under their own private label. Label names are created to identify and gain recognition by consumers for that label. It is interesting to note that many of these retailer brands become known in the minds of consumers as major brands, often competing with major manufacturer's brand names. An example of a successful, nationally known store label is JCPenney's Arizona Jean Company. When a retailer also manufactures merchandise or vice versa, the company is referred to as vertically integrated, because they are performing more than one function in the marketing channel. (See Chapter Four

for an example of a vertically integrated company and Chapter Three for more on private labels.)

How and where private-label merchandise is produced varies from company to company. For example, some retailers who rely totally on private-label merchandise, do so primarily by manufacturing offshore, as The Limited and Gap do. They have specialists, however, in their offshore locations to oversee the smooth operation of business.

Contracting the production of merchandise is a common method of obtaining apparel by both the manufacturers and/or the manufacturer/retailers. A **contractor** is an independent producer who performs aspects of manufacturing, such as sewing, cutting, and finishing. Whether or not to choose a contractor that is domestic or international, exclusive or not, however, must be determined by the manufacturer or retailer who is searching for goods. An **exclusive contractor** is a supplier that only works for a particular company. Exclusive contracting can help or hurt the company a contractor is providing for, or even the contractor itself. For example, dealing exclusively with a producer, a company can be assured of continued consistency and resulting quality. If, however, the contractor is the only producer being used and that contractor runs into trouble, then the company relying on the contractor must also deal with the consequences of that trouble, which very often can hurt their business. Similarly, if something happens to a business that a contractor is dependent on, then the contractor may suffer consequences as well. *Case 24, Chaos of Cancellations* in Chapter Four, is an example of an exclusive contractor who cannot rely on one retailer's private-label manufacturing to provide for the business anymore and must determine what to do to resolve the problem.

The use of key resources by some retailers is one method of containing and narrowing the resource structure. A benefit of this method is that it enables some vendors and retailers to be better business partners than would be possible if retailers had no vendor consistency and different resources were used from season to season. The vendor matrix presented in Chapter Four is one method retailers use to concentrate on purchasing from key resources.

Technology and Sourcing

Technology can play an important and often critical role in the production and delivery of goods. Quick response (QR) and just-in-time (JIT) are terms that describe technologically based strategies that help cut the time from the production of the goods to the sale of the product. Technological linkages between the producer and the retailer speed communication and help to reduce the lead time for receiving merchandise. **Lead time** refers to the amount of time that lapses between the placement of an order and the arrival of the merchandise at the retail establishment. Today, it is critical to obtain merchandise when it is needed and computer technology is a major contributor in doing so. In *Case 43, Quota Limitations,* an importer relies on just-in-time (JIT) manufacturing, which backfires on him because of quota restraints. Other examples of the impact that technology has in reaching and connecting the manufacturer, retailer, as well as the consumer can be found in Chapter Ten.

Domestic and International Sourcing

Merchandise can be procured domestically or internationally. **Domestic sourcing** is the purchasing of merchandise within the borders of the U.S. **International sourcing** is the process of buying goods **offshore,** from countries other than the U.S. Buying merchandise offshore and bringing it into another country to sell refers to importing or purchasing **imports.** There are both advantages and disadvantages to purchasing both domestic and/or imported merchandise, and the retailer must weigh them before deciding how and where to source goods. Such factors as price, quality, and availability are some of the many concerns that must be regarded when evaluating who to use as a resource. The next two sections examine these two types of sourcing.

Domestic Sources

Domestic sourcing can be either advantageous or problematic to the retailer. For example, a faster lead time is usually available with domestic goods, as is more assurance of getting exactly what was ordered. Unfortunately, the cost of goods in apparel is often higher (due to higher labor costs) for domestic merchandise than imports. Even when using only domestic suppliers, there are factors to compare vendors for selection, such as quality, delivery, and cost. Also, close proximity to the source does not always protect against problems. For example, miscommunication and the resultant errors can occur whether two parties are in the same city or on different continents. Similar merchandise is obtainable from two domestic sources and a department store buyer must determine which of the two suppliers would be the most profitable to use in *Case 38, Treadwell's: The Buyer's Decision.* Late delivery of domestic merchandise and the receipt of an odd color assortment and poor-quality fabrics compounds a buyer's problems with a department sales decrease in *Case 33, The Assistant Buyer's Costly Mistake* in Chapter Four.

International Sources

International sourcing can be an invaluable method of obtaining a healthy markup for the retailer. Apparel imports constitute a major portion of clothing sold in the U.S. today. Figure 5.1

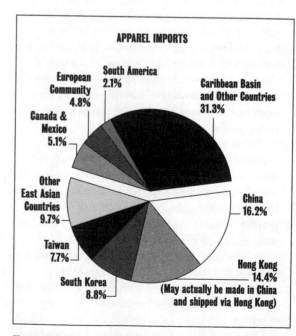

APPAREL IMPORTS

Figure 5.1 This pie chart shows the country-by-country breakdown of apparel imports into the U.S. *Source: U.S. Industrial Outlook, 1994, U.S. Department of Commerce*

shows the countries that provide these imports. Though there are risks and challenges that have to be met, the major advantage to sourcing overseas is that it can help with cost advantage and markup, which often results in better profit. Imports, at one time viewed as inferior and of lesser quality than domestic merchandise, generally are no longer viewed as such, although still can be a major problem. The lead time needed for delivery is often longer for imports than domestic merchandise. Other matters, such as government regulation or the politics of a country can also add to the complexity of determining who and where the best resource is. Trade sanctions and quotas may limit availability of goods, and shipping costs and/or tariff rates may add more cost to goods than make it reasonable. Also, today the ethics of producing in certain countries are paramount in many consumers' decision-making. (See Chapter Twelve for this discussion.) Offshore purchasing is examined in *Case 39, A Color Coordination Conundrum* and *Case 40, To Do or Not to Do Business in China.*

Quotas and Tariffs The limit to the number of units of specified merchandise permitted to be brought into a country for consumption during a specific period of time is called a **quota.** Quotas can be absolute or tariff rate. An **absolute quota** is a limit to the amount of any particular merchandise per year that can be brought into the U.S. A **tariff-rate quota** allows a certain number to be imported at a lower rate and after that threshold has been reached, additional quantities can be imported at a higher tariff rate. Quotas can be a hindrance to manufacturers and retailers alike. For example, if an absolute quota for specific merchandise is filled, no further entries of that type of merchandise into the country is allowed. Therefore, even if retailers and customers have a desire for more of these particular goods, they will be unobtainable and those sales that could have been realized will be lost. Also, when a manufacturer wants to sell goods in a particular country and if the quota for those particular goods has been filled, these goods cannot be imported there. There may be no other avenue to sell the goods

and therefore those revenues are lost. With the passage of the Uruguay Rounds of the **General Agreement on Tariffs and Trade (GATT),** the **Multifiber Arrangement (MFA)**—which places specific quotas on apparel and textile products— will be phased out by the year 2005. Other controls may take its place, however, it appears that importing may become less complex. A manufacturer is caught between the closing and opening of quota categories for some imported merchandise and has to make a difficult choice between the four options in *Case 43, Quota Limitations.*

A visa may be required when importing from certain countries. A **visa** is a document from the exporting country guaranteeing country of origin and is a way for the exporting country to monitor the amount of its exports to the U.S. Tariffs also complicate importing merchandise for the manufacturer and retailer. A **tariff** (also known as **duty**) is a special tax, paid to the government, placed on imported merchandise that adds to the cost of goods. Four rates of duty are:

- **Specific,** which is a rate of duty that is based on a set amount per each unit imported.

- *Ad valorem,* which is a rate of duty that is based on a percentage of dutiable value.

- **Compound,** which is a rate of duty that is a combination of both *Ad valorem* and specific.

- **Free,** which is also a rate of duty, but there is no monetary collection, hence it is called "duty free."

The **U.S. Harmonized Tariff Schedule (USHTS)** itemizes all products subject to the tariff imported from different countries. **Provision 9802 (Item 807** in the old U.S. Tariff Schedule) allows for lower tariffs as it is calculated on only the value that has been added to the product outside the U.S. Generally, U.S. fabric is used and shipped to Mexico or Caribbean countries and the value added there is the sewing that is done. The garments are then exported to the U.S. *Case 40* discusses a similar arrangement with Hong Kong and China. The **U.S. Customs Service** oversees imports involving quotas and tariffs. Their major roles are to collect revenue and to ensure that the trade laws and sanctions that the U.S. government legislates are upheld. These efforts help to ensure that the economic and political goals of the government are met.

Understanding quotas and tariffs is complicated and time-consuming. Manufacturers and retailers who are involved in importing need to clearly understand the policies and procedures so that they can work within the law and work closely with an import broker whose job is to know the complexity of the law and to advise the importer. The paperwork accompanying imported merchandise (and sometimes the actual merchandise) is inspected by Customs to ensure that the importer has complied with the law and has honestly declared those goods that are being imported into the country. If the law is not upheld, or if there has been any dishonesty or errors, serious repercussions may result. These may include confiscation of merchandise, the imposing of fines and/or penalties, or, for the more significant offenses, there may be more serious legal action, such as imprisonment. New importers often can have problems as is shown in *Case 44, The Sweater Dilemma*. Here, two serious importing problems are encountered, which increase the costs of goods and delay delivery time for an importer. First, imported sweaters that did not meet the U.S. Government requirements must be relabeled before release by Customs. Additionally, documentation for the merchandise misrepresents the actual inventory and it appears to Customs that the importer was trying to deceive them.

The Challenges of Selecting Sources

Even with the duties, shipping costs, and complications of imports, they are still often highly competitive with domestic goods or hold a true advantage. Today, most customers look for cost advantages above other advantages, so in many cases, they purchase the less-expensive imports over domestic goods. Figure 5.2 shows a comparison of the costs of manufacturing a pair of casual 100 percent cotton trousers in the U.S., as well as

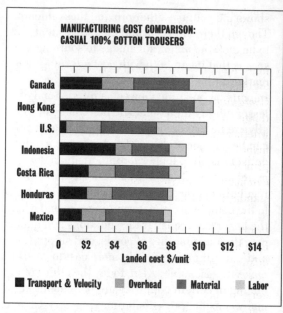

Figure 5.2 This bar chart illustrates the country-by-country manufacturing cost comparison for casual 100% cotton trousers. It is interesting to note that in both Canada and Hong Kong these trousers are more expensive to bring to market than in the U.S. *Reprinted by permission of Kurt Salmon Associates.*

six other countries, including Canada, Mexico, Hong Kong, Indonesia, Costa Rica, and Honduras. As might not be expected, both Canada and Hong Kong cost more than the U.S. in this instance.

Choosing between domestic or offshore resources can often be difficult because of all the factors that must be considered. Sometimes the political situation in a country may cause difficulties and uncertainty of getting the merchandise desired. In *Case 42, How to Produce the Edu-Doll?*, a manufacturer encounters political problems in a country, which result in the elimination of a major production resource. The manufacturer must then quickly find another source for production. A choice needs to be made between a domestic or offshore contractor, which must ensure that the manufacturer will be able to maintain a specific cost for the product.

Even more difficult for some retailers and manufacturers is deciding between countries to use as a source. Both *Cases 39* and *41* involve the sourcing selection between several different countries for offshore production. *Case 39, A Color Coordination Conundrum* profiles the factors related to a retailer's decision in determining whether or not to use a sub-Sahara supplier and manufacturer for private-label merchandise. Of primary concern is whether or not the new resource can meet the retailer's specifications and quality standards. In *Case 40, To Do or Not to Do Business in China,* the opportunities and risks—particularly from cultural, political, and legal considerations—for a manufacturer to invest in a permanent offshore factory are explored.

Often the cost of goods and humanitarian concerns must be considered in resource selection. In many situations, rising costs and the need for more profit is the major deciding factor of where to source. A profit drop has resulted in the need for a lingerie manufacturer to achieve more competitive pricing in *Case 41, Lingerie Incorporated.* Even though offshore sourcing will provide the needed competitive advantage, a choice between two countries must be made. Some factors in the decision-making are equal between the two countries and others are not; therefore, a comparative analysis of all the facts must be undertaken to determine the best choice. The issue of sweatshop labor—and even child and slave labor—in certain countries has raised public concern about the true cost of goods at the expense of exploitation of labor. Many are objecting to the low retail price of much imported apparel, due to the appalling conditions and the pittance workers are paid. (More ethical matters related to retail and manufacturing may be found in Chapter Twelve.)

The choice of where and from whom to source could be an elective decision or it could be imposed upon the business by another party. For example, if a vendor can no longer provide a retailer's needs as a result of changing the way in which the business is done, the retailer must look for a replacement resource—based solely on the need for specific merchandise.

Buying Origination and Merchandise Needs

Accessibility and availability of merchandise in different forms (such as quantities and assortments) are also factors for the merchant to consider in sourcing. The type of merchandise desired and/or reason for the retailer's purchase often narrows down the selection of resources, what type of source to use, and where the buying should originate. A specific determination of needs can assist in the method of buying (centralized vs decentralized), the origination of buying (buying office, market, or direct), place to buy (manufacturers, middleman, or broker), and type of ordering to be done (regular vs off-price). For example, a retailer needs merchandise for a special sale promotion in November. Luckily, this particular retailer can sell Spring merchandise in November, because of the geographical location of the store. Just the fact that sale Spring merchandise is desired—for November selling—can help the retailer determine who the best vendor would be. Such factors as type of merchandise and the styles wanted could also help to further narrow down and target the search.

Types of Orders

Different types of merchandise orders can be placed to cover the specific needs of a retailer and often the origination of the merchandise is determined by placement of different types of orders. A retailer can purchase merchandise by way of several types of orders. These are:

• **Regular orders** are placed for goods purchased in season as part of a regular line of manufacturer's merchandise.

• **Exclusive orders** are those placed for merchandise that can only be sold to one particular store or buyer. Exclusive merchandise is usually a special arrangement between vendor and retailer.

• **Off-price orders** are orders placed for merchandise that is purchased at a price that is below the regular line price. Usually, this is regular merchandise being sold later in the season, or is surplus merchandise.

- **Job lots** are groups of merchandise that are odds and ends of remaining styles, which a manufacturer wants to sell. Often they are broken sizes, colors, and/or styles and are sold at a considerable discount as a group.

- **Prepacks** are assortments of merchandise that are chosen according to a manufacturer's or retailer's direction. These predetermined choices direct that a certain amount of sizes and/or colors of a style or styles are shipped to the retailer.

- **Closeouts** are an assortment of merchandise that is left over from a seasonal line. Usually closeouts include all remaining items and are sold at a discount.

- **Reorders** are purchases placed on merchandise that have been purchased at least once before by the retailer. Reorders are more common with basic merchandise than with fashion items.

- **Promotional orders** are placed for goods at a better-than-regular manufacturer's cost. These are often special purchases from vendors that can be promoted by the retailer at a savings to the customer.

- **Private-label orders** are store brand merchandise that are designed, controlled, and sold by the retailer and are labeled with a store name or brand distinguishing it as its own.

Such resources as **jobbers**—who sell closeouts and job lots—specialize in those kinds of orders. Others may be able to supply a retailer's needs depending on the timing and status of merchandise that they hold, as a major vendor like Levi Strauss would. Levi's sells regular merchandise preseason, reorders and promotional goods inseason, and even closeouts and off-price goods at the end of a season.

Centralized and Decentralized Buying

How a retailer originates the buying (purchasing of goods) is also a decision that has to be made. This is usually dependent on where the merchandising division of the company is located. The two methods of buying are centralized and decentralized. **Centralized buying** entails focusing all the purchasing activities in one place, where it is initiated and overseen by one individual or a group. Many large retailing chains use centralized buying exclusively.

Decentralized buying centers the purchasing activities at the local or retail-outlet level. This method of buying is used less frequently by large retailers; Nordstrom, however, utilizes decentralized buying and some companies like JCPenney use both methods because they feel that better purchases are made when the buyer considers the specific needs and wants of the local or regional customer. Deciding whether or not to strictly utilize centralized buying is the quandary for a chain store president in *Case 45, Should All the Eggs Go in One Basket?*

Buying Offices

Buying offices provide yet another way to supply a retailer with merchandise. Traditionally, a **resident buying office (RBO)** is an organization located in a given fashion market that serves as a retailer's market representative for the procure-

Figure 5.3 Member buyers working with Doneger, the largest U.S. resident buying office. In addition to buying, RBOs can assist retailers in forecasting, finance, advertising and promotion, as well as many other services.

ment of merchandise. The two major types of resident buying offices are independent and store-owned. **Store-owned buying offices** are those offices that are owned and operated by a retail firm or group of retail stores. Years ago, buying offices purchased merchandise for their member retailers and served no other purpose. This is not necessarily true today. Many serve all the varied needs of a retailer. The **independent buying office** is owned and operated separately from its client retailers. Its functions can also include forecasting, finance, personnel, advertising and promotion, as well as providing consultation services and the manufacture of private-label merchandise. Just as there were major shakedowns of stored and mail-order retailers in the 1980s and 1990s, so were there parallel consolidations and buyouts of buying offices. An example is when IRS (Independent Retail Service) merged with Donegar in the 1980s.

There are a variety of buying offices now available that serve almost any type of retailer and their needs. From women's to children's, regular to off-price, bridge to opening price-point lines, men's clothing to women's sportswear—there is a buying office to fill all their needs. Buying offices can help small and large retailers alike, because of the numerous services offered. Sometimes retailers turn all their buying over to a buying office for economic reasons, as is considered in *Case 45*. Not using a buying office probably hindered an assistant buyer on her first market trip in *Case 33* in Chapter Four. A buying office can sometimes complicate matters, as it does in *Case 46, An Overheard Conversation in the Peppermint Dress Showroom.*

Markets

From a retail and merchandising perspective, markets have several definitions and this can cause confusion. A store manager or a market researcher may refer to a "market" as the target customer group (i.e., the target market). To the buyer and manufacturer, however, the **market** is the actual physical place where the retail buyer and seller

come together to purchase or sell goods and services. This marketplace may be at a merchandise mart or trade show, or even a specific city site as in New York City. A market may also refer to a time when buyers and manufacturers come together, such as the Spring market.

Merchandise marts are trade centers built to house manufacturers' representatives and provide a center for retailers and manufacturers to come together to do business. Major marts are located in such metropolitan areas as Dallas, Atlanta, and Chicago. Secondary marts are located in such smaller cities as Charlotte, Pittsburgh, and Seattle.

Trade shows are a means for buyer and seller to meet and do business. Existing facilities are used temporarily to house a trade show and its exhibits, often at convention centers, fairgrounds, or hotels. Figures 5.4 and 5.5 exhibit the exterior and interior of two trade shows. Retailers can also source merchandise directly with vendors, working with them in their headquarters and/or production facilities.

Today's global marketplace is serviced by **international markets,** located all over the world. Paris, London, Milan, and Tokyo are just a few of the larger international markets. **Domestic markets** refer to those in the continental U.S., such as New York City, which also happens to be a major international market. Localized **regional markets,** which may also provide a mart, serve the U.S. retailer as a geographical convenience. Atlanta, Dallas, and Los Angeles are examples of regional markets.

Market calendars publicize the dates (called **market weeks**) and locations of trade shows and markets that are available. Markets coincide with the seasonal delivery of goods by the manufacturer and are set up according to type of merchandise. For example, there are men's wear markets and women's wear markets. The traditional apparel planning seasons of Spring, Summer, Fall, and Winter have been broken down further for more frequent availability and purchasing of goods, because today's fashion customer is looking for newer looks more often. However, there are at least

Figure 5.4 The exterior of the MAGIC (Men's Apparel Group in California) trade show now located in Las Vegas.

Figure 5.5 A vendor's booth inside the International Jeanswear trade show.

five standard seasonal markets for apparel: Spring, Summer, Transition/Early Fall, Fall, and Holiday/Resort. See Figures 5.6 and 5.7 for a market calendar and trade show listing.

The decision to use a specific market depends on the type of retailer and who the target customer is. Some fashion apparel manufacturers break their line releases into further seasonal market time periods that coincide with such specific holidays or events as Back-to-School and President's Day Sales. Liz Claiborne, for example, releases merchandise on a monthly basis, because they feel that their customer wants new merchandise more frequently than the traditional four seasons.

The National Retail Federation (NRF), a major organization of retailers in the U.S., publishes an annual Stores Retail Calendar at the end of each year to aid the retailer in shopping the markets and meeting other specific needs. The calendar lists all monthly events that are related to retail—from regional and international market dates and sites, to trade shows such as NAMSB (National Association of Men's Sportswear Buyers), and conferences on technology, promotion, control, visuals, and fabrics.

1996 Market Weeks

The 1996 general women's and children's apparel market weeks at the various regional marts and in New York are listed below. In addition to these general markets, various specialized events are held throughout the year at some of these venues. Dates are subject to revision, and individual marts should be contacted for confirmation and more information.

LOCATION	SUMMER	FALL I	FALL II	RESORT	SPRING
ATLANTA (Atlanta Apparel Mart)	Jan. 25-29	April 11-15	June 13-15	Aug. 22-26	Oct. 24-28
BIRMINGHAM (Birmingham Jefferson Civic Center)	Jan. 21-22	March 24-25	June 9-10	Aug. 18-19	Oct. 13-14
BOSTON (Bayside Expo Center)	Jan. 14-17	April 14-17	June 16-19	Aug. 18-21	Oct. 13-16
CHARLOTTE (Charlotte Merchandise Mart) (children's market)	Jan. 19-23 Jan. 19-22	March 22-26 March 22-25	June 7-11 June 7-10	Aug. 16-20 Aug. 16-19	Oct. 11-14
CHICAGO (Chicago Apparel Center)	Jan. 26-30	March 29-April 2	May 31-June 4	Aug. 16-20	Oct. 25-29
DALLAS (International Apparel Mart)	Jan. 18-22	March 21-25	June 6-10	Aug. 15-19	Oct. 17-21
KANSAS CITY (Kansas City Market Center)	Jan. 13-15	April 13-16	June 22-24	Aug. 24-27	Oct. 26-29
LOS ANGELES (California Apparel Mart)	Jan. 12-16	April 19-23	June 21-25	Aug. 9-13	Nov. 1-5
MIAMI (Miami Merchandise Mart)	Jan. 14-17	March 16-19	May 31-June 3	Aug. 9-12	Oct. 12-15
MINNEAPOLIS (Hyatt Merchandise Mart)	Jan. 21-24	March 10-12	April 14-17	June 9-11 Aug. 11-14	Oct. 20-23
NEW YORK (For New York updates, contact Fashion Calendar, 212-289-0420)	Jan. 8-19	Feb. 19-March 1	March 25-April 12	July 29-Aug. 9	Oct. 28-Nov. 15
PITTSBURGH (Monroeville Expo Mart)	Jan. 21-23	April 14-16	June 9-11	Sept. 8-10	Nov. 3-5
SAN FRANCISCO (The Fashion Center)	Jan. 6-9	April 13-16	June 15-18	Aug. 17-20	Oct. 19-22
SEATTLE (Seattle International Trade Center)	Jan. 20-23	March 30-April 2	June 8-11	Aug. 3-6	Oct. 26-29

Figure 5.6 A market week calendar from *WWD*, which shows market weeks for the five major seasons in fourteen cities.

DNR Int'l Trade Sh

Dates listed here are subject to change and

Javits Center, NYC

January

11-14 Pitti Uomo
Fortezza da Basso, Florence, Italy
(212) 246-2977

11-14 Surf Expo
Orange County Convention Ctr.,
Orlando, Fla.
(404) 220-2212

12-14 Imprinted Sportswear Show
Long Beach Convention Ctr., Calif.
(214) 239-3060

**12-16 Denver Int'l Western/
English Apparel & Equipment**
Denver, Colo.
(303) 295-1040

13-16 The Fashion Association (TFA)
Hilton/Sheraton hotels, NY
(212) 683-5665

14-16 NAMSB Show
Javits Center, NYC
(212) 986-1811

14-16 Int'l Kids Fashion (IKFS)
Javits Center, NYC
(212) 594-0880

14-17 Florida Men's Apparel Market
Miami Merchandise Mart, Fla.
(305) 261-4921

14-17 National Retail Federation
N.Y. Hilton and Sheraton
Centre hotels, NYC
(202) 783-7971

14-17 Milan Men's Collections
Individual locations, Milan, Italy
39.2/7600-3277

15-20 Bangkok Int'l Fashion Fair
Queen Sirikit Nat'l Conv. Center
66.2/503-2199

16-18 The Print Show
40 W. 40th St, NYC
(914) 722-0406

17-19 U.S. Apparel Solo Show
Tokyo, Japan
(202) 482-4805

**17-20 Hong Kong
Fashion Week**
Convention Center, Hong Kong
(212) 838-8688

19-21 Pitti Bimbo/Teen
Fortezza da Basso, Florence, Italy
(212) 246-2977

20-23 The Exclusive/Eurostyle
Le Parker Meridien hotel, NYC
(212) 315-1495

20-23 MAC of the Carolinas
Charlotte Merchandise Mart, N.C.
(704) 332-2139

**20-23 Men's & Boys' Apparel
Market/ Int'l Western Markets**
Int'l Menswear Mart, Dallas, Texas
(214) 879-8300

**20-23 Pacific NW Apparel Ass'n
(PNAA)**
Seattle Int'l Trade Center, Wash.
(206) 728-6622

**21-23 Designers' Collective/
Mode Coast**
The Plaza hotel, NYC
(212) 759-8055

21-23 The Europeans
The Plaza hotel, NYC
(212) 759-8055

21-23 London Menswear Exhib'ns
Earls Court Exhib'n Ctr., London
44.171/973-8866

23-25 Chicago Men's Apparel Group
Niles, Ill.
(708) 916-1115

24-27 Paris Men's Collections
Individual locations, Paris, France
33.1/426-6664

26-28 MIAS
Milan, Italy
39.2/39215282

26-29 SEHM
Parc des Expositions, Paris, France
(703) 522-5000

**27-30 Southeastern Men's
Collective**
Atlanta Apparel Mart, Ga.
(404) 220-2425

28-Feb.1 Off-Price Specialist Ctr.
Debbie Reynolds Hotel, Las Vegas
(414) 645-7939

30-Feb. 2 MAGIC
Las Vegas Convention Center, Nev.
(310) 393-7757

February

2-4 Int'l Menswear Fair/Inter-Jeans
Cologne Fairgrounds, Germany
(212) 974-8835

4-6 Eurostyle L.A.
Four Seasons hotel, Los Angeles
(212) 315-1495

4-6 Moda In
Milan, Italy
(212) 980-1500

4-7 The Super Show
GWCC, Atlanta, Ga.
(305) 893-8771

5-8 N.Y. Men's Collections
Individual locations, NYC
212) 221-6239

6-9 ColombiaTex '96
Medellin, Colombia
(212) 223-1120

6-9 Int'l Sporting Goods (ISPO)
Munchenermesse, Munich, Germany
(212) 652-7070

8-10 Action Sports Retailer Show
San Diego, Calif.
(714) 376-8144

10-12 Gaudi Barcelona
Barcelona, Spain
34.3/233.3000

10-13 MAC of the Carolinas
Charlotte Merch Mart, N.C.
(704) 332-2139

**11-14 Big & Tall Men's App'l Needs
(B.A.T.M.A.N.)**
Merch. Mart, Miami, Fla.
(305) 255-4163

11-14 Tex-Styles India '96
NSE Complex, Goregaon, Bombay
91.11/332-2819

13-15 Pitti Filati
Fortezza da Basso, Florence
(212) 246-2977

18-20 Eurostyle Too
Le Parker Meridien hotel, N
(212) 315-1495

18-20 Premier Menswear
Nat'l Exhib. Ctr. Birmingham
(212) 745-0495

18-20 Mode Homme Mon
Centre Sheraton hotel, Mon
(514) 488-8853

22-23 Take Off (Interstoff)
Sheraton Airport, Frankfurt,
(404) 984-8016

**23-28 Nat'l Ass'n Unifor
Mfrs. & Distributors (NAU**
Harbor Island, San Diego, Ca
(212) 869-0670

24-26 Int'l Jeanswear & S
N.Y. Coliseum
(212) 921-4177

25-27 Chicago Men's Wea
Chicago Apparel Center, Ill.
(800) 677-6278

28-Mar. 1 Bobbin Contexp
Miami Beach Conv. Center,
(800) 845-8820

Figure 5.7 *DNR* international men's wear trade show calendar for January through June.

...fied **with respective show sponsors.**

DNR, WEDNESDAY, NOVEMBER 8, 1995.

Kolnmesse, Cologne, Germany

...positions, Paris

...remier Coll'ns Moscow
xpocentr
20

rch

l Sportswear Show
tion Center, Fla.

...o

...e MAC
tel, Syracuse, N.Y.

4-7 Ideabiella
Cernobbio, Italy
39.15/84-831

8-10 LOOK: Int'l Sportswear
Convention Ctr., Los Angeles
(800) 225-6278, x231

8-11 Premiere Vision
Parc des Expositions, Paris, France
(212) 755-7197

**9-11 Int'l Travel Goods, Leather &
Accessories Show**
Houston, Tex.
(201) 251-7778

12-14 Interstoff World
Frankfurtmesse, Frankfurt, Germany
(404) 984-8016

13-16 Ideacomo
Cernobbio, Italy
39.15/84831

14-17 MIPEL
Milan, Italy
39.2/89010020

15-17 Bobbin Spring Expo
Sands Expo Center, Las Vegas
(800) 845-8820

17-19 NAMSB Show
Javits Center, NYC
(212) 986-1811

17-20 Int'l Kids Fashion (IKFS)
Javits Convention Center, NYC
(212) 594-0880

**18-20 Int'l Fashion Fabrics
Exhibition (IFFE)**
Javits Center, NYC
(212) 594-0880

18-20 QR (Quick Response) Show
Marriott Marquis hotel, Atlanta, Ga.
(800) 338-0206

**23-26 Men's & Boys' Apparel/Int'l
Western Markets**
Int'l Menswear Mart, Dallas, Texas
(214) 879-8300

26-29 Moda Moscow
Krasnaya Presnya Expocentr, Moscow
(203) 834-1122

29-31 Imprinted Sportswear Show
Philadelphia, Pa.
(214) 239-3060

**30- Apr. 2 Pacific Northwest Apparel
Ass'n (PNAA)**
Seattle Int'l Trade Center, Wash.
(206) 728-6622

April

**2-6 Shanghai Textile Mach'ry/
Fabrics & Accessories Expo '96**
Exhibition Centre, Shanghai
85.2/2865-2633

8-10 Imprinted Sportswear Show
Toronto, Canada
(214) 239-3060

9-11 Florida Men's Apparel Market
Miami Merchandise Mart, Fla.
(305) 261-4921

**13-15 Store Fixturing/
Point of Purchase Show**
McCormick Place, Chicago, Ill.
(800) 241-9034, x 281

13-16 Southeast Men's Collective
Atlanta Apparel Mart, Ga.
(404) 220-2425

14-16 Florida MAC
Miami Merch. Mart, Fla.
(305) 261-4921

25-27 Interstoff Season
Frankfurtmesse, Frankfurt, Germany
(404) 984-8016

29-May 1 L.A. Int'l Textile Show
CaliforniaMart, Los Angeles
(213) 225-6278

May

3-5 SFA: Seoul Fashion Collections
Korea Exhibition Center, Seoul
88.2/551-1117

8-11 Int'l Textile Machinery Show
Korea Exhibition Center, Seoul
88.2/551-1432

**11-14 Int'l Mass Retail Ass'n
(IMRA)**
Wyndham Anatole hotel, Dallas
(202) 861-0774

**18-21 Visual Mktg. &
Store Design**
Javits Center, NYC
(800) 272-SHOW

20-24 Jiangsutex '96 (Silk/Machn'ry)
Jiangsu Exhibition Hall, Nanjing, China
85.2/2541-9196

21-24 Interselection
Parc des Expositions, Paris, France
33.1/47 56 32 32

29-June 1 Matexco
Medellin, Colombia
(212) 223-1120

June

5-8 Garment & Fabric '96
Foreign Trade Centre, Guang-zhou
85.2/2851-8603

**8-11 Pacific NW Apparel Ass'n
(PNAA)**
Seattle Int'l Trade Center, Wash.
(206) 728-6622

23-25 NAMSB Show
Javits Center, NYC
(212) 986-1811

Summary

Determining when and what to buy involves more than might first be realized. The search for the right goods for a retailer's customer, however, is both an easy and difficult undertaking because of the tremendous availability of resources. Selecting where and from whom to source should entail thorough, deliberate decision-making that weighs the advantages and disadvantages to each method and supplier considered. Primary in determining the best merchandise to procure is knowing your company's customers and their wants and needs.

References

American Apparel Manufacturers Association. (1995). *Apparel import digest.* Arlington, VA.: Author.

DNR International Trade Show Calendar Jan–June 1996. (1995, November 8). *DNR*, pp. 8–9.

Diamond, J., & Diamond, E. (1996). *The world of fashion—A global perspective.* New York: Fairchild Publications.

Dickerson, K. (1995). *Textiles and apparel in the global economy.* Englewood Cliffs, N. J.: Prentice-Hall.

Dickerson, K., & Balkwell, C. (1994). Apparel production in the Caribbean: A classic case of the new international division of labor. *Clothing and Textiles Research Journal, 12*(3), 6–15.

Forney, J.C., Rosen, D., & Orzechowski, J.M. (1990). Domestic vs. overseas apparel production: Dialogue with San Francisco based manufacturers. *Clothing and Textiles Research Journal, 8*(3), pp. 39–44.

1996 market weeks. (1996, January 18). *WWD*, p. 15

Ross, J.R. (1992, March). Changes afoot in textile/apparel sourcing patterns. *Global Trade*, pp. 26–28.

Stone, E. (1994). *Exporting and importing fashion: A global perspective.* Albany, N.Y.: Delmar.

Key Terms

absolute quota
Ad valorem tariff
broker
centralized buying
closeout
compound tariff
contractor
decentralized buying
domestic market
domestic source/ sourcing
drop shipper
duty
exclusive contractor
exclusive order
free rate of duty
General Agreement on Tariffs and Trade (GATT)
import
independent buying office
international market
international source/sourcing
jobber
job lot
lead time
manufacturer
market
market calendar
market week

merchandise mart
middleman
Multifiber Arrangement (MFA)
off-price order
offshore
prepack
private-label order
promotional order
Provision 9802 (Item 807)
quota
regional market
regular order
reorder
resident buying office (RBO)
resource
sourcing
specific tariff
store-owned buying office
supplier
tariff
tariff-rate quota
trade shows
U.S. Customs Service
U.S. Harmonized Tariff Schedule (USHTS)
vendor
visa
wholesaler

Case 38
Treadwell's: The Buyer's Decision

Judith Everett, Northern Arizona University

Treadwell's Department Store is a traditional department store that was founded in 1898 by Oliver Treadwell in the American Southwest. Treadwell's has symbolized the spirit of the Southwest for nearly a century, maintaining exclusive merchandise related to the region as well as providing moderate to better apparel, accessories, and home furnishings for the entire family. The regional department store retailer has 18 branch stores located at the major cities in Colorado, New Mexico, Utah, and Arizona. Treadwell's has its buying offices and distribution center in Phoenix, Arizona and sends merchandise to all of its branches from the central distribution center. James Treadwell Stephenson, the great-grandson of the founder, is the current chief executive officer. He is very concerned about maintaining the image of the company as well as the profitability of the firm.

Recently, Tiffany Brentwood has been promoted to the position of buyer of women's sleepwear and loungewear after successfully managing the intimate apparel and children's departments at the Santa Fe branch for four years. She also had held the position of assistant buyer for children's sleepwear and accessories for almost one year. Her long-term professional goals include becoming a divisional merchandise manager and store manager.

After her interview with CEO Stephenson, Tiffany realized the importance of the company philosophy to enhance images of the Southwest yet maintain profitability. She has sought unique merchandise that will reinforce the Southwestern image for Treadwell's. She found a resource for a group of pajamas, nightshirts, and tunics with matching leggings. This merchandise features Southwestern motifs and would fit perfectly with

the goals of the firm to offer such merchandise. She believes that this style is not a passing fad in this part of the country and it should be a staple item in her department.

The merchandise featured tasteful interpretations of traditional Native American blanket designs. The garments were made from 100% cotton knit and produced in fahionable colors. Tiffany was confident that this merchandise would be popular with Treadwell's target customer.

Upon further investigation, Tiffany discovered that similar styles and colors of merchandise were available from two different resources, Southwest Specialties, a vendor in Los Angeles, or JC Enterprises, a local Phoenix vendor.

Southwest Specialties requires a minimum order of $5,000 at cost, offers terms of 3/10, net 30, and does not provide transportation costs. Transportation costs may be estimated at approximately $2.50 per dozen garments. There is a rumor, however, that there may be a trucking strike and Southwest transports by independent truck lines. Southwest Specialties is willing to participate in a cooperative advertising program. This Los Angeles firm assures Tiffany that merchandise will be in stock and available for reorder.

The local vendor does not have a minimum purchase and will deliver the merchandise for free. JC Enterprises also offers terms of 3/10, net 30. This firm is not willing to share in the costs of a cooperative advertisement, since it is a small company. JC Enterprises cannot guarantee immediate delivery. This firm needs a 48-hour delivery notice.

Tiffany decides to bring the merchandise into the stores. She calculates her initial order, which is shown in Table 5.1. Tiffany prepares a financial analysis of the purchase, also taking into consider-

Table 5.1   Tiffany's Initial Order

Quantity	Style	Southwest Specialties Cost	JC Enterprises Cost
12 dozen	pajamas	$174/dozen	$180/dozen
6 dozen	nightshirts	$150/dozen	$155/dozen
20 dozen	tunics	$117/dozen	$120/dozen
15 dozen	leggings	$117/dozen	$120/dozen

ation the discounts and shipping costs that would be applied to her orders to determine which vendor might be the best to purchase from. She studies her analysis, then takes it along with the pros and cons about each vendor, to her divisional merchandise manager. Because Tiffany is new as a buyer, she does not feel confident about making the decision on her own and wants some feedback from her divisional manager.

Major Question

From which vendor should Tiffany recommend purchasing? Why?

Study Questions

1. What is the difference in the total cost of the merchandise from the two different vendors?

2. What factors in addition to price, discounts, and shipping should be considered in making this decision?

Case 39
A Color Coordination
Conundrum

LaDonna Garrett, Fashion Institute of Technology

Global Options (or "GO" as it's known to its customers) is a wildly successful specialty chain retailer, concentrating on better-priced, young misses private-label sportswear. The Global Option motto is "In the know, at the show, gotta GO!" One of the reasons for their success is their "GO Girls"—a batteon of college coeds and young career women used to promote the Global Options lifestyle. GO Girls are prominently featured in all their ads, public relations vehicles, and publicity events.

The other secret to GO's success is their aggressive worldwide sourcing network. Global Options does not own any of the fabric mills or garment fac-

tories used to make their garments and accessories. Instead, Global Options relies on an international network of independent mills and contractors for all of their private-label merchandise. These fabric and production sources work closely with the GO production and product development staff on merchandise assortments. Because GO is a national specialty chain, the smallest quantity usually ordered within an assortment is 8,000–10,000 pieces per style, usually in two to three different colors or patterns.

The GO production staff and product developers have the responsibilities of monitoring quality control, coordinating garment shipment schedules, negotiating prices, and the worldwide coordination of fabrics/colors/prints/patterns. The latter responsibility is the most challenging. Fabric/color/print/pattern coordination means that every garment scheduled to be sold on the retail floor at the same time is color-matched to every other style within the assortment as they would be if they all were produced in the same place—even though different fibers take dye differently. So, whether the fabric is silk or linen or cotton, or the garment came from Hong Kong, Malaysia, Pakistan, or the U.S., each style within the assortment must match a color standard. Moreover, all merchandise within the stock assortment must arrive on time. If any factory is late in shipping its production to GO, then the rest of the stock assortment styles might not sell as well as they would if all pieces were merchandised together.

Production and product developers are constantly trying to identify the next emerging fabric- and garment-producing nation to stay one step ahead of their competition. And the competition in the young misses, better-priced, private-label business is fierce! In the best of circumstances, GO tests new resources by giving them a small trial run. The trial run is a small quantity (200–500 pieces per style) of several styles to see how the new resource performs—quality, adherence to delivery dates, and so forth. The test merchandise is shipped only to the 20 test stores throughout the country. If a new resource's fabric or production meets GO's standards, and the test merchandise performs well at retail, then a regular stock order for all stores is placed with the resource. If GO's standards are not met, GO will not use the new factory. In addition to a trial-run order, sometimes the GO product developers place a reservation order just to reserve production space for a future stock order. The exact styles for production in the stock order could be decided at a later time. There is a risk for the factory with this reservation because if the test run is not successful, GO will not place a full order in the future and other orders from other companies could have been turned away. However, if the test is good (acceptable) and GO places a specific order against the reservation, it is advantageous for both GO and the factory.

Recently, GO's product developers were extremely excited about the potential of an untapped fabric and garment production source. A developing country in the sub-Sahara was eager to begin manufacturing young misses sportswear styles in cotton and linen blends. The quality of raw materials, and the prices and workmanship of sample garments was perfect for the Global Options customer. GO wanted to use two of the sub-Sahara factories to do cotton and linen blend styles for the next season's stock order. GO also planned to place production commitments for different styles in silk and rayon of the same colors from Hong Kong and Malaysian factories to go with the sub-Sahara styles.

GO's product developers have already negotiated prices, distributed style information for production and have given color standards to be matched to the two new sub-Sahara factories. Time is extremely short and this planned stock order assortment is the most critical to making the upcoming season's sales projections. GO would have to make a decision about what to tell the new sub-Sahara factories soon. There are always potential problems with untested resources. GO has several ways of working with new factories.

Major Question
What should GO do?

Study Questions

1. What are some of the potential risks faced by GO if they use the new factories for the stock assortment?

2. How can GO minimize their risks?

3. Would it be better to temporarily postpone doing a program with the two factories? Why or why not?

4. The image of GO is such that customers have a certain expectation of quality in their merchandise. If items from a new factory were offered for sale without meeting color standards, how would this affect customer reactions?

5. How does a company keep costs competitive and quality high?

Case 40
To Do or Not to Do Business in China

Sara Douglas, University of Illinois

Advantage Apparel is a manufacturer of recognized brand-name merchandise for the U.S. market. It is a subsidiary of the Cunningham Company, a one-billion dollar, well-respected, U.S. apparel giant that is based in Seattle. "Hank" Tan, managing director of Advantage Apparel in Hong Kong, is also a member of the board of directors of Cunningham and makes frequent business trips to the U.S. His company is one of the few Hong Kong apparel manufacturers that still has full production operations in Hong Kong. Others that remain in part maintain "high-end" activities in Hong Kong—those production-associated activities that yield reasonably high profits such as marketing, distribution, research, headquartering, and so forth. Advantage is a little different from them, and those differences seem to have served the company well. Its success has not come easily, but hard work has yielded profits and a good reputation.

Advantage has enjoyed its reputation as a large, established Hong Kong apparel manufacturer. In earlier years, the company had four factories on the island of Hong Kong. Now there is only one; but business is good, and there is a clear need for expansion. The one factory remaining in Hong Kong is the site of both company headquarters (with all offices) and production. About 1,000 people are employed in this facility.

It is not easy to expand in Hong Kong. The island is literally out of space. Buildings are going up higher and higher, and so are real estate prices and rent. Labor costs have also climbed with unbelievable rapidity. If Hank expanded facilities here, it will mean adding more floors to his six-story factory or trying to find land on which to build. Both these options are so costly that Hank can only shake his head when he considers them. Additionally, he would have to find workers and—even worse—pay them about ten times more per hour than he did just five years ago.

Hank believes an "Outward Processing Arrangement" (OPA) seems to offer more opportunities to the company right now. Outward processing is a British/European term with approximately the same meaning as "offshore sourcing" in the U.S. OPA was legitimized in Hong Kong recently and so is a strategic option for manufacturers there. In essence, while Hong Kong manufacturers are being encouraged to continue to maintain high-return activities in Hong Kong, they now are able to move some of the lower cost activities offshore. Cunningham operates in a similar manner in the U.S.—sometimes contracting offshore, especially in the Caribbean nations or Mexico, and sometimes making more permanent investment arrangements. At this point, Hank prefers directly investing in China by purchasing land and building manufacturing facilities rather than increasing Advantage's contractual arrangements. Advantage already has some contracting work done in other countries, including China; and, given the company's current expansion needs, he believes it makes more sense to think about

direct, foreign investment in a nearby country where he could obtain both land and labor at significantly lower prices than he could in Hong Kong. Nearby China and its Guandong Province—the closest to Hong Kong—seem the obviously appropriate choice. A subregional trade agreement exists between Hong Kong and China. What the countries offer each other in this arrangement is complementarity; essentially, China provides to Hong Kong necessary low labor and land costs, and Hong Kong provides large available quota allocations from the U.S. plus marketing and distribution expertise and infrastructure. Again, these arrangements are quite familiar to Hank's fellow board members at Cunningham because of their similarity to 9802 (807) offshore operations undertaken by U.S. firms. Agreements are negotiated for tariff reductions or total abolition in order to move goods between the countries.

But OPA has some very clear disadvantages. First, it is extremely bureaucratic. Numerous photos and detailed documentation are required for every job. That alone takes a minimum of five to six working days, a time period that is significant enough (when added to the fact that Hong Kong must import its piece goods, which takes about one month) to decrease Hank's competitive advantage with U.S. companies that are constantly improving their pipeline times with Quick Response and other strategies. Hank figures it would take about five months from receipt of order to shipment. There are also difficulties that come with coordinating assembly lines in two countries. It is not the most efficient process.

Could Hank just cut the garments in Hong Kong and send them off to China for assembly, as many U.S. companies do with their Caribbean Basin partners? Then China could ship them back to Hong Kong for finishing and export to the U.S. Such an arrangement would make an efficient production loop. It would be perfect!

Hank knows it is not so simple. There are at least two problems: one old and one new. First, doing only cutting in Hong Kong is not a possibility because Hong Kong policy disallows it and requires that some assembly be done in Hong

Kong. Second, the General Agreement on Tariffs and Trade (GATT)-Uruguay Round Bill that was passed in the U.S. in December 1994 changed the definition of "major product transformation" from garment cutting to garment assembly. Apparel country of origin had been determined by where "major product transformation" of the garment has occurred. Since 1984 the U.S. has considered major product transformation to be where the garment is cut. For that reason, cutting has been done in Hong Kong in order that the garments can have a "made in Hong Kong" label and be shipped to the U.S. using Hong Kong's quota allocations from the U.S. (which are more plentiful than China's). The cut parts are then shipped to China where partial assembly occurs (for example, collars and cuffs); and, finally, to comply with Hong Kong policy, the final product assembly is done in Hong Kong. The U.S. change of definition will have a major effect on apparel manufacturers, importers, and retailers. It is controversial in the U.S., and Hank is uncertain about what changes in the rule might occur before it is finally implemented. If country of origin is defined by where the products are assembled and if Hong Kong manufacturers plan to use their quota allocations, Hank's company must assemble the garments in Hong Kong. Minor assembly and perhaps cutting and finishing could be done in China. The production loop still would be workable.

A big challenge is that Hank must comply with not only various onerous U.S. policies but also onerous Hong Kong policies. In his words, "The U.S. government ties my hands, and the Hong Kong government ties my feet." "Actually," he adds, "it may be more simple when the new country of origin rules are in place. As it has been, in order to ship my goods and use Hong Kong's quota allocations from the U.S., the U.S. requires me to cut garments in Hong Kong. The Hong Kong government requires me to do final assembly here. So I had to do two major transformations in Hong Kong. With the new country of origin rules maybe I'll just have to do one—plus exporting the finished garments, of course. Still, orders that

Advantage accepts will have to continue to be limited carefully to those that are manageable in terms of lead times and other requirements."

All these considerations don't include certain other challenges presented simply by doing business in China. While Hong Kong business persons have some cultural ties to China that Americans don't and they have definite language advantages, China certainly presents many disadvantages. The Chinese government continues to act in ways that frequently throw its trade and business partners off guard. Individual officials there often interpret laws and regulations in different ways, which disrupts planning. China's leaders have been criticized by the U.S. for being negligent of human rights and paying too little attention to fair wages, long hours, child labor, and safe working conditions. "Free" prison laborers, put to work under harsh conditions, have been used for production. Chinese officials often are equally negligent of international regulations regarding Customs, labeling, and quotas. So, too, are factory managers themselves. Further, local talent in China would need to be developed because Hank cannot afford to send many managers to China for very long. It would be too expensive.

Among all these troubling facts, in Hank's mind the most significant concerns center around wages and factory conditions, and Hank is well aware that these issues also trouble his associates on the Cunningham board of directors. Levi Strauss halted production in China entirely because of what it considered "systemic labor inequities." Also, last year there was a devastating fire in a small apparel factory in China. It was much worse than the toy fire in Bangkok a year earlier but news of it leaked out of China slowly. The real cause of the fire is suspected to be negligence and extremely poor conditions, but no one talks about what really happened. It is frustrating to Hank not to know the answers to his questions or be able to find out what he would like to learn. This particular fire was preceded by two others, both (evidently) smaller; but information about them is scarce as well. What would something like that fire do to Advantage's image and reputation?

Still, China's economy is currently growing at an annual rate that exceeds all other countries, and there are numerous potential advantages and opportunities for companies that move into China at this time. One of the most important would be the ability to tap the huge market that China offers, and China is willing to negotiate reasonable joint ventures. Advantage could have a 50/50 ownership deal. In addition to the ownership deal, China will provide the land and will build the necessary roads and factories. However, China demands a 50-year lease, after which the land, roads, and factories revert to complete Chinese ownership. In the world of joint ventures, however, these arrangements are considered liberal, and numerous Hong Kong companies have taken advantage of them, not to mention all the Japanese companies that also are eager to do business there. Clearly, there is opportunity in China—as well as risks. Hank keeps arguing with himself, thinking and rethinking about these factors.

Major Question

What is your recommendation, regarding whether Hank should do business in China?

Study Questions

1. What kind of support or criticism do you think Hank would receive from the company's publics—composed, for example, of Cunningham's board of directors, the U.S. Commerce Department, the human rights committee of the International Labor Organization, U.S. labor and human rights groups, the Hong Kong Department of Trade, the International Association of Chambers of Commerce, U.S. importers and retailers, and any other groups that have some kind of interest in the company if he made a certain decision? How would this affect his business?

2. What are the long-term advantages and disadvantages of investing in China?

Case 41
Lingerie Incorporated

Molly Eckman, Colorado State University
Diane Frey, Bowling Green State University

Lingerie Incorporated is a family-owned company that was founded by the grandparents of Randall and Amanda Miller, the current owners who are brother and sister. Randy and Mandi hope to pass the business on to their own children. The medium-size domestic apparel business has been producing women's lingerie for 40 years within the U.S. Currently, their annual sales volume is $30 million. The primary customers are upscale national retailers seeking lingerie that displays uniqueness in fabric, design, and quality. Randy and Mandi recognize that the lingerie industry is becoming increasingly similar to the fashion apparel industry in the fact that responding quickly and efficiently to market trends is becoming more and more important.

Although profits have been climbing steadily over the last five years, the rate of increase in profit is declining annually. Randy and Mandi attribute the drop in profit to the increased quantity of lower-priced lingerie that is exported to the U.S. each year. This trend has made it more difficult for Lingerie Incorporated to compete on price while maintaining the high level of design detail for which their garments are known in the market.

Lingerie Incorporated has identified two strategic goals. Goal one is to increase the company's production capacity and profits by identifying additional sources of manufacturing for selected lingerie apparel. Traditionally, the company has placed contracts only with domestic contractors who have a reputation for being cost conscious and efficient. Goal two is to achieve higher sales and profits by changing the merchandise mix from the current ratio of 80 percent/20 percent (basic to fashion merchandise) to 60 percent/40 percent (basic to fashion). The company hopes to achieve this goal while maintaining its reputation for value by offering high-quality goods with unique design details at a moderate price.

Additionally, at Lingerie Incorporated, quality will never be sacrificed to make a product cheaper. Timely delivery of merchandise is also a priority. Efficient communication systems, transportation, and production operations contribute to having appropriate inventory for customers.

Randy and Mandi have decided that moving a portion of their production offshore is necessary to enable them to be more price competitive and to achieve their goals. Randy and Mandi have done much research and have narrowed their offshore sourcing options to Honduras or Mexico. They realize that the firm's optimal strategy, at least at first, is to work through contractors. A contractor, fluent in the native language and English, has been identified in both countries. Not only are the contractors familiar with their culture but they are skilled at managing personnel and understand local production and business practices. The contractors are equally qualified; therefore, this has not been a consideration in selecting where to source Lingerie Incorporated's garments.

An employee of Lingerie Incorporated has gathered information on both Honduras and Mexico for Randy and Mandi to consider when making their decision. Additionally, comparative data between the two countries is contained in Table 5.2.

Honduras—General Information
The government of Honduras is a democratic republic and the official language is Spanish. The population is approximately 5.17 million, with an annual growth rate of 2.8 percent. The literacy rate is 65 percent. Due to free elections of government officials, Honduras enjoys political stability that is rare among Central American countries. Honduras is one of the largest countries in Central America, yet is also one of the least developed in the Western hemisphere.

Characteristics of the Labor Force
Approximately 50,000 Hondurans work in the sewn-products industry; 181 apparel manufacturers operate in Honduras. Most apparel production plants employ 350 to 700 employees. A majority of apparel production takes place in the vicinity of San Pedro Sula, the second largest city in Honduras. Extensive training programs and incentives have encouraged the development of a stable and efficient pool of apparel workers. Worker wages and benefits are among the lowest in the Western hemisphere; however, the wages and benefits that are paid by U.S. firms are higher than the minimum wage. Honduran law provides for seven days of wages for five-and-one-half days of work, paid on a weekly basis. Workers receive 13 months of wages for 12 months of work.

Trading Trends
Honduras participates in the Caribbean Basin Initiative through Provision 9802 (807) production. This trade regulation offers several advantages to U.S. apparel manufacturers who produce apparel in the Caribbean. If a U.S. firm ships fabric produced and cut in the U.S. to Honduras for assembly, the finished product may be subject to quotas when shipped back to the U.S. However, duty is paid only on the value added to the garment during assembly. The close proximity of the Caribbean to the U.S. is attractive to U.S. manufacturers because they have greater control over production, quality, and quick turnaround than when goods are produced in other international locations. Due to Provision 9802 production, apparel exports to the U.S. have increased.

Infrastructure and Business Incentives
A local family, the Kattans, began the Honduran apparel manufacturing industry in the 1920s. Today, the family owns seven plants, the majority of which are joint ventures with U.S. firms. While other apparel manufacturing companies are emerging in Honduras, most of the major U.S. companies manufacturing in Honduras (e.g., Warnaco and Phillips-Van Heusen Corporation)

Table 5.2 Comparative Facts Concerning Honduras and Mexico

	Honduras	Mexico
Government	democratic republic	federal republic
Language	Spanish	Spanish (English widely understood)
Population	5.17M	90.4M
Annual population growth rate	2.8%	2.0%
Labor force	1.8M	25M
Number employed in apparel production	50,000	200,000
Number of apparel firms	181	5,000
Unemployment	15%	11%
Literacy	65%	87%
Real GDP growth rate	5.6%	2.6%
Minimum wage U.S. $	$2.00 to $3.50 per day	not available
Working week	44.0 hours	45.5 hours
GDP per capita U.S. $	$665	$4,275
GNP U.S. $	369.8B	323.5B
Telecommunications infrastructure scale 1 = lowest 10 = highest	3.30	4.35

work with the Kattans. A majority of apparel manufacturing takes place in free trade zones. Because of the strong infrastructure for apparel manufacturing in San Pedro Sula, Honduras has become an attractive source of apparel for U.S. firms. Thus, joint ventures with U.S. companies are common, as is sharing U.S. technology that is essential for producing goods to meet U.S. quality standards. These strong joint ventures with U.S. companies have resulted in a network of strong contractors for apparel production in Honduras.

Local energy crises have been reported to make it necessary to avoid the use of power for half of the workday. The power shortage is due to higher demands resulting from increased manufacturing and deforestation that have lowered water levels in the dam that runs the country's hydroelectric plant. This is a problem not previously encountered in Honduras and most plants now have their own generators. A complete transfer of high technology may not be effective because workers, who are paid low wages, have generally not been trained for highly technical jobs. Locating mechanics for maintenance has also been difficult.

Costs of Manufacturing and Transportation
Honduras has four international airports. With sea-coasts on both the Atlantic and Pacific oceans, Honduras is accessible to the U.S. by sea within three days.

Opinions of Industry Experts
Regardless of concerns about sourcing in Honduras, for individuals who are experienced in apparel production there are positive assessments of the future of Honduras as a source of apparel. Companies that source apparel from Honduras include JCPenney, Jockey, OshKosh, Phillips-Van Heusen, and Warnaco.

Mexico—General information
Mexico is a highly centralized federal republic and the official language is Spanish. Mexico is the largest Spanish speaking country in the world with a population of 90.4 million. Literacy rate is 87 percent. Political uncertainty continues due to recent assassinations and a peasant revolt in the state of Chiapas. High inflation and the unstable peso have resulted in a shaky economy. The fluctu-

ating value of the peso may result in shifts in hourly wages and difficulty in estimating other production costs.

Characteristics of the Labor Force
The more than 5,000 apparel firms employ about 200,000 workers, usually with 15 or fewer per plant. Approximately 60,000 workers are involved in Provision 9802 plants, most of which are located in free trade zones along the U.S. border. The remaining employees are located in central Mexico (Mexico City, Guadalajara, and Leon). Unskilled and semi-skilled labor is plentiful in Mexico. It is estimated that by 1997, 90,000 new apparel employees will be working in Mexican plants, many of which will replace those in other parts of the world, particularly Asia. Training programs are described as adequate. However, both high absenteeism and turnover make investment in training and management critical, increasing employment costs from $2 per hour to $10 per hour. Additional labor costs include severance pay for involuntary retirement, profit sharing, social security, and payroll taxes for housing. Fringe benefits comprise a higher percentage of workers' salaries in Mexico than in the U.S.

Trading Trends
As a result of the North American Free Trade Agreement (NAFTA), imports of apparel from Mexico are increasing and the trend is expected to continue. Several reasons for this change include the progressive phasing out of tariffs and quotas and the relative low wages of Mexican workers, which are advantageous for the labor-intensive production of apparel. Other benefits of NAFTA include the potential for fabric to be cut in Mexico, and less paperwork. The opportunity for U.S. companies producing apparel in Mexico to sell goods directly to the Mexican market is attractive because this is not currently an option for apparel produced under Provision 9802. Also, some predict a growth of middle class consumers in Mexico as a result of increased economic activity under NAFTA. This new middle class is expected to be a lucrative market for American goods.

Infrastructure and Business Incentives
The infrastructure is developing rapidly. Experts predict that at least $1 billion will be invested in Mexican apparel plants and equipment by 1997. However, substantial investment resources are needed to achieve full quality and productivity. The cost of electricity is 25 percent higher than in the U.S. The network of contractors is strong in Mexico, primarily due to the maquiladoras (i.e., factories) located along the border with the U.S.

Costs of Manufacturing and Transportation
When labor, material, overhead, and transportation are considered, it may be appropriate that Mexico be a source for selected apparel products. An attractive feature of apparel production in Mexico is the close proximity to the U.S., resulting in lower transportation costs, particularly when compared with other areas, such as Asia.

Opinions of Other Industry Experts
Market research experts predict that despite the relative low wages, with proper training, Mexican workers can meet productivity and quality standards that are comparable to those in the U.S.

Major Question
Assume the role as a consultant who has been hired by Lingerie Incorporated to make the decision for the location of new offshore production. Should offshore production be done in Honduras or Mexico? How would you advise Randy and Mandi?

Study Questions
1. Using the facts in Table 5.2 that compare Honduras and Mexico, which part of the data is most important in making this sourcing decision?

2. What are the pitfalls involved with switching from domestic sources to those in another country?

References

Cedrone, L. (1994, November). Honduras on the move. *Bobbin,* pp. 33–38.

DeWitt, J.W. (1995, February). NAFTA: One year later. *Apparel Industry Magazine,* p. 34.

Dickerson, K. (1995). *Textiles and apparel in the global economy.* Englewood Cliffs, N.J.: Prentice-Hall.

International Strategies, Inc. (1995). *Export hotline market information service.* Boston: Author.

Riley, S. (1994, November). New thinking for off-shore manufacturing: The Muff Mills story. *Bobbin,* pp. 64–71.

Silva, F. (1993, August). Mexico: The making of a new market. *Bobbin,* pp. 38–46.

Stone, E. (1994). *Exporting and importing fashion.* Albany, NY: Delmar.

Case 42
How to Produce the Edu-Doll?

Diana Rosen, California State University

The Edu-Doll Company manufactures educational dolls. The owner of the company, Mary Foster, developed the dolls through her job with the State Board of Education where she is responsible for developing reading skills methods for underprivileged children. She began producing dolls that were based on her illustrations for a book that she had developed and illustrated. Her dolls sell all year round, but over 60 percent sell between October and December, when sales are for the Holidays.

The entire product is packaged and assembled in the Philippines where Mary set up her factory with the help of local laborers. The doll consists of a plastic die-cut head made of PVC. The body is sewn and stuffed using knit tricot synthetic fabric. The doll is dimpled by hand, which is a labor-intensive process. The doll's hair is also manufactured in the Philippines and must be woven through the doll's hair follicles. The shoes are manufactured in Korea where leather is inexpensive and labor is skilled in the manufacturing of shoes. The doll's clothing is manufactured in a local sewing shop in the Philippines. There are five different types of dolls that are produced. They represent different nationalities. There is an Asian doll, a Hispanic doll, an African doll, and two blue-eyed blond American dolls. They are packaged in a large cardboard box with a plastic front showing the doll. The accompanying book is displayed at the side of the doll. All of the packaging has been sourced out of the Philippines. Only English is used for the book and written packaging information.

Unfortunately, local political turmoil proves to be detrimental when the Philippine factory production manager is killed. The plant now sits idle. The workers are afraid to return to work.

To survive, Edu-Doll Company must find a safer and more predictable place to manufacture its product. Mary has employed a local U.S. consultant who specializes in product development to investigate the possibility of producing the dolls in the U.S. or to consider other alternative sites. For countries that are being considered, the areas of investigation will be: 1) lead time; 2) political problems; and 3) the overall cost of manufacturing this product, including labor costs, travel to these locations to oversee production, and employment of an outside agent to assist in the manufacture of the doll. In addition to the U.S., Mary is interested in marketing the dolls in Europe.

Mary can salvage the doll's head die-cuts (the metal "cookie cutter" type form that standardizes the doll's head) from the Philippine factory, and has found a factory in China that can produce the heads at a comparable cost. The shoes will continue to be made in Korea as there are few problems with the current set up in Korea. The problem is that the sewn doll and the doll's clothing need to be produced at a reasonable cost either in the U.S. or in another country. Assembly and packaging must also be done at the main production site.

The doll must retail for $50. This leaves the actual raw cost (materials and labor) to be no more than $10 for the doll, the packaging, the book, and all other costs included. The doll wholesales for $25 to accommodate a $15 per unit overhead. Retailers will double that price to cover their own costs.

Major Question

Where and how should the dolls be assembled, produced, and packaged?

Study Questions

1. How seasonal is the doll market? Will the majority of the production need to be manufactured by October in time for pre-Holiday deliveries? Will changing production locations impact quota restrictions, which could jeopardize the timely delivery of the doll?

2. What about cultural and other local considerations, such as holiday periods, monsoons, work cycles, ethics, and so forth in other countries being considered for production?

3. Is marketing in the U.S. different than marketing in Europe? Should the graphics and language used on the packaging of the European doll be different than those that would appeal to the U.S. consumer? Is that an important issue to consider for this particular market?

Case 43
Quota Limitations

Nancy Anabel Mason, United States Customs Service

M-Wang Enterprises is a manufacturer and importer of women's wearing apparel and textile items for the home. During the past ten years, Jerry Lee, the owner of M-Wang has struggled to remain competitive in the clothing and textile industry in the U.S. Maintaining his competitive position has been difficult and has required many changes and swift decisions by management.

Table 5.3   Reference Chart/Comparison Textile Quota, Visa Requirements and Duty Rates

Country of Origin	Quota Y/N	Visa Y/N	Duty Rate
Canada (NAFTA qualifying)	N	N	2.8%
Costa Rica	Y	N	9.4%
El Salvador	Y	Y	9.4%
Israel	N	N	0.0%
Korean Republic	Y	Y	9.4%
Macedonia	N	N	9.4%
Malaysia	Y	Y	9.4%
Mauritius	Y	N	9.4%
Mexico (NAFTA qualifying)	N	N	6.8%
Peru	N	Y	9.4%
Sri Lanka	Y	Y	9.4%
Turkey	Y	Y	9.4%
Vietnam	N	N	90.0%

This is an illustration of the different rates of duty, quota restrictions, and visa import document requirements for the Women's Night Dresses made of cotton USHTS 6208.21.0020, category 351 for the above countries, as of October 1995.

The goals of M-Wang include maintaining flexibility in selecting the countries and specific locations in which to establish manufacturing facilities and to nurture relationships with major retailers. Jerry is continually working to establish new accounts, while at the same time delivering goods as contracted which requires clearing merchandise through the U.S. Customs Service without delays. To meet these goals, M-Wang employs an individual who is responsible for studying manufacturing trends. This person must be aware of statutory changes made in Washington D.C. and quota policy establishment, as well as be able to identify the most cost-effective manufacturing locations. See Table 5.3 for information on each country regarding quotas, visa requirements, and duty rates.

Originally, Jerry operated factories in Thailand, the Philippines, Hong Kong, and China. Today, his staff works aggressively to establish operations in countries with low wages and countries that are not subject to U.S. quotas. Such countries as Canada, Costa Rica, El Salvador, Israel, Korean Republic,

Table 5.4   Rates of Duty

Item	Quantity	Value	Duty Rate	Duty
Nightdresses (Category 351)	100 Dozen (1,200 pieces)	$8,400.00	9.4%	$789.60
Pillowcases (Category 369)	100 Dozen (1,200 pieces)	$3,000.00	23.5%	$705.00

Macedonia, Malaysia, Mauritius, Mexico, Peru, Sri Lanka, Turkey, and Vietnam are all potential new manufacturing locations. Currently, Vietnam is subject to column two rates of duty, which are prohibitively high, although trade agreements may change in the future and allow column one duty rates (i.e., lower rates) and a competitive manufacturing location without quota limitations. To control costs associated with clearing merchandise through U.S. Customs, M-Wang has developed a small inhouse import department managed by an individual who has a Customhouse Broker's License.

One of the significant challenges, as well as potentially disastrous obstacles to importing popular clothing and textiles, is import quotas. Quota class merchandise can be defined as any imported merchandise subject to limitations under an absolute quota or a tariff-rate quota. The majority of clothing and textile items are subject to absolute quotas. Quotas permit a limited number of units of specified merchandise to be entered or withdrawn for consumption in the U.S. during specified periods.

In an attempt to retain profit margins and meet the competitive pricing of the retailing environment, Jerry Lee has established a form of just-in-time inventory. The merchandise is delivered immediately to the retail establishment or retail warehousing facility upon clearance through U.S. Customs. This practice requires precise planning, transportation coordination, knowledge of U.S. Customs requirements, and luck. It also limits liability and overhead, reducing time for the disposition of merchandise, and reducing or eliminating prolonged warehousing costs.

One of Jerry's largest clients ordered 100 dozen pieces of women's nightdresses (pyjamas) and 100 dozen pieces of pillowcases (bedding items) with an embroidered Holiday theme. These apparel and textile items are classified in the U.S. Harmonized Tariff Schedule (USHTS) in Chapter 62, articles of apparel and clothing accessories, not knitted or crocheted, and Chapter 63, other made-up textile articles, needlecraft sets, worn clothing and worn textile articles, rags.

100 percent cotton woven embroidered nightdresses from China are classified as 6208.21.0020 and dutiable at a 9.4 percent rate of duty. Embroidered pillowcases from China, made from 100 percent woven cotton are classified as 6302.31.5040 dutiable at 23.5 percent. (See Table 5.4 for the resulting duties on orders for 100 dozen nightdresses and 100 dozen pillowcases.)

The contract specifies a delivery date of no later than November 25. Based upon past experience, Jerry is aware that quota categories start to reach threshold and are at risk of closing in November or December, the last two months of the quota cycle. His items have special embroidered holiday theme phrases, "Happy Holidays," "Happy New Year," and "Peace On Earth." A major retailer is planning to advertise and merchandise these items together, positioning them as special gift ideas for the holidays.

Production of the nightdresses and pillowcases is complete. Labeling, packaging, and invoicing documents have been prepared. Visas have been obtained from China and transportation has been scheduled. The merchandise enters the Port of San Francisco. The import manager, David DeMarcio, prepares the required clearance documents and submits them to Customs for release of the goods. Upon input quota processing in the Automated Commercial System (ACS), Alva Bostick, a Customs officer, discovers the nightdress (pyjama) quota category has been closed.

When merchandise is caught between the closure and opening of specific quota categories, the consequences can be disruptive and expensive. The importer must choose one of the following options:

- DESTROY THE MERCHANDISE UNDER CUSTOMS SUPERVISION.

- ENTER THE MERCHANDISE INTO A FOREIGN TRADE ZONE.

- EXPORT THE MERCHANDISE.

- WAREHOUSE THE MERCHANDISE.

If one of the above options is not chosen the articles will go General Order (GO). This happens when articles are taken into Customs custody and placed in a public store or general order bonded warehouse by a Customs Port Director at the risk and expense of the consignee. The shipment will be designated General Order thirty calendar days after the arrival of the importing vessel. The duration of a general order period is six months from the date of importation (Customs Federal Regulations 19 §127.1). After the general order period is exceeded, Customs may exercise the right to auction or destroy the merchandise.

Jerry has been notified by Customs that the nightdress (pyjama) quota category is closed.

Major Question

Given the above options, what should Jerry Lee do?

Study Questions

1. In the future, how can M-Wang guard against this problem?

2. What are ways of ensuring your merchandise will arrive before the closing of a quota category?

3. What other risks are there in importing merchandise into the U.S.?

4. How should this serious problem be disclosed to the retailer?

References

Black, H.C., Nolan, J.R., & Nolan-Haley, J.M. (1990). *Black's Law Dictionary Sixth Edition.* St. Paul, MN.: West Publishing Company.

USITC Publication 2831. (1995). *Harmonized Tariff Schedule of the United States.* Washington, DC.: U.S. Government Printing Office.

Code of Federal Regulations 19. (1992). *Parts 1 to 199, Revised as of April 1, 1992.* Washington, DC.: Office of the Federal Register National Archives and Records Administration.

Taylor, S., Mishulskis, J.V., & Penn, M., (eds.) (1995). *Introduction to Customs Brokerage.* Allegan, MI.: Boskage Commerce Publications.

Case 44
The Sweater Dilemma

Teresa Braswell Robinson, Middle Tennessee University

Chloe Gallagher, of Smith & Cooley Apparel Associates, an importer, has been assigned the new South American territory. Because of the wool resources that are abundant in that area of the world, Chloe's assignment is to develop a new wool ladies' handknitted sweater line, at better price points. As a part of her research, Chloe has located numerous potential resources, and has traveled to these areas twice to network and establish contact with potential suppliers/vendors. She has located several reputable suppliers who will provide her company with reasonable minimums, yarn procurement, design assistance, as well as allow her company to maintain the overseas production without assigning someone permanently to that country for day-to-day operations.

After considerable investigation of quality, prices, and so forth, Chloe has selected two major suppliers, one that can provide basic traditional looks and a second, which can provide more fashion-forward looks. Both looks are important to the development of the sweater line.

In selecting her resources, Chloe was assured that the designs created for her company would not be offered to any other potential competitors, allowing her exclusivity. In viewing sweater samples, which were examples of designs produced for other companies, she ran across one style which would be ideal for her own company's line. Upon questioning the suppliers, she was informed that she could also use the same design for her line. Because the sample had been produced for a well-known, nationally branded company, Chloe was sure that this item would be a huge success for her company. Because her company works on a tighter than normal markup and profit margin, she could successfully undersell her competition. Without question, she adopted the item into her company's sweater line.

Starting a new line of imports, however, was not without problems. Initially there were language problems, because Chloe did not speak the native Spanish. This resulted in some misinterpretations regarding sizing, measurements, labeling, and shipping. For example, despite careful tracking, the first shipment of sweaters was lost in transit. The reputable air shipping agent chosen—an international airline—lost the entire shipment, and its tracking system was unable to determine the routing of the products after they had been landed on U.S. soil. After seven days of searching, the goods were located in an airport dock in New York City, despite the fact that the original U.S. destination was Miami. This, of course, meant that shipments to retail accounts, which had already placed orders at market, were delayed for at least seven days.

Upon location of the goods, the shipment had to clear U.S. Customs. Then upon inspection of the goods, two problems were discovered. The documentation provided by Jane Ashley, the supplier, misrepresented the contents of the shipment. The manner in which the inventory was described, which is typically used by Customs to determine duty rates, was deceiving, thus appearing to be an attempt for assessment of lower duty rates. Although Jane Ashley had provided the documentation, it was still the responsibility of the importer, Smith & Cooley Apparel Associates, to assure proper information for U.S. Customs.

Also it was discovered that Jane Ashley had used the wrong labels. Chloe's company had designed and manufactured several thousand labels, which had been left with the supplier for proper insertion into the sweaters; however, they had used other labels with information that was insufficient to meet U.S. requirements. U.S. Customs normally would not release the goods to Chloe's company with incorrect labeling. However, because this was their first problem with U.S. Customs, the agent agreed to release the goods on a Friday, with the condition that the entire shipment be returned to Customs on Monday, with the proper labels affixed. Otherwise, Customs would seize the goods. (The alternative was to send someone to the Customs office who would sew in the labels, at that location). This meant another four-day delay in shipping the sweater orders to the already unhappy retail accounts.

Major Question
What suggestions would you make that might reduce the potential for these problems in labeling and documentation occurring in the future?

Study Questions
1. In what order should the problems be handled and how?

2. With all the problems with importing, why would a buyer want to go overseas to source?

3. Do you think exclusivity of designs would be an advantage to an importer such as Smith & Cooley? Why or why not?

Case 45
Should All the Eggs Go in One Basket?

Judy K. Miler, University of Tennessee
Nancy J. Rabolt, San Francisco State University

Lawrence Collins is the president of Blake's, a chain store operation, consisting of nine moderately priced stores located in West Virginia. He founded the stores over 25 years ago, and feels fortunate that they are still doing well. The company has been built on loyal customers and loyal employees. Collins considers his company his second family (as a matter of fact, he named the chain for his deceased wife, Blake). Most employees remain until they retire, as everyone seems to get along very well and morale is excellent. Blake's company office is in Charleston and operates with four buyers who visit the New York market four or five times a year. The exception is Rose Rockwell who handles dresses and sportswear—she is in New York every two months because her departments are the most fashion oriented. The total volume of the dress and sportswear departments is $600,000 a year (about 40 percent of the total company volume), of which dresses contributes $250,000.

Even though Rose's formal training is limited, having come up from the ranks as a salesperson, she has paid her dues and Rose is considered a dedicated, fairly knowledgeable merchandiser. Rose works with the company's New York corporate buying office sometimes, but essentially makes all the merchandising decisions herself, including what goods to buy.

Collins, although satisfied with Rose's performance, believes that the chain is not obtaining its full share of volume potential in her areas, as compared to industry figures that show women's sportswear usually bringing in about 50 percent of the total sales volume of comparable retailers. He

has never entertained the thought of replacing Rose because he is essentially a small-town man who believes in loyalty and appreciates that trait in all his employees—especially buyers. In fact, Rose is unmarried and considers her job the biggest, most important part of her life and she always puts the company first.

Collins was in New York last week and was reviewing his operation with the management staff of the corporate buying office, Associated Small Stores, Inc. In addition to Collins, Leonard Carroll, the buying office president, and Marvin Black, the buying office merchandise manager of moderately priced apparel, were present. During the meeting, Carroll—a dynamic businessman, whom Collins has worked with for a number of years—suggested that the Blake's chain switch to the buying office's unit control service as so many of their other retail groups had. This move would probably free up management for other concerns. Carroll concluded his compelling suggestion by stating, "The central operation is a way for a smaller group like your stores to save expenses. We can do all your buying so your buyers are not needed, and the fee is only two percent of net sales. You can make your buyers department managers, who then can concentrate on the stores' site business. We can almost guarantee a better business in dresses and sportswear by controlling the merchandise plans, buying, and designing ads. Above all, your stores will be stocked with all the latest, freshest merchandise in demand, because we are in the market and our buyers work the market every morning finding new resources and the latest trends."

Carroll's arguments were so powerful and logical that Collins's sense of loyalty to his employees and particularly Rose, began to waiver. He was on the verge of saying, "Okay, we'll try centralizing buying for a year," but his business acumen dictated a cautious approach. He decided to mull it over before coming to a conclusion.

He then sought out his corporate controller and trusted, long-time friend, John Slattery, a level-headed pragmatist. Collins explained his predicament to him. After listening to what had transpired, Slattery said, "The economics of the situation are probably just as presented by Associated Small Stores; we might be better off in the long run using their buying service. However, you realize that there are two negative points. One, you're going to 'destroy' Rose Rockwell who will never accept the job of department manager, like your other buyers probably will; and, two, what does a New York office really know about the local conditions in West Virginia? Having Rose where the customers are provides the advantage of her being on top of the local customers' needs and wants. She even has the opportunity to meet and talk to her customers, giving them personal attention."

Collins replied, "John, you're saying just what I've been thinking, and I'm feeling like I'm up a creek without a paddle. I'll have to give this matter some more careful consideration in weighing the pros and cons."

Major Question
If you were Lawrence Collins and these facts were presented to you, would you decide to switch to corporate centralized buying? Why or why not?

Study Questions
1. What are the advantages and disadvantages of merchandising centralization? Decentralization?

2. Should the size of a retailing operation be a factor in determining whether centralized or decentralized buying and control be used? Why or why not?

Case 46
An Overheard Conversation in the Peppermint Dress Showroom

Faye Y. Gibson, University of North Carolina

Delores Long is the divisional merchandise manager and Becky Wall is the moderate dress buyer for Bell Department Stores, a seven-store group, which is one of several store groups comprising a 300+ store conglomerate located in the Southeast. Delores and Becky were planning a buying trip to the New York market to place their annual fall purchases. Before drafting detailed market plans, Delores and Becky always followed the required management procedures. First they talked with the store managers and department managers in each store to obtain opinions concerning the merchandise mix in the department, the best-selling vendors, styles, colors, and fabrications in each store, as well as to pinpoint the high markdown subclasses and poor-selling styles.

Additionally, they requested from the department managers detailed information pertaining to customer requests, dislikes, and wanted brands not carried by the store. Next, they analyzed all computer printout information confirming the best-selling SKUs and high markdown subclasses plus vendors maintaining low and high gross margins and adequate maintained markups. Also, vendors were evaluated for timeliness of deliveries, substitution rates and return of merchandise percentages. Then Delores and Becky compiled a report of all information to discuss with Bill Carden, the general merchandise manager, and Allen Bell, the group executive vice-president, before developing the buying and assortment plans for each of the seven stores.

After evaluating the moderate dress departments in each store for the same season of the previous year and after ascertaining current selling patterns in the departments, Delores realized that the moderate dress category had a larger sales decrease and higher markdowns than previously anticipated. Many of the vendors were shipping poorly, substituting fabrications, and sending badly constructed merchandise. Others had gone bankrupt or closed their doors in mid-season. To further complicate matters, one of the store managers, Ted Youngblood, was very critical about the poor selection and quality of merchandise in his store. He even talked with Bill Carden and Allen Bell about the poor performance of his store's moderate dress department.

Allen scheduled a meeting with Delores. In the meeting, Allen requested that he and Ted review the preliminary six-month merchandise plans and assortment plans, and that he authorize the detailed market buying plans. Delores and Becky worked on the required plans for over two weeks. While working on the plans, they realized that during the third and fourth quarters they would normally cover four major promotional events. They knew that they did not have adequate open-to-buy to cover Back-to-School, Autumn, Anniversary, and Holiday promotions. After discussing the problem with Allen Bell, a decision was made to promote only the Anniversary Sale. Allen then requested that Delores and Becky review the Anniversary Sale merchandise purchased by the corporation's New York buying office's moderate dress buyer, Cindy Nipper, and to purchase additional quantities of the same merchandise as it had a higher markup than usual. Both Delores and Becky were very disappointed at the vice president's request, because this buyer's merchandise was usually not targeted to their Southeastern customer nor did it usually maintain a good sell-through percentage.

However, at the request of Bell and before leaving for market, Delores called the New York Office to schedule an appointment with Cindy Nipper and to request that Cindy's staff arrange market appointments for her group during market week.

Upon arriving in New York, Delores and Becky went directly to the buying office to meet with Cindy. Cindy was very upbeat and excited about market offerings, even though her area was very depressed and not performing well. She informed Delores and Becky that the dress market lacked trendy merchandise or newness and direction in styling and fabrication. However, she had found new resources and fantastic buys in her most recent market appointments.

Cindy announced that she would join Delores and Becky for the morning market appointments. When the group arrived at each showroom, they were greeted by smiling sales representatives who showed only the garments Cindy requested, instead of the entire dress line. If Delores or Becky inquired about other merchandise in the showroom, or, as was usual market procedure, if they requested to inspect samples and in-stock merchandise, they were told that Cindy had selected the top-selling styles with the best delivery dates and discouraged them from pursuing these requests further. The sales representatives always agreed with Cindy's opinions and told her what a fantastic job she had done working their lines for the buying office purchases.

At lunch time, Cindy excused herself and returned to the buying office. Delores and Becky arrived early at the Peppermint Dress Showroom, their next scheduled market appointment, to find that their sales representative, Henry Edwards, was unavailable. The showroom receptionist asked them to be seated and provided lunch while they waited.

Not realizing that clients were in the showroom, Henry Edwards and the president of the company, Richard Neff, were discussing their latest shipment of merchandise delivered from one of their major contractors. While eating their lunch in a corner of the showroom, Delores and Becky overheard Richard Neff tell Edwards that the dresses just delivered were not the fiber content specified nor the normal quality of the contractor and that these were the dresses that Cindy Nipper had purchased for the 300+ store conglomerate. Neff was in a quandary as to what to do, but Edwards just laughed and told him not to worry, because Cindy would not know the difference in fiber content anyway. He would be glad to call Cindy and tell her how great the dresses were that she had selected. To make matters worse, these were the dresses purchased for the Anniversary Sale; and, by instructions of Allen Bell, Delores and Becky had been told to buy additional quantities of the merchandise for the sale.

Major Question

If you were Delores or Becky what course of action would you take?

Study Questions

1. What should be the relationship between the store buyer and the buying office buyer?

2. What are the normal duties of a buying office?

Chapter Discussion Questions

1. Explain the opportunities and challenges of international sourcing. Compare and contrast it with domestic sourcing. Use case examples from this chapter to reinforce your discussion.

2. How can types of orders fulfill specific merchandise needs of retailers? Incorporate examples from the chapter cases differentiating the types with needs.

3. Compare and contrast centralized and decentralized buying. Note examples from cases that support your arguments.

4. Discuss the importance of careful research and decision-making in the selection of resources and merchandise. Explain how the customer helps retailers select their products.

5. How has exclusive private labeling altered sourcing practices of many retail chains today, for example Gap and The Limited, from traditional sourcing? Explain the advantages and disadvantages of private labels to retailers, whether they are exclusive users (e.g., Gap) or partial users (e.g., JCPenney).

6. Discuss the reasons that retail buyers search globally for the best-value merchandise.

6

Retailer/Vendor Relationships

Chapter Objectives

- Stress the importance of good retail/vendor partnerships.

- Present the reasons for negotiations between buyer and seller.

- Identify and explore major problems and resolutions between vendors and retailers.

- Distinguish between types of ordering methods.

Retailing success may be due in part to the kinds and types of relationships that a retailer has with suppliers. The building or formulation of retailer/vendor relationships is of critical concern because the type of relationship and partnership between a retailer and vendor often can make or break a business. Building an open, honest working relationship through mutual understanding, resolution of problems, communication, and partnerships, helps both realize their goals. Today, retailers look to their vendors for help in meeting or exceeding sales goals by partnering with them to build business. The smart vendor knows, of course, that if they help the retailer do well, they too will have success. In today's marketplace, new ways in which the retailer and vendor can work more efficiently are constantly being created to gain the competitive edge in meeting the consumer's satisfaction with the goods and services they desire. Speed is of primary concern in all phases of the marketing distribution channel and technology is the major force providing it—from negotiations through to order processing and delivery. Interactive links between customer, retailer, and manufacturer result in speedy delivery of the desired goods and services to the customer, which also helps ensure an effective, positive working relationship between retailer and vendor.

Vendor Partnerships

Effective working relationships between a retailer and resource are often the result of a partnership. A **partnership** is a working relationship that is formed to achieve a mutually beneficial goal. Today, even vendor and retail planning is often part of a partner relationship, because managing merchandise is no longer just the retailer's job. The supplier and retailer can no longer afford to work independently but must partner for success. Many manufacturers (for example, Levi Strauss) invest in and use leading technology that benefits not only their business, but their retail accounts. Many vendors today take the leading role in training and/or supplying retail sales help, as well as instore merchandising support. This is done in an effort to ensure that the vendor's merchandise is presented in the manner in which it was intended. A vendor may also supply support fixturing and signage for their goods to help present their merchandise.

Hard work, time, and energy is needed to build solid, open, and mutually beneficial relationships between retail companies and their vendor representatives. Sometimes, however, problems create the need for reworking an established relationship. The next section examines some of the circumstances involved that can create conflicts between retailers and vendors.

Causes of Partnership Conflicts

There are a number of difficulties that can arise between manufacturers and retailers that must be resolved to continue working together effectively. A 1996 *DNR* survey reported that about 64 percent of the manufacturers who responded believe that current supplier/retailer problems are the result of changing market conditions and suppliers are equally at fault with retailers. A majority of retailers (51 percent) believe that the major cause of troubles between the two are due to retail consolidations. Some of the most common specific causes of conflicts between retailers and vendors are:

- Cancellation of merchandise by the retailer.

- Substitution of merchandise by the vendor.

- Merchandise returns and adjustments.

- Delivery and transportation.

- Exclusivity.

- Special orders, reorders, and minimum orders.

- Discounts and allowances.

- Unreasonable conduct and dishonesty.

The following is a brief examination of each of these critical, problem areas.

Problems can occur when merchandise orders are canceled (i.e., not accepted) by the retailer or when substituted merchandise is shipped by the resource. This is particularly true if the action (i.e., cancellation or substitution) is taken without informing the other party. For example, a vendor with an almost too-good-to-be-true product disappears between the placement of an order and the delivery of the goods, leaving a buyer without promotional merchandise in *Case 50, The Source that Didn't Supply*.

Sometimes unauthorized **returns to vendor** (**RTV**) on the part of a retailer create difficulties between a resource and the retailer. These returns may be due to not liking the merchandise or inherent problems (e.g., poor quality) in the product; following proper procedures, however, might prevent bad feelings. **Adjustments** to the cost of goods may also be requested and sought by the retailer, because of problems with the merchandise or because the items were returned. This can also create ill will if retailers do not go through the proper procedures to remedy the situation or if vendors do not fulfil their end of the bargain.

Delivery of the goods from the manufacturer to retailer may be another source of difficulty and conflicts, if communication is unclear or incorrect delivery information is given (e.g., wrong delivery dates, the method of transportation, late shipments, and so forth). Specific and clear instructions should be stated upfront, in order to lessen the chance or type of error and the resultant problems in delivery and/or transportation.

As discussed in Chapter Five, exclusivity of merchandise or territory may be requested and promised to a retailer but not delivered by the vendor, which in turn angers and upsets the retailer. Exclusivity is under consideration in two cases in which negotiations need to be conducted. In *Case 48, Tying One On*, a retailer must determine the best action to take after being pressured by a resource to either accept a cost increase—and subsequently raise the retail price—or lose merchandise exclusivity. In *Case 49, Exasperations with Exclusivity*, a vendor has to decide whether or

RTV REASON CODES

REASON: Three letter code identifying the reason the merchandise is being returned to the vendor **AND who pays the freight charges outbound**.

Reason	Description	Frt. Out/HC Responsibility	Frt.-in* Respons.
DAM	Damaged Merchandise	VENDOR	VENDOR
WRG	Wrong Merchandise	VENDOR	VENDOR
NOR	Not Ordered	VENDOR	VENDOR
CAN	Order Cancelled	VENDOR	VENDOR
LAT	Received Late	VENDOR	VENDOR
AGV	Agreement—vendor pay	VENDOR	N/A
AGS	Agreement—store pay	STORE	N/A
SMV	Sample—vendor pay	VENDOR	N/A
SMS	Sample—store pay	STORE	N/A
JBV	Job Out—vendor pay	VENDOR	N/A
JBS	Job Out—store pay	STORE	N/A

*Freight In will be charged back to the vendor ONLY if the store payed the original inbound freight.

Figure 6.1 A department store's RTV reasons codes. Many times, unauthorized returns to vendors cause difficulties between retailers and vendors. A list such as this can help both the vendor and the retailer follow the proper procedures, thus avoiding problems in the vendor/retailer relationship.

not to sell to a retailer's competitor, which will result in the retail account losing exclusivity of the vendor and the possibility that the vendor may also lose the retail account.

Special orders (those that are placed with a vendor generally for a specific customer), reorders (an order that has been placed previously), and **minimum orders** (a specific amount of merchandise that must be placed) are other situations that can cause relationship conflicts. For example, if a vendor cannot fill special orders or reorders when it has been previously stated that they can, unhappy retailers and their unsatisfied customers result. A reorder cancellation creates a difficult situation for

a manufacturer who had already produced goods for a retailer in *Case 51, Plant a Seed: A Lack of Leeway Inventory*. Additionally, **discounts and allowances,** which are price concessions given by the vendor to the retailer in return for certain actions that the retailer is taking and which may not be what was originally arranged. When an invoice arrives at the retailer and there is a discrepancy or variation to an agreed-upon discount or allowance, it can create conflict and distrust between a vendor and a retail account.

Unreasonable conduct and dishonesty on the part of either party can also be a major problem or can build tension between the people involved in a transaction. Retailer/vendor partnerships must rely on trust and honesty in order to be a successful alliance.

All of the matters discussed (i.e., cancellation and substitution of merchandise, merchandise returns and adjustments, delivery and transportation problems, exclusivity, special orders, reorders, minimum orders, discounts and allowances) could be initially negotiated to arrive at what both the buyer and the vendor want or they could be issues that can create conflicts and then will need to be resolved through further negotiations.

Negotiations

A partnership is often dependent on **negotiations** because the parties involved may not be seeking the exact same outcome and are looking out for their own best interests. Negotiations can result in a settlement and mutual agreement between two or more parties on any matter. This settlement is based on communication and the satisfaction of a goal of one or more of the parties. From a retailer's or manufacturer's perspective, negotiations are often undertaken to solve problems, resolve conflicts, reduce costs, and/or improve profit. The means to do this, however, are numerous. Often a compromise is realized when negotiations occur and the "best" (i.e., the most workable, most equitable) settlement is worked out.

A retailer negotiates with many people for various reasons. Negotiations might be undertaken with a vendor for a certain delivery or cost. A retailing manager might negotiate with sales employees of the company to increase sales. Knowing when and what to negotiate—as well as how—ensures successful negotiations. Negotiating for what is desired may begin a good working relationship, help a failing alliance, or even salvage an association that is not beneficial to one or both parties. Being an effective negotiator is often a learned skill that takes years of practice and listening. See Table 6.1 for nine techniques of successful vendor negotiations.

Some matters that are frequently negotiated between the retailer and resource in an effort to help improve the retailer's bottom line are:

Table 6.1   Nine Techniques of Successful Vendor Negotiations

1. *Act Collaboratively, Not Competitively.* Negotiation is not "me against you." Recognize that the other party has to come away with a benefit, too. Show them how giving you what you want will help them get what they want.

2. *Prepare.* Do your homework about the other party; gather as much information about them as possible. Even rehearse and outline your remarks.

3. *Know What You Want.* Being able to state specific proposals or plans gives you strength. Don't wait to "see what they offer us." Know in advance what you must have, and what you can afford to give up. Each time you make a concession, get something in return.

4. *Don't Let Your Ego Get in the Way.* When you think of the negotiating process as winning or losing, you have too much ego involved. Don't get sidetracked by personalities or emotions. Stick to the issues.

5. *Learn to Make Time Your Ally.* Time is at the heart of every negotiation. Learn to make it work for you. Try to learn the other party's deadline without giving away yours. Most concessions occur at somebody's deadline.

6. *If You Can't Agree on Point One, Go to Point Two.* Agree even in small increments. Don't get hung up on one issue. It is easier to come back to an issue after you have reached some agreement, and the other person has invested time and energy in working with you.

7. *Be a Creative Risktaker.* If you are known to not take risks, you are predictable and can be easily manipulated. Create your own solutions; there is usually more than one way to get the results you want.

8. *Closing the Negotiation: Wrap it Up.* Don't stay around and chat after you have reached an agreement. If you have what you want, close the negotiation. Don't linger too long, or it may unravel.

9. *Develop Long-term Relationships.* Focusing on long-term goals will keep both parties from being sidetracked by short-term frustrations. Knowing you are both in for the long haul means you can solve any problem that arises.

Prepared by Elizabeth Tahir, former retailing executive, now president of Liz Tahir Consulting, a retail marketing and management consulting and training firm in New Orleans, Louisiana.

- Obtaining specific merchandise (for promotions or other specific needs).

- Extra markup or markdown money (to help with profitability).

- Transportation and delivery charges (to reduce costs).

- Cooperative advertising (for media costs or instore promotions).

- **Terms of sale** (conditions in a purchase agreement between retailer and vendor that include discounts, delivery, and transportation costs).

- **Dating** (a predetermined amount of time during which discounts can be taken and the invoice is to be paid; for example, 8/10 EOM means the retailers can take an eight percent discount if the invoice is paid by the 10th day of the month).

Additionally, other sales, marketing, and merchandising needs are negotiated when necessary.

In *Case 47, Negotiating the Coat Closeout Purchase,* rock-bottom prices are thought to have been obtained by a group of stores and their buying office, yet the divisional merchandise manager discovers that the quoted cost prices are higher than the initial order in season. Sometimes personal and professional behavior causes problems between vendors and retailers. A buying decision has to be made by a buyer in *Case 52, Is the Product Worth the Rep?* because of the pressure being exerted on the buyer by the rep, as well as the rep's rude behavior. At other times, ethics come into play as in *Cases 47, 50,* and *52.* (Also see Chapter Twelve, *Ethical and Legal Behavior in Retail Management.*)

Negotiations can occur between the retailer and resource, but often specifically between a manufacturer's representative and the retailer's representative.

Sales Representatives

A **sales representative** is an individual who represents a manufacturer's product. Often, sales representatives are the major link between the retailer and the manufacturer. Sales representatives can provide invaluable information to the

Figure 6.2 A sales rep showing a line of clothing to retail buyers. Often, a manufacturer's representative will negotiate the terms of sale with buyers.

retailer, in the same way that retailers can help relay information about their customers to the manufacturer through the sales rep.

The type of vendor and the sales representative determines the type of partnership that exists between the retailer and resource. An **independent rep** may be under contract to a specific company as their sales agent, but may also represent other firms. Arnold Helman, for example, represents many major dress manufacturers as shown in Figure 6.3. **Company reps** or **corporate reps** are those persons who work exclusively for a supplier and are company employees. There are fewer and fewer independent reps today par-

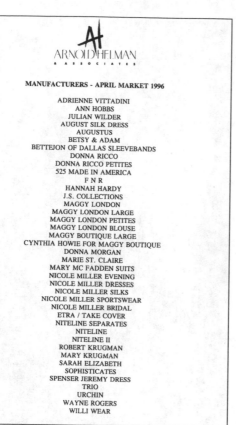

ARNOLD HELMAN
& ASSOCIATES

MANUFACTURERS - APRIL MARKET 1996

ADRIENNE VITTADINI
ANN HOBBS
JULIAN WILDER
AUGUST SILK DRESS
AUGUSTUS
BETSY & ADAM
BETTEJON OF DALLAS SLEEVEBANDS
DONNA RICCO
DONNA RICCO PETITES
525 MADE IN AMERICA
F N R
HANNAH HARDY
J.S. COLLECTIONS
MAGGY LONDON
MAGGY LONDON LARGE
MAGGY LONDON PETITES
MAGGY LONDON BLOUSE
MAGGY BOUTIQUE LARGE
CYNTHIA HOWIE FOR MAGGY BOUTIQUE
DONNA MORGAN
MARIE ST. CLAIRE
MARY MC FADDEN SUITS
NICOLE MILLER EVENING
NICOLE MILLER DRESSES
NICOLE MILLER SILKS
NICOLE MILLER SPORTSWEAR
NICOLE MILLER BRIDAL
ETRA / TAKE COVER
NITELINE SEPARATES
NITELINE
NITELINE II
ROBERT KRUGMAN
MARY KRUGMAN
SARAH ELIZABETH
SOPHISTICATES
SPENSER JEREMY DRESS
TRIO
URCHIN
WAYNE ROGERS
WILLI WEAR

Figure 6.3 A list of the merchandise lines carried by Arnold Helman & Associates, an independent sales representative company.

tially because of the merging of retailing operations into mega-corporations. These giant corporations (e.g., Federated, Dayton Hudson) are now becoming major accounts to many suppliers. Major accounts often work corporately with the principals of the suppliers, rather than through a sales representative because they are such an important part of the resource's business. For example, Wal-Mart made a major change away from dealing with reps to only working with the principals of their suppliers, which, of course, angered many reps. Even the numbers of corporate reps have diminished within some resources because of this trend.

After the buyer (or other authorized retail representative) determines what to buy, from whom, and has negotiated the conditions and terms of the sale, the order is placed. A **purchase order** (**PO**) is the legal contract that binds the buyer and seller. All pertinent information that must be relayed between the two parties for the purchasing of merchandise should be contained on this document, as shown on the example in Figure 6.4. A purchase order ensures that what the retailer wants is being requested and it also verifies any special requests that have been negotiated.

As discussed in Chapter Five, the type of merchandise and/or vendor helps to determine the type of order that is placed. This—the method of ordering—is an issue that needs to be addressed by both the buyer and seller, and is dependent on their relationship and partnership. Additional ordering methods (other than regular or **standard orders**) that a merchant can use to ensure that needs are met are:

• **Open orders,** which allow a manufacturer the discretion of shipping merchandise when deemed necessary, rather than locking into a set delivery date. Open orders may also specify a dollar amount that must be purchased, but not always the specific styles, sizes, or colors.

• **Advance orders,** which commit the retailer to a long-term delivery because of the nature of the merchandise or the needs of the retailer. Often imported goods and seasonal merchandise require advance orders.

• **Back orders,** which are full or partial orders that are still outstanding (i.e., not shipped) by the manufacturer, but will be completed when the merchandise (or the balance of the merchandise) is available.

• **Blanket orders,** which are those that do not have specific information spelled out, but which commit the retailer to a certain number of units or dollars that will be detailed at a later date.

Open, advance, and blanket orders are methods of placing forecasted orders in advance to help ensure availability and timely delivery of the merchandise the retailer desires by committing to merchandise ahead of need.

DATE SHIPPED	TO BE SHIPPED FROM	DELIVERY DUE	F.O.B.	FREIGHT ALLOWED	TERMS
				Charges on shipments bought FOB New York or our premises must be prepaid	Dating Is From Date of Receipt of Goods

CLASS.	HOUSE # STYLE # LOT #	DESCRIPTION	1	2	3	4	5	6	7	8	9	QUAN.	UNIT COST	TOTAL COST	UNIT RETAIL	TOTAL RETAIL

TOTAL

M.U.%

THIS ORDER IS PLACED SUBJECT TO CONDITIONS ON BOTH SIDES

Signed _____ DEPT. MANAGER

Countersigned _____ MDSE. MANAGER

Date _____ 19 _____

Figure 6.4 An example of a purchase order form. Note that the copy on the back of this particular form is very explicit in spelling out all the instructions, shipping terms, and general terms that are acceptable to the retailer. Many times, these terms, if not followed, can cause problems between a vendor and a retailer. (See next page for back of form.)

SHIPPING TERMS AND INSTRUCTIONS (ANY DEVIATIONS AT VENDOR'S RISK AND EXPENSE).

1. Follow all routing instructions. Note routing guide referred to on face of order.
2. An unextended packing list must accompany each shipment (showing breakdown of color and size where applicable).
3. Risk of loss or damage in transit to PARCEL POST shipments shall be upon the Vendor, notwithstanding who pays shipping costs.
4. Do not ship before or after dates on face of order. Violation of this requirement will subject Vendor to (a) storage and handling charges of 5% of the gross value of the invoice or (b) merchandise will be returned to Vendor with charge-back of inbound and outbound transportation and handling charges incurred by J & Y.

The following applies where Purchaser pays transportation charges in absence of different instructions in Routing Guide:

5. If there is sufficient volume available and freight charges will be less, ship as carload or truckload.
6. Two or more shipments being forwarded to the same delivery point on the same day must be combined and shipped on the single bill of lading irrespective of departmental variance.
7. Merchandise must be packed, shipped and described on bills of lading in accordance with applicable freight tariffs. Differently rated commodities must be in separate containers and be separately described on the bill of lading.
8. In absence of contrary instructions, do not insure shipments, and do not declare value on express shipments for benefit of J & Y.

GENERAL TERMS

1. Vendor warrants and represents that it has the right to sell the merchandise purchased hereunder and agrees to indemnify and save the Purchaser harmless from and against any and all suits, actions, claims or demands that may be brought against Purchaser and from and against all liability, loss, damages, costs and expenses, including attorney's fees, incurred by Purchaser by reason thereof, on the grounds that the purchase or sale of any of the merchandise covered by this order constitutes unfair competition or infringement of patent, copyright or trademark or an invasion of the rights of any person or corporation, and Vendor further agrees at its own cost and expense to defend, upon the request of Purchaser, any such suits, action, claims and demands.
2. In addition to the warranties set forth in Sections 2-312 (1) and (3), Section 2-313 (1), Section 2-314 of the Uniform Commercial Code, Vendor warrants that the goods are fit for the purpose of retail sale, and Vendor represents that it is a merchant with respect to the merchandise, and that no express or implied warranties have been excluded by examination of the goods or otherwise.
3. All electrical appliances and devices must comply with the requirements and bear the seal of Underwriters' Laboratories, Inc.
4. The time stated for delivery hereunder is of the essence hereof.
5. Purchaser reserves the right to cancel this order if the terms and conditions hereof are not fully complied with. Purchaser further reserves the right to refuse any merchandise and to cancel all or any part of this order if Vendor fails to deliver all or any part of the merchandise in accordance with the terms of this order. Acceptance of any part of the order shall not bind Purchaser to accept future shipments, nor deprive it of the right to return merchandise already accepted. Payment of all or any part of the purchase price shall not be construed as a waiver of any claims of the Purchaser for defects or delay in delivery or for breach of the contract, and any and all such claims shall survive payment.
6. Vendor represents that the merchandise covered by this order has been manufactured and labeled in accordance with the requirements of all applicable Federal, State and Municipal laws, rules and regulations, including but not limited to the Fair Labor Standards Act, the Wool Products Labeling Act, the Fur Products Labeling Act, the Textile Fiber Products Identification Act, the Flammable Fabrics Act, the Federal Hazardous Substance Labeling Act, and the Federal Food, Drug and Cosmetic Act. Vendor's invoice shall bear the separate guarantees provided for under any of such acts or shall contain the appropriate statement that a continuing guarantee has been filed in accordance with such acts and applicable rules and regulations of the Federal Trade Commission and other governmental agencies with jurisdiction in the premises.
7. Vendor agrees to deliver the merchandise at prices stated herein or at ceiling or prevailing price at the time of delivery, whichever is lower, and Vendor warrants that no other purchaser from Vendor is receiving more favorable terms than J & Y.
8. Purchaser's failure to insist in any one or more instances upon the strict or timely performance of any of the terms, provisions or conditions of this instrument shall not be considered as a waiver or a relinquishment in the future of the requirements of such terms, provisions and conditions, or of Purchaser's rights based upon Vendor's failure to perform any of such terms, provisions or conditions, but the same shall continue in full force and effect. This Agreement may not be modified or terminated orally, and no modification or termination nor any claimed waiver of any of the provisions hereof shall be binding unless in writing and signed by the party against whom such modifications, termination or waiver is sought to be enforced. ADDITIONAL OR DIFFERENT TERMS IN ANY INVOICE OR OTHER DOCUMENT ISSUED BY VENDOR SHALL NOT BE BINDING ON PURCHASER.
9. All costs incurred by Purchaser because of non-compliance with the terms and conditions of this order (including Shipping and Billing Instructions) will be charged to Vendor.
10. By signing a copy of this order or making any shipments, Vendor shall be deemed to have accepted this order. FAILURE OF VENDOR TO GIVE NOTICE OR REJECTION WITHIN REASONABLE TIME SHALL CONSTITUTE ACCEPTANCE OF THIS ORDER.
11. INDEMNITY AND INSURANCE

    Vendor shall protect, defend, indemnify and save Purchaser harmless against any and all claims, demands or causes of action of every nature whatsoever arising in favor of any person, including both Vendor's and Purchaser's employees on account of personal injuries or death or damages to property occurring, growing out of, incident to, or resulting directly or indirectly from the performance by Vendor hereunder, whether such loss, damage, injury or liability is contributed to by the negligence of the Purchaser or its employees, or by the premises themselves or any equipment thereon whether latent or patent, or from other causes whatsoever, except that the Vendor shall have no liability for damages or costs incident thereto caused by the sole negligence of Purchaser.

    Vendor agrees to obtain and maintain, at its expense, a policy or policies of products liability insurance, with a limit of liability of not less than One Million Dollars, and with broad form Vendor's endorsement naming Purchaser, in such companies and containing such other provisions which shall be satisfactory to Purchaser covering merchandise sold to Purchaser hereunder. All such policies shall provide that the coverage thereunder shall not be terminated without at least thirty (30) days prior written notice to Purchaser. Vendor agrees to promptly supply Purchaser with evidence satisfactory to Purchaser, upon demand by Purchaser, of the existence of said aforementioned policy or policies.

Summary

Building positive relationships between retailers and vendors takes time, energy, openness, and honesty; however, the benefits result in more business success for both. The possible difficulties a retailer and resource may encounter are numerous today due to many factors, but particularly the complexity of business and the interactive nature of the marketing channel. Resolving the problems mutually may depend on partnerships between the parties involved. In some instances negotiations may be necessary to settle a matter of concern and aid in ensuring that the benefits desired are achieved.

References

Berman, B., & Evans, J.R. (1995). *Retailing management: A strategic approach.* Englewood Cliffs, N.J.: Prentice-Hall.

Biesel, J.H. (1993). *Contemporary retailing.* New York: Macmillan.

Morgenstein, M., & Strongin, H. (1992). *Modern retailing: Management principles and practices.* Englewood Cliffs, N.J.: Prentice-Hall.

Schneiderman, I. (1996, May 27). Vendors view retail relationships. *DNR*, pp. 2–3.

Key Terms

adjustments	negotiations
advance orders	open orders
back orders	partnership
blanket orders	purchase order (PO)
company rep	returns to vendors (RTV)
corporate rep	sales representative
dating	special orders
discounts and allowances	standard orders
independent rep	terms of sale
minimum orders	

Case 47
Negotiating the Coat Closeout Purchase

Faye Y. Gibson, University of North Carolina

The Bell Department Store Group, which is one of several store groups comprising a 300+ store conglomerate in the Southeast, always plans a market trip to New York in early November. This trip is planned to search the market and to purchase the best price/value coat closeouts in the industry. This particular store-group is recognized by both its competition and its New York private buying office for locating a wide assortment of merchandise in the market, for developing shrewd merchandising techniques, and for maintaining a large sales volume plus excellent gross margin in the coat category. In fact, the divisional merchandise manager, Kavonna Davis, had been appointed to buying office committees to select merchandise for company-wide special promotions, and three of the five stores had received awards for outstanding sales in the "Coat Classification." Additionally, Bill Carden, the general merchandise manager of the group, prides himself on being the best negotiator of closeout coat prices in the entire organization.

On this particular annual closeout trip, Kavonna, Bill, and the coat buyers (Jennifer Berke and Amelia Lopez) visited the New York buying office to discuss market conditions, the best vendors, and current sales trends with Pearl Wall, the buying office buyer. The New York buying office buyers are responsible for advising all stores in the selection of their merchandise mix and establishment of price points. They are also responsible for planning sales promotions, developing special events and the supporting advertisements for these events, and providing training seminars for the store buyers. Therefore, Allen Bell, the executive vice president of the Bell Department Store Group, always insists that the buying office be contacted on each buying trip and to also be notified of all market orders placed by the Bell Group.

After reviewing the vendor matrix—a listing of approved key vendors recommended by the New York buying office—and discussing available closeout offerings in the market, the group decided to visit Wellmade Coat, the top sales volume coat house for Bell Department Stores. There are very few moderate-price, high-quality, domestic coat vendors who could supply a substantial quantity of closeouts for immediate delivery, so Bill requested that the store group purchase a substantial package of goods. Consequently, one-quarter of the group's initial open-to-buy was allocated to Wellmade. Bill also requested that the sales promotional events and advertisements be planned while in the New York showroom.

Upon arriving at this well-respected Seventh Avenue coat house, the group was greeted by its regular sales representative, Howell Buntington, who always promises the group the "lowest" prices in the market. At times, Howell has even gone into the president's office to obtain permission to sell a particular fabrication to the group at a lower-than-established market cost.

After reviewing the closeout line and "cherry picking" the most appropriate styles, colors, and fabrications, Bill negotiated with Howell for what he considered to be rock-bottom prices. Many of the styles were identical or similar to coats purchased initially at the beginning of the season and the stores had a good track record with this merchandise, which sold well even at regular prices. Howell invited Wellmade's president, Martin Gordon, to come into the showroom to meet the group and to assure Bill that no one in the market had received these same low prices on this particular merchandise. However, the group must leave "paper" (i.e., place a detailed order before leaving) because there was a limited quantity of the coats. Upon hearing of the limited availability, Bill requested that the store buyers write the orders immediately. He then made it known that he was off to visit the Adorn Coat showroom, which was

located in an adjacent building, and that he planned to negotiate an additional coat closeout purchase there.

After working in the Wellmade showroom for over two hours and while assisting the buyers in calculating orders, planning markups, and developing advertisements, Kavonna reviewed copies of previous orders and realized that Howell had quoted higher cost prices ($1.00 to $3.00 per coat) for the closeouts than for the initial, beginning-of-the-season orders on the same coats. To further complicate matters, the group had not developed a detailed market plan to establish total cost dollars to be spent, total quantities to be bought, or expected markups and gross margins to be acheived to meet planned company goals. Thus, Kavonna was very coy and asked Jennifer and Amelia to give her the orders. She then told Howell that she would not leave paper immediately. Howell became very upset, as did the president of the company, but Kavonna insisted that she had to confer with Bill again because she was missing some essential information. She then left, but felt that she would have a great deal of explaining to do because she went directly against Bill's orders.

Major Question
If you were Kavonna, what course of action would you have taken in regard to Bill Carden's orders for her to leave a detailed order in the showroom before leaving? How would you present your findings of the cost-price discrepency?

Study Questions
1. What business ethics should be considered or questioned when analyzing the negotiation process?

2. Would you continue to do business with this vendor? Why or why not?

3. What preplanning is necessary for a successful market trip, and who should be responsible for this preplanning?

Case 48
Tying One On

Judy K. Miler, University of Tennessee
Nancy J. Rabolt, San Francisco State University

Kendall's Department Store is located in Memphis, Tennessee and caters to an upper-middle income clientele. In all the departments, and particularly in the ones dealing with fashion merchandise, the buyers are under constant orders from the general merchandise manager, and especially from their divisional merchandise managers, to be on the lookout for highly original, exclusive merchandise. Alexander Henley, the general merchandise manager, has made it a practice to have all such merchandise privately labeled either as *Made Exclusively for Kendall's* or *Designed Exclusively for Kendall's*.

One of Henley's favorite departments is the men's furnishings department (he is a big customer at 40 percent off). Even though Kenneth Mackay is the divisional merchandise manager for men's and boys' wear, Henley himself keeps a close eye on many of the merchandise segments in the men's furnishings department because of his own personal shopping preferences. Henley is forever sending Francine Woods—the men's furnishings buyer—memos, clippings, and ads, all intended to prod Francine into investigating and buying new lines or styles. It is an awkward situation for both Kenneth and Francine, but one that they tolerate with good humor.

One of Henley's chief contributions to the men's furnishings department is his encouragement and approval of buying from relatively unknown designers—especially men's ties. These designers are usually young and ambitious and they generally do well with Kendall's. Probably the best-selling designer of ties in this *Designed Exclusively for Kendall's* merchandise is Theo Moore. Henley is one of the most avid collectors of Moore's highly original tie designs.

When Moore began to sell exclusively to Kendall's, the store was charged $25 per tie, which was retailed for $50. As Moore's ties became more popular, his price was raised by $3 each and Kendall's passed on this increase to their customers, who did not seem to mind paying higher prices for these one-of-a-kind tie creations. By the end of Moore's second year with Kendall's (after yet another cost-price increase), customers were paying $60 per tie.

Now, halfway into his third year as an exclusive Kendall's designer-resource, Moore is getting restive, and a bit demanding, and is now commanding $35 (cost-price) for the ties, which are still selling quite well at $70 each. Moore recently has had offers to sell his ties to Kendall's competitors under his own name (as opposed to the *Designed Exclusively for Kendall's* label). This would help him gain name recognition and obtain a wider, healthier distribution for increased volume.

After Moore had received the third offer to sell his ties to another store, Theo arranged for a meeting with Francine. At this meeting, Theo laid his cards on the table and told Francine that the alternative to going to another store (i.e., staying with Kendall's) would be another substantial increase in the cost-price to make up for the lost potential volume. He then told Francine that he would be asking $40 per tie. This would translate into $80 per tie for Kendall's customers.

Francine considers Theo's merchandise valuable both to the store and to her department, but wonders if another price increase—and a substantial one at that—will cause Moore's customers to shy away from buying more ties. Either losing Moore or sharing him with another retailer—the other alternative—is not an appealing idea to Francine.

Major Question
If you were Francine Woods, how would you resolve this with Theo Moore?

1. Discuss some instances of negotiations that you think should result in compromise between a retailer and vendor. What instances do you think would not result in compromise?

2. Do you think maintaining retail price levels is important to maintaining customers? Why or why not?

Case 49
Exasperations with Exclusivity

Judy K. Miler, University of Tennessee
Nancy J. Rabolt, San Francisco State University

The Seasonless Store is located in Kennebunk, Maine and prides itself on the better merchandise that it carries for an affluent clientele. While the store's name indicates merchandise of a nonseasonal nature, The Seasonless is a specialty store with the emphasis on fashion merchandise that can be worn all year long. Like many specialty stores, there is at least one outstanding merchandising area for which it is widely known—in this case, the dress department. Oscar Shepherd is the well-respected divisional merchandise manager of the misses and women's departments and has been with The Seasonless for over 25 years. Sybil Duncan is the women's dress buyer and is also highly regarded.

One of the women's dress department's key resources is the Dixie Dress Company. Dixie has showrooms in New York City, Atlanta, and Los Angeles and a magnificent, new manufacturing facility in Flatrock, North Carolina. Sybil brought the Dixie Dress line with her when she came to The Seasonless from her last position in Chicago. She has close ties to Dixie Dress and its sales manager, Garret Evans, because they are both from the same town in Georgia. Sybil felt that Dixie Dress

shipped a very well-made garment that was styled particularly well for the larger, more matronly woman. Evans had agreed at the beginning of the relationship with The Seasonless that Sybil's department would be the exclusive distributors for Dixie Dress in her trading area. In return for this exclusivity, The Seasonless invested a large portion of its advertising space and money over the three years that Dixie Dresses had been featured. Sales, also, had come along splendidly after Kennebunk and the surrounding area's customers (including day-trippers from Portland) began to appreciate the fine fabrics, well-fitting designs, and excellent finishing details of Dixie dresses. Sybil's annual volume with Dixie had increased to well over 1500 dresses with an average cost of $95, which translated to almost $300,000 at retail for The Seasonless. As a result, Dixie Dress now accounted for a sizable portion of the women's dress department's volume.

This ideal arrangement came to a grinding halt one day when Ike Plunkett, the sales representative for Dixie Dresses, called from Portland and asked to meet with Oscar and Sybil. Actually, Garrett Evans should have called for this meeting, but his personal ties to Sybil embarrassed this courtly southern gentleman. Hence, Plunkett drew the "dirty work" assignment.

In essence, Plunkett brought this message from the Dixie Dress management:

• Dixie Dress needs more sales volume. The firm is in an expansion cycle and it was looking for more outlets for its merchandise and more cash flow.

• Dixie Dress is approaching stores they had refused to sell to before because of their previous policy of granting exclusivity to the best store in a trading area.

In The Seasonless's trading area, Woodward's Department Store has long sought to buy some of Dixie's lower-priced lines but had never succeeded. Woodward's was a full-fledged department store with highly promotional merchandising policies. At times, its ads give the impression that it is a discount organization. While The Seasonless's emphasis is on quality and service, Woodward's image, as reflected by its ads and other communications, shouts "PRICE!"

Oscar was livid. "You mean to tell me, after all this time, effort, and money, you want us to share your merchandise with that 'cheap' store?"

Uncomfortably, Ike Plunkett pointed out, "Mr. Shepherd, we have definite assurances that with their overall sales volume, we can more than double our sales in this area."

"Do you know what this will do to The Seasonless's customers?" Sybil asked. "The status associated with the dresses will most certainly be lowered."

Plunkett assured her that this would not happen because each store would have exclusive rights to certain styles that would be confined to that store. Additionally, there would be less chance of conflict because Woodward's price zones would confine its buyers to those numbers that The Seasonless never bought anyway.

"Have you ever seen Woodward's ads?" Oscar queried. "They scream PRICE, PRICE, PRICE! They frequently cut prices at the slightest pretext. With a nationally known name like Dixie Dress, they will damage your reputation as an upscale manufacturer."

Both Oscar and Sybil continued to argue, plead, and cajole, but it soon became apparent that Ike Plunkett was only the "messenger" who was there to deliver the message from Garrett Evans.

Major Question

What should The Seasonless Store do in regard to the decision by Dixie Dress to sell merchandise to one of their competitors?

Study Questions

1. Discuss the reasons why a retailer would want exclusivity from a vendor. Are there any reasons to not want such an exclusive arrangement with a manufacturer?

2. What might be negotiated by a retailer for obtaining exclusivity of a brand?

Case 50
The Source that Didn't Supply

Doris Kincade and Cynthia L. Regan, Virginia Polytechnic Institute and State University

Dorilee Mason has worked as an assistant buyer for the men's casual shirt department for one year at the Huntington Department Store. Many of Dorilee's fellow trainees have had more buying responsibilities than she had. However, all trainees knew that Mark Castleton, the men's casual shirt buyer, was a challenging and difficult boss to work for. Dorilee felt that she had learned well by following in Mark's footsteps.

The men's casual shirt stock assortment has a high percentage of foreign-sourced, private-label goods. Mark, who is responsible for buying all of the casual shirt stock, was known in the industry as being a tough, but fair negotiator when he dealt with shirt vendors. Dorilee's responsibilities include analyzing the markup reports, talking to the sales representatives to troubleshoot problems with merchandise delivery, and proofreading advertisements for the department.

Mark has emphasized to Dorilee the importance of attaining a big markup. She knew from reading the markup reports that last year's average cumulative markups for the men's casual shirt department were 35 percent for domestic goods and 45 percent for foreign goods. Business has not been strong for the last six months, and Mark has authorized a number of markdowns to get merchandise moving. A review of the men's casual shirt markup report for the last six months shows that the department's average cumulative markup was down to 30 percent.

In a conference, Mark told Dorilee that he was pleased with her overall performance, even through the retail business was tough right now. He wanted to give her the responsibility of buying one of the shirt classifications—men's T-shirts. Dorilee was very excited at her first real "buying" responsibility and silently vowed to work hard to make buying the men's T-shirt classification successful.

Mark travelled to the New York market in Spring and would be out of the office for a week. He gave Dorilee strict orders to find some T-shirt merchandise for the annual Father's Day Sale. He emphasized that the T-shirts be a good buy, have a low wholesale price, and have a potential for larger than usual markups. This way they could potentially increase the department's depressed average markup.

Dorilee decided that she would call the domestic vendors from which Mark had previously purchased and a few new foreign source vendors to come into the buying office to show her their T-shirt lines. Spending two days reviewing the seasonal lines, Dorilee realized that there was only one way to get exciting merchandise at a low cost—buy from the importers! Dorilee had surmised, after reviewing the markup reports, the lower the price—the better! The Indigo Shirt Company had a new sales representative, a real charmer, who told Dorilee that his products were wonderful because they came from such exotic countries as Macao and Sri Lanka. Dorilee had never been to Macao or Sri Lanka, but she felt that the more exotic or foreign sounding a country was, it was a sure sign that the price was right, and the rep promised that his T-shirts had high quality construction and materials. Dorilee was sure that she could get a 65 percent markup on the T-shirts so she ordered 500 for the Father's Day Sale. She was sure that Mark would be happy with her performance. Instead, when Mark came back from New York, he was quite irritated that Dorilee had not purchased from his regular vendor. He said he meant it when he gave her the responsibility for the classification, but would be watching her performance very closely. Dorilee started to become nervous. "Maybe I should have bought from the domestic supplier," she thought, "but then again, those T-shirts usually only brought in a 40 percent average markup." Dorilee decided she had made the right decision.

The T-shirts were going to be advertised in Huntington Department Store's Sale Flyer, and when the T-shirt photo samples first came into the buying office, Mark said that the T-shirts appeared to be as good as the brand they usually bought. Dorilee proofread the newspaper advertisement and the catalog flyer and thought everything was going smoothly.

The T-shirts were to arrive ten days before the Father's Day Sale. As that day approached, Dorilee went to review the Daily Merchandise Release Report that indicates which merchandise has been received into the distribution center and released to the branch stores. The vendor for the T-shirt merchandise was not listed. Dorilee thought that maybe they were only one or two days late. The advertisement didn't break for a few days. As the week progressed, however, Dorilee became very anxious and she checked the reports daily and still the T-shirt shipment was not on the daily merchandise release. Dorilee called the distribution center just to make sure it wasn't being held up there. The distribution center manager told her that her shipment had not arrived. When Father's Day was only three days away, Mark demanded that Dorilee find those T-shirts. Dorilee pulled out her purchase order and the sales rep's telephone number. As she dialed the phone number, she thought about the smiling salesman and wondered what would be his excuse for the late shipment. "Fire in the warehouse, ship was lost at sea." Dorilee realized she had been staring into space and the phone was ringing and ringing. She thought that it was odd that no one answered. It was 3:30 in the afternoon, so perhaps they had quit early. Panic set in the next day as Dorilee continuously called the vendor unsuccessfully throughout the day. Panic was fueled by an angry Mark with a few words about who was responsible for buying the T-shirts.

The sale flyer reached Huntington Department Store charge customers two days before the Father's Day Sale. A few customers came in inquiring about the special promotion T-shirts. Efrem Robbins, a department manager, called Dorilee inquiring about the T-shirts. He said that several customers were excited about the T-shirts they had seen in the flyer. She nervously told him that she was working on it, but the shirts had not arrived yet. Efrem asked, "What happens if the shirts aren't here and my customers want them? Should I make a substitution?" Dorilee shouted, "You'll have them!" as she slammed the receiver on the phone.

A call to the local phone company confirmed Dorilee's worst fear. The Indigo Shirt Company had not paid their bills for the past two months and their service would be terminated tomorrow. What was she going to tell Mark? He would be furious with her. What was she going to do with the customers coming in expecting the special promotion T-shirts? Would she be fired? She had so wanted to make a good impression on her boss . . .

Major Question

What can Dorilee do to remedy the situation?

Study Questions

1. How can markup be increased? Why is lowering the cost of product not always the best way to increase markup?

2. What are the problems involved with using international vendors?

3. What safeguards should buyers use when sourcing internationally?

4. What are the similarities between international sourcing and domestic sourcing?

5. Why is timing so critical with advertising and catalog mailers?

6. What type of information about a new vendor should be sought before ordering?

Case 51
Plant a Seed: A Lack of Leeway Inventory

Diana Rosen, California State University

Plant a Seed Company designs and manufactures 100 percent cotton maternitywear aimed at the baby-boomer market. Joan Jefferson, the owner, started the company 15 years ago. She has a background in dance and kineseology. Plant a Seed developed a reputation for good-quality, cotton knit maternity apparel with a fashion-forward look. Because of her background, Joan was able to develop a unique design that supports the unborn baby, while at the same time gently forcing the mother's body into proper alignment. In addition to the unique design, another interesting aspect of the company is that they have taken an aggressive fabric purchasing position because reorders are two times the quantity of the initial orders.

Because of a nationwide recession, consumer confidence took a nosedive, the price of houses dropped dramatically, and consumers stopped buying discretionary items as more and more people became unsure of their future job status. Suddenly, many retailers began to cancel orders. Many small retailers were either not paying their bills or were going into Chapter 11 bankruptcy protection from creditors. One large department store, which owed Plant a Seed a great deal of money, did just that. The result was devastating for Plant a Seed, as the best-selling basic styles had already been produced for the anticipated large reorders. Plant a Seed then had the job of selling off the excess yardage and the merchandise already produced in order to avoid having to pay taxes on existing inventory.

Because of the uncertain business climate, Sheila McGuire, the purchasing manager, and Joan decided to cut garments for the next season based on actual orders and only built in a 5 percent leeway for unexpected reorders rather than the large reorder business that normally had been achieved. This worked for two seasons. Yesterday, however, an existing account of chain maternity stores has requested an immediate reorder of 1500 pairs of pants. At two yards per garment, Sheila will have to come up with 3000 yards of a 9 1/2-ounce black jersey for an immediate delivery. All of the mills that she currently is using are quoting three to five weeks lead time. The pants can be sewn in three weeks by the sewing contractor, which makes it six to eight weeks for reorder delivery. Sheila is begging a mill to push production knowing full well that the quality may suffer.

Both Joan and Sheila know that the retail market is unpredictable and unforgiving. If they cannot fulfil this order, the maternity chain will go to another vendor.

Major Question

What can Joan and Sheila do to be able to respond more quickly to unexpected reorders during uneasy financial times?

Study Questions

1. What are the issues the company must face?

2. What new policies should be set to accommodate the change in the retail climate?

3. Can the company use the concept of Quick Response and Just-in-Time to accommodate these changes?

Case 52
Is the Product Worth the Rep?

Teresa Braswell Robinson, Middle Tennessee University

Claire Sanchez, the women's plus-size buyer for her family owned ladies' specialty store, has a vendor problem. The family retail business—Jazzy Lady—sells budget-priced apparel for ladies, offering junior, misses and plus-size sportswear, dresses, outerwear, and accessories. Jazzy Lady is fortunate that there is minimal competition from mass merchandise chains or other stores in the area. They have therefore built up a loyal customer base over the course of the twenty years that Jazzy Lady has been in operation. The Sanchez family has been running the business since its inception and has built a reputation as an honest business whose owners are greatly involved in the commu-

nity. The retail business is located in a small city in the Midwest (with a population of approximately 150,000); their target customer is 35–65+ years of age, with low to moderate income. Her typical customer is interested in budget-priced, sure fashion trends.

Claire has been buying for four years. Prior to that, she helped sell and stock, open and close the store, as well as learning from her sister (the former plus-size buyer) the ins and outs of buying for the store. Because she was raised in the business, she came to buying with advantages of knowing the business and her customers. But buying differs from running the store, and Claire is still learning about her role and the responsibilities associated with it. As in any retail business, each day brings new opportunities and challenges to face.

In recent seasons, sales trends have indicated a growing percentage of volume in the area of women's plus sizes. While available resources are limited in this area, Claire does have a few key vendors from which lines are typically purchased each season.

During the last visit to her regional market, Claire met with one of these key resources, Beautiful Blouse, a plus-size blouse manufacturer. Because Claire has been buying this line regularly for several years, she knows Jim Lane, the sales rep, and she thought that she had a good working relationship with him. However, she has noticed during the last few market trips that Jim's attitude toward her seemed to have changed and he wasn't as friendly or as cooperative in helping meet her buying needs. At the most recent market, she found him to be quite rude, insisting that she had not been buying sufficient volume from his line, despite the fact that she has always met Beautiful Blouse's minimum order requirements. Her invoices have always been promptly paid and her account is always current.

Jim was quite adamant that certain style numbers should be purchased, some of which Claire knew were just not right for her typical customer. He even suggested that the future of Jazzy Lady's account with his company would be in jeopardy if an increased volume of orders was not placed (in other words, he would not continue to sell the line to her business). Additionally, after returning home from market and prior to placing orders, Claire received a letter from Jim reiterating his stance toward her account.

Jim is an independent, multiple-line rep working on straight commission. He has been selling for over twenty years and would like to retire in the next five years. To him, selling just isn't what it used to be. He is the only sales representative assigned to Claire's territory and he is entitled to a sales commission for all sales that are generated from accounts in his region. He is the only sales rep who shows/sells the Beautiful Blouse line at the regional market that Claire attends. Claire has never encountered a problem like this with a rep and is not sure how to proceed.

Major Question

What are Claire's options in handling the pressure and rude behavior from Jim, her sales rep?

Study Questions

1. Was Jim correct in his actions? Why was he requiring more than the manufacturer's minimum orders?

2. What are Claire's rights as the retail buyer?

3. How is an independent rep different from a company rep in terms of salary and commission?

4. What expenses does an independent rep have?

Chapter Discussion Questions

1. Discuss the major causes of problems between vendors and retailers and how negotiation may help to resolve these difficulties. Specify those matters that are most frequently negotiated.

2. Why are "good" retail/vendor partnerships and relations particularly important in the apparel industry today? Justify your answers with examples from the cases in this chapter.

3. How are the types of merchandise and/or vendors related to the determination of the types of orders placed by retailers? Use examples of order types in your discussion.

4. What can exclusivity do for a retailer? Discuss the pros and cons of negotiation with this type of arrangement.

7 Sales Promotion and Advertising

Chapter Objectives

- Present the methods of communication between retailers and customers and discuss their effectiveness.

- Define promotional mix and relate it to media selection.

- Relay the types and importance of advertising, promotional planning, and budgeting.

Appropriate communications with customers are one of the keys to successful business. To communicate effectively with their target audience, companies must plan and coordinate promotional mixes to reach customers and project clear images. A promotional budget typically is divided among various elements, which include: sales promotions (which provide for short-term objectives), special events (which are planned by the company to attract large amounts of customers into a retailing environment), institutional advertising (which achieves long-term objectives of goodwill, service, and prestige), displays (which capture the customer's interest at point-of-sale and promote on-the-spot purchases), and visual merchandising (which serves to present salable merchandise in different settings and also promotes consumer purchases). These elements (along with publicity and public relations), when used effectively, efficiently, and in a timely fashion, can help a retailing operation reach their target market and even expand it. By reaching and increasing their customers, a company can expect to achieve more recognition, greater numbers of customers, and, therefore, more profit.

Communications

Communications with a company's target market and potential new customers take many forms and are primary to attracting customers and making sales. Communications can be personal or non-personal, and can be paid or unpaid. Table 7.1 illustrates the relationship between these four factors. Generally, unpaid communications hold more credibility with consumers than those that are paid. Also testimonials and blind tests by everyday consumers are believable, whereas commissioned sales associates often are thought of as saying anything to make a sale. **Publicity** is information reported in the media by a source outside the company with no vested interest. This is the primary method of generating unpaid communications. A firm's **public relations** department is responsible for creating public impressions about the company. They are responsible for press releases and press conferences to release facts about a company.

Store location communicates a great deal about a store without any additional effort from the retailer. Certain shopping areas have an image or reputation, such as Union Square in San Francisco, Madison Avenue in New York City, The Champs Elysees in Paris, or Oxford Street in London. Often locations come with association dues, which support and promote area activities. One successful boutique owner in Union Square in San Francisco indicated she has no promotional or advertising budget as she sees her location as all the advertising she needs.

Promotion and Special Events

Sales promotion is thought of, in the broadest sense, as all the efforts that attract consumers, build customer loyalty, and overall contribute to generating sales. The purpose of sales promotion is to inform, persuade, or remind customers about the business and its product. A company's **promotional mix** can include personal selling (see Chapter Eight for more on personal selling), advertising, displays, publicity, and/or special events. **Promotional campaigns,** overall focused efforts, often attempt to communicate a message to consumers in various ways. These can include: television, radio, and print advertising, store and/or mall signage, and articles written in local newspapers about an event. The more coverage, the more apt the message is to get to the customer. Having the same message on television, radio, and print for example, can be effective because they all reinforce each other. See Table 7.3 for a comparison of the advantages and disadvantages of various advertising media.

Special events can be classified as paid/personal communication and can include demonstrations, trunk shows, fashion shows, celebrity

Table 7.1	Methods of Communications with Customers	
	Impersonal	Personal
Paid	Advertising Store Atmosphere Visual Merchandising Sales Promotion	Personal Selling
Unpaid	Publicity	Word-of-Mouth

Source: Levy and Weitz, 1995

appearances, or other events, which are used to gain the interest of consumers. Manufacturers' personnel often are involved with such special events. Demonstrations require a knowledgeable person to show the correct usage of a product, for example, cosmetics, cooking implements, or household tools. **Trunk shows,** which are presentations of apparel lines by designers or vendors to store personnel or to customers, have become very popular. For some designers, trunk shows have provided the bulk of their sales in some stores. **Fashion seminars** (a presentation and discussion of new fashions) and **fashion shows** can attract large audiences into both stores and malls and can be very effective forms of promotion of new, seasonal merchandise.

Retail stores often have annual or monthly sales and promotions, which their customers come to expect. Table 7.2 lists the dates of some common promotions, although individual stores usually have a special time for such annual promotions as Anniversary Sales or Founder's Day Sales. Nordstrom, for example, only has their Anniversary Sale and Half-Yearly Sale, while Macy's and other department stores have sales once a month or even more often—depending on the competition. These sales have all sorts of names, for example, January White Sales, Big Sales, One-Day or Three-Day Sales, Customer Appreciation or Sales Associates Appreciation Day, and some discount stores run Dollar Day and Buy-One-Get-One-Free Sales. Some sales are planned in conjunction with other promotional events such as for Mother's Day or Christmas. *Case 54, The Founder's Day Special,* illustrates a prob-

Figure 7.1 This Ralph Lauren fashion show is an example of an instore promotional special event. Note that the event was held in the Ralph Lauren boutique within the store.

Table 7.2	**Typical Sales Promotions by Month**
January	White Sales, Winter Clearance, After-Holiday, Super Bowl Specials
February	President's Day (Weekend) Sale, Valentine's Day
March	Easter/Spring, St. Patricks Day
April	Easter/Spring, Pre-Summer
May	Mother's Day, Memorial Day, Bridal, Graduation
June	Father's Day, Vacation
July	Summer Clearance, Fourth of July, Dog Days
August	Summer Clearance, Dog Days, Back-to-School
September	Labor Day, Autumn
October	Octoberfest, Halloween, Columbus Day
November	Thanksgiving, Resort, Election Day, Pre-Holiday
December	Holiday, After-Holiday

Table 7.3 Advantages and Disadvantages of Different Advertising Media

Medium	Advantages	Disadvantages
Television	• Most powerful, versatile medium • Some flexibility; can be changed on short notice	• Expensive to produce and air • Local TV not available in rural areas • Cannot target specific audiences except with cable
Radio	• Can target particular demographics • Spoken message more persuasive than print • Can be changed on short notice	• Less impact than television • Message is short-lived • Cannot show or demonstrate product
Magazines	• High quality photographs show product to best advantage • Can target specific markets and regions	• Expensive • Ads must be placed far in advance • Large wasted circulation
Newspapers	• Often used as shopping guide • Ads can be purchased or changed quickly • Products can be shown	• Cannot target specific audience • Color reproduction poor • Short life of individual issues
Direct Mail	• Can address very specific target market • Low total cost • Complete control over timing of message	• High cost per person contacted • Requires appropriate mailing list • Often seen as "junk mail"
Outdoor/Billboards	• Frequent exposure • Low cost per impression delivered • Can target specific region	• Much wasted exposure • Very little text possible • Unwilling audience; some resentment
Internet	• Combines visuals, audio, and text • Low cost after initial investment; unlimited "hits" • Can be revised at any time • Well-educated, high-income target market	• Customer must initiate contact • Security concerns limit direct credit card orders • Reaches only people with computers

lem between a buyer and a merchandise manager with the selection and pricing of merchandise for a retailer's annual sale.

Advertising

Any form of paid/impersonal communication from a company is called **advertising.** Manufacturers may advertise to retailers, which is called **trade advertising,** for example in *WWD* or *DNR.* Manufacturers offer advertising directly to consumers, which is called **national advertising,** as illustrated by Levi's ads on television, or fragrance ads in magazines. Retailers advertise to consumers—called **retail advertising**—and, generally, is in more local media, with specific information of place, dates, and prices.

Advertising has two main objectives: 1) to sell a product, which is called product or promotional advertising; or 2) to sell an image, which is called institutional advertising. **Product ads** promote immediate consumer action, that is, the ad urges the consumer to come into the store and buy that specific product. **Institutional ads** are concerned with building a company's reputation or image rather than selling a product. They may illustrate the good deeds a company is doing in the community, the services it offers, or the prestige it maintains or desires. Some examples are oil company ads, which promote the idea that the oil company is helping to protect the environment; store ads, which show the store support of local school programs or offer special services for the elderly or handicapped; or department stores, which offer top designer merchandise (if fashion leadership is the image to be projected). Nordstrom, Target, and Wal-Mart all run institutional ads for these purposes. Calvin Klein, Guess?, and Benetton are well-known for their image advertising, which is also a form of institutional advertising. This type of image advertising has brought Benetton especially a great deal of notoriety. In the 1970s and early 1980s Benetton concentrated on product ads, while in the late 1980s and 1990s it changed to pure image advertising, which usually depicted a social situation with no product at all, just the Benetton name.

Their purpose was consciousness-raising in regard to social issues, while promoting the Benetton name. Some critics feel their ads were and are exploitative and inappropriate but they were successful in reaching consumers and establishing more name-recognition for the company. *Case 55, Sandini's Corporate Image* presents a case of similar, controversial image advertising.

Cooperative (coop) advertising normally involves retailers and suppliers sharing the costs of advertising. Generally, retailers are reimbursed for part of the cost of the ad by vendors upon receipt of tear sheets (copies of the ad). Another type of coop advertising is when a group of merchants cooperate and run one ad that benefits all of the retailers. Coop advertising is often utilized when considering the advertising/promotion budget. However, the addition of advertising dollars to a budget through coop advertising should not be the foremost consideration when choosing the right merchandise for a retailer's customers. *Case 56, The Coop Advertising Fiasco,* illustrates a situation in which coop ad money was used to supplement an advertising budget in an unorthodox way, which ultimately backfired on the buyer.

Media Selection

Companies must choose the medium (i.e., television, newspaper, tabloid inserts, magazine, radio, direct mail, and so forth) to use for advertising. Media selection is key to a successful advertising/promotion plan because it is vital that advertising messages reach their intended market. The next five sections briefly examine the common forms of media used by retailers and manufacturers for advertising and promotion.

Print Media Newspapers, magazines, flyers, and direct mail are all included in **print media. Newspapers** are the most widely used media for retailers because they are the most flexible and have a wide circulation. Because most newspapers are daily, advertisements can be very timely. These ads are called **run of press/newspaper (ROP)** ads, and often are used for weekly store specials. **Tabloid**

Co-op Advertising Offer

This offer is the official Co-op Advertising Plan for the OshKosh Mens Wear Division, effective November 1, 1993. It replaces the plan printed in 1992. This offer is the only means by which our retailers may obtain the advertising assistance available from OshKosh B'Gosh, Inc.

Who is eligible for the OshKosh Men's Wear Co-Op Offer?

Co-op funds are available to every men's wear retailer who buys first-quality men's wear directly from OshKosh. This co-op offer is available to all competing retailers on a proportionately equal basis.

Our co-op offer applies to advertising or sales promotions executed January 1 through December 31. Unused funds from one year cannot be carried over into the following year.

How are funds accrued?

Co-op funds will accrue in an amount equal to 3% of the net billing price of first-quality OshKosh men's wear products excluding off-price items, close-out merchandise and products purchased from OshKosh B'Gosh, Inc., licensees.

Your OshKosh net purchases from the previous calendar year will be compared with those made during the current calendar year. Your co-op fund is calculated on the amount that is greater. Accrual information is continually upgraded as the year goes on. To assist you in budgeting, the previous year's net purchases are used as a baseline until they are exceeded by the current year's net purchases.

Credit will not exceed, in any calendar year, your accrued advertising allowance applicable to that year.

How will you be reimbursed?

Spelled out on pages 5 through 8 are the basic content and documentation requirements an advertisement or sales promotion must meet in order to qualify for reimbursement. When these requirements are satisfied, you will be reimbursed with a credit memo. We will reimburse 50% of the net media and/or merchandising/sales promotion costs (less discounts and rebates) — providing the reimbursement does not exceed the limit of funds accrued.

If there are insufficient funds to pay a claim in full, it will be paid to the limit of the funds available. The balance will be a "pending" file so it can be paid when sufficient funds become available. If the claim has not been fully paid by the end of the calendar year, it will be paid to the limit of the funds available at that time, then closed.

Obtaining reimbursement is as easy as 1-2-3!

1. To receive reimbursement, submit your co-op claim within 75 days of the end of the month in which your advertising or sales promotion occurs. For example, if you run an ad on January 15, you will have until 75 days from January 31. Therefore, you must submit your claim by April 15. Extensions are available under special circumstances, with the approval of the OshKosh Co-op Department. Please do not send a co-op claim to your OshKosh sales person or OshKosh corporate headquarters. This could result in a lost or misdirected claim, and delayed payment.

2. Along with your claim, include the required documentation as specified in the Print Advertising, Broadcast Advertising or Sales Promotion, Merchandising & Other Advertising sections of the OshKosh Co-op Offer.

Figure 7.2 OshKosh's cooperative retail advertising program.

Developing Your OshKosh® Advertising Plan

Your Media Mix

Each medium has strengths and weaknesses. It will take a combination of media to reach your target market most efficiently. You'll need to study each medium to determine the media mix right for you. The following media charts summarize the strengths and weaknesses of each medium in five crucial areas and explain how each medium is sold. You can use the charts as a quick reference to aid in your advertising decisions.

Media Tips

- Running an ad smaller than full-page, but big enough that no one else can advertise on the page, is a good way to get exclusivity.
- Always request a proof of your print ad prior to publication to make sure it's correct.
- Include easy-to-follow directions to your store in your broadcast and print advertising.
- Outdoor advertising requires long lead times, from 45 to 70 days. So plan well ahead. Billboards require prior approval of location, layout, timing and estimates of costs should you desire OshKosh® co-op reimbursement.
- A direct mail envelope that hints at the offer is better than a "blank" envelope.

Your Results

Advertising objectives set earlier allow you to evaluate your results. Increased sales is the most obvious measurement of your advertising. It's not always the most accurate, however, especially if you only count the sales immediately after you ran the ad or spot. You should also consider increased floor traffic and how that might affect your sales in the long run.

Set up a permanent scrapbook or file for the ads you run. Measure their pulling power by counting floor traffic a few days before and a few days after the advertising has run. (Remember to take note of weather conditions or competitors' advertising that appeared when yours did. They could have a bearing on how well your advertising pulled.) You'll soon learn which approaches and appeals bring prospects into your store.

Once you have established a regular advertising program, you'll be able to measure the pulling power and sales success of one ad or commercial against another. Soon you'll know exactly which ingredients work and which don't.

Advertising Efficiently

Planning not only makes advertising more effective, it can also make it more efficient. Most media will give discounts when you buy a regular planned schedule.

"Regular" doesn't have to mean every day or every week. Smart advertisers often "flight" their ads — they run a good solid schedule for two weeks, take a week or two off, then start up again. It's a good way to stretch an advertising budget while maintaining visibility. Try not to stop advertising altogether. Removing your name from the marketplace also removes it from consumers' minds.

If you have a small budget, it's better to do a few things well and create a big impact over a few shorter periods. Don't spread yourself too thin. Never put just a little bit everywhere. Concentrate your efforts in the right places. And remember, cost is a big factor, but don't ever buy the wrong medium for your target audience just because you got a "deal."

Putting It All Together

With this Ad Planner as your guide, you can coordinate your advertising across all media. Projecting the same image and tone throughout your OshKosh advertising will result in a multi-media campaign that has a consistent look and message. This consistency will help the consumer immediately recognize you as an OshKosh retailer.

Figure 7.3 OshKosh's advertising plan tips to retailers.

inserts—often called **preprints**—are printed separately from the regular newspaper and are usually inserted into Saturday or Sunday papers. These can be done in color and are cheaper than the ROP. **Magazines** are generally geared to a national audience and are relatively expensive, but provide good-quality print and color that are usually missing from ROP. Many national magazines, however, produce regional editions in which an ad can be targeted to local retailers. Because they are often published monthly, these ads are generally more image related than geared toward immediate customer reaction.

Direct Mail and Marketing A broad concept, **direct marketing** is utilized today by retailers and manufacturers. This term refers to the various ways a company can communicate directly with potential customers. This can include the use of "800" numbers, telemarketing (those dinnertime calls trying to sell you something), catalogs, television shopping programs, and other forms of electronic interactive retailing.

Direct mail (which is also a type of print media) is used by both retailers and manufacturers, to send flyers, catalogs, or other literature to target customers. Catalogs increased tremendously in the 1980s and 1990s as busy families found less time to go downtown or to the mall. With such improved customer service as Spiegel's easy method of returning merchandise and the use of 24-hour "800" numbers for ordering, some of the disadvantages of catalog shopping are being eliminated. Neiman Marcus, for example, has become so well-known for its Christmas catalog that it is sold to the public at newsstands and is a major form of advertising for the store.

Broadcast Media Television and radio encompasses **broadcast media.** Generally television is used the most by retailers, while radio is used the least. This is understandable in that a product often sells better if the target consumer can see it. However, for special events advertising (e.g., fashion shows, celebrity appearances, and so forth), radio advertising can be quite effective. Television

reaches a mass audience and is expensive, but it can create dramatic results not easily achieved in other types of media. Generally, only such large retailers as Sears, Wal-Mart, and Kmart utilize national television advertising. However, the use of local television and cable shows is increasing, lending itself for more use by local and regional companies and is succeeding in reaching more specifically targeted audiences.

Outdoor Advertising Billboards, the roving billboard (on wheels!), posters at train and bus stations, and on the buses, trains, and subways themselves are all included in **outdoor advertising.** In larger cities, kiosks are used to advertise retailers, manufacturers, banks, performances, and other city events. San Francisco has recently utilized 90 JCDecaux kiosks, which are expected to provide three million dollars of advertising revenues per year. These revenues are intended to help pay for the upkeep of matching sidewalk toilets, similar to those in Paris. Also, in cities, sides of buildings are sometimes utilized for advertising, for example, Adidas, Samsung, Barney's, Levi's, and DKNY all have ads painted on the sides of New York City buildings. These ads are variously institutional, product, retailer and manufacturer/designer ads. Similarly, in rural areas or along the sides of highways, the roofs or sides of barns are often utilized in similar ways to either advertise products or to direct drivers to attractions. Companies have used other such non-conventional places to advertise as ball parks and stadiums. For example, Gap's name appears prominently in the sports section of newspapers as it is captured in the background of photographs of ball games and other sporting events.

Electronic and Video Displays **Video walls** (i.e., many television screens displaying the same visual and/or large screen projections) are being used more and more by large retailers. They make a dramatic display and are effective in gaining consumer attention. Smaller stores utilize videos from designers to showcase their latest collections.

Figure 7.4 Levi's big screen creates a dramatic effect at their 57th Street store in New York City. This screen can help promote and advertise merchandise in the store or provide entertainment for shoppers.

Additionally, **online advertising** through the Internet is gaining popularity. For example, new e-mail software such as Juno is free to users because the service is accompanied by advertising. Many retailers are developing home pages for the purpose of advertising. (See Chapter Ten for more on the use of new technologies in retailing.)

Effectiveness of Promotions and Advertisements

Advertising effectiveness is measured by achievement of the objective. For example, product advertising is supposed to sell a product, therefore, the success of such an ad is measured in relation to the amount of sales generated by the ad.

Experimentation with alternative promotional events at different times, using different media, or targeting different groups can be used to evaluate methods. When a company has a complex promotional mix, it is difficult to separate the parts to evaluate the effectiveness of each part because they often work together in creating results. Institutional ads are also hard to evaluate because the results are not produced immediately. Additionally, evaluation can be difficult because such outside factors as the economy or other competing events can affect the results also. *Case 53, Back-to-School Fashion Flop* illustrates how another event can draw customers away from a promotion that otherwise might have been successful.

Some ads are sensational and even objectionable to consumers, but are these the ones people remember? Calvin Klein has pathed the way for cutting-edge fashion advertising starting in the 1980s with Brooke Shields stating, "Nothing comes between me and my Calvin's." Since then he has continued to remain controversial with ads featuring Marky Mark, Kate Moss, and Christy Turlington. Some of his more controversial ads have included his Obsession ads, a naked Kate Moss lying on a couch (also Obsession), and his CK One ads depicting groups of young people, who are paired off in ways that suggest alternative sexualities. Some critics think he went too far by using what some called soft-porn images of teenage boys and girls, which ignited debates about sex, youth, and gender roles. His ads continue to be the most recognized and remembered and he shows no sign of changing his highly successful strategy. He was, however, challenged on whether he used under-age models for his ads, but no charges were brought against him for child pornography. The ads, nevertheless, were pulled by Klein after a very short time.

Visual Merchandising

Visual merchandising is a general term that is used to describe everything that is seen when a customer enters a store. This includes the exterior appearance of the store, window displays, signage, and all interior displays of merchandise on fixtures and lighting that are used to create an overall effect. Effective visual merchandising can sell the

Figure 7.5 Another controversial ad from Calvin Klein. This ad is for CKOne, a genderless fragrance. Note that the groupings of young people in various forms of dress and undress suggest not only alternative lifestyles, but also alternative sexualities and relationships.

Figure 7.6 Barney's extravagant and often offbeat Christmas windows draw many shoppers to the store during the Holiday season. This humorous window depicts Coco Chanel and Karl Lagerfeld and an Eiffel Tower decorated like a Christmas Tree.

merchandise without any other type of promotion. It can draw customers into an establishment and create the desire for purchase, encourage impulse buying, and provide self-service. With the trend of less personal sales assistance in many stores—especially department stores—effective visual merchandising is especially important. Such stores as The Limited use an instore approach for the majority of their promotion rather than utilizing media advertising. Often corporate offices develop strict standards to create merchandise presentation consistency in all stores. See Figures 7.7–7.9.

Window displays are an important part of visual merchandising. Window displays can be open or closed. Traditional store window displays are enclosures with solid backings that isolate the merchandise to be presented. These are called **closed** or **closed-back window displays.** Often stores use **open window displays** enabling the viewer to see directly into the store through the display. Effectiveness is often more challenging to achieve in an open window display, however, because the interior of the store competes with the display. Open window displays are more common in malls where there are no outside windows, while department stores in downtown areas most often use closed window displays. These closed window displays perform a selling function even when the store is closed, in addition to pure entertainment for "window shoppers." Henri Bendel and Bergdorf Goodman have extremely effective closed window displays and Barney's New York has become well-known for its creative, entertaining, unconventional windows in which nothing is sacred and often common objects are used in offbeat ways. Some stores (e.g., Barney's, Lord & Taylor, Saks Fifth Avenue, among others) have become known for their elaborate Christmas displays, which bring large numbers

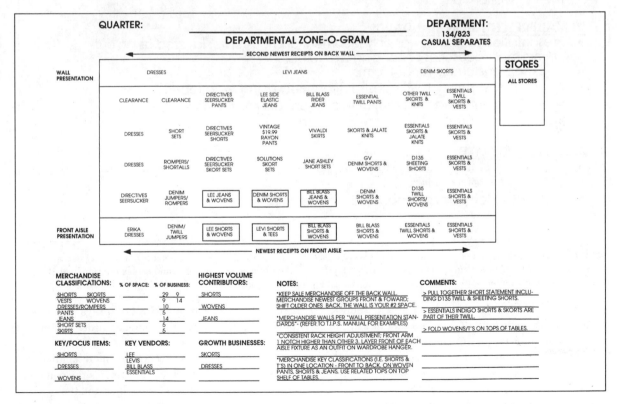

Figure 7.7 A typical departmental presentation plan from a major department store chain. Note how merchandise has been grouped together or in close proximity in order to promote selling between lines. (See Figure 7.8 for a department store's visual merchandising standards.)

VISUAL MERCHANDISING BASIC STANDARD

DIVISON: Moderate Sportswear
DEPARTMENT 127,121
CLASSIFICATION: "Innovation"/Career Related Separates
FIXTURE STANDARD: Face out, Flat bar (for side hanging merchandise), Presentation shelf. T-stands, Small capacity four-way racks, Fourth arm displayer with abstract mannequin (prototype), "Innovations" sign wardrober (prototype)/or mannequins.

MERCHANDISE PRESENTATION STANDARD:
- Merchandise as a collection by fashion trend.
- Divide floor by fashion trends, according to quarterly zone-o-gram.
- Utilize flat bar for side hanging under presentation shelves, or post out.
- Walls without valances should be broken up by using buttons, or broken up by use of presentation shelf.
- Consistent rack height adjustment, front arm one notch higher than rear and side arms.
- Nortan McNaughton, Chaus and Chaus Sport should be merchandised within the Innovations area.

VISUAL PRESENTATION STANDARD:
- Presentation shelf with wall enhancement and costumer layered as an out-fit, minimal accesories or hanging wall forms.
- Rack top costumers /or 3/4 forms.
- "Innovations" sign unit with abstract mannequins/or wardrober.
- Layer face outs and front arm of floor fixture as would be worn.
- Place acrylic forms in sets of three on focal wall.

SIGNING STANDARD:
- "Innovations" floor fixture sign (prototype).
- 11"x14" key item signing.
- 7"x5 1/2" price point signing, where applicable.

Figure 7.8. An example of corporate visual merchandising standards. This particular example comes from a major department store chain; the information contained in this report is relayed to all the branches of the chain and each store is expected to comply with these standards. (See Figure 7.7 for a departmental zone-o-gram.)

of shoppers just to view them. This is a time when many retailers try to "out do" one another in window presentations under the presumption that the more people that view the Christmas windows, the more customers that will come in the store and purchase. Figure 7.6 is an example of a Barney's Christmas window featuring humorous caricatures of Coco Chanel and Karl Lagerfeld.

Effective **interior product displays** help customers locate merchandise and can illustrate how the merchandise is used or worn. Additionally, product displays can show how the merchandise can be accessorized, which encourages the consumer to purchase that merchandise and the accessories. Most displays have a sales (product) objective; some displays, however, project an image

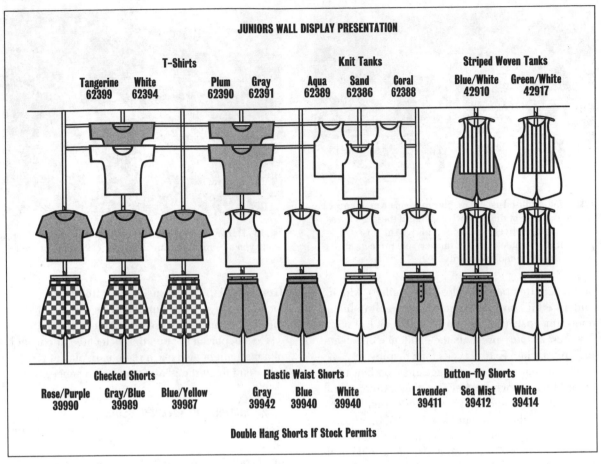

JUNIORS WALL DISPLAY PRESENTATION

T-Shirts

Tangerine	White		Plum	Gray
62399	62394		62390	62391

Knit Tanks

Aqua	Sand	Coral
62389	62386	62388

Striped Woven Tanks

Blue/White	Green/White
42910	42917

Checked Shorts

Rose/Purple	Gray/Blue	Blue/Yellow
39990	39989	39987

Elastic Waist Shorts

Gray	Blue	White
39942	39940	39940

Button-fly Shorts

Lavender	Sea Mist	White
39411	39412	39414

Double Hang Shorts If Stock Permits

Figure 7.9 A junior fashion wall display plan, which shows how to present several types of shorts and tops. Note how the colors and prints are grouped, which can suggest various combinations to the customer.

of prestige without a sales objective (this is a type of institutional display, which serves much the same purpose as an institutional ad). For example, a very expensive designer gown with limited stock (or no stock at all) may be displayed for prestige and not a sales purpose. The various types of interior displays include:

• **Counter top** or **point-of-purchase displays** in which the merchandise can be touched and self-selected by the customer.

• **Showcase displays,** which are often used for small or expensive items. These are usually enclosed and locked.

• **Wall** or **ledge displays,** which utilize dead or unused space to show merchandise.

• **Aisle displays,** in which merchandise might be layered and accessorized and then hung at the end of the display case (often these are the items that sell first!).

Any of these types of displays can be either open or closed. Open-selling displays are those that enable customer self-service, but which have a higher potential for shoplifting. **Closed-island displays** provide less customer access, which results in fewer thefts, but also possibly fewer sales. Closed displays also require a salesperson to

Figure 7.10 A closed-island display of Donna Karan's accessories. Because of the expensive nature of these goods, as well as their relatively small size, this type of closed display not only protects against thievery, but projects an image of quality and exclusivity.

Figure 7.11 In contrast to a closed display, this open-selling display in a Nordstrom store allows for easy customer self-service.

be present (to open and close the display), which under certain circumstances could result in higher operating costs (i.e., employee salaries). *Case 57, The Best Display* presents the challenge of selecting appropriate fixture types for a display.

Often customers need suggestions on how to put apparel items together because they cannot visualize this for themselves. The employee display, or modeling of the merchandise, is one of the most effective selling tools. In stores in which such "employee racks" are used, those items sell out the fastest. Also visuals from vendors can show how merchandise is intended to be worn or used.

There are many elements for creating productive, effective displays. Props, signage, and lighting are important components for creating displays. Other principles to remember when planning a display include:

1. Select the most in-demand merchandise.

2. Plan for installation time.

3. Consider the timeliness of the goods and display.

4. Keep the display clean.

5. Keep the display appropriate to the store's image.

6. Use elements and principles of design properly.

7. Change the display often.

Remote displays are used away from a store's location. These free-standing units can target tourists because they are often placed in hotels, while a department store that is located at one end of a mall might also use a remote display at the other end to alert customers of its presence.

Promotion and Advertising Budgets

Retailers and manufacturers develop **promotional plans** by carefully considering their budgets. They must consider what percent of their budget will be spent on the type of promotion and then choose the appropriate type of media to utilize. Often a percentage of sales is used to determine the amount to be spent on promotion. This could be a percentage of either past or anticipated sales. For example, with last year sales of $200,000 and 5 percent of sales allocated for promotion, the promotion budget is $10,000. That amount would be divided among television, magazine, and newspaper ads, special events, publicity, displays, and other general promotion items according to plan. In addition to allocating monies to departments, some companies divide budgets on a seasonal or monthly basis. Another method some small stores use is the "all-you-can-afford" method, which allows for promotions only if there is available cash. Sometimes the "meet-the-competition" method is also used when needed, i.e., when a direct competitor has a sale or promotion, a retailer might meet that competition with its own promotion.

Some unpaid communications cost nothing; however, companies do incur costs to stimulate them, especially for some forms of publicity. Developing events worthy of media coverage can be costly, even if they are very effective. Macy's annual Spring Flower Show, Fourth of July Fireworks display, and Thanksgiving Day Parade receive a great deal of media coverage but are extremely expensive to produce. Word-of-mouth may be the best promotion (if it is positive) and it is free; however, negative word-of-mouth information can be very detrimental to retailers and manufacturers. That is why most companies care about the impression customers are left with after transactions.

Retailers should allot promotional dollars first to their **primary trading area,** which is the area in which it can serve its customers in terms of convenience better than its competitors, and then to its **secondary trading areas,** which yield customers despite a competitor's location advantage. Generally, there is a maximum distance that customers will travel to shop at a certain retailer or mall. A primary trading area is usually three to five miles from the site, while a secondary trading area is seven or more miles away. This, of course, varies from state to state and city to city. A retailer's promotional efforts should be geared toward those consumers that are most likely to shop at the retailing establishment.

Summary

Sales promotion and advertising are vital components of a retail business as they convey specific and general information to potential and current customers. Companies plan and budget a promotional mix to communicate their message, which can consist of paid, non-paid, and personal and impersonal types of communication. Whatever the method, promotion and advertising are essential elements to a successful, growth-oriented business.

References

Anguin, J. (1996, May 28). Advertisers finally discovering kiosks. *San Francisco Chronicle*, pp. B1, B6.

Bell, J. (1988). *Silent selling: The complete guide to fashion merchandise presentations.* Cincinnati, OH.: ST Publications.

Colborne, R. (1996). *Visual Merchandising: The business of merchandise presentation.* Albany, N.Y.: Delmar.

Diamond, J., & Diamond. E. (1996). *Fashion advertising and promotion.* Albany, N.Y.: Delmar.

Drake, M.F., Spoone, J.H., & Greenwald, H. (1992). Retail fashion promotion and advertising. New York: MacMillan.

Levy, M., & Weitz, B. A. (1995). *Retailing management.* Chicago: Irwin.

Pegler, M. (1995). *Visual merchandising & display, third edition.* New York: Fairchild Publications.

Phillips, P.M. (1996). *Fashion sales promotion: The selling behind the selling.* Upper Saddle River, NJ: Prentice-Hall.

Spitzer, H., & Schwartz. F.R. (1982). *Inside retail sales promotion and advertising.* New York: Harper & Row.

Winters, A.A., & Goodman, S. (1984). *Fashion advertising and promotion.* New York: Fairchild Publications.

Key Terms

advertising	magazines
aisle display	national advertising
broadcast media	newspapers
closed/closed-back display	online advertising
closed-island display	open window display
cooperative advertising	outdoor advertising
counter top display	point-of-purchase display
direct mail	preprints
direct marketing	primary trading area
fashion seminar	print media
fashion show	product advertising
institutional advertising	promotional campaign
interior product display	promotional mix
ledge display	promotional plan

publicity
public relations
remote display
retail advertising
run of press/newspaper
   (ROP)
sales promotion
secondary trading area
showcase display

special events
tabloid inserts
trade advertising
trunk show
video wall
visual merchandising
wall display
window display

Case 53
Back-to-School Fashion Flop

Anne M. Duskin, Santa Barbara Museum of Art

Peninsula Mall is the largest mall in San Mateo County and is not far from San Francisco. It has 150 specialty shops, plus Nordstrom, Macy's, Sears, and Mervyn's. Recently remodeled, Peninsula Mall has also added such upscale stores as Lillie Rubin, bebe, Cache, and Nine West to its tenant mix. These new stores, along with its "popular-price" merchant selection and list of department stores, position Peninsula Mall as an upscale fashion center. The mall's goal is to attract the upscale customer in addition to its current "popular-price" clientele.

Peninsula Mall is located in an affluent county with a consumer base posting a median age of 36, owning a home, and having 2.3 children. To appeal to this more discriminating, affluent customer, Peninsula's marketing department—with the approval of the Mall Tenant's Association—has created a new "fashion forward" ad campaign and special events calendar.

The "Back-to-School" retail buying period is generally promoted in the month of August. In an effort to merchandise the apparel and accessory shops during this period, an extravagant traffic-generating event was scheduled for the second Saturday in August. Mall management had planned an exciting "Back-to-School" fashion show. This was something that had never been held before at the Peninsula Mall and was a major marketing undertaking. It was to take place in the center core area of the mall and included participation from most of the apparel and accessory stores, highlighting, however, two junior apparel stores—Wet Seal and Pacific Sunwear.

To enhance the event, *Sassy*, a popular national magazine, was asked to sponsor the event. *Sassy* was selected over *Mademoiselle* and *Glamour*, because market research indicated *Sassy* was the fastest-growing subscription magazine for young women. Sponsorship from *Sassy* did not come cheaply, however. As host of the fashion show, *Sassy* was paid a $6,000 fee by the Mall Association, which covered the expenses of: 1) a *Sassy* fashion editor (flown from New York to San Francisco with one-night hotel stay) to MC the show and advise the fashion show coordinators on the latest teen fashions; and 2) audience giveaways such as *Sassy* magazines, advertiser coupons, and *Sassy* T-shirts, as well as a grand prize of a beach vacation trip for two. *Sassy* also gave Peninsula Mall a free listing in the Special Events column of the magazine, which afforded them national exposure! The planners of the event thought that perhaps new visitors to the area would also seek out Peninsula Mall as a destination because of the publicity.

The mall was responsible for models, stage, backdrop, fashion show coordinator, and music. Additionally, Peninsula Mall planned to expend a large advertising budget to promote the event on a regional level (Bay Area wide). In other words, the mall was going all out on this campaign.

Utilizing the beautiful new ad campaign format, an ad was produced that ran in the *San Francisco Chronicle* and the *San Mateo Times*. Additionally, radio spots—with special music supplied by *Sassy*—ran on KGO talk radio, the Bay Area's top radio station. The two junior apparel stores agreed to supply the labor to pass out flyers to their customers.

The day of the event was the hottest Saturday of the year—but it was a clear, beautiful day. The county fair was taking place across the street from the mall at the county fairgrounds. It looked as if record numbers of people were flocking to both the fair and the fashion show. Mall management was excited, as were the retailers, expecting a super shopping day. By noon, the mall parking lot was quickly filling up with both shoppers and county fair goers.

The fashion show was scheduled for 2 pm. Excitement was building as 2 pm rapidly approached. The show music began early to help create interest and attract a crowd. Volunteers in oversized Sassy T-shirts passed out programs. At show time, however, only twenty passersby had assembled for the show. The mall marketing director was terribly disappointed. The participating stores and *Sassy* could not figure out what went wrong.

Major Question

How could the mall marketing director, *Sassy*, and the participating stores have improved their promotional efforts in order to attract a "sellout" crowd for the fashion show?

Study Questions

1. Do you think the back-to-school promotion should have been scheduled for another time, when the county fair was not being held? Why or why not?

2. Analyze the participation by *Sassy*. Can you recommend any changes that could have improved the promotion?

3. What type of back-to-school events are most successful with children and parents? What about teenage girls?

4. Suggest additional methods for a mall to advertise its special events.

Case 54
The Founder's Day Special

Nancy J. Rabolt, San Francisco State University
Judy K. Miler, University of Tennessee

Every October, the Young Company, a department store in Orlando, Florida, runs a Founder's Day Sale, which is a storewide clearance sale. The event lasts for one week and features stock goods ranging from 25 to 40 percent off regular prices. The yearly event, which has been held for the past 20 years, has become a store tradition and has always been highly successful. From the store's point of view, it is an excellent sale because: 1) it helps to clear merchandise from the store and brings the inventory levels down to accommodate for new Holiday merchandise; and 2) it yields customer satisfaction because of the great bargains that can be found.

The Young Company advertises this sale through an ad and a flyer. The flyer is sent directly to credit card customers and is also available in the local paper on the Sunday before the sale begins. The ad is run every day in the local paper during the week before the sale. The flyer and ad consist of a list of every sale item in the store. Every buyer submits a list of items to be included in the ad and flyer. The list describes the merchandise, the regular retail prices, and the new reduced prices. This strategy creates a large amount of traffic through the store and the sale has become the largest revenue producer of all the Young Company's promotions.

Ethel Frommer, the coat buyer, who has been with the company for five years, submitted her list to her divisional merchandise manager, who reviewed it for sufficient quantities, original values, and new price levels. They were satisfactory and approved. Two days before the ad was to appear, Sidney Smith, the general merchandise manager, visited the department with a proof copy of the first series of ads.

He said, "Ethel, I'd like to review the merchandise and check it against the copy." "Fine," replied Ethel, and she followed him to the stock room.

Sidney and Ethel entered the stockroom off the selling floor and checked each group to get a feeling for the bargain aspect of the merchandise. As he was nearing the end of his research, he spotted one group of coats originally priced at $100 marked down to $50.

"Ethel, didn't you run these coats at $50 last month?"

"Yes, I did," she replied.

"And wasn't it a bust—about four coats out of seventy-five?" he retorted.

"You have a fine memory; that's the case."

"Well, you aren't going to run them again. We don't repeat failures," he stated in no uncertain terms.

"Please, Sidney, market conditions have changed; cold weather and sparse market supply make these coats worth $100. In fact, if I had to fill in colors and sizes, I'd have to pay the regular $60. At $50, the customers are getting the bargain of the season," Ethel pleaded.

"Sorry," Sidney responded, "go up to the advertising department and change the price to $40. First, of course, be sure to take the markdown and enter the reduction in the system."

Ethel was extremely angry. She felt the decision was arbitrary and without respect for her judgment.

Major Question

What should Ethel do regarding Sidney's request to reduce the promotional coats to $40 and run them in the ad?

Study Questions

1. What factors make a successful sale?

2. What factors enter into the pricing of a sale item like these coats?

Case 55
Sandini's Corporate Image

Janice Rosenthal McCoart, Marymount University

Antonio Sandini, corporate king of the global fashion empire Sandini, is thinking of changing his corporation's promotional image. The Italy-based apparel business has been gaining notoriety for an advertising campaign that uses shock-tactic themes. Ever since the campaign started, it seems as if Sandini is constantly being barraged by individuals and/or groups that oppose this style of advertising. There have also been lawsuits and threatening letters to corporate officers and their families. Perhaps life would be easier if a new image were adopted (and the socio-cultural "waves" were stilled). Antonio does know that his life would certainly be calmer if the company were to forgo their controversial campaign. He must also consider the other employees that have also suffered as a result of the backlash from the publicity. Sandini wonders, however, how much of their successful sales history can be attributed to the publicity that the company gets from their nontraditional advertising.

Such themes have nothing to do with the origin of the company. Sandini began as a knitting business; handmade sweaters were sold directly to Italian shops using no middleman. Antonio offered discounts to retailers who paid cash on delivery. As the business grew, he bought knitting machines to make the sweaters. Out of that purchase, factories developed, first in Europe, then others in the U.S., South America, South Korea, and Japan. Foreign factories meant Antonio could avoid import taxes, and cut transport time and costs. He also used subcontractors to do some of the manufacturing, which limited the necessity for employees and helped to circumvent union and government controls.

As in the case of the advertising campaign that brought public attention, Sandini attempts to be at the cutting edge in all aspects of its business. At the business' headquarters, designers work with the most up-to-date computer and knitting technology to develop the samples. Even the packing and circulation of goods inside the warehouse is computerized. Technology aids in the adjustment to sudden changes in production and mid-season reordering.

Sandini has several thousand licensed stores in over 100 countries, including Japan, China, Russia, Czechoslovakia, Poland, Turkey, Egypt, as well as the U.S. The company sells its goods at wholesale prices to stores that agree to sell Sandini's merchandise exclusively. The product line is extending into men's wear, children's wear, infant apparel, shoes, underwear, perfumes, watches, and sunglasses. Any financial risk rests entirely on the shop owners. They pay no fees or royalties to the Sandini corporation and do not share their profits. Sandini therefore is not limited by regulatory franchise laws. The shop owners are selected by several worldwide agents who are often part owners of the shops in their region. Most of these agents are Italian. They also book orders and monitor standards.

Sandini does not actually make up a garment until it is ordered. It takes 80 percent of the orders nine months before the season starts for its two yearly collections—Fall/Winter and Spring/-Summer. Their most important target market is fifteen- to twenty-five-year-old females with considerable disposable income. But this market is expanding to include many thirty- to fifty-year-olds. Because of its first priority market, Sandini began to advertise in teen and rock magazines, and then in career and fashion magazines.

Sandini uses a Paris firm to develop its advertising. The first campaign highlighted models of various skin colors, emphasizing society's multi-ethnicity. At that time, the firm decided to omit copy in the ads, except for the corporate name Sandini. That campaign received a lot of praise from the public. There was also an increase in the quantity and quality of editorials featuring Sandini's merchandise in the leading magazines.

Then the Paris advertising firm tried another approach. It chose to run productless ads, a method meant to market company philosophy or designer image. Without emphasis on product characteristics, the ads attempted to predispose the consumer to what makes one manufacturer distinctive from another. Without any merchandise or copy, the impact of the ads rested solely on the unexplained visual image.

What followed was a series of artistically composed ad layouts, featuring images meant to reflect problems in contemporary society in regard to perceived equality between peoples. These images touched on race, religion, birth, illness, death, among other relevant aspects of life. These were met with negative reactions from some minority, religious, and parents' groups—confirmation that the campaign attracted attention.

The first ad pictured two male arms, one white and one black, handcuffed together at the wrists, both garbed in light-blue, denim workshirts. American civil rights groups complained that handcuffs do not convey brotherhood. The United Kingdom would not run the ad.

Table 7.4 Sandini's Sales by Region	
France and the United Kingdom	38%
Italy	31%
Japan, Korea, and China	15%
U.S.	6%
Russia, Czechoslovakia, Poland, Turkey, Egypt	6%
South American Countries	4%

Another ad was rejected by U.S. publications. It featured a black woman nursing a white infant. The rejection partially came from an American awareness of conditions before the Civil War when black women were forced to nurse white children while their own went hungry. The other negative reactions were in response to the woman's bare breast being shown in the ad.

In the midst of a Persian Gulf conflict, another ad pictured a cemetery with one white star of David among a field of white crosses. In Italy, a Milan jury deemed it offensive to religion.

A more recent ad made use of a photograph that earned an international journalism award. It portrayed a family grieving at the bedside of a young man who has just died of AIDS. The public wondered whether the ad raised awareness of the disease or exploited it. As a result of other ads that referred to the same illness, a French court found Sandini guilty of exploiting the illness and ordered the company to pay damages to a national AIDS organization, which was responsible for the suit.

Regardless of the controversy, Antonio is generally pleased with the attention the ads are receiving. Despite economic problems and lawsuits during the campaign, the corporation's net earnings increased 21 percent, largely because of licenses for new merchandise in the product line and expansion into new countries. Sales in Italy, France, and the United Kingdom (two regions) account for nearly 70 percent of Sandini's total volume. Two other regions contribute 6 percent each to the total sales and the sixth region constitutes the lowest amount—4 percent. Sandini's sales by region appear in Table 7.4.

Major Question

Should Antonio Sandini change his corporation's promotional image? How might he accomplish the task?

Study Questions

1. Has the existing ad campaign attracted the company's target market?

2. Examine corporation sales by region. Could the advertising campaign have hindered sales in some locations? What else might influence quantity of sales volume?

3. Is political or social comment appropriate within the scope of a fashion ad campaign?

Case 56
The Coop Advertising Fiasco

Nancy J. Rabolt, San Francisco State University
Judy K. Miler, University of Tennessee

Howard Peterson, the moderate dress buyer for Perkins Apparel, was having his weekly meeting with Paul Jacobs, the ready-to-wear merchandise manager. Perkins is a large, privately owned specialty department store located in New York City. They have been successful for over thirty years, but competition from the large chains makes it tougher and tougher each year to make the profit that they require.

This particular meeting took place at the beginning of the month. Paul, while reviewing the department's figures, remarked to Howard, "Say, you'll have to come up with a big promotion to meet and hopefully beat your last year's figures for the last week of this month. Last year you were lucky and latched on to an item that was hot, and it was responsible for last year's tremendous figures. I don't see any strong trends in sight at this time, so you better go out and find one."

Howard replied glumly, "You're right, there's nothing really hot that I'm aware of. And, to tell you the truth, I've been worrying about those figures for awhile now myself. My key resources do not seem to be in a position to even give me a promotional buy, so I'm not sure what to do.

All of a sudden, Paul's face lit up. He had an idea of how to help Howard. "Tell you what—the way I figure it, you need to get three thousand dresses to sell for about $49.99 each to make your figures. To meet your last year's record, you should pay about $24, no more. I'll get you about $72,000 in open-to-buy for the event and also arrange for extra advertising money for a full-age ad in two papers. That ought to do the trick; but, Howard, you better get some good merchandise at a price...the ads have to generate a sellout for us if we're to come out all right."

The next day, Howard went to Goodman Dresses, a dress manufacturer who had been after him for a long time and who was very eager to get his foot into Perkins's door. Previously, Howard had made several unimportant purchases from Goodman Dresses and had found the dresses to be nicely made. Thinking (and hoping) that this was his big chance to become a key resource with Perkins, Sam Goodman went all out in shaving his prices and ensuring delivery well in advance of the promotion.

Shortly after the purchase was made, Paul called Howard and told him that a small problem had arisen. "Howard, I hate to tell you that the general merchandise manager was not able to come across with the whole $12,800 we need for the ads. We can't cut the ads—we need all the ad space we can buy to make the ad scream PRICE! I was only able to get half the ad money, we'll need $6,400 to pay for the rest."

Howard was incredulous because the inference was unmistakable. Paul wanted him to get a $6,400 coop ad contribution on a promotional purchase, and he knew that was almost impossible. However, he dutifully went to Sam Goodman and asked him for the money to help pay for the ad. Goodman looked at Howard as if he was nuts; he swore that he was losing money on each of the three thousand dresses he had already sold to Howard. Sam pointed out what Howard already knew: he was taking this deal only because he was hoping to do business later with Perkins on a more profitable basis.

Howard reported back to Paul and informed him of his inability to get the ad money. "There is only one way out," Paul replied. "We'll have to load the invoice. Instead of $24, we'll ask Goodman Dresses to bill us at $26.15 per dress; and then we'll retail them for $54.99 instead of the $49.99 we originally planned. Also, ask Goodman to throw in some dresses that can genuinely be sold at retail for $100 so that we can legitimately advertise 'VALUES UP TO $100 FOR $54.99.' We'll then charge the manufacturer back $2.15 for each garment to cover the $6,400 we need for the ad money. In the final analysis, we'll get the volume and sacrifice a little markup."

And so it went. The merchandise arrived at the store in time and was ticketed at $54.99. The ad was to appear on Wednesday evening, for the big Thursday to Saturday sale.

After dinner on Wednesday evening, Howard went to buy the morning paper. He found his full-page ad and was quite pleased with the way it looked. But, to his horror, he discovered that on the page following his big promotion there was one from Sommers Specialty Store, their chief competitor. The Sommers ad appeared to feature the identical merchandise, but the dresses were priced at $49.95 each. Both ads had photographs illustrating what appeared to be very similar merchandise.

Howard ran to the phone and called his merchandise manager at home, exclaiming, "Paul, we've been killed—did you see the ads?"

Paul replied, "Howard you selected the merchandise. Who told you to buy from someone who could not be trusted to not sell the same dresses to another store in our market?"

The next morning Howard stopped at Sommers Department Store on the way to work and looked at the merchandise on sale. Of course, it was the same—style numbers, colors, sizes. No customer in her right mind could fail to see that it was the same merchandise at $5 lower than it was at

Perkins across the street. It is well-known in the trade that the moderate dress customer is a very smart shopper who does not impulse buy, but shops around before purchasing.

When Howard arrived at his desk there was the expected message to see Jacobs at once. Paul went right to work on Howard.

"You, as a seasoned buyer, should have known how to select a resource, negotiate your needs, and then buy a promotional purchase. I don't see how this happened!"

Major Question

If you were Howard Peterson, how would you reply to this criticism, and how would you propose to remedy this situation?

Study Questions

1. When do manufacturers offer cooperative advertising money? In what situation should a retailer accept it?

2. Why did the retailer end up in this situation? Should he deal with this vendor in the future?

3. How will customers view this price war?

4. Is it ethical to "load" the invoice as was done in this case? Is that standard business practice?

5. Is Paul Jacobs culpable in this situation?

Case 57
The Best Display

David Ehrlich, Ghostwriters

Recognizing that its first-floor selling fixtures had become outmoded, a major department store set aside funds to renovate. The main floor hadn't been changed appreciably since the store was built in the 1920s. There were a number of hand-

From *Retailing Management* by Michael Levy and Barton Weitz. Reprinted by permission of Richard D. Irwin. Copyright © 1995. All rights reserved.

some mahogany-paneled counter islands, which had always given the store an aura of tasteful elegance.

Jim Lewis, director of store fixturing, was debating the merits of several possible display systems. The selling departments that would be affected by the renovation were cosmetics; fine and costume jewelry; women's handbags, scarves, and belts; men's shirts, ties, and furnishings; women's sweaters; and gifts.

As Lewis saw it, the two major issues surrounding his decision were incompatible. On the one hand, the store wanted to make merchandise as accessible to customers as possible. On the other hand, experience indicated that open-selling fixtures inevitably lead to more shoplifting.

As an experiment, the store had tried substituting self-service fixtures in its upstairs sweater department a year earlier. Sales jumped 30 percent, but inventory shrinkage in the department had gone from 2 percent to almost 5 percent.

A further consideration was that the size and quality of the staff on the selling floor had declined dramatically. In 1929, there were always two salespeople behind every counter. Customers could count on never having to wait for service. But, due to escalating selling costs, the store's staff was now less than half what it had been then. Furthermore, the store had instituted modern point-of-sale cash registers that enabled every salesperson to ring up a sale from any department in the store at any register. Most clerks were paid minimum wage and were only working there until something better turned up. Although some could provide useful selling information to the public, most could do little more than ring up sales.

The kind of open-selling fixtures Lewis was considering were contemporary and very attractive. They allowed the customer to pick up, unfold, or unpackage merchandise; try it on if appropriate; and then return it to the fixture. Such fixtures would unquestionably lead to more sales, especially since the customer could merely look for any salesperson or perhaps go to a central cashier to pay. But, equally questionable, such easy access to merchandise—especially to small goods—would encourage shoplifting and would increase the need for ongoing stock keeping.

Another disadvantage to the new type of fixturing was that, besides being contemporary, it is somewhat trendy, so it would have to be replaced in a few years—adding to capital costs.

An alternative system would be to retain the old counter islands or a portion of them but to put more goods on the countertops to encourage a measure of self-service. The disadvantage here, of course, would be blocked sight lines. Salespeople couldn't see customers, customers couldn't see salespeople, and the store security personnel couldn't see either. There would also need to be more policing by the store's display and merchandising staff to be sure the countertops looked inviting at all times. Manufacturers often contribute countertop displays to stores as part of the merchandise buying, and many of them might not be in harmony with the store's overall appearance.

Lewis recognized that he would have to make some compromises. Every affected department has its own peculiarities, and his job was to minimize those differences rather than allow them to get out of hand. Some merchandise, such as fine jewelry, would obviously have to remain behind glass, but other departments would probably do much better by opening up their stocks to the public.

Major Question

What display system would you recommend for each of the affected departments? Why?

Study Questions

1. How can shoplifting be controlled?

2. Compare display systems in well-known stores and discuss the relationship between them and security systems.

3. How should fixturing relate to level of service in a store?

Chapter Discussion Questions

1. Compare types of promotion and advertising of well-known retailers. What media is used? What image is presented to the public? Explain what methods might be more effective for different types of retailers. Use case examples from the chapter to reinforce your decisions.

2. Compare institutional and product ads, and institutional and product displays at various stores. Which stores use mostly institutional? Which use mostly product? How does this relate to fashion leadership and the type of retailer?

3. What type of promotion is used by manufacturers, catalog companies and other non-stored retailers? How is this different from stored retailers?

4. How can a retailer be assured that a particular promotion will be successful?

5. Discuss promotional mix and how it relates to media selection. Why is it important for companies to have a promotional mix?

6. Compare and contrast the various types of interior display and suggest what types of merchandise might be best suited for each.

8

Personal Selling and Customer Relations

Chapter Objectives

- Emphasize the importance of customer service and the role of personal selling at retail.

- Examine the various aspects of customer service relations, compensation, and selling incentives.

- Define product knowledge and explain its importance in the selling process.

- Discuss the methods and importance of effective sales training and evaluation of retail sales personnel.

Today's retail customers are highly educated and sophisticated. Because they often shop with only their needs in mind, without time to waste, they are looking for good service to help them obtain what they want—when they want it. The retailers and manufacturers that address the issue of customer service can help make the sales experience a positive one that brings the customer back to shop again and again. After all, service is often at the crux of sales. More and more today, vendors are playing an active role in attracting and keeping retail customers. In many cases, they are partnering with retailers through training, to work cooperatively toward the same goal—to sell merchandise. Selling skills are crucial to retail success. Effective selling is reliant on a number of factors. For example, having a good, effective sales force to motivate customers not only to buy, but to come back to a retailer is paramount. Sales associates that are courteous, knowledgeable, and ready to serve and sell to the customer can do the job they were hired to do with confidence. This can be achieved through the proper hiring and training of the sales force. Most experts agree that the relationship between a satisfied employee and customer is closely linked, so both the customer and the retailer benefit when a well-trained sales associate performs well.

Sales and Profit

Sales lie at the base of retailing, because without sales, there would be no resulting profit and no point in being a retailer. Ironically, this crucial fact is often ignored by retailers themselves. Also, the service that should work hand in hand with selling to the customer is often disregarded. Most authorities agree that service and selling must be combined in an effort to run a successful, integrative, customer-driven business.

Improving sales and customer relations at retail should be an ongoing process that is attempted by retailers and manufacturers alike through various means. New technology, merchandising techniques, and customer service policies, in combination with pricing, have all been used by retailers to gain the competitive advantage in building good customer relations.

Sales often rely on promotion (as discussed in Chapter Seven) and personal selling is a major component of sales promotion. Because of its importance, personal selling warrants separate attention in this chapter.

Personal Selling

Selling is the person-to-person (most often face-to-face) contact between the retailer and customer, or between the manufacturer and customer, which results in a purchase by a customer. Personal **direct selling** involves direct sales contact with the customer. This includes two major kinds of selling: 1) wholesale selling; and 2) retail selling. **Wholesale (or contact) selling** involves the customer purchasing directly from the manufacturer. **Retail selling** involves using an actual physical location, for example, a store for the customer and retailer to conduct business. Retail selling can be one of three types: 1) **house-to-house**; 2) **mail** and electronic (e.g., telephone, television, and computer); and 3) **over-the-counter.** Today, the majority of retail sales still occur over-the-counter but mail order is the fastest growing method of selling in the U.S. Stored retailers rely on **sales personnel** (**sale associates**) at a store location to sell merchandise to the customer. Non-stored retailers rely on various other types of personnel to service the customer (although there may be sales representatives at some level in the marketing channel, and very often there are guest hosts and telemarketer/order takers instead of traditional salespeople).

Retail selling has always been an interactive and communicative process between buyer (customer) and seller (retailer). In its early days, shopping at a department store was a form of entertainment that included listening to concerts, attending art exhibits, and enjoying a fine meal at the store itself; therefore, visiting a department store was not done only to shop and buy but was a social occasion. Today, the interactive nature of television and electronic retail has elevated shopping once again to a new level of entertainment—one of fun, in which window shopping can be done without even purchasing. Part of the fun is researching and exploring what there is to buy, as the presentation of merchandise is enjoyable in and of itself for those who have and take the time to do so. The mega-malls (for example, Mall of America) have become vacation entertainment destinations with much more to do than purchase goods. From food to fashion, once again, retail has become a form of entertainment for all ages.

The responsibility of directing the sales staff varies from retailer to retailer. Most large stored retail organizations direct and manage sales at the store level. Merchandising plays both a direct and indirect role in selling. Some large retailers, such as JCPenney and Nordstrom and the majority of small independent merchants, clearly integrate the buying and selling functions at the store level. Store merchandisers at these retailers actively participate in the purchasing, presentation, and subsequent sale of merchandise through the supervision and direction of the sales staff and working directly with their buyers. Other retailers—particularly large chains—have their merchandising and selling functions clearly delineated. These retailers have management that is responsible for sales at the store or non-store distribution location and/or operations headquarters. Their buyers are attached to a merchandising division and are indirectly responsible for sales, because they do not supervise the sales personnel. (See Chapter Nine for more information on store management and organization.)

To achieve success today, retailers and their suppliers are working together to gain the sales that both desire and require. In some instances, a retailer's selling staff may actually be a part of the manufacturer's payroll. Some vendors, for example, Liz Claiborne (who was one of the first to do such), may furnish the sales staff to sell their goods at the retail establishment. In doing so, vendors can be assured that the sales staff is trained and knowledgeable about their products.

Expanding the Customer Base

Maintaining and expanding a retailer's customer base is necessary for growth. There are many ways for retailers to expand their customer base to ensure positive growth and sales increase. They could open more stores, expand into new markets, or diversify their merchandise assortments. However, the major way to expand customer base and stimulate sales at the retail location level without expansion or remerchandising is to encourage sales personnel to meet or exceed established **sales goals** and/or **sales quotas,** which are sales plans that are set by the retailer. Usually, the retailer hopes to either achieve or exceed these sales goal or quota plans. For example, *Case 58, The Clientele Specialist: Banana Republic* profiles a sales specialist for a specialty chain who believes, as does her company, that no type or level of service is too much for the customer. This specialist's sales are a result of establishing a strong relationship with her clients. Part of her job goal is to continuously expand her customer base by meeting a monthly clientele recruitment quota.

Incentives

Both the retailer and vendor often create incentives or motivators to stimulate sales at the retail level. Nordstrom managers, for example, often work the store handing out rewards to their employees when they see them deliver good service. **Retail-induced incentives** are those motivators that are produced or provided by the retailer to encourage sales personnel to sell, while **vendor-induced incentives** are those furnished by the supplier to the retailer or directly to the sales employee. Retail-induced incentives include compensation and recognition. **Compensation** rewards employees for work they have accomplished and/or goals that they have met or have exceeded. This compensation may be direct or indirect. **Direct compensation** is the awarding of such monetary payment as salaries or wages, **commissions** (monetary reward based on achievement of goals and usually a percentage of sales), **bonuses** (extra rewards), and **prizes** and **awards. Indirect compensation** involves non-monetary rewards, which include paid vacations, paid insurance, parking, retirement, and other perks. **Perks** are non-monetary rewards that express gratitude for work done or a position that is held by the employee. Free lunches or the right to use a company-owned vacation home (an example of a perk Esprit provided for employees) are sometimes given as perks. While recognition could include compensation, it is primarily concerned with emotional well-being. An example of employee recognition would be a salesperson being honored as employee of the month, thereby acknowledging that person as an outstanding employee.

Often, retailers use a combination of compensation methods to reward sales employees. For example, many retailers pay a minimum wage salary, but also award a commission if a sales objective for a certain time period is met or exceeded. They may also run sales contests that further reward personnel and perhaps even give free parking to outstanding salespeople. Additionally, the vendor could participate in providing an incentive for sales. In efforts to strive for high sales, salespeople at Nordstrom are encouraged to compete against each other through contests and high sales goals. The company culture is definitely one of competition within the company and amongst the employees, to achieve the sales goals of the company. A settled lawsuit brought against Nordstrom by employees, however, questioned the fair treatment and equitable compensation of the employees for the customer service they rendered. (See *Case 64, parts 1 and 2.*)

What type of monetary compensation to pay sales personnel—whether salary, wages, or commission—is often a difficult decision for retailers to make. Paying only salary or wages often results in complacency and lack of motivation in many salespeople. Commissions, on the other hand, are sometimes just the boost some salespeople need to strive harder to generate more sales. They may, however, create a harder selling (i.e., more pushy and aggressive) retail environment than some customers like. Also, figuring out how to divide up a commission can occasionally present a problem for which there is no easy solution. For example, a retail owner must determine if and how to split a commission between two sales associates who jointly served a customer in *Case 59, Wedding Gown Commission Blues.*

Vendor-induced incentives may also include the same variety of compensation methods as already mentioned under retail-induced incentives, but often they supplement the incentives that the retailer uses. **Spiffs** or **push money** are sometimes provided to retailers by vendors. These are incentives that compensate the salesperson, thereby providing motivation to try to sell particular items. In addition to monetary rewards, various other forms of vendor support and incentives include: training, trunk shows, educational material, and contests. The vendor may also supply personnel sales training and/or educational materials. Contests to win items or trips may also be vendor provided to help encourage strong sales. Additionally, some of these incentives are promotionally oriented (see Chapter Seven).

Training and Evaluating the Sales Associate

Having well-trained and knowledgeable salespeople helps to ensure that retailers communicate well with their customers. Communicating a retailer's particular message to the customer also relies on training. Periodic reviews of the salesperson's performance evaluates the job being done and helps to rectify any problems that occur, as well as providing rewards for a job well done.

Training

The people that do the selling within an organization are the most important tool a company has with which to run and improve a business. These salespeople, however, must know the goals of the company and receive instruction in what their particular role is in accomplishing these goals. **Goals** are the objectives for which a company and its employees strive. Job descriptions should clarify what is expected of employees, but training is often the means to ensure that goals can be met by teaching employees what to do. Sales personnel should be taught how to perform their jobs in the best, most productive manner according to company policy and procedures, and their particular selling methods and customer-service orientation. Policies and procedures are guides for companies to run their business how they so desire. **Policies** set governance guidelines and rules as to specific ways in which a company wants to accomplish its goals. **Procedures** are the methods—or steps—and therefore the means for a company to reach a goal. A company's procedures should be within the established policy guidelines. Training can be time-consuming and expensive and is a very serious matter to many retailers. Because it is of the utmost importance, however, it can be the basis for success or failure of a business.

The **human resources** (or **personnel**) **department** often plays a major role in training and evaluating the retailer's sales personnel, particularly when the retailer is large enough to have a separate division or department for this function. The specific role human resources plays within a retailer varies, depending on the size of the company and staff but in general it is involved with employee matters. A small retailing operation might employ a single individual who handles all personnel tasks. Conversely, a large, multi-unit department store chain might have a large human resources staff in which the various functions are divided amongst the personnel of that department. Four major functions are usually allocated to the human resource department no matter who does the job or how many people are in the department: recruiting, training, evaluating, and rewarding. Hiring and firing may also be done centrally by this department or it may be done at the retail outlet level, depending on the policy of the retailing establishment. If help in sales training (or any of the other personnel functions) is not available within an organization, professional training assistance can usually be found outside the company.

Sales training varies in type and style and from retailer to retailer but is always concerned with readying salespeople to sell products and/or services that are being offered. Some organizations realize the importance of sales training; others do not. Parisian (a retail chain), for example, invests 43 hours of new employee training before an individual is allowed on the sales floor. Instruction in excess of one week may seem like overkill to some retailers, but Parisian takes pride in its high level of service and salespersonnel, who are very professional.

Types of training, along with methods and levels of training, differ depending on the mission and goals of the retailer. The retailer's image and the types of services offered should also play a role in determining what type and level of training that employees receive. Training may be formal or informal, on-the-job or in the classroom, or even a combination of types. These types of training methods are explored in the following sections.

Formal Training Structured training that involves teaching specific tasks, methods, and/or other objectives is called **formal training**. This method of training relies on a person(s) and/or written instructions, which is used to relay the information to be taught. Sometimes formal training may be taught in a classroom in much the same way as school. Another example is a salesperson learning from a sales manual with instructions on how the job is to be performed.

Sales manuals are used by numerous retailers to convey the expectations of the company to the sales associates. Sales manuals are written procedures or directions and policies that a company wants to ensure their employees follow. Sometimes, salespeople are tested on the material found in a sales manual, which they are expected to know after training is completed. Additionally, some sales manuals are written specifically for a retail operation and incorporate all policies and procedures; these are called **store manuals.**

Major formal methods of training salespeople include:

- Lecture (and/or oral presentation)
- Demonstration (a showing of capabilities of a product)
- Videos (or films)
- Meetings, seminars, and conferences
- Role playing (i.e., acting out situations and simulations)
- Case analysis

Informal Training The **informal training** approach relies on employees learning skills as they work (i.e., **on-the-job training**) and as they need to learn specific skills. In this type of training, employees are often solely responsible for learning what they believe they need, rather than what their employer thinks is necessary. This method of training can often present problems, because how can new employees know what is expected, or how their jobs should be performed?

Many retailers today find that a combination of both formal and informal training methods works best. This combination of training methods helps to ensure that the company policies and procedures are relayed; at the same time, the employee can get a "feel" for the job and learn it while actually practicing it. The degree and mix of methods depends on the type of retailer and its philosophy or mission.

Whatever the method of training, effective selling is usually the major emphasis in training sales associates. They are trained on the mechanics of selling as well as the techniques. There are six recommended sequential steps to complete a sale. These are:

1. Approaching and greeting the customer.

2. Determining the needs and wants of the customer.

3. Presenting the merchandise and/or service to the customer.

4. Relaying product information and answering questions.

5. Suggestive selling of merchandise that may be related to that which the customer is already interested in, or stimulating interest in another product or service.

6. Closing the sale.

In addition to selling, salespeople usually have other duties tied to their job that may also have to be taught, for example, housekeeping, display, stock, pricing, and merchandise handling. These tasks may also be taught formally or informally.

Training should be considered an investment in people for a better return on financial investment (i.e., profit). Employee turnover, particularly at the sales and entry level management positions, is an unfortunate major financial problem for retailers, which is always being examined by retailers in order to improve it. **Employee turnover** is the percentage of employees that begin with a company at a certain time period, but do not remain employed at the end of that set time period. This percentage figure is usually calculated on an annual basis. Generally, healthy turnover is considered 40 percent, while 70 percent is considered unhealthy by retailers and their researchers as reported by Kabachneck (1996). This is a wide range indeed, but it is seemingly quite high even on the "healthy" low end. Kabachneck also states that many times employee turnover is due to the mismatching of people to jobs, companies, and people. Hiring and training the right people can help improve a company's employee retention level and return on investment.

As mentioned previously, partnerships are sometimes made between the retailer and supplier for training sales staff and management about merchandise. Traditionally, this was done for products that needed special instructions or fit. Today, however, it is important to relay product knowledge from sales to customer no matter what the category of merchandise. The variety and quantity of goods available today have created competition among both manufacturers and retailers that requires a higher level of product knowledge than ever before in order to win the customer's patronage. For example, if a salesperson can knowledgeably answer a customer's question about a product at one store, while at another store the salesperson cannot answer the query, the customer is more likely to purchase at the store where the question was answered.

Sales training should not only communicate exactly what the job is, it should also motivate salespeople to do the best job they can toward improving sales and customer service. When salespeople understand what is expected of them and feel confident and happy about doing their jobs, their positive attitude is usually relayed to customers. Some retailers train sales help only once, after they are hired. Others believe that training should be ongoing, because business and the customers change and the salespeople should be prepared to meet those changes. It may also be necessary to change procedures and policies to meet the changes that a particular business encounters, and this must be relayed to employees through training.

Evaluation of the Sales Associate

The **evaluation** of sales associates helps monitor their work and also informs the employee of job performance. Additionally, the evaluation of salespeople's performance can aid in bettering the work that is done, and this contributes to the improvement of the retailer's performance.

Evaluating salespeople should include a **performance review** on a regular basis. Reviewing work performance can be formal or informal, and some retailers use both methods. **Formal reviews** use time set aside on a periodic basis to meet one-on-one with the salesperson to go over their accomplished work. Additionally, feedback can be given on performance at these formal reviews. **Informal reviews,** however, consist of feedback given at any time it is needed. Some experts believe that this is the more effective means of evaluation, because it is given at the same time as the incident that warrants the feedback. The performance of salespeople is measured primarily on the sales goals and quotas they have been given, along with their customer service behavior. Evaluations, whether formal or informal, should be used to provide performance feedback and to reward, help, and/or promote that employee—if warranted.

Sometimes a sales associate's poor performance or problematic behavior requires evaluation by a supervisor in order to find a resolution. In *Case 60, Jeremy's Problem: A Possible Drug Situation,* a department manager tries to determine (evaluate) just what lies at the root of a problem with a sales associate who performs quite well but has personality problems with other staff members, who refuse to work with him.

Product Knowledge

Some say a good salesperson can sell anything. Others say that a salesperson must know and believe in the product in order to sell it. No matter what the truth is, the more knowledgeable a salesperson is about a product, the easier it is to explain it to others, who may then more readily purchase that product. **Product knowledge** educates sales associates, which enables them to educate their customers, help interpret their needs, and in turn (through the sale of that product), provide for those needs. Information about a product often sells the merchandise. Retailers and vendors alike supply information to the salespeople about merchandise that helps them answer questions and resolve problems knowledgeably.

Some products require more selling and product knowledge than others, and often the vendor must help provide the information for a salesperson to relay to the customer. Additionally, warranties and guarantees may help convince the customer that the product is what it should be and therefore will help to close a sale. A **warranty** ensures the integrity and life of a product for a specific period of time usually in writing, while a **guarantee** ensures that a product will perform as it is supposed to or the customer will be compensated.

Figure 8.1 Adrienne Vittadini Look Book pages. This type of vendor-provided product knowledge helps to educate retailers and their salespeople about Vittadini's line of merchandise by showing combinations of the various apparel pieces, as well as suggesting display and advertising possibilities.

Unfortunately, sometimes all this training and product knowledge does not achieve the results that are expected. For example, a product knowledge seminar does not stimulate sales in *Case 61, The Product Knowledge Seminar that Didn't Work;* in spite of efforts at conveying information and educating the salespeople about a new product line, a lack of knowledge still remains and sales do not improve. Because of this, other methods of relaying product knowledge and stimulating sales must be determined and then initiated, which could result in successfully selling the line.

Customer Service

Many retail experts say that **customer service** is an overused and misused term. Simply stated, it is assisting customers by providing retail activities. Prompt and courteous service is what most customers look for from retailers today because this type of effective customer service supplements the value received from a retailer. Some retailers and customers say service beyond a customer's expectations is what "good service" is all about (Kennedy, 1996). Therefore, knowing what the customer wants in regard to customer service is vital when trying to provide it. Nordstrom has a reputation for superior-quality customer service, to which they partially attribute their overall success. Employees are given the empowerment and the freedom to do almost anything it takes to satisfy customers—from delivering merchandise to accepting any product return without question.

Customer service should supplement and facilitate sales. The service given and offered to customers plays a very real role in creating the customers' perception of the store and the image they have of the retailer. It also contributes greatly in making the shopping experience positive or negative. Convincing customers to return to a store to purchase again is key to the success of a retailer. It is often not just dependent on having the merchandise a customer wants, but is also directly related to how the customer is served. Castner Knott's customer service definitions emphasize their high service orientation (see Table 8.1).

Table 8.1	Castner Knott's Customer Service Definitions

1. Greet, smile and acknowledge customers even walking through the store.
2. Listen to customers' needs.
3. Satisfy customers' needs and offer more—suggestive merchandise.
4. Go out of our way to appease unhappy customers so they will always want to come back!
5. Mention their last name.
6. Offer extra services if needed such as deliveries, gift wrap, alterations, etc.
7. Always make customers feel important as if they are the only one.
8. Being ready and willing to help every customer, being cheerful and helpful. Call other stores for additional merchandise.
9. Be willing to transfer merchandise or send something out to customer.
10. Say "Thank You" and "Have a Good Day."
11. Say "Hello, how are you?" not just "May I help you?"
12. Always smile and be excited which will make the customer feel good.
13. Do not point to the customer where to go, show them!
14. Follow through!
15. Take the time to meet the customer's needs.
16. You should be able to help a customer find what they want, which means knowing your merchandise.
17. Start talking about what customer is looking at to get conversation going and draw customer to you.
18. LISTEN to the customer.
19. Ask questions that will help you make suggestions.
20. Give benefits that the customer will receive from the purchase.
21. Treating each customer as they are the person you've been anxious to serve = special.
22. Do move around departments to assure customers you want to service them.
23. Follow up whenever possible, call or ask if you see them again how they are enjoying their purchase.
24. Going the extra mile is what will separate Castner Knott from our competitors.
25. Smiles and a positive attitude will be a plus for any customer.

Levels of Service

The manner in which a retailer sells (stored and/or non-stored) helps to determine what level of customer service the merchant should provide. Self service, limited service, or full service are terms used to describe the levels of service available to the customer. The next paragraphs briefly describe these different levels and their implications for the retail establishment.

Self service is minimal service, for example, when customers are first expected to find the merchandise they want, then take it to a service desk (cashier) to purchase it. **Limited service** provides a modicum of assistance to the customer beyond the self-serve level, but still in restricted amounts. For example, a store that has hours from 10 to 5, has a small sales staff, takes credit cards, does not gift wrap or deliver merchandise but has alterations available can be described as having limited service. **Full service** gives the customer the maximum amount of services that can be expected. These services include basic and secondary services, as well as all possible transactional services. A full-service department store today, for example, would provide cash and credit, returns, exchanges, delivery, alterations, private dressing rooms, restrooms, personal shoppers, gift wrap, and probably a restaurant or snack bar; customers would expect all regular department stores to provide these services.

The types of services available are numerous. **Essential services** (also called **primary** or **basic**) are those services that most retailers provide. Some retailers today, however, neglect supplying what is considered basic and essential service by everyone—for example, mirrors, dressing rooms, parking, and someone to ring up your sale pleasantly. **Ancillary services** are also referred to as **support services** or **secondary services.** These ancillary services usually include merchandise transfers between stores, gift wrap, valet parking,

Figure 8.2 Levi's 57th Street in New York City store provides an upbeat, trendy, self-service retail environment for its customers.

Figure 8.3 Macy's full-service retail environment, in which customers expect salespeople to assist them with their purchases.

alterations, and delivery. What is considered basic service for one store, however, may be considered support services for another—depending on the company. Services may also be tangible or intangible. **Tangible services** are those that provide such concrete assistance as personal shoppers, child-care, and delivery service. **Intangible services** are those abstract activities provided that cannot be touched physically, for example, assistance with decision-making and merchandise selection. These intangibles can be product-use displays, convenient store hours, and personal assistance. The purchased merchandise is, of course, tangible, but the aid from the display or the salesperson is not.

Customer-service philosophies and policies vary from retailer to retailer and are often dependent on the type of retailer, although this is not always predictable either. Again, what is full service to one retailer may differ from another and is often defined by company policies and procedures as well. At one time, it was rather predictable as to the kinds and levels of service that could be associated with the type of retailer. Today, it is not as easy to typecast because everyone seems to be concerned with providing service to the customer. An example of this is that at one time, all factory outlet stores were self-service stores that had only one or two employees to ring up sales and customers were on their own to decide what to buy. There were certainly no services such as gift wrapping or instore restaurants. The first department stores were full service and had everything from lounges, restaurants, libraries, and post offices, in addition to a high ratio of sales personnel to customers. Today, many factory outlets and discount stores may rival the full-service stores of the past, whereas, some department stores often provide only limited service and sometimes even seem like self-service outlets.

In addition to helping a customer with a purchase, customer service also includes ways of accommodating the purchase. These are called **transactional services,** for example, credit or charge cards, layaway, returns, and exchange adjustments. **Credit** is an alternative to paying cash. It allows the customer to buy on time, getting merchandise now, but paying for it later. Many stores find that issuing their own **charge cards** (in which an account is established in a customer's name and purchases are billed to their address) is a successful way to issue credit to their customers and increase sales. **Layaway** is another way of delaying payment for goods. Payment amounts are scheduled to be made on merchandise that is held by the store until all the payments have been received and then the customer takes ownership of the goods. This method enables customers to purchase goods ahead of need and obtain clear title with possession.

When exchanges and returns are made to a retailer, there are various ways to handle these transactions. Service includes the policies and means by which these actions are handled. For example, does a store only give credit for merchandise returned or does it give cash as well? Or, is cash only rendered if the customer has a sales receipt that proves that the merchandise was purchased with cash? Today, more and more customers want transactions handled in the manner that is preferable to them, and many times they equate a retailer's level and type of service with this accommodation to their requirements. Exemplifying this, a customer might perceive an excellent level of service at Target, because it was easy to find pleasant, helpful sales assistance, yet no tangible services were used or given.

The way in which employees behave toward the customer is also an indicator of the type of customer service a retailer provides. According to customers, customer service often is judged primarily on how the sales associates have treated the customer—it is an emotional response—rather than being reflective of tangible services. Consequently, it is wise for retailers to remember that no matter what type and number of actual services they provide—from delivery to repairs—if the customer is not treated well, these services do not mean much. Consumers today have enough stress in their lives, so eliminating stress from the retail environment certainly helps to make the customer want to stay and shop. So, even if a retailer offers full service, it may not be perceived as providing good service, and conversely, if a retailer provides limited service, it may be perceived as providing the highest level of excellent service.

Professional behavior is a term used to describe employees utilizing a businesslike manner in their interaction with other employees and/or customers. When one is unprofessional, the actions are usually those not in accordance with company policy and/or procedure. Not only is professional behavior important for sales associates to model for success, but holding the values and beliefs necessary to behave toward customers in a positive manner that is appropriate for types of merchandise, environments, and customers is also important. Sales associates' behavior is said to be the major cause of customer dissatisfaction with a retailer according to a national survey of retail management and sales personnel (Kabachneck, 1996b). Results of this survey indicate that such characteristics as friendliness, enthusiasm, and being outgoing (which are usually thought of as being the most important to effective selling) are not effective without "the qualities that indicate a belief and value system aligned with [the] sales and service" (p. 6) of the company for which the salesperson is working. So determining the selling styles of individuals, which reveals their values, attitudes, and strengths, will make a better match of seller to customer from a behavioral perspective, thereby creating more success in sales.

Two cases in this chapter examine poor customer service and unprofessional behavior in regard to the treatment of customers. Retailer policies and procedures must be reviewed and possibly adjusted because of a customer service problem in *Case 63, Customer Relations and the Black Vest.* This case involves a customer who is impatient and unhappy because of the lengthy and unprofessional manner in which an exchange is handled by a salesperson. Repeated attempts by the department manager have not resolved a problem with a strong sales producer who has weak customer service skills and demonstrates unprofessional behavior in *Case 62, Mary's Problem: Improving Her Customer Service.* Wanting to retain the employee because of her good sales record further complicates the decision-making.

The customer of today is said to be "time-poor" and either does not have extra time or does not want to use it to spend hours and hours shopping.

Consequently, speed in the sales transaction is essential. The time involved in completing a sale, along with the manner in which it is accomplished is very important to the customer. Customers regard standing in line the biggest time waster of all (Pagoda, 1996). If help is needed to expedite a purchase, the customer wants that service. Even more disturbing to the customer is when a store that is known and counted on for good customer service fails to provide it. Unhappy customers may result and can be harmful and even devastating to a retailer. Figure 8.4 depicts the consequences of 100 dissatisfied customers.

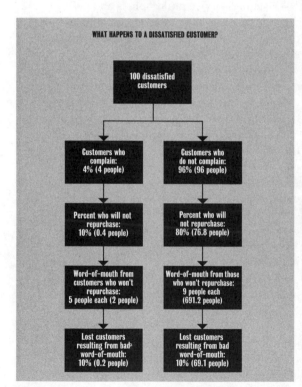

Figure 8.4 Of 100 unhappy customers, only 4 percent complain, and of the 96 percent who do not complain, some researchers estimate that up to 80 percent (i.e., 76 people) will not repurchase from the company. Theoretically, each person who won't repurchase will tell 9 other people of their negative experience (this translates to approximately 691 people) and 10 percent of those (i.e., 69 people) will be lost customers. Thus, a few complaints may represent only the tip of an iceberg: for every four complaints registered, there may be 69 lost customers due to bad word of mouth.

Summary

One major outcome of good, effective, courteous customer service is that customers will want to return to a retailer to shop. Building customer loyalty is important if a retailer wants to ensure the return of the customer, and loyalty can be partially built from good customer service. Providing good customer service today involves much more than just having sales associates wait on customers. It also involves learning the skills and product knowledge necessary to sell the merchandise and services offered to the customer. This may be provided to the sales associate through various training methods. Another important aspect of customer service is being attuned to the customer's needs and wants and providing a pleasurable environment to shop and purchase. Relaying this through personal selling helps to reinforce positive customer relations. Successful retailers must provide the best training, incentives, and evaluations for their sales personnel to stimulate and create customer loyalty and patronage. Retailers must also pay attention and address their customer's needs, wants, and values; if they do not, there are many other retailers that can (and will) satisfy their customer's desires.

References

Anton, J. (1996). *Customer relationship management: Making hard decisions with soft numbers.* Upper Saddle River: Prentice-Hall.

Blueprint for retail skills: New standards help prepare employees for sales floor success. (1995, February). *Stores,* pp. 24–26.

Cronin, J.J., & Taylor, S.A. (1992, July). Measuring service quality. *Journal of Marketing,* pp. 55–68.

Davidow, W.H., & Uttal, B. (1989). *Total customer service.* New York: Harper & Row.

Dutka, A. (1993). *AMA handbook for customer satisfaction.* Lincolnwood, IL.: NTC Publishing Group.

Kabachneck, T. (1996a, January). The true cost of turnover, *WWD,* Special Atlanta Report, p. 52.

Kabachneck, T. (1996b, May). *DNR,* Specialty Stores/The Men's & Boy's Newsletter, p. 6.

Katz, B. (1987). *How to turn customer service into customer sales,* Lincolnwood, IL.: NTC Business Books.

Kennedy, E. (1996, January). Excellent customer service means exceeding expectations. *WWD,* Special Atlanta Report, p. 51.

Nordstrom defines services. (1990, January). *Retailing Today,* p. 3.

Pagoda, D.M. (1996, April). It's a matter of time: Stores keep traffic moving, cash flowing. *WWD,* p. 1, 8, 12.

Phillips, P.M. (1996). *Fashion sales promotion: The selling behind the selling.* Upper Saddle River, N.J.: Prentice-Hall.

Plymire, J. (1991, March/April). Complaints as opportunities. *Business Horizons,* pp. 79–81.

Reda, S. (1996, January). Seven keys to better service. *Stores,* pp. 32-34.

Schneiderman, I.P. (1995, February 20). Taking the price tag off of value, *DNR,* p. 62.

Shulz, D., Robinson, W.A., & Petrison, L.A. (1993). *Sales promotion essentials,* Lincolnwood, IL.: NTC Business Books.

Zeithaml, V., Parasuraman, A., & Berry, L.L. (1990). *Delivering service quality.* New York: The Free Press.

Key Terms

ancillary service	employee turnover
awards	essential service
basic service	evaluation
bonus	(of sales associates)
charge card	formal review
commissions	formal training
compensation	full service
contact selling	guarantee
credit	house-to-house selling
customer service	human resources
direct compensation	department
direct selling	indirect compensation

informal review

informal training

intangible service

layaway

limited service

mail selling

on-the-job training

over-the-counter
    selling

performance review

perk

personnel department

policies

primary service

prizes

procedures

product knowledge

push money

retail-induced
    incentive

retail selling

sales goals

sales manual

sales quotas

sales training

secondary service

self service

selling

spiff

store manual

support service

tangible service

transactional service

vendor-induced
    incentive

warranty

wholesale selling

Case 58
The Clientele Specialist: Banana Republic

Kathryn Osgood, Levi Strauss & Co.

Meet Maria Canseco. She is a clientele specialist for the Banana Republic retail stores. A clientele specialist is a full-time, service-oriented position that is based in the store but also requires working outside the store. The specialists are in charge of building repeat customers who spend several thousand dollars each season on new merchandise. This is achieved by establishing a relationship with clients and working to meet their fashion needs. The needs of customers can be met through walk-in store visits, by appointment, or even by visitation to the customer's home. The specialists send postcards or call customers when new items come in. They may also order specific items for customers or bring new collections to their homes and allow them to shop at their convenience.

The clientele specialists can also offer such additional services as suggesting other stores that offer shoes and accessories that coordinate with the Banana Republic merchandise the customers have purchased; suggesting hair styles and/or hair salons that may help the customers complete their look; and even make dinner reservations. It is not unusual for clientele specialists to set up the fitting rooms with outfits for these customers and then bring in beverages for them. No service is too much for the clientele specialists. For all these special services, clientele specialists receive a higher hourly salary than sales associates and are offered an incentive if they make their monthly sales goals.

Both the store and Maria's position are sales-goal driven. Most of the employees of the store are part-time, and their responsibilities do not include customer follow-up. All employees are expected to work well as a team, and this is one of the reasons they are not on commission. Excellent customer service is stressed as a major company philosophy. When an employee is not working and one of his or her regular customers comes in to shop, it is expected that another employee will take over and provide the high level of customer service that the absent employee would have performed.

Maria is a full-time employee and, as such, is an unofficial manager of client customer service responsible for all follow-up to clients. Therefore, when part-time sales associates sell to new customers, they are expected to inform Maria of the sale and the store is in turn assured of follow-up. Needless to say, Maria holds a very important role in gaining repeat customers and loyal clientele.

Maria is a veteran sales associate who is perfectly suited for this position. She is, however, a part-time student, on top of a full-time job. She has worked from her assigned store for over three years. As a sales associate, she led all other salespeople in sales volume and she did so with great enthusiasm. She was promoted to client specialist where she generally meets her monthly sales volume goal, but has difficulty adding new clients. The more clients she adds, the more volume she does and the higher her incentive payouts are. Her job is not in jeopardy if she does not meet her client goal; however, if she continually misses this goal, she could be replaced in this position with a more productive worker.

Meeting the client goal is not easy. She needs to add ten new clients monthly as part of her new goals. Occasionally, a new client will just walk into the store, enjoy the service he or she has been given, and be interested in shopping with Maria again in the near future. The challenge with gaining walk-in clients is that many of her store's customers are either tourists or customers interested in sale merchandise only. Other sales associates have helped Maria with her job by suggesting the program to their good customers. Because Maria isn't always in the store to remind them to look for potential customers, she only gets a new name every couple of weeks from them. Maria, however, planned a strategy to achieve her goal.

As a means to accomplish her goals, she planned and held a fashion show with a local private Catholic school. Coordinating all the outfits and fitting the models required a lot of time. Maria did a great job, and the show was well received. Several customers responded to the merchandise they saw in the show. As a result of the show, Maria added two new clients, both with daughters in high school, which limited their time and available disposable income. This event was not quite the success she had hoped it would be. Next, she attended a meeting of a local business women's organization. That night there was a long-winded guest speaker, and Maria did not have the opportunity to speak in front of the group. She did locate the group's chair after the meeting and set a date to present some of the latest fashions to the group, but it would not be scheduled for another month. She needs to find at least five new clients by the end of this month, which is exactly one week away.

Major Question
What should Maria do to find new clients?

Study Questions
1. What are other ways that a store can increase its customer base besides using a clientele specialist?

2. What types of incentives can a retailer provide its sales staff to increase sales?

3. What is the difference between a bonus system and commission?

4. How might Banana Republic's management help encourage a team-oriented store culture?

Case 59
Wedding Gown Commission Blues

Paula R. King, Southeast Missouri State University

Charlene Keithley operates a bridal specialty shop in Houston, TX. Houston is a huge metropolitan area in both population and geographical area so the market for bridalwear is large. Many small businesses compete for customers. Charlene offers a full range of bridal goods and services, as well as excellent customer service. She stresses customer service in all store advertising. Charlene's employees are expected to happily go out of their way to serve the customers and this gives her store a competitive edge in the market.

Two sales associates work for Charlene—Elaine Rhodes and Pat Slack. Elaine has worked in various retail clothing establishments for twenty years and considers herself to be an "old pro." She is an older worker, dependable and available to work a variety of hours. Elaine is very protective of her break times and strictly regulates her efforts in store tasks to what she considers fair. She is also very aggressive in pursuit of commission-paying customers. Pat is younger and relatively new to retail. She is less aggressive with customers and is more likely to do such routine tasks as cleaning and fixing the displays around the store. Elaine and Pat have a good working relationship, but they are not friends outside of work. Both salespeople work for a salary plus commission on customer orders and they are responsible for ensuring that their customers are taken care of throughout the whole sales transaction.

Elaine's customer, Nancy Cuthbertson, ordered her wedding gown, veil and headpiece, bridesmaids' dresses, and silk floral arrangements from Charlene's store. Nancy's gown needed fairly extensive alterations and because she ordered it during a very busy season, the gown was taken to a seamstress off the premises. Elaine made an appointment with Nancy for a fitting at 1:00 on the second day of May. Nancy called to confirm the appointment on that morning. Pat took the call.

When Pat could not locate the gown in the storage area reserved for completed alterations, she asked Elaine what she should tell Nancy. Elaine, who was with another customer, said "I haven't had time to pick up that gown. Ask Nancy to reschedule. May 4th or 5th would be good." Pat relayed the message to Nancy who became furious. "I had to make special arrangements to leave work to keep this appointment! I had to drive myself to work rather than car pool, which meant that my mother had to give me her car for the day. This is the only day I can come!" Nancy continued to berate Pat for several minutes.

Pat listened to Nancy's complaints, then decided to go get the gown herself, even though she had to leave work to do so. She calmed Nancy, told her to come at the appointed time, then explained her decision to Elaine. Elaine was very critical of Pat for "giving in to a customer's unreasonable demands" and further criticized her for leaving the store shorthanded, while she went to get the gown from the seamstress. Nevertheless, Pat got the dress and Nancy came in for her fitting.

Charlene, who had been away from the store on May 2, was unaware of the situation until she received a letter of apology and appreciation from Nancy, who was embarrassed about her outburst on the phone and very grateful for Pat's efforts. Because Charlene wants to encourage good customer service by her sales associates and understands the benefit of good word-of-mouth advertising, she approached both Elaine and Pat with the idea of splitting the commission for Nancy's sale between the two of them. Elaine, not surprisingly, was not pleased. "I worked with Nancy for a long time on the whole wedding. Pat doesn't deserve pay for work that I did." Pat was reluctant to accept any plan that would make working with Elaine difficult, although the extra money would be very welcome.

Major Question

If you were Charlene, how would you handle the question of splitting the commission between Elaine and Pat?

Study Questions

1. Was Pat's decision to leave the store to pick up the dress an appropriate one? What other options might she have considered?

2. In a business that is strongly service oriented, is a customer's demand ever unreasonable? Was Nancy's anger an unreasonable response?

3. What steps can Charlene take to encourage good future customer service by her sales staff?

Case 60
Jeremy's Problem: A Possible Drug Situation

Peggy Gorbach, Evergreen Valley College
Nancy J. Rabolt, San Francisco State University

Jeremy Christopher, at the age of 23, has worked for three years in the men's department at Robinson's, a moderate Southern California department store. His job performance rating is excellent because of his high sales records and he does all the different aspects of his job completely and accurately. Jeremy rarely misses a day when he is scheduled to work and he always stays for his entire shift. However, at times Jeremy is rude to fellow employees and he appears to have severe mood swings from time to time. This behavior never shows in his manner with customers who he treats courteously and professionally. Lately Jeremy's mood swings have become more extreme, provoking constant conflicts with other sales associates. These conflicts include disagreements over department displays, miscommunication regarding merchandise that

has been placed on "hold" by customers, rotation of customers, follow-ups on special orders and store transfers, and the responsibility for mark-downs. When Peggy Kerns, the department manager, finally asked him about his behavior, Jeremy had a reason for his actions and blamed the other associates. After a month of conflicts, fellow employees no longer wanted to work with him and asked to be scheduled on opposite days. Suzi Tepper and Claire Morgan, new employees, have gone so far as to call in sick on the days they were scheduled to work with Jeremy.

At first, Peggy thought Jeremy was becoming bored with his job but because of Jeremy's dramatic mood swings, Peggy suspected he had a drug problem, but had no proof. She repeatedly tried to find the source of his problem; but Jeremy never came forth with any information, only denial of drug usage or any problem with his private life. Jeremy's answer was always related to other people, not to himself. Robinson's policy was dismissal of employees—on the spot—if they were found to be using drugs at work. The store had no mandatory drug testing for new or current employees; therefore, there was no chance of physical evidence.

Because Jeremy is an effective salesperson and customers like him, there appeared no reason to dismiss him. But there still was the big problem of the fact that no one wanted to work with him. Peggy approached the store's human resources department about this particular situation and consequently a company policy was developed. This new policy stated that if an employee had a drug problem and if the employee came forward with it, everything possible would be done to assist the employee if he or she would go into a drug rehabilitation program at the company's expense. An employee would be able to take sick leave, vacation time, and any other necessary time off to complete the rehabilitation program and keep his or her job. Upon implementation of the company policy every employee received a leaflet explaining the program and ensuring complete confidentiality. Also in the flyer was an explanation of the company policy regarding employee drug usage. (If an employee was found to be using drugs and didn't come forward with the problem, he or she would be terminated.) Employees were asked to sign a statement that they understood store policy and the program that was available to them.

After the new program was in place and known throughout the store, Peggy again approached Jeremy. She spoke to him about his continued abusive actions toward the other associates and their complaints about him. She advised him that if he was using drugs he would lose his job. Again, Jeremy denied any use of drugs. He said "You have a very active imagination," and turned and went back to the sales floor. Peggy was dumbfounded.

Major Question

As a department manager, what should Peggy do about Jeremy's abusive, erratic behavior toward the other employees?

Study Questions

1. What could be the cause of Jeremy's behavior?

2. What types of activities and conflicts can lower the morale of employees in the workplace?

3. What criteria should the human resources department use when firing an employee with a problem like Jeremy's?

Case 61
The Product Knowledge Seminar that Didn't Work

S. Lee and Mary E. Boni, Kwantlen University College

Urbanite is a privately owned retail operation. The store has been very successful to date because of the ability of the owners and managers to predict trends in advance of larger chains, to provide excellent customer service, and to offer good value for the money. The store is promoted as a one-stop store, selling a total head-to-toe look, offering helpful advice from knowledgeable sales staff, and coordinating accessories to an outfit. Urbanite's market is primarily working women, from age 25 to 60, who want distinctive and contemporary fashions made with quality fabrics. The average customer has some knowledge of fashion, but relies on the experience and guidance of the sales staff when she shops. To date, the company has carried such lines as Jones New York, Anne Taylor, Steilman, and Ellen Tracy. The sales staff is a mixture of seasoned and new employees whose interest in and knowledge of fashion and retail varies with age and experience.

Recently, the company introduced the Anne Klein II line into its store. The line, with its emphasis on quality fabrics, finishing details, and forward design, fits in very well with the store's image. The current Anne Klein II line features top-quality natural and state-of-the-art synthetic fabrics, with a new microfibre being used for outerwear that is unique to them this season. The wool for suiting has been blended with Lycra in a waffle weave, resulting in a textured lightweight, comfortable fit. Egyptian cotton—in a finer waffle weave than the suiting—is being used for tops. The line is extremely well-constructed, with unusual finishing details, and the silhouette is flattering and fashionable. The colors coordinate with trend predictions for upcoming seasons, and are combined in a manner that is unusual, but versatile. Further coordination of the look comes from the Anne Klein II accessory line, which Urbanite also carries. To enhance sales, Urbanite arranged a product knowledge seminar with the Anne Klein II representative. Employees had been requested to attend the seminar, which was held after work at the sales representative's office.

Pamela Benjamin, the sales representative, had set aside time after work for her presentation, but was running late and started the meeting feeling tired and a bit rushed. Her office is small, and when the Urbanite employees arrived it felt cramped and stuffy. Pamela spoke enthusiastically, but quickly, and rarely paused to allow questions. She showed story boards and illustrations of the line the store currently carries. She talked about the history and success of the company, and discussed her own success in promoting the line. Her talk focused more on her area of expertise—sales—rather than a detailed discussion of the garments. The employees who attended listened carefully, but also were tired from a long day's work, and when Pamela asked for questions, she received little response. Pamela thought she had sufficiently explained the line, but in fact many of the Urbanite employees left the seminar having gained little information or product knowledge, and in the resulting weeks, their lack of knowledge about the product affected the sales of the Anne Klein II line.

Heather Holland, a new employee, has had particular trouble selling the line. Although able and courteous, she is weak in her knowledge of fashion trends, and gained little useful information from the product knowledge session. To her, the Anne Klein II line seems similar to other lines, but considerably more expensive. Being unaware of its superior quality and distinctiveness, she finds it hard to justify the increased cost to customers. She makes a few attempts to show the line, but when she meets with resistance to the price she cannot discuss the quality and uniqueness of the garments. Consequently, she has been losing sales and is turning off the product—which only makes it harder for her to make a sale.

Judy Abdul, a more seasoned employee, has a good grasp of fashion trends and is somewhat familiar with the Anne Klein II line. However, she left the seminar without determining what angles she could use to promote the line. She has shown the line to her customers, but when she encounters resistance to the higher price, she did not have sufficient knowledge to justify the difference. When showing the line, she talked about its relation to current trends in terms of silhouette and color. For her customers, this is not enough reason to spend more on a garment that they perceive as being very similar to a less-expensive item. When faced with

such resistance, and without having a strong counter argument, Judy fell back on the technique of promoting less costly garments. Her sales record is quite good, but not with the Anne Klein II line, and she has begun to feel frustrated when she tries to sell it.

Samantha Holloway, on the other hand, has had success with the line. Her sales of the line are extremely good, and she frequently adds to her sales by promoting the Anne Klein II accessories. However, her knowledge of the line comes from previous experience in selling it in another store, coupled with her own avid interest in fashion. She is highly aware of the quality of the clothing, and makes her sales pitch from that angle.

The manager, dissatisfied with the Anne Klein II sales figures, has talked with each of the three employees, and has recorded their observations and frustrations. The owners and manager have met and discussed the problem. They decided that lack of sound product knowledge is preventing the employees from making a strong presentation to the customer. To justify the price, customers must be convinced that they are buying distinctive, well-crafted, fashionable garments that will last due to their design and construction. To convince Urbanite's customers to buy the Anne Klein II line, the sales staff must be convinced themselves and must be extremely knowledgeable about the value of both the apparel and the accessory lines.

Major Question

What can the management of Urbanite do to ensure the success of the Anne Klein II line in their store?

Study Questions

1. How could the employees be motivated to attend a second product knowledge session? Is it necessary?

2. How could the first product knowledge session have been more successful?

3. How can employees become knowledgable about any product they sell?

Case 62
Mary's Problem: Improving Her Customer Service

Melissa M. McCune, Carolee Designs, Inc.

Mary Franklin has been employed with Rosenberg's Department Store as a sales associate for over sixteen years and until quite recently has never caused any concern. Everyone on the staff really likes Mary. She is on time, flexible, has high sales per hour, is meticulous with paperwork, and works well with other sales associates. Recently, however, her performance in customer service has been poor. For the last few months, customers have constantly complained that she is rude and short with them. Many of the customers who are complaining are long-time, regular customers of Rosenberg's and many have been working with Mary for a number of years. They are concerned, because they think something must be wrong to create such a change in her. They are remaining loyal to Mary and Rosenberg's, however, and, for the time being, are continuing to buy as usual.

Steve Kim, the department manager, has already spent quite some time with her discussing and trying to resolve this new problem. He has explained that she must be polite, respectful, and professional when dealing with all customers on the selling floor, as Rosenberg's takes pride in valuing their customers and treating each one as an important individual. Mary still continues to act unprofessionally, regardless of his intervention and her early training on how Rosenberg's expects sales associates to treat their customers. Something is going on that Steve cannot put his finger on.

Mary does not seem aware that her behavior is offensive to the customers, stating that they must be overreacting, because her sales are still high. It is unusual that her sales per hour are high given this type of behavior toward customers and Steve feels that before too long her sales will decline. Steve has tried to deal with Mary's problem one-on-one, instead of getting upper management involved because she has been an excellent sales associate for sixteen years. The problem has still continued after several discussions, so he has recommended that Mary go through the company's retraining program to help her improve her professional skills with customer service. This retraining program is designed for employees who are having some difficulty with customer service and has proven to be successful for others who have attended; therefore Steve feels that this is all Mary needs to get back on track.

Mary accepted Steve's recommendation and she went through the two-week training program, which concentrated on professional customer service. The instructor of the training program explained how to act when dealing with customers in various circumstances on the selling floor. The steps in completing a successful sale, suggestive selling, and even approaches to handling irate customers were also covered in the training. Mary was told that giving excellent customer service involves respect, politeness, and excellent communication skills—including, of course, listening to the customer. The instructor also recommended creating a strong clientele book, which should be done by developing well-established, one-on-one relationships with customers. After returning to the store, Mary mentioned to Steve that she felt it had been a good program and she now felt that she actually understood just what good customer service is. Steve felt that perhaps the problems were resolved.

Following the program, Steve watched Mary very closely when she was on the selling floor to see if she made improvements in her behavior. The first week after the program Mary did seem to improve, but after that week, she again started acting unprofessionally toward customers. At this point, Steve was very frustrated and almost at his wit's end. Not knowing what to do, he decided to speak to the store manager as soon as possible about the problem with Mary. He hated the fact that he couldn't resolve the problem without getting the store manager involved, but it was time to take strong action on the problem. After Steve and Fred Reicher (the store manager) talked, Fred advised Steve to set up a meeting with Mary, Steve, and himself. Steve and Fred thought this meeting would give Mary an indication of the seriousness of the matter, as well as give her the incentive to try harder to be professional when dealing with customers. The actual meeting went well as Mary finally acknowledged that she was having some problems and seemed willing to improve her weaknesses. Fred was very optimistic about the situation, because he thought that Mary now would finally improve her work performance. Surely the combination of the training program, the discussions, and the meeting would actually help Mary resolve her interpersonal skills. The results, however, were once again less than expected as Mary's performance toward customers still remained unsatisfactory.

Steve, Fred, and the entire management at Rosenberg's were now very discouraged about resolving Mary's problem. Steve had yet another meeting with Mary to indicate to her that strong actions—including letting her go—would be taken if she didn't change her performance, as it could not continue. Steve doesn't want to let Mary go because of her other assets including her dependability and high sales performance. Also, Mary has been a loyal employee of Rosenberg's and Steve feels that she is at least owed something for that. Firing her may be necessary if improvement does not occur, however, because it is most likely just a matter of time until her sales performance will decline as a result of her behavior toward the customers—even though many are still putting up with her rudeness.

Major Question

What recommendation(s) would you give Steve in regard to Mary's unprofessional behavior toward her customers?

Study Questions

1. How is good customer service defined?

2. Why is it important to treat customers courteously?

3. Could other sales associates help Mary learn how to deal with customers?

4. How do the relationships that sales associates have with customers affect the customer's opinions and attitude about the store?

Case 63
Customer Relations and the Black Vest

Carol F. Tuntland, California State University

Robinsons-May has just had their "Big Spring Sale" with major markdowns on all items in the store. Business had been brisk in the misses departments during the two weeks of the sale. One of the items that had been on sale in the misses sportswear department was a black, crinkle-fabric, front-buttoned vest. This vest coordinated with black pants in the same fabric and with similar items in two additional black/brown/white print fabrics. The sell-through on the black items had been very good. Only a few vests in broken sizes remained at the end of two weeks. The department, however, was still crowded with merchandise.

The day after the sale ended, a customer returned a black, crinkle-fabric vest in size 12 that had holes in the fabric at the shoulder. The damage to the fabric had been caused by improper handling of the merchandise at the manufacturing or distribution levels, rather than by poor construction techniques. This customer wanted a replacement vest in black. There was only one salesperson on the floor—in the register area. Her name tag identified her as Bette. The customer asked Bette if there were more vests on the floor in the size needed, but Bette just indicated where to look and did not move from behind the register to check the merchandise in the department. The customer found the merchandise on the floor herself and reported to Bette that there was one additional size 12 vest on the rack of pants and vests—but it was also damaged. When the customer asked if there was any back stock, Bette replied, "All the stock is on the floor." At this point, the customer asked, "Would any of your other stores have this vest?" Bette indicated that the other stores might have it and reluctantly agreed to call the other stores in the area to see if the vest was available from any of them.

While the customer waited, Bette began to call other stores, but was called away to deal with another situation on the selling floor. Bette, however, did enlist the help of a salesperson from another department to continue the search for merchandise while she was gone. The customer decided to search other racks in case the merchandise was available but misplaced. They discovered three additional vests on other racks with similar damage, indicating that there was a consistent problem with this particular merchandise. After approximately fifteen minutes, Bette returned to the register area to continue calling additional stores. She continued to call for an another ten minutes. Salespeople at two of the stores were busy and refused to check for merchandise at the time.

The tenth store on the list had the vest but was approximately 30 miles from this store. When Bette relayed this information, the customer asked to have it sent to the local store for pickup. Bette requested the customer's driver's license and informed the customer that there would be a $3 charge for the delivery of the merchandise to the customer's home, unless she wanted to drive to the other location to pick up the vest herself. When the customer requested that the merchandise be transferred to this store for pick up, she was informed that there was no mechanism for a transfer of merchandise between stores. The customer's choices were to pay the $3 service charge for delivery to her home or drive to the other location for the merchandise. The customer quickly calculated that it would be more efficient to pay the $3 charge than to drive to the other location and agreed to the delivery.

Bette gave the information to the salesperson at the other location, used the customer's charge card, and added that the charge for this particular delivery was to be $3. When the salesperson at the other location questioned the delivery charge, Bette was forced to leave the telephone to seek a department manager to verify the delivery charge. The customer began to grow impatient, but continued to wait, drumming her fingers while the salesperson and the department manager haggled with the salesperson at the other location. They finally agreed on the $3 charge, and the transaction was completed. When the customer asked when the transfer process for merchandise was discontinued, Bette casually replied, "Oh, a long time ago, before I began to work here." When questioned further by the customer, Bette was clearly peeved by the questions and informed the customer that, "Normal delivery charges are $6.00. This is a special case because you are exchanging merchandise so you have to pay only half of the delivery charge."

Bette then credited the customer for the damaged goods and thanked her for her business. The transaction was complete. Bette did not suggest other merchandise, but smiled pleasantly and turned to help the next customer. The return for damaged goods took 45 minutes for both Bette and the customer.

Major Question

How could this transaction have been accomplished to reflect a better customer service orientation on the part of the salesperson (Bette) and the store?

Study Questions

1. Could the situation have been averted by prior checking of merchandise for damages and removing damaged merchandise from the floor? Who is responsible for these problems?

2. Do you believe that the salesperson provided good customer service ? Why or why not?

3. Why was the driver's license requested?

4. Why is merchandise sent directly to the customer rather than transferred between local stores?

5. How can retailers provide good customer service and keep expenses down?

6. Because the customer was exchanging defective merchandise, should she have been charged any amount of money for the delivery of the replacement vest?

Case 64, part 1
The Nordstrom Way

J. Barry Mason and Morris L. Mayer, University of Alabama
J.B. Wilkinson, Youngstown State University

Nordstrom, a fashion specialty retailer headquartered in Seattle, Washington, sells mainly apparel, accessories, and shoes. Sales have grown tenfold in the past decade. Competitors have taken notice and now benchmark their customer support programs against Nordstrom. They recognize that competent service and an experienced sales staff are keys in customer satisfaction.

Nordstrom's merchandise is the same as in most large upscale chains. The look is classy. The selection is limited to styles with broad appeal. Nordstrom outlets stock many of the most popular designer lines such as Calvin Klein, Anne Klein, and Donna Karan. They typically do not feature designers with their own in-store boutiques in the belief that such a move would draw attention away from the Nordstrom name.

Nordstrom's primary competitive advantage in merchandising comes from its enormous inventory and regionalized buying system. Merchandise is available in every conceivable size and color. Some Nordstrom stores stock more than 10,000 pairs of shoes. The stores are replete with small amenities such as real piano players and baby grands. The dressing rooms are large, and the merchandise doesn't carry large antitheft apparel tags.

Nordstrom stores typically have as many as 50 percent more sales associates on the floor than competitors of similar size have. Salespeople receive a continuing stream of morale-boosting and attitude-shaping messages. Associates write notes to customers thanking them for their business. Merchandise is accepted for return without question and, often, without receipts.

Nordstrom creates an intensely competitive atmosphere by setting ever-higher sales goals and pitting employees against one another in contests. "People that respond to that kind of pressure are our kind of people," says Bruce Nordstrom.[1] Store managers, for instance, must publicly declare their sales goals at regional meetings. Then a top executive unveils what he calls the "secret committee's" sales target for each store. Unlucky managers who set goals below the committee's are booed. Those who exceed them are cheered. To egg on the crowd, the usually reserved John Nordstrom sometimes dons a letterman's sweater emblazoned with a big N.

The executives also hand out monthly cash prizes to stores that provide the best service. The choice is made on the basis of scrapbooks bulging with letters from customers, copies of thank-you notes salespeople write to their customers, and notes called "heroics" that associates write about each other.

Sales associates who do especially well are honored monthly as All-Stars. A Nordstrom executive shakes their hands and gives them $100 and the right to big discounts in the store. The most productive are inducted annually into the Pace Setters Club, which also entitles them to big discounts. And the best managers get their names engraved on a plaque in the executive suite.

To promote service, employees are given the freedom to do almost anything to satisfy shoppers. Billie Burns, a former men's clothing department manager, once got a call from a regular customer who was racing to the airport and needed some clothes. Mr. Burns gathered up a bag full of blazers, slacks, and underwear; charged them to the customer's account; and met the man's car outside the store for the handoff. A sales representative at

---

[1] The remaining portions of this case are quoted from Francine Schwadel, "Nordstrom's Push East Will Test Its Reknown for the Best in Service," *The Wall Street Journal,* August 1, 1989, p. 1. Reprinted by permission of *The Wall Street Journal,* ©1989 Dow Jones & Company, Inc. All Rights Reserved Worldwide.

the same store once soothed a frantic executive with a run in her stockings by delivering some nylons to the woman's office in time for her to change for a big meeting.

Today, the Nordstroms, unlike other retailers, require virtually everyone to start on the sales floor, where they themselves started by stocking shoes. They attract career-oriented college graduates partly by paying, in combination with an hourly wage, commissions ranging from 5 to 10 percent after employees meet certain sales quotas. The average Nordstrom sales associate earns around $25,000 a year, compared to less than $20,000 for associates at other stores where commissions normally aren't paid. A top performer at Nordstrom can make more than $80,000.

The Nordstrom culture does have its eccentric moments. Former employees in certain regions say that, in motivational seminars, they were encouraged to write and repeat upbeat statements called "affirmations." While still a sales associate, for instance, one former store manager told himself repeatedly, "I enjoy being a store manager at Nordstrom." Associates have also focused on such phrases as "I feel proud being a Pace Setter." Some employees consider it pop psychology, but others embrace the idea, writing chants aimed at changing their lives.

Major Question[1]

What elements of the Nordstrom culture result in such an obsessive focus on customer service?

Study Questions

1. What role does merchandising play in Nordstrom's drive to deliver superior customer service?

2. How does Nordstrom manage to survive and prosper when its stores have many more sales associates than the typical competitor and offer amenities not found in similar retail outlets?

---

[1]Please note: Do not use alternative analysis format for this case.

Case 64, part 2
Labor Strife Clouds Nordstrom's Service Policy

J. Barry Mason and Morris L. Mayer, University of Alabama
J.B. Wilkinson, Youngstown State University

Everything was going just fine for Nordstrom. With its smiling employees who offered legendary customer service, the Seattle-based retailer was hailed as the perfect role model for department stores everywhere.

But then came nasty allegations that some employees were never paid for all those special Nordstrom touches. Nordstrom sales associates, it seems, were dropping off those purchases at shoppers' homes and dashing off thank-you notes to loyal customers on their own time. Some of the employees didn't think that was right. As one ex-Nordstrom associate told the *Wall Street Journal*: "Granted, the customer gets treated like a hundred bucks. And Nordstrom gets rich off it. So nobody loses—except the employee."

As part of a class-action suit against Nordstrom, the United Food and Commercial Workers Union collected more than 1000 complaints from employees who claimed to have worked an average of 8 to 10 hours a week "off the clock." Nordstrom got more bad news when the state of Washington's Department of Labor and Statistics said Nordstrom had violated state law by not keeping accurate records of employee overtime.

The controversy began when Nordstrom introduced a policy making union membership optional in six stores in the Seattle and Tacoma areas. The union fired back with a class-action suit that would

---

require Nordstrom to keep records of all labor time. The suit also asked that Nordstrom be made to pay employees for all overtime worked in the past six years as well as penalties, attorney fees, and court costs. The suit covered employees in every state in which the chain operates.

Joe Peterson, president of Local 1001 (Seattle) of the United Food and Commercial Workers Union, contended Nordstrom employees had a "directive" to report overtime. If they reported the extra hours, however, their sales-per-hour figure went down. That meant they might miss out on getting the best shifts or even risk being fired.

"It's a trade-off. The best companies are not always the easiest employers," said David Hadad, president of Mighty-Mac, one of Nordstrom's apparel vendors. "They want to be on top." Nordstrom, without question, is tops in understanding customers' needs and providing customer satisfaction, he said. It demands optimum performance from its employees and is very competitive. But Nordstrom also gives its sales associates the chance to make more money than they would with the competition.

Nordstrom eventually signed National Labor Relations Board orders settling all outstanding issues stemming from the unfair labor practice complaints.

Major Question

What type of customer service activities would you recommend Nordstrom initiate and/or alter in order to avoid problems like those they have had with employees? Employee procedures?

Study Questions

1. What are the attributes of successful Nordstrom salespeople? What types of individuals are not likely to succeed in the Nordstrom environment?

2. Discuss the differences between hourly and salaried personnel.

3. What expectations of a retailer are reasonable of an hourly associate?

Chapter Discussion Questions

1. How can personal selling be directly related to providing good customer service? What roles do training and evaluations of sales personnel play toward the goal of good customer service?

2. Why is it imperative that apparel retailers and resources partner for the benefit of good customer service? Explain some methods of doing such, in addition to those described in the chapter cases.

3. Compare and contrast formal and informal sales training. What are the benefits and shortcomings of both methods? Case examples may support your discussion.

4. Explain why product knowledge is important for sales. How is it related to customer service?

5. Discuss the relationship between employee compensation, sales incentives, and customer service. How do these relate to good and/or poor customer service? Cite case examples and specific methods to support your arguments.

9

Management Roles and Responsibilities

Because change is such a major part of the world today, business organizations must prepare their management to react and adapt to change. Managers plan, organize, direct, and control businesses and should possess effective communication skills and leadership traits to do their jobs in the best possible manner. Successful and effective managers today must also be flexible, open-minded, and visionary in order to lead their companies and employees. Managers are very often responsible for supervising, training, and evaluating employees who report to them. This makes it just as important for their roles and responsibilities to be as clear as those that they manage. Through the proper training and evaluation methods, retail organizations can help ensure that management is prepared to succeed. Organizational charts are tools used to help clarify positional structure within an organization. These help delineate authority and reporting associations, as well as organize the work functions.

Chapter Objectives

- Describe retail management's roles and responsibilities.

- Emphasize the methods and importance of effective training and evaluation of retail management personnel.

- Explain organizational structure, delegation of authority, and chain of command.

Managers and Management

Management is "the process of getting activities completed efficiently and effectively with and through other people" (Robbins and Coulter, 1996 p. 8). **Managers** are the people who have been given formal authority and power to direct, supervise and motivate employees to complete those activities that ensure that a company's needs are met. A business usually has at least three management aspects: 1) the business; 2) the employees; and 3) the operations. Managers may supervise one or more of these aspects. For example, a divisional merchandise manager directs the business within a specific domain, but also supervises and directs the buyers who are under this position. Another example is that of a store manager who not only

Rich's/Lazarus/Goldsmith's
Management Philosophy

"We have a concept, held by all levels of management that the elements of good human relations are more essential to the success of a business than any one single thing. The development of people...the job satisfaction of people...are more important than anything that one can buy or sell or make." Richard Rich (1950)

In keeping with these words of wisdom, Rich's/Lazarus/Goldsmith's strives to create a working atmosphere which contributes to maximum productivity. In so doing, each & every associate has the equal opportunity to reach his or her fullest potential. The policies below create a safe, pleasant & rewarding environment for all. It is essential that all associates at every level know & abide by these policies. It is through these very basic concepts that each of us can obtain the rewards of our efforts.

Equal Employment Opportunity:

Rich's/Lazarus/Goldsmith's is committed to equal employment opportunity for all individuals without regard to race, color, religion, national origin, age, sex, marital status or disability. These opportunities include, but are not limited to, recruitment, hiring, training, transfer/promotiion, compensation, benefits & all other terms & conditions of employment. Employment related decisions are made & based on job related criteria & policies & procedures establish within the Company. Each associate is encouraged & expected to contribute to the organization the full value of their knowledge & experience. Any actions contrary to this policy, whether by management or co-workers, should be reported immediately to the Human Resources Manager.

Sexual Harassment:

Rich's/Lazarus/Goldsmith's is committed to work environment free of sexual harassment. It is the policy of Rich's/Lazarus/Goldsmith's to prohibit sexual harassment of any kind. Sexual harassment is defined as "unwelcomed" sexual advances, requests for sexual favors, and/or other verbal or physical conduct of a sexual nature when:

A. submission to such conduct is made either explicitly or implicity a term or condition of an individual's employment, or;

B. submission to or rejection of such conduct by an individual is used as the basis for employment decision's affecting such individual, or;

C. such conduct has the effect of unreasonably interfering with an individual's work performance or creating an intimidating, hostile or offensive working environment.

It is the responsibility of each & every associate to conduct themselves in a manner consistent with professional behavior. Any concerns of this nature should be reported immediately to the Human Resources Manager.

Open Door Policy:

Every Rich's/Lazarus/Golsmith's associate has both the privilege & the responsibility to express ideas, suggestions or issues of concern to a supervisor, Human Resources member or any other appropriate executive. Our Company is a diverse one with a varied background. Each associate at every level is encouraged to share their experiences so that we all may grow as a team. it is only through this open discussion that sound ideas can become practices & concerns become resolved quickly & efficiently.

Legal Compliance:

Rich's/Lazarus/Goldsmith's is committed to obeying all laws which affect the company, but we need your help.

If you are aware of any violation of applicable law at Rich's/Lazarus/Goldsmith's, please report it to any member of senior management immediately.

We will not tolerate violations of applicable law, & any such conduct may result in disciplinary action or termination of employment, & could carry state/federal penalties for any involved associate as well as the company. Likewise, we will not tolerate retaliation against associates who report violations.

Supervisors should create a work climate where everyone is expected to obey laws which affect the company.

Each & every one of our associates has the responsibility to abide by these policies. To do so creates a working environment where we are winners. Complete policies can be reviewed in your Associate Handbook or in the Human Resources Department. We encourage you to take the time to read them carefully.

Russell Stravitz, Chairman   Susan Kronick, President

Figure 9.1 Rich's/Lazarus/Goldsmith's management philosophy, which expresses the company's policies on equal employment opportunity, sexual harassment, open door policy, and legal compliance.

oversees the store employees, but also runs the store operations and the company business. The organization of the business guides management toward realizing goals. Communication lies at the base of effective management from clarifying roles and responsibilities, to the training and evaluation of personnel. Many companies have philosophies or missions that help to clarify and relay the objectives of the organization, as is shown in Figure 9.1.

Roles and Responsibilities

There are a myriad of management positions in retailing today and with these management positions come roles and responsibilities that must be adopted in order to achieve success. To be effective, however, managers must first understand the goals of the company and the role they play toward achieving this shared goal. As a manager, generally, the position includes four basic functions:

1. Planning

2. Organizing

3. Directing

4. Controlling

Creating and/or maintaining company policies and procedures is another major role of management. Personnel decision-making also lies at the base of a manager's position. The retail manager may undertake numerous specific duties and decisions while planning, organizing, directing, and controlling staff. These duties may include:

- Planning goals and such events as promotional sales.

- Organizing, scheduling, and assigning work.

- Leading, instructing, informing, training, and assisting employees.

- Motivating, directing, and supervising staff.

- Monitoring, disciplining, and counseling employees.

Influencing people to act in a certain way or persuading them to do certain work is dependent on a stimulus—**motivation**—which is the drive to stim-

ulate action. Managers are usually responsible for motivating others, based on the needs or goals of the company. Often motivation is tied to rewarding the employee. These rewards can be intrinsic or extrinsic and sometimes management plays a role in determining what rewards are given and to whom. **Intrinsic rewards** are those personal rewards that fill an individual's need such as self-esteem. **Extrinsic rewards** are those tied to material gain, for example, raises, promotions, and recognition within a company. Job roles and responsibilities are given to company employees to clarify what their jobs are and to help to guide them. **Job roles** designate the part an employee plays for an employer, while job descriptions spell these roles out and clarify them. **Job titles** may also help to identify those roles and responsibilities that a particular position denotes. (See Chapter Eight for more discussion of non-management job descriptions and roles.) For example, an operations manager would be responsible for the running of the company (operations) and a merchandise manager would be in charge of all merchandising functions.

Repercussions of not clarifying roles are evident in *Case 66, part 1, Many Tasks, Few People: Lullaby Begins.* Here, family members, who are unsure of their roles and responsibilities at their store, are creating frustration, disagreement in decision-making, cross-over in management duties, and general confusion. Clarification of roles and the assignment of authority is necessary, but how to implement it amicably is the challenge.

The types and numbers of managers within an organization vary depending on the kind of company and the goals of that organization. Management style (or the way in which managers conduct themselves while managing), also varies from one individual to another, reflecting the way individuals interact and manage others. Managers can be authoritative and dictatorial or they can be caretaking, group builders. Some like to work alone, others as a team. Some are delegators, others are not. Many retail managers practice **management by walking around**, a technique that places the manager in the work site, interacting directly with employees. A good example of this is Nordstrom store managers who reward excellent customer service given by sales associates by distributing dollar bills to them on the spot while working the store. Some upper managers also call out anything that is irregular, which requires department managers to give explanations for department conditions. Some retail managers do this, but others do not spend much time on the selling floor, instead directing activities primarily from an office.

Although job titles may help describe the job an employee holds, often the job titles of managers vary from company to company creating confusion as to roles. For example, at Bloomingdale's, all management personnel are called "executives," while at another similar organization, management personnel are referred to as "managers." Some retailers have assistant store managers, yet another may have "second keys." (This term refers to the fact that the store manager holds the first set of keys and the assistant holds the second set.) There may also be "merchandise managers" at one company, who are the people who oversee and manage a merchandise division, the buyers and their assistants. However, another company's merchandise manager may be working at the store level, involved with the day-to-day operations and merchandise presentation and sales. It is, therefore, not always easy to define a particular manager's job just by the title that has been given to them.

Three major levels of management may exist within an organization. These, with typical corresponding job positions follow:

1. **First-line, entry-level managers**, which include supervisors and assistant managers.

2. **Middle managers**, which include department heads, managers, divisionals, and buyers.

3. **Top, upper-level managers**, which include officers and top executives, for example the president and vice president of a company.

A **supervisor** is usually a first-line, entry level manager and is any person who is responsible for the conduct of others in the accomplishment of a task. Supervisors can be managers or vice versa. A **leader** has qualities and/or abilities that emerge to influence and direct others. Leaders may not be

managers within an organization, but it would be ideal if all managers were leaders. Unfortunately, this is not always the case. Types of managers and leaders vary from company to company and even within companies. (Leaders as entrepreneurs are discussed in Chapter Eleven.)

Figure 9.2 presents a list of nine general attributes, which would be ideal if all executives possessed them. How these ideal attributes translate into a retail executive perspective are also presented. Often a manager becomes a role model to other employees, who then strive to emulate that manager. Consequently, if a manager is helpful, encouraging, patient, and understanding to fellow employees and still succeeds in the achievement of company goals, they are modeling positive attributes to those they supervise and are providing a good example of how to effectively manage. On the other hand, a poor management role model might be demanding, impatient, unkind, unmotivating, and might not exemplify the best traits for a good manager to possess. Future managers can suffer horribly if not exposed to a positive management role model. Therefore, the development of positive leadership traits are essential for successful, good management.

"An organization is a systematic arrangement of people to accomplish some specific purpose" (Robbins and Coulter, 1996, p. 4). **Organizational structure** describes how a company is set up and directed. The organizational structure aids in monitoring and managing work to be done by assigning accountability for that work. This, in turn, facilitates companies to reach their objectives and goals. To aid in this, **organizational charts** are used by many retailers to model the structure of their companies. These charts depict the **hierarchical structure** (pecking order), **chain of command** (who reports to whom), and the relationship between the parts of the company and the whole through **line** (direct authority and responsibility) and **staff** (advisory and support) components. Usually the divisions, departments, and even positions within an organization are pictured on a company's organizational chart along with who reports to whom. Paul Mazur (1927) is credited with introducing the four-function department store

A RETAIL EXECUTIVE CHECKLIST

Attributes Required	ability	desire	In the Retailing Environment
Analytical Skills: ability to solve problems; strong numerical ability for analysis of facts and data for planning, managing, and controlling			Retailing executives are problem solvers. Knowledge and understanding of past performance and present circumstances form the basis for action and planning.
Creativity: ability to generate and recognize imaginative ideas and solutions; ability to recognize the need for and to be responsive to change.			Retail executives are idea people. Successful buying results from sensitive, aware decisions, while merchandising requires imaginative, innovative techniques.
Decisiveness: ability to make quick decisions and render judgments, take action and commit oneself to completion.			Retail executives are action people. Whether it is new fashion trends or customer desires, decisions must be made quickly and confidently in this ever-changing environment.
Flexibility: ability to adjust to the ever-changing needs of the situation; ability to adapt to different people, places, and things; willingness to do whatever is necessary to get the task done.			Retail executives are flexible. Surprises in retailing never cease. Plans must be altered quickly to accommodate changes in trends, styles, and attitudes, while numerous ongoing activities cannot be ignored.
Initiative: ability to originate action rather than want to be told what to do and ability to act based on conviction.			Retail executives are doers. Sales volumes, trends, and buying opportunities mean continual action. Opportunities for action must be seized.
Leadership: ability to inspire others to trust and respect your judgment; ability to delegate and to guide and persuade others.			Retail executives are managers. Running a business means depending on others to get the work done. One person cannot do it all.
Organization: ability to establish priorities and courses of action for self and/or others; skill in planning and following up to achieve results.			Retail executives are jugglers. A variety of issues, functions, and projects are constantly in motion. To reach your goals, priorities must be set, work must be delegated to others.
Risk-Taking: willingness to take calculated risks based on thorough analysis and sound judgment and to accept responsibility for the results.			Retail executives are courageous. Success in retailing often comes from taking calculated risks and having the confidence to try something new before someone else does.
Stress Tolerance: ability to perform consistently under pressure, to thrive on constant change and challenge.			Retail executives are resilient. As the above descriptions should suggest, retailing is fast-paced and demanding.

Figure 9.2 A checklist of ideal attributes for retail executives. Not all executives will have all of these attributes, but a majority of these qualities make for better managers/leaders. Reprinted by permission of Macy's.

organizational chart, which is used as a basis for most retail organizational charts.

The **Mazur plan** divides retail activities into four divisional areas. Descriptions of the responsibilities of the four major **retail divisions** are:

1. **Merchandising,** which is the buying and selling of goods and services for a profit. This includes the planning, pricing, and control of sales and inventory.

2. **Publicity,** which is concerned with promotion and advertising, display, special events, and public relations.

3. **Store (operations) management,** which involves the operations of the retail store, selling, customer service, and all such physical concerns for the store as maintenance and receiving.

4. **Accounting and control (finance),** which is concerned with all the financial aspects of the business, including credit, collection, budgets, control, bookkeeping, and even security.

A fifth divisional area that most retailers include is human resources (or personnel). This division has the responsibility of monitoring employee concerns, such as hiring, training, bene-

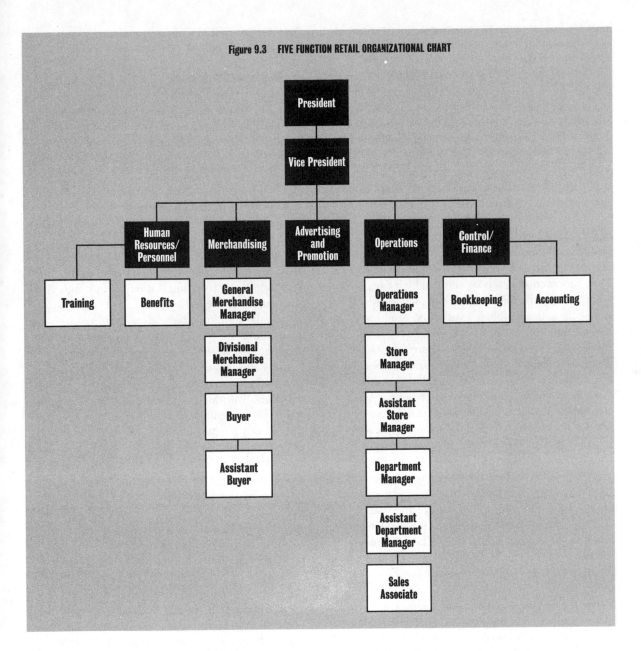

Figure 9.3 FIVE FUNCTION RETAIL ORGANIZATIONAL CHART

fits, and sometimes payroll. A five-function organizational chart is depicted in Figure 9.3.

Retailers vary the configuration of their organizational charts from the four-function chart to accommodate the size and type of their company and how their company is structured. Specialty chains, for example, may differ from department stores in structure and composition. Some retailers may also have a sixth divisional area to account for and handle their branch stores. Yet others may be organized according to regions and/or divisions. All retailers, however, must have at least two functional areas—merchandising and store operations management—to run the business; by very definition, in a retail company a product and/or service must be offered and a method of selling that offering is essential.

Case 66, part 2, Out of Control: Lullaby, Fifteen Years Later, examines organizational structure, chain of command, and responsibility from a private, family-owned and operated specialty store perspective. Line and staff positions, roles and responsibilities are clear, but employee morale is low and turnover is very high, and therefore a solution is sought to remedy the problems. The maintaining of employee morale, which is the responsibility of management, may take time and effort. **Morale** refers to the state of enthusiasm and happiness of employees. It is often very difficult—if not impossible—to keep all employees happy, because of the nature of individuality. Research shows, however, that high morale in a company contributes to happier employees, which translates to the customers, very often resulting in higher sales and greater profit. Conversely, low morale is rarely conducive to company success. Morale is reflected in the attitude of employees and this attitude is relayed to other employees and/or customers, creating a kind of chain reaction. A positive attitude helps to create better customer service, which, in turn, helps to retain customers. Managers can play a direct role in developing high morale within an organization. All people like to be appreciated and valued and employees are no exception. A good manager can behave and act in ways that relay appreciation and value to those they supervise. Whether it is a pat on the back or a prize, there are many ways for management to help boost employee morale. Because employee morale can directly impact a business, it is an important issue for all managers to understand.

Sometimes management may not take its responsibility and may assign inappropriate responsibilities to others. In *Case 65, The Difficult Manager,* a manager assigns a supervisor the responsibility of trying to make a sales associate quit. The supervisor does not feel the request is appropriate or fair for the manager to make. The supervisor is angry, upset, and in a quandary as to who and where to turn. The responsibilities of managers may be clearly designated through their job descriptions, however, training is often neces-

sary to ensure that managers understand the tasks that relate to their responsibilities.

Management Training

Generally, training prepares personnel to do a certain job. Management personnel often needs to be trained, just as non-management does in specific job tasks. However, training other employees is often a major part of a manager's job. For example, a buyer who has an assistant buyer should be training that assistant to become a buyer at a later date. Management training can also be directed by human resources just as sales training may be. (For more on sales training and training in general see Chapter Eight.) Training can be structured (formal) or unstructured (informal). **Informal management training** is the type in which managers are expected to learn their job "on-the-job," taking the initiative themselves. Informal training is used in *Case 68,* Apropos: *Managing a Multi-Aged Staff.* **Formal management training** is usually supervised or directed, and follows a program that involves the accomplishment of certain set goals. Training can involve working with new employees or entail working with employees who are already a part of the company, but who may be changing positions. Employees are often promoted to new positions and need to learn skills that are associated with them. For example, those employees who have worked their way up to management or higher levels of management may not know what their new position entails specifically.

Training can be new training, retraining, or even such specific forms of training as management training or buyer negotiations. Management training prepares managers for their job roles and varies from retailer to retailer, just as sales training does. Some companies employ management training programs to prepare employees to become first-level managers. Others believe that "working your way up through the ranks" is the best way to prepare for management. Nordstrom and *Apropos* are examples of retailers, who believe that all managers should begin their professional careers on the sales floor (see *Case 68*). Training challenges vary from large organizations to small, family-run retailers as in *Case 66, parts 1 and 2.*

Most large department and specialty store chains, such as Federated and Dayton Hudson, use structured executive training programs to ready recent college graduates for entry-level management positions. Not very frequently, however, some retailers even provide self-directed management training programs, as is described in *Case 70, The Case of Tardy Trainee.*

Internships are another structured method of training employees to become managers, while students are still enrolled in college. A highly structured, rigorous, and extensive Gap coop/internship program is described in *Case 67, Gap's Student Manager Training Program.* Management/executive training and internship training can be classroom and/or on-the-job, at headquarters and/or at the retail-outlet level. Additionally, **continuing (ongoing) education** and training is an effective way in which successful retailers help to motivate, refresh, and assist management to advance into higher management levels. Continuing education can be in the form of a seminar or classes, which teach specific job skills or product knowledge. Usually, this type of ongoing training is done as the need arises.

Advancement and Promotion

Progressive management advancement is the most common way for employees to be promoted within a company. An employee moves through the management level ranks of a company to higher levels by phases and structured management training programs. These programs vary in design and scope, but usually begin with the formal training of recruits who progress in position, stage-by-stage, through evaluation and promotion. Many times **career ladders (career paths)** are utilized in which progression of rank and position is planned in stages. Two examples of retail career paths can be found in Figures 9.4 and 9.5.

Job promotion occurs when an employee is advanced into a higher level position. It often presents unexpected challenges and circumstances for a manager to face that may not have been addressed before. The new role can cause frustration and concern as it does in *Case 68,* Apropos: *Managing a Multi-Aged Staff.* New

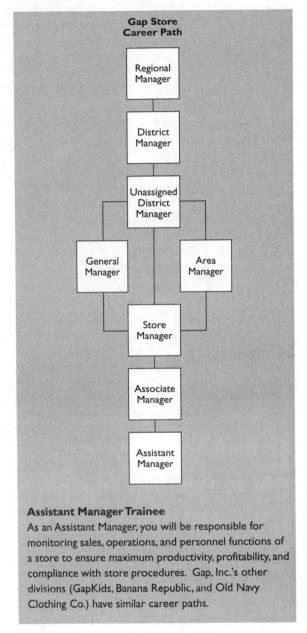

Assistant Manager Trainee

As an Assistant Manager, you will be responsible for monitoring sales, operations, and personnel functions of a store to ensure maximum productivity, profitability, and compliance with store procedures. Gap, Inc.'s other divisions (GapKids, Banana Republic, and Old Navy Clothing Co.) have similar career paths.

Figure 9.4 Gap store career path for assistant manager trainees.

managers often encounter specific problems, such as supervising for the first time, balancing a professional and personal life, directing and delegating work, and evaluating others. New managers often turn to others for help in large

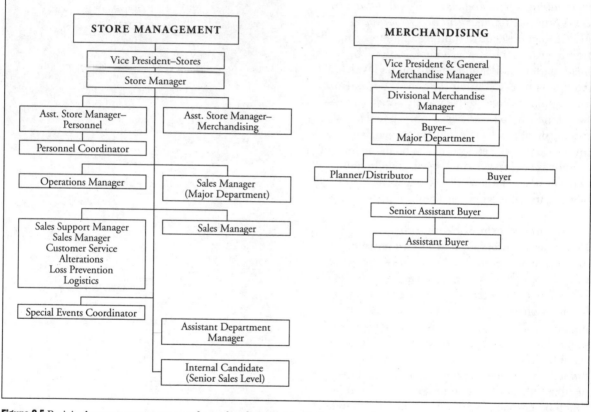

CAREER OPPORTUNITIES AT PARISIAN

It is Parisian's desire and practice to advance associates whenever possible. These career advancements are based on merit and not seniority.

A typical career growth pattern has been developed for those associates interested in management or merchandising careers. Associates who reach the Senior Sales Associate level are eligible to be promoted to Sales Consultant or apply to enter the Executive Development Program.

STORE MANAGEMENT

- Vice President–Stores
- Store Manager
- Asst. Store Manager–Personnel
- Personnel Coordinator
- Asst. Store Manager–Merchandising
- Operations Manager
- Sales Manager (Major Department)
- Sales Support Manager
  Sales Manager
  Customer Service
  Alterations
  Loss Prevention
  Logistics
- Sales Manager
- Special Events Coordinator
- Assistant Department Manager
- Internal Candidate (Senior Sales Level)

MERCHANDISING

- Vice President & General Merchandise Manager
- Divisional Merchandise Manager
- Buyer–Major Department
- Planner/Distributor
- Buyer
- Senior Assistant Buyer
- Assistant Buyer

Figure 9.5 Parisian's store management and merchandising career paths.

companies just as the manager does in *Case 62* in Chapter Eight. A new store manager has to resolve a morale problem with inherited multi-age employees in *Case 68*. Luckily the manager can turn to her district manager for help in resolving the problem. In small, privately owned companies, the manager would have to resort to outside help if some is desired. In *Case 70, The Case of the Tardy Trainee*, a manager is plagued with a management trainee who reports to work late, has excessive absences, and does not turn in work that is requested.

Often the difference between doing well and being promoted, or not doing well and not being promoted is putting in extra effort and going beyond the expected duties. The buying trainee in *Case 69* does not realize the important fact that balancing a personal and professional life is essential. Keeping family matters separate from business is a problem for many new managers as is shown in *Case 65*.

Effective communication between management and non-management is crucial for a retailer to succeed and developing good communication skills should be a goal of all managers. The effectiveness is dependent on the clarity of the relayed message. Information can be communicated from management to employees in a number of ways. It may be written, oral, or non-verbal. Some of the most frequently used methods of communicating within an organization are: 1) individual and/or group meetings; 2) memos; and 3) letters. For communication to be effective it should be two-way; there must be ways for non-management to communicate back to management. Some methods instituted by companies to encourage this are suggestion systems and open-door policies. An **open-door policy** is a practice in which a superior allows others to interact with him/her—as the need arises—as if their office door were always open. Even with the best efforts by management for open communication, there may be problems due to barriers of one kind or another that need to be overcome.

How to handle specific problems and/or difficult employees is a challenge many first time managers encounter. In *Case 71, Internal Relations,* a new employee is neglecting the responsibilities of her job. The new manager must decide whether or not she can or should fire this individual. Along with training, measures should be employed that ascertain whether or not a manager is effectively carrying out his/her job and responsibilities. One manner in which this can be done is through management evaluations.

Management Evaluation

The **management evaluation** (or **review**) should be done by the manager's immediate supervisor as a means to communicate how that manager is performing. As stated in Chapter Eight, these can be **formal evaluations** (or structured) and/or **informal evaluations** (or unstructured) and should provide feedback on the work that is being completed. This evaluation may occur after a task is completed or after a specific period of time. Formal evaluations of employees are usually held annually or semi-annually and they are often tied to rewards and promotions. Sometimes, as in *Case 67*, evaluations are given after various training periods. Additionally, a probationary period may be used for a new employee evaluation as shown in *Case 71*.

A troublesome manager conducts an annual review of an employee in *Case 65*. This manager gives the employee a (much) worse-than-expected evaluation because the employee did not do what the manager had wanted her to do—even though the employee felt the request was unfair. In *Cases 69* and *70*, management has problems evaluating store employees because of complicating circumstances.

The evaluation procedures and methods for management personnel may entail more than non-management personnel evaluations. (See Chapter Eight for evaluations on selling staff.) For example, it is not unusual for managers to help set their own job goals that are used in their evaluations. The **management by objectives** (**MBO**) method of evaluation is a common way of involving management in monitoring their own progress and success on the job. In this method managers play an active part in setting their own management goals.

Summary

Because managers often supervise, train, and evaluate employees it is essential that their roles and responsibilities be clearly defined in order for them to manage effectively. Proper training and evaluation methods also help ensure the success not only of management, but also of their employees and the entire retail organization. Such tools as job descriptions, organizational charts, and career ladders can clarify management positions within an organization by delineating duties and responsibilities, as well as helping to organize the various functions being managed. Reward systems, either extrinsic or intrinsic, can also assist managers in providing incentives to the people that they manage, thereby helping a manager (or a department or a store) to reach the goals set by the company. Additionally, personal management style plays a large part in the success or failure of a manager. Knowing whether or not to push to achieve goals, whether to rally or regroup, and whether to fire or retrain an employee are vital characteristics of an effective manager.

References

Anderson, C.H. (1993). *Retailing concepts, strategy and information.* St. Paul, MN.: West Publishing.

Berman, B., & Evans, J.R. (1995). *Retailing management: A strategic approach.* Englewood Cliffs, N.J.: Prentice-Hall.

Donnellan, J. (1996). Educational requirements for management level positions in major retail organizations. *Clothing and Textiles Research Journal. 14*(1), 16-21.

Dunne, P.M., Lusch, R.F., & Gable, M. (1995). *Retailing.* Cincinnati, OH.: SouthWestern Publishing.

Levy, M., & Weitz, B.A. (1995). *Retailing management.* Chicago, IL.: Irwin Publishing.

Mazur, P. (1927). *Principles of organization applied to modern retailing.* New York: Harper and Bros.

McDonald, J.O. (1981). *Management without tears,* Lincolnwood, IL.: NTC Business Books.

Morgenstein, M., & Strongin, H. (1992). *Modern retailing: Management principles and practices,* Englewood Cliffs, N.J.: Prentice-Hall.

Robbins, S. P., & Coulter, M. (1996). *Management.* New Jersey: Prentice-Hall.

Key Terms

accounting and control

career ladder

career path

chain of command

continuing education

extrinsic reward

finance

first-line, entry level manager

formal evaluation

formal management training

hierarchial structure

informal evaluation

informal management training

internship

intrinsic reward

job promotion

job role

job title

leader

line

management

management by objectives (MBO)

management by walking around

management evaluation

management review

manager

Mazur plan

merchandising

middle manager

morale

motivation

ongoing education

open-door policy

organizational charts

organizational structure

progressive management advancement

publicity

retail divisions

staff

store (operations) management

supervisor

top, upper-level manager

Case 65
The Difficult Manager

Susan Wegleitner-Taplin, J.C. Penney Company, Inc.
Kim K.P. Johnson, University of Minnesota

Kathy Kincaid has worked for a major department store for the past five years. She began her career as a commissioned sales associate in women's shoes. During that time, her manager noted that she was always pleasant and willing to work with her customers to find "just the right fit." Other sales associates would complain that customers were taking up too much of their time but Kathy did not mind if she spent over an hour with a single customer.

One way in which employees receive recognition is through customer service letters. These letters are written by customers who are pleased with the service they have received while shopping in the store. While working in women's shoes, Kathy received four customer service letters, a higher-than-average amount.

From women's shoes, Kathy was promoted to a supervisory position. Her responsibilities included hiring and managing customer service representatives, supervising switchboard operations, authorizing refunds, and package pickup. While she was in this position, she received an "employee of the month" award. Her department manager, Chris Hampton, described her as "hard-working, flexible, dependable, and cooperative. When the going gets tough—we can always count on Kathy." After Kathy had held this position for two years, Chris was promoted to a position in another store and she began working with Keith Meyers. From the start, Keith appeared to want total control of everything. First, he began by taking responsibilities away from Kathy. She was no longer involved in hiring decisions and he was changing other aspects of the department's procedures. Kathy's initial reaction was that he was the

department manager and he had the right to run the department as he saw fit. But then, after awhile, other things began bothering Kathy about Keith's management style.

When the department was running smoothly, Keith was eager to take the credit. Kathy and two colleagues had developed a store flyer indicating a procedure for processing refunds. Kathy overheard the store manager commenting to Keith on the clarity and usefulness of the flyer, to which Keith responded, "Thanks...I spent a lot of time on that...." And there was the time when Sarah Daniels, a sales associate, had a suggestion for securing leather and fur coats and Keith presented the idea to the store manager as his own. Also, Kathy's colleagues were beginning to complain to her about Keith. They complained that they no longer liked coming to work and that Keith did not set a very good example. Before Keith took over, the undercover investigators and the customer service representatives worked as a team. They kept their office doors open so that everyone knew what was happening and how to work to help each other. Although it seemed like a small thing, Keith closed the doors between the offices and that action, Kathy believed, was an indication that Keith was trying to break up the team.

Kathy was also uncomfortable with what Keith said about his wife. He made comments including, "She's such a bitch." He told the representatives to take messages whenever she called—even when he was available. Everyone in the department wondered what he said about them if he talked this way about his wife to his colleagues and employees.

It was obvious to Kathy that morale in her department was declining quickly. She was even beginning to feel that her job was not what it used to be. Then the annual reviews came up and Kathy became really upset. Employees were rated as either excellent, very good, good, fair, or poor. Keith stated that his standards were much higher than all the other managers and what they considered to be excellent work, he felt was average. For the past two reviews, Kathy had received a rating of excellent. In this review, Keith rated her as "good." According to Keith, her rating was such because Kathy did not carry out her "responsibilities." The responsibility that Keith was referring to was his request that Kathy talk to Eleanor, a retired school teacher, who had worked for the store for ten years and recently experienced the death of her husband. Eleanor had been anxious lately and had made some minor clerical errors. Kathy assumed that Eleanor was upset about the death of her husband and just needed some time to cope with it. Keith specifically stated that Kathy was to "try to work on her so she would quit." He gave no specific directions on how to achieve this, however. Kathy thought this was an inappropriate request. She told Keith that if he wanted Eleanor to quit, he needed to talk to her himself. Kathy was angry, frustrated, and not sure where to go for help, but she knew she could not follow his orders. The store manager, Mr. Mathews, thought Keith was a good producer—someone who got things done. Kathy was uncertain if he would even listen to her concerns about what Keith was doing. She had worked at the store for five years, but she was young, in her early twenties.

Major Question

What would you recommend that Kathy do?

Study Questions

1. What do you think the real problems are? What options are available to Kathy to help her work effectively with Keith?

2. How can Kathy help to raise the morale of her subordinates?

3. Should Kathy contest her annual evaluation to Mr. Mathews? Why or why not?

4. What are some of the characteristics of a good manager?

Case 66, part 1
Many Tasks, Few People: Lullaby Begins

Marcia Morgado, University of Hawaii

John Chang is a graduate of the University of Hawaii, where he majored in accounting. For five years, he worked in the central accounting office of the Honolulu Sears store, and then became the assistant manager of his division. John's wife, Jennifer, received a degree in fashion merchandising from the University of Hawaii three years ago. She completed an internship at Liberty House (a Hawaii-based specialty store) while in college, and continued with the firm for a time after graduation. Since then, Jennifer has held various positions, including buying office clerical, assistant department manager, and assistant buyer.

Recently, John and Jenny decided to give up the security of their respective positions and open their own small fashion retail store. Their market research indicated that upscale maternitywear was not readily available in Honolulu, and that both the resident and tourist market for this merchandise was rapidly expanding. John and Jenny found space for a shop on the ground floor of Ward Center, a small, centrally located, upscale, destination mall. Although the space was expensive, the location was in high demand, and the couple determined they should move quickly to secure it.

The Changs signed a five-year lease, and named the new shop "Lullaby." Jenny's mother, Martha, an experienced interior designer, provided 30 percent of the funds they required for the business venture, and they were able to secure the balance with a bank loan. They purchased merchandise fixtures and a cash register, selected a tropical green and warm peach color scheme to use throughout the store, placed an order for stationery, gift wrap, and paper bags, and flew off to New York to review merchandise lines and to place orders for the opening inventory.

Martha served as a silent partner in the business, which normally means that she would participate in 30 percent of the profits or losses without further input. However, she offered to help out by overseeing the refurbishing of the shop during the Changs' market visit. She offered, as well, to continue working in the store on a casual basis, without compensation. Although John was not enthusiastic about working with Martha (he finds her domineering and overly critical), he was willing to accept her offer. After taking all costs into account, the Changs determined they would be able to afford only two full-time, minimum-wage employees to help them with all the activities necessary to merchandise, manage, and operate the store. Upon Jenny's insistence, John realized Martha's offer was an opportunity to acquire additional help and expertise—without extra expense.

Their first market trip was a frustrating experience. Although they agreed that the merchandise offerings were exciting, John and Jenny found themselves in continuous disagreement over which lines to select and what quantities to order. John insisted on purchasing only from vendors who offered cash discounts or allowances or who would accept small or random assortment orders. Jenny was not insensitive to economic advantages, but was strongly committed to developing shallow assortments with an emphasis on lines that offered unique and unusual styling details. John felt it essential that the shop carry nationally advertised goods, arguing that Lullaby's upscale market would want—and would expect to find—these represented in the inventory. Jenny was adamant about avoiding nationally advertised lines, arguing that such merchandise was widely available and would detract from the shop's unique, upscale image. Although shaky compromises were reached, neither looked forward to receiving the goods, nor to the grueling tasks of unpacking, counting, tagging, pressing, hanging, and displaying the merchandise.

The Changs returned to find other problems awaiting them. In their absence, Martha had ordered a change in the color scheme. The walls were painted and the carpet installed, but the sophisticated green and peach palette had been replaced with pastel yellow and deep blue. A strange young woman, who introduced herself as the "assistant manager," and who apparently had a key, was inside the store drinking coffee and eating a fast-food, carry-out meal on an obviously new, unfamiliar, brocade sofa. A note from United Parcel Service informed the couple that repeated attempts to deliver COD packages were unsuccessful, and that those parcels had been returned to senders. Excess lumber and empty paint cans were piled in the delivery lane behind the rear security door, and a warning notice from the mall management admonished the Changs for defaulting on their obligation to keep access lanes free from obstruction.

Jenny took the circumstances in stride. Although the color scheme was not as they intended, it did "work," and the couple could now concentrate on developing inventory control and financial accounting systems. Jenny was also hopeful that the "assistant manager" would work out, and that if Martha stayed on, they could escape the costs of an additional employee. Quietly, she hoped the returned parcels contained merchandise that John had selected, and that the trash blocking the delivery lane was simply an oversight on the part of the contractor. But John was furious. Although he admitted the color scheme "wasn't bad," he argued that Martha had no right to make independent decisions affecting the business, was not authorized to hire employees, and that she should have had the common sense to accept the COD deliveries and to arrange for removal of the trash. Martha's efforts, John said, were simply complicating what was obviously becoming an overwhelming venture.

Jenny and John are exhausted and concerned about the future of their business. Because both are equal partners in the business, neither has final decision-making authority. Because they have comparable educational backgrounds and professional experience, neither outranks the other. Because personal, as well as financial relationships, are involved, it is important that solutions be amicably reached—soon.

the store. Deadlines were established between Danielle and the Gap supervisor. The college supervisor worked with the supervisor from Gap and Danielle. Her work schedule would be 12 to 20 hours per week, yet it was emphasized that school was still to be her number one priority.

Phase 1 (March to May or June of Junior year)

Danielle was oriented with the company's history and philosophy at the onset of Phase 1. The objective for Phase 1 was relayed to her as instore and out-of-store activities. Instore activities included everyday operations, which stressed customer service and meeting the customer's needs. Product knowledge was also concentrated on in order for Danielle to familiarize herself with Gap merchandise. Product movement and merchandise flow, from receiving incoming shipments to floor set up to markdowns, were also evaluated.

The out-of-store activity was entitled "The Sales Generation." Danielle had to select three stores for this assignment: the first, which is a direct competitor to Gap; the second, which is a specialty clothing store; and the third, which is not a clothing retailer. Her task was to evaluate the stores based on customer service criteria, including courteous, prompt, and attentive service; determining the needs of the customer; suggesting merchandise to meet the customer's needs; product information given; attentive service in the dressing room for the apparel stores; giving a disabled customer the same quality of service as other customers; recommending additional items that will create an outfit for the apparel stores; and thanking and welcoming back customers.

Danielle visited her three stores and completed "The Sales Generation" project. Next, the finished project was presented to the store manager (with an emphasis on positive and negative characteristics) and was documented, along with a recommended action plan of how customer service can be improved in Gap stores. The store manager then evaluated Danielle's project. As Danielle completed Phase 1, the store manager again evaluated all of her work and made his first decision concerning Danielle's progress.

Phase 2 (June to August)

Danielle succeeded in making the transition from sales associate to assistant manager. She received the keys to the store, symbolizing her movement up to management, and was able to work full time for the summer. The project during this stage was a management development program. The district manager set up intern classes to take place during one eight-hour day per week for three weeks, which Danielle, other interns, and any new managers with the company attended. Classes included such topics as sales generation, payroll, loss prevention, communications, recruiting, interviewing, planning and setting priorities, delegating and follow-up, and how to access reports made available to the store. Small projects were also assigned for the interns to do with each topic.

Phase 3 (September to January)

The transition into Phase 3 can be a difficult one. Danielle returned to school and had to once again reduce her working hours to between 12 to 20 per week. For the Phase 3 project, Danielle was given eleven scenarios that could occur during the holiday season. She had to:

- Choose four to six scenarios.
- Develop an action plan.
- Present action plan.
- Receive feedback.

To complete the work, Danielle had to work on the assigned scenarios while on the sales floor, which caused her store manager some difficulties because he needed her to cover the floor. Danielle felt guilty, too, because she was having trouble working on the scenarios and attending to the customers at the same time. She felt she couldn't turn away customers, but she was under pressure to finish the written work. Additionally, as a part of Gap's training program, her college-supervised internship began in October full time for eight weeks. Gap's busiest season is the holiday season, and her manager evaluated Danielle on whether she could handle the pressure.

As a last assignment for Phase 3, a set of management case studies was presented. Danielle and the other interns were required to analyze the cases, which would be discussed at a final meeting in January.

Phase 4 (February to May)

At the beginning of Phase 4, Danielle met with the store manager and district manager to express her interest in staying with Gap upon graduation. She continued to develop as an assistant manager, working 12 to 20 hours per week in addition to going to school full time. Four projects were completed during Phase 4. The first was a merchandising project, in which Danielle had to plan and implement the instore merchandising of a new line received into the store. All of the corporate communication in regard to the merchandise must be understood and a plan-o-gram drawn to show fixtures needed and the space required to place it on the selling floor. Upon completion of this project, the store manager reviewed Danielle's work.

The second project in this phase was a mentoring project. Danielle was paired with a Phase 1 intern (Toby Green) and became his "buddy." This gave Danielle additional experience with training someone and experience in evaluation techniques. After Toby, Danielle was assigned to Amy Kovacs, another new intern.

The third project was on performance issues. For this project, fourteen scenarios that describe particular performance problems must be reviewed. Six to eight of these must then be prepared for discussion.

The fourth project was a meeting with the district manager to discuss and evaluate Danielle's progress and the program's objectives. Danielle successfully completed all four phases and has been offered a full-time job upon graduation. A Gap graduation ceremony was also planned for all interns who completed the program.

Major Question

If you were a district manager, how would you evaluate Gap's intern/coop management training program, based on Danielle's experience? What recommendations would you make to improve it?

Study Questions

1. Do you think that more projects should be included in the program? If so, can you recommend some?

2. What would you do in regard to the problem Danielle was having working the floor and with the customers?

3. What do you think are the advantages and disadvantages to a part-time coop management training program? What about a full-time internship program?

Case 68
Apropos: Managing a Multi-Aged Staff

Judith Everett, Northern Arizona University

Apropos is a chain of twenty-five specialty stores, featuring better and designer merchandise. Several branches are located in Los Angeles, San Francisco, and San Diego and one branch is out-of-state in Phoenix, Arizona. This company targets an affluent female customer generally between the ages of 25 and 65, who is career oriented or who is the spouse of a successful professional. She has a relatively high clothing budget—typically spending between $6,000 and $12,000 per year on clothing and accessories.

The buying and merchandising operations for *Apropos* are centralized in Los Angeles. Employees who are interested in an executive or professional career with the company are promoted from within the firm. All personnel start as sales associates. The first executive position is as an assistant store manager, which involves learning the successful operation of a branch store and hands-on training to become a manager. After successfully completing this training, an individual is assigned his or her own store to manage. It is expected that a manager will remain in that position for a minimum of two to five years. In addition to the supervision duties, store managers are given sales responsibilities. With the company expansion plans, it is realistic to expect to be a district manager or return to the central offices as a merchandise planner or assistant buyer after working as a store manager. *Apropos* typically asks management personnel to transfer to another branch when they accept promotions. This is done to avoid any problems associated with managing former peer employees.

Jennifer Hudson has recently been promoted from the assistant manager of the Horton Plaza store in San Diego to the manager of the Biltmore Shopping Center in Phoenix, Arizona. Jennifer completed a Bachelor of Science degree in Fashion Merchandising while she served as the assistant store manager. Sandy Cohen, the district manager saw excellent executive potential in Jennifer despite her young age of 21. Normally managers of *Apropos* are 25 years old or older, because of the nature of the target customer, who tends to expect service from an older sales associate. Jennifer's enthusiasm, her ability to handle school with a high grade-point average, in addition to working full time as the assistant manager in San Diego reminded Sandy of herself at that same age.

The store at the Biltmore Shopping Center has been open for nearly twenty-five years. It is the only branch of *Apropos* located in the Phoenix market. Two of the full-time sales associates, Blanche Darcy and Elsie Scheiner, and Sophie Rostoff, the assistant manager, are nearing retirement age. They have been with *Apropos* as long as the store has been open in Phoenix. They take pride in the store, their customers, and the fact that several of the previous store managers from that store have been promoted into the executive ranks and now serve as buyers and other merchandise executives. Sophie feels that because of her leadership and training skills as the assistant manager most of the former Biltmore store managers have been promoted and achieved success as company executives. Because she is close to retirement and wants to spend more time with her grandchildren and hobbies, Sophie wants to cut back on her responsibilities and hours. All three of these older employees enjoy their work

at *Apropos,* but are not assertive in sales, nor motivated to rise careerwise within the company. Sandy has asked Sophie to remain as assistant manager, however, during Jennifer's transition to manager of the Phoenix store.

The remaining sales staff is younger than Blanche, Elsie, and Sophie. They are between 35 and 42. Kathy Acres, Andy Wright, and Mickey Malone have bachelor degrees in liberal arts or education. All three of these younger associates would like to move up in the company as managers, but each is aware of the transfer policy. They are assertive salespeople and are extremely competitive. Kathy, who is 35 years old, has been with the firm for four years and is married with two children. Her husband is a well-respected physician in Phoenix. Because of her family responsibilities it is impossible for her to leave the area. Mickey has also been with the firm for four years. She started a Master of Business Administration degree on a part-time basis and will complete it in two years. Andy is a single woman with aging parents who live in Sun City—a nearby retirement community. She has been working at *Apropos* for eight years. This group of employees is resentful and jealous that a young "21-year-old girl" has been given the manager's position. They all feel that the company policy of "asking" employees to transfer after accepting a promotion is unfair and unrealistic in a market such as Phoenix, which has only one branch. Kathy, Andy, and Mickey each feel that they should have been eligible for the manager's position at the Biltmore store.

When Jennifer arrived in Phoenix she detected a serious morale problem in the store. The enthusiasm she has seen in all other *Apropos* stores she has visited or worked in seems to be totally absent. The older employees are very friendly, personable, and rather matronly, helping her adjust to the new city. But these women don't seem to have much work enthusiasm, and she feels that she cannot really motivate them. The younger employees seem efficient in their job tasks, but they are not very friendly toward her at all. They are distant and cool, causing Jennifer to feel somewhat uncomfortable. It seems as if the employees resent Jennifer, and she is uncertain as to why. Jennifer is familiar with the *Apropos* policy in regard to promotion and transfer, and she figures that everyone else was told about the policy at the onset of their employment with *Apropos* as well, so she doesn't consider this to be a problem that would contribute to the low morale of her staff. Jennifer is concerned because she has never had a problem getting along with fellow employees, and is particularly proud of the way in which she has motivated others to work for the benefit of the total company in the past. Working for *Apropos* has always been fun and Jennifer wants it to continue to be. Attitudes have continued to deteriorate, however, during her first few months on the job, regardless of Jennifer's various attempts to try to build enthusiasm and motivate everyone to work together as a team.

This is the first time that Jennifer has lived this far from her friends and family. Therefore, she does not have a personal support group to brainstorm with in regard to her personal concerns. Although San Diego is only a couple of hours away by plane, Jennifer never seems to have the time to visit. Because she is so busy learning her job and managing the Phoenix branch, she has had little time to socialize and meet new friends and is therefore very lonely in this new town. This loneliness, along with her frustration at her futile attempts to motivate her staff, is beginning to seriously worry Jennifer about her capabilities as a store manager.

During a spring trend meeting in Los Angeles, Jennifer decides that she must discuss her problems of motivating her multi-aged staff with Sandy, because she knows no one else to turn to. Jennifer is extremely discouraged with her sales associates and their generally poor attitudes and hopes that Sandy can give her some insight and recommendations to help her improve morale.

Major Question

What recommendations should Sandy make to Jennifer in regard to the lack of motivation and poor morale of her staff?

Study Questions

1. How can Jennifer motivate her multi-aged staff and learn to balance her professional life with some type of social life?

2. Was Jennifer promoted too quickly?

Case 69
Generations Apart: Training the Executive Trainee

Shirley A. Lazorchak, West Virginia University

The Galleria is known as one of the most innovative department stores in the U.S. They excel at customer service and are national leaders in competitive merchandising strategies. They adopt new technologies at a rapid pace, are aggressive in their quest for business, and are known for their distinctive merchandise. Because of their well-deserved reputation in the marketplace, the organization has no trouble recruiting the best and brightest students from the nation's leading schools for inclusion in their buyer training program.

Sean MacGregor, a twenty-one-year-old trainee, is one example of the high-caliber trainee that the Galleria regularly hires. He earned a high grade-point average in college, was actively involved in both leadership and service roles as an undergraduate, and gained experience in the field by working for two different retailers while still in college. Because of his outstanding background, Ellen Silverstone, director of executive training, was surprised to hear complaints about Sean's performance from Shirley Brown, Sean's fifty-year-old supervising buyer.

To gain a consistent, thorough understanding of the nature of the problem(s), Ellen decided that the best approach was to schedule individual meetings with both Sean and Shirley. After the conferences, she reviewed her notes. It was apparent to Ellen that Shirley's review of Sean's performance centered around the following complaints:

1. Although Shirley was impressed with Sean's eagerness to learn the retail apparel business by asking questions in regard to open-to-buy, import buying, and the six-month merchandise plan, she was distressed that such routine matters as gather-

ing sales data, picking up the mail, ordering supplies, unpacking merchandise, packing boxes, and paper filing were still neglected—even after repeated reminders.

2. Shirley realizes that Sean has the skills to one day be an outstanding merchant; however, she is tired of Sean pressuring her to recommend him for a promotion to assistant buyer with only two months of experience under his belt.

3. Shirley agrees that Sean is a very hard worker, but he does not show a willingness to complete the job over and above the call of duty. For example, fifteen minutes before closing, a shipment of merchandise arrived on the selling floor. The merchandise was featured in an ad that would appear in the evening newspaper. Sean, however, did not offer to stay and help Shirley rearrange the selling floor to accommodate the new merchandise. Shirley was disturbed by this lack of initiative.

Sean viewed the situation differently:

1. Although he appreciated Shirley's willingness to answer his questions in regard to the administrative aspects of her job, as a college graduate, he felt that the routine matters were easily performed by the sales staff and therefore he delegated many of those duties to them.

2. Sean admits that he has been persistent in his request to Shirley to recommend him for early promotion, but he points out that even Shirley admits that he has the skills and talent to succeed at the next level. Sean wants to know why he cannot be promoted now.

3. Sean admitted that he knew that the merchandise arrived in support for an ad; however, he thought that there would be time in the morning to participate in the floor move. Sean admitted that he does not see the benefit in working past regular business hours, because loyalty and extra effort are rarely rewarded in today's business world.

After a review of her notes, Ellen began to uncover the source of their disagreements; many of Sean's and Shirley's differences emanate from perceptual differences between generations. In other words, "baby boomers (older workers in their thirties and beyond) see the world differently from "generation Xers" (younger workers in their twenties). In fact, one of her publications stated that "a combination of clashing workplace values and the sour economic scene is creating lasting tensions...."

Ellen remembered that the generational issue had been extensively covered in many of her trade and professional journals. She also remembered that baby boomer bosses perceived generation Xers as cocky, unwilling to pay their dues, disloyal, and uncommitted to their employers. Generation Xers felt that baby boomer bosses were workaholics who sacrificed quality of life issues, actually preferred a hierarchical management style although they said they supported a participatory approach, and were technologically inept. Generation Xers admitted that they were less interested in paying their dues and exhibiting loyalty because recent downsizing of companies revealed that employment security was an idea of the past. Ellen read that the number one predictor of job satisfaction for Xers was work that was considered fun. Also, Xers tend to need feedback and recognition because many grew up in homes where the family unit was not strong.

Major Question
With all these generational differences operating in her department, how should Ellen begin to resolve Sean's and Shirley's disagreements?

Study Questions
1. Which viewpoint will lead to a win-win situation for both Shirley and Sean?

2. Discuss those generational differences that could explain the conflicts between Sean and Shirley.

Reference
Ratan, S. (1993, October, 4). Why boosters hate busters. *Fortune*, pp. 56–58, 62, 64, 68, 70.

Case 70
The Case of the Tardy Trainee

Laura Bliss, Stephens College

The Metro-Day department store, located in downtown Seattle, specializes in better-made clothing, and up-to-the-minute kitchen items and home furnishings. Of the six Metro-Day stores around the country, the Seattle store is ranked #1 in terms of sales volume and store standards. It is also the home of the company's executive training program, which is used to train future store managers.

Max Murphy is a "rising star" with Metro-Day. Max graduated from the training program himself only two years ago and has done well with his first two assignments with other Metro locations. When an opening presented itself in the Seattle store, Max jumped at the chance—and was enthusiastically hired. Not only would he be promoted to sales manager of the kitchen and home furnishings department, but he would be allowed to teach that section of the training program, as well. Max had done well in the training program and had gained the reputation of being a sharp, creative manager with both of his assignments prior to the Seattle promotion.

The first few months of managing the new department went very smoothly. Max had resolved and mediated the usual personnel gripes and disputes and had familiarized himself with the existing stock. He also remerchandised the stock in his area to boost sales 20 percent over last year's figures. The first batch of two trainees came through the program with high marks, singing Max's praises. They stated that not only was he a smart merchant but he was also a fair, honest, and caring trainer. Max prided himself on the successful development of these "new recruits" into competent managers using his trainer as a role model.

There were four trainees going through the second training program, twice the normal number; and Leslie Joplin, one of the new trainees, presented Max with concerns. Leslie often showed up to work late or worked on written homework when she was supposed to be managing sections of the sales floor with the other trainees. Max knew that he needed to sit down and have a talk with Leslie in the first two weeks of working with her as the manager in his training program had done; but, whenever he had a chance to talk with her, she was either absent—she was often sick or was somewhere other than the department. With the three other trainees in the department—plus preparing for Christmas—Max was very busy. The trainee program was also commonly referred to as a "self-directed" program: the more one put in the more one got out.

Max finally cornered Leslie and spoke to her about her performance, highlighting his concerns. Leslie seemed to take the conversation very personally. She said that Max didn't understand that she had car problems and allergies and that, not being a parent himself, he would not understand her responsibilities when her two children were sick, and also that, when she was on the sales floor, he was not around. Max tried to be sympathetic to Leslie's situation but made it clear that she had responsibilities to the store, as well. The conversation ended with both parties agreeing to try to do better.

Midway through the program, all trainees were to turn in progress sheets to Max to be initialed and rated. All did so—except Leslie. Max asked Leslie for the report twice, but she never could seem to get the report to Max. By the end of the program, Max had to turn in a final report on all of the trainees. Now, finally at the end of the program, Leslie came through with her midway review sheets. Both of Max's reports on the trainees—the midway and final—would need passing marks for the trainee to move on to the next section of the store. Leslie's work on the second half was "passable" but just barely. Looking over the review sheet for the first part of the program after so much time had passed and the problems with Leslie's attendance and work performance made it almost impossible, in Max's mind, to evaluate Leslie fairly. However, he honestly didn't believe that Leslie had successfully completed the program.

Max feels responsible for Leslie's failure in not pushing her harder to get her work turned in. Max feels Leslie's failure is his failure. Furthermore, a negative supervisor's report generally meant dismissal from the program. Max knows Leslie needs to keep this job to support herself and her children.

Major Question

What should Max do in regard to evaluating Leslie's work performance?

Study Questions

1. What methods could be initiated to help Max evaluate the performance of his employees more easily and fairly?

2. Are there recommended actions that Max could have taken that may have remedied Leslie's problems from the onset? How could these have been undertaken?

3. How do more formal training programs differ from this type of program?

Case 71
Internal Relations

Laura Neumann, Eagle's Eye

Poly Sport, a private-label design studio in Manhattan, consisted of ten employees: two designers, two assistants, one production coordinator, two patternmakers, two sample sewers, and a receptionist. Poly Sport designs misses sportswear exclusively for Second Skin, an apparel retailer. The designers at Poly Sport receive a commission from Second Skin, which is involved with the product development of all garments and has uncommon influence over the organization of the design studio. Second Skin's influence over Poly Sport is a direct result of the exclusive design arrangement between the two companies. A decision was made by Second Skin to require Poly Sport to hire a business manager to reorganize the studio. The apparel manufacturer, which manufactures Poly Sport's designs for Second Skin, and Poly Sport agreed with Second Skin's decision and a business manager, Larissa Boskov, was hired. After analyzing the design studio business environment, Larissa decided to replace the two assistants, both of whom had little knowledge or talent in the apparel field, with experienced personnel. Larissa further determined that a resource coordinator and an assistant designer with knowledge and experience in the field should replace the two former assistants. The resource coordinator would source all buttons, trims, and fabrics. The assistant designer would produce all the artistic work (e.g., theme boards, flat sketches, illustrations) and answer questions from the production coordinator whose main responsibility was to move the design from sketch to production sample.

The assistant designer, Tom Yukosato, was hired first as the result of an advertisement in *WWD* for the position. Another advertisement was then placed in *WWD* for a resource coordinator. Over 50 resumés were faxed or hand delivered to the studio. Resumés were reviewed and telephone interviews were made to 22 applicants. Seven of these 22 were chosen to be interviewed personally. Although there were lingering doubts, one of the seven, Alison Perry, was judged to be the most qualified for the position. This candidate had some experience in several apparel areas including designing, sourcing, and merchandising. Larissa called all three of Alison's references. Two were positive; one, however, raised some questions regarding Alison's work and interpersonal skills.

Alison was hired, despite the questionable reference, and everything seemed to go smoothly at first. Before long, however, it became apparent that there were going to be some problems. After a week of on-the-job training regarding her specific duties, Alison still was unable to recognize and identify the specific fabric that was used for 80 percent of the studio's volume. It was clear that she did not have the former product knowledge nor was she gaining knowledge that a fabric sourcer should have to do the job well. One month later, improvements were still not evident. In addition to her apparent incompetence in her position, her attitude and her interpersonal skills with the rest of the team were poor. She often promoted arguments and created tensions. Of even more concern, her relationship with vendors was reportedly not professional—according to witnesses, who heard her on the phone or saw her interact with vendors face-to-face. Although Alison's job responsibilities were outlined in writing and had been reviewed with her when she was hired and during her training, some of her responsibilities were repeatedly neglected. Surprisingly Alison seemed to believe she was doing well!

Although Alison was articulate, outgoing, and appeared to be well educated, her primary strength seemed to be that she interviewed well, not that she could do her job. Fulfilling the job responsibility of resource coordinator was clearly a wise choice for making the studio function better; Alison, however, was a poor choice for someone to fill that position. As time went on, the daily morale in the studio was becoming worse. Larissa was considering terminating Alison, but the studio needed to be careful because further investigation about Alison's background revealed that she had a history of suing former employers. Since Alison's first week of employment with Poly Sport, Larissa had documented Alison's behavior and had carefully tracked her daily work performance. Larissa also wished they had delved deeper into Alison's past performance record before deciding to offer her the job. Larissa knew that legally there exists a 90-day window in which a new Poly Sport employee can be terminated without major documentation, because all new employees are hired on a probationary basis. Today is day 89. Larissa must make a decision now whether or not to fire Alison. She does, however, remember how difficult it was to find someone with even Alison's meager qualifications and questionable references.

Major Question
What would you recommend Larissa do, fire or keep Alison? Why?

Study Questions
1. How can an employee be assured that a candidate for a position will be a productive employee?

2. What other types of measures could Poly Sport have used to find a more suitable employee?

3. After Alison was hired, could training have solved this problem?

Chapter Discussion Questions
1. What are some attributes that make a "good" retail management executive? Explain how these attributes would readily translate into specific job roles and responsibilities.

2. How are organizational charts beneficial to retail managers? What are the basic divisional areas and their functions?

3. Discuss why training and evaluation is such an important part of a manager's role. Incorporate some case examples (both good and poor) in your discussion.

4. Name and explain the four basic functions of a management position. Use a management case example to explain how the responsibilities of that particular position modeled these roles.

5. Explain the differences and similarities between supervisors, managers, and leaders. Categorize individuals from case examples into these various positions and relate how the person "fits" (or doesn't fit) the job.

10 Technology in Retail Merchandising

Chapter Objectives

- Emphasize the importance of technology at the consumer, retail, and manufacturing levels.

- Describe the major technological systems that aid retail merchandising.

- Examine the interaction of technology at the manufacturing and retail levels.

All aspects of manufacturing and retailing are being impacted by technology enabling both to work smarter and faster, leading to competitive companies that are cost-effective and profitable. Such new technologies as quick response and just-in-time, and sophisticated software are being used to help companies monitor sales, stock, and profitability. Customers benefit by getting what they want, when they want it. Technology is also allowing companies to individualize the customer's shopping experience with such items as custom-made apparel and individualized created catalogs, in both paper and online formats. Although there are advantages and disadvantages in the application of computer technology to manufacturing and retailing, most experts agree that it is here to stay and that we will continue to see the creation of new venues, which will change business as we know it today.

The Impact of Technology

Technology is probably the most important environmental factor affecting retailing, manufacturing, and consumers today. Technology plays a major role in providing service to the customer at all levels of the marketing and retail channel. The retailer has joined in a partnership with the manufacturer, who has joined with suppliers in an effort to make service the number one priority, as the pipeline from supplier to consumer is shortened.

Technology can be applied to all levels of retailing and manufacturing operations to increase efficiency and provide information to improve the quality of decision-making. The management of data and information is improved with the use of high technology. Much of the technology used by retailers today is also used by their resources, therefore technology fulfills both sets of needs to fulfill customer needs. At times, however, one or the other plays the lead in implementation of the technology.

Technology at the Manufacturing Level

Technology plays three major roles at the manufacturing level: production, distribution, and selling. Although many manufacturing concerns incorporate technology in all aspects, some have only limited technological input in production and processing of merchandise. The manufacturer who wants to compete, however, must use some of these technologies to keep up with competitors. The three major roles that technology plays at the manufacturing level are examined in the following sections.

Production and Technology

New production technologies being used today include just-in-time (JIT) supply deliveries, computerized design, cutting, and sewing, agile manufacturing, and mass customization (which allows for individualized sizing incorporated into regular production). Robotic sewing systems and digital customized printing are also used but at different stages of mass utilization. **Textile Technology Corporation (TC²)**, an effort between education, industry, and the U.S. Government, is taking the lead in the area of technology that is applied to the manufacturing of apparel. Its concepts of agile manufacturing, long-distance learning, and the virtual factory are examples of demonstrated applications of the newest technologies to lower costs and maintain international competitiveness.

Just-in-time (JIT) is a concept used in manufacturing to lessen costly inventories. Communications and partnerships with suppliers enable fabric and other supplies to be delivered to the manufacturing site "just-in-time" for production. *Case 43* in Chapter Five illustrates a problem that can happen with this technology when an importer utilizes this concept a little too closely and finds the quota category closed.

Figure 10.1 A computer-aided design (CAD) system. The marker making (pattern layout on the left screen) and grading (pattern sizing on the right screen) are easily created on a computer.

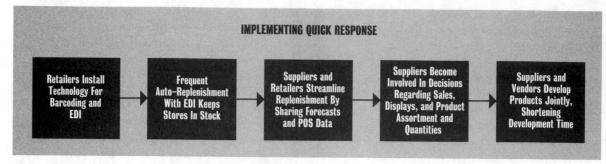

Figure 10.2 Stages in the implementation of a quick response system for a retail operation in conjunction with vendors.

Computer-aided design (CAD) and computer-aided manufacturing (CAM) have enabled manufacturers to significantly speed up the production process. Computerized grading and marker making are most commonly used; however, cutting controlled by computer, lasers for specialized cutting, and robotics are all currently being utilized to lower the use of manual labor. These latter technologies however, are not widely used yet. Generally, it is only the large manufacturers that utilize this sophisticated technology because of the initial high capital investment. However, smaller companies can take advantage of some parts of this technology by working with contractors specializing in such processes as CAD or computer marker making.

Agile manufacturing, incorporating modular production rather than the traditional piece goods line method, allows for special orders at the last minute without disruption. Similarly, **mass customization** allows for individualized sizing to be incorporated into regular mass production. This is currently being implemented by Levi's Customized Fit program called Levi's Personal Pair™ Jeans. For a nominal fee, test stores are offering customers an opportunity to order custom-made jeans. Customers are measured at the waist, hips, inseam, and rise in addition to their choosing between types of fit and leg styles. Actually this is not a revolutionary change in manufacturing because it utilizes the same current system; other technology, however, has made it feasible for computers to quickly choose one of over 4000 possible combinations of these variables to arrive at a "custom fit."

This is a whole new way of offering choices to customers, which if successful, will be more readily available from Levi's. To implement actual mass-customized, made-to-measure apparel, body scanning or 3D personal measuring systems and CAD made-to-measure drafting systems would have to be implemented, but these are not economically feasible today.

The **virtual factory** incorporates communications technologies, which allow different stages of production to be completed in various remote locations. Using this technology, a garment could be designed in California, cut and sewn in Texas, and the product drop shipped to retail establishments in Florida—all controlled from a computer system that is headquartered in New York City.

Distribution and Technology

Electronic data interchange (EDI) is a communications system that electronically transfers information from one point to another via computer. An important application is the transfer of purchase orders between manufacturers and retailers. This is one way that vendors and retailers can respond instantaneously to quickly changing consumer demands.

Quick response (QR) shortens the pipeline of getting a product from its conception to the retail consumer by capitalizing on EDI. Quick response was developed as a strategy to fight imports because domestic manufacturers have the advantage of proximity to the marketplace over the offshore manufacturer and therefore have the capability to deliver faster. It also serves as a competitive advantage for domestic manufacturers competing with each other. QR is effective if manufacturers and retailers are true partners, in which retail sales data are shared with the manufacturer who then can automatically arrange for **automatic replenishment** of stock. For example, LeviLink is a program offered to retailers selling Levi's to maintain a model stock program where stock is replaced when sold. Some small retailers, however, found the investment in the equipment was too high for them. (More information on QR is presented later in this chapter.) However, no matter what the name of the technologically based system of distribution, the primary objective is the same—get the goods to the customer when wanted—fast.

Selling and Technology

Selling merchandise through technology also helps speed up the process from production to delivery, in addition to lowering costs. Sales representatives can be linked electronically to customers and corporations alike, being the conduit of effective, rapid business. Some large manufacturers have developed such good reprographic images of their merchandise lines on computers that sales reps have used these images rather than actual samples to show the lines to retailers. This realizes a major cost savings each season. Some manufacturers are using the computer to present their lines with such software systems as ERIC and Image Info Pro.

Sales reps using **electronic mail** (**e-mail**) can effortlessly communicate with headquarters to determine exact availability of goods (i.e., quantities, styles, and sizes for each ship date) and lock in and guarantee an order on the spot when working with customers. Some companies are using systems that can be hooked up to any phone jack and that allow reps to access the company mainframe. This speeds up the time of order processing tremendously from conventional mail.

The concept of **narrowcasting** is permeating all levels of selling. Companies implementing mass customization use this term to mean serving one customer's needs in a very specific manner. Catalogs—based on narrowcasting—may be avail-

able in the future in which special, individualized catalogs containing specifically selected merchandise will be printed and sent to consumers. The technology of digital printing and the specialization of direct marketing data bases will be used to implement these individualized catalogs. Currently, national advertising campaigns can be customized to fit regional needs and artwork digitally sent to those specific regional locations. This can be utilized at the manufacturing or retail levels.

Technology at the Retailing Level

As previously mentioned, much of the technology used at the manufacturing level is also used at the retail level, which necessitates a partnership concept because it ties the two levels together. For example, Wal-Mart has a customized QR program that is linked to their suppliers, who can access detailed information through their Retail Link technology. Retail Link downloads information from Wal-Mart computers to the vendor's computer, which includes point-of-sale data by SKU and by store, warehouse movement, forecast analysis, electronic mail, and so forth. This enables vendors to micro-manage, that is, to customize assortments according to region and even by store. The information that is gathered by Retail Link drives vendors' planning and replenishment systems. In other situations, the manufacturer, for example, Levi Strauss, has taken the lead in technological partnerships with retailers.

There are special technology applications that retailers alone may utilize; however, according to an Ernst & Young 1995 survey (Edelson, 1996), generally retailers are not investing in high technology at the early innovative stage. Primarily, they have been followers, not leaders in the adoption of new technology, with the exception of grocery retailers. However, the most successful retailers are utilizing the best technology available. Wal-Mart, JCPenney, and Sears are examples of those retailers that are successfully using high technology. Sears has developed an automated footwear distribution center to store 5 million pairs of shoes, which should quickly meet their customers needs.

Figure 10.3 Image Info Inc.'s computerized merchandise stock status report, which is used by manufacturers to communicate product availability to retailers.

Point of Sale and Control

Point of sale (**POS**) systems are the major technological control that retailers use today to track inventory and sales by the use of computer software programs. Additionally, information systems and communications technologies have improved retail productivity and profits. These include **universal product coding** (**UPC** magnetic bar coding) and EDI, which are utilized at point of sale. In retailing, there has been an increase in computerized POS systems and a decrease in manual cash registers during the last decade. Although it is a major capital expense, stores are investing in sophisticated POS terminals that provide up-to-the-minute information on sales at all locations of a company. Sales data are captured instantly at the terminal and, in a quick response relationship with vendors, are then relayed to the vendor for automatic reordering.

The UPC system is becoming widely used by apparel manufacturers and retailers today. It creates a unique code to identify a product according to manufacturer, brand, style, size, and/or color. A magnetic base is read (scanned) at the POS terminal, which captures sales and inventory data and tracks the movement of merchandise within a retail organization. This gives the retailer such instant information as what is selling best and what is not selling, which leads to better and faster decisions in regard to reorders and markdowns. Controls must be input by the retailer and/or supplier, however, to effectively use the data. An automatic replenishment system can save many manual inventory and reorder hours but there must be an excellent relationship between vendor and retailer for this system to work effectively and efficiently. The vendor must clearly understand the needs of the retailer and the nature of the business. (See Chapter Six for more on retail/vendor relationships.) One pair of brown shoes that is purchased may not necessarily mean an automatic reorder of that shoe as is shown in *Case 72, The Case of the Brown Shoe Epidemic: Quick Response Technology*, which is an example of quick response gone haywire.

In addition to QR, the 1990s introduced **product data management** (**PDM**) technology that speeds up the product development cycle and reduces the time it takes to bring products to market. This new software by Gerber is being used by large retailers such as JCPenney, Talbots, and J. Crew, along with such apparel manufacturers as OshKosh. PDM not only joins computer to computer, but also people to people by way of e-mail.

Retail Pro is an example of sophisticated software packages used by retailers and manufacturers to control inventory in addition to obtaining other information including historical product performance, sale analysis, labor analysis, and open-to-buy calculations. In many instances, sales and inventory data are cross linked to productivity and other organizational functions for a comprehensive data base. *Case 74, Computer Wizardry in St. Croix,* illustrates how this technology can easily analyze profitability by department.

But what about small retailers? How can they apply advanced technologies on their budgets? Many options are available at minimal cost for small retailers to utilize the latest technology. One option is a **turnkey system,** that utilizes a computer to perform specific, exclusive functions already programmed and ready for use. Personal computer programs, on the other hand, are more versatile and varied to meet the many different needs of retailers. However, those often need customizing, which may take the expertise of a computer consultant. *Case 73, Canine Computer Caper,* describes the difficult decision of a small company in regard to its computer needs for inventory control.

Selling and Promotion

Electronic retailing offers products through such electronic media as computers and television. Shopping on the **Internet** is the newest technological retail format of online retailing. (See *Case 75, //WorldWideWeb.Trinkets.com/* and *Case 76, The World Wide Web: Opportunities and Threats for a Catalog Company* for examples of retailing on the Internet.) What catalogs were to the 1980s, online is projected to be in the 21st century. Consumers will be able to shop actual or virtual malls, known retailers or electronically created ones, and even search data bases for specific goods, at prices they desire.

Michael Rollens, co-founder of an interactive network on the Internet, explains the major consumer paradigm shift that he sees in the near future

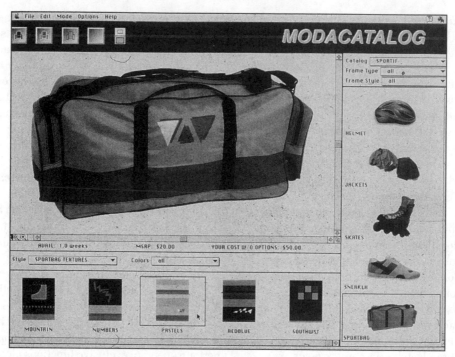

Figure 10.4 A screen (frame) from Modacatalog (by Modacad), which is a versatile interactive product that can be used on the Internet as consumer information, instore for stock checking, or on a laptop computer for use by company salespersons. Different colors and fabrics can be draped to view the desired product before ordering. In the future, consumers may design their own personal products and order them with such software.

(Rollens, 1996). Shopping in tomorrow's virtual world would be like shopping in today's physical world. Technology will allow us to immerse ourselves in this new electronically created world, not only to shop, but to visit friends, be entertained and be informed as we have already begun to do. Rollens forecasts that the television generation will be replaced by the interactive generation, who will spend more and more time in the cyber world, taking away time from the physical world. This, of course, will have a tremendous effect on the way today's manufacturers and retailers do business. Imagine no more traffic, parking, or rude sales associates when Christmas shopping, which takes place in a virtual re-creation of a Vermont village and in which the consumer is in control. Why not? This may be our retailing future, designed specifically for the individual consumer.

Examples of companies currently on the Internet are Wal-Mart and Eddie Bauer. Wal-Mart has teamed up with Microsoft to offer their mer-

chandise online using their current low-priced leader status. For Eddie Bauer it's a quick move from paper to online catalog because photos and catalog copy can be easily replicated online. Eddie Bauer's shop on America-On-Line's Marketplace page can be accessed at any time by AOL's 5 million subscribers. They even have a second store on the World Wide Web in a mall called Dream Shop. Both companies feel, as does Rollens, that the future is on the Internet.

Not all business usage of the Internet is for selling, however. Such retailers as JCPenney are utilizing the net as a relatively inexpensive way of sharing information between employees and training internally. This phenomenon has been labeled "Intranet." Other companies, for example, Levi Strauss and Joe Boxer, have home pages that both educate and entertain the consumer. A spokesperson for Express indicated they had no intention of selling online; they are only interested in promoting its presence and educating consumers. Often, however, an online presence is the first step towards online sales. Also this presence and education may lead to store sales. Perhaps when credit card security—the one major concern of buying and selling on the Internet—is guaranteed, more companies (and consumers) will jump on the online bandwagon. Actually, some experts feel it is the perception of a security risk that is the problem, as there are as many safeguards on the Internet as in any other credit card transaction.

Television shopping, such as the Home Shopping Network and QVC, and other forms of electronic shopping (which got a slow start in the 1980s), along with the Internet, may replace the mail order catalog of the 1980s and 1990s. *Case 78, Home Shopping Dilemma* and *Case 79, Spotlight on On-Air Sales* give insights into the problems with this venue of retailing. They share some of the same problems as direct mail because customers cannot try on the merchandise and are hesitant to buy. Additionally, colors and even styles often look different at home than on the television, which can lead to a high number of returns. This has implications for the type of merchandise and the sizing chosen for TV shopping. Small/medium/large, or better yet, one-size-fits-all might be better than conventional sizing for this type of promotion.

Other forms of electronic retailing include **interactive kiosks** (free-standing computerized units), which enable retailers to carry smaller

Figure 10.6 Levi's customer service touch screen. Interactive kiosks give consumers information on product ordering and availability.

inventories than conventional stores. Some manufacturers are using interactive kiosks as an outlet in stores to better represent themselves. Using a computer through an interactive kiosk, customers can find out immediately if the company has their size in stock, feed in order information, and have a finished product shipped either to the store or to a residence. Tommy Hilfiger uses interactive kiosks, which utilize CD-ROM technology in his New Generation shops. They provide customers with product information and wardrobing tips, in addition to such entertainment information as new music releases, concert information, video clips, and sports updates. CD-ROM updates are delivered to the stores monthly and, after the technology is set up, are an inexpensive way of giving up-to-the-minute information to consumers. Mixing fashion with entertainment enhances the designer's image and can increase sales.

Merchandise **video catalogs** in which the retailer reproduces a printed catalog on a videocassette or videodisc and then sends it to their customers was the precursor to online shopping. At-home shoppers watch the catalog using a VCR and then telephone their orders to the retailer. Speigel was one of the first to produce such a "videolog." Another precursor is the CD-ROM shopping format, of which The Merchant is a popular example. Eddie Bauer, along with their Internet stores, is also continuing the use of CD-ROM.

Figure 10.5 QVC television selling screen. Home shopping programs are popular with many consumers due to both the convenience and entertainment value.

Figure 10.7 The Merchant is an example of a CD-ROM shopping catalog that consumers can use on their home computers.

Consumers use their personal computers to view graphic or pictorial representations of merchandise with text descriptions and ordering information on videotexed programs. *Case 77, Retailing by Telecommunications,* explores the methods of these types of electronic shopping.

Fashion information is disseminated faster than ever with electronic technology. Such fashion and lifestyle programs as America Online and Capital Cities/ABC's joint venture will allow fashion reporting in a more immediate way than ever before. Tommy Hilfiger's live broadcast via satellite from his shop at Macy's San Francisco, during which he discussed fashion, sports, and music with celebrities in New York, is another example of companies applying current technologies to their own unique needs.

Customer service applications at retail are also evolving with the use of technology. One example is Gap's Old Navy stores, which began having sales associates use wireless headset communication devices to relay merchandise needs from the sales-floor to the stock room, thus enabling the associates to remain on the floor to help customers, yet still obtain the needed merchandise out of the stock room. Low cost pagers also are being used by other retailers on the selling floor to expedite customer service.

Summary

Today's technology of electronic retailing still generally utilizes one-way information systems, different from the two-way interactive shopping experience visualized for the future where consumers are empowered to control their own individual environments and choices. But the future may not be far off, if the speed of progress is similar to what we are experiencing today. Fifty years ago, it could not have been predicted what we have today, so it is almost impossible to predict what lies ahead. Computers seem to have permeated all aspects of business today, leading to efficiencies and spurring new ways of doing business. Retailing direct from the manufacturer to the consumer and bypassing conventional venues (which we see on the Internet) may be one of those changes.

References

Antley, J. (1995, September). Surfing the Net, part one: A beginner's guide to exploring the Internet. *Bobbin,* pp. 139–144.

Antley, J. (1995, October). Surfing the Net, part two: A look at apparel industry-specific resources. *Bobbin,* pp. 63–66.

Antley, J. (1995, November). Surfing the Net, part three: The basics of publishing on the Internet. *Bobbin,* pp. 99–103.

Cole, D., & Moazami, M. (1996, March). Technology in the new millenium. Special Report Quick Response/EDI, *Bobbin,* pp. 36–44.

Custom manufacturers suit up with technology. (1995, April). *Bobbin,* pp. 10–14.

Edelson, S. (1996, June 26). Selling in cyberspace: Retail execs debate potential of the web. *WWD,* pp. 1, 8, 9.

Emert, C. (1996, February 27). Hooked into the Net: Retailers large and small. *WWD,* pp. 14–15.

Internet shopping new competitor or new frontier. (1996, February). *Stores* (special research report supplement), pp. MC1–MC23.

Kincade, D. (1995). Quick response management system for the apparel industry: Definition through technologies. *Clothing & Textiles Research Journal, 13*(4), 245–251.

Lockwood, L. (1996, June 21). The web snares fashion. *WWD*, pp. 12–13.

Nannery, M. (1996, March 14). Fashion industry using Internet for in-house communication forum. *WWD*, pp. 12, 13.

Retailing in the nineties: The age of information. (1996, May 8). *WWD*, pp. 2, 18.

Rollens, M. (1996, January). Shopping in the virtual world. *Arthur Anderson Retailing Issues Letter.* Texas A&M University: Arthur Anderson.

Reda, S. (1994, April). Floor ready merchandise: DCs implement QR technology as retailers set FRM guidelines. *Stores,* pp. 41–44.

Ross, J.R. (1996, June). Standards seek to counter kiosks' consumer problems. *Stores,* pp. 52–56.

Seaver, M. (1996, Feb./March). Tommy Hilfiger cuts loose with cutting edge POP. *Point of Purchase Magazine,* pp. 22–24.

Window on the interactive future. (1995 April). *Stores,* pp. 57–90.

Latamore, G.B. (1996, March). Electronic commerce: Window of opportunity. *Bobbin,* pp. 46–50.

Key Terms

agile manufacturing

automatic replenishment

computer-aided design (CAD)

computer-aided manufacturing (CAM)

electronic data interchange (EDI)

electronic-mail (e-mail)

electronic retailing

interactive kiosk

Internet

just-in-time (JIT)

mass customization

narrowcasting

point of sale (POS)

product data management (PDM)

quick response (QR)

television shopping

Textile Technology Corporation (TC2)

turnkey system

universal product code (UPC)

video catalog

virtual factory

Case 72
The Case of the Brown Shoe Epidemic: Quick Response Technology

Doris Kincade and Cynthia L. Regan, Virginia Polytechnic Institute and State University

John Markowitz was an experienced store manager for Shoe Box Chain Stores. John described himself as a manager who came from the "old school." John took pride in knowing all of his customers personally. He was familiar with his inventory and enjoyed negotiating with sale representatives. He also liked the autonomy that Shoe Box Chain Stores gave him as a store manager. Sales representatives called on him personally so that he could place orders for goods that he best felt met his consumer market needs.

Ten years ago, the Shoe Box Chain Stores had started a manual model stock program for reorder basic stock items. Each week John was responsible for counting and sending to the main buying office a model stock report for his basic stock of reorder athletic shoes, work boots, and plain dress pumps. He always dreaded filling out the reorder forms as he had to count the shoes out on the floor and the back stock room for each size and for each individual SKU. Usually during the middle of counting he would be interrupted by one of his sales clerks and would have to recount the shoes. It always took four weeks to get replenishment. Every week when he wrote in the current stock amount, he thought the effort did not seem to have any benefit because the store never got the reorderable goods in time. "Even though I send it in every week, it just sits on some clerical's desk who never seems to get around to placing the order in a timely manner," John thought. Additionally, he always seemed to be out of basic athletic shoes, which was disturbing to his customers and meant many lost sales to him.

Shoe Box Chain Stores announced a month ago that they were going to implement a new replenishment program called quick response (QR). John was hopeful that this QR system would be better than the old manual model stock program. He had just come back from a QR training session that was promoted as a new management strategy. The QR strategy emphasized partnership with vendors and new systems using computers. At the training session, John had been given several articles about new model stock programs and automatic replenishment systems. All of the articles praised this type of system as a way to lower investment costs, to increase return on investment, and to keep stock fresh.

John received his first call from U.S.S. Factory, one of his "oldest" vendors, about setting up the QR automatic ordering program in his store. He had been buying women's dress pumps and athletic shoes from them for about 15 years. John figured that if he were in "partnership" with anyone, the people at the U.S.S. Factory were the ones he could trust. He set up a conference call, and on Monday, the U.S.S. Factory sales manager, Camille Duncan, John, and the store's top salesperson, Steve Belmont, conversed to iron out all of the details. Camille assured John that not only could they predict the inventory needs for the store based on their past sales, but they could also set up a new model stock program. The inventory deliveries would be adjusted on a weekly basis depending on the daily point of sale (POS) data. Deliveries would be made every Tuesday. John was excited that he didn't have to do any more of the weekly counting. Camille also assured John the inventory stock could be lowered by 45 percent because of increasing stock turnover and the stock would be kept fresh and up-to-date with this system.

The Shoe Box Chain Stores had spent thousands of dollars buying updated POS terminals and dedicated phone lines. After the initial installation of the equipment and with the employee training for the POS terminals and the stock room, the routine seemed established. Sales were fine—maybe even a little up for the first month. About the middle of the third month on the new system, however, John was walking through the stock room and noticed that things were not quite right. He began to walk down each aisle in the department and each row in the stock room. Yes, he was correct, more than 80 percent of the store's inventory—both out front in the store and in the stock room—was brown or tan. Brown and tan shoes were everywhere: boots, dress shoes, even athletic shoes. He checked with the sales staff as they changed shifts at 3:00 pm. Yes, several of them had noticed quite a number of brown and tan shoes when they were unpacking stock. Two of the sales clerks who worked evenings said several of the store's best female customers had come to buy shoes, but left complaining about the lack of color choice among the dress pumps. John was confused. He felt as if he had lost touch with his stock. In his 22 years of selling shoes, he had never seen such a mess. For two days he went around complaining about computers and how they had a mind of their own. He figured that this new QR program was no better than the old model stock program.

On Friday, when he sat down to examine the weekly sales, he saw that the sales were down about 23 percent from this time last year and 33 percent from last week. With this new information, he raged, "Where are those people who wrote those articles and claimed about 150 percent return on investment, with six months pay back? At this rate I will be lucky to be in business in six months!" As he sat at his desk mumbling and fuming, he looked back over the sales figures for the last three months and saw that about six weeks ago a local high school choral group had purchased 30 pairs of brown pumps one day, just as they did every year. Additionally, the high school drill team had bought 30 pair of tan athletic shoes. The high school was one of his best customers. He liked working with the school, he gave them a discount, and the publicity was good for the store.

As John reviewed his sales and inventory figures for the past three months, John turned from mad to confused. He had lost sales, the Shoe Box Chain had spent a substantial amount of money, and this QR thing did not work. John's annual performance review was in two weeks and he was worried that he would be heavily criticized for the store's weak sales. John decided to call one of his colleagues, Clara Bruno, another Shoe Box Store manager. John asked Clara if she was having any problems with the new QR program. Clara laughed as she said "Do I have problems! All my new shoes are blue!" John breathed a sign of relief and said "Maybe we can work out a trade . . . "

Major Question
What can be done to improve the immediate condition in the store's stock?

Study Questions
1. How is a model stock plan established in a traditionally managed store?

2. What information do computers need to forecast sales for this retailer? How well can computers predict fashion trends?

3. What are some safeguards that should have been used for control and evaluation, when implementing a new technology into the Shoe Box Chain?

4. What role can salespeople have in establishing buying plans?

5. How can John, the store manager, determine the success or failure of this new system?

6. What will happen to the lost sales and dissatisfied customers?

Case 73
Canine Computer Caper

Antigone Kotsiopulos and Molly Eckman, Colorado State University

Kara Jules owns a pet store that sells pet supplies and also provides animal grooming and training services. She loves animals, has worked for several kennels in the area, and is now the proud owner of her own business. She has a good location in a strip mall not far from a major city street. In addition to some already established local competition, she had also heard that a large chain pet store may be expanding into the area. However, she felt confident that her combination of products and services along with a more personal touch, would attract a good following. Furthermore, she has a very supportive husband and family who could assist in times of crises and served as a sounding board on business issues.

Kara was right—the business did grow. She expanded her training space and hired someone to handle client scheduling and retail sales. She now spent most of her time grooming and training dogs. Her new employee, Jane, is also her daughter. Jane is a young, aggressive college graduate, who was very enthusiastic about seeing the business grow.

At the close of her second year of business, Kara asked Jane to complete a physical inventory of all retail merchandise. Jane was not thrilled with the idea. After all, she had just completed a bachelor's degree and was capable of more than counting the number of bottles on a shelf. Furthermore, she had learned about computers in college and felt a machine should be doing the counting, not her. It was her first experience with taking a physical inventory and while her mom had given her some tips and guidelines, she became even more frustrated with the process while still trying to serve customers. She decided to push her mom harder to purchase a computer.

Kara listened to Jane's recommendation to install a computer system for inventory control and discussed the idea more extensively with her husband. Kara's husband, a college professor, knew a little about computer applications and thought it was worth checking out the idea. The family sought input from a number of people including local computer retailers, vendors at trade shows, and a fellow college professor who taught merchandising.

Kara was now totally confused after hearing a variety of recommendations while her husband and daughter remained excited about the turnkey system. At opposing ends of the spectrum were the trade show salesman and the merchandising pro-

fessor. The trade show salesman had a turnkey system (hardware and software) that would do everything from point of sale to accounting at a cost of $12,000. The turnkey system was specialized for pet stores but there was no local sales representative in the community. It would also be difficult to resell or use the turnkey system for anything but a pet store. The computer salesman was very thorough in pointing out all the benefits of computerization including detailed reporting and business analyses, many of which contained data and terms that were not familiar to Kara or Jane. The salesman also reported that the accounting system typically made it possible to greatly reduce daily bookkeeping costs.

The merchandising professor argued that the business was too small for such an investment, as annual sales are less than $200,000. She also believed that good manual records would serve as an effective first step in analyzing the business. If they did want to purchase a computer, the professor recommended a personal computer and printer, at a cost of around $4,800. This computer could serve other such business and personal needs as word processing, spreadsheets, development of a client list, and desktop publishing for advertising and mailings. There were several retailers in the area which sold and supported personal computers and most knew of software that could be modified to generate customized reports.

Both the turnkey system and the personal computer would require some training, however, and Jane did know something about the latter from her college courses. Lists of satisfied customers for both the turnkey system and the personal computer were available from the salesman and other retailers.

Major Question

What would you recommend to Kara in regard to computerization of her pet store?

Study Question

Are there any other items you believe should be considered by the Jules to help them make a decision about their computer needs?

Case 74
Computer Wizardry in St. Croix

Jim Meisler, Retail Technologies International

Jennifer Mollier owns a small boutique on the island of St. Croix in the Virgin Islands. She has done moderately well, with most of her business coming from tourists on cruise ships, who, after disembarking, are led to her store by guides. (She pays a small fee to the guides for this privilege.) In anticipation of growth, she recently purchased and installed a new computer system that uses Retail Pro software. It has excellent reporting capabilities, such as best/worst sellers, stock distribution, profit contribution, GMROI, stock turn, and sell-through by department, vendor, or style. How to best utilize the system and its reports, however, requires some careful thought on Jennifer's part.

Jennifer's store sells summer resortwear all year, and she is interested in tracking her merchandise more effectively and efficiently, in order to catch problems and increase sales. The store had four major departments, but has just launched the merchandising of men's and women's swimwear,

bringing the number of departments to five. Surprisingly, the original four departments, which were cosmetics, perfume, women's accessories, and men's accessories, had been doing quite well and Jennifer hadn't needed to go into apparel. Now, however, she felt the timing was right.

With her expansion into swimwear, and no previous experience, she felt a better tracking system was needed. As Jennifer saw it, the basic problem to be resolved was finding a way to determine which department had the best return on investment and how she should apportion her buying amongst the five departments. It is always difficult comparing relative profitability for each department, because by nature they are very different from each other. Cosmetics are very cheap (at cost), perfumes are a bit more expensive, and accessories are very expensive—for example, fancy purses, wallets, Rolex watches, and so forth. The swimwear business, however, was another animal altogether. Quick feedback was needed on its profitability and return on investment because it was being launched at the expense of the other departments. In other words, Jennifer was not investing additional money into the inventory, but was reapportioning it to accommodate for the department.

The first step in setting up her new software was to take a physical inventory and reconcile it with her book inventory. Then all the data had to be entered into the new system. Finally, after several

Table 10.1 Average Monthly Inventory Data from Retail Pro Spreadsheet

Department	COS	MAC	PER	SWI	WAC	Total
$ at Cost	4,500	9,000	18,000	4,500	9,000	45,000
% of Total Inventory	10	20	40	10	20	

Table 10.2 Retail Sales Data for One Month from Retail Pro Spreadsheet

Department	COS	MAC	PER	SWI	WAC	Total
$ Retail Sales	9,200	3,680	14,720	1,840	7,360	
% of Total Sales	25	10	40	5	20	

Using Retail Pro, Jennifer could generate various reports. The samples displayed here let her compare the sales and on-hand inventory. She could also compare sales activity to her inventory on hand in terms of units, dollars of sale, and dollars of margin. This analysis provided a clear-cut picture of which departments were most viable. An explanation of abbreviations used in both tables are COS (cosmetics), MAC (men's accessories), PER (perfumes), SWI (swimwear), and WAC (women's accessories).

months of input, all the inventory was entered, and there were now three months of sales history recorded on file. Jennifer compared each department's total sales and profit to get a percent "weighting" (contribution) for each department. She compared these contributions to the on-hand cost value to see what the current investment was. The Retail Pro analysis found that men's accessories comprised 20 percent of inventory and yielded 10 percent of all profits, while cosmetics were 10 percent of inventory and resulted in 25 percent of profits. She also found they had 40 percent invested in perfume, which yielded 40 percent of the profits and women's accessories were 20 percent inventory and 20 percent profit. As for swimwear, she found that she had invested 10 percent and the profits were 5 percent. (See Tables 10.1 and 10.2.)

Major Question

Was the new swimwear line worth the investment? If not, how should the buying be restructured?

Study Question

Which product categories were the most profitable?

Case 75
//WorldWideWeb.
Trinkets.com/

Diane Frey, Bowling Green State University
Marsha A. Dickson, The Ohio State University

The World Wide Web (Web) is one of the newest technological innovations linking business to consumers via computer for purposes of information, feedback, marketing, advertising, and/or sales. The power of the Web is its ability to provide global access to information in a variety of formats, including text, graphics, video, and audio in combination with user-friendly computer programs. The hypermedia capabilities of the Web hold promise for increased consumer awareness and sales with direct relevance to the apparel industry.

Many believe that dramatic growth of Web sites is occurring. In *Business Week*, a Yankee Group Survey reported one-half of companies in the study are using the Internet for external communications with increased usage projected; advertising and selling products are the greatest growth areas. Currently, 8 percent of companies surveyed use the Web for advertising while 5 percent are selling products with an expected participation in the range of 35 percent. Kurt Salmon Associates predicted that 55 percent of total retail sales in 2010 will be through non-store channels.

From a customer point of view, a high level of satisfaction from Internet shopping has been reported. It should be noted, however, that the purchases involved little risk in terms of potential manufacturing defects, style, color, size, or fabric. In the sample group of 378 customers, nearly two-thirds of the purchased goods were in categories of software, books, music, magazines, and computer hardware. Clothing purchases ranked low: men's clothing 6 percent, women's clothing 3 percent, and children's clothing 1 percent of total purchases.

Without some creative developments, the product categories that consumers are now buying on the Web are not likely to change. In the apparel industry, prior uses of computer technology were limiting because suitable visual images were not possible. Steady improvements in digital imaging have allowed advertising and product sales to become more effective for apparel retailing because of expanded color palettes and quick display of high resolution images.

The Web is being used for promotion as well as sales by department stores, specialty stores, mail order companies, market centers, and discount stores. Let's take Wal-Mart as an example: the Wal-Mart Web site (http://www.wal-mart.com) provides consumer information about store locations, products in the current store circular, company background information, charts of the chain's stock performance, and career opportunities. The JCPenney company (http://www.jcpenney.com) offers scanned images with product and pricing information. Bridal and baby registry pages, as well as career information and historical information about JCPenney is available. L.L. Bean, Inc. (http://www.llbean.com) offers images of products with additional product information, site index, free catalogs, directions for ordering by the Web, as well as providing contact with the company, even feedback to the consumer.

Anticipated outcomes for developing a Website and/or investing in an infrastructure when funds are limited will be expanded markets and increased sales, as well as increased customer interaction. While business experts believe that current users of the Web should not expect immediate profits, those who adopt the technology now will position themselves to take advantage of increased consumer demand for quick and customized service that can best be satisfied with Web technology.

Similar to instore business, non-store retailing will rely on understanding customer demographics. The overall number of consumers who currently access the Web for shopping purposes is small; more often users access the Web for product and company information or entertainment than for making purchases. Users are a small elite group that typically spend more than six hours per week browsing the net. *Chain Store Age* and *Direct Marketing* profile Web users as predominately male (approximately 80 percent), in their mid-thirties, college educated, earning salaries over $60,000. From a selling standpoint, men are not as inclined to shop as are women, making the future of Web shopping somewhat dependent on its ability to attract the female consumer.

Lisa Lawrence, owner of Trinkets, a successful women's specialty store on the Pedestrian Mall in downtown Iowa City, Iowa, is considering new strategies for marketing that will result in increased sales. A small shop established since 1988, Trinkets has offered merchandise to an upscale customer who appreciates fine suits,

officewear, and casual sportswear from natural fibers or novelty fabrics. In-state customers travel to Iowa City because of the unique and high-quality styles offered at Trinkets. Out-of-state customers visit the store after attending sporting events and professional conferences at the University of Iowa. However, the core customer is the professional career woman.

Even though Trinkets has developed a loyal customer base, sales have leveled off during the last two years. Lisa has watched other established entrepreneurs fail in the increasingly competitive retail environment. Lisa continues to plan for growth, even to consider various strategies, among which is to build a Web site. She is unfamiliar with the Web, but her sixth grade son has been "surfing the net" at his school and talks about it at home to Lisa who ponders this technology for potential marketing.

Major Question[1]

Lisa has asked you, in the role of consultant, to plan and evaluate the use of the Web specifically for Trinkets. The particular considerations of your report are:

The Plan

• Identify the kind of information to be included.

• Describe the target market for the Web site and explain the process to be implemented that will attract these customers.

• Develop a plan for informing the customers about the Web site.

• Develop a rationale for the selection of products offered on the Web (products now sold instore or new products).

• Make a recommendation for the level of direct interaction with customers.

• Make a recommendation concerning updating the Web page.

---

[1]Please note: Do not use alternative analysis format for this case.

- If support costs should become excessive even though being on the Web has boosted product sales, note other options that are available.

- Identify and evaluate the merits of alternate media systems.

The Evaluation

- How will Trinkets measure the success of the Web site?
- What evidence will indicate whether the purposes of the Web site are being met?

References

Eng, P.M. (1995, June 26). Big business on the net? Not yet. *Business Week*, pp. 100–101.

Fox, B. (1995, September). Retailing on the Internet: Seeking truth beyond the hype. *Chain Store Age Executive*, pp. 33–46, 68, 72.

Fram, E.H., & Grady, D.B. (1995, October). Internet buyers: Will the surfers become buyers? *Direct Marketing*, pp. 63–65.

Case 76
The World Wide Web: Opportunities and Threats for a Catalog Company

Jennifer K. Meyer, Gardner Publications, Inc.
Bruce Klopfenstein, Bowling Green State University

History of the Web

The Internet ("the Net") is a global computer network of networks that links computers through a common communications system. The World Wide Web (WWW or the Web) was invented to make the Internet much easier to use. The WWW is a hypertext-based system for allowing easy access to information on the Internet. "Browser software" allows users to traverse the Web easily using the computer mouse "point and click" interface.

If a marketer's aim is to maintain a presence among their consumers, then the World Wide Web may offer such a place for doing so. Usership of the Web has grown exponentially—world wide. Some say it continues to grow at a rate of over 40 percent per month. These figures, however, have been fluctuating uncontrollably because it is difficult to estimate the numbers of Web users. Forrester Research in Cambridge, Massachusetts, predicts that by 1998, there will be at least 11.2 million World Wide Web users.

Commercial Development of the Web

Although the old Internet did not allow commercial (advertising) applications, that restriction ended in the early 1990s with the privatization of the Internet. Today the WWW is an enticing new medium for commercial transactions. Its interactive nature makes it a particularly attractive medium for catalog companies. Catalog marketers have already created sophisticated graphics and other existing resources that may be applied in digital form on the Web. Other advantages include:

- Ability to use existing resources, images, and so forth.

- The similarities to their print medium.

- The potential to be more dynamic in offering promotions than print catalogs.

- More easily and regularly updated than print catalogs.

- Being lower in cost because of increases in printing and postal costs of existing print catalogs.

There are catalog company motivations for going online. The problem with catalog shopping today isn't the concept—it's the medium. Catalog marketers have found the costs of getting their catalogs to consumers soaring. There have been large rises in paper costs, as well as increases in postal rates. For a company such as Lands' End that mails out 191 million catalogs yearly, these increases could add at least $15 million to its costs of printing, producing, and mailing catalogs. Furthermore, information provided on a Web catalog could be kept more current because it can be updated fairly easily and an online presence is cheaper than CD-ROM catalogs, which are less expensive than print catalogs. Given these positive Web attributes, why wouldn't a marketer be anxious to go online?

The Web provides a medium to catalog marketers where there are tremendous graphics capabilities, an elimination of printing and postal costs, ease of updating material, and most interesting—its demographics. Taking a profile of a typical catalog consumer and comparing it to one of a typical Web user, many similarities are revealed. In fact, 82 percent of computer shoppers also buy from catalogs. Additionally, 71 percent of Web users buy from catalogs and of those individuals, 68 percent have made purchases over the Internet.

Research has shown that catalog shoppers are better educated, work in professional and managerial capacities, earn more money, and are more comfortable with modern technology and stocks and bonds than non-catalog shoppers. Also more than two-thirds of catalog shoppers have attended college and more than half earn between $30,000 and $99,000 annually. These are positive demographics that might someday soon be Net shoppers.

In comparing the previously mentioned catalog user statistics to the following Web user statistics drawn from the preliminary results of the Commerce/Nielsen Internet Demographics Survey, there are striking similarities:

- 25 percent of Web users have an income of $80,000 or more.

- 51 percent are in professional or managerial capacities.

- 64 percent have had at least four years of college.

As of 1996, Web demographics compare quite favorably to those of the average catalog shopper demographics. On the other hand, there appear to be more male than female Web users; however, some women may be using an account registered in the name of a man (e.g., a husband); in such cases, surveys might incorrectly show fewer women online than there really are.

Web Page Maintenance

On first glance it would appear that there are no major disadvantages to being "on the Web." The best Web home pages, however, require a significant commitment of resources. Experience has shown that people will visit Web sites only if they are frequently updated. The Web is an interactive medium, so simply placing existing, static, print-based media content on the Web is not a good idea. Some original content usually must be created for a viable presence on the Web. A Web site also costs money in the form of a provider's own networked computer or monthly fees paid to an "Internet Service Provider" who instead maintains the equipment.

Women's Resortwear is a privately held mail order company whose primary merchandise is women's swim and resortwear. The target audience for their products is women aged 35 to 65 who come from households with a combined household income of over $100,000. This major catalog company mails catalogs to more than four million households per year. Unlike other catalog companies, Women's Resortwear has not experimented with such new media as CD-ROM or interactive television. The company has been satisfied with focusing exclusively on the printed catalog as their sales vehicle. As members of the direct marketing industry, however, the company has become well aware of the potential for the Web to maintain or increase sales.

Women's Resortwear has two marketing managers who have been asked to make recommendations to the vice president of marketing on how they should respond to the Web (e.g., as threat or opportunity). The first executive, Anna Williams, is cautious. She believes Women's Resortwear will not reach their target audience with an online catalog.

The second executive, Simone Moses, is excited about the possibilities of the Web for Women's Resortwear. The younger, more vital Web "surfer" represents a new potential customer with whom the company can establish and perhaps maintain a lifelong electronic relationship. Simone and Anna have met several times to discuss this subject, but have not been able to come to an acceptable agreement about the Web.

Major Question

Should Women's Resortwear place its catalog on the World Wide Web? Should they continue their paper format catalog? What other options do they have?

Study Questions

1. Why is the catalog industry an especially interesting one to examine in the context of this new communication medium?

2. What are the costs of Women's Resortwear placing its catalog on the Web? What are the benefits of Women's Resortwear placing its catalog on the Web? Consider the intangible costs and benefits.

3. What can the company do to accommodate both executives' concerns? Can you produce a scenario in which Women's Resortwear attempts to use the Web without overextending itself?

4. Should Women's Resortwear take its existing catalog and digitize it for Web access? Is this a desirable use of the Web? Why or why not?

References

Braun, H.D. (1993, March). The catalog shopper of the '90s. *Direct marketing*, pp. 15–18.

Evans, C.R. (1994). *Marketing channels: Infomercial and the future of televised marketing.* Englewood Cliffs, N.J.: Prentice-Hall.

Hoffman, D.L., & Novak, T.P. (1995, October 30). Measuring the Internet: Preliminary results of the commerce/Nielsen Internet demographics survey. *Project 2000: Research program on marketing in computer-mediated environments.* From http://www2000.ogsm.vanderbilt.edu/novak/CN.prelim.results.oct30.html.

Jones, T. (1995). Marketing guide to the Internet: The executive guide to marketing on the new Internet. From http://www.industry.net/guide.html.

Koelsch, F. (1995). *The infomedia revolution: How it is changing our world and your life.* Whitby, Ontario, Canada: McGraw-Hill Ryerson Limited.

Press, L. (1994, November). Commercialization of the Internet. *Communications of the ACM*, pp. 17–21.

Rickard, L. and Raiston, J. (1995, July 10). Catalogers order changes to beat costs. *Advertising age*, pp. 1, 10.

WebLink Design Services. (1995). *WWW Demographics* (From Hermes WWW users survey 1995). From http://www.serix.com/weblink/demogr.html.

Williamson, D.A. (1995). Building a new industry: There is a business, but defining it is like lassoing jell-o. *Ad Age. It's all about marketing.* From http://www.adage.com.

Case 77
Retailing by Telecommunications

Melvin Morgenstein and Harriet Strongin, Nassau Community College

---

Telecommunications, combined with other advanced technologies, can transform retailing from stores to non-store systems. The rapid growth of non-store retailing is beginning to take a larger share of sales away from the traditional stores.

Reasons for the growth of non-store selling include the following:

- Exclusive offering through TV of many products, such as hardware specialties, records, and the like.

- Increased use of catalog shopping.

- Increase in mail shopping using credit cards.

- Large volume of telephone and mail order retailing done by traditional stores.

- Use of cable TV to order merchandise.

Advanced technology makes it possible for customers to shop at home for a variety of products. The use of the computer and an in-home video catalog enables consumers to order goods and services. Retailers equipped to do business via telecommunication merchandising systems can deliver merchandise without seeing the customer. This method of operation affords the retailer access to larger trading areas, benefits of reduced operating costs, no traditional store overhead, lower inventory costs (stock can be replenished as needed), and a 24-hour/7-day-a-week operation.

Retailers that utilize this type of operation include Video Tex, a computerized shopping service with computer and telephone link-up, with customers ordering goods shown on their television screens. Comp-U-Card is another computerized shopping service that operates a video service on cable television. Also, video catalogs and video ordering are currently used on a small scale by traditional retailers such as Sears, JCPenney, and Bloomingdale's.

Growing numbers of consumers are interested in the system for a variety of reasons:

- It is a time-saving convenience.

- Television clearly illustrates the product in action.

- It saves the cost of car use and gasoline.

- Consumers can avoid crowded shopping areas and the carrying of products from store to home.

- In-home use of several catalogs is an ideal way to comparison shop.

In conclusion, if cable TV systems offer consumers the possibility of ordering at home, having the product delivered, and paying through financial transfer systems, all that is needed to produce a retail revolution is large-scale acceptance of non-store shopping by consumers.

Major Question

How should traditional retailers change or adjust to meet the competition of electronic retailers?

Study Questions

1. Will there be a need for retail stores in the future?

2. What effect will the system have on small, independent stores that sell convenience products?

3. As consumers place more value on their time, which types of stores might be endangered most?

4. Can this system actually replace personal shopping?

Case 78
Home Shopping Dilemma

Janice Rosenthal McCoart, Marymount University
Judy K. Miler, University of Tennessee

Michele Lansburg is a buyer for a major network home shopping television program called "Fashion Sampler." Her program focuses on soft goods, and she is responsible for women's apparel. Several other programs focus on selling jewelry and such hard goods as sports equipment, small appliances, and tools.

Although her merchandise is termed "fashion," she knows, along with the other program employees, that her merchandise cannot be the highest fashion, as her target consumers are not primarily fashion leaders, but followers. The majority of the Fashion Sampler consumers are middle income homemakers, with a lot of disposable time on their hands. Most have children at home, are married, spend leisure time outdoors, and attend their children's sporting and other extracurricular activities. They are also involved with their neighborhoods, volunteer work, and are health conscious. The profile of the Fashion Sampler customer is clearly atypical of what research indicates the majority of home-shopping viewers are, as she does not like hot trends, nor is she a stay-at-home mom. She seems to be a new, emerging type of television shopping customer that represents another market.

At this time, Michele must select merchandise to sell during the last fifteen minute segment of a one hour program (5:00 pm EDT/2:00 pm PDT) of a Thursday afternoon show, planned to air during the upcoming Spring season. The program is slated to run between the "Collectible Gifts" and "World's Best Dolls" programs. (See Table 10.3, Program Guide.) She has done some preliminary planning work, and has narrowed the product choices down to three apparel merchandise groupings. Her task now is to determine which of the three apparel groups would be the best to sell.

One of the products under consideration is a sporty scarf hat in four colors: navy, bright green, turquoise, and fuchsia. These scarf hats can be arranged into three different styles on the head, and their poly/cotton fabric is an easy care, year-round weight. Additionally, one size adjusts to fit all heads, and they are manufactured by a major accessory resource, whose brand-name hats are in all the major department stores at a retail price of $15 each.

Table 10.3 Home Shopping Program Guide

What's new on homeshopping television?
Look here for Thursday's listings.
Please note: Hosts and shows are subject to change.

EDT	PDT	THURSDAY	HOSTS
12:00 am	09:00 pm	The Jewelry Connection	Celia Harris
01:00 am	10:00 pm	The Latest in Electronics	Ted Hanson
02:00 am	11:00 pm	The Latest in Electronics	Ted Hanson
03:00 am	12:00 am	Baseball Hall of Fame	Will Smith
04:00 am	01:00 am	Car Shop	Will Smith
05:00 am	02:00 am	Car Shop	Will Smith
06:00 am	03:00 am	Clever Cookery	Jean Cohn
07:00 am	04:00 am	Work Out Today	Fred Haley
08:00 am	05:00 am	Work Out Today	Fred Haley
09:00 am	06:00 am	Northern Home	Suzanne Ames
10:00 am	07:00 am	Northern Home	Suzanne Ames
11:00 am	08:00 am	Beauty and Skin Care	Suzanne Ames
12:00 pm	09:00 am	Time on Your Hands	Audrey Friend
01:00 pm	10:00 am	Collectable Gifts	Audrey Friend
02:00 pm	11:00 am	Collectable Gifts	Audrey Friend
03:00 pm	12:00 pm	Fashion Sampler	Trish Parsons
04:00 pm	01:00 pm	Fashion Sampler	Trish Parsons
05:00 pm	02:00 pm	Fashion Sampler	Trish Parsons
06:00 pm	03:00 pm	World's Best Dolls	Fran Stoessell
07:00 pm	04:00 pm	Travel Ease	Fran Stoessell
08:00 pm	05:00 pm	Sideline Sports	Jim McKay
09:00 pm	06:00 pm	Sideline Sports	Jim McKay
10:00 pm	07:00 pm	The Best of Gold	Celia Harris
11:00 pm	08:00 pm	The Jewelry Collection	Celia Harris

Another product considered for selection consists of separate tunic tops and slim skirts. The tops are solid colors and the skirts are matching pastel prints. They are the network's private label, sized small, medium, large, and have an average retail of $30 a unit.

The third group of merchandise to be considered is a signature line of golf apparel from a women's golf circuit pro. The coordinates of the licensed golf activewear manufacturer include: polos, skirts, shorts, and cardigans. The golf apparel is cotton knit, in solid red, white, and navy along with argyle pieces that mix and match. Sizes of the golf wear are misses, 8 to 16 and the retail for each item in this line runs in the $20 to $35 range.

Michele's considerations in selecting what to sell differ somewhat from a conventional store buyer. She has to not only worry about profitability, return rates, and other traditional merchandising matters, but she also has to be accountable for the additional cost of air time and/or attendant staff and production of the show as factors reflected into her bottom line profitability. She knows that merchandise sold on television requires specific broadcasting and selling skills in the presentation to motivate customer purchasing. Additionally, information about the print, color, silhouette, price, and fabric should be effectively communicated, as these are factors that sell the goods. A lesson well learned by Michele, through trial and error, is that certain prints and colors do not show to advantage on television, especially stripes or close shades of a color. Program positioning is another consideration in determining what merchandise will sell best, because carryover watchers could very easily become customers. Michele must also consider the demographics of her customer audience. Then the merchandise must be picked, packed, and sent without error. She hopes to plan the right amount of inventory—not too little or too much—of the best merchandise.

Major Question

If you had Michele's responsibility, which of the three merchandise selections would you decide to promote and sell? Why?

Study Questions

1. As a buyer, what are some of the merchandising considerations upon which you would base your decisions to purchase any product?

2. What other information could be obtained to help make Michele's decision easier?

3. Why might it be harder to sell apparel on TV than at a store?

Reference

Edelson, S. (1995, November 8). Fashion reevaluates flickering fortunes of TV home shopping, *WWD*, pp. 8–9.

Case 79
Spotlight on On-Air Sales

Laura Neumann, Eagle's Eye

Imagine taking orders for over 18 million dollars worth of merchandise in 24 hours. Spotlight, a major electronic television retailer, shipped over 39 million packages, received more than 55 million calls and sold over 1.4 billion dollars in one year. Spotlight's major competitor's yearly sales are 1.1 billion dollars. This compares to Spiegel's annual sales of 2.7 billion dollars and Lands' End with sales at .9 billion dollars. Programming for Spotlight runs 24 hours per day, 7 days a week, reaching over 50 million households. The studio, buying, and administrative offices are located on the East coast of the U.S. with additional telecommunication centers in the East, South, and Southwest. Four distribution centers (i.e., returns, warehouse, shipping, receiving) are located primarily in the East and Southeast. Approximately 6,100 people work for Spotlight including 104 buyers in four areas—apparel, home furnishings, electronics, and jewelry. Internationally, Spotlight has joint ventures in Mexico and England.

Approximately 250 new products are sold each week. It is unusual for Spotlight to markdown an item. However, when they do, two markdown opportunities are utilized: 1) a 10 percent markdown for items that are aired the two days following Christmas; and 2) "first time pricing." With this second method, occasionally, Spotlight will offer a price reduction on an item the first 12 times it is aired, after which the item is sold at full retail price. Additionally, everyday there is one new product that is featured at a "bargain" price. After that initial bargain offering, the new product never again returns to that "bargain" price.

In successful electronic retailing, product development is the first step. Buyers, assistant buyers, and merchandise specialists assist the vendors and designers with the development of apparel products. Negotiating price, writing the purchase orders, and working the open-to-buy are the major responsibilities of the buyer. The assistant buyer works with the buyer, helps develop the product, and assists in computer sales and inventory forecasting. Merchandise specialists enter purchase orders into the computer and assist in administrative tasks (i.e., filing and faxing). Directors oversee the buyers and sign off on purchase orders. One divisional vice president manages and leads each product category (i.e., apparel, home furnishings, electronics, jewelry). Additionally, this person approves purchase orders with large dollar volumes.

After the product is developed and ordered, the buyers no longer have full responsibility for the product. Programmers take the merchandise ordered by the buyers and allocate air time for the merchandise. Producers manage the on-air time and direct the models, technical staff, and program hosts. Program hosts are on-air for three hour time blocks and adlib their presentations with the exception of an information card that lists the product's price, color, spec, and style number. Program hosts spend time with the buyer learning detailed information about each product. They are paid a salary and utilize the theme of quality products at a good value.

Live models are utilized to display apparel products. Typically three to four models are hired for each show: three size medium and one size extra large (1X). Product shows can vary in length of time and number of products sold. Apparel products typically air for six minutes, with ten products per hour. A show could be one to three hours in duration. At times the program host will be joined on-air by a designer so that more product detail can be provided to the customer. Orders are taken by order-entry personnel and by an automated order-entry system. Customers with touch tone telephones can place their order using the automatic order entry system without requiring the assistance of an order-entry representative. Customer service is available to answer any questions. After an item is ordered, it is shipped from a warehouse within three to ten days. All returns are sent to a facility allocated exclusively for that purpose.

DeShaundra Dews, an apparel designer located on the East coast—who works exclusively for Spotlight—has had tremendous success by combining a good product with an excellent talent for selling the product on television. DeShaundra was willing to take some risks in building a business with Spotlight. The first order, over five years ago, was for only 20 dozen units. The product was a success and DeShaundra was magnificent at selling the product on-air. Now, five years later, DeShaundra recently sold 2.2 million dollars in retail sales in three hours, one-quarter of the total network sales volume for the 24-hour day. DeShaundra is the only designer who contracts with Spotlight to have a full, one-hour program each week and additional miscellaneous hours throughout each month.

DeShaundra has recently been asked to build a joint venture business with Spotlight in England. Very little information exists on the new joint venture. She has learned that the styles ordered by the retail buyers in England would be exactly the same as those purchased by the Spotlight buyers in the U.S. Having no history or other business records to examine, it would be trial and error as to whether the English market would accept U.S. styles.

Sizing would have to be adjusted for the English customer. For example, a size "medium" in the U.S. would be a "small" in England. In order to meet England's spec requirements, DeShaundra would also have to add one size range, 3X (28/30), equaling a 4X using Spotlight's U.S. sizing. This sizing would incur a one-time specification expense that would be an added expense for the cutting of new sizes for the English customer. DeShaundra's current major concern is that the orders would be too small to make a profit. Additionally, the designer would have the expense and time commitment of traveling to England approximately six times per year. Further, there is no guarantee that DeShaundra's product line—so popular with Spotlight's American customer—would be similarly appealing to English television apparel shoppers. Also, DeShaundra wonders whether her domestic business would suffer from her attention to the new British market. She now works about as hard as she feels she can and is hesitant about taking on more responsibility and work. From DeShaundra's perspective, there is much to consider. Are the risks worth the potential success?

Major Question

From DeShaundra's perspective should her arrangement with Spotlight be developed for the English at-home shopper?

Study Questions

1. What type of research should DeShaundra do before making this decision?

2. Besides size, what other differences might there be between U.S. and English markets to consider?

3. Would prices be different in the two markets? If so, why?

4. Would there be different considerations relative to expanding the business, for the television retailer and the conventional store business?

Chapter Discussion Questions

1. Discuss the major technological applications that are used at the apparel manufacturing and retail levels today. Name the benefits that retailers, manufacturers, and consumers realize from this technology, using case examples to support your discussion.

2. Discuss how quick response and other computer applications link the manufacture and the retail processes.

3. How is the consumer affected by the new technologies? How do you think the consumer shopping environment will change in the future?

4. How is retail merchandising specifically impacted by the advances in technology today? Support your answers with examples from the cases in this chapter.

5. Which new technologies do you believe will survive into the next century? Which will not? Why do you think this is true?

6. Assess the future of the Internet for businesses and consumers.

11 Entrepreneurship and Small Business Ownership

Chapter Objectives

- Describe entrepreneurship and present the characteristics of successful entrepreneurs.

- Relate leadership to entrepreneurship.

- Explain the process and challenges of starting your own business.

- Distinguish between an entrepreneurial and a non-entrenpreneurial small business.

The U.S. business base was founded on entrepreneurism and small businesses. Today we see developing countries following in these footsteps with many new successful businesses, particularly in the apparel and textiles fields, bringing continual competition to established American companies. Entrepreneurs are future-oriented risk takers who have shown leadership in developing new businesses. Many large, successful companies started out small—with a single creative leader. However, not all small business owners are entrepreneurs, nor are they leaders. Starting your own business takes a great deal of time, energy, planning, and self-sacrifice, and is not for everyone; but it can be a rewarding undertaking that leads to success. Careful consideration and decisions must be made along with self-analysis of strengths and weaknesses to determine one's entrepreneurial aptitude and direction relative to small business ownership.

The Realities of Entrepreneurship

Starting your own business is the dream of many people, but how many are really prepared for the realities of business ownership? More small businesses fail in the first year than survive. Entrepreneurs often fail in their first attempt, but the successful ones do not give up even in the face of several failures. Successful entrepreneurs have a vision for their business that is carried through to completion. Consider the case of Allen Breed who developed the air bag and waited twenty years to convince the automobile industry of its usefulness; or Sam Walton and Rowland H. Macy, whose first attempts at retail businesses failed.

There are many definitions of **entrepreneur.** S/he can be considered as a person who is a leader, is a visionary, and has the ability to see and evaluate business opportunities, bringing together the factors of production in such a way that new wealth is created as their business grows. Some feel an entrepreneur also must possess a certain inventive genius.

Many of today's successful retail and manufacturing giants started out as small businesses. Today the majority of U.S. retailers and apparel manufacturers are small businesses, and many of these may be tomorrow's successful entrepreneurs. Table 11.1 profiles leading retail entrepreneurs, the originators of Wal-Mart, The Limited, Petrie Stores, Lands' End, and Mrs. Fields Cookies, all of whom started with small businesses.

Being an entrepreneur means combining personal characteristics, knowledge, financial means, and resources. Entrepreneurs are all unique and each has an individual style; therefore, it is difficult to list all the personal characteristics required to be successful. What works for one person may not work for another. However, one trait they all have in common is that they are visionary: they perceive what others have not seen and act upon that perception. Some personal characteristics that frequently surface in successful entrepreneurs include:

- The ability to make their own decisions.

- The ability to organize.

- The ability to lead.

- The ability to get along with people.

- The acceptance of responsibility.

- The possession of willpower, self discipline, good time-management skills, self confidence.

- The possession of originality and flexibility.

- The capacity for hard work, long hours, and physical stamina.

Table 11.1   Profiles of Leading Retail Entrepreneurs

Sam Walton	He opened his first retail store shortly after World War II; his first Wal-Mart discount department store was opened in 1962. In 1995, Wal-Mart had over 2,900 store and sales volume in excess of $193 billion. Sam Walton was the richest man in America before his death in 1992.	Gary Comer	In 1963, he founded Lands' End, a mail-order company. Prior to that, Comer was an advertising copywriter for Young & Rubicam. Lands' End became a publicly held corporation in 1986 with circulation of 200 million catalogs and sales of over $1 billion in 1996.
Leslie Wexner	He borrowed $5,000 from an aunt to start a ladies' clothing store in the early 1960s. In 1994 his firm, The Limited, Inc., had almost 5,000 stores (including The Limited, Express, Structure, Victoria's Secret, Lerners New York, and Henri Bendel among others) and had annual sales of over $7 billion.	Debbi and Randy Fields	In 1977, at age twenty, Debbi Fields opened a small cookie store in Palo Alto, California. Today, there are more than 700 company-owned Mrs. Fields' Cookies stores, with outlets in thirty-seven states and Australia, Canada, Great Britain, Hong Kong, and Japan. The personal wealth of Debbi Fields and her husband, Randy, is estimated at between $50 and $100 million.
Milton Petrie	He started in retailing as a $10-per-week department store clerk in Indianapolis. In 1995, Petrie Stores' medium-priced clothing chain with a teen emphasis had over 1,700 stores and annual sales of over $1.2 billion.		

- The enjoyment of competition.

- Being task-result oriented.

- Being a risk-taker.

- Being future-oriented.

- Having a strong desire to be independent and to succeed.

Knowledge or technical information needed for success might include:

- Knowledge about products or services sold.

- Finding the target market, selling techniques, and how to promote the product or service.

- Knowledge of personnel management, record keeping, and inventory controls.

- Experience or formal training, depending on the area.

It is important to remember, however, that not all entrepreneurs possess these characteristics.

The **entrepreneurial process** can be seen in one of five ways: 1) introduction of a new product or of improved quality; 2) introduction of a new method of production; 3) opening of a new market; 4) conquest of a new source of supply of materials; and 5) carrying out a new organization of an industry.

Brown and Smith (1986) offer this advice for would-be entrepreneurs:

- Avoid businesses that are oversaturated.

- Originality isn't always necessary; improving on a well-established business type can be successful.

- Concentrate your research on filling a need or niche.

- Start a business cautiously with sufficient capital. And don't expect to get rich overnight.

What an Entrepreneur is Not

A person who merely owns a company or gives orders is not necessarily an entrepreneur. A **venture capitalist** or **financier** is a person who supplies money and takes a financial risk, but this person is not necessarily an entrepreneur—s/he can be merely an investor. These roles have often been confused. A person who creates in the literary or artistic sense is not an entrepreneur; that person would need to recognize an innovative idea or creation and capitalize on it to be an entrepreneur. Merely being self-employed also is not necessarily being an entrepreneur because an element of growth is required that leads to innovation, job creation, and economic expansion. Not all small firms are entrepreneurial, but most entrepreneurs start out in small firms. In this chapter, *Case 80, Wal-Mart: Strategies for Market Dominance, Case 81, Growing Pains for Baubles, Bangles & Beads*, and *Case 82, Amber's Wave*, all discuss retailers and manufacturers that are small businesses or started out as such, but all may not be thought of as entrepreneurs.

The Owner as Leader

Being a leader is a prerequisite to entrepreneurship. **Leadership** is the process of moving a group in a direction that is in their long-term best interests. The leader must demonstrate strength and the ability to carry the followers. Common characteristics of a leader include having a realistic, clear vision of a goal, the means to accomplish it, and the ability and means to communicate the vision to inspire others. Most believe that people are not born leaders; leadership skills can be learned. Shefsky (1994) developed a list of 23 recommended skills to help develop entrepreneurial leadership, as shown in Table 11.2. In addition to these 23 skills, number 24 should be caring. Perhaps Sam Walton is one of the best examples of this, as he visited hourly employees at the stores showing how important the business was to him while undergoing chemotherapy for bone cancer. They knew he cared, and they responded in kind.

Leaders are not always managers. Some people are both, but many managers are devoid of leadership. Managers instruct people on what to do, but leaders help them decide what to do. (For more on managers, see Chapter Nine.) A leader is not necessarily the best at doing what needs to be done;

Table 11.2   23 Recommended Entrepreneurial Skills

1. Keep your perspective.	14. Take responsibility for their mistakes.
2. Know why you want to lead.	15. Select the birds you flock with.
3. Identify your targets (dream); know when to shoot.	16. Give.
4. Be clear and fixed.	17. Keep your goal in sight.
5. Observe when people listen to you.	18. One-to-one is the same as 1-million-to-1-million (some people won't take risks).
6. Leverage your small successes.	19. Trust.
7. Be tough, not mean; use carrots, not sticks.	20. Communicate to inspire.
8. Let them see you err.	21. Be a cheerleader.
9. Show you are willing to pay the price.	22. Remember what they wish they were.
10. Create positive-sum games. (Create something.)	23. Do windows, but not details. (Do anything to make the dream happen, but know your strengths and weaknesses.)
11. Withstand temptations.	
12. Study your opportunities.	
13. Select the right followers.	

but s/he motivates others. As small companies grow large, the originators often find they are not good managers. Companies often find they have outgrown their founder's skills and their ability to integrate other talented people. That was the case with Apple Computer as Steve Jobs and Steve Wozniak went on to other ventures; this also happened when Banana Republic's originators sold to Gap. On the other hand, Bill Gates, owner of Microsoft, and Sam Walton, owner of Wal-Mart, stayed with their companies as they grew large and successful. Most attribute the success of Wal-Mart to the entrepreneurial spirit of Sam Walton which he maintained throughout his life (see *Case 80*).

Entrepreneurial leaders have a dream. They start without followers and proclaim their beliefs publicly, risking being wrong. They are inspirational. If they believe wholeheartedly and can demonstrate that to others, followers will join in the dream. People want to associate with those who can give them a positive experience.

Starting Your Own Business

As previously mentioned, not all small businesses are entrepreneurial, but most entrepreneurs start out in small businesses. Who knows which small enterprise will be the next Levi Strauss or Wal-Mart? With today's large businesses downsizing, we are seeing an increase in the creation of small

Figure 11.1 Paying off a bet, Sam Walton, chairman of Wal-Mart Stores, does the hula in New York's financial district on March 15, 1984. Walton, who calls his employees "associates," promised all 65,000 of them that he'd do a hula dance on Wall Street if they showed an 8 percent pretax net profit for 1983 in an industry in which 3 percent profits were average. In 1983, Wal-Mart's 642 stores in 19 states wound up with a pre-tax net of 8.04 percent and Walton (keeping his promise) came to New York to do his wriggling. *Photo courtesy of UPI/Bettmann Newsphotos.*

companies. The **Small Business Administration (SBA)** defines a small business differently depending on the industry, however, for retailing it is sales of less than $5 million and for manufacturing it is defined as less than 500 employees. Small businesses have advantages and disadvantages over larger companies and corporations. Advantages include being your own boss and decision-maker, the freedom to do what you want when you want, and the satisfaction of knowing you were responsible for your success and the employment of other people. Disadvantages include not being able to be all things or possess all the skills necessary to run your business, limited capital, time and energy, and being responsible for the things that go wrong, which perhaps result in the loss of the livelihood of others. The positive aspects of business ownership may be a detriment to others. For example, being the sole decision-maker may be stressful to some, which could result in poor decision-making at times.

Small business owners have other options besides starting a new business. They may buy an existing business as in *Case 84, parts 1 and 2, Amy's Fashions on First,* or they could buy into an independent or corporate business and become a partner with another person already in that business, or they could buy a franchise. Of course, there are dangers in these options too. *Case 5, Cironi's Sewing Center Loses a Franchise* in Chapter One, shows the dangers of owning a franchise, as a sewing machine company withdrew the franchise without much notice.

New small business owners may need assistance as usually no one holds all the skills and knowledge necessary to run a successful business. The legal aspects of starting or buying a business may necessitate the services of a lawyer for assistance in complying with local laws and ordinances. Accountants may be necessary to develop a system of record-keeping, including payroll, sales, and tax reports. First-time apparel store owners may need help developing merchandise plans or even shopping the market. In *Case 84, part 1,* Amy went to market for the first time with no idea of how much

merchandise to order or how much money to spend.

It takes an incredible amount of time and personal sacrifice starting a business as Jane Jeffries discovers in *Case 81, Growing Pains for Baubles, Bangles & Beads.* Putting all of your time into a business very often leaves little time for a personal life. Going into a new venture with your eyes wide open will help to increase your chance of success.

Planning

Planning is the anticipation and organization of what tasks need to be done to reach an objective or goal. A business plan is an important part of the overall planning for a new business. It should include a marketing plan, financial plan, and legal considerations. Additionally, a merchandise plan may be necessary if goods are to be sold (Chapter Four explains merchandise planning and its importance). A **marketing plan** includes an analysis of the business environment that should support the definition of the designated target market. Generally, small businesses need to find a niche market that is not completely filled. *Case 83, The Home Shopping Heartache*, profiles a small manufacturer producing unique hats, one of only a few in the country. A **financial plan** includes an estimate of start-up costs and the amount of financing required. It should include performance objectives, estimated sales, and cash flow. Legal requirements include a basic understanding of the laws affecting the business such as permits, licenses, and regulations. This information can be procured from the SBA, local chamber of commerce, or department of economic development.

Access to Capital

While many businesses can be started with little money, most businesses need some capital to get started. Access to capital—a perpetual problem for the entrepreneur and new business owner—can take several forms. Having your own money is the easiest way of financing your business, but that is not always possible. Some borrow from family and other personal sources who may want to invest.

Case 66, part 1 in Chapter Nine, illustrates a situation with a young couple starting a business using personal and family funds to get started.

If small business owners can prove credit worthiness, generally through a proven track record, they may be able to secure a loan to start their business. Loans are possible through the SBA, a federal agency with special programs for minority business development and for the economically disadvantaged. Another source of income is through venture capitalists, individuals who invest money in someone else's business. For a substantial part of the profits, the venture capitalist provides financial backing for the company to get started. Many well-known designers have such financial backing. It can be risky business for both the backer and the designer. If profits are not as anticipated, the financial backer may pull out of the deal, leaving the designer no way to continue in business. Designers have been known to even lose their trademarked name when their business went bankrupt. Entering into a partnership is another way of procuring funds for a small business. A partner contributes financial support and shares in the profits or losses.

Most new businesses need start-up costs. These vary, of course, from business to business. Stores often require interior and/or exterior remodeling that can take considerable funds unless one is creative and can "beg or borrow" to get started. A direct mail or electronic retail business does not require such investment; however, start-up costs would be required for the paper or on-line catalogs and distribution. Part of start-up costs goes toward procuring inventory (if merchandise is sold). Some retail companies can start out with **consignment** or "on memorandum" merchandise in which the supplier is paid for only those items that are sold. Some retailers refer to these as "goods on wheels!" The owner does not take title to the goods, and hence does not need to have funds up front to purchase the merchandise as most retail does. Other costs incurred for a new business include rent, supplies, employee wages, advertising, utilities, insurance, taxes, delivery costs, and so forth.

Environmental Influences

The economic and political environments play crucial roles in the survival and growth of new and small businesses. High inflation and interest rates can be devastating to a new, struggling business. The effect of most governmental regulation is generally most severe on small businesses. For example, the small pharmaceutical company has all but disappeared due to the high costs of testing requirements imposed by the Food and Drug Administration (FDA). The FDA also monitors the cosmetics industry, which has come under attack for claims that cosmetics affect the functioning of the body, thus defining the product as a drug. Small companies may not be able to survive such legal battles. The Federal Trade Commission (FTC) regulates unfair competition including deceptive advertising and has the power to remove products from the market if suspected of trademark infringement or to effect changes in advertisement claims if warranted. Additionally, the Consumer Product Safety Commission (CPSC) has the power to recall products in the marketplace if they have been proven to be a safety risk or hazard. *Case 94, The Bean Bag Case* in Chapter Twelve, illustrates this as the company verges on bankruptcy. (U.S. governmental regulatory agencies are discussed further in Chapter Twelve.)

The competitive environment can also be difficult for a new small business. With tight resources and many roles to occupy, new owners may not find time to evaluate their competition and keep on top of trends as they should. This appears to have happened in *Case 82* where strong growth suddenly slows.

Small Business Performance

Many people can start a business if they possess the desire to do so. Achieving success, however, is another story. Individuals wanting to own their own businesses should possess similar personal characteristics as entrepreneurs, for example, sufficient knowledge, skills, interest, and financial means; however, as mentioned earlier, not all owners are necessarily entrepreneurs. Many small businesses fail for many reasons. *US News & World Report,* ("Checklist for small business," 1989) cited ten major reasons for small business failures:

1. Insufficient profits.

2. Poor growth.

3. Too much debt or too little equity.

4. Inexperience.

5. Heavy operating expenses.

6. Industry weaknesses.

7. Internal factors such as high interest rates, poor location, or competition.

8. Neglect.

9. Fraud.

10. Poor planning.

   Case 84, parts 1 and 2, is an example of a small business owner with several of the above problems, not the least of which was a fire that destroyed all the stock in her store. She has to decide whether or not to start up the business again after the fire. On the other hand, some small companies with good ideas and new niches can be phenomenally successful. Despite inexperience in the retailing field, Mel and Patricia Ziegler founded Banana Republic company as a "no-nonsense" travel and safari clothing company. After five years, they sold Banana Republic to Gap for $535 million. *Case 81* is another example of a successful company making one-of-a-kind jewelry that grew faster than the owner could manage.

Summary

Most businesses in the U.S. are small and there are many success stories of small companies becoming leaders in the economy. Such is the American dream. These small businesses often were started by entrepreneurial leaders who may or may not have been successful in their first venture. Entrepreneurs are risk-takers and visionaries who are dedicated to long hours of work to realize their dreams as they create something new. Not all small business owners are entrepreneurs, but they are the backbone of our economy. Starting a new, successful business takes careful research, analysis, and planning in addition to sufficient capital.

References

Apparel shop entrepreneurship. (1990). Stillwater: Center for Apparel Marketing and Merchandising (CAMM), Department of Design, Housing and Merchandising, Oklahoma State University.

Berman, B., & Evans, J.R. (1989). *Retail management: A strategic approach.* New York: Macmillan.

Brown, P.B., & Smith, G.N. (1986). *Sweat equity: What it really takes to build America's best small companies—by the guys who did it.* New York: Simon & Schuster.

Checklist for small business. (1989, October). *U.S. News & World Report,* pp. 72–80.

Dun and Bradstreet (annual publication) *The business failure record.* New York: Author.

Franchise opportunities: A business of your own. (1989). New York: Sterling.

The hottest entrepreneurs in America: Our seventh annual entrepreneur of the year awards. (1995, December). *Inc.,* pp. 35–37+.

Redden, T. (1989). *Franchise buyers' handbook.* Glenview, IL.: Scott, Foresman.

Shefshy, L.E. (1994). *Entrepreneurs are made not born.* New York: McGraw-Hill.

Small Business Administration, Office of Business Development, various publications. Washington, D.C.: U.S. Government Printing Office.

Thirteenth CFR (Code of Federal Regulations) Part 120. (1996). Federal Register, National Archives & Records Administration. Washington, D.C.: U.S. Government Printing Office.

Case 80
Wal-Mart: Strategies for Market Dominance

James W. Camerius, Northern Michigan University

"I didn't sit down one day and decide that I was going to put a bunch of discount stores in small towns and set a goal to have a billion-dollar company some day. I started out with one store and it did well, so it was a challenge to see if I could do well with a few more. We're still going and we'll keep going as long as we're successful."

—Samuel M. Walton (1918–1992)

An Emerging Organization

In 1996, Wal-Mart Stores, Inc., with corporate offices in Bentonville, Arkansas, operated stores under a variety of names and retail formats including: Wal-Mart discount department stores; Sam's Wholesale Clubs, which were wholesale/retail membership warehouses; and Supercenters, which are large combination grocery and general merchandise stores. In the international division, it operated in Canada, Mexico, Argentina, Brazil, and Asia.

The Sam Walton Spirit

Much of the success of Wal-Mart was attributed to the entrepreneurial spirit of its founder and chairman of the board, Samuel Moore Walton. One of the most influential retailers of the century, Walton died on April 5, 1992, at the age of 74 years. "Mr. Sam," as some referred to him, had traced his down-to-earth, old-fashioned, home-spun, evangelical ways to growing up in rural Oklahoma, Missouri, and Arkansas. Although he was remarkably blasé about his roots, some suggested that it was a simple belief in hard work and ambition that had "unlocked countless doors and showered upon him, his customers, and his employees... the fruits of... years of labor in building [this] highly successful company." "The reason for our success," he noted, "is our people and the way that they're treated and the way they feel about their company." Many have suggested it is this "people first" philosophy that guided the company through the challenges and setbacks of its early years, and which allowed the company to maintain its consistent record of growth and expansion in later years.

For all that Walton's success had been chronicled, its magnitude is difficult to comprehend. Sam Walton was selected by the investment publication *Financial World* in 1989 as the "CEO of the Decade." He had honorary degrees from the University of the Ozarks, the University of Arkansas, and the University of Missouri. He also received many of the most distinguished professional awards of the industry like "Man of the Year," "Discounter of the Year," "Chief Executive Officer of the Year," and was the second retailer to be inducted into the Discounting Hall of Fame. He was recipient of the Horatio Alger Award in 1984 and was acknowledged by *Discount Stores News* as "Retailer of the Decade" in December of 1989. "Walton does a remarkable job of instilling near-religious fervor in his people," said analyst Robert Buchanan of A.G. Edwards. "I think that speaks to the heart of his success." In late 1989, Sam Walton was diagnosed to have multiple myeloma, cancer of the bone marrow. He planned to remain active in the firm as chairman of the board of directors.

The Marketing Concept: Genesis of an Idea

Sam Walton started his retail career in 1940 as a management trainee with JCPenney in Des Moines, Iowa. He was impressed with the Penney method of doing business and later modeled the Wal-Mart chain after many Penney principles.

Following service in the U.S. Army during World War II, Walton acquired a Ben Franklin variety store franchise in Newport, Arkansas, which he operated successfully until losing the lease in 1950. He opened another store under the name of Walton's 5 & 10 in Bentonville, Arkansas, the following year. By 1962, he was operating a chain of fifteen stores.

The early Walton retail stores were variety store operations. They were relatively small operations of 6,000 square feet, were located on a "main street," and displayed merchandise on plain wooden tables and counters. Operated under the Ben Franklin name and supplied by Butler Brothers of Chicago and St. Louis, they were characterized by a limited price line, low gross margins, high merchandise turnover, and concentration on return on investment. The firm, operating under the Walton 5 & 10 name, was the largest Ben Franklin franchisee in the country in 1962. The variety stores were phased out by 1976 to allow the company to concentrate on the growth of Wal-Mart Stores.

Foundations of Growth

Sam Walton became convinced in the late 1950s that discounting would transform retailing. His theory was to operate a discount store in a small community offering name-brand merchandise at low prices and friendly service. He tried to interest Butler Brothers executives in Chicago in the discount store concept, but they rejected the idea. The first "Wal-Mart Discount City" opened in late 1962 in Rogers, Arkansas.

Wal-Mart stores would sell nationally advertised, well-known brand merchandise at low prices in austere surroundings. As corporate policy, they would cheerfully give refunds, credits, and rain checks. Management conceived the firm as a "discount department store chain offering a wide variety of general merchandise to the customer." Early emphasis was placed on opportunistic purchases of merchandise from whatever sources were available. Heavy emphasis was placed upon health and beauty aids and "stacking it high" in a manner of merchandise presentation. By the end of 1979, there were 276 Wal-Mart stores located in eleven states.

The firm developed an aggressive expansion strategy as it grew from its first, 16,000-square-foot discount store in Rogers. New stores were located primarily in towns with populations of 5,000 to 25,000. Store sizes ranged from 30,000 to 60,000 square feet, with 45,000 being the average. The firm also expanded by locating stores in contiguous areas, town by town, state by state. When its discount operations came to dominate a market area, it moved to an adjoining area. While other retailers built warehouses to serve existing outlets, Wal-Mart built the distribution center first and then spotted stores all around it, pooling advertising and distribution overhead. Most stores were less than a six-hour drive from one of the company's warehouses. The first major distribution center, a 390,000 square-foot facility opened in Searcy, Arkansas, outside Bentonville in 1978.

National Perspectives

At the beginning of 1991, the firm had 1,573 Wal-Mart stores in thirty-five states with expansion planned for adjacent states. The stores offered a wide variety of general merchandise to the customer. They were designed to offer one-stop shopping in 36 departments, which included family apparel, health and beauty aids, household needs, electronics, toys, fabric and crafts, automotive supplies, lawn and patio, jewelry, and shoes. Additionally, at certain locations, a pharmacy, automotive supply and service center, garden center, or snack bar were also operated. "Everyday low prices" were stressed as opposed to emphasizing special price promotions. Each store was expected to "provide the customer with a clean, pleasant, and friendly shopping experience."

Although Wal-Mart carries similar merchandise at similar prices and operates stores which look much like the competition, there are many differences. Wal-Mart employees wear blue vests to identify themselves, aisles are wide, apparel departments are carpeted in warm colors, a store employee follows customers to their cars to pick up their shopping carts, and the customer is welcomed at the door by a "people greeter" who gives directions and strikes up conversations. In some cases, merchandise is bagged in brown paper sacks, rather than plastic bags because customers seem to prefer them. A simple Wal-Mart logo in white letters on a brown background on the front of the store serves to identify the firm. The chain is particularly adept at striking the delicate balance

needed to convince customers its prices are low without making people feel that its stores are too cheap. In many ways, competitors like Kmart, sought to emulate Wal-Mart by introducing people greeters, by upgrading interiors, by developing new logos and signage, and by introducing new inventory response systems. In 1996, sales-per-square-foot at Wal-Mart were $307. Kmart, in contrast, sold only $192 per square foot that year. Each Wal-Mart store is encouraged to initiate programs that will make it an integral part of the community in which it operates. Associates are encouraged to "maintain the highest standards of honesty, morality, and business ethics in dealing with the public.

The External Environment

Industry analysts label the 1980s and early 1990s as eras of economic uncertainty for retailers. Many retailers were negatively affected by increased competitive pressures, sluggish consumer spending, slower-than-anticipated economic growth in North America, and recessions abroad. In 1995, Wal-Mart management felt the high consumer debt level caused many shoppers to reduce or defer spending on anything other than essentials. Management also felt that the lack of exciting new products or apparel trends reduced discretionary spending. Fierce competition resulted in lower margins and the lack of inflation stalled productivity increases.

Many retail enterprises confronted heavy competitive pressure by restructuring. Sears became a more focused retailer by divesting itself of Allstate Insurance Company and its real estate subsidiaries. In 1993, the company announced it would close 118 unprofitable stores and discontinue the unprofitable Sears general merchandise catalog. It eliminated 50,000 jobs and began a $4 billion, five-year remodeling plan for its remaining multi-line department stores, realigning its merchandise strategy to meet the needs of middle market customers, focusing on product lines in apparel, home, and automotive. The new focus on apparel was supported with the advertising campaign, "The Softer Side of Sears."

By the early 1990s, the discount department store industry had changed in a number of ways and was thought to have reached maturity by many analysts. Several formerly successful firms like E.J. Korvette, W.T. Grant, Zayre, and Ames had declared bankruptcy and as a result either were liquidated or reorganized. Regional firms began carrying more fashionable merchandise in more attractive facilities and shifted their emphasis to more national markets. Specialty retailers such as Toys "R" Us, Pier 1 Imports, and Oshmans were making big inroads in toys, home furnishings, and sporting goods. The "superstores" of drug and food chains were rapidly discounting increasing amounts of general merchandise. Some firms had withdrawn from the field by either selling their discount divisions or closing them down entirely.

Several new retail formats had emerged in the marketplace to challenge the traditional discount department store format. The superstore, a 100,000- to 300,000-square-foot operation, combined a large supermarket with a discount general-merchandise store. Originally a European retailing concept, these outlets were known as "malls without walls." Kmart's Super Kmart Center, American Fare, and Wal-Mart's Supercenter Store were examples of this trend toward large operations. Warehouse retailing, involving a combination of warehouse and showroom facilities, used warehouse principles to reduce operating expenses and thereby offer discount prices as a primary customer appeal. Home Depot combined the traditional hardware store and lumber yard with a self-service home improvement center to become the largest home center operator in the nation.

Some retailers responded to changes in the marketplace by selling goods at price levels 20 to 60 percent below regular retail prices. These off-price operations appeared as two general types: 1) such factory outlet stores as Burlington Coat Factory Warehouse, Bass Shoes, and Manhattan's Brand Name Fashion Outlet; and 2) such independents as Loehmann's, T.J. Maxx, Marshall's, and Clothestime, which bought seconds, overages, closeouts, or leftover goods from manufacturers

and other retailers. Other retailers chose to dominate a product classification. Some super specialists like Sock Appeal, Little Piggie, Ltd, and Sock Market, offered a single, narrowly defined classification of merchandise with an extensive assortment of brands, colors, and sizes. Others, as niche specialists, like Kids Mart (a division of F.W. Woolworth), and McKids (a division of Sears), targeted an identified market with carefully selected merchandise and appropriately designed stores. Some retailers like Silk Greenhouse (silk plants and flowers), Office Club (office supplies and equipment), and Toys "R" Us (toys) were called "category killers" because they had achieved merchandise dominance in their respective product categories. Such firms as The Limited, Victoria's Secret, and Banana Republic became mini-department specialists by showcasing new lines and accessories alongside traditional merchandise lines.

Wal-Mart became the nation's largest retailer and discount department store chain in sales volume. Kmart Corporation, the industry's third largest retailer and discount department store chain, with over 2,100 stores and $34,389,000 in sales in 1995, was perceived by many industry analysts and consumers in several independent studies as a laggard, even though it had been the industry sales leader for a number of years. In the same studies, Wal-Mart was perceived as the industry leader, even though according to the *Wall Street Journal:* "they carry much the same merchandise, offer prices that are pennies apart and operate stores that look almost exactly alike." "Even their names are similar," noted the newspaper. The original Kmart concept of a "conveniently located, one-stop shopping unit, where customers could buy a wide variety of quality merchandise at discount prices," had lost its competitive edge in a changing market. As one analyst noted in an industry newsletter: "They had done so well for the past 20 years without paying attention to market changes. Now they have to." Wal-Mart and Kmart sales growth over ten years is reviewed in Table 11.3. A competitive analysis is shown of four major retail firms in Table 11.4.

Table 11.3 Competitive Sales & Store Comparison[1] 1985–1995

	KMART		WAL-MART	
Year/Sales	Sales (000)	Stores	Sales (000)	Stores
1995	$34,389,000	2,161	$93,627,000	2,943
1994	34,025,000	2,481	82,494,000	2,684
1993	34,156,000	2,486	67,344,000	2,400
1992	37,724,000	2,435	55,483,771	2,136
1991	34,580,000	2,391	43,886,902	1,928
1990	32,070,000	2,350	32,601,594	1,721
1989	29,533,000	2,361	25,810,656	1,525
1988	27,301,000	2,307	20,649,001	1,364
1987	25,627,000	2,273	15,959,255	1,198
1986	23,035,000	2,342	11,909,076	1,029
1985	22,035,000	2,332	8,451,489	882

[1]Number of general merchandise stores.

Table 11.4 An Industry Competitive Analysis 1995

	Wal-Mart	Sears	Kmart	Target
Sales (Millions)	$93,627	$34,925	$34,389	$15,007
Net Income (1000s)	$ 2,740	$ 1,801	$ (571)	$ 1,047
Net Income/Share	$ 1.19	$ 4.40	$ (1.08)	$ N/A
Dividends Per Share	$ .20	$ .92	$ .36	$ N/A
% Sales Change	13.0%	5.8%	5.8%	16%

Table 11.5 Number of Stores in Competing Chains

Wal-Mart & Subsidiaries
Wal-Mart Stores—2,218
SAM's Clubs—470
Supercenters—255

Sears Roebuck & Company (all divisions)
Sears Merchandise Group
Department Stores—806
Hardware Stores—108
Furniture Stores—138
Sears Dealer Stores—375
Auto/Tire Stores—1051
Auto Parts Stores
Western Auto—392
Parts America—190
Western Auto Dealer Stores—900

Kmart Corporation
General Merchandise—2,161
Specialty Retail Stores
Builders Square Home Improvement—167

Dayton Hudson Corporation
Target—670
Mervyn's—295
Department Stores—64

Some retailers like Kmart had initially focused on appealing to professional, middle-class consumers who lived in suburban areas and were likely to be price sensitive. Other firms like Target, which had adopted the discount concept early, generally attempted to go after an upscale consumer, who had an annual household income of $25,000 to $44,000. Fleet Farm and Menard's served the rural consumer, while firms like Chicago's Goldblatt's Department Stores returned to their immigrant heritage to serve African-Americans and Hispanics in the inner city.

In rural communities, Wal-Mart success often came at the expense of established local merchants and units of regional discount store chains. Hardware stores, family department stores, building supply outlets, and stores featuring fabrics, sporting goods, and shoes were among the first to either close or relocate elsewhere. Such regional discount retailers in the Sunbelt states as Roses, Howard's, T.G. & Y, and Duckwall-ALCO, all of which once enjoyed solid sales and earnings, were forced to reposition themselves by renovating stores, opening bigger and more modern units, remerchandising assortments, and offering lower prices. In many cases, such stores as Coast-to-Coast, Pamida, and Ben Franklin closed upon a Wal-Mart announcement to build in a specific community. "Just the word that Wal-Mart was coming made some stores close up," indicated a local newspaper editor.

Corporate Strategies

The corporate and marketing strategies that emerged at Wal-Mart to challenge a turbulent and volatile external environment were based upon a set of two main objectives that had guided the firm through its growth years. In the first objective, the customer was featured, "customers would be provided what they want, when they want it, all at a value." In the second objective, the team spirit was emphasized, "treating each other as we would hope to be treated, acknowledging our total dependency on our associate-partners to sustain our success." The approach included: aggressive plans for new store openings; expansion to additional states;

upgrading, relocation, refurbishing and remodeling of existing stores; and opening new distribution centers. The plan was to not have a single operating unit that had not been updated in the past seven years. The 1990s were considered a new era for Wal-Mart; an era in which "we plan to grow to a truly nationwide retailer, and should we continue to perform, our sales and earnings will also grow beyond where most could have envisioned at the dawn of the 80s."

Several new retail formats were introduced by Wal-Mart in the 1980s. The first Sam's Wholesale Club opened in Oklahoma City, Oklahoma in 1983 and was an idea that had been developed by other firms earlier, but which found its greatest success and growth in acceptability at Wal-Mart. It featured a vast array of product categories with limited selection of brand and model, cash-and-carry business with limited hours, large (100,000 square foot), bare-bone facilities, rock-bottom wholesale prices, and minimal promotion. The limited membership plan permitted wholesale members who bought membership and others who usually paid a percentage above the ticket price of the merchandise. At the beginning of 1991, there were 470 Sam's Wholesale Clubs in operation.

The first Wal-Mart Supercenters, a 222,000-square-foot superstore that combined a discount store with a large grocery store, a food court of restaurants, and other such service businesses as banks or video tape rental stores opened in 1988 as Hypermarket*USA in the Dallas suburb of Garland. A smaller, scaled down version of Hypermarket*USA was called the Wal-Mart Supercenter, similar in merchandise offerings, but with about half the square footage of hypermarts. These expanded store concepts also included convenience stores, and gasoline distribution outlets to "enhance shopping convenience." The company proceeded slowly with these plans and later suspended its plans for building any more hypermarkets in favor of the smaller supercenter concept.

Several programs were launched to "highlight" popular social causes. These included the "Buy American" program, green retailing concept, brand name emphasis, and a sophisticated inventory control system.

The "Buy American" program was a Wal-Mart retail program initiated in 1985. The theme was "Bring It Home To The U.S.A." and its purpose was to communicate Wal-Mart's support for American manufacturing. In the program, the firm directed substantial influence to encourage manufacturers to produce goods in the U.S. rather than import them from other countries. Vendors were attracted into the program by encouraging manufacturers to initiate the process by contacting the company directly with proposals to sell goods that were made in the U.S. Buyers also targeted specific import items in their assortments on a state-by-state basis to encourage domestic manufacturing. According to Haim Dabah, president of Gitano Group, Inc., a maker of fashion discount clothing that at one time imported 95 percent of its clothing and now makes about 20 percent of its products here: "Wal-Mart let it be known loud and clear that if you're going to grow with them, you sure better have some products made in the U.S.A." Farris Fashion, Inc. (flannel shirts); Roadmaster Corporation (exercise bicycles); Flanders Industries, Inc. (lawn chairs); and Magic Chef (microwave ovens) were examples of vendors that chose to participate in the program.

From the Wal-Mart standpoint, the "Buy American" program centered around value—producing and selling quality merchandise at a competitive price. The promotion included television advertisements featuring factory workers, a soaring American eagle, and the slogan: "We buy American whenever we can, so you can too." Prominent instore signage, and store circulars were also included. One store poster read: "Success Stories—These items formerly imported, are now being purchased by Wal-Mart in the U.S.A."

Wal-Mart was one of the first retailers to embrace the concept of "green" retailing. Shoppers were offered the option of purchasing products that were better for the environment in three respects: manufacturing, use, and disposal. It was introduced through full-page advertisements in the *Wall Street Journal* and *USAToday*. Instore signage identified those products that were environmentally safe. As Wal-Mart executives saw it, "customers are concerned about the quality of land, air, and water, and would like the opportunity to do something positive." To initiate the program, 7,000 vendors were notified that Wal-Mart had a corporate concern for the environment and to ask for their support in a variety of ways. Green and white store signs, printed on recycled paper, marked products or packaging that had been developed or redesigned to be more environmentally sound.

Wal-Mart had become the channel commander in the distribution of many brand-name items. As the nation's largest retailer and in many geographic areas the dominant distributor, it exerts considerable influence in negotiation for the best price, delivery terms, promotion allowances, and continuity of supply. Many of these benefits could be passed on to consumers in the form of quality name brand items available at lower than competitive prices. As a matter of corporate policy, management often insisted on doing business only with a producer's top sales executives rather than going through their representative. Wal-Mart had been accused of threatening to buy from other producers if firms refused to sell directly to it. In the ensuing power struggle, Wal-Mart executives refused to talk about the controversial policy or admit that it existed. As a representative of an industry association representing a group of sales agency's representatives suggested, "In the Southwest, Wal-Mart's the only show in town." An industry analyst added, "They're extremely aggressive. Their approach has always been to give the customer the benefit of a corporate saving. That builds up customer loyalty and market share."

Another key factor in the mix was an inventory control system that was recognized as the most sophisticated in retailing. A high-speed computer system, linked virtually all the stores to headquarters and the company's distribution centers. It electronically logged every item sold at the checkout counter, automatically kept the warehouses informed of merchandise to be ordered and directed the flow of goods to the stores and even to the proper shelves. Most important for management, it helped detect sales trends quickly and sped up market reaction time substantially.

Decision-Making in a Market Oriented Firm

One principle that distinguished Wal-Mart was the unusual depth of employee involvement in company affairs. Corporate strategies put emphasis on human resource management. Employees of Wal-Mart became "associates," a name borrowed from Sam Walton's early association with JCPenney. Input was encouraged at meetings at the store and corporate level. The firm hired employees locally, provided training programs, and through a "Letter to the President" program, management encouraged employees to ask questions, and made words like "we," "us," and "our" a part of the corporate language. A number of special award programs recognized individual, department, and division achievement. Stock ownership and profit-sharing programs were introduced as part of a "partnership concept."

The corporate culture was recognized by the editors of the trade publication, *Mass Market Retailers,* when it recognized all 275,000 associates collectively as the 1989 "Mass Market Retailers of the Year." "The Wal-Mart associate," the editors noted, "in this decade that term has come to symbolize all that is right with the American worker, particularly in the retailing environment and most particularly at Wal-Mart..." The "store-within-a-store" concept, as a Wal-Mart corporate policy, trained individuals to be merchants by being responsible for the performance of their own departments as if they were running their own businesses. Seminars and training programs afforded them opportunities to grow within the company. "People development, not just a good 'program' for any growing company but a must to secure our future," is how Suzanne Allford, Vice President of the Wal-Mart People Division explained the firm's decentralized approach to retail management development.

"The Wal-Mart Way," was a phrase that was used by management to summarize the firm's unconventional approach to business and the development of the corporate culture. As noted in an annual report referring to a recent development program: "We stepped outside our retailing world to examine the best managed companies in the United States in an effort to determine the fundamentals of their success and to 'benchmark' our own performances." The term "Total Quality Management" (TQM) was used to identify this "vehicle for proliferating the very best things we do while incorporating the new ideas our people have that will assure our future."

The Growth Challenge

David Glass, 53 years old, assumed the role of president and chief executive officer of Wal-Mart, the position previously held by Sam Walton. Known for his hard-driving managerial style, Glass gained his experience in retailing at a small supermarket chain in Springfield, Missouri. He joined Wal-Mart as executive vice president for finance in 1976.

Wal-Mart Stores, Inc. had for over twenty-five years experienced tremendous growth and as one analyst suggested, "been consistently on the cutting edge of low-markup mass merchandising." Much of the forward momentum had come from the entrepreneurial spirit of Samuel Moore Walton. The company announced on Monday, April 6, 1992, following Walton's death, that his son, S. Robson Walton, Vice Chairman of Wal-Mart, would succeed his father as chairman of the board. David Glass would remain president and CEO.

And what of Wal-Mart without Mr. Sam? "There's no transition to make," said Glass, "because the principles and the basic values he used in founding this company were so sound and so universally accepted." "As for the future," he suggested, "there's more opportunity ahead of us than behind us. We're good students of retailing and we've studied the mistakes that others have made. We'll make our own mistakes, but we won't repeat theirs. The only thing constant at Wal-Mart is change. We'll be fine as long as we never lose our responsiveness to the customer."

The post-Sam Walton era in the company's history brought a number of new challenges. In early 1993, Wal-Mart management confirmed that sales growth for stores open more than a year would likely slip into the 7 percent-to-8 percent range in 1993. Analysts were also concerned about the increased competition in the warehouse club business and the company's move from its roots in Southern and Midwestern small towns to the more competitive and costly markets of the Northeast. Wal-Mart Supercenters faced more resilient rivals in the grocery field. Unions representing supermarket workers delayed and in some cases killed expansion opportunities. Some analysts said that the company is simply suffering from the high expectations its stellar performance over the years has created. In early 1996, management acknowledged that 1995 had not been a "Wal-Mart Year." After 99 consecutive quarters of earnings growth, Wal-Mart management said profit for the fiscal fourth quarter ending January 31, would decline as much as 11 percent from the year before.

Major Question[1]

Identify and evaluate the marketing strategies that Wal-Mart pursued to maintain its growth and marketing leadership position. What factors should a firm consider in the development of its marketing strategy?

Study Questions

1. Discuss the importance of changes in the external environment to an organization like Wal-Mart.

2. What conclusions can be drawn from a review of Wal-Mart's financial performance since the 1980s. From this review, what can you conclude about the financial future of the firm?

3. Speculate on how much impact the "absence" of Samuel Moore Walton will have on the forward momentum of the organization. What steps should be taken to continue Mr. Sam's formula for success?

4. What evidence is there to suggest that the marketing concept was understood and applied at Wal-Mart?

---

[1]Please note: Do not use alternative anaylsis format for this case.

References

Barrier, M. (1988, April). Walton's mountain. *Nation's Business*, pp. 18–20.

Glass is CEO at Wal-Mart. (1988, March). *Discount Merchandiser*, pp. 6+.

Helliker, K., & Ortega, B. (1996, January 18). Falling profit marks end of era at Wal-Mart. *The Wall Street Journal*, p. B1.

Huey, J. (1991, September 23). America's most successful merchant. *Fortune*, pp. 46–48+.

Trimble, V.H. (1990). *Sam Walton: The inside story of America's richest man.* New York: Dutton.

Annual Report. (1996). Bentonville, AR: Wal-Mart Stores, Inc.

Case 81
Growing Pains for Baubles, Bangles & Beads

Evelyn Brannon, Auburn University

Jane Jeffries began making one-of-a-kind jewelry and selling it at arts and crafts shows to earn money for college. As her confidence and skills grew, she became more sophisticated in her design and manufacturing approach. In the early 1980s, she landed her first account with a department store and began doing trunk shows at other stores in the chain. Soon after, she met a sales representative at a regional apparel mart who became her mentor and helped her become established in the world of wholesale selling and the accessories business.

Jane named her company Baubles, Bangles & Beads because her jewelry blends beads, charms, and other novelties. The logo she developed—an Egyptian-style cat wearing necklaces and earrings—helps buyers and customers recognize and recall her whimsical line based on magic, myth, and mystic themes. She became known for assembling a lavish number of beads and charms on each item and for off-balance necklaces and mismatched earrings. Over the years, novelty looks in jewelry gained in popularity and Jane's company was in the vanguard of the movement. The line featured design options from extravagant, theatrical looks to more wearable, scaled-down versions. Because so many companies knocked off her designs, she started a line of less elaborate, lower-priced jewelry targeted at volume retailers.

Jane's company grew quickly. With sales representatives nationwide, Baubles, Bangles & Beads reached customers through 3000 stores, about 75 percent of them specialty stores. Annual sales now top $3 million and the company is growing at about 30 percent per year. Jane's company owns an 11,000-square-foot building in her hometown where she manufacturers all her designs. She oversees an operation that employs over 70 people.

As the company grew, Jane hired people to manage various aspects of the business. One woman, Pia Savitch, is in charge of ordering all the beads, charms, and novelties and also maintaining an inventory of the items needed to manufacture the line. Another employee, Frank Merrill, oversees all packing and shipping of the completed items. An accountant, Maury Zamarin, handles tax matters from reports generated by inhouse bookkeeping. Supervisors manage the day-to-day manufacturing. Jane, however, interviews all people hired by the company. Recently she hired a marketing director, Hillary Wingate, to assist her in advertising in fashion and trade magazines and in showing the line at markets and to buyers.

Jane is the sole designer and is responsible for a wholesale line of approximately 350 styles of earrings, 100 pins, and 50 necklaces, priced from $8 to $50. She does five markets a year. The design task includes a constant search at gift shows and stores for inspiration. Because she manages manufacturing, marketing, and financial aspects of the business, Jane must retreat to a secluded site to work on designs. She needs to be undisturbed to maintain the creative side of the business. Future plans call for Jane to expand into other such accessory lines as handbags and belts. She will contract

out the manufacturing but will finish these items with the style of embellishment that has become her trademark.

Jane is a confident, high-energy person. Her drive, ambition, and need for control can be annoying to the people around her. People who leave the company say that she is hard to work for. There is frequent turnover in all job categories.

At age 30, Jane has achieved a success she once only dreamed about. But, there is a downside to success. Basing the business in her hometown has brought Jane the gratitude of some townspeople and the envy of others. As a successful entrepreneur, Jane has become a kind of local celebrity and popular speaker at civic events. Her success has produced tension between Jane and some old friends and family members. Jane would like to move to a metropolitan area where she could have access to the social and cultural opportunities lacking in her hometown. However, the financial advantages of owning her own building and ready access to skilled, affordable labor keep her tied to her present situation.

Jane has close friends in her hometown. She is close to her parents and they work in the business. Business contacts have turned into friendships and these friendships are important to Jane and her company. Jane would like to marry and have a family someday but, for now, all her time and energy is devoted to growing her business.

Jane has always been creative, but lately she is feeling a little burned out. She often says that the designing is easy compared to running the business. The pressure to continue to grow the business is intense and Jane feels responsible for the jobs the business provides.

A recent incident has caused Jane to reconsider the way she does business. A key associate—Pia Savitch, the employee in charge of ordering all the beads, charms and novelties for Baubles, Bangles & Beads—left the company to work for a competitor. The sourcing of components was a skill Pia (along with Jane) had developed over the years. Essential contact information was lost when Pia took her phone records and therefore the company's sourcing contacts. Jane had not thought to create a company list too, and it is not unusual for employees to take their contact records with them when they leave employment. Jane, however, was able to recover most of the information and recreate her contact list by dropping all other activities for two weeks to comb through packing slips and invoices and by phoning suppliers.

Jane started the business based on her talent as a designer. She has worked hard to learn the business side of being a wholesale jewelry manufacturer. Rapid growth has made the business increasingly complex. Jane's business now seems to have outgrown her ability to manage it.

Major Question

What changes should Jane make in company management to ensure continued business growth while clearing more time for the creative side of the business she most enjoys?

Study Questions

1. How can Jane ensure in the future that key employees and the information they control are not lost to the business?

2. Do you believe that only so much growth and expansion should occur for some businesses? Why or why not?

3. Are there specific controls that can be implemented to help an owner more easily manage a business like Baubles, Bangles & Beads?

Case 82
Amber's Wave

Nancy A. Oliver, Northern Arizona University

Amber Marcel has a $1.5 million apparel manufacturing business and a problem. Amber started making her own accessories in high school when she couldn't find the "right" belt to wear with a dress for the Junior Prom. She went to a fabric store, bought fabric, trim, and binding and made a belt that was the highlight of her outfit. With the success of her first belt, Amber started making more accessories. By the time she was in college she had expanded to designing and making her belts, earrings, and vests.

Amber's career goal was to own a specialty store. To help her reach this goal she majored in merchandising with a minor in business. She planned to graduate, work for a large department store for five to seven years and then open her own business. Financial backing for a speciality store was a concern but she was determined and decided she could make it work.

Amber was a good student and during her Junior year received a scholarship from the Women's Business League. The organization enjoyed meeting the young women to whom they awarded scholarships and invited each recipient to a luncheon in September.

Because of the uniqueness of her accessories, Amber continuously received compliments and inquires about items she was wearing. It was no different at the Women's Business luncheon. After Amber explained to two women that she had made the items herself, the women asked if she made accessories for other people. Amber had not considered going beyond her own personal production and hesitated with her answer. Before she could give a response one woman suggested she would pay Amber $35 to make a belt like the one she was wearing. Amber quickly made a mental calculation of the cost of materials and time and realized she could make a 50 percent profit. She readily agreed.

So began the visual advertising of her belt. Other women quickly began to ask about the belts and the possibility of other accessories. Between classes, nights, and weekends Amber started a cottage accessory business. At times the demand became so great she hired several friends to form assembly line production of belts and earrings.

During her Senior year Amber officially established a small business. She had a phone number, business card, bank account, and a name: Amber's Wave. Her last name was French for wave so it seemed appropriate. As the popularity of the accessories continued, she decided to market the product to a larger area. With samples of belts, earrings, and vests, Amber visited five towns within a 200-mile radius of her location. She had researched the best specialty shop in each town and, acting as her own sales representative, presented the items to the owners. Many of the owners selected several designs and some requested designs exclusively for their stores. Again the appeal of her accessories resulted in a growth surge in the business.

Within two years of her college graduation, Amber's Wave had five employees dealing with the management and the corporate end of the business. She also employed two sales representatives who promoted Amber's Wave merchandise and had a subcontract with a manufacturing plant in Mexico to produce the accessories based on her samples and specifications.

Throughout the growth of the company, Amber used her knowledge of merchandising, research, and lifestyles to determine the changes in the style and design of her products. This technique proved successful.

Seven years after Amber's college graduation she expanded into the mail-order business. In addition to the accessory line, Amber's Wave also had expanded into several lines of apparel. The catalog contained styles that were not as fashion forward as in the retail stores but contained classic designs of merchandise. Currently, the catalog is in the third year of production and, as of last year, was doing well.

Amber's Wave uses technology for as much of the decision-making process as possible. Because the actual production of the garments is not done inhouse, being efficient is paramount. An automated computer system was installed at corporate headquarters to itemize all the materials used in the garment. Using the historical data for sales projections for the coming year and the specifications of raw materials for each item in the line, the computer system generates the amounts of fabric, notions, thread, and so forth, needed to produce garments for the coming season. This information is then forwarded to the subcontractor with all specifications for garment production.

The merchandise is displayed at two major apparel marts on a biannual basis. The sales representatives keep the corporate office aware of what retailers are saying about the products. They also give input about projections of items that might do well in the catalog.

Amber has created a $1.5 million dollar business within ten years. She is in all geographic regions of the country, as well as 200 specialty stores, she has a major account with at least one large department store in the fifty largest cities, and she has a mail-order catalog and a reputation for innovative, quality products.

However, Amber has a problem. She has just met with Kelly Whitehurst, her leading sales representative for speciality stores in the Southwest. Kelly informed Amber that there is a major problem and that her accounts are not buying the new merchandise. This is a serious concern as the Southwest has always been the leader in sales and acceptance of her new product lines and they have been an indication of what she can expect for total line sales each season. Could this be a predictor of a trend with other areas of the country? Kelly indicated that the owners don't seem to be excited by the merchandise and feel it is similar to previous designs. This seems to be true with the accessories, as well as the vests and other clothing items.

After meeting with Kelly, Amber decided to check for rumblings elsewhere in the company. She first looked at a computer printout of sales during the last month, six months, and year. There was definitely a downward trend in sales. Amber looked at the mail-order division. Again, sales were showing a decline from last year's figures.

She next contacted Jennifer Logan. Jennifer is in charge of department store accounts in the Southwest and Northwest. Amber explained Kelly's concerns about the lack of specialty store acceptance of the new lines. She then asked for input about the department store response to her new merchandise. Jennifer mentioned that although responses were positive at the last apparel show, she did not receive as many orders as she thought she would. And she has not received a single reorder. According to Jennifer, sales are often slow with new merchandise, especially accessories. Also, Jennifer mentioned that consumers seemingly have to be excited about the clothing items and trends before they get interested in accessories, and the clothing items this season were not sparking as much interest as they had in the past, so this may be why the accessories are not selling well either. Amber contemplated the situation. It was possible that sales of her lines were off because the merchandise designs were stale and out-of-date. If this is true, would she have to rethink her company? Amber pondered her problem all night long, jotting down ideas, only to throw them away.

Major Question

As an entrepreneur who owns her own successful business, what direction should Amber take to rethink and refresh her accessories and clothing lines?

Study Questions

1. How should Amber go about deciding on changes to be made, if any?

2. Has the company grown too fast?

3. If indeed the new styles are not different from previous seasons, is this necessarily a problem? Could the Amber's Wave look become a basic in a retailer's merchandise mix? Does Amber's Wave merchandise need to be different each season?

Case 83
The Home Shopping Heartache

Laura Bliss, Stephens College

Jill Whitmore is a designer/manufacturer of women's moderately priced hats. Her business is called Top Cappy and reflects the whimsical, humorous nature of her designs. Jill's factory, one of a handful of hat manufacturers in the U.S., is located in a very small town outside Kansas City, Missouri. Jill has been in the hat business for more than a few years and has had steady business in the past—mainly from nationally known specialty department stores and a variety of smaller boutiques. Though the company is rather small, it is quite versatile and produces straw, fabric, and felt hat bodies in various styles. In the past, Jill has had close relationships with major department store buyers and has been successful developing private-label programs to meet their needs. Jill has also been successful producing small specialty orders for unique mom and pop boutiques throughout the Midwest and the West Coast.

Though business has been good, during the last year it has been difficult for Top Cappy to make ends meet. Jill's once steady department store accounts have, in many cases, cut back on their orders or dropped them altogether. The overall effect is that Jill's factory can no longer rely on her old accounts to stay in business.

During the past year when business had been slow, Jill researched new markets for her product. She attended several industry seminars and trade shows and came to the overwhelming conclusion that she needed to pursue global exporting, as well as television and Internet sales. Being unfamiliar with these markets, Jill was somewhat at a loss on where exactly to begin. Then, miraculously, Jill heard that one of the major home shopping networks, "Home Buying Club" (HBC) was searching for new products from small manufacturers from every state. Jill was excited; this seemed to be an opportunity tailor-made for Top Cappy.

Jill contacted the network and within a week had received a large packet of information explaining exactly what she needed to do to enter her hats as samples for consideration by HBC buyers. Being a frequent viewer of HBC, Jill had a good idea of what types of hats would best suit the HBC customer. She eagerly began designing the samples for her upcoming HBC entry.

Months passed, and soon the big day arrived when the HBC buyers came to the Mackinaw Convention Center in Kansas City to evaluate the local Missouri product samples. Jill's booth was set up and ready to go. She felt good about her entry and, in viewing the competition, felt very confident that her hats were among the very best items on display. The day was long, but good. She enjoyed talking with the other manufacturers and felt that the buyers had been suitably impressed with her product. At the end of the day, 15 winners were announced. To Jill's disappointment, her hats had not been chosen. Jill was crushed. Though the sting of the rejection on a personal level was bad, the rejection on a financial level was even worse. Jill needed this account, or a similar one, to keep her factory in business.

Major Question

If you were Jill Whitmore, how would you proceed? Is there a way she could still sell to HBC, or is this pursuit futile?

Study Questions

1. Is there anything else you would recommend that Jill do to improve her business?

2. Do you think Jill should pursue Internet sales? Why or why not?

3. How would you recommend pursuing a global market for the sale of women's hats?

Case 84, part 1
Amy's Fashions on First: A New but Tenuous Beginning

LuAnn Ricketts Gaskill, Iowa State University

Maple Bluffs is a quaint farming community of about 7,000 residents located in northeastern Iowa. It sits in a gently sloping valley surrounded by acres of corn and beans. Like many rural Iowa communities, the town offers local residents a variety of small businesses, including several clothing stores, as an alternative to a major shopping area some 75 miles away.

Amy Jensen, a long-time resident of Maple Bluffs, grew up in a close-knit, well-respected, successful farming family. Her college years were spent out of state at a major Midwestern university pursuing a four-year degree in fashion merchandising along with an interior design minor. She was able to help with her educational expenses by working part-time in sales at a major department store located near the university. In her Senior year she interned with a chain store in Omaha, Nebraska. The experience was invaluable to her; but, after her summer in Omaha, Amy realized she wasn't cut out for city life and returned to Maple Bluffs after graduation.

Joselyn's, located on First Street in downtown Maple Bluffs, was a small retail business that offered a broad assortment of moderately priced, larger-sized women's clothing. The seven-year-old business was owned and operated by Martha Stout and Eileen Alloway, two ladies nearing their 70s. Their health failing, they offered to sell Amy their 2,000-square-foot store including its existing fixtures, current inventory, and outstanding orders, which would complete her merchandise needs for the coming Spring/Summer season. Amy and her parents reviewed the current financial records for

Joselyn's and noted that the initial financial investment would be fairly modest. With financial backing from her parents, Amy purchased the business. After all, the timing was right: she had just finished her college education and wanted to begin a career in or near her hometown of Maple Bluffs.

Martha and Eileen stayed on for two months to orient Amy to the store. Amy's mother voluntarily assisted Amy full-time at the store where she was kept busy doing the accounting for the store, which was no doubt a challenge because she had no formal training in accounting. Although Amy had hired three part-time salespeople, she spent much of her day on the selling floor.

By the following Spring, it was apparent that sales were not at the level Amy had hoped for, and she determined that a new merchandising strategy was necessary. Before attending the Spring market, she decided to refocus Joselyn's from primarily larger-sized merchandise to moderately priced misses sportswear. By doing such, she would be targeting a middle-aged market, and would also offer a line of misses petites, for the smaller proportional woman.

Amy operated Joselyn's with two selling seasons, Fall/Winter and Spring/Summer, which required her to attend only two markets annually. The Spring market was Amy's first real experience at the regional apparel mart, although she had visited market week as part of a class project during her senior year in college. Having no knowledge as to how much merchandise to order for the upcoming Fall/Winter season, she conferred with several small local apparel retailers and learned from them that they had placed orders in the range of $30,000 to $35,000 (cost) during their last market trips.

Spring market was an exciting experience for Amy, but the realities of small business ownership soon set in. Because Amy still owned and operated the business under the original business name, Joselyn's, she was not able to establish a line of credit with any of the market vendors. Over the years, Martha and Eileen had been negligent in paying their invoices; vendors wanted all purchases sent to Joselyn's shipped C.O.D.

Immediately after the Spring market experience, Amy had the store name legally changed to Amy's Fashions on First. She also sent out credit applications to her vendors and had the First Iowa Bank in Maple Bluffs run a credit history on her and her family. She had no further problems placing orders on credit. She followed the other local retailers' example and placed Spring orders in the range of $30,000 to $35,000. She would continue this practice of placing orders in the $30,000 to $35,000 range at both Spring and Fall markets during the next two years.

During the summer months, Amy worked constantly on the selling floor and made mental notes of what was and was not selling. She maintained a suggestion box for her customers to let her know what they particularly wanted. During these months of continued slow sales, she recognized a growing trend of older customer clientele, although she offered only a narrow merchandise selection that appealed to them. By Fall, Amy determined that the store needed to start targeting an even older clientele than she had been targeting earlier. The new target market was identified as an older customer (60+) who valued active, comfortable, easy-care clothing. Orders placed during the Fall market were placed with this change in mind. Amy even had the store remodeled to reflect the new, more mature woman's focus.

Fall/Winter shipments arrived offering new, moderately priced sportswear for the mature, older customer in misses and petite sizes. Although Amy's Fashions on First was still heavily inventoried with Spring/Summer goods, the new items added some excitement. Mixed in the store's current inventory were the remaining large-sized apparel including lingerie, bras, girdles, and so forth, which were carried over from the previous owners. Clearing out the old seasonal goods took on top priority, so that space could be made for the newly arriving orders. Based on the space available on the main floor, there was no alternative but to clear out the store's basement and establish a bargain area for all but the current Fall/Winter inventory. Basement merchandise was marked 30 percent to 75 percent below original retail.

Response was sluggish initially; but, after local radio advertisements promoting the basement and associated sale prices, traffic increased. The idea was effective in helping to move some of the old inventory out, but margins were negligible if at all, and very little exposure was given to the main selling area where the current, regular-priced inventory was located. It appeared that most everyone entering the store went directly to the basement.

By the next Spring, customer interest in what remained in the basement had declined significantly. Customers, however, frequently asked Amy when the next big sale would be taking place. Amy heard from a few customers that the previous owners ran monthly clearance sales at 50 percent off current prices. Responding to their requests, Amy began an aggressive pricing campaign in the local media that lasted most of the year.

During this year, the bargain basement was still in operation although much less successful. Spring/Summer merchandise arrived, followed later by Fall/Winter orders, both accompanied by heavy markdown advertising. Although no formal merchandise planning or control was in place and record-keeping was minimal, Amy knew that the business was losing money—and lots of it!

Major Question

What recommendations would you make to Amy to improve her business to achieve profit?

Study Questions

1. What is the best way to determine the amount of merchandise to buy at market for a small store?

2. What guidelines could Amy have used for promotional campaigns?

3. How should Amy determine her target market?

4. What are reasons for the store's loss of profit?

Case 84, part 2
Amy's Fashions on First: Moving Forward and Planning for the Future

LuAnn Ricketts Gaskill, Iowa State University

No one knows what time the fire started, but it probably was around 11:00 pm. The local fire chief determined that it started as the result of a faulty furnace. Smoke, water, and fire damage to Amy's Fashions on First resulted in complete loss of inventory. Amy's insurance company, Statewide Mutual, settled by reimbursing the cost value of all merchandise existing in the store. Amy was able to salvage most of the fixtures. Fixing up the interior of the store would require some work, but most of the interior was surprisingly intact and her design background would come in handy.

It was not an easy decision for Amy and her family to make; but, after considerable debate and with the encouragement of her parents, Amy decided to reopen the business on March 15, but help was sought. With advice from Small Business support groups, Amy made the following changes to her business.

She continued with the age 60+ market but began a simple, effective record-keeping system so she now knows when merchandise (by specific style number) arrives, how long it is on the selling floor before it moves, what the final selling price is, and so forth. With this information she has a much clearer picture of what is selling and is able to develop assortment plans that reflect sales trends. Purchases are based on sales plans, existing inventory, and open-to-buy. Now Amy says she wouldn't think of going to market without her merchandise plan. Amy talks of some day purchasing a computer to help her track sales and inventory. But for now, she is comfortable with her manual tracking system, calling it her "bible."

With her commitment to record-keeping and inventory documentation, she now spends much more of her time off the selling floor. She also relies much more on her mother and the part-time salespeople to work with the customers.

Although customer service was always important, Amy has become increasingly committed to letting the community know how much she values their patronage. Thank-you letters are sent to customers after each purchase. She makes a more conscientious effort to involve herself in community events and to make herself visible in town, if for no other reason than to remind people that she's a business owner in Maple Bluffs.

Advertising has continued using the same media (radio and newspaper) as before the fire, but the focus of the ads has changed. She is now promoting the image of the store and merchandise quality rather than low prices.

Amy has hired an accountant who supplies her with monthly profit and loss statements. The accountant will soon teach her how to develop profit and loss statements, so she can generate her own for the store. Amy and her mother are paying themselves full-time salaries. The loan from her parents has also been paid off.

While the fire and insurance settlement offered Amy a chance to begin again, the year has not been without problems. The store is currently running about $2,000 a month less than the previous year. Business, overall, in Maple Bluffs is slow. Only time will tell if Amy's business or others in Maple Bluffs will pull out of the downward trend.

When asked what her biggest mistakes were before the fire, Amy took a deep breath and replied, "Not paying close enough attention to what was selling and not better researching the store. We didn't look at any information other than the current books at Joselyn's. We have since learned that the owners had been losing money for years and were continuously infusing money in the store. They paid themselves no salaries."

No one knows what the future holds for Amy's business. Perhaps in a few years the store will be profitable and operating in the black, or perhaps another type of business will have taken its place.

Amy's opinion is that, "If it doesn't turn around, we may not be here next year; but I'd like to stay in business."

Now, Amy must determine whether or not fate, or she herself, will decide whether Amy's Fashions on First will remain in business for the long run. She knows very well that some improvements must be made, but she is not certain what specific undertakings should be initiated. Because she had success previously with the consultants from the Small Business Administration, she decides to seek advice from them once again.

Major Question

What advice do you think the Small Business Administration should give Amy in regard to recommendations to help ensure her continued success?

Study Questions

1. How typical is this actual business's experience to other small business owners?

2. In light of the existing revised business strategies, what are her chances of small business success?

Chapter Discussion Questions

1. Describe the characteristics of successful small business owners.

2. What extra qualities does a small business owner need to be thought of as an entrepreneur?

3. What are the challenges and opportunities for starting your own small business?

4. Explain how planning is a vital part of the process of starting a business. Cite case examples to support your position.

Ethical and Legal Behavior in Retail Management

Chapter Objectives

- Explain ethics and social responsibility of retailers and manufacturers.

- Discuss the ethics involved with sourcing and selling.

- Identify and examine legal considerations within which retailers and manufacturers operate.

Awareness of ethical and socially responsible business behavior has increased today as consumer advocacy has become more prevalent and also because there are more methods available to do business. With increased affluence to meet our basic needs, we expect more socially responsible behavior from business and industry. For example, we can now afford to have a clean environment, and society is demanding that businesses contribute toward that goal. Laws explicitly outline appropriate business conduct to protect the consumer and maintain fairness, while ethical and socially responsible behavior go beyond the law to include the further expectations of society. Globalization has introduced increasingly complex issues regarding cross-cultural values, such as intellectual property and use of labor. Also, the highly sophisticated and competitive nature of retail today raises new potential ethical issues. Therefore, strong personal and business codes of ethics applicable to many situations may be more important today than ever before.

What are Ethics?

Ethics are rules or standards based on moral duties and obligations by which society evaluates conduct. They furnish criteria for distinguishing between right and wrong. Some people use the terms ethics and morals interchangeably; however, morals most often are referred to as personal beliefs that are more closely tied to religious tenets, whereas ethics deal with living up to society's principles. In either sense, ethics are forms of "dos and don'ts." Guy (1990) explains how ten core values are central to ethical choices and interpersonal behavior (see Table 12.1).

Table 12.1 Ten Core Values

Caring
Honesty
Accountability
Promise Keeping
Pursuit of Excellence
Loyalty
Fairness
Integrity
Respect for Others
Responsible Citizenship

Source: Guy (1990)

Most of us have both personal and business ethics, which are the basis for business decisions. An individual may have different standards for personal ethics and business ethics, which can cause conflicts for that person. Others may share personal and business ethics. **Business ethics** deal with what is right or wrong for the company, while **personal ethics** deal with an individual's own personal beliefs and principles. In some instances, corporate standards may be higher than an individual's own. In other instances, company goals of growth and profit may conflict with personal ethical standards. For example, in *Case 87, To Go or to Stay: Ethics in the Workplace,* a young buyer wrestles with her personal ethics as she considers corporate requests to cancel merchandise orders, which she knows have already been produced for her company, and which will result in financial hardship and possible bankruptcy for the vendor.

A business may have a written **code of ethics** that states what that company has decided is ethical and unethical behavior. Similarly, associations have a written code of **professional ethics.** For example, The American Marketing Association has set forth a clear and extensive statement of their professional code of ethics that deals with responsibilities of the marketer, honesty and fairness, and the rights and duties of those in the exchange process, which include promotion, distribution, pricing and market

research, and organizational relationships. An example of an explicit code of **corporate ethics** is the public notice run in apparel trade papers during the holidays by such retailers as TJX Companies to their suppliers. Their public notice was in regard to their policy of prohibiting employees to accept any gifts—without exception. Written codes of corporate ethics should refer to practices specific to the company, for example, accepting gifts, kickbacks, or false record keeping, and should be supported by top management. Sometimes a company's statement of philosophy incorporates their code of ethics. James Cash Penney, the founder of JCPenney, was a religious man and used the "Golden Rule" in his philosophy statement for his company, merging personal and corporate ethics. See Table 12.2 for the "Penney Idea."

Other companies have an implicit code of ethics, which is an unwritten but understood set of standards of moral and ethical responsibility. Whether implicit or explicit, corporate ethics are important guidelines in decision-making, especially for those issues that are not clearly defined by law.

Table 12.2 The "Penney Idea"—JCPenney's Philosophy Incorporating an Ethical Stand

1. To serve the public, as nearly as we can, to its complete satisfaction.
2. To expect for the service we render a fair remuneration and not all the profit the traffic will bear.
3. To do all in our power to pack the customer's dollar full of value, quality and satisfaction.
4. To continue to train ourselves and our associates so that the service we give will be more and more intelligently performed.
5. To improve constantly the human factor in our business.
6. To reward men and women in our organization through participation in what the business produces.
7. To test our every policy, method and act in this wise: "Does it square with what is right and just?"

THE TJX COMPANIES, INC.
Framingham, Massachusetts 01701

To Our Manufacturers And Suppliers: Statement of Policy Concerning Gifts

We are taking this opportunity to restate our policy concerning gift-giving, not only during the forthcoming holiday season, but at all times of the year, on any occasion. Gifts, no matter how well intentioned by the donor, tend to shake the moral structure of the firmest business foundations by substituting subjective emotions and motives for objective judgement based on service, quality and price.

Accordingly, for the mutual protection of our suppliers, our employees and the Company, we prohibit our employees from accepting gifts, gratuities, payments or favors of any kind. Any gifts received by our employees will be returned to the donor or donated to charitable organizations. Our employees are advised that violation of this policy is considered to be a grievous matter.

We call upon you to assist us and our employees by refraining from giving or offering such gifts. Your awareness of and cooperation with this policy will foster the continuation of fair business practices that favor our close association.

Best wishes for a happy holiday season and a prosperous New Year.

Sumner Feldberg
Chairman of the Board

Bernard Cammarata
President and Chief Executive Officer

Newton Buying Corp./T.J. Maxx
Hit or Miss, Inc.
Chadwick's of Boston, Ltd.
Winners Apparel, Ltd.
HG Buying, Inc./HomeGoods, Inc.

Figure 12.1 An example from TJX Companies of an explicit code of corporate ethics regarding a no-gift policy. TJX prohibits any gift-giving from suppliers to employees, while other companies do permit such gifts as lunches or dinners.

Anderson (1995) outlines a three-part framework for understanding ethical decision-making:

1. ***Prima facie* duties** (or moral obligations), which some feel are universal, include such things as keeping promises, telling the truth (see *Case 89, The Perilous Promotion*), honoring warranties and abiding by agreements or understood guidelines (see *Case 21* in Chapter Three), not taking abnormal credit extensions or making unjust retail cancellations (see *Case 87*), and ensuring product safety (see *Case 94, The Bean Bag Case*). Pricing policies fall under this concept, for example, the setting of unfair prices, maintaining the same price after a lowering of quality of the products that were previously ordered, taking excessive markups, and gaining unfair advantage because of a retailer's or manufacturer's size and/or power.

2. **Proportionality framework** relates to decisions that focus on actions rather than consequences, that is, the ends do not justify the means. For example, high profits should not be achieved by deceiving customers or by exploiting employees. As an example, *Case 11* in Chapter Two presents a situation in which employees appear to be stealing the ideas of their colleagues under the pressure of coming up with new lines each season.

3. **Social justice framework** means everyone should be treated equally and no group should be taken advantage of, for example, the dumping of unsafe products in third world countries.

Utilitarianism, another ideal that could be added to such a framework, can be thought of as doing "the greatest good for the greatest number." A cost-benefit analysis can assess the viability of this and is generally used in business and governmental decision-making. For example, an improvement to a process will only be made if the benefits are greater than the cost of making that improvement. Therefore, those who may have benefitted will not if the cost is too high.

Ethics in Sourcing and Working with Vendors

Global sourcing and international retailing today have stimulated more interest and concern for humanitarian rights. These concerns often cause dilemmas because of the differences between cultures. Should one country impose its ethical standards on another? For example, should a manufacturer hire a third world contractor that uses prison or child labor? In the extremely price-competitive apparel business, many companies use such contractors to keep labor expenses down (see *Case 86, To Work, Study, or Starve: Bangladesh Child Labor*). It is an ethical issue that more and more companies are facing, especially with increased public awareness of apparel assembly locations and conditions around the world. Levi Strauss & Co., the world's largest apparel manufacturer, has set the "standard" guidelines for the apparel industry when choosing business partners. These business partners are defined as contractors and subcontractors who manufacture or finish Levi Strauss products and suppliers who provide material utilized in the manufacture and finishing of their products (see Table 12.3).

Sometimes large companies that have such strict policies are caught in a "catch 22" situation when they cancel a contract because of labor abuses. Monitoring human rights at foreign contractors is complex to say the least. For example, Gap pulled its business from an El Salvador contractor amid accusations of serious human rights abuses at the plant that were reported by the people working there. After Gap was unable to determine the truth, it canceled the contract, which was followed by loud protests that the company was punishing the all-female workforce for speaking up about the abuses. As Gap did not want to participate in producing its product in an abusive environment, many felt it had an ethical obligation to ensure that changes were made at that plant. A similar situation happened in Honduras in a Liz Claiborne plant. Both companies (i.e., Gap and Liz Claiborne) reinstated their contracts and worked with the plants to improve conditions.

Table 12.3 Levi Strauss' Business Partner Terms of Engagement

1. *Ethical Standards*: We will seek to identify and utilize business partners who aspire as individuals and in the conduct of all their businesses to a set of ethical standards not incompatible with our own.

2. *Legal Requirements*: We expect our business partners to be law abiding as individuals and to comply with legal requirements relevant to the conduct of all their businesses.

3. *Environmental Requirements*: We will only do business with partners who share our commitment to the environment and who conduct their business in a way that is consistent with Levi Strauss & Co.'s Environmental Philosophy and Guiding Principles.

4. *Community Betterment*: We will favor business partners who share our commitment to contribute to the betterment of community conditions.

5. *Employment Standards*: We will only do business with partners whose workers are in all cases present voluntarily, not put at risk of physical harm, fairly compensated, allowed the right of free association and not exploited in any way. In addition, the following specific guidelines will be followed.

- *Wages and Benefits*: We will only do business with partners who provide wages and benefits that comply with any applicable law and match the prevailing local manufacturing or finishing industry practices.

- *Working Hours*: While permitting flexibility in scheduling, we will identify prevailing local work hours and seek business partners who do not exceed them except for appropriately compensated overtime. While we favor partners who utilize less than sixty-hour work weeks, we will not use contractors who, on a regularly scheduled basis, require in excess of a sixty-hour week. Employees should be allowed at least one day off in seven.

- *Child Labor*: Use of child labor is not permissible. Workers can be no less than 14 years of age and not younger than the compulsory age to be in school. We will not utilize partners who use child labor in any of their facilities. We support the development of legitimate workplace apprenticeship programs for the educational benefit of younger people.

- *Prison Labor/Forced Labor*: We will not utilize prison or forced labor in contracting relationships in the manufacture and finishing of our products. We will not utilize or purchase materials from a business partner utilizing prison or forced labor.

- *Health & Safety*: We will only utilize business partners who provide workers with a safe and healthy work environment. Business partners who provide residential facilities for their workers must provide safe and healthy facilities.

- *Discrimination*: While we recognize and respect cultural differences, we believe that workers should be employed on the basis of their ability to do the job, rather than on the basis of personal characteristics or beliefs. We will favor business partners who share this value.

- *Disciplinary Practices*: We will not utilize business partners who use corporal punishment or other forms of mental or physical coercion.

Source: Levi Strauss & Co.

The U.S. Congress is attempting to mandate that manufacturers be responsible for the actions and conditions of the contractors they use. Federal investigators have repeatedly found wage and safety violations in cut-and-sew operations in New York City, Los Angeles, and other major apparel-producing cities. For example, a nationwide government crackdown on sweatshops that exploit workers was spurred by the discovery of Thai apparel workers in slave-like conditions at El Monte, in southern California. Holding manufacturers, retailers, and even name licensees such as Kathie Lee Gifford accountable for these contractor abuses has been a controversial issue because small manufacturers say the expense of regulating their contractors would bankrupt them. Likewise, large manufacturers (as do large retailers who produce private labels) do not feel they should be held accountable for the busi-

Figure 12.2 Kathie Lee Gifford and New York Governor George Pataki at a press conference after the discovery that part of her Wal-Mart licensed apparel was produced in Honduran and New York City sweatshops. Subsequently, Kathie Lee became a crusader for the anti-sweatshop movement. Governor Pataki announced a proposal for "hot goods" legislation for New York State, already enforced in other states, which prohibits the sale of goods made in plants violating labor laws.

ness dealings of contractors that they utilize. Jessica McClintock's use of a small San Francisco contract shop, which eventually went out of business before paying their employees, brought her company a great deal of negative publicity from local workers who insisted that she pay their back wages, even though she had paid the company and had not used that contractor for over a year. The workers' insistence was based on a moral obligation they felt she had because of the previous profits she had enjoyed from their work. See *Case 85, Ethical Considerations*

for Sourcing: The Case of Esprit de Corps for a similar situation that happened with that company in the early 1990s. As the U.S. Department of Labor works toward a resolution of these problems, they have also rewarded 31 retailers and manufacturers—including Levi Strauss, Jessica McClintock, and Gap—by very publicly praising them as "Fair Labor Fashion Trendsetters." This distinction was given for their work on eradicating sweatshops and protecting garment workers. As good citizenship is good business, perhaps such positive reinforcement will be an effective method of reducing and eventually eliminating labor abuses.

A **kickback** is the return of part of monies received, which has been prompted by a threat or secret agreement, and is illegal. Some people say this type of corrupt behavior is happening more and more today and on a larger and larger scale. It also happens in smaller related ways, for example, suppliers that offer meals or gifts to buyers in efforts to secure orders. Because of these variations, it is hard to know where the line is between ethical and unethical behavior in regard to kickback-type favors. Additionally, kickbacks, or inducements, are legal and sometimes expected in many countries; therefore, these standards and expectations vary around the world. This can be a real problem because so many buyers now source internationally and deal with people from different cultures who hold different values, morals, and ethics. Some retailers explicitly prohibit employees from accepting anything from a supplier; others allow a few such items as meals. Wal-Mart, the largest U.S. retailer, may have the strictest standards as they do not allow their employees to accept anything from a vendor—not even a cup of coffee. *Case 88, Today's Woman: The Buyer's Personal Decision,* explores the conflict of interest—or the illusion of a conflict—of giving an order to a personal friend.

Ethics in Selling and Management

Should a salesperson withhold information about a product from customers, sell them merchandise (or a service) that does not meet their needs, or use high pressure, manipulative sales techniques to secure a commission? Some industry analysts feel that if sales associates are paid commission or have high sales quotas, this type of selling behavior, which is seen as unethical by some, will continue. As an example, consider the stereotypical reputation of the used car salesperson.

Sharing responsibilities on the sales floor is considered appropriate conduct for sales associates; however, with several generations working together today, value systems and individual work ethics can clash. *Case 69* in Chapter Nine is an example of an eager, young manager-trainee who feels he deserves a promotion without "paying the appropriate dues" in the eyes of older workers.

The misuse of company assets by employees is unethical, but there are certainly different degrees and interpretations of what is right or wrong behavior. Stealing merchandise or money from an employer is illegal, but what about taking a pen? Or an extra break? Or making long distance personal calls on the company telephone? These are all forms of employee theft and may be considered by some companies as unethical behavior. *Case 90, To Tell—Or Not to Tell* poses the problem of a young store manager who leaves the store after clocking in; a manager who lies and places blame elsewhere to protect her reputation is explored in *Case 89*. A new employee who uses confidential information from a previous employer is also considered unethical. Is it also unethical for a company to lay off employees because they make high salaries and replace them with younger, lower-salaried employees or to lay off an employee before pension benefits become available? This appears to be happening in the 1990s with many companies downsizing. Thus, potential unethical behavior can originate from both employee and employer behavior.

Social Responsibility

Closely related to ethics is **social responsibility,** that is, a company's duties and obligations to society that extend beyond ethics and legalities. Robin and Reidenbach (1989) differentiate between ethics and social responsibility based on the level of structure. As social responsibility is related to a loose social contract between business and society, ethics requires more structured rules of moral

behavior. Often the two concepts lead to the same decision, but sometimes they do not. Retailing and manufacturing often suffer from a consumer perception of being profit oriented and not particularly caring about the individual or community. However, there is a trend toward returning to an increased business involvement in society as the early retail pioneers did. Actually, the public expects business to be part of the community and to act responsibly. Because of this sentiment, many companies have found that ethics and social responsibility are good business.

Some tangible responses to the needs of society are the giving programs conducted by many retailers and manufacturers, as well as their involvement in educational and environmental programs and assistance to the disadvantaged. Levi Strauss and Koret of California, for example, have extensive foundation programs, in addition to community involvement. Dayton Hudson has been making charitable contributions to communities since 1917 with little fanfare. Environmental and social programs are supported by many retailers and manufacturers today including Levi Strauss, Gap, Esprit, Patagonia, Body Shop, and Wal-Mart. *Case 85* discusses the social responsibility award given to Esprit de Corps. Although this case looks critically at possible ethical problems at Esprit, it is one of the companies best known for having a corporate social conscience by supporting programs that promote AIDS awareness and protection of the environment. Notably their E-collection line of **environmentally friendly** apparel attempted to incorporate only environmentally safe methods and materials in its production. More and more retail buyers are seeking out vendors who specialize in "green" products, which do not harm the environment when they are produced. OWear and products using Sally Fox's FOXFIBRE®, a naturally colored cotton fiber that eliminates the need for toxic dyeing processes, are examples of green products. As more consumers gain a social conscience about the environment, these products will be in higher demand. Meanwhile, companies find they can be expensive to produce, and although consumers have started to have an interest in buying these environmentally sound products, they also want style, fashion, and a

Figure 12.3 An example of a trade ad from Anatomy, an environmentally friendly company. More apparel manufacturers are appealing to consumer concern for the environment.

Figure 12.4 Protests against the killing of animals for the production of fur coats are becoming more and more common, causing the apparel industry to reconsider the use of fur in garments.

reasonable price. It can be difficult for a company striving to balance social responsibility with profits.

Today, more and more consumers are holding companies accountable for their behavior and are acting as watchdogs in pressuring businesses to be more socially responsible. The day after Thanksgiving—traditionally one of the busiest retail days of the year—seems to be a designated day for animal rights protests and boycotts against such retailers as Fendi and others who sell furs as fashion. For years, both Europeans and Americans have lodged loud complaints against the slaughter of animals for the beautification of consumers. Because of consumer pressures and the resulting decrease in consumer demand (which go hand in hand), many retailers such as Nordstrom have closed their fur salons. *Case 91, Betty Campbell: Confronted with a Consumer Protest* describes a demonstration by anti-fur activists who are protesting the selling of fur coats by a department store and urging other shoppers boycott the store. The event was effective enough to get media coverage, which created significant negative press for the store.

Government Regulation

In addition to ethics and social responsibility, retailers and manufacturers cannot make decisions without regard to the laws of their resident country if they want to stay in business. Laws represent the

formalized set of ethical standards of a country, region, or population center. However, legal and ethical behavior are not necessarily the same, and some unethical behavior may very well be legal. Often, laws do not change as quickly as they should to meet the needs of the times. The legal environment includes federal, state, and local laws and ordinances. Because the latter two can vary widely from area to area, companies must become familiar with them to be in compliance. At the federal level, independent regulatory and other government agencies monitor such unfair business practices as price fixing, bait and switch, misleading advertising, and provide other consumer protection provisions. Table 12.4 lists the legislation that impacts the manufacture, distribution, and retailing of merchandise.

Legalities of Pricing

Price discrimination occurs when two retailers buy identical merchandise from the same supplier but pay different prices. The purpose of the law against price discrimination is to protect competition by ensuring that retailers are treated fairly by suppliers. Regulatory laws can be complicated and very confusing for non-lawyers. *Case 92, The Robinson-Patman Dilemma* illustrates this as a buyer is totally confused in regard to what type of price negotiations are legal—and which are not—under this act.

Price fixing creates monopolies and is considered illegal and a restraint of trade. It occurs when a group of competing retailers (considered horizontal price fixing) or a retailer and manufacturer (considered vertical price fixing) agree to maintain the price of merchandise. Vertical price fixing is called price maintenance, which is a violation of the Sherman Antitrust Act. This does not mean that manufacturers cannot recommend a price at which they would like to see their product sold. Hence, we see "suggested retail price" on price tags. However, until 1975 with the passage of the Consumer Goods Pricing Act, **fair trade laws** were in effect. These laws formerly had protected the small retailer from larger retailers as they both sold the same goods at the same price, since large retailers were not allowed to receive a discount for

Table 12.4 Selected Federal Legislation Affecting the Manufacturing, Retailing and Distribution of Merchandise.

Sherman Antitrust Act (1890): Banned "monopolies or attempts to monopolize" and "contracts, combinations, or conspiracies in restraint of trade" in interstate and foreign commerce.

Federal Trade Commission Act (1914): Established the Federal Trade Commission with broad powers to investigate and to issue cease-and-desist orders to enforce Section 5, which declares that "unfair methods of competition" in commerce are unlawful.

Clayton Act (1914): Adds to the Sherman Act by prohibiting specific practices (e.g., certain types of price discrimination, tying clauses) "where the effect . . . may be to substantially lessen competition or tend to create a monopoly in any line of commerce."

Resale Price Agreement (1931): Legalized resale price maintenance between manufacturers and retailers.

Unfair Practices Act (1935): Prohibited sales below cost.

Robinson-Patman Act (1936): Amends the Clayton Act. Adds the phrase "to injure, destroy, or prevent competition." Defines price discrimination as unlawful and provides the FTC with the right to establish limits on quantity discounts, to forbid brokerage allowances except to independent brokers, and to ban promotional allowances or the furnishing of services or facilities except where made available to all "on proportionately equal terms."

Miller-Tydings Act (1937): Legalized certain resale price maintenance contracts.

Food, Drug and Cosmetic Act (1938): Expanded the responsibility of the Food and Drug Administration to include cosmetics and therapeutic devices, by amending the 1906 act.

Wheeler-Lea Amendment of the FTC Act (1938): Prohibits unfair and deceptive acts and practices regardless of whether competition is to the injured.

Fair Labor Standards (1938): Established minimum wages.

Wool Products Labeling Act (1939): Required that products containing wool carry labels showing the fiber content.

Antimerger Act (1950): Amends Section 7 of the Clayton act by broadening the power to prevent intercorporate acquisitions where the acquisition may lessen competition.

Fur Products Labeling Act (1951): Required that all fur products carry labels correctly describing their contents.

McGuire Act (1952): Validated specific price maintenance contracts.

Flammable Fabrics Act (1953): Prohibited the manufacture or sale of fabrics or wearing apparel that were dangerously flammable.

Textile Fiber Product Identification Act (1960): Required fiber content identification on all apparel.

Kefauver-Harris Amendment to Food, Drug and Cosmetic Act (1962): Required that all drugs be tested for safety and efficacy.

Child Protection Act (1966): Amended the Hazardous Substances Labeling Act (1960) to ban all hazardous substances and prohibit sales of potentially harmful toys and other articles used by children.

Fair Packaging and Labeling Act (1966): Makes provision for the regulation of the packaging and labeling of consumer goods. Permits industries' voluntary adoption of uniform packaging standards.

Flammable Fabrics Act (1967): Amended the 1953 act and expanded textile legislation to include the Department of Commerce Flammability Standards for additional products.

Truth-In-Lending Act (1968): Requires lenders to state the true costs of a credit transaction. Established a National Commission on Consumer Finance.

Fair Credit Reporting Act (1970): Regulated credit information reporting and use.

Care Labeling Act (1971): Required all apparel selling for over $3 to carry labels with washing or dry-cleaning instructions.

Consumer Product Safety Act (1972): Established the Consumer Product Safety Commission and empowered it to set safety standards for a broad range of consumer products and to impose penalties for failure to meet these standards (includes flammable fabrics regulations)

Equal Credit Opportunity Act (1974): Insured that financial institutions engaged in the extension of credit make credit available without discrimination on the basis of sex or marital status.

Magnuson-Moss Warranty/FTC Improvement Act (1975): Empowers the FTC to determine rules concerning consumer warranties and provides for consumer access to means of redress, such as the "class action" suit. Expands FTC regulatory powers over unfair or deceptive acts or practices.

Consumer Goods Pricing Act (1975): Outlawed legalized resale price maintenance. (Fair trade laws)

Fair Debt Collection Practice Act (1978): Made illegal to harass or abuse any person and make false statements or use unfair methods when collecting a debt.

Amendment to the Wool Products Labeling Act (1980): Required that products containing recycled wool carry labels showing the content.

Amendment to the Care Labeling Act (1984): Expanded requirements on apparel labels to include water temperature, bleaching, ironing requirements.

Amendment to the Textile Fiber Product Identification Act (1984): Required apparel labels to indicate country of origin to include Made in the USA.

Source: Dunne, Lusch & Gable, 1995; Bohlinger, 1993.

quantity purchases. The Consumer Goods Pricing Act repealed all resale **price maintenance laws** and enabled retailers to sell products below the suggested retail prices that were set by manufacturers. Although this ended protection for the small retailer, it allowed consumers to buy at the lowest possible free-market price. Price maintenance laws and rules, however, change with the sentiment of congress, the justice system, and presidential administration. For example, in 1988, the Supreme Court ruled that manufacturers can refuse to sell to retailers that sell below the manufacturer's suggested retail price, to protect the manufacturer's reputation.

Predatory pricing, a situation in which a retailer prices a product below cost with the intent to drive out any competition, is also illegal. Not all below-cost selling is illegal or considered predatory pricing, as some end-of-season goods are sold at a loss to clear out old merchandise. Wal-Mart has been accused and acquitted in court of predatory pricing, as they have driven small retailers out of business. Wal-Mart claims the intent of its pricing is to provide low prices for consumers, not to hurt competition. There appears to be a gray area here as that certainly was not the interpretation of the situation by the bankrupt small retailers.

Legalities of Distribution
Retailers and manufacturers are also subject to laws that affect the distribution of goods. **Tying contracts,** a situation in which suppliers force retailers to buy unwanted merchandise in order to purchase other desired merchandise, is illegal. Collusion between manufacturers and retailers to exclude competition is also illegal if this collusion restrains trade. The case in this chapter that explores this type of illegal activity is *Case 93, Collusion to Catch Anti-Trust Offenders,* in which a supplier sold only to one large retailer, the result of which pushed out several smaller stores.

The Legal Aspects of Advertising
The **Federal Trade Commission (FTC)** monitors the legal aspects of business advertising. **Bait and switch** is a form of deceptive advertising in

which a product is promoted at an unrealistically low price to serve as bait. After a consumer arrives to buy this advertised product, the retailer attempts to switch the customer to a higher-priced item. A retailer must have the stock on hand that is advertised and in sufficient quantity. For example, an advertised item with a stock of one piece stored in an inaccessible place would be suspect of a bait and switch scheme. **Misleading advertising** is another form of consumer deception that is illegal. If a manufacturer's claims are untrue or misleading, a cease and desist order can be issued, putting a halt to such claims.

Special Apparel Regulations
The FTC and the **Consumer Product Safety Commission (CPSC)** are independent regulatory agencies charged with overseeing the area of consumer protection and restraint of trade and have the specific responsibility of apparel regulation. Within the purview of the FTC are labeling requirements for apparel. These include: the Textile Fiber Products Identification Act, which requires generic fiber identification, manufacturer identification, and country of origin; the Permanent Care Labeling Act, which requires care labels to be placed in most apparel items; and legislation covering fur and wool products labeling. Even though there has been no new legislation related to care labeling since 1984, the FTC has considered adding alternative care labeling to the current recommended care labeling requirement. *Case 95, The Flannel Fiber Fiasco* presents a circumstance in which a supplier provides fabric that has a different fiber content than that which had been contracted. This was done without notifying the manufacturer, who, unknowingly, had been labeling garments incorrectly. When the deception was discovered, the manufacturer knew it was not in compliance with the law and something had to be done to rectify the situation.

The CPSC regulates flammability requirements of both apparel and home furnishings. Strict requirements for children's sleepwear decrease the risk of young children being burned from highly flammable fabrics. From time to time, this agency has also considered more stringent requirements for adult sleepwear. All apparel must meet basic standards for flammability, and no dangerous fabrications are allowed to be sold or imported into the U.S. for sale. Similar to toy recalls for safety purposes, occasionally apparel is also recalled. An example of this is when there was a recall of a popular, sheer-cotton skirt that had been made in India.

CPSC also monitors other product safety, which is the subject of *Case 94*. In this case, popular children's bean bag cushions were recalled by this agency after there were several instances of young children who died as the result of inhaling or swallowing the plastic beads that filled the cushion. This company finds itself in a situation of being ordered to reimburse retailers for stock and disposing of its unsold inventory with the real possibility of going bankrupt in the process.

Intellectual Property Protection

Patents, copyrights, and trademarks are considered a company's **intellectual property**. Infringement of any of these is illegal. A U.S. **patent** grants to the inventor the right for 17 years to exclude others from making, using, or selling that invention. The applicant makes a complete disclosure of the invention, which is published and which moves into the public domain when the patent expires.

There are few patents granted to developers of fashion because one small alteration in a design can negate its originality; however, patents are granted if a unique process or material is developed in textiles or special purposes in apparel. For example, Ultrasuede®, a patented fabric, developed in Japan and now copied by other companies (because the patent has expired), simulated suede as no other fabrication previously had. In apparel, a small maternity manufacturer in San Francisco called Japanese Weekend received a patent for products called the OK belt and pant that was a new concept for maternitywear. This apparel utilized a belt under an unborn baby for support, and which left the mother's stomach exposed rather than covering it with a large expanse of fabric as had always been done in previously designed maternity pants.

A copyright is protection for original creative writings or works of art. From time to time, an apparel designer will procure a copyright on a design, which is designated on the label by the copyright symbol. For example, Karen Alexander copyrighted her sleeve design. She published notices in the trade papers warning would-be copiers that she would prosecute those who infringed upon the copyright. Most copyright infringement today is on videos, audio tapes, and computer software.

A **trademark** is any word, name, or symbol that has been adopted and used by the owner to identify a product and distinguish it from others. The first person to use the trademark in conjunction with a product has ownership of the trademark and can exclude others from using it. This is not the case, however, in other countries where often it is the person who registers it who holds the trademark; therefore, companies trading overseas may not have rights to use the trademark they use in the U.S. Knowing the local laws is extremely important. Also, if consumers cannot separate a specific trademarked product (such as Levi's) from a generic product (such as jeans), the company can lose the exclusive rights to their trademarked terminology. Therefore, companies use a generic name with their trademark to remind consumers that theirs is a special type of that product. So even though it seems awkward and redundant, we see the use of Kleenex facial tissue, Xerox photocopies, Jacuzzi whirlpool baths, and Levi's jeans.

Counterfeiting

Counterfeited merchandise violates a company's intellectual property rights. The Anti-Counterfeiting Coalition, which is strongly supported by Levi Strauss & Co., was instrumental in gaining the federal legislation in 1984 that makes trademark infringement a crime. As discussed in Chapter Three, knockoffs, or close copies of designs, are common in the fashion industry. Some companies' knockoffs, however, come dangerously close to being **counterfeits.** The law states that a protected

THESE YOU CAN BORROW.

THESE YOU CAN'T.

Only Levi Strauss & Co. is entitled by the U.S. Patent and Trademark office to use the Arcuate Stitching Design®, Tab Device® or the Two Horse Design® trademarks. Our lawyers agressively pursue every legal means at their disposal to protect our trademarks. So if you're thinking of borrowing something, it's probably best to stick with tools and stuff.

Figure 12.5 Levi Strauss & Co. vehemently polices its trademarks and informs the industry of this policy in this trade ad.

trademark or copyright cannot be copied and offered for sale by another company. As an example, Express was found guilty of infringing on the copyright of Banff's Aran fisherman's sweater. Express attempted to have this judgment overturned; but this case is a good example of the fact that one person's idea of a knockoff is another's idea of a counterfeit. Designers often fight in court over whose idea was first. Yves St. Laurent sued Ralph Lauren for copying his tuxedo dress, which was then claimed to have been designed by Bernard Perris five years earlier, which had already been copied by the "king of copycats"—Victor Costa! As fashion is interpretation and often is inspired by earlier designs, many times it is hard to know who is the originator of a particular design. Levi Strauss has been actively involved for years in the pursuit of protecting its trademarks, many of which are counterfeited and sold mostly overseas. They were one of the first to use technology to ensure authenticity for their retailers. For example, a tracking system has been developed that codes the inside label of the jeans with a serial number; through a computer-generated light beam, it can detect whether the merchandise is legitimate or counterfeit.

Gray market goods also plague both the cosmetics and apparel industry. These are not illegal, but are imports that are unauthorized by the company owning the trade name. Often such goods are sold at discounters with no warranty or with older dates than those through authorized channels. Fragrances, for example, may have been on shelves for longer than the recommended product life. The prices, however, are lower, which benefits the consumer. There is an ongoing campaign to make gray goods illegal.

Other Regulations
The **Food and Drug Administration (FDA)** is responsible for regulating the food, drug, and cosmetics industries in regard to the safety of and disclosure of ingredients of products. Cosmetics claiming to have effects that permanently change the skin have come under fire by the FDA because such claims define the product as a drug, which would also carry the requirement of effectiveness

in addition to safety. If the FDA didn't become involved over such claims, the FTC would then intervene with a misleading advertising charge as the cosmetics' permanent change claims have not been proven.

Summary
Successful businesses conduct themselves in a legal, ethical, and socially responsible manner. As retailing and manufacturing expand globally, this type of behavior becomes more complicated as laws and standards vary from country to country. Much attention and public awareness has been focused on the use of labor throughout the world to produce products that we buy at low prices. Some companies formulate strict ethical standards and policies; others stay within the letter of the law. At the same time, government debates mandating certain behavior, which many have considered overly ethical. So, whatever a company's ethical standards may be now, as we move toward the new millenium, ethics and socially responsible behavior will continue to grow as issues for businesses. Those companies that can find a way to comply with both the law and with society's dictates, and still offer their customers a good product at a good price, will succeed.

References
Anderson, C.H. (1995). *Retailing concepts, strategy and information*. Minneapolis: West Publishing Co.

Barchak, W., Conan, Liebowitz, & Latman. (1986). A trademark is not a patent or a copyright. *Executive newsletter*, No. 39, U.S. Trademark Association.

Barrett, J., & Ramey, J. (1996, June 6). Sweatshop-buster Charles Kernaghan: Fashion hits its nader. *WWD*, pp. 1, 6, 7.

Bohlinger, M.S. (1993). *Merchandise Buying*. Boston: Allyn and Bacon.

Cedrone, L. (1995, February). On the road to flexibility Oshkosh takes many paths. *Bobbin*, pp. 26–36.

Dunne, P., Lusch, R., & Gable, M. (1995). *Retailing.* Cincinnati: South-Western Publishing Co.

Friedman, A. (1996, June 11). Fashion's blame game: Is retail price squeeze reviving sweatshops? *WWD*, pp. 1, 8, 9.

Fuller, D.A. (1994). Shopping centers and the environment: Recyling strategies for the 1990s, An exploratory investigation. *Journal of Shopping Center Research, 1*(1), 7–37.

Graphics artists guild handbook of pricing & ethical guidelines. (1994). New York: Author.

Gordon, M. (1992, April 22). The greening of SA. *WWD*, pp. 10–11.

Guy, M.E. (1990). *Ethical decision making in everyday work situations.* New York: Quorum Books.

Hartnett, M. (1994, May). Community commitment: Kenneth A. Macke receives American Spirit Award. *Stores*, pp. 49–66.

Henderson, V.E. (1992). *What's ethical in business?* New York: McGraw-Hill.

McNamara, M. (1994, May 18). Ecology goes mainstream. *WWD*, p. 10.

Net, A.J. (1996, February). Patagonia pursues pure cotton. *Bobbin*, pp. 62–65.

Ottman, J.A. (1994) *Green marketing: Challenges and opportunities for the new marketing age.* Lincolnwood, IL.: NTC Business Books.

Ramey, J. (1996, March 18). Apparel's ethics dilemma, *WWD*, pp. 10–12.

Ramey, J. (1996, June 7). Kathie Lee to push Wal-Mart on cleaning up sweatshops. *WWD*, p. 16.

Robin, D.P., & Reidenbach, R.E. (1989). *Business ethics: Where profits meet value systems.* Englewood Cliffs, N.J.: Prentice Hall.

Trademark Counterfeiting Act of 1984 becomes law. (1984, Aug.–Sept./Oct.–Nov.). *Anti-Counterfeiting Coalition Newsletter*, pp. 1–2.

U.S. Department of Commerce. (1986). *General information concerning trademarks.* Washington, D.C.: U.S. Government Printing Office.

Key Terms

bait and switch

business ethics

code of ethics

Consumer Product Safety Commission (CPSC)

corporate ethics

counterfeit

environmentally friendly

ethics

fair trade laws

Federal Trade Commission (FTC)

Food and Drug Administration (FDA)

gray market goods

intellectual property

kickback

misleading advertising

patent

personal ethics

predatory pricing

price discrimination

price fixing

price maintenance laws

prima facie duties

professional ethics

proportionality framework

social justice framework

social responsibility

trademark

tying contract

utilitarianism

Case 85
Ethical Considerations for Sourcing: The Case of Esprit de Corps

Diane Frey, Bowling Green State University
Molly Eckman, Colorado State University

Esprit was founded by a husband and wife team, Doug and Susie Thompkins, in 1979. Susie was responsible for apparel design and Doug concentrated on marketing. Since the Thompkinses began Esprit, the company has grown from just a few employees to more than 4,000. Esprit is a successful manufacturer of trendy, casual clothing and accessories. In the 1980s, their target market was unclear as a rift between the Thompkinses arose over Susie's wish to target a more mature consumer, while Doug favored maintaining their focus on younger styles. When Susie acquired the majority of the company, Esprit changed its target from exclusively juniors to include not only children, but career adults.

Esprit is known for more that just producing fashion merchandise. Company policies are guided by a social conscience and support for diverse issues of global concern, including arts education, women's issues, and environmental responsibility. Although Susie understands that Esprit cannot change the world, she believes that company policies can contribute in a positive way. Susie's vision for the company is to reflect corporate responsibility by inspiring employees, doing more in the community, and making a more conscientious product. Employees are encouraged to become involved in community organizations through paid leave time. The owners' interest in the environment is evidenced by the development of an experimental ecologically oriented sportswear line called Ecollection. The Ecollection line of clothing was a result of collaboration with organic farmers, fabric manufacturers, dye chemists, finishing technicians, anthropologists, and craftspeople to produce "environmentally friendly" clothing. Through their association with Aid to Artisans, Esprit assisted indigenous artisans in developing countries and economically depressed areas of the U.S. by sourcing handcrafted clothing for the Ecollection, which incorporated the artisans' crafts. Thus, Esprit supports the philosophy of Aid to Artisans, which is helping people help themselves through identifying markets for products incorporating traditional crafts. Despite higher production costs for Ecollection, the line was priced comparably to the conventional Esprit lines. Since the introduction of Ecollection, the company has mainstreamed many of its concepts of using environmentally safe materials into its regular lines. This was the original intent of Ecollection.

Esprit has staffed an "Eco Desk" through which Esprit employees work to educate consumers and employees about environmental issues. In 1990, they ran an advertisement beseeching their customers to consume responsibly. The message of the advertisement was to encourage consumers to buy for vital needs, avoid frivolous purchases, and attempt to balance their lives. The advertisement was run despite the fact that the message, which seems to be incongruent with the philosophy behind fashion, made the retail stores that sell Esprit goods somewhat uncomfortable. Esprit was also one of the first major fashion firms to address AIDS and to develop advertisements to educate consumers about the disease. Susie's reasoning behind supporting these causes is that when offered the choice, consumers will purchase goods from an environmentally and socially conscious company. Some compromises, however, have been made in Esprit's production decisions. For example, Esprit clothing is made from both natural fabrics as well as synthetics—which are petroleum based. However, Esprit justifies their use of synthetics by stating that apparel made from synthetics is easy to care for and practical.

Esprit clothing is designed and produced to reflect a sense of value, simplicity, and elegance that is in tune with today's world. While the focus

in the 1980s was on style, the 1990s is about substance and values. Susie believes that Esprit
customers display confidence as well as a personal
style through their choice of clothing. Her target
market is the woman who is responsible and sensi-
ble and not concerned with clothing that exudes
power and flash. Susie has described her merchandise as simple, eclectic, and human.

Because image is so important to Esprit, the
company attempts to control all aspects of distribution. Most Esprit clothing is produced in Asia, but
some is made in the Western hemisphere.
Merchandise is sold in Esprit-owned retail stores
nationwide, as well as in better department and specialty stores. For their department store business,
Esprit has relied on their "shop-within-a-shop" concept, which allows them some control of their
presentation within the department store setting.
The company also is expanding its outlet business
in order to manage the sale of their leftover merchandise, in addition to providing another retail
venue for their merchandise.

In 1972, the company opened a garment factory
in San Francisco's Chinatown that employed
approximately 100 people. Employees' attempts to
unionize the factory were thwarted and eventually
the plant was closed when Esprit was threatened
with unionization. The court ordered the company
to pay workers back wages. To date, no union has
been successful in organizing Esprit workers.

In the early 1990s, the Department of Labor
(DOL) raided a shop that Esprit contracted for
apparel production. The DOL found that Esprit
owed the workers over $120,000 in back wages.
Additionally, the contract shop was not paying the
current U.S. minimum wage, nor were they paying
overtime. Through the contracting system, manufacturers may be insulated from individuals who
are employed by them indirectly through contractors. Furthermore, poor communication between
manufacturers and contractors has sometimes
resulted in manufacturers being uninformed about
contractors' employment practices. Regardless, the
DOL has taken the position that clothing manufacturers are responsible for contractors' hiring
practices because the garment workers are sewing
the manufacturer's garments.

Recently, the DOL has increased its efforts to
ensure that apparel contractors comply with federal wage and hourly regulations. Contractors who
are found to be in violation of labor laws are forced
to pay back wages or face stoppage of shipments.
In an effort to avoid a reputation for exploiting
workers, a group of apparel manufacturers has vol-
unteered to fund independent auditors to monitor
their contractors in Los Angeles. Under this agreement, approximately 50 percent of all L.A.
contractors will be audited. The goal of these sponsors is to generate a "culture of compliance" with
agreements concerning overtime pay, prearranged
prices for contractors, and licensing requirements
of the contractor.

Esprit has been recognized for their activities
related to community service and has received the
1992 Corporate Conscience Award given by the
Council on Economic Priorities. The award was in
recognition of Esprit's efforts to advance the wel-
fare of minorities and women and promote
environmental programs, including Ecollection, its
environmentally friendly line of clothing. Despite
these recognitions, Esprit has faced ethical challenges directed at their employment practices. To
overcome these challenges and criticisms Esprit's
sourcing director has been asked to analyze the
company's contracting and employment policies
and practices. The criteria to be used to assess the
ethical nature of a decision are:

1. Does the decision conform with the legal system?

2. Will the decision remain sound, even in the
face of an audit?

3. Does the decision follow standard corporate
practices?

4. Does the decision remain within the corporate
code of ethics?

5. Does the decision comply with general rules of
human conduct?

6. Does the decision promote the general well
being of the company?

7. Does the decision increase the corporation's
economic efficiency?

8. Does the decision maintain the corporate image?

9. Has the decision been made in good conscience?

10. Does the decision augment the decision-maker's reputation?

11. Does the decision follow previous managerial behavior?

Major Question

If you were Esprit's sourcing director, what corrective measures in the company's contracting and employment policies and practices would you recommend for Esprit? State which ethical criteria have been used in your analysis.

Study Questions

1. Analyze the firm describing factors that shape Esprit's company culture.

2. Describe the ethical violations attributed to the Esprit company.

3. In light of the eleven ethical criteria, describe the ethical nature of Esprit's contracting policies.

References

Benson, H. (1991, February). Reinventing Esprit. *San Francisco Focus,* pp. 41–45.

Marlow, M. (1990, September 10). Susie's Esprit: New looks, new outlook. *Women's Wear Daily,* pp. 1, 6.

Saeks, D. (1992, September). Always true in her fashion. *Metropolitan Home,* pp. 37–44.

Monitoring effort in L.A. expanding. (1995, June 21). *WWD,* pp. 2, 15.

Udesky, L. (1994, May 16). The 'social responsibility' gap: Sweatshops behind the labels. *The Nation,* pp. 665–668.

Case 86
To Work, Study, or Starve: Bangladesh Child Labor

Kitty Dickerson, University of Missouri

Ted Jonas is involved in global sourcing for a major retail chain, Dazzlemore. He travels a good portion of the time, going from country to country to find good potential contractors to produce the lines developed in his company's product development department.

Ted has found many of his prospects for contractors in less-developed countries. Many of these countries offer good quality and will produce apparel at costs that are attractive to Dazzlemore. One of the countries Ted often visits is Bangladesh, one of the poorest countries in the world. When he has visited factories there, he has noticed that some of the workers looked more like children than adults. At least when he has been present, he has seen no evidence that these young people were held against their will or abused. He suspected, however, that the youngsters probably worked very long days, just as the older operators did.

At the same time, Ted is aware of the poverty, the malnutrition, and the poor health conditions of many—both old and young—in Bangladesh. In Dhaka, the capitol of Bangladesh, he has also noticed the number of children who were running in the streets, often in physical danger as they peddled trinkets and gum. He has seen few schools to accommodate the large number of children who seem to be everywhere.

When Ted was back in the U.S. for a meeting, he happened to see an exposé on television about a major U.S. retailer doing business with a Bangladesh supplier who appeared to be using child laborers. In the weeks that followed, Ted followed the repercussions of this exposé about child workers. Members of the U.S. Congress were sensitized to the issue, and bills were introduced to regulate the importation of products made by children. Congress adjourned before passage of the bills.

When visiting with European colleagues, Ted learned that the issue of child labor in developing countries had also been featured in the media there. As in the U.S., some European policy makers were launching an effort to place a ban on products made with child labor. In another visit with a European, Ted learned about an organization, Kids in Deficient Situations (KIDS), that had a very different approach. This group, which had many informed, caring parents among the membership, advocated that banning child labor entirely was doing a disservice to starving children in some of the poorest Third World nations. This group voiced the opinion that factory work was far safer for children than running in the streets, and that earning a wage was better than starving—even if the wage earner happened to be younger than developed country standards for minimum age workers. The KIDS group collected donations for Third World families so they might send their children to school for at least three years.

Meanwhile, back in the U.S., a group called the Child Labor Coalition developed plans for a boycott of Bangladesh apparel unless Bangladesh manufacturers agreed to eliminate child labor. UNICEF and the International Labor Organization also supported the boycott.

Finally, the Bangladesh Garment Manufacturers and Exporters Association agreed to ban workers under 14 in apparel factories. Estimates of the number of children under 14 in the country's large industry were as low as 8,000 and as high as 50,000. The agreement required that schooling be provided for the children who would be dismissed because of the agreement. Coalition leaders heralded the agreement as a breakthrough for the child labor issue in the Third World.

Ted followed the results with interest. He pondered his own position on this issue. He agrees that abusive child labor conditions should be eliminated. He knows that children generally have no

advocates in those situations and are, therefore, easily exploited. He also knows the dire poverty in Bangladesh and the alternative activities for children. He understands the position of the KIDS advocates. He agrees that the safe confines of a factory, as unacceptable as that may be to many westerners, might also be safer than dodging in and out of traffic. He also knows that far too few schools exist in Bangladesh to believe that all the children denied factory work would be sent off cheerily by their mothers to school each day.

Ted searched his heart for an answer to what he expected to confront in future visits to potential contractors in Third World countries.

Major Question
What should Ted do when he sees children at work in the factories he contracts from?

Study Questions
1. How can apparel and retail companies stay competitive when some companies utilize contractors with employment practices less than ethical (using Western standards)?

2. What ethical considerations are involved with choosing contractors?

3. Does a buyer have the power to decide what contractors a large retailer uses for their private-label merchandise?

Case 87
To Go or to Stay: Ethics in the Workplace

Kitty Dickerson, University of Missouri

When Janice Heitler landed a job after graduation in the buyer training program at retailer BuyBest, she believed her career dreams were close to being fulfilled. Although she had limited experience with the company through an internship, she was particularly fortunate to be hired immediately into the BuyBest's buying office. Typically, potential buyers spend at least two years in a BuyBest store before having an opportunity to go to the headquarter's buying offices.

Janice plunged quickly into her work as a buyer trainee at BuyBest. Although she was given a relatively limited amount of training and guidance in her new job, Janice learned quickly. She soon earned the respect of her colleagues and the vendors with whom she worked. Before long, Janice was given limited opportunities to do some of the actual buying for her area. As her experience increased, so did her responsibilities for buying. In what was a relatively short period of time for a buyer in training, she was made buyer of her own area. Although this first buying area was relatively low profile, the multiple stores represented in the chain meant that the dollar volume for which she bought was fairly significant.

As Janice continued her successful performance, she was rewarded with higher dollar volume areas for which to buy. Within less than three years, she was buyer for two merchandise areas and was responsible for a staggering dollar volume for a person of her age and experience. Although somewhat uneasy at times because of her fast promotion, Janice continued to perform well. Her areas were successful and she was a valued employee of BuyBest.

As the economy changed in the early 1990s and consumer apparel expenditures declined, Janice's satisfaction with her job began to wane. Although her own buying areas were doing reasonably well, the company as a whole was less profitable than in prior years. Many of BuyBest's buyers had merchandise on order with manufacturers and found that consumer demand was not adequate to sell all the merchandise ordered. Many of Janice's buyer peers canceled their orders with manufacturers.

As Janice's buying areas began to show lackluster performance, she began to be pressured from her superiors to cancel orders for merchandise not yet shipped. She understood why her superiors wanted her to cancel the orders; however, she felt it was unethical treatment of the manufacturers with

whom she had developed trusted relationships. Because Janice was buying a substantial volume of merchandise for the multiple stores in the BuyBest organization, she was sensitive to what this meant to those vendors. For many small suppliers, in particular, the volume she ordered could make or break the manufacturer. For those companies with whom she had placed orders, the fabrics and others supplies would have been purchased by the manufacturers, and in several cases, production was already in progress. This also would mean the manufacturer would have incurred labor costs at that point. In short, the losses associated with canceled orders from BuyBest could put some of her vendors out of business or seriously cripple them.

Janice found herself torn between her conscience and the expectations of her employer. To stay in her job, she must cancel orders to meet BuyBest's financial expectations for her area. To do so, Janice knew she would be seriously hurting vendors with whom she had developed good relationships, and she had become friends with several. Additionally, she knew that she might need to place orders again with those companies— if they were still in business—and she was uncertain if they would sell to her again if she treated them in this manner.

Janice's superiors were very much aware of the implications of canceled orders on vendors. They, too, were responding to pressure from their superiors. Janice could not be sure how high in the corporate structure the decisions were being made.

Janice saw some of her buyer peers leaving BuyBest. Although she was troubled by her dilemma, she knew she would not likely find another job with comparable opportunities at this stage in her career.

Major Question
What should Janice do?

Study Questions
1. What other factors, besides an economic downturn, would cause a retailer to cancel orders so close to delivery dates?

2. What are the retailers' rights regarding cancellations?

3. What can the vendor do to protect itself against last-minute retail cancellations?

Case 88
Today's Woman: The Buyer's Personal Decision

Judith Everett, Northern Arizona University

Diane Mather has recently accepted the position of buyer of suits for Today's Woman, a women's specialty chain. Previously Diane was the regional manager for the southwest division. This promotion required relocating to New York City where the corporate headquarters is situated.

Diane had a strong record as a hard worker and had been promoted regularly since graduating with a degree in fashion merchandising eight years ago. Diane set high standards for her personal and ethical performance. She expected no less from her staff. She always met or exceeded her sales and performance goals, and moved quickly up the ranks from assistant manager to branch store manager. Her next promotion was to Southwest regional manager. This job included training store managers, providing budget and inventory information to the personnel in her region and to the buyers at corporate headquarters, and completing product and consumer demand analysis. She watched the changing consumer demands in her region and reported the trends in consumer behavior to the buying offices. The merchandise demands for the southwest region emphasized a more casual styling, with a new emphasis on "Friday Wear." This trend allowed managers to wear more casual, yet professional clothing on Fridays. Demand was growing for less rigid and traditional suits; blazers with slacks or skirts and polo shirts were quickly becoming the norm for "Friday Wear." When Diane took over the buyer's job, it was clear that the trend occurring in her homebase of the southwest region was a national trend. Women all over the country were seeking non-traditional suits and more casual attire for the office.

Today's Woman is a national chain store with nearly 300 branches. It targets an audience of working women between the ages of 21 and 65. The company has aggressive growth plans, opening several new branches each year. The suit buyer has a significant position in the firm because all other buyers must coordinate their purchases to the colors and silhouettes selected by the suit buyer. The company sells women's suits, coordinated separates, blouses, and such accessories as belts, handbags, briefcases, shoes, and jewelry. The company has recently added a line of casual separates to the merchandise mix. Suits account for 60 percent of annual sales for Today's Woman. The company has traditionally purchased 90 percent of their suits from one manufacturer, Ben Ross.

Ben Ross is a manufacturer of good quality suits in the moderate to better price range. The company has been producing suits for nearly 50 years. The owner of the firm has provided excellent service through fair pricing and reliable delivery. The styling of the merchandise is quite traditional and conservative, serving the traditional business woman very well for the past 50 years.

After arriving in New York, Diane has been invited to many social events sponsored by the senior executives at Today's Woman, her college alumni association, and the Fashion Group International, a professional organization for women executives in the fashion industry. She has learned to love living in the "big city." At Diane's college alumni association annual banquet she met George Robinson, a sales representative for Hunting Brothers, a men's apparel manufacturer with retail outlets on the east coast. Diane and George were immediately attracted to each other and began dating. They have attended several

Broadway shows together and have enjoyed dining at some of the great restaurants in New York.

Hunting Brothers has a reputation for innovative men's apparel and has recently expanded into manufacturing women's suits. The women's market is a very small part of the company at this point, but the firm's products have tested very well in the East coast retail stores owned by Hunting Brothers. The firm does not plan on opening retail stores in other parts of the U.S. at this time. Hunting Brothers plans to expand the market share of the women's suits by selling to other retailers.

George has given Diane several suits as gifts. She thought that the suits had a nice, up-to-date fashion appearance. They fit well and are of excellent quality. The fabric and styling would fit the growing "Friday Wear" merchandise segment as well as the traditional suit categories.

After several months of dating, George suggests that Diane drop Ben Ross as the primary suit vendor and purchase most of her merchandise from Hunting Brothers. Diane recognizes the quality of the product and the more fashionable styling but fears that her supervisor will question why she is buying her suits from her "boyfriend."

Major Question

What should Diane do?

Study Questions

1. What are the ethical considerations in this situation?

2. What should be the criteria for vendor selection?

Case 89
The Perilous Promotion

Laura Bliss, Stephens College

Jacob Henry is an internationally recognized retailer of sophisticated, updated classics for men, women, and children. The retailer also carries fine accessories and home furnishings. After graduating at the top of her class from a reputable state university, Paige West began her career with Jacob Henry, selling men's suits in the Vermont store. She literally took the company by storm, increasing sales in the area by nearly 30 percent in a three-month period. When an opening as an assistant manager in the Vermont store presented itself, management thought of Paige first. Paige worked diligently with her new assignment and succeeded in much the same way as she had in men's suits, increasing sales significantly. Upper management took notice of Paige's efforts and again were impressed. It was not surprising that, when a new store was scheduled to open in Paige's home state of Illinois, she was eager to seize the new challenge and opportunity to become an actual store manager.

Unfortunately, the opening of Paige's store in Illinois got off to a rocky start. Heavy rains flooded the store twice before opening, and merchandise and store fixtures did not arrive as planned. Additionally, her new district manager, Liz Holzman, had never before actually managed a store. Rumor had it that Liz was a "friend" of a corporate executive and was owed a favor. Liz and Paige got along amicably, but it was evident to Paige that she could not really count on Liz for sound advice. Being slightly insecure of her own abilities, Liz often became defensive and made snap decisions when she felt that her authority was being threatened. Paige began to notice this pattern and, rather than making waves, simply took the blame for any misunderstanding and tried to immediately make the situation right.

Even with all these obstacles, the store opened on time and had done very well, exceeding an ambitious plan by 23 percent. Both Paige and Liz looked like heroes in the company's eyes. As this was Liz's first store opening and it had gone so well, Liz's career was off to a good start regardless of the rumors of how she had been promoted. She had essentially "proven" herself and had the beginnings of a great career with Jacob Henry.

Time passed, and Labor Day was a few days away. Liz arrived at the store for her monthly visit to review the sales floor with Paige and help her prepare for the big Labor Day sale—specifically in home furnishings. As Liz and Paige walked the sales floor, Liz noticed that there were many styles of sheets and assorted bedding that were not selling. Liz asked why the sheets weren't marked down. Paige replied that they were not on the suggested SKU markdown list and that she already had bath sheets and summer beach towels on sale that must be sold. Paige tried to explain that if she marked the sheets down, her markdown percentage in home furnishings would "go through the ceiling." Liz was agitated and reacted quickly to Paige's remarks. Liz claimed that the reason Paige wasn't getting any new merchandise was because these abundant (and ugly!) styles that weren't being marked down were "clogging up" the inventory. According to Liz, Paige was undermining her store's business by not taking action to move the sheets. Liz demanded that Paige mark down the sheets to $5.99 a piece—a price that was sure to move them out. Paige was aghast and tried to explain why this wouldn't be a good idea. Liz cut her off and said, "Just do it." Liz also wanted signs made up specifically for the "dump table" and for the store windows to help move these products more quickly. Against her better judgment, Paige followed Liz's orders.

Liz went back to the corporate offices in New Jersey, and the sale started two days later. Paige's Labor Day business was brisk, but the store was not as crowded as she had hoped; sales were good but not great. Of all the items moving out of the store, the $5.99 sheets were going the fastest. This concerned Paige, as she feared there were not enough full-priced items being sold to mask the huge markdown which was being registered. An hour later Paige received a call from DeAnne Magnus, the Jacob Henry home furnishings buyer. DeAnne had been following the sales results through her computer terminal at the main office and had noticed that Paige's store was taking unapproved markdowns. DeAnne began screaming at Paige for placing merchandise on sale that was not authorized and for "blowing her markdown dollars" on the sale. She demanded that the sheets be taken off sale immediately and promised that Paige's store would not receive any new goods because it was obvious that Paige could not follow simple directions and could not be trusted with other goods. Paige was dumbfounded. She stammered, tried to explain, and finally said that she had followed strict orders from Liz to mark the sheets down. Besides, they were being heavily promoted in her store as they spoke. DeAnne acted confused and told Paige to hang on for a second. A few minutes later Liz was on the phone, claiming that she had not told Paige to mark those sheets down as they were not specified on the SKU markdown list.

Major Question
What should Paige do about her district manager's lie, and how would you recommend she take the sheets off sale?

Study Questions
1. Is there a way for Paige to save her reputation without ruining her relationship with her district manager or the home furnishings buyer?

2. What would you recommend Paige do to try to prevent similar problems from occurring in the future?

Case 90
To Tell—Or Not To Tell

Carolyn Olsen, Southeast Community College

The Purple Shop, a small but spacious, fashion-forward junior's shop, is located in a downtown Midwest mall. After proving herself by working through the ranks, Kathy Morgan had recently been promoted to manager at this store. Kathy received her degree from a nearby community college in fashion and her alma mater was quite proud of her accomplishments.

During her first quarter in school, Kathy, an intelligent student, had experienced some academic as well as drug problems. After the first quarter, her "friends" had failed academically, but with the help of her advisor, Kathy had improved her grade average, going on to graduate with outstanding marks. She had been working at the Purple Shop since it opened and it seemed to her family and advisor that she had overcome all of her past drug and peer-pressure problems.

Now, Kathy appeared to be handling her new position in management equally well. Sales had increased at the Purple Shop, and the store was flourishing. The district manager (DM) gave her the go-ahead to hire some more part-time employees in addition to the two that she currently employed.

In an attempt to make her part-time staff even more professional, Kathy turned to her alma mater to hire a student. Claire Lundquist, the selected student, was currently on a work-study program called cooperative education in which she received academic units for this work experience. She had set very clear goals and objectives for her quarter's work in Kathy's store. Working fifteen hours per week and going to school full-time, Claire decided to work most of her required hours on the weekends.

Because this was a fall quarter, football mania hit the city and business was brisk. Claire found herself working nearly every Saturday and realized that Kathy was also coming to work on football Saturdays. Kathy would often meet her boyfriend, a long-haired ex-jock (with a reputation for doing drugs), and leave from the store for the afternoon games nearby. After awhile, Claire noted that Kathy did not always clock out of the store before leaving for the game. But because Kathy usually returned to close the store after the game, Claire decided not to ask about this practice. However, Claire did note that Kathy was on the worksheet as manager for the day. Claire also was not sure how Kathy was paid (by the hour or by the month) so she decided to forget the clocking-out incidents, although she did mention it to her instructors at the community college.

Claire received excellent marks in her cooperative education program and made the decision to remain at the Purple Shop. Christmas trade had become very heavy when she again noticed that Kathy was clocking in and then leaving the store. Claire's fellow workers said Kathy often did this, and they felt she did so in order to shop their competitors. Again, Claire decided to keep silent about the problem because there seemed to be a logical answer to her misgivings.

In addition to the "paid breaks," Claire was also concerned by the fact that Kathy often worked alone in the shop, instead of hiring extra help or asking one of the other workers to work more hours. From her classes, Claire realized that this was a good way to encourage shoplifters and there had been several incidents of theft in the mall. Additionally, Claire knew that the store policy called for two or more employees to be on the floor during store hours.

This time, Claire decided to ask Kathy about the rule infringement. When asked about working alone, Kathy said that she was careful to never leave the floor and that a security guard was on duty in the lower level of the mall. At this time, she also indicated that she would never ask Claire to work alone as Claire was relatively inexperienced. She also indicated that because she was the manager, working alone during slow periods was a way for her to stay within her allocated budget of floor coverage hours and still allow her to allocate hours that her employees wanted. Again, Claire decided to remain silent because she liked the shop and her regular customers. But in her retail management class at college, she brought up her problems and quite a lot of discussion followed. None of the discussion made Claire feel any more at ease with Kathy, and she began to feel quite stressed by all of the pressures of work and school.

One Tuesday, the DM was scheduled to visit the store. Kathy and Claire worked very hard the night before to prepare for her visit. As Claire worked preparing for the visit, she noticed some merchandise missing and remarked on it to Kathy. Kathy replied that she had sold most of that line the night before. Claire accepted this answer with some hesitation as she had made the bank deposit and had not thought sales had been that good. Kathy had worked alone that evening, so there was really no one else to ask.

The big day arrived, and the store was spotless with every item correctly merchandised. The DM was impressed! On the premise that she wanted to interview Claire for possible promotion, the DM asked to speak to Claire alone.

The private time began as a regular interview with some of those old, tired questions like, "Tell me a little about yourself!" and "Are you happy with our store?" and "Where do you see yourself in five years?" Suddenly the tenor of the questions changed, and the DM's queries became more specific about the conditions in the store. These questions included:

• Do you or anyone else ever work alone in the store?

• Have you or anyone else ever neglected to clock out when leaving the store?

• Have you ever seen anyone taking merchandise from the store?

Major Question
How would you advise Claire to answer these questions?

Study Questions
1. Are there possible ethical compromises on the part of both Claire and Kathy?

2. Is there possible illegal behavior? If so, what should be done?

Case 91
Betty Campbell: Confronted with a Consumer Protest

Sandra Skinner Grunwell, Western Carolina University

It was the day after Thanksgiving, typically the biggest selling day of the year for Hatties' Department Store. Betty Campbell was excited. This was her first Christmas season with Hatties' as the buyer for ladies' coats. Last spring she had bought for the fall season, and her selections had brought much success for Hatties'. In October she made a special trip to market to buy for the holiday season and had gotten an excellent buy on a line of fur coats.

Although Hatties' had always had a small fur salon as part of the coat department, it had never received much recognition. Betty felt that the great buy on furs was a perfect opportunity for her to boost her success as buyer and promote Hatties' as a fashion leader by offering a luxury item to her customers at a price they could afford.

Betty knew she needed to sell the furs early in the Christmas season, otherwise there would be major markdowns. She was confident, however, that with the additional advertising dollars and window display space allotted to her department for the Christmas season, she would have no trouble selling the majority of the furs at full price. With a full page ad in the previous Sunday's paper and three window displays on Main Street promoting the furs, Betty was sure that this first day of the

From *Retailing Concepts, Strategy, and Information (3rd ed.)* by Carol H. Anderson. Reprinted by permission of West Publishing Company. Copyright © 1993. All rights reserved.

Christmas selling season was going to be her most successful selling day of the year.

Soon after the store opened at 10:00 am, a sizable group of consumers gathered outside the store's main entrance protesting Hatties' selling of furs. Slogans on posters such as "Fur is Dead," "Get a Feel for a Fur Coat; Slam a Door on Your Hand," "Buy a Fur and Slip into Something Dead," "Fur: The Look that Kills," and "It Takes up to 40 Dumb Animals to Make a Fur Coat But Only One to Wear It" decorated the street in front of the main entrance into Hatties'. Protesters distributed leaflets informing passersby of the gruesome story behind the making of fur coats. One protester, dressed in a fox costume, read the leaflet over a megaphone.

The leaflet was entitled "The Fur Industry: An Ugly Business." It stated that millions of animals killed for fur garments each year in the United States were caught in traps, including the steel-jaw leghold trap, which more than 70 countries had banned because of its extreme cruelty. Animals caught in the trap could suffer for hours or days before trappers returned. The intense pain and terror caused many animals to escape by chewing off their limbs. Animals that remained trapped faced freezing, starving, and predator attack unless the trapper arrived first to kill them by clubbing, stomping, or drowning. Traps also maimed and killed millions of what trappers called "trash" animals each year, including birds and companion dogs and cats.

The pamphlet also condemned fur "ranches." It stated that ranched furbearers suffered from crowding and confinement, which induced contagious diseases as well as self-mutilation and even cannibalism. Selective breeding techniques produced painful genetic defects. The open sheds in which the animals were raised were usually not heated or cooled. Killing methods on fur farms included poisoning with strychnine or hot, unfiltered automobile or lawnmower exhaust; neck-snapping; gassing; decompression; and anal electrocution.

Across the street in front of Nobel's Book Store, a video was being shown from a mobile unit. The video depicted animals suffering in steel jaw leg-

hold traps, and "ranched" animals living in tiny, cramped, dirty cages. It showed the animals being killed by inhumane methods that would not damage the furs. At the end of the video, celebrities disapproving of furs were interviewed. Protesters at the mobile unit passed out flyers promoting a "Rock Against Fur" concert scheduled for Saturday night and urging consumers to boycott Hatties'.

By midday the media had arrived to cover the event. Reporters had interviewed the protesters and were beginning to seek out the store manager for statements. The store manager, Mr. Cohen, was seeking out Betty. By this time both Mr. Cohen and Betty were quite upset over the negative publicity the store was getting. Mr. Cohen approached Betty asking, "What were you thinking about when you made the decision to do an all out promotion on furs, especially since it is such a sensitive issue with the public? Two other department stores in the area have recently closed their fur salons."

Betty responded heatedly, "What is wrong with furs? Man has worn fur since time began. Besides it is a luxury item that is now affordable to the average woman. It is a status symbol; it represents success. These people are just being emotional. I like furs; they feel great."

She showed Mr. Cohen a booklet on furs she had been given by one of the fur sales reps entitled "Fur the Renewable Resource." The booklet stated that the majority of furs came from ranches where the furbearing animals were raised for their fur. Ranched animals, such as mink and fox, were scientifically bred to obtain superior quality and more colors. These animals were humanely raised in spacious settings and fed excellent diets—how else could the furs look so good?

In regard to the trapping of animals, the booklet said it was a well-regulated activity and was necessary to prevent starvation and diseases, such as rabies, in wild animal populations. The booklet pointed out that everyone involved in conservation, including the fur industry, had agreed the present traps were not perfect, but they were the best available. The money from trapping licenses went toward conservation to maintain an ecological balance of nature. The booklet also mentioned that the fur industry promoted wildlife conservation and supported the protection of endangered species in every way.

"Obviously," Betty told Mr. Cohen, "the public is just misinformed."

"Certainly someone is misinformed," replied Mr. Cohen. "We need to straighten this situation out or Hatties' sales for the holidays are going to suffer. You got Hatties' into this dilemma. By tomorrow morning I want you to come up with a plan to get us out of it."

Major Question

If you were Betty, what would be your proposed plan to Mr. Cohen?

Study Questions

1. What type of information could Betty have considered before developing the fur promotion?

2. What other types of products/services have consumers boycotted? Are these boycotts successful?

Case 92
The Robinson–Patman Dilemma

Roger Dickinson, University of Texas

Ann Reider has just taken over as handbag buyer for a ten-store chain of women's fashion outlets called Ansonia Stores, located in a large eastern metropolitan area. She had been the assistant buyer in the handbag department, and prior to that she was department manager of one of the largest of the 10 stores.

Reider was superbly qualified for her job. She even had an M.B.A. from a leading business school. At school, she had been exposed to the Robinson–

Patman Act. Her impression at that time was that it was illegal for a buyer to solicit discounts from suppliers unless the buyer was sure that other stores were also being offered the same discount.

Since coming to Ansonia Stores, Reider had not heard much discussion of the Robinson-Patman Act. Irma Schultz, the buyer for whom she had worked, had never mentioned it. Reider knew that Schultz bargained very aggressively; but she did not know how, if at all, her activities were altered by the Robinson-Patman Act. As assistant buyer this did not bother her. Now, however, she is the buyer. According to the way business is conducted at Ansonia Stores, Reider has all the responsibilities for negotiation.

Reider decided that she would find out about the law. A reasonable first step was to read it. She finally located a copy of the law in the back of a book. Section 2(a), she discovered, suggested that price discrimination by the supplier was illegal if, and only if, in addition to other things, the effects of such discrimination were anticompetitive. Furthermore, Section 2(b) of the act permitted suppliers to meet competition in good faith. Reider felt that this would justify almost any action by a domestic supplier, since all other suppliers were doing almost anything imaginable to get the business, particularly with the threat of imports. Reider also found that Section 2(f), which was directed toward buyers, applied only to the prohibitions of Section 2(a), which alluded only to price discrimination. Reider felt assured that all her activities were probably legal.

Soon after her promotion, Reider ran into an attorney friend of hers at a party. During their conversation, he stated that the courts had basically ignored the anticompetitive provisions of the act. Furthermore, while the act has held buyers responsible only for price violations of the act, the courts have held that buyers were indeed responsible for other aspects of negotiation, such as advertising and services. Lastly, while the need to meet competition was a defense against violations, it was a very difficult defense for a buyer to use, mainly because much of the data on meeting competition was in the supplier's hands.

Reider was now confused. What should she do? She did not want to break the law, but what was it? She knew that bargaining was a key element in the handbag industry, and she had tried to find out the practices of other buyers. But there was no way that she could find out what other buyers in her competitive area were paying for anything. As she thought about her problem, there appeared to be three general approaches that she might use.

First, she need not bargain at all. This procedure appeared safe legally, although the Robinson-Patman Act implied that she could still be held liable because of its suggestion that it is unlawful "knowingly to induce or receive a discrimination in price which is prohibited by this section." One need not induce a discrimination; receiving the discrimination under certain condition would be enough. There were other ways to be safe within the Robinson-Patman Act. For example, a buyer might deal with suppliers who qualified in the legal sense as dealing only in intrastate traffic. She might also deal only with suppliers who sold exclusively to large stores. Presumably, the problem would not then be as important. Indeed, she might try to become the only account of a few firms, although Ansonia was probably too small a chain for this. A clear alternative was to try to develop private brands. While these did not exclude one from the Robinson-Patman Act in and of themselves, goods not of "like grade and quality" are exempt from the provisions of the act.

Another alternative that occurred to Reider was to bargain vigorously but in a manner that was likely to be considered legal. But for this it was necessary to become fairly knowledgeable about the Robinson-Patman Act. Reider would have to find out things like: (a) What does it mean for a supplier to meet competition? (b) Could a supplier meet an illegal price? (c) Who bears the burden of proof? In instances where the burden of proof is on the government, it is unlikely that any buyer would be caught. (d) What types of legal defense were permitted for the various kinds of discrimination? For example, cost defense was permissible under several conditions.

A third alternative was to disregard the Robinson-Patman Act in some intelligent manner. Most buyers did not understand it very well anyway; they lacked either the time or the legal training, or both. Reider thought most buyers bargained aggressively. But few were investigated. Nevertheless, she would conduct herself with discretion.

Major Question

Which alternative would you have chosen if you had been in Ann's position?

Study Question

Do you think buyers should have legal training? If so, how much?

Case 93
Collusion to Catch Anti-Trust Offenders

Nancy J. Rabolt, San Francisco State University
Judy K. Miler, University of Tennessee

Guido Paolluci Knitwear Company is a very successful manufacturer of medium to better knit garments. They feature knit jacquard design motifs that are produced on Italian knitting machines in the U.S. The two principals of the firm are Irving Copeland, who is "inside" handling production, purchasing, and so forth, and Bill Samuels, who is "outside"—in charge of marketing and sales functions. The firm's merchandise is well known in its field as a result of years of regular advertising in a variety of fashion magazines as well as in repeated store (cooperative) ads. The company has also received "good press" from the excellent work of its public relations agency. Guido, as the company is frequently called, is sold in many large department and specialty stores and in hundreds of better independent stores throughout the country. They have over two thousand accounts and a sales volume approaching $10 million per annum.

Meryl Alexander is the misses sportswear buyer for Benson's, a prestigious retailer in Spokane, Washington. Meryl came to Benson's from a fine specialty store in the Midwest because her husband had been transferred to his firm's new offices in Spokane. Benson's felt extremely fortunate to get someone like Meryl, who was known in her market as a fashion innovator, as well as a good promotions authority.

On one of her early buying trips to New York, Meryl went to the Guido Paolluci showroom and had a reunion with Bill Samuels. After exchanging hearty greetings and nostalgic reminiscences, Meryl got down to business and went over the line with Bill.

Benson's, in addition to its main store, has nine branches in the surrounding suburban areas. Many of the branch stores were in upper-middle class sections of the metropolitan area.

Guido had never sold to Benson's before, but Meryl, an old customer, knew the firm well and had done an excellent job with its merchandise in the past. Her first thoughts were possibilities of exclusivity of the Paolluci knits. Large retailers frequently seek to control the distribution policies of manufacturers in an effort to eliminate as much competition as possible. This is in exchange for the opportunity granted by the large store to permit the manufacturer to use the order to influence other stores in purchasing the line. When a store is not sure about carrying a line, the success of a well-regarded retailer with the line helps reinforce to the unsure store that "what is good enough for so and so, is good enough for me."

When she had reviewed the line, Meryl turned to Bill and asked a simple question: "Bill, who do you sell to in my area, and who do you intend to sell to in the immediate future?" In reply to her question, Bill told Meryl that there were six independent stores in her area that were currently carrying the Guido line. Meryl indicated that her opening order for Benson's and its branches would be much greater than those six stores' total annual purchases combined, and, of course, there was the undeniable prospect of sizable reorders.

Overcome by the probable size of the forthcoming Benson's business, Bill rapidly lost his sense of loyalty to the six independent stores. After doing some rapid mental arithmetic, Bill came to an understanding that Benson's with its branches probably would buy about two thousand pieces for the season, whereas the six smaller stores would each wind up with an average of sixty to one hundred pieces for the same period. Although Bill would like to continue to sell to the six independent stores as well, he knew that he could not have his cake and eat it, too!

He and Meryl agreed that he could not cancel the independent stores' orders because this would be a direct violation of Federal anti-trust statutes, and it was still fresh in his memory that three of the most prestigious fashion stores in the country had recently been found guilty of just such a violation. Accordingly, he agreed to kick their orders around until they "got lost" for the current season. In the future, he promised, he would dream up further measures designed to discourage the local stores from ordering the Guido line.

Soon after, the merchandise began to arrive at Benson's, and, as expected, it did very well. About this time, Jerry Peters, owner of Peter's Fashions, and Harold Tillman of Milady's, accidentally met in the bar at Rudi's, a well-known eating establishment. Being friendly non-competitors (Peter's Fashions was located in a nearby suburb, while Milady's was a downtown competitor of Benson's main store), they had a drink and decided to dine together.

During the course of the meal, Harold asked Jerry how business was and particularly how the new Guido Paolucci merchandise was moving.

"How could I know? I never received one piece of it," Jerry replied.

"Son of a gun, neither did I," mused Harold. "I wonder what's going on?"

"Hey, wait a minute, Hal," interjected Jerry, "Did you see that Benson ad on the Guido merchandise? I'll bet that's the answer—they're trying to squeeze us little guys out."

To avoid any semblance of collusion, before they parted company that evening, Harold and Jerry decided to begin simultaneous but independent action to rescue their Guido merchandise orders. They agreed to call Bill at separate intervals and, if they received no satisfaction, to have their attorneys threaten him with civil, as well as criminal, action.

They also agreed to check the other four independent stores to see if they were in the same boat.

When Jerry reached Bill in New York, he accused Guido of giving Benson's preferential treatment which, of course, Bill denied. Bill professed ignorance of the order and said he would look into the matter. Jerry then reported this conversation to Harold.

Another call to New York from Harold brought a similar response—ignorance of the order and the promise of investigation. Both men agreed that there must be collusion between Benson's and Guido's and now was the time for action.

Major Question

If you were advising Jerry and Harold, how would you go about handling this situation?

Study Questions

1. Do you think the actions of the knitwear company and retailer were illegal? Unethical?

2. What is more profitable for the manufacturer; selling to one large retail account or several smaller ones? Which is safest for the manufacturer relative to any of the companies going out of business?

3. Can you cite a recent example of small retailers being squeezed out of the market by a large retailer?

4. How can the law protect against collusion between a manufacturer and retailer to discriminate against a small retailer?

Case 94
The Bean Bag Case

Catherine Porter, University of Massachusetts

Rob and Sandy Miller own the ABC Toy Company. They manufacture foam floats and pool toys and other large items for children's playrooms. One of their most popular products has been a bean bag cushion for a young child's playroom. These bags are filled with plastic (polyethylene) beads the size of small marbles. The popular bags are covered in two layers of plastic. The inner layer is virtually puncture proof unless pierced with a very sharp object applied with force. The outer layer is a heavy duty vinyl and comes in a variety of colors.

Because the bags have been selling so well since introduced into their toy line two years ago, production has been increased to the point that the ABC Toy Company has an inventory of 15,000 ready for the Christmas selling season. Each bag is sold to the retailer for $10 with the average retail price in most stores listed at $25. The total value of the inventory at cost is $150,000.

In August, Rob and Sandy were contacted by a representative from the Consumer Product Safety Commission (CPSC) of the federal government with a formal order to stop both production and sale of the bean bag cushion. According to the CPSC representative, five children allegedly had died as the result of inhaling or swallowing the plastic beads that fill the cushion of their beanbags. The CPSC ordered a recall of every bag the company has sold to retailers around the country and that retailers in turn must recall all of the bags they have sold to their customers. The CPSC also required that the Millers give full credit to retailers for unsold inventory as well as full reimbursement for the retail price of all bags which were sold. The number of bags in stores or the homes of customers is approximately 10,000 or $100,000 in value at cost plus an additional $15 for each bag that had been sold. The Millers estimated that 9,000 bags had been sold which would mean another $225,000 in losses ($15 markup per bag above the $10 cost). In addition, the Millers are prohibited from selling any of the 15,000 bags in stock. The following illustrates the estimated loss of the recall (see Table 12.5). If the Millers stop production of the popular bean bag cushion they would have to shut down part of their operation and possibly lay off 15 employees ($\frac{2}{3}$ of their total work force of 25). They do not believe they can make up their losses by expanding the pool toy line at this time. If they are forced to abide by all of the CPSC regulations, their business would eventually have to close.

Table 12.5 Estimated Loss of Recall

	Number	Total Value
Warehouse inventory	15,000 @ $10	$150,000
Store inventory	1,000 @ $10	10,000
Sold to customers	9,000 @ $25	225,000
ESTIMATED LOSS		$385,000

Major Question

What should the Millers do?

Study Questions

1. What is the purpose of the CPSC? What type of products are they responsible for monitoring?

2. Is it fair that a government agency can interfere with a private company and put them out of business?

3. How can a company guard against such problems?

4. In addition to the financial loss the Miller's will take, what other types of losses may they possibly incur?

Case 95
The Flannel Fiber Fiasco

Connie Ulasewicz, CU Productions

Lewis & Lee is a contemporary clothing manufacturer of a line of whimsical layette items and accessories for the infant to 4T set. The line includes hats, booties, blankets, and bibs offered in bright, novelty stripes, prints, and solids. The Lewis & Lee layette collection is marketed as a 100 percent cotton, gift packaged, flannel program. The layette items are continually available for stores to reorder 12 months of the year. Lewis & Lee products have national distribution and are carried in a variety of stores including Macy's, Saks, Lullaby Lane, Bellinis, and hospital gift

shops. The manufacturer is successful because they deliver a high-quality, well-priced, natural-fiber product.

One of the fabrics with wide customer acceptance in the layette line is a 100 percent cotton flannel. Moms seem to love the softness next to their babies' skin and are willing to pay a higher price for an all cotton receiving blanket, cap, and booties from Lewis & Lee vs a polyester cotton blended flannel from their competition. Based on the success of their flannels, the company offered a second product line this past year: corduroy hats and booties lined in flannel. The products are quite sturdy and still have the softness of 100 percent flannel next to the infant's head and toes.

Finding a consistent quality of 100 percent cotton flannel available year round in solids, prints, and matching yarn dyes at an affordable price is a real challenge. The responsibility of the Lewis & Lee fabric merchandiser, Kayla Woolsey, is to swatch, sample, and test fabrics from many different resources. The fabric tests performed are for shrinkage and colorfastness. Both finished garments and fabric squares are tested. When Kayla approves a quality, an order is placed. Most of the solids and basic prints are ordered three to five months in advance through a fabric distributor in Portland, Oregon. The lead times are long because the flannels are manufactured in China. This requires long-range planning, but it has been worth it for the ability to reorder the same color and prints throughout the year and the great price received when purchasing in large quantities.

One day while taking the fabric inventory of a recent shipment, Kayla discovered a fiber content label reading 60 percent cotton/40 percent polyester stuck inside one of the rolls of fabric. The fabric and color number on the tag was the same as the flannel she had been ordering for four seasons. After looking inside several more tubes she discovered three more of these 60/40 content labels. She was shocked. Was there an error? She had order confirmations for 100 percent cotton flannel. Had she been sold 60 percent cotton/40 percent polyester goods all along with the assumption she would not know it was not 100 percent cotton? She

Glossary of Key Terms[1]

A

absolute quota is a type of *quota* in which there is a limit to the amount of any particular merchandise per year that can be brought into the U.S. (See *Chapter Five.*)

accounting and control (See *Mazur plan.*)

adjustments are reductions in the cost of goods to the retailer because of problems with the merchandise or because the items were returned. (See *Chapter Six.*)

Ad valorem **tariff** is a rate of duty that is based on a percentage of dutiable value. (See *Chapter Five.* Also see *tariff.*)

advance orders commit the retailer to a long-term delivery. Often imported goods require advance orders, as well as seasonal merchandise. (See *Chapter Six.*)

advertising is any form of paid/impersonal communication from a company. (See *Chapter Seven.*)

agile manufacturing is a new technology that incorporates modular production rather than the traditional piece goods line method and allows for special orders at the last minute without disruption. (See *Chapter Ten.*)

aisle display is a display in which merchandise might be layered and accessorized and then hung at the end of the display case. (See *Chapter Seven.*)

anchor store is a large retailing establishment that attracts considerable numbers of people to a mall and is usually located at the end of the mall (hence the term "anchor"). (See *Chapter One.*)

ancillary service (**support service/secondary service**) usually includes such services as merchandise transfers between stores, gift wrap, valet parking, alterations, and delivery. What is basic service for one store, however, may be ancillary services for another. (See *Chapter Eight.* Also see *essential service.*)

assortment is the selection of merchandise offered in a store at any given time. Descriptions of assortments are often presented in terms of breadth (i.e., number of styles) and depth (i.e., number of sizes and colors available for each style). (See *Chapter Four.*)

assortment planning is the plan for mixture of merchandise found in a store. It regards not only what vendors to carry, but the number of units and stock levels, price ranges, styles, sizes, colors, fabrics, and even the level of fashion. (See *Chapter Four.*)

automatic replenishment is a part of *quick response* in which the retail sales data gathered by computer automatically arranges for stock to be replaced when stock levels are low. (See *Chapter Ten.*)

awards are given as a type of direct compensation, which is based on recognition of a employee's meeting or exceeding a company's goal. In retail

---

[1]Within this glossary, we have cross-referenced to other glossary terms and to the appropriate chapter. These cross-references are shown in *italic* typeface.

organizations, awards are usually given to sales-people for exceeding *sales goals.* (See *Chapter Eight.* Also see *compensation.*)

B

baby boomers are those 76 million Americans born after World War II between the years 1946 and 1964. They are the largest group of consumers ever. (See *Chapter Two.*)

back orders are either full or partial orders that are still outstanding (i.e., not shipped) from the manufacturer, but will be completed when the merchandise (or the balance of the merchandise) is available. (See *Chapter Six.*)

backward integration is a form of *vertical integration* in which a company acquires another or develops a function that serves as its supplier. As an example of backward integration, The Limited acquired Mast Industries, which manufactures The Limited's apparel. (See *Chapter One.*)

bait and switch is a form of deceptive advertising in which a product is promoted at an unrealistically low price to serve as bait to the consumer. After a consumer arrives to buy this advertised product, the retailer attempts to switch the customer to a higher-priced item. (See *Chapter Twelve.*)

basic service (See *essential service.*)

basics (**staples**) are products that generally have a stable customer demand. Some examples of basics are pencils, shoelaces, jeans, T-shirts, and hosiery. (See *Chapter Three.*)

basic stock method is a merchandising method that relies on having a minimum level of stock, as a reserve stock level and also enough stock to meet projected sales each month. Basic stock is equal to the average stock for the season minus the average monthly sales. (See *Chapter Four.*)

basic stock planning is a system of developing assortment plans that involves staple merchandise. (See *Chapter Four.*)

better goods are merchandise offerings at price points between *bridge* and *moderate goods.* (See *Chapter Three.*)

big box store (See *category killer.*)

blanket orders are those that do not have specific information spelled out, but which commit the retailer to a certain number of units or dollars that will be detailed at a later date. (See *Chapter Six.*)

bonus is an extra monetary reward given to an employee, which is a type of direct *compensation* that is based on recognition of a employee's meeting or exceeding a company's goal. (See *Chapter Eight.*)

bottom-up planning involves goal setting at the lowest levels of management—and even sometimes non-management—which then filters plans up the organizational structure to the highest management level. An example of bottom-up planning is when sales volume is being predicted by the sales associates, who relay this information to the department manager, who then tells the store manager, who finally relays this to top management. (See *Chapter Four.* Also see *top-down planning.*)

boutique is a small specialty store, often owned or franchised by designers. Boutiques can offer both accessories and apparel. (See *Chapter One.*)

brand is a known name associated with a specific product or group of products carrying with it an expectation of such perceived values as style and image, quality, price, fit, reliability, consistency, and confidence that you'll look good. (See *Chapter Three.*)

breadth is a term used to refer to the number of different product lines, styles, or brands that are carried in a retailing establishment. (See *Chapter Four.*)

bridge is a merchandise level price point between *designer* or couture and *better goods.* (See *Chapter Three.*)

broad is a term that describes a merchandise assortment featuring numerous styles. (See *Chapter Four.*)

broadcast media is a type of media that includes television and radio. Broadcast media is used by retailers and manufacturers for advertising and promotion. (See *Chapter Seven.*)

broker is a *middleman* who helps negotiate business between the buyer (retailer) and seller (manufacturer). (See *Chapter Five.*)

budget goods (**popular goods**) are products sold at the most inexpensive price point, usually at discount department stores and mass merchandisers. (See *Chapter Three.* Also see *opening price point.*)

business ethics are *policies* (both written and unwritten) that deal with what is right or wrong for a company. These can be part of a company's mission statement or management philosophy. (See *Chapter Twelve.* Also see *code of ethics* and *corporate ethics.*)

buyer is an individual given formal authority to undertake the purchasing for a retailer. (See *Chapter Four.*)

buying is the purchasing of goods and/or services for the retailer to sell to the ultimate consumer. This function can be separated out as a division, as is most often the case in large organizations, or it may be combined with the operations function, as it often is in smaller companies. (See *Chapter Four.*)

C

career ladder (See *progressive management advancement.*)

career path (See *progressive management advancement.*)

catalog showroom sells merchandise from a catalog or floor samples in a warehouse-style operation. (See *Chapter One.*)

category is a major grouping of merchandise that includes all types of *departments, classifications,*

and *sub-classifications* that a particular type of customer would shop, for example, women's or men's apparel. (See *Chapter Four.*)

category killer is a specialty discounter that focuses on one product and has the best selection at the best price. This effectively "kills" the competition. (See *Chapter One.*)

centralized buying entails focusing all the purchasing activities in one place, where it is initiated and overseen by one individual or a group. Many large retailing chains use centralized buying exclusively. (See *Chapter Five.* Also see *decentralized buying.*)

chain is defined as multiple retail units, which are under common ownership and usually has centralized buying and management. Some define a chain as the same ownership having at least two stores; however, chains generally have more than two outlets. Department stores are often chains, but they may not have the same degree of corporate control as other specialty chains. (See *Chapter One.*)

chain of command (See *organizational charts.*)

charge card is a store credit account that is established in a customer's name and purchases are billed to their address. Many stores have found that this is a successful way to issue credit to their customers and, ultimately, increase sales. Also, many stores benefit financially from the interest charged on this type of account. (See *Chapter Eight.*)

class (See *classification.*)

classification (**class**) is a group of items (or the same general type of merchandise that is housed within a department), for example, sportswear or eveningwear. (See *Chapter Four.*)

closed/closed-back display is a traditional store window display or enclosure with solid backings that isolate the merchandise to be presented. (See *Chapter Seven.*)

closed-island display is a type of display in which the merchandise is enclosed (and sometimes locked) behind glass. It provides less customer access, which results in fewer thefts, but also possibly fewer sales because of the intimidation factor. (See *Chapter Seven.* Also see *showcase display.*)

closeout is an *assortment* of merchandise that is left over from a seasonal line. Usually closeouts include all remaining items and are sold at a discount. (See *Chapter Five.*)

code of ethics is a written policy that states what a company has decided is ethical and unethical behavior. (See *Chapter Twelve.*)

commissions are monetary *awards* based on achievement of goals. These are usually given to salespeople as an incentive to achieve a *sales goal* or to increase sales. Commissions are generally based on a percentage of sales. (See *Chapter Five.*)

company rep (**corporate rep**) is a *sales representative* who works exclusively for a supplier and is a company employee. (See *Chapter Six.*)

compensation rewards employees for work they have accomplished and/or goals that they have met or have exceeded. This compensation may be direct or indirect. Direct compensation is the awarding of such monetary payment as salaries or wages (cash payment), *commissions* (monetary rewards based on achievement of goals and usually a percentage of sales), *bonuses* (extra rewards), and prizes and *awards* (recognition). Indirect compensation involves non-monetary rewards, which can include paid vacations, paid insurance, parking, retirement, and other *perks*. (See *Chapter Eight.*)

compound duty/tariff is a rate of duty that is a combination of both *Ad valorem tariff* and *specific tariff.* (See *Chapter Five.*)

computer-aided design (**CAD**) is a computer technology that enables products (e.g., apparel) to be designed and augmented on a computer. This technology can significantly decrease production time for a company. Generally, it is only the large manufacturers that utilize this sophisticated technology because of the initial high capital investment. However, smaller companies can take

advantage of some parts of this technology by working with contractors specializing in such processes as computer marker making. (See *Chapter Ten.*)

computer-aided manufacturing (**CAM**) is a computer technology that enables manufacturers to significantly decrease production time by using computers to do formerly labor-intensive work. Computerized grading and marker making are most commonly used; however, cutting controlled by computer, lasers for specialized cutting, and robotics are all currently being utilized to decrease the use of manual labor. Generally, it is only the large manufacturers that utilize this sophisticated technology because of the initial high capital investment. However, smaller companies can take advantage of some parts of this technology by working with contractors specializing in such processes as *computer-aided design* or computer marker making. (See *Chapter Ten.*)

consignment is a term used for merchandise not paid for by a retailer until it is sold. Usually the retailer will keep a percentage of the price and the consignee retains the remainder. (See *Chapter Eleven.*)

Consumer Product Safety Commission (**CPSC**) is an independent regulatory agency charged with overseeing consumer protection. The CPSC regulates flammability requirements of both apparel and home furnishings and monitors other product safety. (See *Chapter Twelve.*)

contact selling (See *wholesale selling.*)

continuing education can be in the form of seminars or classes, which teach specific job skills or product knowledge. Usually, this type of ongoing training is done as the need arises. It is an effective way in which successful retailers help to motivate and to refresh management and/or assist employees to learn and to advance into higher management levels. (See *Chapter Nine.*)

contractor is an independent producer who performs specific aspects of manufacturing, such as sewing, cutting, and finishing. (See *Chapter Five.*)

controls are the methods employed to help a retailer track the business to see how it is doing and how effective the merchandising strategies are. (See *Chapter Four.* Also see *Mazur plan.*)

convenience goods are products that are purchased with relatively little evaluation as compared to *shopping goods* and *specialty goods.* (See *Chapter Three.*)

cooperative advertising normally involves retailers and suppliers sharing the costs of advertising. Generally, retailers are reimbursed for part of the cost of the ad by vendors upon receipt of tear sheets (copies of the ad). Another type of coop advertising is when a group of merchants cooperate and run one ad that benefits all of the retailers. (See *Chapter Seven.*)

corporate ethics refer to practices specific to the company, for example, accepting gifts, kickbacks, or false record-keeping. Sometimes a company's statement of philosophy incorporates its *code of ethics.* (See *Chapter Twelve.* Also see *business ethics.*)

corporate rep (See *company rep.*)

corporation is a firm owned by one or more persons, each of whom has a financial interest. A corporation allows capital to be raised through the sale of company stock and does not allow legal claims against individuals, as is the case with sole proprietorships and partnerships. (See *Chapter One.*)

counterfeit is a type of merchandise that violates a company's intellectual property rights. The law states that a protected trademark or copyright cannot be copied and offered for sale by another company. (See *Chapter Twelve.*)

counter top display is a merchandise display in which the merchandise can be touched and self-selected by the customer. (See *Chapter Seven.*)

credit is an alternative to paying cash. It allows the customer to buy merchandise now, and pay for it later. There are many national and regional credit companies that issue credit cards that are widely accepted by retailers. Even though the

stores do not benefit financially from the interest charged on these accounts (as they do with *charge cards*), acceptance of these cards is a convenience afforded to their customers that can ultimately increase patronage and sales. (See *Chapter Eight.*)

customer segmentation (See *target marketing.*)

customer service is assisting customers by providing retail activities. Prompt and courteous service is what most customers look for from retailers today because this type of effective customer service supplements the value received from a retailer. Customer service should also supplement and facilitate sales. The service given and offered to customers plays a very real role in creating the customers' perception of the store and the image they have of the retailer. (See *Chapter Eight.*)

D

dating refers to setting a predetermined amount of time during which discounts can be taken and the invoice is to be paid; for example 8/10 EOM means the retailers can take an eight percent discount if the invoice is paid by the 10th day of the month. (See *Chapter Six.*)

decentralized buying centers the purchasing activities at the local or retail-store level. (See *Chapter Five.* Also see *centralized buying.*)

deep is a term that refers to a merchandise *assortment* of many colors and sizes. (See *Chapter Four.*)

demographics are used to identify and count groups of people, including population factors of age, gender, income, education, marital status, religion, family size, life-cycle stage, ethnicity, and mobility, among others. Demographics are used by retailers because they are often linked to marketplace needs and are relatively easy to access. (See *Chapter Two.*)

department is a segment of a retailing establishment that groups *classifications* of merchandise together that are complementary to one another, such as a junior department or a men's department. (See *Chapter Four*.)

department store is a large retailer that carries an extensive assortment of merchandise organized into separate departments. The U.S. Bureau of Census uses three criteria to define department stores: 1) at least 25 employees; 2) must carry dry goods and household items, family apparel, and furniture and home furnishings; and 3) $10 million in sales with some stipulations. Both the traditional department store like Macy's and the full-line discount store, such as Kmart, qualify for this definition. However, today we often refer to other specialty stores such as Nordstrom and Saks Fifth Avenue as department stores—even though they don't carry furniture. (See *Chapter One*.)

depth refers to the number of units within a product line, style, or brand. (See *Chapter Four*.)

designer collection is the most expensive, high-end line produced by a designer. (See *Chapter Three*.)

destination store is a type of retailer that a customer shops because only it can provide the product or service that the customer wants. *Discount Store News* defines this as a "magnet" for customers, distinguishing it from other retailers that customers also patronize. Customers make special efforts to go to destination stores. (See *Chapter One*.)

direct compensation (See *compensation*.)

direct mail is used by both retailers and manufacturers, to send flyers, catalogs, or other literature to target customers. (See *Chapter Seven*.)

direct marketing is a broad term that includes many forms of non-personal communication, for example, mailed catalogs, flyers, radio, magazine, and newspapers. It also includes forms of personal communication, such as telemarketing and TV home shopping, in which customers call "800" numbers to order merchandise. (See *Chapters One* and *Seven*.)

direct selling involves direct sales contact with the customer. This includes two major kinds of selling: 1) *wholesale selling*; and 2) *retail selling*. (See *Chapter Eight*.)

discounts lower the retail price to a consumer. At retail establishments, discounts are commonly given to employees and special customers. (See *Chapter Four*.)

discounts and allowances are price concessions given by a vendor to a retailer in return for certain actions that the retailer is taking, which may not be what was originally arranged. (See *Chapter Six*.)

discount stores sell merchandise at prices lower than other traditional department and specialty stores due to lower operating costs. Generally, they offer self-service and large quantity purchases to lower costs. Kmart and Wal-Mart are considered discount stores. (See *Chapter One*.)

division is the largest breakdown of merchandise for a retailer. It contains *categories, departments, classifications,* and *sub-classifications*. Examples of divisions are: soft goods, hard goods, women's and children's. (See *Chapter Four*.)

dollar plan forecasts the merchandising activities for a department or store for a specific period of time. Dollar planning is regarded as the money budget preparation of retail dollars to meet sales plans. (See *Chapter Four*.)

domestic market refers to a *market* in the continental U.S., such as New York City. (See *Chapter Five*. Also see *international market* and *regional market*.)

domestic source/sourcing is the purchasing of merchandise within the borders of the U.S. (See *Chapter Five*. Also see *international source/sourcing, sourcing*.)

door-to-door selling is also referred to as direct-to-home selling and includes personal contact with consumers in their homes and through telephone solicitations. Cosmetics, household goods, encyclopedias, and vacuum cleaners are often sold direct to consumers without a retail store middleman. (See *Chapter One.*)

drop shipper takes title to merchandise, but does not take actual possession of the goods. A drop shipper just arranges shipment of the goods to the retailer. (See *Chapter Five.*)

duty (See *tariff.*)

E

electronic data interchange (**EDI**) is a communications system that electronically transfers information from one point to another via computer. An important application is the transfer of purchase orders between manufacturers and retailers. This is one way that vendors and retailers can respond instantaneously to quickly changing consumer demands. (See *Chapter 10.*)

electronic-mail (e-mail) is a technology that can help companies to effortlessly communicate with headquarters or other companies to determine exact availability of goods (i.e., quantities, styles, and sizes for each ship date) and lock in and guarantee an order on the spot when working with customers. Some companies are using systems that can be hooked up to any phone jack and that allow reps to access the company mainframe. This greatly speeds up the time of order processing from conventional mail. (See *Chapter Ten.*)

electronic retailing offers products through such electronic media as computers and television. Shopping on the *Internet* is the newest technological retail format of on-line retailing. (See *Chapter 10.*)

employee turnover is the percentage of employees that begin with a company at a certain time period but do not remain employed at the end of that set time period. This percentage figure is usually calculated on an annual basis. Generally, healthy turnover is considered 40 percent, while 70 percent is considered unhealthy by retailers and their researchers. Employee turnover, particularly at the sales and entry level management positions, is an unfortunate major financial problem for retailers, which is always being examined by retailers in order to improve it. (See *Chapter Eight.*)

entrepreneur/entrepreneurial leader is a person who is a leader, is a visionary, and has the ability to see and evaluate business opportunities, bringing together the factors of production in such a way that new wealth is created as their business grows. Some feel an entrepreneur also must possess a certain inventive genius. Entrepreneurs have a dream. They start without followers and proclaim their beliefs publicly, risking being wrong. They are inspirational. If they believe wholeheartedly and can demonstrate that to others, followers will join in the dream. (See *Chapter Eleven.* Also see *leader* and *leadership.*)

entrepreneurial process can be seen in one of five ways: 1) introduction of a new product or of improved quality; 2) introduction of a new method of production; 3) opening of a new market; 4) conquest of a new source of supply of materials; and 5) carrying out a new organization of an industry. (See *Chapter Eleven.*)

environmental factors come from both an internal (inside) and external (outside) perspective. External environmental factors include aspects of technology, the economy, society, and culture, along with political and legal issues that impact the business and the customer being considered. Internal environmental factors include information from store records to the store's particular culture and vendors. (See *Chapter Four.*)

environmentally friendly is a term that refers to products that are made with an attempt to incorporate only environmentally safe methods and materials in its production. (See *Chapter Twelve.*)

essential services (**primary services/basic services**) are those services that most retailers provide, for example, mirrors, dressing rooms, parking, and someone to ring up your sale pleasantly. (See *Chapter Eight.* Also see *ancillary services.*)

ethics are rules or standards based on moral duties and obligations by which society evaluates conduct. They furnish criteria for distinguishing between right and wrong. (See *Chapter Twelve.* Also see *business ethics, code of ethics, corporate ethics,* and *personal ethics.*)

evaluation (of sales associates) helps to monitor their work and also informs the employee of job performance. Additionally, the evaluation of a salesperson's performance can aid in bettering the work that is done and this contributes to the improvement of the retailer's performance. Evaluating salespeople should include a performance review on a regular basis. (See *Chapter Eight.* Also see *formal review* and *informal review.*)

even priced is a term used for prices ending with numbers that can be divided evenly. Odd price point endings, such as .95 or .99, often reflect sale merchandise, while .00 or evenly divisible numbers usually indicate non-sale prices. (See *Chapter Four.*)

exclusive contractor is a supplier that only works for a particular company. (See *Chapter Five.*)

exclusive orders are those orders that are placed for merchandise that can only be sold to one particular store or buyer. Exclusive merchandise is usually a special arrangement between vendor and retailer. (See *Chapter Five.*)

expenses are the costs incurred by a business to generate sales. (See *Chapter Four.*)

extrinsic rewards are those tied to material gain, for example, raises, promotions, and recognition within a company. (See *Chapter Nine.* Also see *intrinsic rewards.*)

F

factory outlet is a manufacturer-owned store that sells the manufacturer's closeouts, overruns, canceled orders, discontinued items, and irregulars. (See *Chapter One.*)

factory outlet mall is a mall composed of several *factory outlet* stores. (See *Chapter One.*)

fair trade laws formerly protected the small retailer from larger retailers when both were selling the same goods at the same price, since large retailers were not allowed to receive a discount for quantity purchases. In 1975, the Consumer Goods Pricing Act repealed all resale price maintenance laws and enabled retailers to sell products below the suggested retail prices that were set by manufacturers. Although this ended protection for the small retailer, it allowed consumers to buy at the lowest possible free-market price. (See *Chapter Twelve.*)

fashion cycle (product life cycle) represents the stages of a product's life cycle and the adoption level of consumers of a particular style at each stage. (See *Chapter Two.*)

fashion followers are consumers who adopt a new fashion after the *fashion leaders* do; they are also sometimes called emulators. (See *Chapter Two.*)

fashion forward is a term used to describe designers, retailers, consumers, and merchandise that represent the newest, latest styles. (See *Chapter Two.*)

fashion goods are thought of as something new, in demand, or popular—at any particular time. They are less stable, have a short life span, and therefore are more risky (financially) than basics. (See *Chapter Three.*)

fashion leaders are the first group of consumers to adopt new fashions. (See *Chapter Two.* Also see *fashion followers* and *fashion forward.*)

fashion seminar is a discussion of new fashions in order to attract audiences into stores and malls, and to promote new, seasonal merchandise. (See *Chapter Seven.*)

fashion show is a live presentation of new, seasonal merchandise. (See *Chapter Seven.*)

Federal Trade Commission (FTC) is an independent regulatory agency charged with overseeing the area of consumer protection and restraint of trade. Within the purview of the FTC are labeling requirements for apparel. These include: the Textile Fiber Products Identification Act, which requires generic fiber identification, manufacturer identification, and country of origin; the Permanent

Care Labeling Act, which requires care labels to be placed in most apparel items; and legislation covering fur and wool products labeling. The FTC also monitors the legal aspects of business advertising. (See *Chapter Twelve.*)

finance (See *Mazur plan.*)

financial plan is a part of a merchandising plan that includes an estimate of start-up costs and the amount of financing required. It should include performance objectives, estimated sales, and cash flow. (See *Chapter Eleven.*)

financier (See *venture capitalist.*)

first-line, entry level manager is the lowest level of management and which includes supervisors and assistant managers. (See *Chapter Nine.*)

Food and Drug Administration (**FDA**) is a federal agency that is responsible for regulating the food, drug, and cosmetics industries in regard to the safety of and disclosure of ingredients of products. (See *Chapter Twelve.*)

forecasting is a term used to describe the prediction of styles and trends. These predictions assist retailers in making both long- and short-term merchandising decisions. (See *Chapter Four.*)

formal evaluation (See *management evaluation.*)

formal management training is usually supervised or directed, and follows a program that involves the accomplishment of certain set goals. Training can involve working with new employees or can entail working with established employees, but who may be changing positions. (See *Chapter Nine.* Also see *informal management training.*)

formal reviews use time set aside on a periodic basis to meet one-on-one with the salesperson to go over their accomplished work. Additionally, feedback can be given on performance at these formal reviews. (See *Chapter Eight.* Also see *evaluation* and *informal review.*)

formal training is structured training that involves teaching specific tasks, methods, and/or

other objectives. This method of training relies on a person(s) and/or written instructions, which is used to relay the information to be taught. Sometimes formal training may be taught in a classroom in much the same way as school. Another example is a salesperson learning from a *sales manual* with instructions on how the job is to be performed. (See *Chapter Eight.* Also see *informal training.*)

forward integration is a form of *vertical integration* in which a company acquires another company or develops a function that serves as its customer. Examples include manufacturers that have retail outlets for their products. (See *Chapter One.*)

franchise is a contractual arrangement between a franchisor (the entity selling its name) and a franchisee (the owner). A franchise combines independent ownership with franchisor-management assistance, which includes a well-known name and image. The franchisee pays royalties for the privilege of using the company name. (See *Chapter One.*)

free rate of duty is a rate of duty in which there is no monetary collection, hence it is commonly called "duty free." (See *Chapter Five.*)

full service is a type of overall customer service that is provided to the customer by a retail establishment. Full service implies the maximum amount of services that can be expected. These services include *essential* and *ancillary services,* as well as all possible *transactional services.* A full-service department store today, for example, would accept both cash and *credit* (or provide their own store *charge card*), provide for returns, exchanges, delivery, alterations, private dressing rooms, restrooms, personal shoppers, gift wrap, and probably a restaurant or snack bar; customers would expect all regular department stores to provide these services. (See *Chapter Eight.*)

G

General Agreement on Tariffs and Trade (**GATT**) is a multinational agreement regarding global trade policies. In international trade of textiles and apparel, GATT allows for the use of *tariffs* to protect domestic industries and for quantitative limits (*quotas*) on the entry of certain textile and apparel merchandise in the U.S. from specified countries during a specified period of time. (See *Chapter Five.*)

generation X is a term used to describe the population group born following the *baby boomers*. (See *Chapter Two.*)

goals are the objectives for which a company and its employees strive. (See *Chapter Eight.* Also see *sales goals.*)

gray market goods is a term used to describe merchandise that is not illegal, but is an unauthorized import. Often such goods are sold at discounters with no warranty or with older dates than those through authorized channels. Fragrances, for example, may have been on shelves for longer than the recommended product life. The prices, however, are lower, which benefits the consumer. There is an on-going campaign to make gray goods illegal. (See *Chapter Twelve.*)

gross margin is the difference between the net sales and the cost of goods sold and usually is an indicator of profit. (See *Chapter Four.*)

guarantee is issued by a manufacturer and ensures that a product will perform as it is supposed to or the customer will be compensated. (See *Chapter Eight.* Also see *warranty.*)

H

hard goods include home furnishings, appliances, electronics, and so forth. (See *Chapter Three.* Also see *soft goods.*)

hierarchical structure (See *organizational charts.*)

high fashion is apparel that is produced and priced for that small percentage of the population who want something new and different from mass fashion, with the added panache of exclusivity. High fashion products are generally high-priced because of these factors. (See *Chapter Three.*)

home party is a non-stored retailing format consisting of merchandise showings in the home to guests or customers. (See *Chapter One.*)

horizontal integration is one company buying, merging, or forming another company that is different than its customer or supplier. (See *Chapter One.*)

house-to-house selling (See *retail selling.*)

human resources department (**personnel department**) often plays a major role in training and evaluating the retailer's sales personnel, particularly when the retailer is large enough to have a separate division or department for this function. The specific role human resources plays within a retailer varies, depending on the size of the company and staff, but in general it is involved with employees and their well being/problems. Four major areas are usually allocated to the human resource function: recruiting, training, evaluating, and rewarding. Hiring and firing may also be done centrally by this department. (See *Chapter Eight.*)

I

identity is a consistent, well-articulated company mission, including the nature, purpose, and direction of the company. (See *Chapter Two.*)

image is a term used to describe the perception customers have of a company or a product. (See *Chapter Two.*)

imports are goods and services that are purchased from other countries. (See *Chapter Five.*)

impulse goods are goods that are purchased with little or no planning on the part of the consumer. (See *Chapter Three.*)

income statement (See *profit and loss statement.*)

independent buying office is owned and operated separately from its client retailers. Its functions can also include forecasting, finance, personnel, advertising and promotion, as well as providing consultation services and the manufacture of private-label merchandise. (See *Chapter*

Five. Also see *resident buying office, store-owned buying office.*)

independent rep is a *sales representative* who may be under contract to a specific company as their sales agent, but who may also represent other firms and is paid a commission on sales. (See *Chapter Six.*)

independent store is a single retailing unit owned by an individual or a group of individuals, but is not connected to any chain of stores. (See *Chapter One.*)

indirect compensation involves non-monetary rewards given to employees, which can include paid vacations, paid insurance, parking, retirement, and other *perks.* (See *Chapter Eight.* Also see *direct compensation.*)

informal evaluation (See *management evaluation.*)

informal management training is the type of training in which managers are expected to learn their job "on-the-job," taking the initiative themselves. (See *Chapter Nine.* Also see *formal management training.*)

informal reviews consist of feedback given at any time it is needed. Some experts believe that this is the more effective means of evaluation, because it is given at the same time as the incident that warrants the feedback. (See *Chapter Eight.* Also see *management evaluation* and *formal review.*)

informal training relies on employees learning skills as they work (i.e., on-the-job training) and as they need to learn specific skills. In this type of training, employees are often solely responsible for learning what they believe they need, rather than what their employer thinks is necessary. (See *Chapter Eight.* Also see *formal training.*)

institutional advertising is concerned with building a company's reputation or *image* rather than selling a product. They may illustrate the good deeds a company is doing in the community, the services it offers, or the prestige it maintains or desires. (See *Chapter Seven.*)

intangible services are those abstract activities provided by a retail establishment that cannot be touched physically, for example, assistance with decision-making and merchandise selection. These intangibles can be product-use displays, convenient store hours, and personal assistance. The purchased merchandise is, of course, tangible, but the aid from the display or the salesperson is not. (See *Chapter Eight.* Also see *tangible services.*)

intellectual property includes patents, copyrights, and trademarks. Infringement of any of these is illegal. (See *Chapter Twelve.*)

interactive kiosks are free-standing computerized units that enable retailers to carry smaller inventories than conventional stores. Some manufacturers are using interactive kiosks as an outlet in stores to better represent themselves. Using a computer, customers can find out immediately if the company has their size in stock, feed in order information, and have a finished product shipped either to the store or to a residence. (See *Chapter Ten.*)

interior product displays help customers locate merchandise and can illustrate how the merchandise is used or worn. They include *counter top* or *point-of-purchase displays, showcase displays, wall* or *ledge displays, aisle displays, open selling displays,* and *closed-island displays.* (See *Chapter Seven.*)

international market is a *market* that could be located anywhere in the world and that draws buyers from around the world. Paris, London, Milan, and Tokyo are just a few of the larger international markets. (See *Chapter Five.* Also see *domestic market* and *regional market.*)

international source/sourcing is the process of buying of goods *offshore,* from countries other than the U.S. (See *Chapter Five.* Also see *import, domestic source/sourcing, sourcing.*)

Internet is an on-line, worldwide network of computers, which is used for the exchange of information. The Internet is being used by retailers to market and advertise products, as well as to sell them. This technology ultimately works in much the same way as a store, however, it is generally used the consumer on a home computer. Shopping on the Internet is the newest technological retail format of online retailing. (See *Chapter Ten.*)

internships are structured methods of training employees to become managers, while students are still enrolled in college. Management/executive training and internship training can be classroom and/or on-the-job, at headquarters and/or at the retail store level. (See *Chapter Nine.*)

intrinsic rewards are those personal rewards that are given to employees and which fill that individual's needs such as self-esteem. (See *Chapter Nine.* Also see *extrinsic rewards.*)

inventory (stock) planning entails the determination of the stock levels necessary to meet the sales plan. Note: the terms inventory and stock are used interchangeably. (See *Chapter Four.* Also see *basic stock planning* and *model stock planning.*)

J

jobber is a resource that sells *closeouts* and *job lots.* (See *Chapter Five.*)

job description (See *job roles.*)

job lot is a group of merchandise that is odds and ends of remaining styles, which a manufacturer wants to sell. Often it consists of broken sizes, colors, and/or styles and is sold at a considerable discount as a group. (See *Chapter Five.*)

job promotion occurs when an employee is advanced into a higher level position. (See *Chapter Nine.* Also see *progressive management advancement.*)

job roles designate the part an employee plays for an employer, while job descriptions spell these roles out and clarify them. Job titles may also help to identify those roles and responsibilities a particular position denotes. (See *Chapter Nine.*)

job title (See *job roles.*)

just-in-time (JIT) is a concept used in manufacturing to lessen costly inventories. On-line communications and partnerships with suppliers enable fabric and other supplies to be delivered to the manufacturing site "just-in-time" for production. (See *Chapter Ten.*)

K

key resource list (See *vendor matrix.*)

keystone markup is a *markup* that doubles the cost of the merchandise. Essentially, it is a 50 percent retail markup. (See *Chapter Four.*)

kickback is an illegal return of part of monies received in a business deal, which has been prompted by a threat or secret agreement. (See *Chapter Twelve.*)

kiosk is a small stationary facility used as advertising venue or sometimes has the capability of customer ordering of merchandise through a computer. (See *Chapter One.* Also see *interactive kiosk.*)

knockoff is a copy of a new (or *fashion forward*) style that has been accepted by consumers. It is usually made with less-expensive fabrication and detailing and is produced and sold at lower-price points. (See *Chapter Two.*)

L

layaway is a way of delaying payment for goods. Payment amounts are scheduled to be made on merchandise that is held by the store until all the payments have been received and then the customer takes ownership of the goods. This method enables customers to purchase goods ahead of need and obtain clear title with possession. (See *Chapter Eight.*)

leaders are people who have qualities and/or abilities that emerge to influence and direct others. Common characteristics of a leader include having a realistic, clear vision of a goal, the means to accomplish it, and the ability and means to communicate the vision to inspire others. (See *Chapters Nine* and *Eleven.*)

leadership is the process of moving a group in a direction that is in their long-term best interests. *Leaders* must demonstrate strength and the ability to carry the followers. (See *Chapters Nine* and *Eleven*. Also see *entrepreneur/entrepreneurial leader*.)

lead time refers to the amount of time that lapses between the placement of an order and the arrival of the merchandise at the retail establishment. (See *Chapter Five*.)

ledge display utilizes dead or unused store ledge space to display merchandise. (See *Chapter Seven*.)

licensed goods carry the name of a famous person, character, or company. In this arrangement, a company allows a marketer to sell a product with its registered trademark or logo (for example, Mickey Mouse nightshirts). (See *Chapter Three*.)

lifestyle is a term that is used to describe how people spend their time and money. (See *Chapter Two*.)

limited assortment store (See *specialty store*.)

limited service provides a modicum of assistance to the customer beyond the *self-service* level, but still in restricted amounts. For example, a store that has hours from 10 to 5, has a small sales staff, takes credit cards, does not gift wrap or deliver merchandise but has alterations available can be described as having limited service. (See *Chapter Eight*. Also see *full service*.)

line (See *organizational charts*.)

long-range planning entails looking toward the future for a business and projects goals of five or more years. (See *Chapter Four*.)

loss leader is a term used to describe merchandise that is priced at or below cost to attract customers. (See *Chapter Four*.)

M

magazines are publications that are generally geared to a national audience and provide good-quality, expensive print and color for ads. Many national magazines, produce regional editions in which an ad can be targeted to local retailers. Because they are often published monthly, these ads are generally more image related than geared toward immediate customer reaction. (See *Chapter Seven*.)

mail order is a form of non-store retailing in which customers typically purchase products from a catalog. Mail order can be an extension of a store's business for example. (See *Chapter One*.)

mail selling (See *retail selling*.)

management is the process of getting activities completed efficiently and effectively with and through other people. A business usually has at least three management aspects: 1) the business; 2) the employees; and 3) the operations. (See *Chapter Nine*.)

management by objectives (**MBO**) is a method of *management evaluation* that is a way of involving managers in monitoring their own progress and success on the job. In this method *managers* play an active part in setting their own *management* goals. (See *Chapter Nine*.)

management by walking around is a *management* technique that places the *manager* in the work site, interacting directly with employees. (See *Chapter Nine*.)

management evaluation/review should be conducted by the manager's immediate supervisor as a means to communicate how that manager is performing. These evaluations can be formal evaluations and/or informal evaluations and should provide feedback on the work that is being completed. This evaluation may occur after a task is completed or after a specific period of time. Formal evaluations of employees are usually held annually or semi-annually and they are often tied to rewards and promotions. (See *Chapter Nine*.)

managers are the people who have been given formal authority and power to direct, supervise, and motivate employees to complete those activities that ensure that a company's needs are met. (See *Chapter Nine*.)

manufacturers offer goods for sale that they have produced. Manufacturers are also referred to as vendors, suppliers, or resources, and these terms often are used interchangeably.

markdown is a lowering of a retail price. This can be either *promotional* or *permanent* and will either adjust the initial retail price downward temporarily or set a new retail price, respectively. (See *Chapter Four.*)

market is the actual physical place where the retail buyer and seller come together to purchase or sell goods and services. This marketplace may be at a *merchandise mart* or *trade show,* or even a specific city site as in New York City. A market may also refer to a time when buyers and manufacturers come together, such as the Spring market. Markets coincide with the seasonal delivery of goods by the manufacturer and are set up according to type of merchandise. For example, there are men's wear markets and women's wear markets. (See *Chapter Five.*)

market calendar publicizes the dates (called market weeks) and locations of trade shows and *markets* that are available. (See *Chapter Five.*)

marketing plan is a part of a business plan that includes an analysis of the business environment that should support the definition of the designated target market. (See *Chapter Eleven.*)

market research includes the collection and analysis of data relating to such issues as store location, target-market profiling, the determination of the target consumer's needs and wants, company image, promotion, and so forth. Research provides data on which to base decisions and thus reduces some risks. Market research should be a continuous process providing information for planning and decision-making. (See *Chapter Two.*)

market week (See *market calendar.*)

markon (See *markup.*)

markup cancellations adjust the amount of *markup* that was put on an item originally, thereby lowering the retail price. (See *Chapter Four.*)

markup (**markon**) is the difference between the manufacturer's cost and the retail price offered to the customer. To realize profit, a retailer must sell merchandise for more than it costs. (See *Chapter Four.*)

mass customization allows for individualized sizing to be incorporated into regular mass production. (See *Chapter Ten.* Also see *narrowcasting.*)

mass fashion appeals to the majority of consumers and is produced and distributed at moderate or *opening price points* at both discount and department stores. Consumers who buy mass fashion are not *fashion leaders,* but still want to be in fashion. (See *Chapter Three.*)

mass merchandiser is a large discount store that serves the mass market. (See *Chapter One.*)

Mazur plan divides retail activities into four divisional areas. Descriptions of the responsibilities of the four major retail divisions are: 1) merchandising, which is the buying and selling of goods and services for a profit. This includes the planning, pricing, and control of sales and inventory; 2) publicity, which is concerned with promotion and advertising, display, special events, and public relations; 3) store (operations) management, which involves the operations of the retail store, selling, customer service, and all such physical concerns for the store as maintenance and security; 4) accounting and control (finance), which is concerned with all the financial aspects of the business, including credit, collection, budgets, control, and bookkeeping. Retailers vary the configuration of their organizational charts from this four-function chart to accommodate the size and type of their company and how their company is structured. Some retailers may also have a fifth divisional area to account for and handle their branch stores. Others may be organized according to regions and/or divisions. All retailers, however, must have at least two functional areas—merchandising and store operations management—to run the business. (See *Chapter Nine.*)

merchandise budget is a monetary plan that forecasts the merchandising activities for a department or store for a specific period of time. (See *Chapter Four.*)

merchandise mart is a trade center built to house manufacturer's representatives and provide a center for retailers and manufacturers to come together to do business. Major marts are located in such metropolitan areas as Dallas, Atlanta, and Chicago. Secondary marts are located in such smaller cities as Charlotte, Pittsburgh, and Seattle. (See *Chapter Five.*)

merchandise mix (See *assortment.*)

merchandise planner is an employee of a retail organization whose sole responsibility is to predict, distribute, and control merchandise at their stores. (*See Chapter Four.*)

merchandise planning is a broad term that describes those retailing activities that are based in planning. It directly involves the five "rights" of merchandising that Mazur brought to our attention. These are: purchasing the right merchandise, at the right time, at the right place, in the right quantities, and at the right price. (See *Chapter Four.*)

merchandiser (See *purchasing agent.*)

merchandising is the buying and selling of goods and/or services for the purpose of making a profit. (See *Chapter Four.* Also see *Mazur plan.*)

middleman is a term used to describe an agent who processes goods in one way or another from the manufacturer to the retail distributor. For example, a manufacturer produces a garment and does not do the finishing or packaging but sends the garment to another company (the middleman) for these steps. (See *Chapter Five.*)

middle manager is a management position that includes department heads, managers, divisionals, and buyers. (See *Chapter Nine.*)

minimum orders designate a specific amount of merchandise that must be purchased from a vendor in order to place an order. (See *Chapter Six.*)

misleading advertising is a form of consumer deception and is illegal. If a manufacturer's claims

are untrue or misleading, a cease and desist order can be issued by the *Federal Trade Commission,* putting a halt to such claims. (See *Chapter Twelve.*)

model stock planning sets a determination of merchandise levels according to factors important to the buyer, for example, fabric, price, style, and so forth. A model stock plan is for fashion and/or seasonal merchandise within a particular merchandise category. (See *Chapter Four.*)

moderate goods are lower in price and quality than better goods and are sold at many department stores. (See *Chapter Three.*)

mom and pop store is a small, privately owned, independent store that is owned and operated by the proprietor with perhaps a few employees. Often these stores are run by a husband and wife, hence "mom and pop." (See *Chapter One.*)

morale refers to the state of enthusiasm and happiness of employees. It is often very difficult—if not impossible—to keep all employees happy, because of the nature of individuality. Research shows, however, that high morale in a company contributes to happier employees, which translates to the customers, very often resulting in higher sales and greater profit. Conversely, low morale is rarely conducive to company success. Morale is reflected in the attitude of employees and this attitude is relayed to other employees and/or customers, creating a kind of chain reaction. A positive attitude helps to create better customer service, which, in turn, helps to retain customers. *Managers* can play a direct role in developing high morale within an organization. A good manager can behave and act in ways that relay appreciation and value to those they supervise. Because employee morale can directly impact a business, it is an important issue for all managers to understand. (See *Chapter Nine.*)

moral obligations (See *prima facie duties.*)

motivation is the drive to stimulate action. *Managers* are usually responsible for motivating others, based on the needs or goals of the company.

Often motivation is tied to rewarding the employee. (See *Chapter Nine*. Also see *extrinsic rewards* and *intrinsic rewards*.)

Multifiber Arrangement (**MFA**) is the general framework for international textile trade that operates under the authority of *General Agreement on Tariffs and Trade* and allows for the establishment of bilateral agreements between trading partners. The MFA will be phased out by the year 2005 and will bring the textile and apparel industry under the jurisdiction of the newly formed World Trade Organization. (See *Chapter Five*.)

N

narrow refers to a type of assortment plan characterized by offering relatively few different styles. (See *Chapter Four*.)

narrowcasting means serving one customer's needs in a very specific manner. In the future special, individualized catalogs—based on narrowcasting—which contain specifically selected merchandise will be printed and sent to consumers. (See *Chapter Ten*. Also see *mass customization*.)

national advertising refers to manufacturers advertising directly to consumers. (See *Chapter Seven*. Also see *retail advertising* and *trade advertising*).

negotiations can result in a settlement and mutual agreement between two or more parties on any matter. This settlement is based on communication and the satisfaction of a goal of one or more of the parties. From a retailer's or manufacturer's perspective, negotiations are often undertaken to solve problems, resolve conflicts, reduce costs, and/or improve profit. (See *Chapter Six*. Also see *Table 6.1, Nine Techniques of Successful Vendor Negotiations* by Liz Tahir.)

newspapers are publications that are the most widely used media for retailers because they are the most flexible and have a wide circulation. Because most newspapers are daily, advertisements can be very timely. (See *Chapter Seven*.)

niche is a term used to describe a narrowly defined customer segment. Because niches have very specific needs, niche retailers offer deep assortments of one particular type of merchandise. A company could also serve a niche by defining its market in narrow geographic terms; that is, a retailer might serve only one small neighborhood, meeting many of its needs. (See *Chapter Two*.)

non-seasonal is a term that describes products that sell steadily year-round. (See *Chapter Three*.)

O

odd priced goods have prices ending with an odd number. Odd price point endings, such as .95 or .99, often reflect sale merchandise, while .00 or evenly divisible numbers usually indicate non-sale prices. (See *Chapter Four*.)

off-price orders are orders, which are placed for merchandise that is purchased at a price below the regular line price. Usually, this is regular merchandise being sold later in the season, or is surplus merchandise. (See *Chapter Five*.)

off-price store sells *brand* merchandise at lower than department store prices due to low overhead and such special purchases as overruns or end-of-the-season merchandise. (See *Chapter One*.)

offshore is a term used to describe buying or manufacturing goods in countries other than the U.S. (See *Chapter Five*. Also see *international sourcing* and *import*.)

ongoing education (See *continuing education*.)

online advertising is advertising accessed on personal computer via the Internet and the World Wide Web. (See *Chapter Seven*.)

on order refers to goods that have been ordered but have not yet arrived. (See *Chapter Four*.)

on-the-job training (See *informal management training* and *informal training*.)

open-door policy is a practice in which a superior (manager) allows employees to interact with him/her—as the need arises—as if his/her office door was always open. (See *Chapter Nine.*)

opening price point is the most inexpensive, low-end price point. (See *Chapter Three.* Also see *budget goods.*)

open orders allow a manufacturer the discretion of shipping merchandise when deemed necessary, rather than locking into a set delivery date. Open orders may also specify a dollar amount that must be purchased, but not always the specific styles, sizes, or colors. (See *Chapter Six.*)

open-to-buy (**OTB**) is an adjustment to the planned purchases that takes into account what is already *on order* (i.e., what is due in). It is calculated on a frequent basis and aids the buyer in making necessary adjustments throughout the season to help control inventories and profitability. (See *Chapter Four.*)

open window displays enable the viewer to see directly into the store through the street window display. (See *Chapter Seven.*)

organizational charts are used by many retailers to model the structure of their companies. These charts depict the hierarchical structure (pecking order), chain of command (who reports to whom), and the relationship between the parts of the company and the whole through line (direct authority and responsibility) and staff (advisory and support) components. Usually the divisions, departments, and even positions within an organization are pictured on a company's organizational chart along with who reports to whom. Retailers vary the configuration of their organizational charts from the Mazur four-function chart to accommodate the size and type of their company and how their company is structured. Some retailers may have a fifth divisional area to account for and handle their branch stores. Yet others may be organized according to regions and/or divisions. All retailers, however, must have at least two functional areas—merchandising and store operations management—to run the business. (See *Chapter Nine.* Also see *Mazur plan.*)

organizational structure describes how a company is set up and directed. The organizational structure aids in monitoring and managing work to be done by assigning accountability for that work. This, in turn, facilitates companies to reach their objectives and goals. To aid in this, *organizational charts* are used by many retailers to model the structure of their companies. (See *Chapter Nine.*)

outdoor advertising includes billboards, the roving billboard, and posters at train and bus stations, and on the buses, trains, and subways. In larger cities, *kiosks* are also used to advertise retailers, manufacturers, banks, performances, and other city events. (See *Chapter Seven.*)

over-the-counter selling (See *retail selling.*)

P

partnership is a term that can refer a firm owned by two or more persons, each of whom has a financial interest. A partnership is also a working relationship that is formed to achieve a goal, which is mutually beneficial. Today, vendor and retail planning is often part of a partner relationship, because managing merchandise is no longer just the retailer's job. (See *Chapters One* and *Six.*)

patent grants to the inventor of a product or process the right for 17 years to exclude others from making, using, or selling that invention. The patent applicant makes a complete disclosure of the invention, which is published and which moves into the public domain when the patent expires. (See *Chapter Twelve.*)

percentage variation method is a stock method that determines stock for a high turnover rate (six or more per year). This method allows for stock fluctuation and is based on the premise that the variation of monthly stock from average stock should be half as much as the percentage variation in monthly sales from average sales. (See *Chapter Four.*)

performance review (See *evaluation (of sales associates).*)

periodic inventory is a method of stock control in which the retailer physically counts merchandise at designated time periods. Many apparel retailers take periodic inventories twice a year, in July and January. (See *Chapter Four.*)

perk is a non-monetary reward that expresses gratitude for work done or a position that is held by the employee. Free lunches or the right to use a company-owned vacation home are sometimes given as perks. (See *Chapter Eight.* Also see *indirect compensation.*)

permanent markdowns refer to permanent lowering of the initial retail price, setting a new retail price. (See *Chapter Four.*)

perpetual inventory is a term that describes a type of stock control method that provides a continuous record of the movement of incoming and outgoing merchandise. (See *Chapter Four.*)

personal ethics deal with an individual's own personal beliefs and principles, as opposed to the company's *code of ethics.* (See *Chapter Twelve.* Also see *business ethics* and *corporate ethics.*)

personnel department (See *human resources department.*)

planned purchases are the difference between what is needed and what is on hand. The amount of planned purchases that is projected is based on the planned sales, BOM and EOM inventory levels desired, and the amount of reductions that are being planned. (See *Chapter Four.*)

planning is a means of control that helps to provide the buyer with information to make the best decisions in purchasing, which generally results in a profit. (See *Chapter Four.*)

point-of-purchase displays are displays in which the merchandise can be touched and self-selected by the customer. (See *Chapter Seven.*)

point of sale (POS) is technology that retailers use to track inventory and sales by the use of computer software programs that are implemented at the point of sale (i.e., traditionally the cash register).

These information systems and communications technologies have improved retail productivity and profits. (See *Chapter Ten.*)

policies set governance guidelines and rules as to specific ways in which a company wants to accomplish its goals. (See *Chapter Eight.* Also see *procedures.*)

popular goods (See *budget goods.*)

positioning refers to the image of a company relative to its competition in the marketplace. (See *Chapter Two.*)

predatory pricing is a situation in which a retailer prices a product below cost with the intent to drive out any competition, which is illegal. Not all below-cost selling is illegal or considered predatory pricing, as some end-of-season goods are sold at a loss to clear out old merchandise. (See *Chapter Twelve.*)

prepack is an assortment of merchandise that is chosen according to a manufacturer's or retailer's direction. This predetermined choice directs that a certain amount of sizes and/or colors of a style or styles are shipped to the retailer. (See *Chapter Five.*)

preprints (See *tabloid inserts.*)

price discrimination occurs when two retailers buy identical merchandise from the same supplier but pay different prices. The purpose of the law against price discrimination is to protect competition by ensuring that retailers are treated fairly by suppliers. (See *Chapter Twelve.*)

price fixing creates monopolies, is illegal, and is a restraint of trade. It occurs when a group of competing retailers (horizontal price fixing) or a retailer and manufacturer (vertical price fixing) agree to maintain the price of merchandise. Vertical price fixing is called price maintenance, which is a violation of the Sherman Antitrust Act. (See *Chapter Twelve.*)

price maintenance laws (See *fair trade laws.*)

pricing strategy is the determination of the type of pricing policy a buyer or retailer will use along with the practices the buyer or retailer will employ. It involves understanding not only who the target customer is and what their needs and/or wants are, but also a number of other such factors as the image and identity that a retailer wants to project. (See *Chapter Four.*)

prima facie duties (moral obligations) include such responsibilities as keeping promises, telling the truth, honoring warranties, abiding by agreements or understood guidelines, not taking abnormal credit extensions or making unjust retail cancellations, and ensuring product safety. Pricing policies fall under this concept, for example, the setting of unfair prices, maintaining the same price after a lowering of quality of the products that were previously ordered, taking excessive markups, and gaining unfair advantage because of a retailer's or manufacturer's size and/or power. (See *Chapter Twelve.* Also see *business ethics, code of ethics, corporate ethics,* and *personal ethics.*)

primary service See *essential service.*

primary trading area is the area in which a retailer can serve its customers better in terms of convenience and location than its competitors. A primary trading area usually extends three to five miles from the site, while a *secondary trading area* can be seven or more miles away. (See *Chapter Seven.*)

print media includes newspapers, magazines, flyers, and direct mail. (See *Chapter Seven.*)

private label is a term used to describe goods that are produced and named by the retailer that sells them. Private labels may carry names other than the store's name, however, unlike *store brands.* (See *Chapter Three.*)

private-label orders are orders placed for merchandise that is designed, controlled, and sold by the retailer and is labeled with a store name or brand distinguishing it as its own. (See *Chapter Five.*)

prizes (See *awards* and *compensation.*)

procedures are the methods—or steps—and therefore the means for a company to reach a goal. A company's procedures should be within the established policy guidelines. (See *Chapter Eight.* Also see *policies.*)

product advertising promotes immediate consumer action, that is, the ad urges the consumer to come into the store and buy that product. It is designed to sell a product rather than promote a company's *image.* (See *Chapter Seven.* Also see *institutional advertising.*)

product data management (PDM) is technology that speeds up the product development cycle and reduces the time it takes to bring products to market. PDM not only joins computer to computer, but also people to people by way of *e-mail.* (See *Chapter Ten.*)

product differentiation is distinguishing a product from a competitor's in order to avoid competing for the same customer. (See *Chapter Two.*)

product knowledge educates sales associates, which enables them to educate their customers, help interpret customer's needs, and, in turn (through the sale of that product), provide for those needs. Information about a product often sells the merchandise. Retailers and vendors alike supply the information to the salespeople about merchandise that helps them answer questions and resolve problems knowledgeably. Some products require more selling and product knowledge than others, and often the vendor must help provide the information for a salesperson to relay to the customer. (See *Chapter Eight.*)

product life cycle (See *fashion cycle.*)

professional ethics identify what is ethical and unethical behavior within a particular industry. Trade associations often have a written code of professional ethics. (See *Chapter Twelve.* Also see *business ethics, code of ethics, corporate ethics,* and *personal ethics.*)

profit results when operating expenses are less than the *gross margin*. (See *Chapter Four.*)

profit and loss statement (P&L/income statement) summarizes the financial workings of a business during a certain period of time and documents whether or not there is a profit or loss. (See *Chapter Four.*)

progressive management advancement is the most common way for employees to be promoted within a company. An employee moves through the management level ranks of a company to higher levels by phases and structured management training programs. These programs vary in design and scope, but usually begin with the formal training of recruits who progress in position, stage-by-stage, through evaluation and promotion. Many times career ladders (career paths) are utilized in which progression of rank and position is planned in stages. (See *Chapter Nine.*)

promotional campaigns attempt to communicate a message to consumers in various ways. These can include: television, radio and print advertising, store and/or mall signage, and articles written in local newspapers about an event. (See *Chapter Seven.*)

promotional markdowns are temporary reductions in the initial retail price. (See *Chapter Four.*)

promotional mix is a term used to describe a company's use of the various advertising and promotional venues. It can also include personal selling, advertising, displays, publicity, and/or special events. (See *Chapter Seven.*)

promotional orders are orders that are placed for goods at a better-than-regular manufacturer's cost. These are often special purchases from vendors that can be promoted by the retailer at a savings to the customer. (See *Chapter Five.*)

promotional plan is a determination of what percent of the budget will be spent on various types of promotion in the appropriate media. Often a percentage of sales is used to determine the amount to be spent on promotion. That amount would be divided among television, magazine, and newspaper ads, special events, publicity, displays, and other general promotion items. (See *Chapter Seven.*)

promotional pricing means offering goods at sale prices. (See *Chapter Four.*)

proportionality framework describes an area of ethical decision-making relating to decisions that focus on actions rather than consequences, that is, the ends do not justify the means. For example, high profits should not be achieved by deceiving customers or by exploiting employees. (See *Chapter Twelve.*)

Provision 9802 (Item 807) is a part of the *U.S. Harmonized Tariff Schedule,* which allows for lower *tariffs* as they are calculated on only the value that has been added to the product outside the U.S. (See *Chapter Five.*)

psychographics is a term used to describe data that is related to the activities, interests, and opinions of the target consumer. (See *Chapter Two.*)

publicity is information reported in the media by a source outside the company with no vested interest. This is the primary method of generating unpaid communications. (See *Chapters Seven* and *Nine.*)

public relations is a part of a corporate structure that is responsible for creating public impressions about the company. They are responsible for press releases and press conferences to release facts about a company. (See *Chapter Seven.*)

purchase order (PO) is the legal contract that binds the buyer and seller. All pertinent information that must be relayed between the two parties for the purchasing of merchandise should be contained on this document. A purchase order ensures that what the retailer wants is being requested, and it also verifies any special requests that have been negotiated. (See *Chapter Six.*)

purchasing refers to *buying* at the manufacturing level, i.e., obtaining the materials to make the end product. (See *Chapter Four.*)

purchasing agent is the individual given buying authority at the manufacturing level. Sometimes this position is called a merchandiser or sourcing agent. (See *Chapter Four.*)

push money (See *spiffs.*)

Q

quality is often thought of as "degree of excellence." In apparel it is determined by many aspects, which are comprised of many aesthetic and functional features. Aesthetics include appearance, fit, design, fabrication, construction, and details or decoration. Functional features include such attributes as durability and serviceability. (See *Chapter Three.*)

quality control is done at the fabric manufacture, garment manufacture, and retail levels. Normally, the manufacturer is responsible for checking the quality of materials before production. (See *Chapter Three.*)

quick response (**QR**) shortens the pipeline of getting a product from its conception to the consumer by capitalizing on *electronic data interchange*. Quick response was developed as a strategy to fight imports because domestic manufacturers have the advantage of proximity to the marketplace over the offshore manufacturer. It also serves as a competitive advantage for domestic manufacturers competing with each other. QR is effective if manufacturers and retailers are true partners, in which retail sales data are shared with the manufacturer who then can arrange for *automatic replenishment* of stock. (See *Chapter Ten.*)

quota is the limit to the number of units of specified merchandise permitted to be brought into a country for consumption during a specific period of time. Quotas can be absolute or tariff rate. (See *Chapter Five.* Also see *absolute quota, tariff-rate quota,* and *sales goals.*)

R

records are documents or electronic data that help management to follow and guide businesses to success. Retailers generate various reports to help monitor their businesses, which may include many types of planning reports and records. Reports on units, dollars, assortment, pricing, fast or slow sellers, sell-through analysis, vendors, and other information desired are frequently used methods of retail control. (See *Chapter Four.*)

reductions are a provision used by retailers to reduce the retail price of merchandise and to encourage the sale of stock so that it can be replaced with fresh, new goods. *Markdowns, markup cancellations,* and *discounts* are all types of reductions that a retailer should plan to incur. (See *Chapter Four.*)

regional market is a smaller type of market that serves U.S. retailers as a geographical convenience. Atlanta, Dallas, and Los Angeles are examples of regional markets. (See *Chapter Five.*)

regular pricing refers to prices on merchandise that is not on sale, and are not promotionally priced. (See *Chapter Four.*)

remote displays are product displays that are not located at the actual store. These free-standing units can target tourists because they are often placed in hotels, while a department store that is located at one end of a mall might also use a remote display at the other end to alert customers of its presence. (See *Chapter Seven.*)

reorders are orders that are placed on merchandise that has purchased at least once before by the retailer. Reorders are more common with *basics* than with *fashion goods.* (See *Chapter Five.*)

resident buying office (**RBO**) is an organization located in a given fashion market that serves as a retailer's market representative for the procurement of merchandise. The two major types of resident buying offices are independent and store-owned. (See *Chapter Five.* Also see *independent buying office* and *store-owned buying office.*)

resource (See *manufacturer.*)

retail advertising is advertising by retailers directed at consumers. (See *Chapter Seven.* Also see *trade advertising* and *national advertising.*)

retail divisions (See *Mazur plan.*)

retail-induced incentives are those motivators that are produced or provided by the retailer to encourage sales personnel to sell. Retail-induced incentives include *compensation* and recognition. (See *Chapter Eight.*)

retail selling can be one of three types: 1) house-to-house; 2) mail and electronic (e.g., telephone, television, and computer); and 3) over-the-counter. Today, the majority of retail sales still occur over-the-counter but mail order is the fastest growing method of selling in the U.S. (See *Chapter Eight.*)

returns to vendor (**RTV**) occur when a retailer returns goods to a manufacturer for any reason, for instance not liking the merchandise or inherent problems (e.g., poor quality) in the product. (See *Chapter Six.*)

run of press/newspaper (**ROP**) advertisements are ads in daily newspapers, usually used to promote weekly specials. (See *Chapter Seven.*)

S

sales goals (**sales quotas**) are sales plans that are set by the retailer. Usually, the retailer hopes to either achieve or exceed these sales goals or sales quotas. (See *Chapter Eight.*)

sales manuals are used by retailers to convey the expectations of the company to the sales associates. Sales manuals are written procedures or directions and policies that a company wants their employees to follow. Sometimes, salespeople are tested on the material found in a sales manual, which they are expected to know after training is completed. Additionally, some sales manuals are written specifically for a retail operation; these are called store manuals. (See *Chapter Eight.*)

sales planning is the first step in developing the merchandise budget and is the estimation of the sales that a retailer will make over a period of time. (See *Chapter Four.*)

sales promotion is thought of, in the broadest sense, as all the efforts that attract consumers, build customer loyalty, and overall contribute to generating sales. The purpose of sales promotion is to inform, persuade, or remind customers about the business and its product. (See *Chapter Seven.*)

sales quotas (See *sales goals.*)

sales representative is an individual who represents a manufacturer's product. Often, sales representatives are the major link between the retailer and the manufacturer. (See *Chapter Six.*)

sales training varies in type and style and from retailer to retailer but is always concerned with readying salespeople to sell products and/or services that are being offered. (See *Chapter Eight.*)

seasonal goods are merchandise that sell best during either the Spring or Fall season. (See *Chapter Three.*)

secondary line is a similar version of a company's own popular item produced in a lower-cost fabrication and generally with lower-cost construction techniques, but keeping the "flavor" of the original design. These products are sold in a different market, at different stores, and to different consumers. (See *Chapter Three.*)

secondary service (See *ancillary service.*)

secondary trading area is the area beyond a store's *primary trading area* that yields customers despite a competitor's location advantage. A primary trading area usually extends three to five miles from the site, while a secondary trading area can be seven or more miles away. (See *Chapter Seven.*)

self service is minimal service, for example, when customers are first expected to find the merchandise they want, then take it to a service desk (cashier) to purchase it. (See *Chapter Eight*. Also see *limited service* and *full service*.)

selling is the person-to-person (most often face-to-face) contact between the retailer and customer, or between the manufacturer and customer, which results in a purchase by a customer. (See *Chapter Eight*. Also see *direct selling*.)

sell-through is the percentage of merchandise sold during a specific time period. It is also a type of sales plan that sets a certain percentage of the amount of merchandise sold as a goal to achieve. (See *Chapter Four*.)

shallow refers to a merchandise assortment with relatively few sizes and colors for each style. (See *Chapter Four*.)

shopping goods is a term used to describe merchandise that is evaluated more by the consumer than *convenience goods* and include most clothing purchases. (See *Chapter Three*.)

short markup is a markup smaller than a *keystone markup*, i.e., one that creates a retail price that is less than double the cost of the goods to the merchant. (See *Chapter Four*.)

short-range planning involves looking at the most immediate concerns and setting goals of the business to achieve them. Two examples of short-range planning include such subjects as what to do about a sale that is a week away or how to meet a sales plan for the week. (See *Chapter Four*.)

showcase displays are often used for small or expensive items. These are usually enclosed and locked. (See *Chapter Seven*. Also see *closed-island display*.)

SIC (Standard Industrial Classification) codes is an industry-wide coding system that categorizes types of merchandise and general types of retailers such as apparel and department stores. (See *Chapter One*.)

silver-streakers are the over-50 age population group. (See *Chapter Two*.)

six-month plan is a unit and dollar merchandise plan covering six-month time frames within a calendar year, i.e., Spring/Summer (February-July) and Fall/Winter (August-January). (See *Chapter Four*.)

Small Business Administration (**SBA**) is a federal agency with special programs for minority business development and for the economically disadvantaged. It can provide financial information to small business owners. (See *Chapter Eleven*.)

social justice framework is an area of ethical decision-making determining that everyone should be treated equally and no group should be taken advantage of, for example, the dumping of unsafe products in third world countries. (See *Chapter Twelve*.)

social responsibility describes a company's duties and obligations to society that extend beyond ethics and legalities. The public expects business to be part of the community and to act responsibly. (See *Chapter Twelve*.)

soft goods include apparel and linens and generally have higher turnover and profitability than *hard goods*, which include home furnishings, appliances, electronics, and so forth. (See *Chapter Three*.)

sole proprietorship is a company owned by one person that is fully controlled by the owner, and all benefits and costs accrue to that individual. (See *Chapter One*.)

sourcing is the term used to describe the process of determining how and where goods will be procured. (See *Chapter Five*.)

sourcing agent (See *purchasing agent*.)

special events can be classified as paid/personal communication and can include demonstrations, trunk shows, fashion shows, celebrity appearances, or other events, which are used to gain the interest of consumers and attract them to a retail environment. (See *Chapter Seven*.)

special orders are orders that are placed with a vendor usually for a specific customer. (See *Chapter Six.*)

specialty goods is a term used for merchandise that is a particular brand. (See *Chapter Three.*)

specialty store (limited assortment store) sells a limited type of merchandise, for example, shoes, electronics, or apparel. Generally this type of store provides the customer with special services not often seen in department or discount stores. (See *Chapter One.*)

specific tariff is a rate of duty that is based on a set amount per each unit imported. (See *Chapter Five.* Also see *ad valorem tariff, compound tariff, free rate of duty,* and *tariff.*)

spiffs are incentives provided by vendors that compensate the salesperson, thereby providing motivation to try to sell particular items. Sometimes this compensation is money for merchandise that is being pushed and sold. Spiffs are sometimes called push money. (See *Chapter Eight.*)

staff (See *organizational charts.*)

standard orders are orders that are placed for goods purchased inseason as part of a regular line of manufacturer's merchandise. (See *Chaper Five.*)

standards are a means of measuring performance through accepted guidelines that help to monitor performance. (See *Chapter Four.*)

staples (See *basics.*)

stock keeping unit (SKU) is the smallest unit level of merchandise and includes style, color, size, and any other information that needs to be tracked. (See *Chapter Four.*)

stock-sales ratio method (SSR) is a method of *inventory planning,* which arrives at a planned stock level that is based on what should be on hand at any given time, rather than on an average stock basis. It may be arrived at by multiplying the planned sales for the month by the BOM stock-to-sales ratio. (See *Chapter Four.*)

stock turn (See *turnover.*)

store brand is a term used to describe goods that are produced and named by the retailer that sells them. Store brands literally carry the name of the store. (See *Chapter Three.* Also see *private label.*)

store manuals (See *sales manuals.*)

store (operations) management (See *Mazur plan.*)

store-owned buying office is a buying office that is owned and operated by a retail firm or group of retail stores. (See *Chapter Five.*)

strip center (string street/strip mall) is composed (generally) of a relatively small number of stores set beside each other, with the largest tenant perhaps a grocery store, variety store, or drugstore. Usually the remainder of the stores are convenience stores. These strip malls are not enclosed as are larger malls. (See *Chapter One.*)

sub-classification (sub-class) is the term used to describe a group of merchandise within a classification that is closely related in styling, such as bottoms or tops under the classification of sportswear. (See *Chapter Four.*)

supervisor is usually a first-line, entry level manager and is any person who is responsible for the conduct of others in the accomplishment of a task. Supervisors can be managers or vice versa. (See *Chapter Nine.*)

supplier (See *manufacturer.*)

support service (See *ancillary service.*)

T

tabloid inserts (preprints) are printed separately from the regular newspaper and are usually inserted into Saturday or Sunday papers. These can be done in color and are cheaper than the ROP. (See *Chapter Seven.*)

tangible services are those services that provide such concrete assistance as personal shoppers, childcare, and delivery service. (See *Chapter Eight.* Also see *intangible services.*)

target market is the group of customers that a company seeks to serve. (See *Chapter Two.*)

target marketing (customer segmentation) is identifying one's *target market* by such *demographic* variables as age, gender, income, education, marital status, religion, family size, life-cycle stage, ethnicity, and mobility; *psychographic variables* are also used including activities, interests, and opinions. (See *Chapter Two.*)

tariff is a special tax, paid to the government, placed on imported merchandise that adds to the cost of goods. (See *Chapter Five.* Also see *ad valorem tariff, compound tariff, free rate of duty,* and *specific tariff.*)

tariff-rate quota allows a certain number of specific goods to be imported at a lower rate and after that threshold has been reached, additional quantities of the same merchandise can be imported at a higher tariff rate. See *Chapter Five.* Also see *quota.*)

television shopping is a term used for retailing programs on television, such as the Home Shopping Network and QVC. Customers watch the programs on TV and then phone in (or *e-mail*) their order. This type of at-home shopping, along with the *Internet,* may replace the mail order catalog of the 1980s and 1990s. Television shopping shares some of the same problems as direct mail because customers cannot try on the merchandise and therefore are hesitant to buy. Additionally, colors and even styles often look different at home than on the television, which can lead to a high number of returns. This has implications for the type of merchandise and the sizing chosen for TV shopping. (See *Chapter Ten.*)

temporary retailer is generally a vendor who sets up tables or carts and sells goods—often one-of-a-kind—made by the seller or artist. They usually set up on street sidewalks or walkways of malls. Some larger retailers are also experimenting with temporary stores that sell goods related to

specific events, such as the Olympics or the Super Bowl. (See *Chapter One.*)

terms of sale are conditions in a purchase agreement between retailer and vendor that include *discounts,* delivery, and transportation costs. (See *Chapter Six.*)

Textile Technology Corporation (TC^2) is an effort between education, industry, and the U.S. Government, to take the lead in the area of technology that is applied to the manufacturing of apparel. Its concepts of *agile manufacturing,* long-distance learning, and the *virtual factory* are examples of demonstrated applications of the newest technologies to lower costs and maintain international competitiveness. (See *Chapter Ten.*)

top-down planning involves goal setting at the highest level of the organizational structure and management, then filtering the goals down to the other levels. (See *Chapter Four.* Also see *bottom-up planning.*)

top, upper-level manager is a high-level management position that includes officers and top executives, for example the president and vice president of a company. (See *Chapter Nine.*)

trade advertising is advertising by manufacturers to retailers, for example in *WWD* or *DNR.* (See *Chapter Seven.*)

trademark is any word, name, or symbol that has been adopted and used by the owner to identify a product and distinguish it from others. In the U.S., the first person to use the trademark in conjunction with a product has ownership of the trademark and can exclude others from using it. This is not always the case in other countries, however. (See *Chapter Twelve.*)

trade shows are groups of temporary exhibits of vendors' offerings for a single merchandise category or group of related categories. (*See Chapter Five.*)

transactional service is helping to accommodate a purchase being made by a customer, for example, *credit* or *charge cards, layaway,* returns, and exchange adjustments. (See *Chapter Eight.*)

trunk shows are presentations of apparel lines by designers or vendors to store personnel or to customers. For some designers, trunk shows have provided the bulk of their sales in some stores. (See *Chapter Seven.*)

turnkey system performs specific, exclusive functions already programmed and ready for use. (See *Chapter Ten.*)

turnover (TO) is a term used to describe how many times stock is sold and replaced within a period of time. (See *Chapter Four.*)

tying contract is an illegal situation in which suppliers force retailers to buy unwanted merchandise in order to purchase other desired merchandise. (See *Chapter Twelve.*)

U

U.S. Customs Service oversees imports involving *quotas* and *tariffs*. Its major roles are to collect revenue and to ensure that the trade laws and sanctions that the U.S. government legislates are upheld. (See *Chapter Five.*)

U.S. Harmonized Tariff Schedule (USHTS) itemizes all products subject to the tariff imported from different countries and lists the rates of tariffs imposed on these products. (See *Chapter Five.*)

unit plan is a type of plan that involves the actual physical units and refers most often to the *assortment planning* and qualitative aspects on this plan. Unit planning involves decisions about what types of merchandise (or mix) should be bought and stocked by a retailer down to the number of pieces in inventory. (See *Chapter Four.*)

universal product code (UPC) is a 12-digit number used to track and identify products to the lowest level of merchandise detail. As more vendors use the UPC for item identification, more retailers can reduce their ticketing time and labor, and the stream of merchandise to the selling floor is further accelerated. Because the UPC provides sales data at *point of sale*, retailers are able to make discerning merchandising decisions on-the-spot

including quick adjustment and control of inventory composition and levels. (See *Chapter Ten.*)

utilitarianism can be thought of as doing "the greatest good for the greatest number." A cost-benefit analysis can assess the viability of this and is generally used in business and governmental decision-making. (See *Chapter Twelve.*)

V

value is the relationship between quality and price. (See *Chapter Three.*)

variety store is a retail store that sells a wide assortment of popularly priced goods. (See *Chapter One.*)

vendor (See *manufacturer.*)

vendor-induced incentives are those furnished by the supplier to the retailer or directly to the sales employee. *Spiffs* or push money are sometimes provided to retailers by vendors. These are incentives that compensate the salesperson, thereby providing motivation to try to sell particular items. In addition to monetary rewards, various other forms of vendor support and incentives include: training, trunk shows, educational material, and contests. The vendor may also supply personnel sales training and/or educational materials. (See *Chapter Eight.*)

vendor matrix (key resource list) incorporates the company-approved key vendors from which a buyer is recommended and/or required to purchase. (See *Chapter Four.*)

venture capitalist (financier) is a person who supplies money and takes a financial risk as an investor in a business. (See *Chapter Eleven.*)

vertical integration is a form of diversification that involves a company acquiring another company or developing a function that serves as either its supplier or its customer. (See *Chapter One.*)

video catalog is an electronic form of a catalog in which a retailer reproduces a printed catalog on a videocassette or videodisc and then sends it to customers. This was the precursor to on-line shopping. At-home shoppers watch the catalog using a VCR and then telephone their orders to the retailer. (See *Chapter Ten.*)

video walls (i.e., many television screens displaying the same visual and/or large screen projections) make a dramatic display and are effective in gaining consumer attention. (See *Chapter Seven.*)

virtual factory incorporates communications technologies, which allow different stages of production to be completed in various remote locations. Using this technology, a garment could be designed in California, cut and sewn in Texas, and the product drop shipped to retail establishments in Florida—all controlled from a computer system that is headquartered in New York City. (See *Chapter Ten.*)

visa is a document from the exporting country guaranteeing country of origin and is a way for the exporting country to monitor the amount of its exports to the U.S. (See *Chapter Five.*)

visual merchandising is a general term that is used to describe everything that is seen when a customer enters a store. This includes the exterior appearance of the store, window displays, signage, and all interior displays of merchandise on fixtures and lighting that are used to create an overall effect. (See *Chapter Seven.*)

W

wall displays utilize dead or unused store wall space to show merchandise. (See *Chapter Seven.*)

warehouse store is a discounter that offers food and other items in a no-frills setting. They often concentrate on special purchases of brand-name goods. Generally they are characterized by a lack of such customer services as credit card usage or bagging. Many times these operations require a "membership fee," which the consumer must pay before being able to shop at the store. (See *Chapter One.*)

warranty ensures the integrity and life of a product for a specific period of time, which is usually in writing. (See *Chapter Eight.* Also see *guarantee.*)

week's supply method of *inventory (stock) planning* is used when calculating a needed stock level by week. With this method, planned stock is equal to the average stock in a week's supply multiplied by the planned weekly sales. (See *Chapter Four.*)

wholesaler is a reseller of merchandise. Normally, wholesalers buy merchandise in large quantities, which are then broken down and then sold in smaller quantities. (See *Chapter Five.*)

wholesale selling (**contact selling**) involves the customer purchasing directly from the manufacturer. (See *Chapter Eight.*)

window displays are an important part of visual merchandising. Traditional store window displays are enclosures with solid backings that isolate the merchandise to be presented. These *closed displays* perform a selling function even when the store is closed. *Open displays,* common in malls, enable the viewer to see directly into the store through the display. (See *Chapter Seven.*)

About the Authors

Authors/Editors

Nancy J. Rabolt
Professor, Fashion Merchandising
San Francisco State University

Dr. Rabolt was awarded her Ph.D. from the University of Tennessee. She has served as Chair of the Research and Theory Development Committee for the International Textile and Apparel Association and has edited two special publications for ITAA, *Computer Applications in Textiles and Clothing* and *Global Perspectives Modules for Textiles and Clothing*. She has published articles in many scholarly journals, in addition to trade and computer journals. Currently, she is doing research for Garment 2000, a government/industry/education consortium to support the San Francisco apparel industry. She is also a member of the American Collegiate Retailing Association. Co-author (with Connie Ulasewicz) of Case 2; co-author/editor (with Judy K. Miler) of *Cases 9, 13, 18, 22, 23, 26, 27, 30, 34, 35, 45, 48, 49, 54, 56,* and *93;* co-author (with Diane Cantua) of *Case 21;* co-author (with Peggy Gorbach) of *Case 60.*

Judy K. Miler
Assistant Professor and Merchandising
Coordinator, Human Ecology
University of Tennessee, Chattanooga

Dr. Miler received all her degrees from the University of Tennessee, Knoxville. She brought over 13 years of apparel retail operations and merchandising management experience with her to academia, having worked for such companies as Levi Strauss & Co. and Lord & Taylor. Her experience is in department and specialty stores, from off-price to private label, and corporate to independents. Dr. Miler is a member of ITAA, the Costume Society of America, American Collegiate Retailing Association, and the Popular Culture Association. She also consults for new business startup ventures. Co-author/editor (with Nancy J. Rabolt) of *Cases 9, 13, 18, 22, 23, 26, 27, 30, 34, 35, 45, 48, 49, 54, 56,* and *93;* co-author (with Janice Rosenthal McCoart) of *Case 78.*

Contributing Authors

Laura Bliss
Faculty Member, Fashion Marketing & Management
Stephens College, Columbia, Missouri

Her professional background includes nine years of experience in fashion retailing, visual merchandising, and costume construction/design with such companies as Polo/Ralph Lauren, Toys "R" Us, the Portland Stage Company, and the Santa Fe Opera. She recently completed her fourth year at Stephens College. She is a member of the Fashion Group International, serving as Nominating Chair of the Kansas City region. Ms. Bliss is currently pursuing a Master of Science degree at the University of Missouri focusing on television shopping. Author of *Cases 70, 83,* and *89*.

Maryanne Smith Bohlinger
Professor, Marketing
Community College of Philadelphia

Professor Bohlinger received her Bachelor of Science in Fashion Design and Master of Science in Textiles and Clothing from Drexel University; Ed.D. in Marketing and Distribution from Temple University. She is the author a college-level textbook, *Merchandise Buying* and has experience in the fashion industry as both a consultant and buyer. Presently, she is the owner and president of a fashion and gift boutique called Irresistibles, Ltd. Author of *Case 31.*

Mary E. Boni
Coordinator, Fashion Design & Technology
Kwantlen University College, Richmond, British Columbia

Ms. Boni received her Master of Arts degree from the University of British Columbia. She is a developer of computer-based curriculum and has written software programs for fashion design education. Co-author (with S. Lee) of *Case 61.*

Evelyn Brannon
Associate Professor, Apparel Merchandising and Design
Auburn University

Professor Brannon was awarded her Doctorate degree in Communications from the University of Tennessee, Knoxville. She conducts research on consumer preferences, theories of fashion change, and fashion forecasting techniques. Author of *Cases 11* and *81*.

James W. Camerius
Professor, Marketing
Northern Michigan University

Professor Camerius received his Master of Science degree from the University of North Dakota. His corporate case studies appear in over 30 management, marketing, and retailing textbooks. An international lecturer and award recipient, his work includes several articles on the case writing experience. Author of *Cases 1* and *80*.

Diane Cantua
Instructor, Textiles
San Francisco State University

Ms. Cantua received her Master of Arts from SFSU. She conducts classes at Fashion Institute of Design & Merchandising and at the Academy of Art College, in addition to SFSU. She also has 16 years industry experience including Macy's California, Fieldcrest Mills, and Levi Strauss & Co. She has also been a fabric representative in the OTC trade in the San Francisco Bay Area, as well as having a consulting practice. Co-author (with Nancy J. Rabolt) of *Case 21.*

Kitty Dickerson
Professor and Department Chairman, Textile and Apparel Management
University of Missouri, Columbia

Professor Dickerson has a Masters from St. Louis University and received her Bachelor of Science from Virginia Tech. She is a Fellow, Corporate Development Officer, and former President of International Textile and Apparel Association. She is the author of *Textiles and Apparel in the Global Economy* and co-author of *Inside the Fashion Business.* Author of *Cases 86* and *87.*

Roger Dickinson
Professor, Marketing
University of Texas, Arlington
Professor Dickinson is the former dean of the College of Business Administration, University of Texas, Arlington; former chairperson of Marketing at Rutgers Graduate School of Business; and is a former buyer for A&S. He has also served as the booknote editor for the *Journal of Retailing.* Currently, he teaches a variety of graduate and undergraduate courses in marketing and retailing. Author of *Case 92.*

Marsha A. Dickson
Assistant Professor, Consumer & Textile Sciences
The Ohio State University
Professor Dickson was awarded her B.S. from Kansas State University; M.S. and Ph.D. from Iowa State University. She conducts research related to social responsibility in the international apparel marketing system, focusing on the interrelationships between consumers, retailers, and apparel manufacturers. Co-author (with Diane Frey) of *Case 75.*

Michelle Dolan
Framingham State University, MA
Ms. Dolan received her Bachelor of Science in Clothing and Textiles from Framingham State University, MA. She completed her internship at Gap and is currently working in sales administration for Safety First. Co-author (with Judy Zaccagnini Flynn) of *Case 67.*

John Donnellan
Lecturer, Consumer Studies
University of Massachusetts, Amherst
Mr. Donnellan is the author of *Merchandise Buying and Management,* published by Fairchild. His areas of research include private-label merchandis-

ing, shopping center management, and gift shops in non-profit organizations. Author of *Case 36.*

Sara Douglas
Associate Professor, Textile Marketing and Economics
University of Illinois, Urbana-Champaign
Professor Douglas was awarded her Ph.D. in Communications Research from the University of Illinois. She has lived and taught in Southeast Asia for over five years; her current research interests are in the political economy of the global textile industry. Author of *Case 40.*

Anne M. Duskin
Director of Communications,
Santa Barbara Museum of Art
Ms. Duskin received her Bachelor of Arts in Journalism from San Diego State University. She has been in marketing for eleven years and has previously been Director of Marketing for several shopping centers. She has also won several regional advertising awards. Author of *Case 53.*

Molly Eckman
Assistant Professor, Design, Merchandising, and Consumer Sciences
Colorado State University, Fort Collins
After ten years in retailing, Dr. Eckman received her Masters from Iowa State University and her doctorate from the University of Maryland. She was awarded first place in the International Textiles and Apparel Association Graduate Student Research Competition in 1992. Her research involves understanding how culture influences the consumer's shopping behaviors. Co-author (with Antigone Kotsiopulos) of *Cases 29, 37,* and *73;* co-author (with Diane Frey) of *Cases 41* and *85.*

David Ehrlich
President, Ghostwriters
Mr. Ehrlich received an MBA from Harvard Business School and a Bachelor of Arts from Yale. Currently, he is the president of Ghostwriters, a

writing and editorial firm in Washington, D.C. and is an owner of the Gilpin House Bookshop in Alexandria, VA. In the past, he was a Vice President of the Outlet Company, managed the Smithsonian Institution's mail-order catalog, as well as being an adjunct faculty member at Marymount University for nine years. He has published *Cases in Retailing,* a series of cases for classroom instruction, which was later used in various business schools in Eastern Europe. Author of *Cases 32* and *57.*

Judith Everett
Professor, Fashion Merchandising
Northern Arizona University, Flagstaff
Professor Everett received her Master of Arts degree in Textiles and Clothing from Kent State University; Master of Business Administration from Arizona State University. She is the co-author, with Kristen Swanson, of *Guide to Producing a Fashion Show,* published by Fairchild. Author of *Cases 38, 68,* and *88.*

Terri Faraone
Lecturer and Consultant
California State University, Los Angeles
Ms. Faraone received her Bachelor of Arts degree in Home Economics from California State University, Los Angeles. Formerly Divisional Vice President and Merchandise Manager for May Co., California. She is currently a college lecturer and consultant to the industry. Co-author (with Betty K. Tracy) of *Case 20.*

D. Michael Fields
Professor of Marketing and Coordinator
of the MBA program
Southwest Missouri State University
Dr. Fields received his MBA in 1981 and his Ph.D. in 1985 from the University of Arkansas. He has significant retail experience as both a buyer and as a store manager. His primary research interest is in the area of the turnover of entry-level retail personnel. Author of *Case 28.*

Judy Zaccagnini Flynn
Professor, Clothing and Textiles
Framingham State College, MA
Professor Flynn was awarded her Masters degree in Clothing and Textiles from Kansas State University; Ph.D. in Clothing and Sociology from The Ohio State University. She has taught a "Capstone" case studies course for the past 10 years. Also supervises a field study in a merchandising course and teaches a course in international trade. Co-author (with Michelle Dolan) of *Case 67.*

Gary B. Frank
Professor, Accountancy
University of Akron
Professor Frank was awarded his Doctorate from the University of Illinois. He is the author of 21 journal articles (including "Linking Cost to Price and Profit" in *Management Accounting,* which was awarded the William M. Lybrand Medal for contribution to the literature in management accounting) and numerous conference proceedings and reprints. Co-author (with J.B. Wilkinson) of *Case 5.*

Diane Frey
Associate Professor, Apparel
Merchandising
Bowling Green State University
Professor Frey received her Ph.D. in Textiles and Clothing & Instructional Technology from Iowa State University. Expertise in teaching computer-aided design and concepts in product development. The focus of Dr. Frey's research is technologies used in the apparel industry and the development of computer instruction for a variety of learning styles. Co-author (with Molly Eckman) of *Cases 41* and *85;* co-author (with Marsha A. Dickson) of *Case 75.*

LaDonna Garrett
Assistant Professor, Fashion Buying and
Merchandising
Fashion Institute of Technology
Professor Garrett has held retailing, merchandising, sourcing, and product development positions in the fashion industry with Bloomingdale's, the

Associated Merchandising Corporation, Levi Strauss & Co., and Cygne Designs. She specializes in teaching and consultancies about product development, fashion coordination, and merchandising strategies. Currently, her concentration centers on teaching an advanced computerized product development course she developed using fashion industry software. Co-author of *The Buyer's Workbook*, published by Fairchild. Author of *Case 39*.

LuAnn Ricketts Gaskill
Associate Professor, Textiles and Clothing
Iowa State University
Professor Gaskill has a Doctor of Philosophy degree in Textiles and Clothing with double minors in Human Resource Management and Higher Education Administration from The Ohio State University; Master of Science and Bachelor of Science in Fashion Merchandising from Bowling Green State University. She is a consultant to small business apparel retailers in Iowa and her research related to small business performance has been published both in research journals and by the lay press. Author of *Case 84, parts 1 and 2*.

Aileen Geronimo
Graduate, Clothing and Textiles
University of Hawaii
Ms. Geronimo's studies concentrated on fashion merchandising and she plans a career as an apparel merchandising executive. Co-author (with Karen H. Hyllegard) of *Case 17*.

Faye Y. Gibson
Director Interns, Clothing & Textiles
University of North Carolina, Greensboro
Professor Gibson received her Master of Science in Clothing & Textiles from the University of North Carolina, Greensboro. She has had 22 years in retail with Department and Specialty Stores in the positions of Merchandise Manager, Buyer, and Fashion Director/Trainer. She is now a lecturer in the Textile Products Marketing Area at UNCG. Author of *Cases 33, 46, and 47*.

Peggy Gorbach
Professor, Family and Consumer Studies
Evergreen Valley College, San Jose, CA
Professor Gorbach received her Master of Arts degree in Consumer and Family Studies from San Francisco State University and her Bachelor of Arts in Clothing and Textiles from Long Beach State University. She has taught at community colleges in Northern California for six years. Co-author (with Nancy J. Rabolt) of *Case 60*.

Sandra Skinner Grunwell
Program Coordinator, Fashion
Merchandising
Western Carolina University, Cullowee, NC
Ms. Grunwell received her Master of Science from The Ohio State University; Master of Business Administration from Bowling Green State University. She has published extensively her research on female entrepreneurs in both national and international business journals. Author of *Cases 4 and 91*.

Karen H. Hyllegard
Assistant Professor, Textiles and Clothing
University of Hawaii
Professor Hyllegard received her Master of Arts from Oregon State University. Currently, she is working toward a doctorate in Textiles and Consumer Economics at the University of Maryland. Co-author (with Aileen Geronimo) of *Case 17*.

Kim K.P. Johnson,
Associate Professor, Design, Housing and
Apparel
University of Minnesota
Professor Johnson received her Ph.D. from the University of Wisconsin, Madison. She is chairperson of the retail merchandising program and teaches courses on strategic merchandising, retail promotion, and managerial decision-making. She is co-author, with Mary Ellen Roach-Higgins and Joanne B. Eicher, of *Dress and Identity*, published by Fairchild. Co-author (with Susan Wegleitner-Taplin) of *Case 65*.

Doris Kincade
Associate Professor, Apparel Management
Virginia Polytechnic Institute and State
University, Blacksburg, VA
Dr. Kincade received her Ph.D. from the
University of North Carolina, Greensboro. She is
a TC^2 Fellow and currently teaches apparel man-
ufacturing and fashion merchandising courses.
Her research is on apparel quick response tech-
nologies and strategic business practices.
Co-author (with Cynthia L. Regan) of *Cases 50*
and *72*.

Paula R. King
Assistant Professor and Chair, Human
Environmental Studies
Southeast Missouri State University, Cape
Girardeau
Professor King has a Masters of Science degree in
Clothing and Textiles from Southern Illinois
University; Ph.D. in Human Environmental
Sciences from Oklahoma State University. She
worked as a designer in the fashion jeans industry
and spent seven years in the retail industry before
returning to university teaching in 1992. Author of
Cases 8 and *59*.

Bruce Klopfenstein
Associate Professor and Chair,
Telecommunications
Bowling Green State University
Professor Klopfenstein has a Masters and Ph.D. in
Communication from The Ohio State University. He
currently teaches new electronic media focusing on
the Internet and the World Wide Web. Co-author
(with Ed Krol) of *The Whole Internet: Academic
Edition, 1996*. He also researches WWW users and
the impact of new technology on society. Co-author
(with Jennifer K. Meyer) of *Case 76*.

Antigone Kotsiopulos
Professor and Department Head, Design,
Merchandising & Consumer Science
Colorado State University, Fort Collins
Past President and Fellow of the International
Textile and Apparel Association and co-author of
Merchandising Mathematics, published by
Fairchild. Coordinated the merchandising program
at Colorado State; recipient of the first Award for
Excellence given by the American Textile
Manufacturers Institute. Co-author (with Molly
Eckman) of *Cases 29, 37*, and *73*.

Shirley A. Lazorchak
Assistant Professor, Textile, Apparel and
Merchandising
West Virginia University
Professor Lazorchak earned her Masters degree in
Business at Robert Morris College; her Ph.D. in
Consumer and Textile Science was conferred at
The Ohio State University. Prior to returning to
graduate school, her professional background
included apparel buyer for The May Co. and
Allied Stores Corp. and manager of multiple stores
for The Limited, Inc. She also writes a monthly
column for Pittsburgh Style magazine. Her teaching and research focus on both apparel merchandising issues and social-psychological aspects of
dress and appearance. Author of *Case 69*.

S. Lee
Instructor, Fashion Design and
Technology
Kwantlen University College, Richmond,
British Columbia
Ms. Lee received her Fine Arts diploma from
Alberta College of Art. She teaches Fashion
Drawing and Colour Theory and has a background
in fashion retail sales. Co-author (with Mary E.
Boni) of *Case 61*.

Richard Leventhal
Professor, Marketing
Metropolitan State College, Denver
Prior entering academia, Professor Leventhal
worked for two Fortune 500 Corporations in both
sales and marketing. Currently, he is the editor of
The Journal of Consumer Marketing. His research
has been published in both academic and professional trade journals. He has also written several
cases in the areas of retail marketing, sales management, marketing strategy and marketing
management, which have been published in various marketing textbooks. Author of *Case 7*.

J. Barry Mason
Russell Professor of Business Adminis-
tration and Dean of the College of
Commerce and Business Administration
University of Alabama
Dean Mason is the past Chairman of the Board of
the American Marketing Association and past
President of the Southern and Southwestern
Marketing Associations. He is a frequent contribu-
tor to the literature and is co-author of *Retailing,
Cases and Problems in Retailing,* and *Modern
Retailing: Theory and Practice.* Co-author (with
Morris L. Mayer and J.B. Wilkinson) of *Case 64,
parts 1* and *2.*

Nancy Anabel Mason
Entry Specialist
United States Customs Service
Ms. Mason received her Masters of Arts degree
from San Francisco State University; thesis
research: Apparel and Textile Maquiladora
Industry. She has been with United States Customs
Service from 1991 to the present and is currently
responsible for resolving problems and articulating
Customs regulations to achieve informed compli-
ance. Author of *Case 43.*

Morris L. Mayer
Bruno Professor Emeritus of Retailing
University of Alabama
Professor Mayer taught retailing for more than 30
years and has been inducted into the Retailing
Patronage Hall of Fame and the American
Collegiate Retailing Association Hall of Fame at
New York University. Co-author (with J. Barry
Mason and J.B. Wilkinson) of *Case 64, parts 1* and *2.*

Janice Rosenthal McCoart
Chair, Fashion Design, Fashion
Merchandising
Marymount University
Professor McCoart was awarded her Master of Fine
Arts in Design from The George Washington
University; other study, University of
Massachusetts and Syracuse University. In addition
to having a career in buying women's apparel and
accessories, Professor McCoart is an artist, profes-

sor, and evaluator of fashion design higher education in the U.S. and abroad. Author of *Cases 25* and
55; co-author (with Judy K. Miler) of *Case 78.*

Melissa M. McCune
Account Manager
Carolee Designs, Inc.
Ms. McCune received her Bachelor of Arts degree
in Clothing and Textiles from San Francisco State
University. She is the Account Manager for over
nineteen specialty department stores. She is
involved in promotions, informational seminars,
visual merchandising, and sales and stock analysis
reports. Author of *Case 62.*

Jim Meisler
Public Relations Director
Retail Technologies International
Mr. Meisler's 25-year career as a public relations
professional began in New York City. His work
later took him to England and Europe for 10 years.
His current interests focus on the use of technology
to improve public relations and marketing procedures. Author of *Case 74.*

Jennifer K. Meyer
World Wide Web Specialist/Webmaster
Gardner Publications, Inc.
Ms. Meyer received her Master of Arts degree in
Communications and Bachelor of Science in
Business Administration from Bowling Green State
University; thesis research: Adoption of the World
Wide Web by Marketers for Online Catalogs. She
now maintains and designs the Web site for
Gardner Publications, Inc., a publisher for the
Metalworking and Finishing industries. Co-author
(with Bruce Klopfenstein) of *Case 76.*

Marcia Morgado
Assistant Professor, Textiles & Clothing
University of Hawaii
Professor Morgado received her Master of Arts
Degree and continues her Doctoral work in
American Studies at the University of Hawaii, with
emphasis in American Art and culture. She spent
10 years in apparel buying and retail management

prior to joining the University faculty. Author of *Case 66*, parts *1* and *2*.

Melvin Morgenstein
Professor Emeritus
Nassau Community College
Professor Morgenstein is currently an adjunct professor for the Department of Accounting and Business Administration. His degrees are Bachelor of Business Administration, Master of Arts, and Doctorate of Education. His areas of interest are in marketing, retailing, finance, and educational consulting. Co-author (with Harriet Strongin) of *Cases 6* and *77*.

Laura Neumann
Private Label Brand Manager
Eagle's Eye
Ms. Neumann was awarded her Master of Science in Textile Marketing from the University of Illinois; Ph.D. in Textile Marketing from the University of Missouri. Employed in apparel manufacturing, she has managed a design studio in New York City for Kellwood Company; currently managing the private label division for Eagle's Eye. Author of *Cases 19, 24, 71,* and *79*.

Nancy A. Oliver
Assistant Professor, Fashion
Merchandising
Northern Arizona University, Flagstaff
Dr. Oliver received her Doctor of Philosophy in Social-Psychology of Clothing from the University of Tennessee. She has been a clothing specialist for the agricultural extension agency, marketing researcher, and university educator. Author of *Case 82*.

Carolyn Olsen
Instructor, Retailing Merchandising
Southeast Community College, Nebraska
Ms. Olsen was awarded her Master of Science degree in Textiles, Clothing and Design from the University of Minnesota. She has been an instructor, advisor, co-op supervisor at the community college in the Business Occupations Division since the late 1970s to the present. Author of *Cases 10* and *90*.

Kathryn Osgood
Production & Scheduling—Dockers Men's Shirts
Levi Strauss & Co.
Ms. Osgood received her AAS from FIT; Bachelor of Science from Cornell University; and Master of Arts from San Francisco State University. During her career in retail sales and management she has worked for Ann Taylor, Gap, Global Kids, and Banana Republic. Current responsibilities include issuing production contracts, maintaining shipments of goods from Asia, assisting in the development of a new software tracking system, and data integrity. Her goal is to channel her knowledge and experience into the apparel production industry with an emphasis on environmentally friendly or "Green" products. Author of *Case 58*.

Catherine Porter
Assistant Professor, Consumer Studies
University of Massachusetts, Amherst
Professor Porter received her Masters of Retailing from the University of Pittsburgh; Ed.D. from the University of Massachusetts, Amherst. She teaches courses related to the textile and apparel industry, professional development, and ethics. Her research has focused on home-based businesses and she is a consultant on customer service for shopping malls. Author of *Case 94*.

Gavin Power
Manager, Communications
Levi Strauss & Co.
Mr. Power is a former columnist with the *San Francisco Chronicle* and has covered the retailing and apparel industries for five years. He holds a degree in economics from the University of California, Santa Barbara. Author of *Case 16*.

Cynthia L. Regan
Ph.D. Candidate
Virginia Polytechnic Institute and State University, Blacksburg, VA
Ms. Regan is currently conducting her dissertation research on concurrent engineering framework for apparel manufacture. She is a United States

Department of Energy Fellow in Integrated Manufacturing. She received her Master of Science degree in Clothing, Textiles and Related Arts from the University of Wisconsin, Stout. Commencing January 1997, Cynthia will be teaching Apparel Merchandising and Management at California State Polytechnic University in Pomona, CA. Co-author (with Doris Kincade) of *Cases 50* and *72*.

Teresa Braswell Robinson
Associate Professor, Textiles,
Merchandising & Design
Middle Tennessee State University
Professor Robinson received her Masters of Science degree in Textiles and Clothing; Doctor of Philosophy degree in Textiles, Merchandising and Design, University of Tennessee, Knoxville. She has an extensive background in apparel retailing. Additionally, she has experience in apparel design, manufacturing, and importing as co-owner of T. Brywn and Associates, an apparel importer. Author of *Cases 44* and *52*.

Diana Rosen
California State University, Sacramento
Ms. Rosen completed her undergraduate studies at San Francisco State University in 1979. She has continued her graduate work in the field of Textiles and Clothing and teaches part-time at California State University, Sacramento. She is also employed full-time as a production manager for Maxit Designs, which specializes in NFL and ski thermal wear. She lives with her two sons, Jared and Joshua. Author of *Cases 42* and *51*.

L. Susan Stark
Professor, Apparel Design
San Francisco State University
Professor Stark received her Masters of Science degree from Pennsylvania State University; Ph.D. from New York University and is a TC^2 fellow. Dr. Stark teaches fashion forecasting, apparel design, and historical influence on fashion. She presently works with the garment industry in San Francisco to optimize methods in clothing construction, is Regional Director of the The Fashion Group International, and is completing research in

apparel manufacturing and production in Brazil and San Francisco. Author of *Case 14*.

Harriet Strongin
Professor Emeritus
Nassau Community College
Professor Strongin is presently an Adjunct Professor for the Department of Marketing, Retailing, Fashion, Apparel, and Interior Design. Her degrees are Bachelor of Science and Master of Arts. Her current areas of interest are in marketing, retailing, fashion, career development, and educational consulting. Co-author (with Melvin Morgenstein) of *Cases 6* and *77*.

Pauline Sullivan
Assistant Professor, Community
Development & Applied Economics
The University of Vermont
Dr. Sullivan received her Ph.D. from New York University and her Masters of Arts degree from San Francisco State University. Currently, she teaches Retail Management, Small Business Marketing, and a seminar in Small Business Marketing and Entrepreneurialism. Dr. Sullivan's research interests focus on out-of-town and cross-border shopping, small businesses, and entrepreneurship. Author of *Case 12*.

K. Denise Threlfall
Assistant Professor, Occupational and
Technical Studies
Old Dominion University
Professor Threlfall received her Doctor of Philosophy in Urban Services-Education from Old Dominion University. She is the Marketing Education Program Leader and coordinator of the Fashion Emphasis at ODU. Author of *Case 3*.

Betty K. Tracy
Professor, Apparel Merchandising and
Management
California State Polytechnic University,
Pomona
Professor Tracy was awarded her Master of Arts degree in Clothing and Textiles from California State University, Los Angeles. She is Director of the AMM

Bachelor of Science degree program with options in Apparel Manufacturing and Fashion Retailing. Co-author (with Terri Faraone) of *Case 20.*

Carol F. Tuntland
Associate Professor, Design, Fashion and Textiles Program
California State University, Los Angeles

Dr. Tuntland received her Doctor of Education in Institutional Management from Pepperdine University; Master of Arts from California State University, Long Beach. Research in articulation of fashion programs among high schools, community colleges, and universities and fashion merchandising program curriculum. She is the author of the *Instructor's Guide* to *Who's Who in Fashion,* published by Fairchild, and the co-author of *The Textiles Handbook.* Author of *Cases 15* and *63.*

Connie Ulasewicz
Educator/Consultant
CU Productions, San Francisco

Ms. Ulasewicz received her Master of Science degree from the University of Maryland. In addition to being an Instructor at San Francisco State University, she is president and founder of CU Productions, which provides production, marketing and sales strategies to textile and apparel businesses. Author of *Case 95;* co-author (with Nancy J. Rabolt) of *Case 2.*

Susan Wegleitner-Taplin
Merchandise Manager
J.C. Penney Company, Inc.

Ms. Wegleitner-Taplin is a graduate of the retail merchandising program at the University of Minnesota. She has over ten years of experience in department store operations and merchandising. Co-author (with Kim K.P. Johnson) of *Case 65.*

J.B. Wilkinson
Professor, Marketing
Youngstown State University

Professor Wilkinson earned her Doctorate from the University of Alabama. She is co-author of *Modern Retailing: Theory and Practice* and has published extensively in such academic journals as *Case Research Journal, Journal of Public Policy & Marketing, Decision Sciences, Journal of Retailing, Journal of Marketing Research,* among others. Co-austhor (with G.B. Frank) of *Case 5;* co-author (with J. Barry Mason and Morris L. Mayer) of *Case 64, parts 1* and *2.*

Case Index[1]

---

[1]Please note that when a case begins with an article such as A, An, or The, these cases have been alphabetized using the second word as the beginning of the title. Hence, *The Knockoff*, (Case 25) is listed as *Knockoff, The,* and is located between the cases *Jeremy's Problem:* A *Possible Drug Situation* and *Labor Strife Clouds Nordstrom's Service Policy.*